URBAN SOCIOLOGY

A Human
Ecological Perspective

URBAN SOCIOLOGY

A Human
Ecological Perspective

WILLIAM A. SCHWAB
University of Arkansas

ADDISON-WESLEY PUBLISHING COMPANY

Reading, Massachusetts • Menlo Park, California
London • Amsterdam • Don Mills, Ontario • Sydney

Library of Congress Cataloging in Publication Data

Schwab, William A.
  Urban sociology.

  Bibliography: p.
  Includes index.
  1. Sociology, Urban. 2. Urbanization. I. Title.
HT111.S315   307.7'6   81-5006
ISBN 0-201-06566-5   AACR2

ISBN 0-201-06566-5
ABCDEFGHIJ-AL-8987654321

to

CHRISTINE

Preface

The idea for this book arose from my experiences in teaching undergraduate courses in urban sociology. Urban sociology is an eclectic field drawing not only from the works of sociology but also from psychology, anthropology, history, and other disciplines. The diversity in approaches and the volume of research make the subject difficult to present to an undergraduate class. This problem is reflected in undergraduate urban sociology texts, many of which are either encyclopedic or very fragmented in their organization of topics

Urban Sociology differs from the other undergraduate texts in that the field of urban sociology is explored in terms of human ecology. This approach provides a common organizational framework for the study of the many facets of urban life. The chapters of this book systematically examine central issues and topics in contemporary urban ecology. Chapter 1, "Urban Sociology from a Human Ecological Perspective," provides a brief overview of the history, theory, terminology, and present state of the human ecological perspective. The other chapters are organized under four broad headings—The Urbanization Process, The Ecology of Urban Regions, The Internal Structure of the Metropolis, and Social Consequences and Social Responses to Urbanization.

PART I: THE URBANIZATION PROCESS

Many Americans assume that the rest of the world lives at a level of urbanization similar to our own. This is a mistaken impression; present United Nations figures show that only about 20 percent of the world's population lives in cities of 100,000 persons or more. Urban growth in the Developing World, however, is occurring at an unprecedented rate, and

rapid growth poses serious adjustment problems for these nations. Therefore, one of the major foci of contemporary ecology is the study of the
urbanization process from a cross-cultural perspective.

Although ecologists have studied the city for more than fifty years,
conceptualization and measurement of the urbanization process are still
problematic. Questions raised in the second chapter, "The Process of Urbanization," are: What criteria are used to define a population concentration
as urban? Does one set a minimum population size—25,000 persons or
more—or include such criteria as density, population composition, and
technological sophistication? Moreover, are the concepts and theories developed to describe and explain the urbanization experience of the West
relevant in the study of the Third World? What is the relationship between
the processes of urbanization and modernization? Is the process of urbanization linked to demographic processes and, if so, how? Answers to these
questions provide policy makers in the Developed and the Developing
Worlds with the basic knowledge necessary for the creation of population
and development polity.

The emergence and rise of cities has long been of interest to the ecologist,
historian, archeologist, and geographer. Chapter 3, "The Origins of Cities,"
is concerned with the why, where, how, and when of the emergence of
man's earliest settlements. In addition, this chapter examines the characteristics and forms of the ancient, preindustrial, and industrial cities of the
18th, 19th, and 20th centuries and the forces that brought about the evolution from one urban form to another.

PART II: THE ECOLOGY OF URBAN REGIONS

From looking at a map of the United States, one might conclude that cities
are distributed in a patterned way across the landscape. What factors determine this pattern? Why will a city spring up at one location and not
another? Chapter 4, "Theories of Location," explores these and other
questions and presents three theories commonly used to explain the location
of cities.

In the United States and other nations of the world, one finds an enormous variation in the size, economic function, and character of cities. In
the second chapter of this section, "City Typologies and the System of
Cities," the ecologist's attempt to uncover the underlying dimension of
cities through the construction of city typologies is discussed. These typologies permit the systematic examination of the differences between the
various forms of urban settlement. In addition, a second topic related to
the literature on city typologies is discussed—the system of cities. Cities
do not exist in isolation but in a complex network of political, economic,
social, and ecological relationships with other cities. The historical development of the nation's system of cities is explored from Revolutionary
times to the present.

PART III: THE INTERNAL STRUCTURE OF THE METROPOLIS

Driving into any large metropolitan area on the interstate highway system, one can view a cross-section of the city. At the periphery, one sees the new low-density suburban housing. Next, the older, well-established suburbs come into view. Closer in, one passes working-class neighborhoods, slums, industrial areas, and finally the high-rise office buildings of the central business district. Clearly, the city is not uniform and undifferentiated but is divided into functionally identifiable subareas. Each of these subareas is distinguished by groups of people and physical structures that are more or less homogeneous.

Part III of this work explores the forces and processes that bring about the sorting of people and institutions into generally homogeneous subareas of cities to form a mosaic of social worlds. Chapter 6, "Social Area Analysis and Factorial Ecology," introduces a model central to the ecological approach, which is based on the close relationship between the social forms in the modern city and the character of the larger containing society. The major emphasis of Social Area Analysis is on the social rather than the physical character of the city.

In Chapter 7, "The Use of Space Within Urban Areas," the physical manifestations of the underlying social organization of society are explored by examining general models of urban geometry including those of Burgess, Hoyt, and Harris and Ullman. Also discussed is the individual's search for a home and a neighborhood and how this decision, combined with millions of others, lends a distinctive character to the various subareas of the city.

In the final chapter of this section, "The Suburbanization Process," the overall suburbanization process is considered. Are suburbs a new post–World War II phenomenon or does their emergence represent the normal development of the city's fringe? What is the popular image of the suburbs—the people who live there and the homes they build—and is this image correct? Do suburbs pay their fair share of central city services or are central city residents subsidizing the suburban way of life? These and other questions central to the study of suburbanization are addressed in this chapter.

PART IV: SOCIAL CONSEQUENCES AND SOCIAL RESPONSES TO URBANIZATION

The focus of the final section of the text is shifted from the ecological forces and patterns which shape the metropolis to the social aspects of urban life. For example, the "community" has been a central theme in sociology for more than 150 years, and this concept is examined in Chapter 9. This chapter first describes the evolution of the concept community through the works of three influential 19th century theorists—Maine, Tonnies, and Durkheim. Second, the influence of these theorists on the works of Robert Park and the Chicago School is assessed. Finally, the community units operating in contemporary urban settings are described along with the participation of urbanites in local community affairs.

Chapter 10, "The Segregation and Location of Groups in U.S. Cities," provides an overview of the most important topic in contemporary ecological research—the segregation of status, ethnic, and racial groups in U.S. cities. Why does segregation occur? The ecological, voluntary, and involuntary factors that operate to concentrate groups in certain parts of the city are systematically analyzed. Special attention is given to the social consequences of these segregation patterns for all of American society.

Population density has been studied by ecologists in two ways. First, some researchers have systematically studied the density-distance relationship, or the tendency for population density to decline as one moves from the city's center to its periphery. The first half of Chapter 11, "Density and Its Consequences," looks at this relationship graphically and shows how density-distance curves differ in cities of high- and low-scale societies and how these curves change over time.

A second group of researchers examines the relationships between high population density and human pathology. The second half of this chapter provides an overview of this literature with emphasis on the major theories and psychological and ecological studies on this topic.

The purpose of this final chapter, "The Structure and Role of Government in the Metropolis," is to examine the role of government in addressing the problems of cities. First, the past and present structure of city government and its position in the nation's federal system are explained. Second, the changing relationships between and within the levels of government are explored. The increasingly important role of the federal government in urban affairs is surveyed. The emerging partnership between the federal government and the cities, often called "cooperative federalism," is explained in terms of federal programs in housing and urban development. Third, the channels through which funds and services flow between governmental units are described. Fourth, the relationship between the structure of metropolitan government and its fiscal affairs is examined with special emphasis on the problems of taxation, spillover of services, and the fragmentation of local government. Finally, the policy alternatives available to the nation's urban areas are explored. Should the administration of cities be centralized in Washington and in regionalized programs, or should control be returned to local governments (decentralization)? Knowledge of the internal structure of the city gained through an ecological perspective is used to evaluate the policy alternatives.

Together, the twelve chapters of this text should give the reader an understanding of the structure and character of the modern city.

Acknowledgments

I began this book in the fall of 1977 thinking that I was embarking on a two-year project; little did I know that the project would last four years. Now that the project is at a close, I would like to acknowledge those people who aided me along the way.

First and foremost there is Ron Hill, my editor at Addison-Wesley, who made this book possible. Ron saw the value of my work and gave the project leadership and direction. Thank you, Ron, I will always be grateful.

On the production side, I would like to thank Cheryl Wurzbacher and the other staff at Addison-Wesley as well as Elydia Siegel and the staff of Superscript Associates for their fine job of producing the book.

Closer to home, there is my past chairman, Elaine O. McNeil, who shared my ordeal from 1977–1980. Elaine is a fine sociologist, and her support for my work and her insightful comments on my manuscript helped immensely. Others, including my present chair, Dan Ferritor, and my colleagues Donna Darden and Don Sieger, deserve recognition for reviewing my manuscript and listening for the past four years. Emily Tompkins also deserves my thanks for her editing and suggestions on early revisions of the book. I would also like to thank Janet Hunter for typing numerous drafts of the manuscript.

Finally, I would like to thank my wife Chris, who is as much a part of this project as I am. I'm sorry for those missed weekends and evenings when I was at the office writing. Thank you for your understanding and support. It is to you, Chris, that I dedicate this book.

Contents

Part One   The Urbanization Process   1

**CHAPTER 1   URBAN SOCIOLOGY FROM A HUMAN ECOLOGICAL
PERSPECTIVE**   **3**
Robert Park and the Chicago school   8
Human ecology today   23
Summary and conclusion   30

CHAPTER 2   THE PROCESS OF URBANIZATION   **35**
Defining urbanization   36
Measuring urbanization   38
United States census definitions of urbanization   41
Global patterns of urbanization   48
Approaches to the study of world urbanization patterns   68
Urbanization and economic development   75
Summary   83

CHAPTER 3   THE ORIGINS OF CITIES   **87**
Human prehistory   90
The earliest cities   95
Other early urban development   99
The preindustrial city   106
The Industrial Revolution   111

American urban history   115
Summary   130

Part Two   The Ecology of Urban Regions   133

CHAPTER 4   THEORIES OF LOCATION   135
Break-in-transportation theory   136
Specialized function theory   145
Central place theory   146
Summary   158

CHAPTER 5   CITY TYPOLOGIES AND THE SYSTEM OF CITIES   161
Single-dimension typologies   163
Multidimensional typologies   174
Uses of city classification schemes   181
The system of cities   183
Summary   208

Part Three   The Internal Structure of the Metropolis   211

CHAPTER 6   SOCIAL AREA ANALYSIS AND FACTORIAL
            ECOLOGY   213
The origins of social area analysis   214
Testing the social area model   238
Factorial ecology   244
Summary   247

CHAPTER 6   APPENDIX   249

CHAPTER 7   THE USE OF SPACE WITHIN URBAN AREAS   257
Theories of residential location   259
Classical theories of urban land usage   270
The decision to move and the search for a residence   284

The search for a new home 288

Summary 299

CHAPTER 8   THE SUBURBANIZATION PROCESS **303**

The suburbanization process in historical perspective 308

The *POET* framework used to analyze suburban growth 321

The suburbanization of business and industry 335

Summary 342

Part Four   Social Consequences and Social Responses to Urbanization   345

CHAPTER 9   THE COMMUNITY—THE SOCIAL ASPECT OF URBAN LIFE **347**

Evolution of the concept of community 348

Robert Park and the Chicago school 355

The social construction of communities 360

Summary 380

CHAPTER 10   THE SEGREGATION AND LOCATION OF GROUPS IN UNITED STATES CITIES **383**

Types of groups 384

Social status segregation 391

Ethnic segregation 399

Racial segregation 410

Summary 428

CHAPTER 11   DENSITY AND ITS CONSEQUENCES **433**

The density-distance relationship 434

Density and the question of pathology 450

Summary 470

CHAPTER 12   THE STRUCTURE AND ROLE OF GOVERNMENT IN THE METROPOLIS **473**

The structure of city government in the United States 475

Intergovernmental relationships 481

The fiscal problems of metropolitan governments 483

The ecological structure of the metropolis and its 491
relationship to fragmented local governments

Policy alternatives 499

Summary 507

REFERENCES **511**

GLOSSARY **537**

AUTHOR INDEX **547**

SUBJECT INDEX **553**

PART ONE

The Urbanization Process

CHAPTER ONE

Urban Sociology from a Human Ecological Perspective

Statement of Objectives

1. The student should understand the relationship between biological ecology and human ecology in terms of shared terminology, theories, and methods.

2. The importance of the work of sociologist Robert E. Park to the early development of the field of human ecology should be known.

3. The value of the Chicago School and its continuing impact on the field of urban sociology should be known.

4. The student should understand Louis Wirth's analysis of the urban way of life.

5. The student should be aware of the criticism of the work of the Chicago School and how this criticism has shaped contemporary human ecology.

6. Two approaches are used in contemporary human ecology—the sociocultural and the neoorthodox. The student should know the differences between these two approaches.

7. The student should review the major topics presently under study by human ecologists.

Urban sociology is one of the broadest and most eclectic fields in the social sciences. Urban sociology overlaps psychology in its emphasis on the "urban personality type" and mental illness in cities, geography in its concern with the spatial distribution of groups and structures, political science in its emphasis on political behavior and decision making, anthropology in its studies of cultural groups, and other fields such as social work, city planning, and urban history. With so much overlapping of interests

3

with other disciplines, how can the study of cities be organized in a systematic and understandable way?

A perspective within urban sociology known as human ecology provides a useful organizational framework for the study of the many facets of urban life. The field of human ecology, introduced in this country by Robert Park more than sixty years ago, has contributed much to the understanding of

Photo 1.1 New York City is viewed from an altitude of two miles in this photograph. From this perspective, one sees the patterned and ordered structure of the city. How these patterns emerge and change through time is a question central to the ecological perspective.

Source: Courtesy Aero Service Division, Western Geophysical Company of America.

how cities grow and change. In fact, some urban sociologists have gone as far as to suggest that the enormous output of empirical research and theoretical essays by human ecologists has provided the closest thing to a systematic theory of the city.

This introductory chapter gives a general overview of the field of human ecology and also provides the background for the remaining chapters of the book. The following questions are addressed: What is human ecology? How is human ecology related to the better-known field of biological (plant and animal) ecology? Historically, how did this field develop? What types of research are human ecologists doing? Finally, how is the human ecology approach used in the following chapters?

Biological Ecology

The word "ecology" is derived from the Greek word *oikos* meaning "house" or "place to live in." Ecology defined in its broadest sense is the branch of science concerned with the interrelationship of organisms and their environment. Ecology is concerned not only with the relationships among members of the same species, but also with the interdependency that develops among members of different species. Ecology also explores how plants and animals collectively adapt to the scarce resources available in the environment.

The field of ecology has its roots in the works of the nineteenth-century English naturalist Charles Darwin. Darwin is best known for his theory of evolution introduced in 1859 in his book *Origin of Species*. Darwin noted that within all species of plants and animals, a certain amount of genetic variation occurs. One can look at any animal species, for example, the horse, and note differences in size, weight, color, and other characteristics. A few members of this species are born with a unique set of characteristics that gives them a slightly better adaptation to their environment. Better adaptation translates into a higher probability that these animals will grow to maturity and pass these characteristics on to their offspring. Animals without these characteristics have a higher probability of dying before they reproduce. Therefore, when Darwin was speaking of the "survival of the fittest," he was referring to the ability of a species to take advantage of such variation over hundreds of generations to change and make a better adaptation to its environment. In other words, a species evolves through time to improve its survival potential (Barzum, 1958, pp. 25–115).

Darwin's theory of evolution is based on his observations of the interrelation and coordination of the numerous and divergent species found in nature. Darwin called this interdependence of organisms in the environment "the web of life," and he demonstrated it in the relationship between the number of cats and the size of the annual red clover crop in England. He found that bumblebees are indispensable to the fertilization of red clover, because other types of bees cannot reach the nectar and so do not visit the flower. If the bumblebee became rare or extinct, the red clover would not be pollenated and it, too, would become rare or extinct. However, the number of bumblebees in any area depends on the number of field mice that destroy their combs and nests (it is estimated that mice destroy more than two-thirds of the nests all over England). Near villages and small towns the nests of bumblebees are more numerous than elsewhere because of the large number of cats that prey on the mice. Thus, the next year's crop of red clover, in certain parts of England, depends on the number of bumblebees in the area; the number of bumblebees depends on the number of field mice; the number of field mice depends on the number of cats; and the number of cats depends on the number of villagers who keep cats (Park, 1961, p.22).

Darwin and other natural scientists discovered many complex food chains. They found that nature exists in delicate balance and that a minor alteration in one link of a food chain can have repercussions for others. For example, the destruction of an animal of prey, such as the fox, at the top of a food chain may enable mouse and rabbit populations to grow unchecked; this growth in turn may have consequences for other plant and animal species.

These early natural scientists established ecology as a separate field with a basic terminology, theory, and method (Park, 1961, pp. 22–28). These scientists' systematic study of natural interrelationships led to the development of an ecological model that accounted for much of the natural world: the impersonal and unexplained forces operating in nature were shown to lead to an ordering of the natural world. Haeckle in 1868 was the first to use the name "ecology" for this study of systems of species, thus giving it the character of a separate science.

Relationship Between Biological and Human Ecology

The word "ecology" in the term "human ecology" is not used arbitrarily; it reflects the close parallel between biological (plant and animal) ecology and human ecology. In many respects human ecology is a straightforward projection of the theories and methods of the plant and animal ecologists. The similarities between the two fields can be seen clearly in their shared terminology.

Shared terminology One of the basic terms used by the ecologist is *environment*. Environment is an area that can be circumscribed on the basis of specific features. Within it the natural processes are studied as part of a natural unit. Examples of environments studied by the biologist are a marsh, lake, river, tideland, or prairie. A biologist could identify these environments by looking at such features as soil type, moisture content of soil, rainfall, and depth of water, and with a certain degree of precision could identify their boundaries. Once these environmental boundaries were located, the ecologist would survey the various species of plants and animals in the environment and then would attempt to discover their interdependence. The environment together with the species of plants and animals that have adapted to it are viewed as an *ecosystem*.

A human ecologist would use essentially the same definition and the same methods to discover and study human environments. A city, for example, could be viewed as a spatial environment. Its boundaries could be identified with a degree of precision from such features as housing and population density. Once boundaries are identified, the same careful methods of observation used by the biologist would be applied to survey the types and numbers of human groups, their interdependence, and their contribution to the functioning of the city's ecosystem.

Within an environment members of the biological community or ecosystem relate to one another on the basis of their likenesses and differences. Biologists and human ecologists have developed terms to describe relationships that have roughly the same meaning to both disciplines. For example, *commensalism* is the competition and cooperation among members of the same species, and *symbiosis* is the interdependency among members of different species.

Commensalism literally means "eating from the same table." Members of the same species compete with each other for the same food and other scarce environmental resources. *Competition* results whenever a species makes demands on the environment for food and water that exceed the supply. In nature this interaction may be very subtle, as in the competition of plants for light and water, or overt, as in the rivalry among wolf packs for the flesh of prey. In human societies competition may be indirect and unconscious, as in the sale of shares on the stock exchange, or direct and conscious, as in that between two businesspeople seeking to purchase the same parcel of land (Hawley, 1950, p. 39). Members of the same species also cooperate to enhance their survival potential. In nature, the hunting organized by a pride of lions is one such cooperative effort. Similarly, our own continued existence is rooted in the cooperative enterprise called society.

Symbiosis, in contrast, refers to the mutual dependency that develops over time among members of different species as they adapt to the environment. In Darwin's red clover example, cats prey on mice, but the mouse population benefits, because cats cull the sick and weak from their number. Both species benefit—the cats have food and the mouse population is kept in balance with its food supply. In human societies, groups and individuals carry out specific functions for society. The interdependency between functionally different groups, say, professors and students, is an example of a symbiotic relationship.

Other ecological principles, *dominance, invasion,* and *succession,* are aspects of commensalism and symbiosis that reflect the structure of relationships of individuals and species within the environment. In every ecosystem there is one or more dominant species. In a plant community this dominance is ordinarily the result of competition among species for light.

For example, in a climate that supports a forest the dominant species is trees; all other plant species have a subordinate position in the ecosystem.

The principle of dominance also determines the ecological pattern of the city and the relationship of the different areas of the city to one another. The areas of dominance in a community are usually the areas of highest land values. High land values reflect the strategic nature of these locations. Industry and commercial institutions normally compete for these locations, because only they have the ability to mobilize the enormous financial resources necessary to purchase such land. The ultimate location of industrial and commercial activities over time determines the main outline of the urban environment. Subordinate land uses—slums, rooming-house districts, middle-class residences—occupy the land that remains. Therefore, subordinate land uses owe their location directly to the dominance of industry and commerce, and indirectly to competition.

Related to the principle of dominance is the ecological process of *invasion-succession*. Invasion-succession refers to the sequence of changes by which one dominant species replaces another in an environment. The term reflects the fact that the relationship between species is in a constant process of change. In nature, a stand of pine trees may age and finally decay to be replaced by a new dominant species, the broad leaf oak. As a city grows, industry and commerce in the downtown business district may gradually invade adjacent residential areas that are undergoing physical decline. The invasion of those dominant activities will eventually cause residential land use to decrease until only commercial land use remains.

The city as an ecosystem The natural ecosystem is a complex set of commensal and symbiotic relationships among a diverse number of plant and animal species. These patterns, moreover, represent a long adaptive process in which those species unable to become dominant find their particular niche in the environment or else become extinct. Once a species finds a niche where it can survive and flourish it will expand its numbers until it encroaches on a species to which it is subordinate. The end result of this process is what some scientists have called a "biological division of labor"—that is, many species of plants and animals use the same environment but each is adapted to a slightly different part of it. Similarly, many people share the environment known as the city, but the individuals who occupy that environment adapt to it in different ways. This ecosystem concept is the basis of the approaches to the study of cities described hereafter.

ROBERT PARK AND THE CHICAGO SCHOOL

Darwin's idea of the web of life and the ecological perspective in general greatly stimulated the imagination of sociologist Robert Park at the University of Chicago.[1] Upon joining the faculty of the Department of Sociology and Anthropology at the University of Chicago in 1914, Park began to

Photo 1.2 Robert Ezra Park (1864–1944).
Source: Department of Special Collections, The Joseph Regenstein Library, The University of Chicago.

formulate a program to study the city of Chicago from an ecological perspective. Park believed the general approach of the plant and animal ecologists could be used to study human societies but that the biological model should be used with caution.

Areas of Agreement

There were certain broad areas of agreement between Park and the nineteenth-century ecologists. First, both saw underlying ecological processes in nature and society, patterns that are recurrent and therefore discoverable through the scientific method. Second, both saw a unity in the natural world, an interdependence among members of the same system as well as a dependence on climate and terrain. Third, both agreed on the "Iron Law of Nature"—a species either adapts to its environment or it becomes extinct. Finally, Park held that nature and society have no ultimate purpose. This notion was in sharp contrast to the ideas of other sociologists who saw society moving to some higher and more complex form.[2]

Areas of Disagreement

Park noted important differences between biological ecology and human ecology. The source of these differences is the nature of human beings and their societies. First, in human society a division of labor and a complex system for the exchange of goods and services lessen the members' dependence on a local environment. A population can trade with people hundreds of miles away for food and other resources, and thus can fundamentally modify its relationship to the environment.

Second, humans through their inventions have the capacity to modify their environments dramatically. The beaver and other animals have this ability, but it is very limited in comparison with that of humans.

Finally, humans have developed language and culture that make possible forms of social organization much more complex than those of any other animal species. Ants, termites, and other species survive because of their social structure, but their systems have a simple division of labor and a rigidity not found in human societies (Park, 1961, p. 28).

The Biotic and Cultural Spheres

To make ecological principles relevant to the study of human society, Park formulated a complicated theory of society as composed of two elements—the biotic and the cultural. According to Park, the *biotic level* is the foundation of society: it is where humans either adapt to the environment or become extinct. The biotic sphere consists of the basic necessities of life such as available water, a particular soil type, and other resources. These factors determine the size of a population in a particular area; they are the resources that the population will be able to use in adapting to the environment. It is on the biotic level that the ecological principles of competition and symbiosis operate. In the struggle for existence, humans compete for the environment's scarce resources, but they also live in a society with a division of labor. Thus competition among humans must always involve an automatic and unplanned degree of cooperation among groups with different functions in society, i.e., symbiosis.

In cities, these unplanned adjustments during the struggle for existence lead to the spatial distribution of people into different areas. Park and his colleagues applied the term *natural areas* to slums, rooming-house districts, wealthy suburbs, and other homogeneous areas of the city because they resulted from unplanned biotic forces. That is, each natural area came into existence through the competition of individuals and groups for space. Once established, these areas provided homes and services for their inhabitants and carried out other functions that contributed to the survival of the entire community.

According to Park and his colleagues, the *cultural level* of society is built upon the biotic level. The cultural level is a structure based on customs, norms, laws, and institutions. It involves the unique aspects of the human species—reason, morality, and psychological makeup.

A working-class neighborhood demonstrates the relationship between the two levels of society. This natural area comes into existence because it is the location in the city where members of the working class can afford to buy housing and still pay the transportation costs to their place of employment—biotic factors. Once established, this natural area develops norms and values as well as institutions such as schools, churches, and fraternal organizations—the cultural level of society.

Park's Research Program

Though Park was aware that the cultural level could affect the biotic (e.g., new technology could permit greater exploitation of the environment), much of the research which he directed was focused on the basic forces within the biotic sphere.

There was good reason for Park's insistence that human ecology should be concerned with the collection of basic knowledge on the city. American cities in the early twentieth century faced a multitude of problems, including massive levels of poverty and social disorganization, deplorable housing and sanitation conditions, and inadequate transportation. Yet little data had ever been collected on this nation's cities. As a sociologist, Park believed that meaningful social reform was impossible unless it was based on verifiable facts. Moreover, he felt that the collection of this information could best be achieved by judiciously applying the rigorous scientific methods of the biological sciences—the ecological perspective.

Park was also aware that social relationships were often reflected in the spatial relationships among areas within the city. Thus, from the beginning, Park emphasized the location and spatial relationships of institutions, groups, and subareas within the city and the processes that modify these patterns over time. As we will see in subsequent chapters, this emphasis continues to shape our study of human ecology.

Park put his beliefs into action in 1916 with the publication of his benchmark work, "The City: Suggestions for the Investigation of Human Behavior in the Urban Environment." In this article, Park outlined a research program that was to occupy the Chicago ecologists for the next two decades.[3] Park listed basic questions whose answers are essential to the understanding of how cities function. A few examples follow (Park, 1969, pp. 91–130).

1. What are the sources of a city's population and how is city growth a combination of natural increase and net migration?
2. What are the city's natural areas and how is the distribution of the city's population among the neighborhoods affected by economic interests such as land values and by noneconomic factors as well?
3. What are the social rituals of various neightborhoods—what things must one do in the area to be fully socially integrated and to avoid being looked upon with suspicion or thought peculiar?
4. Who are the local leaders; how do they embody local interests; how

do they attain and maintain social influence and power; and how do
they exercise control?

5. Do social classes in fact become cultural groups? Do they acquire an
exclusiveness independent of race and nationality?

6. Do children in the city follow in the occupational footsteps of their
fathers?

7. How is social unrest generated and manifested? Are strikes and mob
violence produced by the same conditions that generate financial
panics, real estate booms, and mass movements of the general
population?

8. What changes have taken place in the family? In what areas of family
life has change been the greatest? How has such change been induced by the urban environment?

9. How have educational and religious institutions been modified by the
process of urbanization?

10. Does property ownership affect school truancy, divorce, or crime?
In what areas of the city and among which groups is crime endemic?

Most of these questions appear to be fairly simple. However, in 1916
little was systematically known about population and housing characteristics
or the ethnic and racial groups and the institutions of the city, and even
less was known about how a city actually operated. Therefore, Park's
emphasis on basic research as the focus of human ecology was well founded.

Park made yet another contribution to the field of sociology in the early
years of his career. The field of sociology as it is known today really did
not exist in 1916. Sociologists were involved in either philosophizing about
what society was or should be, or were concerned with social problems
and deviant forms of social behavior. Park's contribution to the field was
in placing the emphasis of his work on the study of "normal" behavior
and in conducting this research empirically. In other words, theories on
how society operated were to be tested in the real world. The character
of Park's research approach is clearly reflected in a quotation from a work
published after his death. Park states:

> I expect that I have actually covered more ground tramping about in
> cities in different parts of the world than any other living man. Out of all
> this, I gained among other things, a conception of the city, the community,
> and the region, not as a geographical phenomenon but as a kind of social
> organism (1952, p. 5).

Publications Park's research program was very successful. By the 1930s
a wealth of research had already been completed that directly addressed
many of the questions raised fifteen years earlier. The first of the studies
to reach book form was *The Hobo,* by Nels Anderson, published in 1923.

Anderson had experienced hobo life first hand before beginning his graduate studies at the University of Chicago in 1921. Park and his colleagues encouraged Anderson to capitalize on his unique experiences while pursuing his graduate studies. They saw in Anderson's research an opportunity to combine the study of a natural area common to most large cities, the hobo area, with the more general ecological and sociological topics of mobility, isolation, and disorganization. Anderson used no formal research technique in *The Hobo,* but rather provided informal descriptions of the hobos' lifestyle and the employment agencies, flophouses, and pawnshops that made up their world. Anderson's work was later augmented with more formal studies such as Harvey Zorbaugh's *The Gold Coast and the Slum,* published in 1929, and Edwin H. Sutherland and Harvey J. Locke's *10,000 Homeless Men,* published in 1936 (Faris, 1967, pp. 64–67).

The Hobo was the first volume in a series of books on urban ecology published by the University of Chicago Press. Books that followed included Fredrick Thrasher's *The Gang* (1927), Louis Wirth's *The Ghetto* (1928), Clifford Shaw's *Delinquency Areas* (1929), Harvey Zorbaugh's *The Gold Coast and the Slum* (1929), Cressey's *The Taxi Dance Hall* (1932), Clifford Shaw's *The Jackroller* (1930) and Faris and Dunham's *Mental Disorders in Urban Areas* (1939). These works taken as a whole give an important insight into the character and functioning of the early twentieth-century city.

Zorbaugh's *The Gold Coast and the Slum*

A good example of the kind of research carried out by the Chicago ecologists is found in one of the better-known works in the series, Harvey Zorbaugh's *The Gold Coast and the Slum,* published in 1929. The title of the book refers to the Near North Side, a one-square-mile area just north of what was at that time Chicago's central business district. Park and his colleagues were deeply interested in the real world, and the Near North Side was a perfect natural laboratory. For example, Zorbaugh found along the Gold Coast area adjacent to Lake Michigan the wealthiest and most influential families in Chicago and a few blocks to the west a concentration of the city's poorest—"Hobohemia." In addition, the Near North Side had a rooming-house district, a Greenwich Village-type of bohemian area, ethnic enclaves of Sicilians and Italians, and a rialto or "bright lights district." Zorbaugh describes the diversity of the area:

> (At this time in the Near North Side) live ninety thousand people, a population representing all types and contrasts that lend to a great city its glamour and romance. . . . (The area) has the highest residential land values in the city and among the lowest, it has more professional men, more politicians, more suicides, more persons in *Who's Who* than any other community in Chicago (Zorbaugh, 1929, pp. 507).

Photo 1.3 (*top*) Lake Shore Drive was photographed in 1926 from the top of the Drake Hotel. During the 1920s, many of Chicago's wealthiest and most influential families lived in the gracious homes and apartments that lined this street. Lake Shore Drive was the hub of the Gold Coast Area studied by Harvey Zorbaugh during this same decade. (Courtesy Chicago Historical Society, IChi-14143). (*bottom*) During the 1950s and 1960s many of the older mansions and apartments along

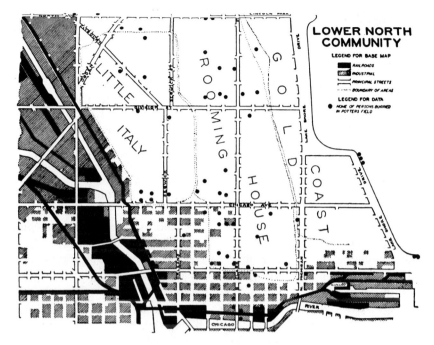

Fig. 1.1 Near North Side, the setting for *The Gold Coast and the Slum.*

Source: Reprinted from "Near North Side" from *The Gold Coast and the Slum* by H. Zorbaugh by permission of The University of Chicago Press © 1929.

Here in one small area was the diversity of a city in an exaggerated form that made it relatively easy to study.

Zorbaugh's approach in studying the area was twofold. First, he conducted a careful census of the number and types of people and institutions in the area to obtain a general picture of its "natural areas" or social worlds. Second, Zorbaugh carried out a form of sociological research known as participant observation—living, visiting, and observing in the various natural areas to gain an understanding of their functioning. As a result, Zorbaugh not only gives a picture of who lived in the Near North Side, but also an insight into the social processes and networks that had emerged there.

Zorbaugh devotes one chapter of his book to each of the six natural areas of the Near North Side. One of the more interesting is the Gold Coast, the area with the greatest concentration of wealth in Chicago.

Lake Shore Drive were demolished, and expensive highrise apartments were built in their place. This photograph taken in 1976 a few blocks north of the Drake Hotel shows the Mies Van Der Rohe Lake Shore Drive Apartments. The Hancock Center on Michigan Avenue is in the background.

Source: ©Paul Sequeira 1976, Photo Researchers, Inc.

The Gold Coast was Lake Shore Boulevard and two adjoining streets where 2,000 of the 6,000 families listed in Chicago's *Social Register* lived. The *Social Register* was a thin blue book containing a "complete list of Chicago's socially acceptable." How did a person become a member of the *Social Register* and therefore of high society? One member suggested that "one must not be employed, one must make application, and one must be above reproach." However, most of the members of high society had no idea how one's name was included in the *Register;* they accepted the "list of the chosen" without question.

Zorbaugh in his research uncovered the "social game" or social process of becoming a member of this exclusive list. It was actually very simple; all one had to do was be invited to a dinner party of one of the "well-established" society families. Having acomplished this feat, one would be included on other lists of social functions, asked to join certain clubs and, at the end of this process, perhaps included in the *Social Register.*

The crucial step in breaking into society was getting the first invitation. Ambitious nonmembers, Zorbaugh found, had developed a number of techniques for doing so. One of the most common techniques was using children as a means of social climbing. The climber would send his/her children to the same schools or move into the same apartment complex as established families with children of the same age. Hopefully a friendship would develop between the children and win an invitation for the parents. Another proven technique was to discover the pet charity of an upper-class woman and devote energy and money to the charity's projects; then, out of gratitude, one might be invited to a social engagement.

This "social game" and the upper-class' idleness; exorbitant expenditures on clothing, automobiles, and homes; and endless rounds of social engagements seem on the surface to be frivolous. Zorbaugh, however, found a more serious side of the Gold Coast inhabitants. In many respects, they were the only people in Chicago with sufficient wealth and leisure to support the arts and charities and to provide unremunerated civic leadership. Gold Coast people were led to such efforts in part by their strong conviction that people of means owed these works to "the less fortunate." Their benevolence, however, was tempered by the need to play the "social game" to retain their social positions.

There was a more disturbing side to this bastion of wealth. Zorbaugh found that the Gold Coast was by no means a true community. There was less group consciousness among members of the *Register* than one would expect. The general pattern was that families would socialize on a regular basis with ten to twelve other families and had little interest in other members of society. One informant, for example, prided herself on having lived next to the same upper-class family for more than twenty-five years without ever having met them. If one views this behavior in combination with the upperclass' continuous travels to Europe, summer retreats to Michigan, and winter vacations in the South, one can easily understand why many of the Gold Coast families suffered—like many of the less fortunate inhabitants of the Near North Side—from the loneliness and anonymity of the city.

Zorbaugh draws a much bleaker picture of the rest of the Near North Side. He describes the rooming-house district with its transient, childless, lonely, and suicide-prone population. On the west were the slums of Little Italy and Little Hell with their newly arrived immigrants eking out a bare existence. The "bright light" district along Clark Street featured open prostitution and tawdry cabarets. To the south on Clark Street were the used-clothing stores, pawnshops, and diners frequented by the derelicts of Hobohemia. The bohemians of the Village, by definition individuals living on the fringes of society, completed the picture.

The only features common to the diverse elements of the Near North Side were an absence of a sense of community and inability of the area to solve its own problems. A recurring problem of all societies is the maintenance of order; order was imposed on the Near North Side by the police and other formal institutions of the city of Chicago. Zorbaugh sums up his view of the Near North Side in the following statement:

> The isolation of the populations crowded together within these few
> hundred blocks, the superficiality and externality of their contacts, the so-
> cial distances that separate them, their absorption in the affairs of their
> own little worlds—these, and not mere size and numbers, constitute the
> social problem of the inner city. The community, represented by the town
> or peasant village where everyone knows everyone else clear down to the
> ground is gone. Over large areas of the city "community" is little more
> than a geographical expression. Yet the old tradition of control persists de-
> spite changed conditions of life. The inevitable result is cultural disorgani-
> zation (Zorbaugh, 1929, p. 16).

Theories and Research of the Chicago School

Titles of the major works of the Chicago School are indicative of the real-world interests of the researchers. For example, Shaw's *The Jackroller* (1930) is about the subculture of the mugger. Cressey's *The Taxi Dance Hall* (1932) explores the operation of the dime-a-dance halls that provided cover for prostitution then, much as some massage parlors do today. *The Hobo, The Gang,* and *The Ghetto* also examine problems still found today.

Taken as a whole, these works give the impression that the Chicago ecologists were interested only in the seamier side of urban life, and to a degree the impression is correct. The small towns and rural areas in which Park and the other major figures in the Chicago School were raised shaped their value systems and impressions of what a community should be (Hinkle, 1954). Their own background clashed with the value systems and conditions in the city they chose to study throughout their professional careers. Chicago in the 1920s was a new city and one of the fastest growing centers in the world. The problems Chicago faced in coping with rapid growth, an ethnically diverse population, and the negative by-products of industrialization led to an interest in the social disorganization and deviancy associated with urbanization. The Chicago ecologists also had strong ties to the reform movements of the day and felt that the knowledge gained in their area studies could contribute to the solution of problems. The limited scope of the area studies eventually led them to shift the emphasis of their work to developing general theories to explain social disorganization and models designed to explain urban growth and change. This work was fundamental to the understanding of processes operating in the urban sphere.

Wirth's Urbanism as a Way of Life

An example of the more theoretical work of the Chicago School is Louis Wirth's essay, "Urbanism as a Way of Life," first published in 1939.[4] Most urban sociologists consider this important essay to be a synthesis of much of the earlier works of the Chicago ecologists. Wirth also provides in this article a general model for the social disorganization studied by his colleagues. Drawing from the rich heritage of the Chicago School, Wirth analyzed the ecological and demographic structure of the city and then considered the psychological or behavioral consequences of living there. These consequences formed a new way of life that Wirth called *urbanism*.

Urbanism is an ideal type. An *ideal type* is a methodological idea first introduced by Max Weber that summarizes the general characteristics of an entire category of phenomena. Ideal types do not attempt to describe each member of a group perfectly but rather they summarize the "essential" characteristics of the group. Researchers use a form of ideal type when they conduct market surveys to determine who the "typical" buyer of a product is. Similarly, in day-to-day life we often make up stereotypes of people and things in our environment to try to make things more understandable. Sociologists do essentially this same thing when they construct ideal types, carefully analyzing the characteristics of a category of social things (in Wirth's case large cities) and then identifying those qualities that best describe the entire group.

To Wirth, the three most distinguishing characteristics of cities were (1) their large size, (2) their great density, and (3) their heterogeneous population. These qualities stand in sharp contrast to the traditional rural-folk societies that Wirth used for comparison. These variables that we term "ecological" in turn explain the unique social forms and psychological patterns found in the city. We should note that although Wirth analyzed the effects of size, density, and heterogeneity as distinct and independent ecological variables, he recognized that the three were interdependent in the real world.

Consequences of size In Wirth's view, as the size of a city's population increases, there is also an increase in the variety of people living there.

Because these diverse types of people are involved in the ecological processes of competition and cooperation, individuals will, over time, come together to form groups similar in their racial, ethnic, occupational, and social-status characteristics. These groups are highly differentiated, yet if the community is to survive they must also be interdependent. The result is that, over time, a complex set of commensal and symbiotic relationships develops among these groups.

Nowhere is this social complexity seen more clearly than in the spatial complexity of the city. Social differentiation leads to increased spatial segregation among the wide variety of racial, ethnic, social-status, and occupational groups found in the city. The city becomes a "mosaic of social worlds" but with a major consequence—this increased social complexity weakens the traditional bonds of kinship, neighborhood, and family. In their place develops a new set of techniques for maintaining order—formal social controls. Therefore, according to Wirth, our laws, courts and police departments, bureaucracies, professional codes of conduct, mass media, and modern corporations are inevitable byproducts of urbanism because they serve essential functions. They order and clarify roles, simplify economic and personal relationships, and structure the complex ecological system called the city.

Accompanying this movement toward increased dependency on formal social controls is a second set of relationships stemming directly from increased population size. Any human grouping, whether it be a city or a college campus, that grows beyond several hundred persons limits the possibility that each member can know all others personally. Although urban dwellers daily come in contact with far more people than their rural counterparts, they have less knowledge of these people and their contacts are often impersonal and superficial. In short, urbanites have many acquaintances, but few friends. Secondary relationships replace primary ones. Most important, people no longer interact with their entire personalities, but rather interaction is limited to those elements associated with a specific role. Consequently, in these relationships people often are considered "things" to be used for some personal end. Gone in these relationships are the pleasures of spontaneous, open, self-expression normally found in primary groups. Gone too, are the obligations and the controls on behavior that primary groups afford—the way traditional societies maintained order. It is the disappearance of this control function of the primary groups, along with the disintegration of a common moral order, that Wirth viewed as a major source of the social disorganization that the Chicago ecologists felt characterized the urban milieu.

Consequences of density Density reinforces the effects of size. For example, a person moving from a small town to a city would experience a shift from mostly primary to a mixture of primary and secondary relationships, informal to formal means of control, as well as an increase in the number of strangers encountered in day-to-day living. Moreover, in the city, strangers are in closer physical proximity because of high density, and according to Wirth this has major consequences.

First, the large number of people living at high density in the city means that the individual is under a constant barrage of stimuli. In order to function in this environment the individual must filter or screen out all but the most important stimuli. The urbanite becomes insensitive to personal differences and becomes increasingly dependent on visual clues to direct behavior. A policeman's uniform, someone's dress and grooming, and other visual symbols of status are used to determine the appropriate behavior in a given social situation. The so-called blasé attitude that characterizes the personalities of many urbanites is both a response to this "stimulus overload" and a manifestation of the desire of urbanites to protect themselves from the personal demands of strangers.

Second, Wirth's work suggests that repeated physical proximity with strangers, combined with the predominance of secondary relationships and the urbanite's blasé attitude, fosters a pervasive spirit of competition and exploitation. Constant crowding among socially distant people gives rise to elevated levels of anxiety that often are expressed as conflicts between individuals (assaults, murders) and violence within—and between—groups (race riots, gang wars).

Third, the nervous tension and anxiety that often accompany the urban way of life are accentuated by the rapid pace and complicated technology of the city. The tempo and technology are necessary so that predictable routines can be followed by the city's mass of unrelated individuals. Without these devices, there would be unchecked competition, and exploitation and chaos would prevail. The clock and the traffic signal are symbolic of the formal technological controls that impose order on an otherwise chaotic situation.

Consequences of heterogeneity The chief social consequence of urban heterogeneity is its impact on the class structure. In folk-rural societies the class structure is rigid; the social class of the family of one's birth determines one's class standing for life. This is not to say vertical social mobility is absent in traditional societies, but it is rare.

In sharp contrast are urban societies where increased heterogeneity leads to increased social interaction among the rich variety of personality types found in the city. The social interaction among these diverse individuals breaks down rigid class distinctions and greatly complicates the social stratification system. Moreover, social mobility is common within the urban milieu. As a result of these changes, traditional ties to family and neighborhood are weaker, and a different pattern of group affiliations emerges.

In traditional societies, membership in one group automatically entailed membership in larger, more encompassing groups. Membership in a family in such societies would automatically confer membership in the clan, village community, and tribe. These memberships, moreover, are compatible and encompass all the roles the individual is expected to play in life. These roles are therefore fixed and compatible and provide the individual with both a stable place in the social order and a stable personality stemming from an absence of role conflict.

In contrast, group affiliations in urban societies are often unrelated and transitory and are based on the interests of the individual. More often than not, membership in one group is totally unrelated to membership in another. For example, a student could be a member of a fraternity or sorority, an honorary society, and a sports team and not share the same group affiliations with any other person on campus. More important is the fact that turnover in these groups is high, and since people define who they are—their "selves"—through these intersecting group memberships, urbanites are in a continual process of defining and redefining who they are. In addition, the urbanite will often find him/herself with contradictory or conflicting roles.

As a result of both a highly mobile social structure, and fluctuating group memberships, the urban personality structure becomes fluid, detached, and disintegrated. The term *anomie* has been developed to describe the state of society in which the normative standards of conduct and belief are weak and individuals suffer from disorientation, anxiety, and isolation.

How does urban society composed of people who have highly fragmented and diverse personality types maintain order? The answer is that a successful society structures itself using the lowest common denominator— institutions and facilities adjust to the needs of the average person. Mass media, mass production, and mass education have all adjusted to mass requirements. This "leveling" tendency of urban society and the accompanying fluid nature of the urban personality were viewed by Wirth as a direct consequence of the increased heterogeneity of the urban population.

In summary, Louis Wirth posited that the growing size, density, and heterogeneity of the urban environment led directly to a variety of changes in the social structure of the city and the urban personality. Most important of these changes were the growing importance of secondary relationships over primary ones and the role of formal social controls in maintaining order within the city. Consequently, the social disorganization that had been a major theme in the early works of the Chicago School was seen as a predictable outcome of the shifts in the three ecological variables—size, density, and heterogeneity.

Critics of the Chicago School

The Chicago School made significant contributions not only to the understanding of the early twentieth century city, but also to the entire field of sociology. Inevitably, the free exchange of ideas led to differences of opinion. During the 1930s and the decades that followed numerous articles were published questioning the concepts and theoretical underpinnings of the classical Chicago School. The role of criticism in the development of any body of knowledge is evident in the works written in response to Wirth's essay.

Critics of Wirth Wirth's theory contends that ecological factors—the concentration of large, heterogeneous populations—lead to the weakening of primary relationships, psychological stress, and dependence on formal means of social control. The ultimate consequences of these processes are alienation, disorganization, and deviant behavior. Yet in the 1940s and later decades a number of urban researchers discovered closeknit primary groups thriving in the centers of the largest cities (Gans, 1962; Jonassen, 1949; Whyte, 1943). Moreover, the "urban villages" appear to have been shaped not by ecological but by nonecological factors such as ethnicity, life cycle, and social class. In general, these researchers took exception to Wirth's theory and argued that no particular social effects could be attributed to ecological factors. There were serious flaws in this nonecological position, however, and nonecological factors alone could not account for the diversity of behavioral and cultural patterns found in the city.

In 1975, Claude Fisher combined the ecological and nonecological positions into a single theory. Fisher suggests that ecological factors contribute to social disorganization, alienation, and deviancy but not in the way hypothesized by Wirth. Fisher posits that ecological factors, instead of having a direct effect on social disorganization and deviancy, are mediated by the nonecological factors of class, ethnicity, race, etc. Urbanism, in other words, brings about a large enough concentration of persons "to maintain viable unconventional subcultures. It is the behavioral expression of those subcultures which come to be called 'deviant' " (p. 1332).

The foregoing point is important and needs elaboration. An increase in the size of a city's population results in an increase in the number and types of groups within its population. Groups similar in occupation, class, stage in the life cycle, etc., through time develop distinguishable subcultures. More important, the social differences that emerge are reflected in the differential use of space within the city. This usage can take the form of an ethnic neighborhood or the exclusive patronage of a bar or restaurant by a subculture, e.g., "gay bars," "singles bars," etc. The urban landscape therefore is a mosaic of social worlds and within each are subcultures with their own beliefs, values, norms, and customs. Subcultures with large populations may even build their own churches, schools, banks, fraternal organizations, and newspapers and thus reinforce the exclusionary character of the group. In this sense the city, rather than being normless, is a complex aggregation of divergent normative systems.

An individual faced with a problem or decision normally would select a solution from his/her immediate social surroundings or subculture. If the solution is the same as the one prescribed by the larger society there is no problem; but if the solution conflicts, the individual's behavior and the subculture that supports it would be labeled deviant. A good example is the juvenile gang. Within the context of this subculture, mugging, purse snatching, and breaking-and-entering would be considered acceptable behavior. From the perspective of the larger society, such behavior would be considered deviant.

Therefore, social disorganization and deviancy are explained largely by nonecological factors, whereas ecological factors (size, density, heterogeneity) are important in explaining subcultures. For example, a small town may have a few delinquent youths, but only in a larger city will there be sufficient numbers to establish a delinquent subculture. In general, the more urban a place, the larger the number of subcultures and the higher the probability of unconventional deviant subcultures.

Critics of the biotic and cultural The Fischer work is one example of criticism of the Chicago School. Other critics disagreed with other concepts and theoretical points. By far the most devastating criticism of the classical position is found in a work by Milla Alihan, *Social Ecology,* published in 1938. Alihan scrutinized the works of the Chicago School and noted in her book that these ecologists could not demonstrate empirically which aspects of human behavior were purely biotic and which were purely cultural. In other words, she could not find the two levels of society hypothesized by Park. Other critics, August Hollingshead (1947) and W. E. Gettys (1940), made the same point and thus weakened the theoretical underpinnings of the classical school.

During the same period Gehlke and Biehl (1934) and Robinson (1950) attacked the research of the Chicago School on statistical grounds. Hatt in 1946 showed that the concept of natural area—such as the Gold Coast and the slum—did not apply to the city of Seattle.

By 1950 the Chicago School had weathered more than two decades of criticism and had been dramatically modified. Some of the theories and concepts had been found to be invalid. The members of this classical school, however, were pioneers in a new and exciting field and had made the mistakes of pioneers. Their work is as readable today as it was fifty years ago and gives a personal insight into the structures and people of a city of the past. The ethnographic studies of this school are also of great value to historians. And more important, the pioneering work of the classical ecologists formed the foundation on which the modern field of ecology is built.

HUMAN ECOLOGY TODAY

During the 1930s and early 1940s interest in human ecology generally declined in the United States. This decline is explained, in part, by the national preoccupation with the events of the Great Depression and World War II.

In addition, in the field of sociology itself, other theoretical approaches were coming into vogue. The underlying soundness of the ecological approach, however, is shown by the reemergence of interest in the field in the late 1940s and early 1950s. By 1950 few researchers agreed with the Chicago or classical ecologists that society is composed of two elements, the cultural and the biotic, but this dichotomy continues to influence contemporary ecology. Those researchers who place primary emphasis on cultural variables are referred to as *sociocultural ecologists*. A second group known as *neoorthodox ecologists* are closer to the classical ecologists in emphasizing ecological rather than cultural factors in their theories (Theodorson, 1961, p. 129).

Sociocultural Approach

The sociocultural approach emphasizes the role of culture and values in explaining the location of groups and institutions within cities. The application of this approach to the analysis of land use patterns is shown in a book by Walter Firey (1947), *Land Use in Central Boston*. Firey argues that the classical ecologists placed too much emphasis on impersonal ecological forces and too little on the role of sentiment and symbolism in human affairs. Specifically, Firey shows how "sentiments" significantly influence the ecological processes in Boston. In a series of case studies, Firey illustrates that the land uses in many areas of Boston differ significantly from predictions made by the classical ecologists. Boston's Beacon Hill, for example, is a residential area only a few minutes' walking distance from the city's central business district. According to the "classical models" this residential area should be declining physically while commercial activities gradually take over. In reality, it is one of the most prestigious residential areas in Boston, inhabited by many of Boston's old, established families. Similarly, both the Boston Common and the King's Chapel Burying Ground areas are centrally located and of great commercial value, but sentiment based on their historic character has prevented more profitable uses being made of the land.

Support for the sociocultural approach has also come from a large number of studies on the spatial patterning of various ethnic groups within the city. Jonassen (1961), Meyers (1961), Gans (1962), and others have shown that both the initial selection of a residential location and the continued existence of ethnic enclaves are related to a host of cultural factors including preferred family forms, religious and political affiliation, and their degrees of acceptance by the urban community. Therefore, members of the sociocultural school maintain that an understanding of the spatial patterning of groups and institutions within cities is possible only if culture and values are made central to ecological theory (Timms, 1971, pp. 91–93).

Neoorthodox Approach

The neoorthodox approach is more important than the sociocultural in contemporary ecology. This approach had its beginning in 1950 with the publication of Amos Hawley's *Human Ecology,* a restatement of the classical or Chicago School's position. In *Human Ecology,* Hawley clarifies concepts and works out the theoretical weaknesses that had been identified by Alihan, Hollingshead, and others some years earlier.

One major weakness of the classical position was Park's insistence that there are two levels of society—*biotic* and *cultural*—and that the biotic is the proper focus of human ecology. Hawley agreed that there are forces and processes over which humans have little control, but disagreed with Park on the notion that cultural phenomena are outside the scope of human ecology. Hawley argued that the human being, like any other animal, must adapt to the environment or face extinction. Ants, for example, have adapted to their environments by developing an elaborate social structure based on a division of labor—as has humankind. People, in addition, have developed sophisticated technologies and other cultural elements in adapting to the environment. Therefore, Hawley viewed human social organization, technology, and culture as nothing more than one of the many types of adaptive mechanisms found in nature.

Hawley's ecological approach differed from Park's in other respects. It focused primarily on the present form and evolution of the *community.* Hawley saw community as the one unit of analysis where all the key elements of society are present in a relatively small geographic area that can be easily studied. Moreover, he defined "community" as the complex system of interdependence that develops as a population collectively adapts to an environment. The key word in this definition is "interdependence." The Chicago School was concerned with social disorganization and conflict. Hawley, in contrast, was impressed with the community's ability to remain in a stable state until disrupted by an outside influence. Hawley therefore provided numerous hypotheses on the structure, functioning, and changes of the community system and in so doing provided the theoretical framework for much of present-day ecological research.

Duncan's POET Approach

Contemporary ecologists' emphasis on the community system is reflected in their use of a research device called the *ecological complex.* The ecological complex is a notion introduced by Duncan in 1959 and involves four reference variables—population, organization, environment, and technology (POET). These categories of variables provide the ecologist with a means of simplifying and identifying clusters of relationships in the initial exploration of any ecosystem (Duncan, 1973, p. 111). As Figure 1.2 sug-

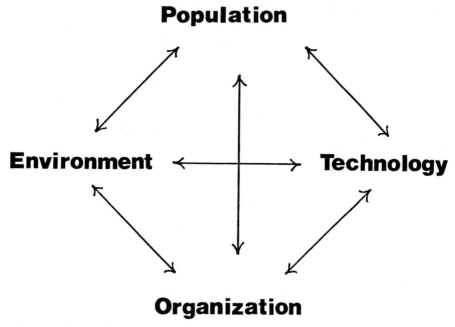

Fig. 1.2 Ecological complex.

gests, the reference variables are a part of a complex interdependent system. With this device the ecologist can follow the direct and indirect effects of change throughout a system. If, for example, the ecologist discovers changes in one element—population—there will be ramifications for the other elements in the complex.

The reference variables are defined very broadly by the ecologist and can be measured precisely only when they are applied to a specific system.

The first variable, *population,* is defined broadly as a structured group of human beings that functions routinely as a unit. The specific character-istics of the population—size and composition—vary with the unit under study. The population of a neighborhood obviously would be very different from the population of an entire community.

The second variable, *organization,* is defined as those structures devel-oped by a population to sustain itself in an environment. Looking at the existing societies in the world, one is impressed by the variety of organi-zational adaptations that different societies have made to overcome the same problems of survival.

Environment is probably the most crucial of the four reference variables, because it determines the broad limits within which populations must adapt. The term "environment" is defined as all phenomena external to a pop-ulation, including other social systems, that influence it. Moreover, the environment is the sole source of raw materials. Ultimately the characteristics of the environment determine the size of a population and the nature of its adaptation.

The environment can be modified drastically by the fourth variable, *technology*. Technology consists of the skills, tools, and artifacts employed by a population in adapting to its environment. A technological artifact such as the telephone or computer can modify organization, which in turn can affect a population's ability to exploit its environment.

To demonstrate the utility of the concepts, the ecological complex can be applied to a present-day problem—a two-year drought in the San Francisco Bay area.

Much of Northern California is classified as semiarid, receiving most of its twenty inches of annual rainfall during the fall and winter months. The large population living in the Bay Area and the intensive agriculture in all of Northern California are made possible only by a complex system of reservoirs, aqueducts, and irrigation ditches which store and distribute water during the dry months. In this case, technology mediates the effects of environment on the population (T→E→P).

The value of the reservoir system is demonstrated by the fact that although a drought began in 1975, the Bay Area had adequate water supplies until the spring of 1977 (T→E). Then, within a few months, reservoir levels dropped dangerously low and water rationing was instituted in many communities (O→P). The rationing guidelines not only limited the number of gallons of water each family could consume, but also restricted and in some cases outlawed the practices of watering lawns, filling swimming pools, and hosing sidewalks (O→E).

The response of residents to water rationing was remarkable. Many families cut their water consumption so drastically that the pumps used to drain the reservoirs could no longer operate (P→T). In turn, low water consumption significantly reduced the income of the water companies, making it impossible for them to meet their operating budgets (P→O). Ironically, many water companies had to actively encourage water consumption during the drought (O→P).

If the drought were to continue, forest fires would ravage Northern California (E→E), farmers would face financial ruin without irrigation water (E→P), and eventually the Bay Area would not be able to support its present population (E→P). A declining population would alleviate environmental pressures (P→E), but would cause major adjustment problems for industry, business, and government (P→O).

The foregoing scenario illustrates the utility of the ecological complex. The POET framework enables the human ecologist to examine systematically a wide range of phenomena. Moreover, the reference variables ensure that the crucial variables operating in any system will be included in the analysis.[5]

Areas of Research

Contemporary human ecology is the area of the social sciences concerned with the interrelationships of the four variables in the ecological complex—population, organization, environment, and technology. Human ecologists study a wide variety of urban phenomena, but their work can be divided into two broad categories. One is the study of the fundamental urbanization process and the relationships that develop through time among cities in the same region. The other is the study of the fundamental processes that shape the internal structure of the city.

The urbanization process The question for one group of ecologists is, "Why cities?" A city represents one of the many adaptations that a population can make to an environment, and the goal of ecologists is to better understand this adaptation process. To this end, a number of ecologists have studied the environmental, technological, and organizational changes that occurred 6,000 years ago to permit the emergence of the first cities. The work of others in this group has been more basic, focusing on the development of urban concepts, definitions, and measures to facilitate the study of the urbanization process. In recent years, ecologists have expanded their research to include the role of urban places in the modernization and economic development process.

Also included in this category are those ecologists who are concerned with the spatial patterning of cities and the complex interrelationships that develop among systems of cities. These researchers have developed theories to explain why a city emerges at one location and not another and why the population of some cities grows and that of others remains unchanged. Other ecologists have tried to analyze systematically the functions of various types of cities and the contribution each makes to the overall operation of a system of cities.

The internal structure of the city A second group of investigators are interested in the distribution of population characteristics, organizations, activities, and behaviors across the urban landscape. These ecologists are not only interested in the spatial distribution of these characteristics but also the processes by which these patterns emerge.[6] A good analogy is to think of the city as a giant chessboard with the city's population as its pieces. The ecologist studies the location and movement of the different pieces to discover the underlying ecological processes.

Much of the research on the internal structure of the city is organized around one of several ecological models. A model, basically, is a simplified representation of some phenomenon. An investigator in constructing a model identifies its key features and determines how these features are interrelated. In the process of building a model, the researcher learns more about the operation of the phenomenon and may also use the model to predict how the larger system operates under certain circumstances.

The dozens of models that describe the form or processes of the city can be grouped according to their focus. For example, some investigators construct models to emphasize the characteristics of urban subareas in terms of their land use or type of neighborhood. Others stress the characteristics of urban subpopulations, the concentration and location of racial, ethnic, and income groups in the city.

Three major groups of models have as their focus the characteristics of urban subareas: (1) classical models, (2) factorial models, and (3) density models. The *classical models* include the concentric zone model, the sector model, and the multiple nuclei model. The models differ, but each attempts to explain citywide land use patterns, that is, why one type of land use is found at the city's center and another at its periphery and how a city's structure changes as its population grows. Although the models predict different urban structures, each is based on the underlying assumption that these patterns are the result of impersonal competition in the urban land market. Moreover, these models are classical in the sense that they were the first, and as such they stimulated much of the present research on the internal structure of the city.

The second group of ecological models, *factorial models,* are based on the mathematical technique called factor analysis. Factor analysis enables researchers to determine the underlying characteristics of neighborhoods in cities around the world. In the United States and the more developed world, subareas of cities can be classified by measures of the areas' social, family, and ethnic characteristics. In Third World cities there are fewer neighborhood types and the classification system is simpler. The major contribution of the factorial models to human ecology has been in the analysis of the relationship between a society's level of economic development and the use of space within its cities.

The third set of models, *density models,* explore the density of urban population at various points in the city. Researchers have found that in all cities in the world, population density declines in a regular fashion from a city's center to its periphery. Investigators have developed sophisticated mathematical models to describe these patterns and their changes through time. In addition, researchers on density have become increasingly concerned with the relationship between population density and human pathology. There is evidence that density levels affect the life styles and well-being of urbanites. As a result, a number of models have been developed to study this relationship.

Two major sets of models are used to study the characteristics of urban subpopulations: segregation models and group location models. *Segregation models* focus on the segregation of racial, ethnic, and status groups across the residential areas of a city. Investigators using these models have found that the social difference among groups is reflected in the physical distances between their residential locations. In other words, the greater the social distance between two groups, the farther apart their neighborhoods. Three factors account for the segregation of a particular group: (1) the social status differences between groups in terms of their income, occupation, and educational characteristics, (2) self-selection, or people seeking out others of the same racial, ethnic, or social status group when searching for a home; and (3) subtle or overt discrimination against a group in the housing market. The majority of the studies on segregation have attempted to measure levels of segregation in cities in the United States and to identify the factors most responsible for the segregation of a particular group.

Group location models represent the physical location of populations in urban space, generally in terms of the position of a particular group in relationship to the city's central business district. The term *centralization* is used in these models to describe the extent to which groups are concentrated in the central city or are dispersed toward the city's periphery. The position of groups in relationship to the city's center is attributed to many of the same factors identified in the segregation models, e.g., social status, self-selection, and discrimination factors. Factors such as neighborhood physical condition, quality and composition of the city's housing stock, and the age of the city are also included in many of the group location models. Segregation and group location models show different aspects of the same phenomenon. Segregation models determine the degree to which groups are concentrated and isolated in a metropolis, whereas group location models determine the groups' relative locations.

Organization of the Text

The following chapters are organized around the topics and models currently of concern to human ecologists. The organization of the text corresponds to the two major research areas of the discipline. Part I and Part II address the urbanization process and the external relationships that develop among cities over time. In these sections, the ecological perspective is applied to the examination of the urbanization process, the origin of cities, and the location and functions of cities. Part III explores the internal structure of the city and three of the major ecological models. Classical, factorial, and group locational models are described with emphasis on United States cities but with a discussion of international patterns. In the final section of the text, the ecological perspective is used to examine the consequences and responses to urbanization. In this section, topics such as the community, segregation, density, and the role of government in dealing with the problems of the city are explored.

SUMMARY AND CONCLUSION

Ecology is the branch of science concerned with the interrelationships of organisms and their environment. The field of ecology has its roots in the nineteenth-century works of Darwin and other natural scientists who discovered the operation of complex interrelated food systems. The terminology, theories, and methods they developed to study these natural systems were later used to study human societies. The close parallel between biological ecology and human ecology is demonstrated in their shared terminology. Terms such as *environment, ecosystem, commensalism, symbiosis, dominance,* and *invasion-succession* have the same meaning in both disciplines.

The father of human ecology in the United States is Robert Park, a member of the Department of Sociology and Anthropology at the University of Chicago from 1914–1933. Although Park believed that the general ecological approach could be used to study human societies, he felt that certain characteristics of human beings required the ecological model to be used with caution. Humankind's culture, reason, and unique ability to use language permit a social organization and intergroup relationships not possible in other animal species. For this reason, Park made a distinction between the biotic and cultural levels of society. The biotic level was viewed as the foundation of society, the level at which society adapted to its physical environment. The cultural level rested upon the biotic foundation and was a system composed of the norms, values, and institutions of society. Park believed that human ecology should focus on the basic adaptive processes of society—the processes that occur at the biotic level.

In his article "The City: Suggestions for the Investigation of Human Behavior in the Urban Environment," published in 1916, Park launched a research program that was to occupy the Chicago School for the next two decades. This research program led to the publication of dozens of books on the city, indirectly addressing many of Park's research questions. The majority of these works were written about groups (*The Hobo*), subareas (*The Ghetto, The Gold Coast and the Slum*), or urban institutions (*The Taxi Dance Hall*). Other articles and books addressed urban theory and process, such as Wirth's "Urbanism As a Way of Life."

The work of the Chicago or classical ecologists drew criticism. In particular, Milla Alihan was able to demonstrate that the biotic/cultural distinction made by Park was wrong and that it did not exist in reality. Although most modern ecologists agree with Alihan's criticism, the biotic/cultural dichotomy continues to influence contemporary ecology. Sociocultural ecologists place primary emphasis on cultural factors in their research, but neoorthodox ecologists are closer to the classical school in emphasizing the role of ecological factors in their analysis of urban structure and change.

The neoorthodox approach is dominant in contemporary ecology. It is largely concerned with the interrelationships of four variables in the ecological complex—population, organization, environment, and technology. Human ecologists use this framework to study two broad aspects of the city. One is the urbanization process and the complex relationships among cities in the same region. This aspect is explored in the chapters on "The Urbanization Process," "The Origin of Cities," "The Location of Cities," and "The Classification of Cities" in Part I and Part II of the text.

The second aspect is the internal structure of the city. Related research is organized around five general ecological models—classical, factorial, density, segregation, and group location models. The chapters in Part III and Part IV examine these basic models, and the final chapter explores the relevance of the ecological perspective to urban policy research.

NOTES

1. Darwin's works also influenced a group of social philosophers called social evolutionists. The social evolutionists sought to use Darwin's scientific principles to explain the operation of the social world. They noted that although human societies are more complex than nature's, human societies are composed of living beings organized into specialized and functionally interdependent groups. More importantly, these groups are organized into a society that maintains order. Hence, the social evolutionists reasoned that if there were an unplanned order in human societies, it must be some type of "biotic" or unplanned natural force. Park was influenced by social evolutionism but applied it cautiously to his own work.

2. Social evolutionism dominated much of nineteenth-century social thought in both the United States and Europe. These social philosophers believed that all societies evolve from relatively simple to increasingly complex forms. Society could be viewed as an organism: social institutions were the organs and citizens were the cells.

3. There is a similarity between Park's article and works published at the same time by the survey movement. The survey movement arose in the late nineteenth and early twentieth centuries when a group of social reformers known as the "muckrakers" began studying the social problems of the cities. Although these studies were not scientifically conducted, they were first-hand accounts of the poverty, government corruption, and deplorable sanitary conditions in the new industrial centers. Among these works were Jacob Riis's *How the Other Half Lives* (1890) and *Battle With the Slums* (1902), which describe slum conditions in New York; Lincoln Steffen's *The Shame of the Cities* (1904), a first-hand observation of government corruption in seven large American cities; and Upton Sinclair's novel *The Jungle* (1906), which describes the conditions of the meat-packing industry. These works profoundly affected American social legislation. They were written, however, by journalists and novelists and were based on personal impressions rather than scientific fact.

   One consequence of muckraking was that some social scientists became convinced that a program of social reform would have to be based on verifiable facts rather than impressions. The work of these researchers came to be known as the "survey movement." In general they used the same research methods in the more than 2,700 projects they completed between 1900 and 1927. Their goal was a collection of minute, verifiable facts as the basis for reform.

4. The discussion of Wirth's article is based in part on the analysis found in Michael P. Smith, "Louis Wirth and Urban Social Order," in *The City and Social Theory* (New York: St. Martin's Press, 1979), chap. 1.
5. For an excellent criticism of the ecological complex, see Sidney M. Willhelm, "The Concept of the Ecological Complex: A Critique," *American Journal of Economics and Sociology* 23, no. 1 (1964): 241–248.
6. The following is based on an article by Kent P. Schwirian, "Some Recent Trends and Methodological Problems in Urban Ecological Research," in *Comparative Urban Structure*, ed. K. P. Schwirian (Lexington, Mass.: D. C. Heath and Co., 1974).

CHAPTER TWO

The Process of Urbanization

Statement of Objectives

1. The student should understand the problems associated with forming the concept of urbanization. Students should know the definition of urbanization adopted for use in this text.

2. The student should understand the problems associated with measuring urbanization.

3. The student should become aware of the problems associated with primate cities, especially when they exist in less developed countries.

4. The student should become aware of the enormous variation in world patterns of urbanization and in the approaches used to study them.

5. The close relationship between the processes of urbanization and economic development should be examined.

6. Some estimate should be formed of the path the urbanization process will take in less developed countries.

Paging through any major work on cities exposes the reader to many new terms—"megalopolis," "metropolis," "SMSA," "urban," and "urbanization." The use of these terms in the literature is often confusing because not all authors use a given term to mean the same things. More than one student of the city has suggested that our inability to cope with urban problems may derive from our inability to define the problems clearly in the first place (Eldridge, 1956; Anderson, 1959; Downs, 1973). This chapter explores the conceptual and measurement problems associated with the urbanization process. In addition, worldwide patterns of urbanization are examined, as well as the relationship or urbanization to the processes of modernization and economic development.

DEFINING URBANIZATION

The conceptual problems associated with the term "urbanization" are not new. In "The Process of Urbanization" (1956), Hope Tisdale Eldridge systematically reviewed the urban sociology literature and found the term "urbanization" used three different ways. At various times, Eldridge reported, urbanization has been defined as (1) a process of diffusion, by which certain characteristics of cities spread to outlying areas; (2) a process of intensification, by which various urban activities or qualities became more frequent; and (3) a process of population concentration.

Diffusion

The *diffusion* definition of urbanization refers to the process whereby urban characteristics spread through time to nonurban areas. These characteristics include norms, values, beliefs, inventions, and innovations. Typically, slang expressions such as "rip-off," fads such as the hula-hoop and skateboard, and dress and hair styles originate in cities but eventually are shared by many Americans.

A use of the diffusion definition of urbanization can be found in a study of birth rates in the USSR (Casetti and Dempko, 1975). Between 1940 and 1965, the Moscow and Leningrad regions showed significant declines in birth rate. Many factors can cause such a decline, but demographers believed that this particular decline reflected a desire on the part of Russian women for smaller families. In 1940, Leningrad had a birth rate significantly lower than that of the surrounding countryside (see Figure 2.1); in general, the greater the distance from Leningrad, the higher the birth rate. Slowly the low fertility norms spread from Moscow and Leningrad, until by 1965 the birth rates had declined by half in the region. The greater the distance from Moscow and Leningrad, the slower the adoption of the low fertility norms. In this context, *urbanization* means the spread of urban traits and characteristics to nonurban areas.

Intensification

The second concept of urbanization Eldridge identified is *intensification,* a notion that originated in the works of various nineteenth-century sociologists and which has been revised in recent years.[1] Emile Durkheim, for example, believed that the concentration in cities of diverse ethnic, racial, and occupational groups leads to a state he called dynamic density (Durkheim, 1949). He suggested that high dynamic density increases the number of contacts between people per unit of time, say, per hour; thus it is conducive to rapid social change or to an intensification of urban traits. Why? If a group of people with diverse skills, education, and heritage are in a state of high dynamic density, the odds are enhanced for ideas coming together to form an innovation. In contrast, in a rural setting where the

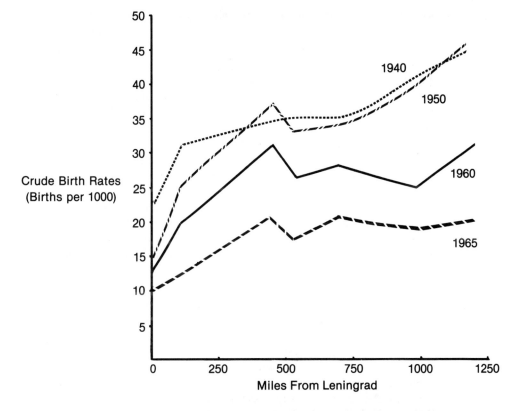

Fig. 2.1 Diffusion of low fertility norms, Leningrad region, 1940–1965.

Source: Adapted from G. Demko and E. Casetti, *A Diffusion Model of Fertility Decline.* Columbus, Ohio State University, 1975, Appendix 2.

population is homogeneous and widely dispersed and interacts infrequently, innovation is less likely to occur. Nor is the need for innovation as great. Innovation is not the only by-product of dynamic density, however; conflict and related urban problems may also ensue.

Population Concentration

The last definition of urbanization Eldridge found in the urban literature is demographic, based on the process of *population concentration*. Urbanization in this sense can proceed in one of two ways—either by an increase in the number of points of concentration (the number of cities) or by population increase in existing cities. This view of urbanization also involves the process of population redistribution—the reshuffling of people between and within urban areas and between rural and urban areas.

This definition may seem overly simple, but it is the one Eldridge and many other urban ecologists prefer. One reason is that a definition of urbanization should describe the process that results in the creation of cities. Both the intensification and the diffusion definitions assume the prior existence of cities; they cannot account for the emergence of the phenomenon they supposedly describe. Another way of looking at it is: what would one call the process of population concentration if not urbanization?

Although one still finds all three definitions used interchangeably in the urban literature, in this book we will consider urbanization to be the process of population concentration.

Therefore, for our purposes, size is the most important criterion for defining a place as urban. Some ecologists, however, argue that it should not be the only one—*urbanism* also must be present. By the most common definition, urbanism refers to the life styles, changes in social structure, and modifications of interpersonal relationships that result from urbanization (Wirth, 1938). These characteristics, however, are difficult and expensive to measure and are seldom included in a country's official definition of urban. Urbanism accompanies the urbanization process, and in future chapters this relationship will be explored.

MEASURING URBANIZATION

Just as urban sociologists lack consensus about the definition of urbanization, they fail to agree how it should be measured. Essentially, two problems emerge when we attempt to measure urbanization. First, how great a population concentration is necessary to constitute an urban place— 2,000, 10,000, or 100,000 people? Second, once a population figure has been agreed upon, how does one go about delimiting the city's boundaries? In short: What is *urban*?

For the past twenty-five years, the United Nations has been attempting to formulate a set of standard measures for urbanization as a basis for international comparisons. This attempt has been frustrated by the more than thirty types of definitions of urban now in use in the world. An analysis of these definitions, however, shows that they fit into three broad categories.

The most widely used definition of urban is based on population size: Approximately thirty-five percent of the countries providing data to the United Nations use a definition based solely on size. The minimum population size considered urban varies considerably from as low as 250 inhabitants to as high as 40,000.

The second type of definition is based on legal or government criteria. In some nations a population concentration is considered urban regardless of size if it is an administrative center—a county seat, for example. Similarly, incorporation—the recognition by the state of a population concentration as a legal entity—also is used as a criterion for defining a place as urban.

The third type of urban definition combines several criteria, usually size and legal or administrative standards. Most state governments in the United States, for example, require a population concentration to reach a predetermined size before it can be incorporated. In other nations, these criteria are combined with other requirements, such as number of inhabitants employed in nonagricultural jobs.

Different Countries' Criteria of Urbanization

In international comparisons, the degree of urbanization frequently is considered simply the percentage of the total population of a country living in urban areas, according to each country's own definition of urban. This approach presents numerous problems, some of which can be seen in Table 2.1. For instance, the wide variation in the definitions used in several

Table 2.1
Urban definition, percent urban by definition, and percent of total population in cities of 100,000 or more and 500,000 or more.

Country	Urban definition	Percent urban by country's definition	Percent of population in cities of 100,000 or more	Percent of population in cities of 500,000 or more
Australia	Population size 1,500 or more	88.5	64.7	58.1
Denmark	Population size 250 or more	80.1	38.3	29.8
United States	Population size 2,500 or more	75.2	58.4	45.1
Netherlands	Population size 6,000 or more	72.2	45.1	23.9
Iceland	Legal-administrative	71.7	0	0
New Zealand	Legal-adminstrative	66.0	45.9	22.1
Canada	Population size 2,000 or more	61.7	49.3	34.8
Spain	Population size 10,000 or more	58.8	33.4	17.7
Italy	Legal-administrative	51.5	29.4	17.3

The influence of the legal definition of a nation's urban population is apparent in this table. In most nations a single criterion—size—is used, but in this table the minimum population size of an urban place ranges from 250 persons in Denmark to 10,000 persons in Spain. In contrast, Iceland and New Zealand consider a place to be urban regardless of size as long as certain legal or administrative functions are carried out within its borders. The problems these conflicting definitions create may be seen by comparing the first column of figures with the last two columns. The resulting discrepancies show that a standard measure must be employed in making international comparisons of urbanization.

Source: Adapted from Davis, K., *World Urbanization 1950–1970, Volume 1: Basic Data for Cities, Counties and Regions.* Berkeley: University of California Press, 1969, Table A.

European and North American countries suggests that Denmark is more urban than the United States and that Iceland is as urban as the Netherlands. This impression is misleading. A method preferred by Kingsley Davis (1969, 1972a) and other ecologists when making comparisons between countries is to find the percentage of each country's population in cities of 100,000 or more inhabitants. This method reveals that Iceland has no cities with population of over 100,000, whereas the Netherlands has 45.1 percent of its population in cities of 100,000 or more inhabitants.

This approach is not without problems, however. A country with a small population and therefore small cities may have the same degree of urbanization as a country with a large population and large cities. Note in Table 2.1 that although Denmark and the United States have similar urban populations, nearly 30 percent of Denmark's population is in one large city (Copenhagen), whereas the United States has thirty-two cities with more than one-half million inhabitants.

Another problem is related to how the cities are distributed. Hypothetically, two countries of the same size, with the same percentage of their populations in cities of 100,000 or more, could have entirely different settlement patterns. Country A might have many cities of the same size, evenly dispersed, and Country B might have one large city that dominates the entire country.

Over the past two decades, ecologists, demographers, and urban sociologists have attempted to come to grips with these measurement problems by developing indices of urbanization (Arriage, 1970; Gibbs, 1961; Mehta, 1963; Subramanian, 1971). These indices have been sensitive to both the size of a nation's urban population and the spatial distribution of cities, yet none of the indices is widely used. The reasons are: in general they are cumbersome and difficult to calculate without a computer, and, more important, the necessary data are simply not available for many nations. Therefore, when making international comparisons, most researchers use the degree-of-urbanization measure (percent of total population in cities of 100,000 or more) despite its major problems.

Delineating Boundaries

Another concern in measuring a country's urbanization is establishing the boundaries of the cities to be measured. Should one use political boundaries or boundaries based on population density and employment? In the United States, for example, the larger urban places have a central city defined by politically established boundaries; but these central cities are surrounded by densely populated suburban areas whose inhabitants are employed in nonagricultural jobs. A case in point is Cincinnati, Ohio, where 385,457 people resided within the political limits of the city in 1980. This figure, however, represents only 28 percent of the population living in the Cincinnati metropolitan area.

The problems in delineating city boundaries have been addressed by many countries, including the United States. The definitions used by the United States Census Bureau in delineating urban places show the lengths to which one must go to define urban boundaries accurately.[2]

UNITED STATES CENSUS DEFINITIONS OF URBANIZATION

Definition of Urban

Until 1950, the official definition of urban used by the United States Census was an incorporated place of 2,500 or larger. This definition was thought to be too narrow, and since 1950 the urban definition has included both incorporated and unincorporated places.[3]

The 1980 definition of urban includes the population living in the following types of population concentrations:

1. Places of 2,500 inhabitants or more incorporated as cities, villages, boroughs, and towns, but excluding those persons living in the rural portions of extended cities.
2. Unincorporated places of 2,500 inhabitants or more.
3. Other territory, incorporated or unincorporated, on the fringes of large cities with a population of 50,000 or more.

Additional detailed rules cover both incorporated and unincorporated areas in New England, Pennsylvania, New Jersey, and elsewhere.

To provide a better distinction between urban and rural population in the vicinity of large cities, the Census Bureau uses four other terms—urbanized area, extended cities, Standard Metropolitan Statistical Area, and Standard Consolidated Statistical Area.

The Urbanized Area

An *urbanized area* is defined by population density. Each urbanized area includes a central city and the surrounding closely settled urban fringe (suburbs) that together have a population of 50,000 or more. The specific criteria used for the delineation of Urbanized Areas are:

1. A central city of 50,000 inhabitants or more in 1970 or 1980; or twin cities such as Minneapolis–St. Paul with continuous boundaries and a combined population of at least 50,000, where the smaller of the twin cities has a population of at least 15,000.
2. Closely settled incorporated territory with 2,500 inhabitants or more; or an incorporated place with fewer than 2,500 inhabitants but more than 100 housing units in a closely populated area. Other areas unin-

corporated or in specialized land use may be included if additional
criteria are met.

The Bureau of the Census's major objective in delineating urbanized
areas is to provide a better picture of urban and rural populations in the
vicinity of our larger cities.

In 1970, 120.7 million (approximately 60 percent) of the total United
States population were living in urbanized areas. More than half this number
(65 million) lived in 340 central cities with roughly 56 million living in the
urban fringe (suburbs). The 1980 population counts showed continued
growth of urbanized areas with the greatest gains made in the urban fringe.
Also of interest is the fact that these areas only covered 36,290 square
miles or about 1 percent of the total land area of the United States.

The Extended City

In the 1980 Census, the Census Bureau gave special attention to extended
cities. During the 1970s there was a trend among cities to annex large
adjacent areas that were rural and not urban in character. To more clearly
delineate rural and urban populations, the Census Bureau closely examined
population density patterns and classified portions of these cities rural.

The Census Bureau defines an extended city as a city that contains one
or more areas, each of at least five square miles and a population density
of fewer than 100 persons per square mile, according to the 1970 Census.
These areas constitute at least 25 percent of the land area of the legal city
or a total of twenty-five square miles or more.

Examples of extended cities that consist of both an urban and a rural
part are Palo Alto, San Diego, San Jose, and Union City, California; and
Jacksonville, Miramar, and West Palm Beach, Florida.

The SMSA

Closely linked to the urbanized-area concept is the concept of the *Standard
Metropolitan Statistical Area* (SMSA). The SMSA is used to identify central
cities, the counties in which they are located, and those adjoining counties
that have economic or social relationships to the central city. There is no
limit on the number of outlying counties in an SMSA. The counties in an
SMSA may even be in different states, if the following criteria are met:

1. One central city with 50,000 inhabitants or more or
2. A central city with at least 25,000 inhabitants, provided that two
   conditions exist:
   a) that the city's population together with that of contiguous places
      totals at least 50,000 inhabitants and constitutes for general eco-
      nomic and social purposes a single community, and

b) that the county or counties in which these places are located has at least 75,000 inhabitants.

The criteria for including outlying counties relate primarily to the residence and employment characteristics of their inhabitants. Three of these criteria are:

1. At least 75 percent of the labor force of the county must be nonagricultural. (There are additional labor criteria.)
2. Fifty percent or more of the county's population must live in minor civil divisions (suburbs, for example) that adjoin the county containing the central city or are part of an unbroken chain of these minor subdivisions.
3. Fifteen percent of the outlying county's work force must live in that county but work in the county containing the central city, or (the opposite pattern) 25 percent of the people working in the outlying county must live in the county holding the central city.

The purpose of the Standard Metropolitan Statistical Area is to indicate the extent of the economic and social integration between the central city and outlying densely populated areas. Political boundaries do not adequately delimit cities because they seldom include the lightly settled areas at the fringe of urbanized areas. In general, urbanized areas are the thickly settled core of the Standard Metropolitan Statistical Area. The balance of the SMSA is the area of low-density settlement. The relationship between the urbanized areas and SMSAs can be seen in Figure 2.2.

1980 Census data was tabulated for 288 SMSAs, plus additional areas that qualified for SMSA status based on 1980 population counts.[4]

The Standard Consolidated Statistical Area

The final category of urban places is the Standard Consolidated Statistical Area (SCSA), and it is employed to analyze data for massive concentrations of metropolitan population. An SCSA includes an SMSA of at least one million people plus one or more adjoining SMSAs related to it by continuously developed high-density population corridors that may be used by commuting workers.

In the 1970 Census, the two largest metropolitan areas in the United States, New York and Chicago, were designated by the Bureau of the Census as Standard Consolidated Areas (SCA). These areas were large metropolitan complexes and are viewed by some students of the city as the settlement pattern of the future—the megalopolis. The New York–Northwestern New Jersey Standard Consolidated Areas include four SMSAs and two additional counties for a total population of 106 million.

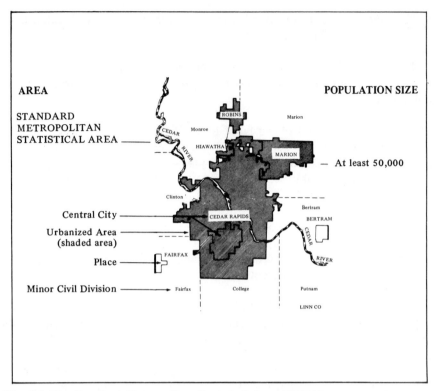

Fig. 2.2 The Standard Metropolitan Statistical Area (SMSA).

Source: Bureau of the Census, *Census '80: Continuing the Factfinder Tradition.* Washington, D.C.: U.S. Government Printing Office, 1980.

The Chicago–Northwestern Indiana Standard Consolidated Area is composed of two SMSAs and has a total population of more than 7.6 million.

In 1976, these two SCAs were redefined to become SCSAs and eleven new SCSAs were identified. These include San Francisco-Oakland–San Jose, California, Cleveland-Akron–Lorrain, Ohio and Houston–Galveston, Texas.

Usefulness of Census Definitions

The definitions and practices of the United States Census Bureau are not without faults. Obviously, many of the criteria used by the Census Bureau are arbitrary and could lead to inaccuracies in classification. For example, a single incorporated place could conceivably have 49,999 inhabitants, and it would not be considered an urbanized area. Most of the classification practices are largely dictated by practical considerations such as time and cost. The question for social scientists is whether the Census's categories are useful in research. In other words, can these relatively simple measures based on population size, density, and employment be used to analyze more

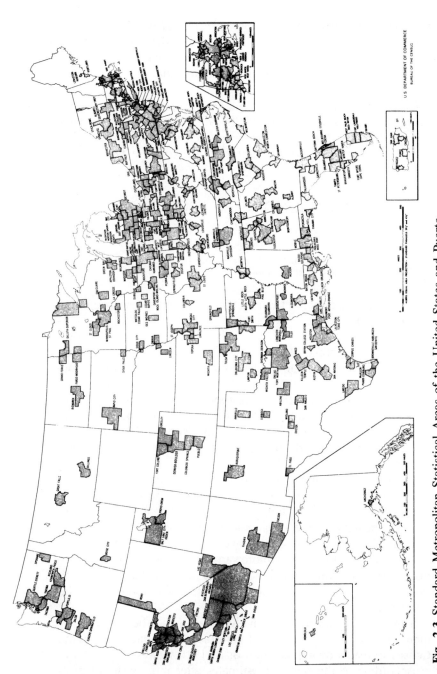

Fig. 2.3 Standard Metropolitan Statistical Areas of the United States and Puerto Rico, 1980.

Source: Bureau of the Census, *Census '80: Continuing the Factfinder Tradition.* Washington, D.C.: U.S. Government Printing Office, 1980.

complex social and economic phenomena? The answer is yes. The definitions reflect a long dialog between the users of the data and the Census Bureau. The Census Bureau appears to provide reliable data that are applicable to the study of a wide range of phenomena.

Problems in collecting basic data on a nation's population are not limited to studies of the less developed world. The following article from the Christian Science Monitor *(June 24, 1980) outlines some of the problems the United States Census Bureau encountered in taking the 1980 Census.*

CENSUS: UNDER FIRE FROM TWO CITIES

By Jonathan Harsch
Staff correspondent of
the Christian Science Monitor, Chicago

If you invite eight people to dinner and a dozen arrive, you could be in trouble.

The trouble multiplies dramatically when you set the table for 221.7 million people—the US Census Bureau's current United States population estimate for 1980—and an extra 5 million show up.

Given the Census Bureau's history of undercounting the US population and the vital role the decennial head count plays in deciding the number of places set at the federal table, two cities have turned to the courts to help ensure an accurate count of their residents.

Detroit is suing the Census Bureau to require an "adjusted" figure to reflect the city's entire population. Chicago's Hispanic-Americans are suing to force the Census Bureau to hire more Spanish-speaking workers immediately to send into entire blocks in West Chicago that are said to have never received census forms.

According to Joseph Baltimore, an attorney for the City of Detroit, greater accuracy and fairness could be achieved by switching from door-to-door head counts to a statistical estimate of the population.

The suits, which lawyers involved feel could be followed by more in New York, Texas, and California, spring directly from the Census Bureau's own evaluation of its 1970 figures.

According to the bureau's estimates after three years of post-census research, it undercounted the US popultion in 1970 by some 5.3 million people, or 2.5 percent. The bureau estimates that its overall 2.5 percent undercount 10 years ago was 1.9 percent among the nation's 180 million whites but 7.7 percent among the 23 million blacks. Others estimate that Hispanics, who were not listed separately in 1970, may have suffered a 15 percent undercount.

Census Bureau spokesman Henry Smith explains that the 7.7 percent undercount among blacks meant that "blacks proportionately lost more" federal funds.

The two cities' legal action follows another suit, filed by the Federation for American Immigration Reform (FAIR), charging the bureau with *overcounting* by including illegal aliens. FAIR's suit is awaiting US Supreme Court action.

Michael Ferrell, staff director for the House subcommittee on census and population, warns that Census Bureau inflexibility could result in "litigating the 1980 census through the next four or five years."

The stakes involved in these actions are high. The final population figures that the bureau delivers to President Carter Dec. 31 will decide how up to $75 billion in funds for housing, education, employment, medical, and other federal programs is to be divided among different parts of the country, between urban and rural areas, and between ethnic groups.

Moreover, population shifts recorded in the 1980 census probably will give the South and West 14 new seats in the US House of Representatives at the expense of the Northeast and Midwest.

With so much money and so many congressional seats on the line, the Census Bureau has been under increasing pressure. Critics charge it with failing to cary out its constitutional duty to make an accurate count of the population every 10 years.

The US General Accounting Office concluded in a 1976 study that it is "doubtful" whether the bureau can reduce its traditional undercount of the population.

The Census Bureau responded to earlier criticisms by starting work on the 1980 census in 1974.

To achieve a more accurate count, the cost of the census is up to $1 billion for 1980—more than $4 a person counted—compared with $221 million for 1970.

Minority groups and the major cities that host large minority populations have been determined not to be shortchanged when federal funds are divided.

Minority leaders emphasized the confidentiality of the census, distributed information in Spanish and other languages, and emphasized that every uncounted person costs his community some $230 in federal funds.

> Mr. Smith stresses that this year's count will continue for another two months as evaluators knock on more doors to find the uncounted.

Comparative studies of urban phenomena are complicated by the fact that the definitions employed by the United States Census Bureau are not used worldwide, and census terminology differs among countries. Nevertheless, in many countries census officials delimit urbanized and metropolitan areas with criteria similar to those of the United States. In Canada, for example, "census agglomeration" is equivalent to the United States Census term "urban area." The British Standard Metropolitan Labour Area is similar to the Standard Metropolitan Statistical Area. The problems in developing comparative international data on urbanization are under study by several international agencies and study groups, but no formal recommendations have been made. At present, every researcher making international comparisons must examine the available data for a correspondence among census units. Although this approach leaves much to be desired, in the absence of universal census definitions it seems likely to continue.

GLOBAL PATTERNS OF URBANIZATION

A question related to the conceptual and measurement problems of urban research is how cities are spatially distributed across a nation's territory. Are all the large cities of a country concentrated in one small region, or are they evenly distributed across the entire country? There are more than 200 countries in the world, with enormous variations in urban spatial patterning. To illustrate the variety of urban patterns, we will compare three countries—Thailand, New Zealand, and Brazil. These countries differ in geographic location, history, culture, topography, but most importantly, in the geographical distribution of their cities. These three countries were chosen out of the world's 200 nations because they exhibit three distinct patterns of urbanization. Equally important was the availability of good census data and of recent ecological studies on the spatial patterns of the urban populations of these nations.

Thailand

Thailand is in Southeast Asia, one of the least urbanized regions of the world. Although Asian countries still have only a small percentage of their population in urban places, Asian cities are growing rapidly. Studying the urbanization process in this part of the world is difficult because modern census techniques have not been widely adopted. Therefore, one of the major research challenges facing demographers and human ecologists is

Photo 2.1 This photograph illustrates the sharp contrast between the old and the new that is often found in the cities of the less developed world. This photo was taken in the city of Niamey, in the Niger Republic.
Source: © 1975 Georg Gerster, Photo Researchers, Inc.

documenting the rate, extent, and character of urbanization in Asia (Goldstein, 1971, p. 205).

Sidney Goldstein, in "Urbanization in Thailand, 1947–1967" (1971), has explored Thailand's urban experience. Thailand is an excellent Asian country to study because it has a census every ten years and also a population register that records vital events such as births and deaths. In 1970, it was estimated that approximately 85 percent of all births and 70 percent of all deaths in Thailand were reported to district officials. These data have been collected with a fair degree of accuracy for the past seventy years.

Urban growth What is Thailand's urbanization pattern? First, one must ask how urbanization is measured in Thailand. As is the case in many countries, the Thai census lacks a clear definition for urban. Three types of municipal areas have population characteristics that can be considered urban—cities, of which there are three, Bangkok, Thonburi, and Chiengami; towns or administrative seats, regardless of population size, of which there are sixty-eight; and communes, designated as municipal areas by the Minister of the Interior, of which there are forty-nine. Goldstein restricted his analysis to the urban population living in municipal areas of 10,000 or more, of which there were seventy-seven in 1967.

Using Goldstein's definition and examining population trends since 1947, one is impressed with the rapid growth of Thailand's urban population. In 1947, 9.9 percent of Thailand's population lived in cities of 10,000 or more. In addition, only thirty-three of Thailand's municipalities had population concentrations in excess of 10,000. By 1967, the number of municipalities with populations over 10,000 had increased to seventy-seven, and more than 14 percent of the country's population lived in these relatively large places (see Table 2.2). During this entire period, urban areas were growing at the rate of 5 percent a year and rural areas were growing at the rate of 3 percent a year.

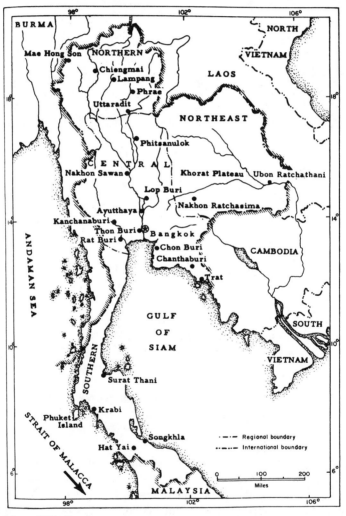

Fig. 2.4 Map of Thailand.

Source: Headerson, J. S. *Area Handbook for Thailand.* (Da Pam 550–53). Washington, D.C.: U.S. Government Printing Office, 1971.

Table 2.2
Ten largest urban places in Thailand—1947, 1960, 1967, and 1980.

1947		1960		1967		1980	
Place and region	Population	Place and region	Population	Place and region	Population	Place and region	Population
Bangkok-Thomburi(C)	781,662	Bangkok-Thomburi(C)	1,800,678	Bangkok-Thomburi(C)	2,614,356	Bangkok-Thomburi(C)	4,999,515
Chiengmai(N)	38,211	Chiengmai(N)	66,823	Chiengmai(N)	81,579	Chiengmai(N)	97,839
Lampang(N)	22,952	Korat(NE)	44,630	Korat(NE)	73,030	Khon Khaen Nakhon	89,925
Korat(NE)	22,340	Hadd Yai(S)	36,197	Hadd Yai(S)	49,327	Ratchasima Nakhon	89,101
Nakhon Pathom(C)	22,007	Lampang(N)	36,002	Udorn(NE)	46,686	Sawan(N)	86,221
Samut Sakorn(C)	20,754	Nakhon Sawan(N)	34,371	Nakhon Sawan(N)	44,851	Ndonthani	79,465
Puket(S)	19,550	Ayuthaya(C)	33,547	Chon Buri(C)	42,141	Songkla(S)	74,728
Songkla(S)	18,662	Chon Buri(C)	33,237	Songkla(S)	40,682	Phitsanulok(N)	73,801
Ayuthaya(C)	17,807	Phitsanulok(N)	33,233	Lampang(N) Nakhon	40,515	Nakhon Sithamarat(S)	65,190
Chon Buri(C)	17,671	Songkla(S)	31,488	Sithamarat(S)	39,426	Ayuthaya(C)	51,179
Total	981,616	Total	2,150,206	Total	3,072,593	Total	5,706,964
Primacy index	20.5		26.9		32.1		51.0

Region symbols: C, Central; NE, Northeast; N, North; and S, South.

Source: 1947, 1960, and 1967 data from Goldstein, S. "Urbanization in Thailand, 1947–1967," *Demography* 8, no. 2 (1971): p. 216. 1980 figures based on unpublished registry data, courtesy of Sid Goldstein, Brown University.

Primacy These general figures give a distorted picture of urban growth in Thailand. Although its urban population grew by more than 213 percent between 1947 and 1967, over 60 percent of this growth was centered in the twin cities of Bangkok-Thonburi. In 1947 greater Bangkok was twenty-one times larger than Chiengmai, Thailand's second largest city. By 1980, Bangkok had grown to more than 5 million people and was fifty-one times larger than Chiengmai. Recent data for Thailand suggest that Bangkok's movement toward primacy is continuing at an accelerating rate (London, 1978).

THE PROBLEM OF PRIMACY

The growth of one large city at the expense of other cities is called the problem of primacy. The terms *primacy* and *primate city* were introduced by Mark Jefferson (1939) more than forty years ago, and they refer to one large city that dominates all other cities in a country and through time "draws away from all of them in character as well as size" (Jefferson, 1939, p. 227). Primacy is measured simply by comparing the population of the largest city with that of the second largest city.[5]

The nature of primate cities and their relationship to economic development has been studied by historians, geographers, ecologists, and demographers for the past forty years.[6] Many of these researchers believe that primate cities in developing nations are "parasitic" and hold back economic development. Why parasitic? Many of the world's primate cities are in countries that have economies based on agriculture rather than industry. Traditional agriculture that uses human and animal power rather than machines differs from industry because it does not produce large profits that can be reinvested in other areas of the economy for development. Cities are expensive to build and maintain; they also tax the limited financial resources of these nations. In other words, money that might have gone into industry, tractors, mining, or irrigation projects is spent on the support of a large urban place.

Another aspect of primate cities exacerbates this problem—the primate city's power of attraction. Large numbers of the rural population, especially the young, are drawn to the city by the prospect of jobs and other opportunities. Although some find jobs, without industry few jobs are available. As a result, a large proportion of the primate city's population remains unemployed or underemployed, continuing the drain on the nation's resources. The term *overurbanized* refers to those nations whose urban population is too large in relation to the level of economic development (Davis and Golden, 1954; Sovani, 1964). The cost of providing food and shelter for this nonproductive population also detracts from economic growth.

Lowering the rate of economic development, however, is not the only consequence of high primacy. Uneven economic development occurs as a government makes large investments in the primate city while ignoring the needs of the other regions of the country. This large investment in the primate city encourages industrial and commercial activities to locate there. Through time, a vicious cycle develops; industrial growth means more jobs, but new jobs also increase the attractiveness of the primate city to new migrants from other parts of the country. This population movement detracts from the growth that might occur in other cities, and economic development in other regions of the country stagnates.

Primacy also has political ramifications. Many primate cities are national capitals and become governmental, educational, and religious, as well as industrial centers. The concentration of a nation's political, business, and religious elites in one city leads to major social and political divisions within a country. The primate city becomes the center of wealth and power and the countryside becomes the habitat of the poor and powerless.

Bangkok's population, which has grown more than 1.8 million persons in the last thirty years, shows many of the problems associated with primacy and overurbanization. Economic development and population growth have been concentrated in this one city in the nation's central region, while the mountainous region to the north and the rich agricultural region to the south have been neglected (see Figure 2.4). "For example, of 2,177 new industries established in Thailand during 1968, more than half were in the metropolitan Bangkok area" (Goldstein, 1971, p. 219).

Thailand is an example of a country that has a small percentage of its population in urban places, but a disproportionate number of urban dwellers in a single primate city. Moreover, the rate of urbanization in Thailand is faster than the rate of change in its economic and social institutions, leading to overurbanization.

Sociologists call this uneven rate of change in various elements of a society, cultural lag. William F. Ogburn (1922) first introduced the concept more than fifty years ago and summarized it as follows:

> The thesis is that the various parts of modern cultures are not changing at the same rate, some parts are changing much more rapidly than others; and that since there is a correlation and interdependence of parts, a rapid change in one part of a culture requires readjustments through other changes in various correlated parts of culture (Ogburn, 1922, p. 200).

The problems of primacy and overurbanization are good illustrations of the concept. Medical technology has been introduced into "developing" societies, but it has not been accompanied by comparable institutions for handling the ensuing "population explosion." Vast numbers of peasants have been pushed off their land through the introduction of high-yield grains and other farm technology, but a comparable number of factory jobs have not been created elsewhere. With nowhere else to go, the surplus rural population migrates to the city where institutions of government often find it impossible to provide basic city services. Thus, the city is only one part in the larger encompassing society, and change in one part of this system will inevitably have an impact on the city. The notion of cultural lag is an integral part of the ecological perspective, and it can be systematically analyzed through the POET framework introduced in Chapter 1. The urbanization patterns of Thailand and its concurrent problems are not an isolated phenomenon but are shared by many developing nations.

New Zealand

New Zealand's economy, like Thailand's, is agriculturally oriented, but it is of a pastoral nature. Dependence on agriculture usually means that a country can support only a small urban population, as we have seen in the case of Thailand. New Zealand, however, is in the paradoxical position of having an agriculturally based economy but one of the highest levels of urbanization in the world, exceeding that of both Canada and the United States. In addition, New Zealand has a low level of primacy, which is unusual for a country its size (Gibson, 1973).

Urban growth Table 2.3 gives the population of metropolitan areas and large towns of New Zealand for the years 1861–1976. As late as 1901, less than 30 percent of New Zealand's population lived in cities of 10,000 or more, and there were no cities larger than 100,000; also, the four largest cities were of roughly the same size. By 1976, this pattern had changed markedly: 62 percent of New Zealand's population was in cities of 10,000 or more inhabitants, and four cities had grown to more than 100,000 people. These four large cities contained more than half of New Zealand's total population. In 1971, for the first time Auckland exceeded the combined populations of the next two largest cities, Wellington and Christchurch.

New Zealand and Thailand are both undergoing rapid urban growth, but from different sources. Thailand's urban population is growing because of rural-to-urban migration and high birth rates of its total and urban populations. Moreover, Thailand's urban and rural populations are both growing at unprecedented rates, 5 and 3 percent, respectively. In contrast, New Zealand's urban population growth is largely the result of rural-to-urban migration; New Zealand still has low birth rates. Between 1960 and 1976, for example, New Zealand's urban population grew by 15 percent while its rural population declined by 13 percent.

Table 2.3
Population of metropolitan areas and large towns of New Zealand, by island: 1961–1976 (in thousands).

Metropolitan area or Town[a]	1861[b]	1881[b]	1901[b]	1921[b]	1951	1971	1976
North Island							
Auckland	11	31	67	158	329	649	743
Wellington[c]	4	21	49	107	208	307	327
Hamilton	—	1	1	11	30	75	95
Palmerston North	—	1	7	16	31	52	64
Napier	—	6	9	14	20	40	50
Wanganui	—	5	7	16	27	36	40
New Plymouth	2	3	4	11	22	34	44
Rotorua	—	—	—	4	11	31	47
Whangerei	—	—	1	4	12	31	40
Hastings	—	—	4	9	17	30	48
Tauranga	—	1	1	2	8	28	48
Gisbonne	—	2	3	11	17	27	32
South Island							
Christchurch[c]	3	31	57	106	174	275	295
Dunedin[c]	7	43	52	72	95	111	113
Invercargill	—	5	6	15	27	47	53
Nelson	4	7	7	9	17	29	42
Timaru	—	4	6	14	21	28	30

— Represents zero or rounds to zero.

[a] The four metropolitan areas (Auckland, Wellington, Christchurch, and Dunedin) and all towns with populations of 25,000 or more at any census are included.

[b] Excludes Maoris.

[c] Metropolitan populations are those shown in census reports, except that Auckland includes Parnell and Newton electoral districts in 1861. The Hutt Metropolitan Area, which has been given separately in the census since 1951, is included with Wellington.

Source: 1861 through 1971 figures from Gibson, C., "Urbanization in New Zealand: A Comparative Analysis." *Demography* (1973) 10, no. 1: p. 75.

1976 figures from New Zealand Department of Statistics, 1976 Census of Population and Dwellings. Vol. 19—Location and Increase of Population, 1977, p. 48.

Primacy New Zealand's urban patterns differ significantly from Thailand's in several ways, but the most important is the level of primacy. New Zealand's primacy is low because of the technology at the time of settlement and historical and geographic factors that have interacted through time. The most important factor is New Zealand's colonial history. New Zealand was conquered and settled by Great Britain in the eighteenth century and is now a part of the British Commonwealth. A common feature of all colonial powers was the use of the city as a tool to administer the colonies.

SOUTH ISLAND

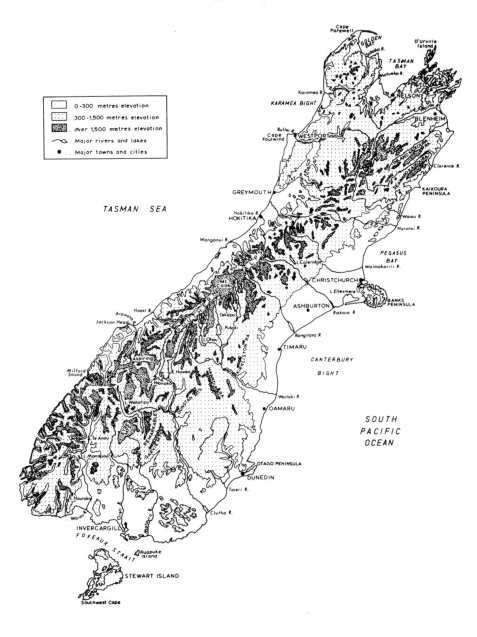

Fig. 2.5 Map of New Zealand.

NORTH ISLAND

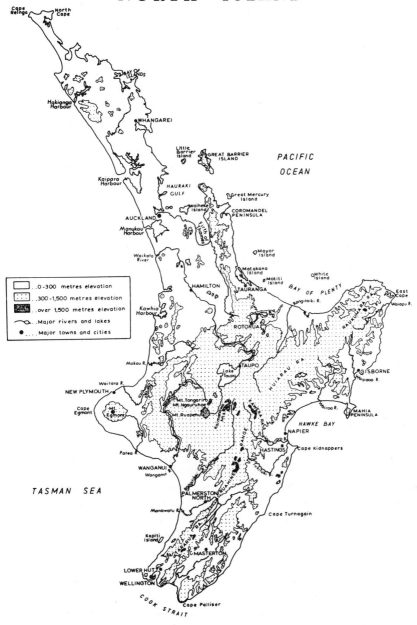

Cape Reinga
North Cape

BAY ISLANDS

Hokianga Harbour

WHANGAREI

Little Barrier Island
GREAT BARRIER ISLAND

PACIFIC OCEAN

Kaipara Harbour

HAURAKI GULF

Great Mercury Island

Waiheke Island

COROMANDEL PENINSULA

AUCKLAND

Manukau Harbour

Waikato River

Mayor Island

Matakana Island
Motiti Island
White Island

HAMILTON

TAURANGA

BAY OF PLENTY

East Cape

Rangitaiki R.

Waiapu R.

Kawhia Harbour

ROTORUA

RAUKUMARA RA.

.0-300 metres elevation
.300-1,500 metres elevation
.over 1,500 metres elevation
...Major rivers and lakes
....Major towns and cities

Mokau R.

Lake Taupo

TAUPO

HUIARAU RA.

GISBORNE

Waipaoa R.

Waitara R.

NEW PLYMOUTH

Cape Egmont
Mt. Egmont

Mt. Tongariro
Mt. Ngauruhoe
Mt. Ruapehu

Wairoa R.

MAHIA PENINSULA

HAWKE BAY

NAPIER

HASTINGS
Cape Kidnappers

Patea R.

WANGANUI
Wanganui R.

RUAHINE RANGE

TARARUA RANGE

TASMAN SEA

PALMERSTON NORTH

Manawatu R.

Cape Turnagain

Kapiti Island

MASTERTON

LOWER HUTT

WELLINGTON

COOK STRAIT
Cape Palliser

20 0 20 40 60 80 100 km

Once the native population was subdued, a colony was divided into administrative districts of manageable size; at the center of each was a city that became the seat of government. New Zealand is a small country, but it has a rugged mountainous terrain. In the nineteenth century communication and travel were slow; railroad construction was difficult and did not begin until late in the period. Therefore, the British found it necessary to build numerous administrative centers to run the colony effectively. These early administrative centers emerged in the twentieth century as the metropolitan areas of New Zealand—Auckland, Wellington, Christchurch, and Dunedin.

New Zealand's combination of an agricultural economy with an urban population has yet to be explained. Gibson (1972), in "Urbanization in New Zealand: A Comparative Analysis," suggests that two factors may be responsible for this paradoxical situation. First, New Zealand's industrial development is hampered by a lack of mineral resources and by the rough terrain. Second, the agriculture on which New Zealand's economy is based is pastoral, and its produce is intended largely for export. Pastoral agriculture (sheep and cattle raising) requires little manpower and thus permits the growth of the urban population.

Brazil

Brazil has a pattern of urbanization very different from that of either New Zealand or Thailand. Brazil is South America's largest country in both land area and population. Its historical development differs notably from that of other South American countries because the early settlers were Portuguese rather than Spanish. However, although Brazil differs culturally and historically from the rest of South America, it shares settlement patterns with the rest of the continent.

Until 1960, most of Brazil's population lived within 200 miles of the Atlantic coast, where the principal cities were situated. The greater part of the country consists of highlands supporting the vast rain forests of the Amazon River Basin that make road and city building difficult. In 1960, Brazil transferred its national capital from Rio de Janeiro to Brasilia, a newly built city in the heart of the country, to symbolize the nation's effort to open up undeveloped lands in the interior (see Figure 2.6). The communication and transportation routes that led to the initial coastal settlement pattern, however, continued to prevail into the 1980s. The planned development of Brazil's interior, pursued for two decades at enormous social and economic cost, has met with only limited success. Most of this country's urban growth continues to be centered in the coastal cities.

Figure 2.6 is a map of Brazil showing the location of this country's territorial divisions and principal cities. Most of Brazil's principal cities are arranged like a string of beads following the Atlantic coastline. Although all the coastal cities underwent remarkable growth during the 1970s and

① **NORTH** ② **NORTHEAST** ③ **CENTRAL-WEST**
④ **SOUTHEAST** ⑤ **SOUTH**

Fig. 2.6 Map of Brazil.
Source: Weil, T. E., *Area Handbook for Brazil.* (Da Pam 550–20) Foreign Area Studies
Division of American University. Washington, D.C.: U.S. Government Printing Office, 1975.

early 1980s, a high percentage of this growth has been in the cities of the
south and southeast (see Table 2.4).

Urban growth Comparing Brazil's urban growth to that of Thailand and
New Zealand is difficult; in Brazil's census a place is defined as urban by
political and administrative, rather than population, criteria. According to
the Brazilian definition, however, the country is undergoing unprecedented
urban population growth. Between 1960 and 1970 its urban population increased from 42 to 56 percent of the total population, or an absolute increase
in the urban population of more than 22 million. During this same period
rural population growth was less than 2 million people. The rural figures
are somewhat misleading because a large proportion of Brazil's rural population has migrated to the cities. For example, São Paulo grew by 3.8
million between 1960 and 1970 to a population of over 6 million. "In the

Table 2.4
Population of national, state, and territorial capitals of Brazil, 1960 and 1970 (in thousands).

Capitals and their political subdivisions	1960	1970	Percent growth 1960–70	1980	Percent growth 1970–80
Porto Velho (Rondonia)	52	89	71	136	52
Rio Branco (Acre)	48	85	77	120	41
Manaus (Amazonas)	175	314	79	736	134
Boa Vista (Roraima)	26	37	42	63	70
Belem (Para)	402	643	60	739	15
Mauapa (Amapa)	47	88	87	141	60
Sao Luis (Maraphao)	160	271	69	448	65
Teresina (Piaui)	145	230	59	378	64
Fortaleza (Ceara)	515	873	70	1,300	49
Natal (Rio Grande De Norte)	163	270	66	956	254
Jose Pessoa (Paraiha)	155	228	47	338	48
Recite (Pernambuco)	797	1,084	36	1,204	11
Maceio (Alagoas)	170	269	58	398	48
Aracaju (Sergipe)	116	187	61	294	57
Salvador (Bahia)	635	1,027	62	1,501	46
Belo Horizanto (Minas Gerais)	693	1,255	81	1,775	41
Vitoria (Espirito Santo)	85	136	60	215	58
Niteroi (Rio de Janeiro)	245	330	35	510	55
Rio de Janeiro (Guanabara)	3,307	4,315	31	5,098	18
São Paulo (Sao Paulo)	3,825	5,977	56	8,491	42
Curitiba (Parana)	361	624	73	1,026	64
Florianopolis (Santa Catarina)	99	143	44	193	35
Porto Alegre (Rio Grande do Sul) .	641	963	50	1,126	17
Cuiaba (Mato Grosso)	58	103	78	216	110
Goiania (Goias)	154	382	148	737	93
Brasilia (Federal District)	93	277	198	420	52

Source: 1960 and 1970 figures from Weil, T. E. *Area Handbook of Brazil,* (DA pam 550–20), Foreign Affairs Division of American University. Washington, D.C.: U.S. Government Printing Office, 1975, p. 28.

1980 figures from "IBGE: populacão é menor porque fecundidade caiu" *Rio de Janeiro,* November 19, 1980, p. 6.

1960s and 1970s as many as 300,000 people a year were pouring into this city, a majority from the impoverished Northeast, and the city proper was girdled by a ring of industrial suburbs" (Weil, 1975, p. 28). Therefore, approximately 70 percent of this growth was the result of rural-to-urban migration (Weil, 1975, pp. 20–47). These trends will unquestionably continue into the 1980s.

THE CHILDREN OF GUAPIRA

By Richard Critchfield
Special to The Christian Science Monitor,
Salvador, Brazil

The greatest problem in the poor two-thirds of the world may no longer be finding enough food, jobs, and shelter.

Rather it could be a cultural breakdown. A generation of urban immigrants is finding that traditional village values have no place in anonymous, slum-ridden, industrial cities.

Here in Salvador (pop. 1.3 million), colonial Brazil's capital from the 16th to 18th century and an Atlantic seaport of lost sugar wealth and present poverty, the issue emerges starkly. In the past five years, massive migrations of villagers from surrounding Bahía State have given Salvador a 7 percent yearly growth rate and led to a decline in the rural population.

Most migrants from the villages find menial jobs and manage to survive or even prosper a little on wages anywhere from $40 to $200 a month. What they do not find is anything to replace the old agricultural moral code.

Recently Dom Avelar Brandão Vilela, the cardinal of Salvador, denounced what he called the "bombardment and violence against the Brazilian family and its values." For this the cardinal blamed northeast Brazil's impoverished economy, the social indifference of its middle and upper classes, and moral confusion among the village migrants themselves.

"Our people have an inexhaustible patience; in their suffering, they somehow endure," he said. "But we cannot abuse this strength. It should not be permitted."

What happens to young villagers when they leave the authority and unity of the village and family to seek work in the modernized cities as individuals, individually paid, in factories or service industries designed not for them but to serve urban society at large?

Recently this reporter surveyed a dozen or so of the Salvador migrants from Guapira village 100 miles away and found all of them experiencing a good deal of cultural confusion.

In Guapira and similar settled agricultural villages, sons and daughters become self-reliant by performing useful chores from earliest childhood. Children of age 6 or 7 help till fields and mill manioc, the main crop, into flour. A boy of 15 is as prepared as a man of 40 to earn a livelihood plowing, sowing, and harvesting.

Marriage comes early. Chastity, early marriage, divorceless monogamy (true not only of Roman Catholic Brazil but also of most Hindu, Muslim, and Buddhist rural societies), and multiple maternity, along with religion and local superstitions, form an agricultural moral code that is nearly universal in the third world.

Salvador's upper 20 percent, partly prospering from new government-aided, capital-intensive industry but mostly wealthy from sugar and cacao plantations, pursue North American life-styles, and the coastal stretch of the city resembles a sort of mini-Miami Beach.

Such life-styles are unattainable, and probably always will be, to most of the other 80 percent, who exist in "favelas" or shantytowns, which extend, like fungus, inland into the surrounding hills.

Marriages are delayed

Guapira's children find their capacity to feed and support a family in Salvador will come much later, probably not until their late 20s or early 30s. Marriages are delayed. Premarital chastity grows harder to maintain.

The authority of father and mother back in the village has lost its economic base. Guapira's children are no longer constrained by the surveillance of the village; sins can be hidden in the protective anonymity of the crowd.

Some of the young villagers pride themselves on a shallow urban sophistication with a cynical, materialistic philosophy; money becomes the prime value.

At home in Guapira, both the church and folk superstition (planting is governed by the moon, crops are said to have humanlike sensitivities) still govern daily life.

The elderly may be abandoned by their families, live in mud-and-wattle huts, and subsist on manioc flour and little else, but religion confers meaning and dignity to their lives.

Guapira has no crime. It is on the rise in Salvador.

In the city Guapira's children face the replacement of Christian with secular institutions. It is the rich man or high government official who counts, rarely the clergyman. At night school (all go, to retake their primary education because the village school was so primitive) and in the newspapers, they are made aware of man's tiny place in the universe, though he possesses the technology to blow up the earth or journey to the moon.

Faith and certainties absent

Holy days become holidays; Salvador's beaches are crowded on Sunday, its churches are half empty. Violent movies of the Kung Fu type and spaghetti westerns set cultural standards of violent behavior. A thousand signs tell Guapira's children that the faith and certainties of their parents are nowhere to be found in the city.

In his 10 years in Salvador, Antônio, 27, has risen from worker to servant to watchman to a $300-a-month job as a driver for a government ministry. He has saved enough to buy a plot of land in an outlying favela and has planted bananas, papaya, and a vegetable garden. He hopes, after three more years, to complete high school at night, build a new house, and afford marriage to Nana, a girl from Guapira. Typical of the migrants, he wants no more than one or two children, as he is determined to educate them.

Antônio's chief concern is his loss of religious faith; he has taken to reading the Bible. His mother back in the village is shocked that one of her sons defends private judgment. She tells the neighbors, "Antônio believes that the most important thing is the God in the heavens."

Antônio is deeply confused. During the pre-Lenten Carnival he used to dance in the streets as did all Guapira's children, losing himself in the heavy, insistent dance of the very African Salvador samba.

Sometimes the drums would beat faster and faster until it was as if thunder were rising from the pavement. Then the tens of thousands of dancers who thronged the streets would break loose, all of them twisting and turning and moving their arms and legs with such violent rhythm that it seemed they would fly to pieces.

In one such crowd, Antônio had seen a man trampled when he lost his balance and fell. No one in the frenzied mob stopped, or could stop. After that, Antônio no longer took part in Carnival.

José Carlos, his younger brother, has done even better in Salvador: He is chef de bar in a luxury beach hotel for international tourists. When guests ask him if he likes his work, his stock answer is, "I wanted to be a civil engineer, but it cost too much money."

He is ashamed to tell them that at 23 he has just entered the third grade. Or that each Saturday in the public market he performs "capoeira," an African fighting dance, with a gang of street toughs who shake down tourists who try to photograph them. To José Carlos the rich long ago became adversaries to exploit, just as they exploit the poor.

A karate expert, he joined the Apaches in Carnival. This group of some 600 poor young blacks from the villages was banned from the streets the last day of Carnival after scattered skirmishes with the police. José Carlos and his friends angrily refused to go home; troops were called out and 125 Apaches were thrown in jail.

Olympia, 17, was too alarmed by Carnival to take part. "Lots of fights," she says. "People drank too much. Big crowds. You could get hurt." Like all Guapira girls in Salvador, Olympia works as a housemaid, earning her keep and $20 a month. She never goes out at night without the company of other girls.

But for all its dangers she finds life in Salvador superior to anything to be found in Guapira. "There's more things to do and more people to see. I don't want to work in the fields all my life."

Guapira's girls, working in the homes of the rich and middle classes, live much better than the boys, who may share a cubicle in some favela or sleep on the construction sites where they work.

Since she had a baby and lost her job as a maid five years ago, Carolina, now 28, has survived by living with a series of men and taking in laundry in Pau Miudo, one of Salvador's poorest slums. When Jorge, a dockworker, abandoned her, she moved in with a woman friend. "We eat," she wrote her mother in Guapira, "but only with the help of the neighbors."

She has two children now and is unable to earn more than $20 a month washing. Carolina's biggest problem has been to find shelter. Recently she joined a mob of some 1,500 people from Pau Miudo who attempted to seize some empty government land near a new low-income housing project.

This squatter's army advanced onto the land, tearing down fences and marking off plots for each family.

At first the police made no attempt to stop them. Carolina was able to build an improvised shack and bring her few possessions: a bare, broken mattress, a box covered with earthenware dishes, a pile of rags, and the means to make a fire to dry the laundry she took in.

A day later troops arrived. As nearly 300 families watched, the soldiers began tearing down their homes.

A neighbor rushed to tell Carolina, sobbing, "I've got eight children, but only two can go to school because I don't have the money. I had to pay 200 cruzeiros [about $20] in Pau Miudo just for one small room. They can't take away this chance. Nobody's using this land."

Then a young soldier appeared in Carolina's doorway. "It's much better you leave now, senhora," he said, "as we are going to tear down everything."

In villages like Guapira the family is the unit of agricultural production, under the discipline of the father and the seasons. Paternal authority has a firm economic basis. Industry and thrift are more profitable than bravery and violence. Children are economic assets.

But the old agricultural moral code breaks down when young men and women from the villages enter the new urban industrial-technological order. The coming generation, the migrants' children who are born and raised in the city slums, are likely to have no cultural moorings at all.

Primacy Brazil's primacy index is in the midrange in comparison with Thailand's and New Zealand's. Table 2.4 gives the population and growth rates of national, state, and territorial capitals of Brazil for the years 1960 and 1980. Note that although São Paulo and Rio de Janeiro are the largest cities, six additional cities have nearly 1 million inhabitants each, and all the midsized cities grew rapidly during the decade.

Brazil, like Thailand, is a developing country, but one that had healthy economic growth during the 1970s and 1980s. Brazil's economic growth is overshadowed by one of the world's highest rates of population growth, over 3 percent a year. As in Thailand, Brazilian cities are growing from both migration and natural increase (births minus deaths), and both have led to serious urban problems. In São Paulo, for example, "traffic congestion has become extremely serious, air and water pollution problems were causing concern, and public services were hard put to meet the growing population demands" (Weil, 1975, p. 27). These problems are not unique to Sao Paulo but are shared by all Brazilian cities. The squatter settlements that have become a permanent fixture of Brazil's cities attest to the problems of overurbanization faced by this country.

World Patterns of Urbanization

Thailand, New Zealand, and Brazil differ greatly in their patterns of urbanization (see Table 2.5). All three countries have agriculturally oriented

Table 2.5
Summary of population, economic, and urban characteristics of Thailand, New Zealand, and Brazil.

	Country		
Characteristics	Thailand	New Zealand	Brazil
Primacy	High	Low	Middle Range
Population Growth Rate	High (3%)	Low/Stable	High (3%)
Urban Growth	Natural Increase/ Migration	Migration	Natural Increase/ Migration
Industrialization	Low	Low	Middle Range
Economy	Agricultural-Extractive	Agricultural (Pastoral)	[a]Mixed Agricultural-Emerging Industrial

[a] Majority of the workforce in agriculture, but industry makes a greater proportional contribution to total GNP.

Table 2.6
Total population and percent of population that is urban in cities of 100,000 or more for the world's regions.

Region and Country	Population Est. Mid-1980 (Millions)	Urban Population (Percent)	Pop. Cities 100,000 or More (Percent)
WORLD	4,410	39	
AFRICA	472	26	11.2
Northern Africa	110	42	21.1
Algeria	19.1	55	13.6
Egypt	42.5	44	—
Sudan	18.7	20	2.9
Western Africa	141	21	7.4
Ghana	11.8	36	17.8
Guinea	5.0	23	5.5
Niger	5.1	11.8	—
Eastern Africa	135	13	4.8
Djibouti	.2	—	
Ethiopia	30.5	13	3.2
Mozambique	10.3	8	4.4
Uganda	13.2	7.7	3.8
Middle Africa	54	29	6.0
Angola	6.9	14.2	6.1
Congo	1.5	39.8	7.2
East Guinea	.3	51	—

Region and Country	Population Est. Mid-1978 (Millions)	Urban Population (Percent)	Pop. Cities 100,000 or More (Percent)
NORTH AMERICA	247	74	57.4
Canada	24	74	49.3
United States	222.5	74	58.3
LATIN AMERICA	360	61	33.5
Middle America	91	59	29.5
Honduras	3.8	31	10.4
Mexico	68.3	65	33.9
Panama	1.9	51	30.0
Caribbean	29.2	50	20.1
Tropical South America	198	60	32.7
Bolivia	5.3	34	15.2
Brazil	122	61	33.8
Ecuador	8.0	43	21.3
Venezuela	13.9	75	36.9
Temperate South America	41	80	52.0
Argentina	27.7	80	61.1
Chile	11.3	80	37.0
Uruguay	2.8	83	53.0
EUROPE	484	69	38.9

Region/Country	(000)		
Southern Africa	32	44	32.0
Lesothe	1.3	4	—
South Africa	28.4	48	31.7
ASIA	2,563	27	15.7
Southwest Asia	98	46	21.7
Israel	3.7	81.9	55.2
Lebanon	3.2	60.1	32.7
Oman	.8	5	—
Middle South Asia	938	21	9.8
Bangladesh	86.5	8.8	
India	650	21	10.0
Iran	35.2	47	23.0
Pakistan	79	26	10.3
Southeast Asia	354	21	12.1
Philippines	47.7	32	16.0
Thailand	47.1	13	7.9
Vietnam	53.7	19	17.5
EAST ASIA	1,173	32	16.1
People's Republic of China	975	26	14.4
Japan	115	76	56.3
Taiwan	17.3	77	37.6
Northern Europe	82	90	58.9
Denmark	5.1	80	38.3
Norway	4.0	44	25.5
Sweden	8.3	83	32.7
United Kingdom	55.8	78	75.3
Western Europe	153	82	46.1
Austria	7.5	52	36.3
West Germany	61.3	92	54.3
Netherlands	14.0	88	45.2
Eastern Europe	110	59	24.3
Czechoslovakia	15.4	67	13
East Germany	16.7	76	22.6
Hungary	10.7	52	24.4
Southern Europe	140	60	29.7
Greece	9.5	65	33.9
Italy	57.0	67	29.5
Portugal	10.0	29	24.1
USSR	266.4	62	31.4
OCEANIA	230	71	—
AUSTRALIA–NEW ZEALAND	17.5	84	61.2
Australia	14.4	86	64.7
New Zealand	3.1	83	45.9

Source: [a] Adapted from Thomas T. Kane and Paul F. Myers, *1980 World Population Data Sheet.* Washington, D.C.: Population Reference Bureau, Inc., 1980.

[b] Adapted from K. Davis, *World Urbanization 1950–1970, Volume 1.* Davis, *Data for Cities, Countries and Regions.* Berkeley: The University of California Press, 1969, Table A.

economies with low levels of industrialization. Thailand and Brazil, moreover, are both undergoing unprecedented population and urban growth, the
latter resulting from natural increase and migration. Despite these underlying similarities, however, differences in terrain, history, culture, climate,
and technology have led to divergent settlement patterns.

Yet these three nations represent only three of the world's 200 countries.
Table 2.6 is a summary of population and urban characteristics of selected
countries in several geographic regions. These data suggest an enormous
variation in the level of urbanization among and within the world's regions.
Asia and Africa are the continents with the lowest levels of urbanization.
The percentage of the population that is urban varies significantly, however,
among the various subregions of the continents. Northern and southern
Africa, for instance, have 40 percent or more of their population in urban
places, whereas eastern Africa has only 12 percent of its population in the
urban category. There are major differences within subregions also. The
level of urbanization in eastern Africa ranges from as low as 6 percent in
Mozambique to as high as 70 percent in Djibouti. Similar differences of
this magnitude are found in all the world's regions except North America.

Another interesting comparison is between various nations' urban population and their population living in cities of 100,000 or more. Although
a nation may have a relatively high percentage of its population in urban
places, this population is not necessarily concentrated in large cities.

APPROACHES TO THE STUDY OF WORLD URBANIZATION PATTERNS

In general, the diversity of the world's urbanization patterns makes their
study difficult. A possible solution to this problem is to group nations
according to some common characteristics like world region, age, or political and economic system. In doing so, generalizations can be made about
groups of nations and systematic comparisons and detailed analyses of these
groups can be made. A discussion of two of the more commonly employed
approaches follows.

Level of Economic Development

A country's level of economic development is the criterion most commonly
used in classification schemes. In Table 2.7 the world's major regions are
divided into "more developed" and "less developed"; each region's total
population in millions is shown in Part A, and the total and percentage of
its population in urban places of 20,000 or more is given in Part B. The
world's population has grown at a prodigious rate during the past half
century, doubling from 1.8 billion in 1920 to more than 4.4 billion in 1980
(Part A). The urban segment of that population, however, has increased
sevenfold during the same period, from 266 million in 1920 to more than

1.7 billion in 1980. The urban population of less developed countries (LDCs) remains low compared to that of developed countries, although both the total and the urban population growth rates of LDCs now exceed the rates in the more developed world.

The comparison in Table 2.7 of total and urban populations by region for the years 1920 and 1980 shows fundamental changes in urban patterns. In 1920, the total population of the less developed countries was double that of the more developed countries, but the reverse was true of the urban populations. By 1980, not only had the total population of the less developed countries grown to three times that of the more developed nations, but the urban population of the less developed countries (reversing the previous trend) now exceeded that of the more developed world.

Absolute figures, giving populations in millions, tell only part of the story. Part B of Table 2.7 also shows urban population figures calculated as the percentage of each region's total population. The 1980 figures suggest that the world is still overwhelmingly settled in rural and small towns; slightly less than 40 percent of the world's population live in cities of 20,000 or more. The percentages for 1980 also show that the more developed regions all have higher levels of urbanization than the less developed world. The only less developed region even approaching the level of urbanization in the developed world is Latin America, with 61 percent of its total population in cities of 20,000 or more.

These percentage figures, however, give a somewhat distorted picture of the changes taking place in the less developed world. The rate of urban growth in the less developed regions greatly exceeds that of the more developed world, even though the less developed regions were only 37 percent urban in 1980. The reason for this is that both the urban and rural populations of many LDCs are growing at a spectacular rate. Thus, in 1980, the cities of the less developed regions contained more people than the more developed regions had in their total populations.

What about future trends? Population projections over a five- to ten-year period have never been very reliable, and projecting urban population changes is even more uncertain. Some relatively conservative United Nations population projections suggest that the world's population will grow to 6 billion by the year 2000. The urban population is also expected to grow rapidly from 1.7 billion in 1980 to 2.3 billion in the year 2000. It is important that 70 percent of the world's urban population (1.6 billion) is estimated to be in the less developed world. One might question whether the world can technologically and environmentally support these tremendous concentrations of population.

The Cohort Approach

A related but somewhat different approach to the study of urbanization patterns is to group countries by cohort. A *cohort* is any group that ex-

Table 2.7
Growth of world population and world urban population by region: 1920–2000.

A. Estimates and projections of the total population of the world and its regions

Area Units	Total population (in millions)				
	1920	1940	1960	1980	2000
World Total	1860.0	2295.1	2990.8	4414	6112
More Developed Major Areas	604.4	729.2	853.5	1020	1266
Europe	324.9	378.9	424.7	484	527
North America	115.7	144.3	198.7	247	354
Soviet Union	155.3	195.0	214.4	266	353
Oceania	8.5	11.0	15.7	23	22
Less Developed Major Areas	1255.6	1565.9	2137.3	3395	4846
East Asia	553.4	634.4	794.1	1173	1287
South Asia	469.8	610.1	857.9	1390	2153
Latin America	89.5	129.9	212.4	360	638
Africa	142.9	191.5	272.9	472	768
More Developed Regions[a]	672.7	820.6	976.5	1131	1441
Less Developed Regions[b]	1187.3	1474.5	2014.1	3283	4671

B. Estimates and projections of the population in urban places (20,000 or more inhabitants) for the world and world regions

Urban population (in millions)

Area Units	1920	1940	1960	1980	2000
World Total	266.4 (14.3)	431.5 (18.8)	760.3 (25.4)	1721.1 (39)	2337 (38.7)
More Developed Major Areas	179.9 (29.8)	267.9 (36.7)	389.5 (45.6)	703.8 (69)	784 (61.9)
Europe	112.9 (34.7)	149.8 (39.5)	187.9 (44.2)	333.9 (69)	290 (56.0)
North America	47.9 (41.4)	66.6 (46.2)	115.3 (58.0)	182.7 (74)	253 (48.0)
Soviet Union	16.0 (10.3)	47.0 (24.1)	78.0 (36.4)	164.9 (62)	222 (62.7)
Oceania	3.1 (36.5)	4.5 (40.9)	8.3 (52.9)	16.3 (71)	19 (59.4)
Less Developed Major Areas	86.5 (6.9)	163.6 (10.4)	370.8 (17.3)	1256.1 (37)	1553 (32.1)
East Asia	39.8 (7.2)	73.7 (11.6)	147.1 (18.5)	375.3 (32)	425 (33.0)
South Asia	26.9 (5.7)	50.6 (8.3)	117.5 (13.7)	403.1 (29)	568 (26.4)
Latin America	12.9 (14.4)	25.5 (19.6)	69.7 (32.8)	219.6 (61)	342 (53.6)
Africa	6.9 (4.8)	13.8 (7.2)	36.5 (13.4)	122.7 (26)	218 (28.4)
More Developed Regions[a]	197.7 (29.4)	303.9 (37.0)	449.6 (46.0)	780.3 (69)	901 (62.8)
Less Developed Regions[b]	68.7 (5.8)	127.6 (8.6)	310.7 (15.4)	952.0 (29)	1436 (30.7)

[a] More Developed Regions refers to Europe, North America, Soviet Union, Japan, Temperate South America and New Zealand.
[b] Less Developed Regions refers to East Asia without Japan, South Asia, Latin America without Temperate South America, Africa, Oceania without Australia and New Zealand.
[c] The figures in brackets are the percentage of the region's total population who live in urban places with 20,000 or more inhabitants.

Source: Adapted from Frisbie, W. P., "The Scale and Growth of World Urbanization." In J. Walton and D. E. Carnes, eds., *Cities in Change.* Boston: Allyn and Bacon, 1977, Tables 3 and 7; and Kane, Thomas T. and Myers, Paul F., *1980 World Population Data Sheet.* Washington, D.C.: Population Reference Bureau, 1980.

periences some event at the same time as another. Countries reaching the same level of urbanization within a few years of each other—for instance, having 30 percent of their respective populations live in urban places—thus can be considered a cohort.

We can divide countries into such cohorts by plotting the percentage of their populations living in urban places over a given period. Countries that began large-scale urbanization in the nineteenth century usually have population curves that take the shape of an elongated S. Assuming that this pattern would also be observed for countries beginning the urbanization process in the twentieth century, it could serve as a criterion for grouping them. In Figures 2.7 and 2.8, for example, one could group the United States with England and Wales at the end of the urbanization cycle; Japan and the USSR would be at the intermediate stage, and China and Kenya would be at the beginning of the cycle. The advantage to analyzing urbanization patterns by cohort is that the historical period when a country begins urbanizing has a profound effect on how urbanization proceeds. The sources

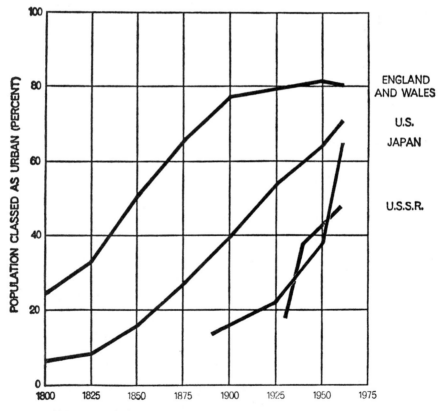

Fig. 2.7 Urban population growth curves for selected more developed countries.

Source: From ''The Urbanization of the Huamn Population'' by Kingsley Davis. Copyright © September 1965 by Scientific American, Inc. All rights reserved.

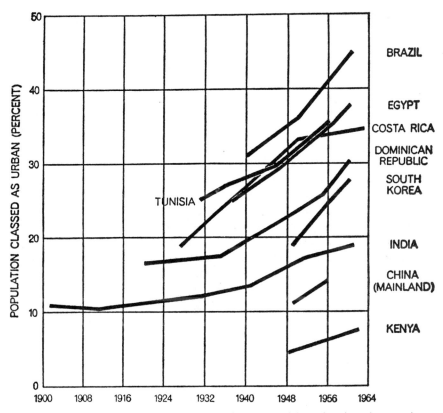

Fig. 2.8 Urban population growth curves for selected less developed countries.
Source: From "The Urbanization of the Human Population" by Kingsley Davis. Copyright © September 1965 by Scientific American, Inc. All rights reserved.

of energy, the level of technology, the nature of the world economy and of the political order have changed dramatically over the past two centuries, and these factors all influence a nation's urbanization.

Industrial-age urbanization England and Wales and the United States are good examples of countries that underwent urbanization during most of the nineteenth century. In the nineteenth century, cities were unhealthy places: mortality levels were so high that urban populations could not reproduce themselves, because deaths exceeded births. Cities during this century grew in primarily one way—by massive rural-to-urban migration. This migration was made possible by vast improvements in agricultural technology that freed workers from the farms. At the same time, burgeoning new urban industries encouraged surplus agricultural labor to gravitate to the cities. At that time, only a few industrial countries were competing in a world market. And underlying their development was an important assumption— the unlimited availability of physical resources. Coal was the major energy source; inanimate power was produced by the steam engine; and the dominant transportation mode was by rail and canal. Therefore, urbanization in this cohort of countries was more or less a gradual process reflecting each country's transformation from agrarian to industrial.

Urbanization in an age of scarcity   In contrast, countries that have only recently entered the first stage of the urbanization process, such as Kenya and China, face an entirely different set of circumstances. The most profound difference is the assumption on which the urbanization process is based. In the past the assumption was abundance; today it is scarcity. There is probably no better example of this point than the effect of the drastic oil price increase in the late 1970s and early 1980s. Urbanization and industrial development require the mobilization of tremendous financial and social resources. Those less developed nations lacking oil resources of their own must purchase oil on an international market, thus sapping the limited foreign exchange capital they might otherwise have available for development. In addition, modern transportation and other technologies differ from those of the last century, as does access to world markets. Many nations in the early stages of urbanization cannot compete successfully for world markets with the more developed nations that have high technology and automation.

Another major difference is the way cities in newly emerging countries grow. Urban growth in these nations is tremendously rapid, surpassing the growth rates of the more developed nations during their ascendancy. For one thing, the importation of modern medicine and public health measures has dramatically lowered mortality rates in both rural and urban areas of the developing world, so that natural increase alone accounts for considerable growth. In the past, cities grew by migration, and the rural-to-urban population movement reduced the population pressures in rural areas. Today, cities in the less developed world grow largely by natural increase. Rural-to-urban migration contributes to urban growth to a lesser degree, and this movement does little to relieve the countryside of its surplus population. Those who do migrate from rural areas to the cities are quickly replaced by new births. Thus, high rates of urban growth reflect high rates of total population growth. Such rapid increase in their urban population quickly outstrips these countries' ability to provide industrial jobs, and urbanization occurs without industrialization and economic development.

In sum, the development environment in the twentieth century—current energy resources, technology, relationship between countries in the international community, world markets, and population dynamics—differs markedly from the scene in the nineteenth century. The two cohorts examined illustrate how countries that entered the first stages of the urbanization cycle in recent years will necessarily have developmental and urbanization patterns different from the patterns of the more developed nations. The final section of this chapter will explore in greater detail the relationship between urbanization and the process of economic development.

URBANIZATION AND ECONOMIC DEVELOPMENT

Social scientists generally agree that the process of urbanization and the process of economic development are linked. But does economic development cause urbanization, or is the reverse pattern correct? The study of economic development, like the study of urbanization, is also complicated by a definition that is less than clear. For example, one finds the terms "modernization," "economic development," "industrialization," and "societal scale" used interchangeably in the literature. In general, economists use "economic development" to refer to what sociologists and other social scientists like to call "modernization." Before exploring the relationship between urbanization and economic development, one must attempt to define what economic development (or modernization) means.

Defining Economic Development

Of the dozens of definitions for economic development, the most common is based on technological criteria. From this perspective, economic development is viewed as occurring simultaneously with industrialization, which is "the extensive use of inanimate sources of power for economic production and all that entails by way of organization, transportation, and communication, and so on" (Moore, 1963, p. 92). Industrialization requires the reorganization of the labor force into more efficient forms that provide a greater output of goods and services for consumption by society. An example is the emergence of the factory system and the gradual elimination of the artisan—the silversmith, the shoemaker, etc. The shift of the labor force into a factory setting and the transformation of, say, shoemaking, from a single skilled worker fabricating a single pair of shoes to a group of unskilled workers assembling shoes on a line, increases efficiency. It is

Source: *The Wizard of Id* by permission of Johnny Hart and Field Enterprises, Inc.

this increase in efficiency or output resulting from the reorganization of the labor force that is considered economic development.

Different social scientists have focused on the social implications of economic growth. Greer (1962) sees these increases in efficiency and output as leading to increasing differentiation of the social structure—the specialization of its functions. Davis (1972b) views economic growth as leading to more complex new forms of social integration. Both writers see changes in the economic sphere of society reflected in a greater social complexity—the emergence of new occupations, interest groups, institutions, and businesses—as well as in more elaborate ways that these new social structures are linked together. Economic growth, then, is one element in a complex process that leads to fundamental modifications of the fabric of society (Smelser, 1963). It is these changes in the fabric of society that sociologists call modernization.

Daniel Lerner (1958) has discussed the individual aspects of modernization, which he defines as the process of social change whereby the less developed societies acquire characteristics common to more developed societies. As a society undergoes modernization, a change occurs in its members' world outlook, values, norms, consumption behavior, and so on.

A final set of theories links economic development (modernization) to energy sources. In one view, economic development is the extent to which a society's members use inanimate sources of power and/or tools to multiply the effects of their effort (Levy, 1967). Others have defined it as the process of using more energy to increase the productivity and efficiency of human labor (Meadows, 1972).

The various definitions suggest that the term economic development can be used to describe numerous broad changes in a society. First, a society's structure changes to permit the more efficient use of resources (the production of greater output). Changes also occur on the social-psychological level, in individuals' attitudes and values. Economic development also entails a change in the sources and the quantity of energy used by the society.

In this text, *economic development* and *modernization* are used synonomously and defined as increases in the aggregate output of a society and the social and cultural changes that occur in the development process. Economic development is a continuing process. Some countries are slowly changing their methods of production and social forms, whereas other countries are rapidly devising new production techniques and forms of organization. There are no such things as "developed" countries, only "more developed" and "less developed." The development scale is a relative one; the position of a country on this continuum changes not only in response to internal changes but in response to the changing positions of other countries. For example, fifty years ago Argentina was a more developed country. Subsequently, progress in the rest of the world caused Argentina to become a relatively less developed country (Hagen, 1968).

Irwin's Model of Modernization

Patrick Irwin (1975) has employed our definition of modernization in a model. Irwin argues that a more developed country uses tremendous amounts of energy (coal, gas, oil and hydroelectricity) in producing goods and services, but these countries use their energy more efficiently than could a less developed country. In other words, during economic development a country undergoes fundamental changes in its social organization that lead to the use of increasing quantities of energy and increased per capita output. The higher the country is on the development scale, the more complex its social organization and the more efficient its use of resources. Rather than studying economic development in terms of organizational complexity, division of labor, and the like, Irwin examines the total input of energy to a country's economy and the resulting output of goods and

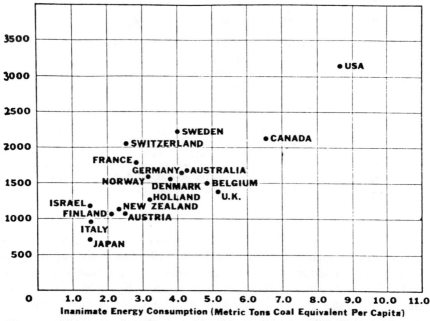

Data on energy consumption and output for most countries in the world are published by the United Nations as Metric Ton Coal Equivalents (MTCE) and Gross National Products (GNP). Metric Ton Coal Equivalent is a standard unit that tells how many BTUs of energy in all forms (oil, gas, coal) are consumed by each country. Gross National product (GNP) is a figure representing the total dollars of goods and services produced by a country in a year.

Fig. 2.9 Per capita GNP by per capita inanimate energy consumption in eighteen more developed countries.

Source: Reprinted from "An Operational Definition of Societal Modernization" by P. H. Irwin in *Economic Development and Cultural Change* 23(4):599 by permission of the University of Chicago Press © 1975.

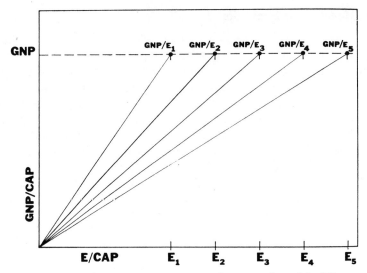

Fig. 2.10 Hypothetical case where the curves for countries with different GNP/E ratios are extrapolated to a constant GNP.

Source: Reprinted from "An Operational Definition of Societal Modernization" by P. H. Irwin in *Economic Development and Cultural Change* 23(4):611 by permission of the University of Chicago Press © 1975.

In this figure five hypothetical countries have the same per capita GNP. According to Irwin, the country with the lowest GNP/energy ratio would be the most highly developed. In this figure, country E_1 would be more developed than E_2, E_2 more developed than E_3, and so on. From Irwin's perspective, development can occur in two ways, (1) increase in per capita output, or (2) increase in energy efficiency in the production of this output. These changes, however, reflect a fundamental modification of the underlying structure of society.

services. The greater the efficiency of a country's economy, the higher the level of development (see Figures 2.9 and 2.10). The Irwin approach thus links resources and technology to broad changes within society. It measures modernization; however, it really does not specify what is involved in gaining increased efficiency. Irwin's research explores the broad social changes taking place within a country that permit its people to utilize resources more efficiently. Irwin, however, does not examine the relationship between urbanization and modernization.

In Figure 2.9 GNP and energy consumption figures are plotted for eighteen countries, providing the basis for some interesting comparisons. For example, find the points of Canada and Switzerland in the figure and notice that the two countries have approximately the same per capita GNPs ($2,000). Now run an imaginary line from the points to the x-axis and note that Switzerland uses less than half the energy used by Canada to reach the same output. Norway-Belgium and Israel-Holland are similar examples.

Relating Modernization and Urbanization

Several social scientists have examined the relationship between modernization and urbanization. Gibbs (1958) takes an ecological position, stating that in the final analysis all societies are organized to provide for material sustenance. That is, a society must provide food, clothing, shelter, and other items of consumption for mere physical survival. However, a country's natural resources are seldom in one place, and are usually widely dispersed. Because no one region is self-sufficient, the country's population must organize itself to exploit the resources and convert them into consumption items for nationwide distribution. One possible approach is to build a complex and expensive road system linking each resource area to all other areas. An alternative is to build a center to act as a transportation hub for the country. This city becomes a place of trade, a center of control over extractive industries, and a locale for processing and combining raw materials. Of the infinite number of ways in which societies can organize for survival, urbanization—organizing into cities—is the most efficient, as is demonstrated by the present dominance of this form (see Figures 2.11A, 2.11B).

The relationship between urbanization and economic development is revealed by examining the relationship between the regions of the hypothetical country in Figure 2.11. Note that the natural resources of this

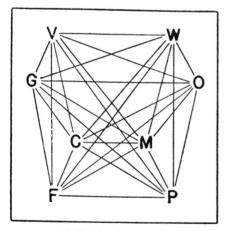 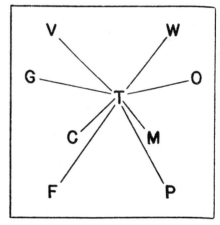

1A. Individualistic Network   1B. Organized Network

C, coal deposits; F, land suited for growing fibrous products such as cotton; G, land suited for growing grains; M, location of metallic substances such as iron; O, oil deposits; P, grazing lands producing animal products; T, transport center; V, land suited for growing vegetables and fruits; W, land areas covered with forests suited for producing wood products.

Fig. 2.11 Alternative transportation connections between areas with different natural resources in a hypothetical country.

Source: Gibbs, J. P., and Martin, W. T., "Urbanization and Natural Resources: A Study in Organizational Ecology." *American Sociological Review* 23, (1958) 266–277.

country are widely dispersed and no one region is self-sufficient. If the country's population is to produce consumption items for nationwide distribution, it must organize itself in such a manner that it may exploit its resources. One approach is depicted in Part A: the country builds a complex road system that links each resource area to all other regions. An alternative approach is to build a transportation center at T as shown in Part B. The way this relationship works can be seen by examining the hypothetical relationship between the coal area, C, and the transportation center, T. Assume that C's area has coal but no other mineral wealth, and strip mining has made it unsuitable for agriculture. Area C therefore would be totally dependent on T for its items of consumption, and the population at T would grow to process the raw material necessary for producing the items of consumption needed by area C. The role of city T in this system, therefore, is pivotal in coordinating the activities of all the regions of this country.

Gibbs and Martin (1958) considered another situation: the country in which most of the raw materials are close to a single center. Such a city would be less dependent on a transport center and as a result this center's population would decline. This situation is fairly common. In general, the degree of urbanization in a country varies directly with the extent of the dispersion of the items it consumes. In agricultural societies, for example, raw materials are evenly dispersed, and the relatively few items of consumption can be produced locally. Thus there is less need for urbanization. Countries that consume many more items and have widely dispersed natural resources will have high levels of urbanization. Urbanization contributes to the efficiency of a society by bringing together at one place the people, capital, and natural resources necessary to manufacture the items consumed. Moreover, the transportation and communication systems centered in cities facilitate the eventual distribution of these objects of consumption.

The link between urbanization and modernization arises from this notion of objects of consumption. The total number of objects produced by a country is its *output*. Modernization or economic development is societal change that permits increased output and increased energy efficiency. It is in the city that this social change takes place; therefore modernization and urbanization are inseparable processes. The expansion of a country's economy through technological development marks a fundamental change in the way a society organizes itself for sustenance.

The Changing Role of Urbanization

In the West, rapid urbanization appears to have been the catalyst that brought about economic development. Urbanization produced an environment conducive to technological invention that fundamentally altered the way people live in western societies. The role of urbanization in development in the less developed world may be different. Cities in the less

Photo 2.2 Pre-emption of land by squatters is apparent in this view of part of Rio de Janeiro. This settlement pattern now characterizes large portions of most cities in the less developed regions of the world.
Source: © Care Frank Photo Researchers, Inc.

developed world continue to be the center of technological change as well as the major point of contact with the more developed world. Whether the changes are diffused to the rest of the society is another question. Population growth in the less developed world is often centered in one or more cities—the phenomenon of primacy and its associated problems. Primacy can lead to a situation in which only the capital city offers the communication, transportation, banking, and other services that Western style commercial undertakings require. Economic development occurs in major cities of the less developed world, but its effects may spread throughout the society.

The rate of urbanization also appears to be different in less developed countries. Their urban populations are growing at an astonishing rate, creating problems of crisis proportions. Less developed countries with limited financial resources are hard pressed to provide basic sustenance for their people. This problem is especially acute in housing; shanty towns and squatter settlements have become a permanent fixture in cities of the less developed world. In Buenaventura, Columbia, for instance, 80 percent of the population is living in uncontrolled settlements. The figures in Table 2.8 indicate the extent of this problem in other regions of the world.

Table 2.8
Extent of slums and uncontrolled settlement in various cities in developing countries.

Country	City	Year	Uncontrolled Settlement Total (000s)	% City Population
Senegal	Dakar	1969	150	30
Tanzania	Dar es Salaam	1967	98	36
Zambia	Lusaka	1967	53	27
Afghanistan	Kabul	1968	100	21
Ceylon	Colombo	1963	305*	44
India	Calcutta	1961	2220	33
Indonesia	Djakarta	1961	725	25
Iraq	Baghdad	1965	500	29
Malaysia	Kuala Lumpur	1961	100	25
Pakistan	Karachi	1964	752	33
Philippines	Manila	1968	1100	35
Rep. of Korea	Seoul	1970	137*	30
Turkey	Ankara	1970	750	60
	Izmur	1970	416	65
Brazil	Rio de Janeiro	1961	900	27
	Recife	1961	396	50
	Brasilia	1962	60	41
Chile	Santiago	1964	546	25
Colombia	Cali	1964	243	30
	Buenaventura	1964	88	80
Ecuador	Guayaquil	1968	360	49
Mexico	Mexico City	1966	1500	46
Peru	Arcquipa	1961	54	40
	Luna	1969	1000	36
Venezuela	Barquisimento	1963	12.5*	41
	Caracas	1964	556	35
	Maracaibo	1966	280	50

*Dwelling units.

Source: U.N. General Assembly, *Housing, Building and Planning Problems and Priorities in Human Settlements.* 1970, p. 55, Annex III.

Shanty towns lead to the paradoxical situation of urbanization without urbanism. Mountjoy (1978) reports:

The expanding shanty towns are becoming re-creations of the village, with narrow streets and alleys not designed for motor traffic, but rather a meeting place, a playground, an area for animals to be tethered or to scavenge. For the majority of rural migrants a change of dwelling does not urbanize them. Tribal and family ties do not become severed by the move to the city for there they tend to coagulate into family and tribal groupings, and they are becoming less and less assimilated into the full urban way of life. Instead they foster a replica of the customs and culture they have grown up with in the village (p. 487).

This situation is not an isolated phenomenon, but is found in most of the cities of the less developed world (Abu-Lughod, 1961; Breese, 1966; Jackson, 1974; Mangrin, 1967; Turner, 1970). When these patterns become institutionalized, the developmental process is impeded.

There is no question that economic development and urbanization are linked, but the exact causal relationship is poorly understood. Rapid urbanization and its associated problems combined with the limited resources of many less developed countries may actually inhibit development. Many questions remain to be answered by students of economic development.

SUMMARY

This chapter has explored a number of issues associated with the process of urbanization. Two of the most important are the conceptual and measurement problems associated with the term *urbanization*. Eldridge, for example, in reviewing the literature of urban sociology, found the term *urbanization* defined as (1) a process of diffusion; (2) a process of intensification; and (3) a process of population concentration. For the purposes of this text, urbanization is considered to be the process of population concentration.

Closely related to conceptual problems is the difficulty of measuring the urbanization process. More than thirty different definitions are used in the world to define a population concentration as urban. The most widely used criterion is population size, followed by legal and government criteria. In making international comparisons, the degree of urbanization frequently is considered simply the percentage of a country's population living in urban areas, according to that country's own definition of urban. This approach presents numerous problems, so most international comparisons use the percentages of each country's population in cities of 100,000 or more inhabitants. In our study of urbanization in the United States, however, we have used the definitions employed by the U.S. Bureau of the Census.

The third section of this chapter explored macro patterns of urbanization. Three countries, Thailand, New Zealand, and Brazil, were examined to show the variety of urban settlement patterns found. A general look at worldwide patterns suggests that the less developed world is urbanizing at an unprecedented rate. In fact, the urban population in less developed countries (LDCs) will soon outstrip the total population of the more developed countries (MDCs). A cohort approach to the study of world ur-

banization was presented in this section. It appears that the urban experiences of LDCs will differ significantly from the MDCs, because the
historical time when a country begins urbanizing has a profound effect on
how urbanization proceeds. The sources of energy, the level of technology,
the nature of the world economy and of the political order have all changed
dramatically over the past two centuries and these factors influence the
urbanization of LDCs.

Finally, urbanization was discussed in relationship to the process of
economic development, modernization, and industrialization. For the purposes of this text, economic development and modernization were used
synonymously and defined as a society's increased output and the social
and cultural changes that occur in the development process. Economic
development is therefore a complex process that leads to fundamental
modification of the fabric of society; urban centers are the places where
this change takes place.

NOTES

1. In recent years, the notion of intensification has been incorporated in the works
   of Greer (1962) and others. Greer in the 1960s introduced the concept of *societal
   scale* which is built on Durkheim's earlier work. This concept is analyzed in
   Chapter 6.
2. It is interesting to note that the United States Census was one of the first
   modern censuses, beginning in 1790. Today it is considered one of the best in
   the world. The United States Constitution originally required the federal government to take a census every ten years in order to reapportion the seats in
   the House of Representatives. Today, Census figures are widely used by business and industry to determine the future locations of factories, stores, and
   other facilities. In addition, government at all levels utilizes the Census in
   formulating land use plans, public policy, and the administration of federal
   programs in revenue sharing, welfare, and housing. The Census is also a major
   tool of social scientists. Urban sociologists and ecologists depend on these
   public data for their research. The definitions used and the accuracy of the
   Census are therefore of vital interest to many spheres of society.
       The importance of these data to the country is reflected in the cost of the
   national Census. The cost of the 1980 Census was estimated to be more than
   four dollars for every man, woman, and child in the United States, or nearly
   a billion dollars.
3. The following section pertaining to Census practices in the United States was
   taken in part (with editing) from U.S. Bureau of the Census, *U. S. Census of
   Population: 1970, PC (1)-A-1* (Washington, D.C.: U. S. Government Printing
   Office, 1972) and updated for the 1980 Census with a work by Charles Pikaplon,
   Thomas Van Valey, and Associates, *Census '80: Continuing the Factfinder
   Tradition* (Washington, D. C.: U. S. Government Printing Office, 1980).
4. Two kinds of changes to SMSAs will take place sometime in 1982 or 1983.
   First, methodological refinements will be introduced into the SMSA definition

through new criteria, and the term "standard" will be dropped to simplify the title to Metropolitan Statistical Area (MSA).

Second, the boundaries of current SMSAs will be examined in light of 1980 Census data on commuting and population density. These data will be used to develop new criteria. In anticipation of the new criteria, to be put in effect after the 1980 Census, the conditions for establishment of a new SMSA in the 1980 Census are (1) its central city reaches 50,000 population; or (2) its urbanized area reaches 50,000 population, and it is located in a county or counties with a 100,000 population. Contiguous counties will be included in SMSAs if they are socially and economically interdependent with the central county of the SMSA (Census Bureau, 1980; pp. 140–141).

5. In the literature, the primacy index is calculated in several different ways: the population of the largest city may be divided by (1) the population of the second most populous city, (2) the combined population of the next two largest cities, or (3) the combined population of the next three largest cities. The first formula, which gives somewhat higher results than the other two, is used herein.

6. For a review of the more important articles on the topic of primacy, refer to the bibliography and the articles of Berry, 1961; Hoselitz, 1955; Jefferson, 1939; Lerner, 1958; Linsky, 1969, Menta, 1969; Owen and Wilton, 1973; and Sjoberg, 1963.

CHAPTER THREE

The Origins of Cities

Statement of Objectives

1. The student should become aware of recent changes in the field of archaeology that have greatly expanded our knowledge of early humans.

2. The rise of the first cities was a long evolutionary process. Students should be aware of changes in each prehistoric period that eventually led to the first cities.

3. The student should analyze the "constellation of changes" associated with the Agricultural Revolution.

4. The student should know the ecological and organizational characteristics shared by all the early urban cultures.

5. The importance of social class in the preindustrial city should be stressed. The student should understand how social class differences influenced the use of space within these cities.

6. The student should be aware of the social, economic, and political changes brought on by the Industrial Revolution.

7. The role of the city in the emergence of American society should be analyzed.

8. The student should become aware of the underlying similarities of the cities of the Atlantic coast, river cities, lake cities, southern cities and cities of the Southwest.

Human beings often ask, "Who am I?" and "From whence did I come?" This concern with origins and identity is a common theme in the comic and tragic literature of many cultures; it is evident today in the growing popularity of genealogy, as well as in the increasingly frequent attempts of adoptees to uncover the identities of their true parents.

The same questions motivate social scientists who are exploring the physiological and social origins of the human species. Research by these scientists during the past thirty years has revolutionized thinking on the evolution of humankind. For example, in the area of research concerned with physical evolution, fossilized remains of early hominids found at Olduvai Gorge and other sites in Africa indicate that the human species originated two to three million years ago—much earlier than previously estimated (Halloway, 1974; Leakey, 1967). Similarly, archeological finds from more recent human history have greatly expanded knowledge of these earliest societies and settlements (Clark, 1965; Jacobsen, 1976; Lamberg-Karlousky, 1971; Schild, 1976; Smith, 1976). Generally, these studies have illuminated the process by which human settlements have evolved to more complex urban forms.

This chapter traces the growth of cities from a historical perspective. Examination of the first agricultural villages 8,000 years ago and their evolution into cities is followed by discussion of the social, political, economic, and ecological characteristics of these early cities and their similarities with other preindustrial cities, whether in Mesopotamia in the third millennium B.C. or in western Europe in the Middle Ages. The emphasis in this section is not on the chronology of historical events per se, but rather on the patterns and processes of urban development. Next, the Industrial Revolution and its impact on urban form and function are explored with emphasis on contemporary urbanization. Finally, the role of the city in American social history is surveyed.

The premise of this chapter is that an understanding of the origins and functions of cities in the past will lead to an understanding of contemporary urbanization. Consequently, the focus is on the broad social changes that made possible the emergence of a unique form of social organization—the city.

The Collection of Evidence

Until recently, knowledge of the origin of cities was based on data gathered from the durable remains of partly explored sites, fragments of writing dating from 3500 B.C., and eyewitness accounts of Mesoamerican cities written by the Spanish during their conquest of the Inca and Aztec empires in the sixteenth century.

Since World War II, new technology has greatly expanded archaeology's data base. Carbon-14 dating techniques, introduced in the 1940s, enable archeologists to place evidence in proper chronological order (Renfrew, 1971). Microscopic analysis of pollen left in storage containers centuries ago gives an inventory of the early human diet (Bender, 1975, pp. 37–64). Rigorous statistical analysis of the frequency and distribution of artifacts at a site, made possible by the high-speed computer, gives insight into the social structure of prehistoric people (Adams, 1966, pp. 1–37). Most important has been the change in the conception of archeology as natural history—the collection, description, and classification of artifacts through inductive reasoning—to a view of it as a deductive social science concerned with theory construction and hypothesis testing (Polgar, 1975). A case in point is the present research on prehistoric societies. The new archeology views human beings as a species of animal and explores the adaptation of this animal to its environment. This ecological approach analyzes the complex interaction among early humans, their technology, and a changing environment and provides a description of the ways social organization has evolved.

Preconditions for Cities

The impact of cities on the modern way of life is so great that it is difficult to realize how "new" cities are in human social history. Archeological evidence shows that the first cities did not appear until about 3500 B.C. (Adams, 1960; Davis, 1973; Sjoberg, 1972). To place the evolutionary process in perspective, one must realize that humankind in its present form, *Homo sapiens,* has existed for approximately 40,000 years but has lived in cities for only 5,500 years, or a little more than 10 percent of the span of human existence (Halloway, 1974; Adams, 1966).

Technological and environmental conditions The emergence of cities, therefore, is a benchmark in an evolutionary process lasting many thousands of years. During these millennia humans gradually accumulated the technical and social inventions necessary for the formation of cities (Harrison, 1954). One of these was the technology to produce a food surplus so that individuals could be freed from food production. This elaborate technology included agriculture, animal husbandry, and a host of related inventions. Also needed was a complex social organization, beyond the ties of family and kinship, to allow the distribution of surplus food for valued social ends. Finally, there was one precondition over which humans had no control—a mild climate. The level of technology in early societies was so low that only the most favorable climatic conditions would allow large permanent population concentrations. Such conditions did not prevail until about 10,000 B.C. when the last stage of the Ice Age came to an end in Europe (Davis, 1973, pp. 11–13).

Necessary social change Pondering these preconditions, one might think that the invention of agriculture would be synonymous with the urban revolution. It is true that permanent settlements require a reliable and intensive agricultural base, but it is incorrect to think of the urban revolution and the agricultural revolution as the same process. Abundant evidence suggests that they were separate processes. For example, the agricultural technology necessary to support an urban population probably had developed several thousand years before the emergence of cities (Adams, 1966, pp. 38–78). The availability of a food surplus therefore does not adequately explain the development of urban forms of human settlement. Cities require not only a food surplus but also the means for its transportation, storage, and distribution for socially valued ends. Thus, a complete change in the structure of society was necessary before cities could evolve. To understand this change one must examine human social evolution prior to the emergence of cities.

HUMAN PREHISTORY

Archeologists have divided human prehistory into three time periods: the Paleolithic or Old Stone Age lasting from 500,000 to 10,000 B.C. in the Near East, the Mesolithic or transition period of the Stone Age lasting from 10,000 to 8000 B.C. in the Near East, and the Neolithic or New Stone Age lasting from 8000 B.C. to the appearance of the first cities in the Near East around 3500 B.C.

The Paleolithic Period

During the half-million years of the Paleolithic period humans lived as nomads—wandering hunters and gatherers with no permanent settlements and a level of technology so low that every individual was required to participate in food gathering. Probably no other form of social organization was possible during this period. The climate during most of the Paleolithic period was much colder than it is today; much of northern Europe, Asia, and North America was covered by glaciers, and the environmental conditions necessary for agriculture were not present.

Technology set limits on both the size and form of Paleolithic societal organizations. Even during the late Paleolithic, when humans were producing flint and bone tools, cave paintings, and sculptured figurines, technology permitted only .025 persons to be supported per square mile (Deevy, 1960, p. 196). Paleolithic people therefore were forced to live in small, homogeneous groups. Because there was no surplus of food there could be no specialized labor beyond that based on age and sex, and without specialization there could be no social classes or other forms of complex human organization (Clark, 1965; Jacobson, 1976; Smith, 1976).

The Mesolithic Period

The last main glacial period in Europe, the Würm, ended around 10,000 B.C. when dramatic climatic changes occurred. As a result of a milder climate, new plants and animals appeared. With the climate change came the onset of the Mesolithic or transition period in human prehistory. The most significant occurrence of this period was the emergence of the first villages. They were based not on agriculture but on a new subsistence strategy of intensive collecting of plants and animals. These villages became a dominant form of human settlement during the Mesolithic period and were widely dispersed from as far north as the Baltic Sea to as far south as India.

Excavation of Mesolithic sites has uncovered an improved bow, scrapers, reapers, and a variety of other specialized tools. Archeologists have concluded, however, that the technology used by each village was related directly to the foodstuffs found in the immediate vicinity. For example, near the Baltic Sea people subsisted on shellfish; in southern Germany, elk; in western Greece, the red deer and plant life; in western Iran, grain. Each population concentration developed a variety of specialized tools to use in exploiting the resources in their environment. Improved technology combined with climatic changes meant that the population that could be supported per square mile increased six-fold—to fifteen persons (Deevy, 1960, p. 196).

The Mesolithic-village form of life was an important step in human social evolution. Sedentism or permanent village life, based on the intensive exploitation of plants and animals, gave people an intimate knowledge of their local environment. Their accumulated experiences with wild wheat, barley, and other food plants, as well as with wild goats, sheep, pigs, cattle, and horses, and the ecological niches where these plants and animals existed, formed the knowledge base from which agriculture would develop (Adams, 1966, pp. 38–78).

The Neolithic Period

The Neolithic period began with the appearance of agriculture. The agriculturally based village originated in about 8000 B.C. in an area of Asia known as the Fertile Crescent that encompasses present-day Israel, Lebanon, Jordan, Syria, northern Iraq, and western Iran. It is a region with a dry climate, plentiful sunshine, mild winters, and abundant water. In addition, in the highlands of the Fertile Crescent were found the ancestors of modern wheat, barley, sheep, goats, and cattle.

The importance of climate cannot be overstated. Neolithic technology was poorly developed, but plentiful sunshine and mild winters provided two or more growing seasons each year, a dry climate permitted the safe and long-term storage of grain and other staples, and abundant water made possible intensive agriculture. Therefore, most early Neolithic settlements of both the Old and the New World were in the tropical latitudes where such conditions prevail.

The Agricultural Revolution

By 8000 B.C. the inhabitants of the hills of the Fertile Crescent had come to know their habitat so well that they were beginning to domesticate the plants and animals they had been collecting and hunting.[1] The food-producing revolution was therefore not an event but a process that occurred

Photo 3.1 This is an aerial photo of Jarmo, one of the early village farming communities located on the slopes of the Zagros Mountains in western Iraq. Jarmo was a permanent, year-round settlement inhabited for several hundred years around 6500 B.C. The village consisted of more than two dozen multiroomed rectangular mud brick houses and a population of approximately 150 persons. The diet of these people was varied and well balanced and included wheat, barley, mutton, goat meat, and probably beef, as well as field peas, lentils, vetchings, and collected pistachio nuts. In many respects the diet of the villagers 8000 years ago was superior to the diet of the present-day inhabitants of the area.
Source: Courtesy of the Oriental Institute, University of Chicago.

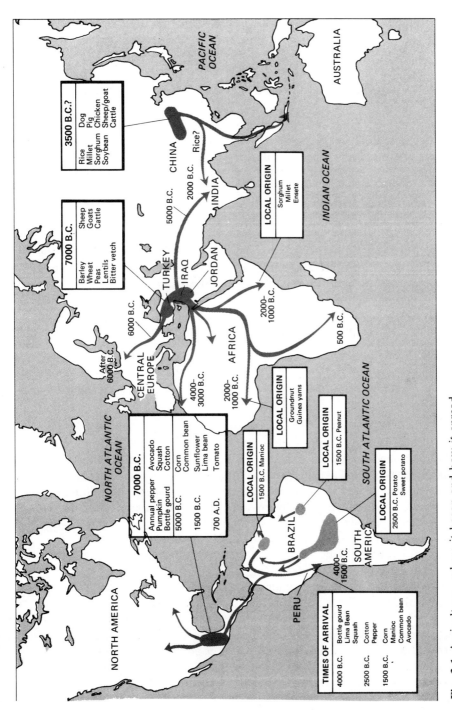

Fig. 3.1 Agriculture—where it began and how it spread.

Source: © 1967 by The New York Times Company. Reprinted by permission.

gradually and followed different courses of development according to different local conditions, even within the Fertile Crescent (Adams, 1966, p. 41). The distinction between plant gathering and plant breeding, moreover, is not based just on the sowing of seeds. For instance, first people had to take wheat from its narrow ecological niche in the highlands and mountains of the Fertile Crescent to open flat areas to which it was not adapted. Second, the removal of certain pressures of natural selection led to strains of wheat more suitable for agriculture. By 7000 B.C. domesticated wheat had been bred and grain culture had emerged. The domestication of cereal grains expanded the environmental range within which these crops could be grown and increased substantially the size and reliability of yeilds.[2] An important quality of grain is its ability to be stored for long periods of time. A large, reliable source of easily stored foodstuffs added physical and, more significantly, social stability to the Neolithic farm village (Bender, 1975; Braidwood, 1960; Harris, 1967; Kimber, 1972; Renfrew, 1973; Solheim, 1972).

Agriculture and animal husbandry were not the only inventions making village life possible. Over the centuries an array of tools, utensils, and cooking techniques had developed to make the plant tissue palatable. In addition, carpentry, masonry, pottery, textiles, polished stone tools, and the plow, as well as the versatile use of wood, hides, and bones, formed a technological complex that augmented the cultural evolution made possible by a food-producing technology.

Agriculture and Cities

In the course of many centuries, the basic elements of the food-producing revolution spread west across the entire eastern end of the Mediterranean and as far east as the Caspian Sea. Eventually the new way of life reached the Aegean and spread into Europe. As in previous ages, indigenous populations selectively borrowed elements of the new technology and adapted them to the conditions of the local environment (Bender, 1975, pp. 89–106; Braidwood, 1960; Harris, 1967; Harrison, 1954). Neolithic villagers, however, did not work at highest efficiency and grew only enough food for their own needs. In order for cities to be formed, both the technology to produce a surplus and institutional mechanisms to motivate farmers to grow and relinquish their surplus were required. By about 4000 B.C. the people of southern Mesopotamia had developed the agricultural technology to produce a large food surplus. Seasonal flooding of the Tigris and Euphrates Rivers and small-scale irrigation had led to a new form of intensive agriculture. Trade appears to have been a major factor in motivating villagers to produce more food than they needed for their own use.

THE EARLIEST CITIES

The Role of Trade

Although Neolithic villages were separated by hundreds of miles of mountains and water, archeological evidence shows that the settlements throughout the Near East were in active communication. Geological studies, for example, indicate that the entire Fertile Crescent region is devoid of obsidian deposits. Nevertheless, substantial amounts of this material have been found at the excavations at Jarmo (more than 450 pounds) and other Neolithic sites.''From this it appears that well before 6000 B.C. Jarmo must have been conducting a thriving trade across the mountains that brought it into contact with the communities to the north of Armenia'' (Dixon, 1968, p. 44).

Obsidian was not the only material traded in prehistoric times. Soapstone, textiles, pottery, and probably perishable items also were traded. By examining artifacts at widely dispersed sites, archeologists are now reconstructing the trade routes of prehistoric peoples. These routes, some of which cross the most inhospitable terrain in the world, linked the early settlements in a communication network that must have influenced their development profoundly'' (Dixon, 1968, p. 45).

The overgrown village Only a few villages out of hundreds had the right combination of terrain, climate, technology, and location in relation to trade routes to become trade centers. The wealth brought to a village through trade permitted it to increase its population and allowed some individuals to become part-time specialists in production and trade. These "overgrown villages covering five to six acres and supporting upwards to 5,000 people began to emerge between 4000–5000 B.C. and became the containers in which the social changes necessary for the emergence of cities occurred'' (Davis, 1973).

The *overgrown village* represents a transition stage in the emergence of the first cities. They were up to ten times larger than the surrounding agricultural villages, and their size permitted a more complex social structure in which the chances for innovation were enhanced. Some of the innovations that indicate a city was forming include: (1) permanent settlement in dense aggregations, (2) nonagriculturalists in specialized functions, (3) taxation and capital accumulation, (4) monumental public building, (5) a ruling class, (6) the technique of writing, (7) the acquisition of predictive sciences—arithmetic, geometry, and astronomy, (8) artistic expression, (9) trade, and (10) replacement of kinship by residence as the basis for membership in the community (Childe, 1950, pp. 4–7). Childe's list is interesting because social innovations rather than technical inventions predominate. Many social forms connected with cities make their first appearance in the overgrown village.

Evolution of Social Organization

The social innovations made possible by the trade surplus in the overgrown village were crucial in the development of cities. For instance, the "cradle of civilization"—Mesopotamia—is not homogeneous in climate, terrain, or rainfall but forms an environmental mosaic. Some areas are well suited for grain cultivation, others for orchards, herding, and fishing. Each ecological niche supported its own specialists, and an early function of the overgrown village was to provide a marketplace for exchange of the diverse agricultural products. Adams (1966) reports that a number of pre-Hispanic cities in Central America became "hyper-developed" markets that had really no other function. More than 60,000 people would gather daily in these cities to exchange and barter (p. 53).

Early formal institutions Early formal institutions had their beginnings in the relationship among the different agricultural specialists. Early temple records suggest that one of the earliest functions of priests was to control and formalize these relationships and even set rates of exchange, e.g., fish-grain equivalents (Adams, 1966, p. 48). The priests, in all likelihood, were also involved in other forms of social control, including keeping herdsmen out of fields during seasonal shortages of fodder and controlling the construction and maintenance of irrigation systems, as well as the distribution of water. In each case, submitting to the control of a centralized authority and paying that authority part of one's agricultural production was an early exchange relationship beneficial to all parties.

Full-time specialists The continued growth of trade and local exchange enabled part-time specialists to become full-time artisans, priests, officials, and warriors. The concentration of these full-time specialists in one place not only encouraged technical innovation but also enabled them to organize and extend their social control. The invention of writing by those specialists led to accurate record keeping that aided commerce. More important, it allowed more complex administrative and legal systems and more rigorous thought. Organizationally, these developments resulted in systematized religious control, linkage of religious institutions with a centralized government, property rights bound to land as a quasi-governmental institution, and an expanded division of labor that facilitated the exchange of goods and services (Adams, 1966). Hence, the cumulative social and technical innovations fostered in the expanded-village environment transformed these villages into the first cities. By 3500 B.C., southern Mesopotamia had evolved specialized groups of producers whose relationships followed the lines of the dominant urban institutions—the palace and the temple. Ultimately the combination of a trade surplus and social specialization ushered in the structured inequality of a more complex social order.

Characteristics of Mesopotamian Cities

Among the earliest cities were Erech, Eridu, Ur, Lagash, and Larsa in the southernmost valley of the Tigris-Euphrates Rivers and Kish and Jemet Nasr in the north (Sjoberg, 1960, p. 34). The first cities were small by modern standards, rarely exceeding 8,000–25,000 persons. The city of Ur, for example, covered only 220 acres and had an estimated total popultion of 24,000. However, these cities were ten to twenty times larger than the Neolithic villages that previously had been the largest settlements, and they must have been awe-inspiring to the rural people of the day.

Ecological and organizational characteristics Interestingly, these cities were very similar in their ecological and organizational characteristics. First, each city was ruled by a king who was also considered a representative of the city's deity and thus its chief priest. Second, they had similar cultures including wheat and barley cultivation; bronze metallurgy; use of wheeled vehicles; the raising of sheep, goats, cattle, and horses; the use of oxen as draft animals; and the production of luxury goods by local artisans from metals and precious stones. Third, these cities were similar in physical appearance. The city's center was a walled zone containing a temple-palace complex devoted to the city-god and the king-priest. Surrounding this core were houses made of dried or fired mud brick, "jumbled together forming an irregular mass broken at intervals by open spaces in front of a temple or governmental building" (Sjoberg, 1960, p. 35). Streets were narrow, winding, unpaved, and inadequately drained. Sanitation was poor; offal and other refuse were simply thrown into the streets. Subareas of the city appear to have been inhabited by various groups of specialists. Agriculturalists lived just outside the city's wall within walking distance of their fields. At the periphery of the city but inside the wall were the poorest inhabitants, who lived in mud and reed hovels. Merchants and artisans lived closer to the city's center, where the nobility, priests, and warriors resided.

Ironically, the opposite pattern characterizes most modern metropolises. High-status groups live at the city's periphery, while the poorest inhabitants live closer to the city's center. This relationship between space and social status will be analyzed in Chapter 7.

Vulnerability These cities shared one other characteristic—vulnerability, both internal and external. Their general tendency to be located on flood plains meant periodic destruction by water. Cooking fires frequently set off conflagrations that leveled large areas of the city. Sanitation was almost totally lacking, and the streets became open sewers, tainting water supplies and breeding disease. The trade on which all the earliest cities relied spread epidemics. Social and economic decay also affected these settlements.

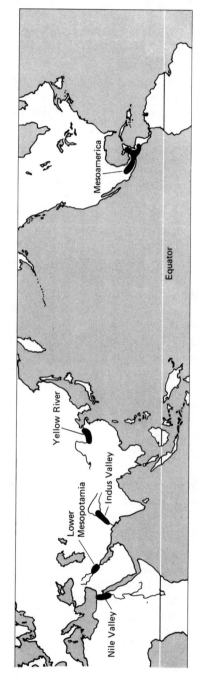

Fig. 3.2 The world's earliest cities first evolved from villages in the lower Mesopotamia. Thereafter cities arose in similar valleys in other parts of the world.

Source: Gideon Sjoberg, "The Origin and Evolution of Cities." Copyright © 1965 by Scientific American, Inc. All rights reserved.

Archeological evidence suggests that many of these early cities fell victim to disease and natural disaster and simply ceased to exist.

The earliest cities were vulnerable to attack from without. Agricultural technology during antiquity was inefficient by modern standards, and an enormous number of agriculturalists were needed to support a small urban population. Hawley (1971) estimates that only 3 or 4 percent of a local population could be supported in urban settlements during this period. Urban populations could grow only when more farmers and producers were brought under the influence of the city. The rise and fall of cities therefore corresponded to the rise and fall of their empires. A city could continue only as long as the ruling elite had the political power to ensure that agriculturalists would give up part of their yield to support city dwellers. The rulers could accomplish this process benignly through trade and taxation or, as was more often the case, through military coercion and the exaction of tribute. Because the urban populations were so greatly outnumbered by the people in the countryside, these settlements were vulnerable to rebellion by angry peasants. The cities also were vulnerable to conquest by other peoples and periodic attack by nomadic raiders. As a result a foe who could seize and destroy the empire's capital city normally brought an end to the empire. In this way many cities and empires fell, never to rise again.

Why the Urban Revolution?

The foregoing sections describe where, when, and how the earliest cities originated. But why did cities evolve? People often think of an invention as a material thing, when in fact the inventions that have had the most pervasive influence on human life have been social in character. Of the numerous ways of defining the term "city," one of the more interesting is to describe a city as a "time-saving device" that enables diverse groups of people to come together to exploit each other. "Some scholars regard the city as second only to agriculture among the significant inventions in human history" (Sjoberg, 1960, p. 1). Cities evolved because they contributed to human efficiency. The major obstacle to exchange and production is distance, and cities reduce this obstacle by concentrating a large population at one place. Thus, they facilitate specialization and exchange and allow for increased productivity at less cost. Because they were a superior adaptation to their environment, cities displaced the Neolithic farm village as the dominant form of organization (Davis, 1973, pp. 14–16).

OTHER EARLY URBAN DEVELOPMENT

The pattern of evolution of the earliest cities in Mesopotamia was repeated in at least four other places in antiquity—in the valleys of the Nile, the

Indus, and the Yellow Rivers and also in Central America. It is generally agreed that Mesoamerican and Mesopotamian cities arose independently, whereas the emergence of cities in other regions of the Old World probably was influenced by Mesopotamian cities.

Early Cities in Egypt

Agriculture, animal husbandry, and other technologies diffused from the Fertile Crescent southwest into the Nile Valley. Cattle, wheat, and barley not indigenous to Africa were incorporated into the Neolithic villages that arose along the lower Nile and its delta around 4000 B.C. By 3500 B.C., a number of these farm villages had grown to the overgrown-village stage and were clustered into several politically independent units each containing large cooperative irrigation projects (Sjoberg, 1960, p. 37). The transition from settled agricultural communities to cities appears to have occurred around 3300 B.C. when the lower Nile was unified under the first Pharaoh, Menes.

The archeological record of Egypt's earliest cities is sketchy before 2000 B.C. The few remaining temples, secular buildings, and written records suggest that Egyptian cities were generally not as large or as densely settled as those of Mesopotamia. One reason for this difference is the early dynastic "practice of changing the site of the capital, normally the largest settlement, with the ascendancy of a new pharaoh" (Sjoberg, 1960, pp. 38–39). Cities simply were not given the opportunity to grow in size or become complex in structure. Another reason was the security provided by the Nile Valley. The Nile is buffered on both the east and west by desert, which was a barrier to invasion. Once the Nile Valley was unified politically, Egyptian cities, unlike Mesopotamian cities, did not require elaborate fortifications and garrisoned troops to protect them from invading armies. Egypt's terrain also had an inhibiting effect on trade. Trade was an essential element in the economics of the earliest cities, and without extensive trade a system of cities could not develop in Egypt.

Another factor was the combination of the religious and political leadership of Egypt in one god/king, the Pharaoh. In Mesopotamian cities, political rule and religious rule were interrelated but not identical. Power was fragmented further by the dispersal of population in city-states. In Egypt, where religious and political power was concentrated in the hands of one person, most full-time specialists were attached to the Pharaoh at his capital. Hence the development of a full civic culture in other urban settlements was retarded (Coulburn, 1959, pp. 67–82).

The combination of environmental and organizational factors in Egypt led to the emergence of cities that diverged from the pattern of those in the lower valleys of the Tigris and Euphrates Rivers. Though it is likely that city-building technology diffused to Egypt from the Mesopotamian city-states, Egypt's indigenous population selectively borrowed items and combined them with the local culture to produce a unique early civilization.

The Harappa Civilization

The next center of civilization appeared around 2500 B.C. in the Indus River system, in what is now western Pakistan. This civilization, known as the Harappa culture, imposed a uniform culture over an area in excess of a half-million square miles. The civilization was distinguished by twin capitals—a northern one, Harappa, in the Punjab, the tributary region of the Indus, and Mohenjo-daro, 350 miles south on the Indus. The uniformity of these cities in layout, size, and population is remarkable.

Each city was laid out in a gridiron pattern with straight, wide streets running north-south and east-west, forming rectangular blocks roughly 1200 feet by 800 feet. These blocks composed precincts, each inhabited by a specific group—potters, weavers, brick makers, metal workers, and working people. Working-people's quarters, for example, consisted of rows of identical two-room dwellings next to the granary and milling works. The elite also were segregated and lived in houses built around courtyards with windowless exterior walls broken only by essential doors. Many of these homes were multistoried and were provided with wells and complex drainage systems. The use of refuse collection bins and a complex underground drainage system suggests a concern for sanitation not shared by other contemporary urban societies.

The cities covered roughly a square-mile area and housed approximately 20,000 persons (Piggott, 1962, p. 167). Centered on the western edge of both cities was a raised citadel, 1200 feet by 600 feet, topped by buildings that appear to have been used for ceremonial or public purposes. The buildings included a great ceremonial bath, a collegiate building, and a pillared hall. This citadel indicates a religious or administrative life of a significant scale.

Centralized control and planning extended beyond the cities to the entire kingdom. After 2500 B.C. the Harappa culture featured a standard of weights and measures, fired bricks of uniform size, mass-produced pottery, and several towns and villages with standardized layouts. The extreme uniformity of material culture throughout the territory suggests that the Harappa kingdom was ruled by a single "priest-king, wielding autocratic and absolute power" from two capital cities 350 miles apart but linked by a river thoroughfare (Piggott, 1962).

This civilization was obliterated by invaders in about 1500 B.C. after being remarkably stable for 800–1000 years. It adopted few material innovations during the millenium of its existence. There is some evidence of trade with the Sumerian states via the Dilmun empire by 2000 B.C., but the unchanging material culture suggests isolation. The writing of this civilization is still undecipherable and is unrelated to Mesopotamian languages. The evidence taken as a whole suggests that the Harappa culture emerged independently. If city-building elements were borrowed by the people of the Indus valley, these people gave them a special cultural flavor (Sjoberg, 1960).

Early Cities in China

The valley of the Huangho (Yellow) River is regarded as the birthplace of another civilization, the Shang, which arose around 1800 B.C. Before 1950, the earliest known city in China was Yin, dated at 1300 B.C. Its ruins are north of the Huangho at the site of the present city of An-yang. From 1928–1937, fifteen seasons of scientific excavations were undertaken in this region by the National Research Institute of History and Philology of China. Archeologists discovered at this site a high culture with mature urbanism and related institutions—class differentiation, trade and currency, chamber burials with human sacrifices, highly developed bronze metallurgy, writing, advanced stone carving, and elegant pottery (Chang, 1968, pp. 209–226). Yin, however, was an enigma to archeologists because it contained no signs of a primitive phase; the material culture was in a highly developed state with no ties to China's Neolithic past. Scholars argued that China's early urban development was the result of advanced technology being diffused from the Near East, where civilization had existed 1500 years before it came to China.

Since 1950, theories on the evolution of China's early civilization have been reinterpreted on the basis of findings from several sites north and south of the Huangho. The discovery of Shang remains in 1950 south of the Huangho and about 100 miles from An-yang filled some of the gaps between civilized and Neolithic eras. Archeologists uncovered a walled city dating from 1650 B.C. with evidence of a large population and a complex social order. The most interesting conclusion from this and other Shang sites of the same period is that individual cities were composed of an organized group or network of villages that shared a single political and ceremonial center. Surrounding but linked to this center were industrial quarters for specialists in bronze, pottery, and bone as well as farm villages, all of whom used the administrative center for exchange and redistribution (Chang, 1968, pp. 240–241). The settlement pattern is without precedent in the early civilizations of Mesopotamia, the Nile, and the Indus. These Shang settlements, however, performed all the essential functions of a city. They represent an organizational nexus that contrasts sharply with the Neolithic villages and can be classified as urban.

Still older sites have been identified since 1960 in an area near the Yi and Lo Rivers, tributaries of the Huangho. The primitive pottery and bronze works found there are unlike the elegantly worked artifacts found at Yin and Cheng-chou. These sites represent "the earliest verifiable phase of a full-fledged Shang civilization with bronze metallurgy, advancing forms of symbols on pottery, a Shang art, large hang-t'u structures, a highly stratified burial pattern, and specialized handicrafts" (Chang, 1968, p. 200).

The remains of these early Shang settlements have been dated at approximately 1850 B.C. Although they are not considered urban settlements, they are indicative of a highly stratified and complex society. More importantly, the findings at these sites demonstrate the close relationship between the Neolithic culture of the area and the early Shang culture.

Although cultural items possibly were diffused from the Near East to the valley of the Yellow River, the distinct phases of the Shang civilization suggest that the transformation from Neolithic to civic culture in China was a gradual one rooted in the cultural history of the Huangho valley.

Urban Development in the New World

In comparison with the time spans of the archeological epochs in the Old World, human history in the New World is very brief. Archeological evidence suggests that people migrated to the Western Hemisphere via Siberia and the Bering Strait a little more than 15,000 years ago. These prehistoric people slowly fanned out from the arctic region to populate both Americas by 1300 B.C. (Clark, 1965). In the southward migration, they came into contact with species of plants and animals very different from those of the Old World. The adaptation of these people to the virgin land led to the emergence of cultures and civilizations that differ markedly from those of the Old World.

Mesoamerica The earliest cities in the New World first appeared around 200 B.C. in Mesoamerica, specifically the area that includes southern Mexico, Guatemala, Belize (formerly British Honduras), and the western parts of Honduras and El Salvador. Domestication of plants began in this region as early as 7000 B.C., but the first agricultural villages did not emerge until 1500 B.C. Mesoamerican peoples therefore were entering the Formative era (a stage roughly equivalent to the Neolithic of the Old World) at a time when Mesopotamian cities had been in existence for nearly two millenia. The nature of New World agriculture was one factor in this late development (Clark, 1965, p. 171). The corn, squash, beans, peppers, and gourds on which the villages depended were more difficult to domesticate than the wheat and barley of the Near East.

The Maya Of the several civilizations—Olmec, Teolihucan, Toltec, Aztec, and Maya—that evolved in Mesoamerica, the Mayan was unquestionably the most culturally developed. The origin of the Mayan civilization is still not well understood, but recent excavations in Belize and other parts of

Central America are rapidly expanding knowledge of this culture. It flourished between 300 and 1000 A.D. and featured mathematics, astronomy, an accurate calendar, a complex hieroglyphic script, and painting, sculpture, and architecture rivaling those of ancient Greece and Rome (Hammond, 1977). Tikal, Vaxactun, Chichen Itza, Mayapan, Copan, and other cities were the centers of small states ruled by a leader drawn from the priesthood. These city-states appear to have been combined into some sort of loose confederation.

The layout of these cities conforms to the internal structure of cities in the other civilizations of early antiquity. At its center were the palaces of temples housing priests and nobility, surrounded by the residences of the wealthy and influential. Toward the periphery were the homes of the lower class. The overall population appears to have been very small, so small that some scholars have argued that these were not cities at all but simply "ceremonial foci to which the rural population flocked on special occasions" (Sjoberg, 1960, p. 47). Maya specialists, however, are coming to believe that they were true urban centers. The highly stratified society that included priests, nobility, soldiers, merchants, and artisans and this society's ability to mobilize the resources necessary to construct ceremonial centers of immense size suggest an urban-based civilization.

The Aztec The Aztec civilization, centered in the high plateau region of southern Mexico, emerged in the 500-year period after the decline of the Mayans around 1000 A.D. The Aztec capital, Tenochtitlan, at the site of Mexico City, probably had a population in excess of 100,000 at the time of Spanish conquest in 1521. This civilization was derived from and was similar to the Mayan in many respects.

The Inca The only other known New World civilization was the Inca of South America, centered in what is now Peru, Bolivia, and Columbia. Agriculture had diffused from Central to South America by 2500 B.C., but at least another 1000 years elapsed before an extensive pattern of farm villages appeared there. The *diffusion* of city-building elements is also likely, but the Inca civilization differed in other significant ways from the Mayan and the Aztec.

Between 100 and 1400 A.D. the Inca conquered most of the central and northern regions of South America, unifying it into an empire linked by more than 10,000 miles of road converging at the Inca capital at Cuzco, in present-day Equador. The empire was administered by a centralized governmental bureaucracy under a god-king. This civilization created elaborate public works such as bridges, canals, terrace systems, and roads, and conducted large-scale social, economic, and city planning. Of interest is the fact that the Inca did not develop writing, although they did have a system of numerical notation using the "quipu," a knotted string. Consequently, mathematics, astronomy, and calendar making were poorly developed. The Inca were conquered in a few months by the Spanish in 1532 (Sjoberg, 1960).

The Spread of the Urban Revolution

The valleys of the lower Tigris, Euphrates, Nile, Indus, and Huangho Rivers and Mesoamerica were the birthplaces of civilization. In succeeding centuries their agricultural, material, and social innovations diffused outward from these centers, profoundly affecting the course of social development in the rest of the world. By the first centuries of the Christian Era, the continents of Europe, Asia, Africa, and the Americas were urbanized to a degree. In Africa, for instance, cities had emerged in the Sudan region by 700 A.D. and were followed in the next 1000 years by urban-based empires in most of the other parts of the continent (Davidson, 1966).

In Europe, those regions closest to the Middle East and most similar to it in climate were predictably the first to develop cities. Trade with the Near East and raids by barbarians on the urban settlements of that region promoted the diffusion of essential city-building elements on the European continent. Mycenaean cities on the Greek mainland and Minoan cities on the island of Crete emerged around 2000 B.C.

By 800 B.C. urban settlements such as Sparta, Corinth, Megara, and Athens dotted the Greek mainland. Urbanization was disseminated to the rest of the Mediterranean Sea basin through the practice of these Greek city-states of establishing sister colonies once the mother-city population exceeded a manageable size. Concurrently, the Etruscans in southern Italy had established urban settlements that eventually led to the most famous civilization of antiquity—Rome.

Rome greatly expanded the scope of urbanization by establishing forts and administrative centers throughout its extensive empire. Modern cities of Europe whose urban beginning can be traced in name, situs, and/or traditions to Roman influence include York, London, Brussels, Ghent, Etrecht, Granada, Seville, Cologne, Strasbourg, Paris, Toulouse, Bordeaux, Basel, Vienna, Zagreb, Sofia, and Belgrade (Sjoberg, 1960, p. 57).

With the fall of the Roman Empire in the fourth century A.D., much of Europe entered a long period of cultural and economic stagnation with subsequent decline in urban populations. Although the Roman Empire ceased to exist, city-building knowledge lingered on to reemerge in the Renaissance cities of Florence, Genoa, Venice, Pisa and others on the Italian peninsula. Although 5,000 years of urban development preceded the rise of these cities, it is interesting to note that cities of the Renaissance have more in common with the earliest cities of Mesopotamia than they do with cities in today's urban-industrial societies. The reason is that Renaissance cities were a part of agricultural societies with a feudal form of social organization.

THE PREINDUSTRIAL CITY

Superficially the earliest cities appear to differ significantly in time and place of origin as well as in the form and character of their cultures. Upon closer scrutiny, one can see that these early cities closely resemble each other in form, especially if they are compared with a modern urban-industrial society. A major work by Gideon Sjoberg, *The Preindustrial City*, (1960), explores the "strikingly similar" social and ecological structures of these nonindustrial cities.[3] Cultural differences impart a unique quality to preindustrial cities, but, according to Sjoberg, the urban patterns of these cities are universal and transcend their cultural boundaries. Therefore, the preindustrial or nonindustrial society spans 5,500 years, from early antiquity to the present time. Remnants in today's developing world include Katmandu in Nepal and Mazar-i-Sharit in Afghanistan. Regardless of time and place, such societies are similar in demographic, ecological, technological, and organizational features and contrast markedly with the urban-industrial world. In the following sections, some of the major characteristics of the preindustrial city are examined.

Pervasiveness of Rigid Social Class

Preindustrial cities are supported by societies described as being feudal. A feudal society's technology was sufficiently well developed to produce a food surplus large enough to support an urban population. A surplus also allowed a more complex social organization that led to the most distinctive characteristic of preindustrial cities and feudal societies—the pervasiveness of social class. A *social class* is defined as a body of persons who occupy a position in a social hierarchy by reason of similar kinship, power, achievements, wealth, or moral and personal attributes. The ordering of social classes in a *system of social stratification* results in the unequal distribution of valued material and nonmaterial items in society and the emergence of institutional mechanisms to perpetuate this structured inequality.

The upper class The social structure of the feudal order was simple. At the top was a literate, leisured elite led by the sovereign—the political and/or religious leader of the society. Everyone else formed the lower class. The elite was composed of the sovereign, his kin, other nobility, and persons who dominated the ranks of the governmental, religious, and educational bureaucracies. It is estimated that the technology of the day could support only a small proportion—5 to 10 percent—of the city's population at high composition levels.

The lower class The lower class was composed of merchants, artisans who provided luxuries for the elite, clerks and scribes in the religious and political bureaucracies, unskilled laborers, servants, burden bearers, and of course the mass of the peasantry. The internal gradation within the lower class was slight in comparison with the extreme distinction between that class as a whole and the elite.

Outcasts One additional group should be mentioned, although it was not present in all feudal societies—the outcasts. The outcasts were often viewed as nonhumans and at best received only a margin of respect. They were slaves and persons performing jobs considered defiling—prostitutes, night soil carriers, actors, dancers. They were shunned socially by the other two groups and often were segregated into the least desirable wards of the city, normally at its fringes.

Hence, feudal society and its preindustrial cities were rigidly stratified and a person's place in society was determined by the social class of the family of his or her birth. There is a degree of fluidity in all societies, but upward mobility was rare in the feudal world. The major reason was that the leisured class, by minimizing their contact with the masses, through time developed their own distinctive dress, speech, and manners. A member of the lower class, having no contact with the elite, found it impossible to learn this subculture and could never hope to pass as a member of the upper class.

Remnants of an upper class subculture are still evident in language, especially the accent of the upper class in urban-industrial societies, e.g., Back Bay Bostonians and "blue-bloods" in Philadelphia. George Bernard Shaw used these linguistic differences as the basis for the plot of *Pygmalion,* which traces the trials of the impoverished Liza Doolittle in learning and finally mastering the language of the "uppers." Mastering the ways of the upper class may be possible in fiction but seldom was achieved in reality. The more common pattern of social mobility in feudal society was the downward slide of members of upper class families into the lower class.

Social Institutions in Feudal Society

Political, economic, religious, and educational institutions also bore the mark of social class. The small upper stratum maintained its privileged position by commanding the key institutions of society. The number of ruling families in most feudal societies was small, yet members of these families would occupy virtually all the strategic positions of power in the social order. Close relatives would fill not only the positions in the capital but also the main bureaucratic posts in the provincial centers. The ruling families used the strong bonds of kinship to ensure the faithful support of key parts of their society.

The importance of kinship and marriage Kinship and marriage therefore were crucial in maintaining the social position of the elite. First, the reputation and position of a family depended on the kinds of marriage partners parents could secure for their children. Second and more important, marriage was based on political considerations—the benefit of the family rather than the happiness of individuals. Two families linked by marriage could dominate an entire community or society by occupying all the key positions in their locale. Parental control of marriage arrangements ensured adherence to tradition and the stability of the feudal class system.[4]

The dominant families in preindustrial societies were therefore able to mobilize the major resources of the society and exert control over the lower classes. The elite were well organized and literate; the masses were illiterate, unorganized, and incapable of knowing what was transpiring in the social system. The elite not only were able to maintain their position of privilege by sheer power, but were also able to legitimize their rule by their control of the religious institutions. The elite were the sole determiners of what was right and good and could appeal to absolutes—the "divine right of kings" or tradition—to justify their superiority over the lower classes.

Demography and Ecology in Preindustrial Cities

The most striking characteristic of preindustrial cities, considering their influence on society, was their small size. The surplus grown by farmers was only large enough to support cities comprising 5 to 10 percent of the total population, and the cities themselves generally consisted of only 10,000–15,000 inhabitants. The population of certain preindustrial cities did grow to more than 100,000, but these cities were few and developed only under special circumstances. Rome, for example, in 200 A.D. may have had a population approaching 1,000,000, but it was the capital of an empire that spanned three continents. Likewise, preindustrial cities in the nineteenth and twentieth centuries often had populations in the millions but only when subsidized by industrial societies.

The Influence of Preindustrial Cities

The preindustrial cities exerted a tremendous influence on their societies despite their small size. Table 3.1 gives the population estimates for several regional centers during the medieval period. Berlin, for example, had a population of only 2,000 inhabitants in the fifteenth century, yet it was an important city in northern Europe. Amsterdam, Antwerp, and Barcelona exerted a similar influence over their regions. This dominance was based on two factors. First, most preindustrial cities were at key break-in-transportation points along trade routes and were able to control the essential commerce of their societies. Second, the urban locations were the site of the key institutions controlled by the elite. The elite required an urban base to sustain their power for several reasons. First, it provided safety unattainable in a rural setting. Second, proximity of key members of the elite in an urban setting facilitated communication among themselves

Table 3.1
Estimated populations of selected medieval cities.

City	Date	Population
Amsterdam	1470	7,476
Antwerp	1437	13,760
Barcelona	1359	27,056
Berlin	1450	6,000
Bologna	1371	32,000
Brussels	1496	19,088
Leipzig	1474	2,076
London	1377	34,971
Paris	1192	59,200
Rome	1198	35,000
Venice	1363	77,700

Source: Adapted from J. C. Russell, "Late Ancient and Medieval Population," *Trans. American Philosophical Society*, vol. 48, pt. 3 (1958): pp. 60–62.

and with operatives in other parts of their kingdoms at a time when travel and communications were slow and sporadic. Finally, face-to-face communication enabled administrative officers to operate the political and religious bureaucracy and to develop cohesive policy. Efficient communication led to effective organization and the ability to mobilize the resources necessary to extract the limited surplus grown by the peasants. The capital city along with provincial and local centers were the focal points of an organizational network that dominated the (feudal) society.

Physical Arrangements in Preindustrial Cities

The social patterns were reflected in the physical land use patterns in cities. The preindustrial city normally was encircled by a wall; additional walls were erected inside the city to form cells and precincts. These well-defined precincts or wards typically were inhabited by specific ethnic and occupational groups having their own social organization. Such groups, like the Jews in medieval European cities, often created a world unto themselves. The word ghetto has its origin in these self-contained areas of the preindustrial city. Craftsmen and merchants not segregated in specific quarters were strung out along certain streets. The various precincts were linked by narrow, winding, poorly drained dirt streets. Major thoroughfares converged on a plaza at the city's center. The plaza was the social and commercial as well as physical center of the city and was bordered by the most important governmental and religious buildings. The plaza itself was multipurposed, serving at various times as a meeting place, market, and ceremonial site for the city's population. The preeminence of the city's center

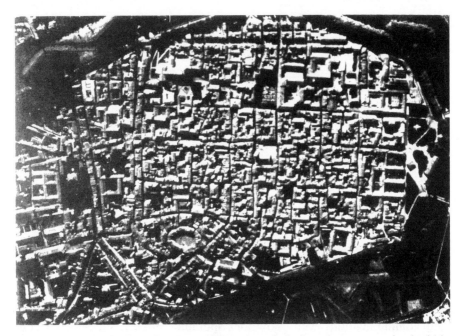

Photo 3.2 A Preindustrial city, Lucca in northern Italy is no longer contained within the bastioned circuit of its walls, which were begun in 1504 and completed in 1645. Note that the outer walls when combined with the gridiron pattern of the streets divides the city into precincts. Four hundred years ago each precinct housed a different segment of society. Then, as today, the physical structure of the city reinforced the social structure of the society.

Source:

over the periphery made it the most highly valued residential location where the nobility and upper class chose to live.

Technology's influence on city structure The physical arrangement of the preindustrial city in many respects was necessitated by the poorly developed technology. Most of the population walked (only the rich rode), and the streets became a mire of mud and refuse after a rain or snowfall. Because of poor transportation combined with the physical barrier of a city wall, people lived very close together and most lived near their place of work. The poor transportation technology also explains the creation of wards and precincts. Merchants, middlemen, suppliers, and retailers, for example, needed to be at one place to conduct business. Similarly, the self-segregation of the elite at the city's center allowed them to isolate themselves from the masses, maintain communication with each other, and have access to the religious and political headquarters of the city. The poor resided on the city's outskirts, the part of the city least protected from attack and farthest from the city's center. Ironically, in today's urban-industrial societies the wealthy live at the city's periphery and the poor near its center. The reasons for these patterns are closely tied to changes brought on by the Industrial Revolution.

THE INDUSTRIAL REVOLUTION

In England during the mid-eighteenth century, a long series of changes began that would profoundly affect the course of that nation and the rest of the world—the Industrial Revolution. The Industrial Revolution commonly is thought of in technological terms—the invention of complex machines and the tapping of inanimate sources of energy—but important cultural, organizational, and population elements also were involved.

Reasons for the Industrial Revolution

The exact reasons for this revolution are still a source of major debate among social scientists. Sjoberg (1960) emphasizes the role of technology in both requiring and making possible certain social forms. He posits that technology is linked to surplus, and the presence or absence and the size of a surplus prescribe the nature of a society.

Weber (1959), Mumford (1961), and others examine nontechnological factors in this change. Weber, in *The Protestant Ethic and the Spirit of Capitalism,* suggests that a fundamental change in Western values and outlook was a prerequisite for the Industrial Revolution. For example, among the artisans in medieval Europe, the notion of profit was an alien concept. The price of an object was set by adding to the cost of materials the fair value of one's labor. Without profit, which is an excess of the selling price of goods over their cost, there could be no large capital formation and hence no industrial societies as they are known today.

The Protestant Reformation fostered a new set of values that stressed rationality, hard labor (the work ethic), and the material rewards of labor. This ethic, originating in small religious sects in northern Europe in the sixteenth century, spread throughout Western society and influenced all religious groups to a degree. This new ethic predates the Industrial Revolution and may have been a necessary precondition for it.

Mumford (1961) suggests a constellation of changes in Western societies originating in the fourteenth and fifteenth centuries as the underpinnings of the Industrial Revolution: the destruction of the feudal order and the rise of nationalism and the modern nation state; the erosion of class barriers and the emergence of an urban-based middle class as a potent force in society; changes in values and outlook; centralized political and economic control; uniformity in taxes, currency, law, and rule; and the rapid expansion of urban population.

The following sections describe the changes in English agricultural technology, manufacturing, and social structure brought about by the Industrial Revolution. These changes form the basis for the emergence of the present-day urban-industrial world.

Changes in English Agriculture

In the preindustrial world, only a small percentage of the population was urban, and the cities themselves were small by modern standards. The level of agricultural technology was a major determinant of this patterning, for without an increase in the food supply there could be no growth in the percentage of the society's population in cities. The American colonies provide a good example. Just before the American Revolution only one out of twenty-six Americans lived in cities, 85 to 90 percent of the labor force was engaged in agriculture, and nine farm families were needed to support just one urban family. In contrast, by 1970, one American farmer supported forty-five other people and less than 5 percent of the total workforce was engaged in agricultural occupations. Clearly an important precondition for urban-industrial societies was the removal of the constraints placed on population concentrations by the food supply.

Changes in English agriculture began to occur at a rapid rate during the first half of the eighteenth century. At the beginning of that century, the average English farmer practiced three-crop rotation whereby fields were divided into fourths and one parcel was left fallow each year to replenish itself. Pasture lands were held in common by the local village, as were woods and water rights. Moreover, the average farm was small. The farmer grew only for his own needs and had little left over for sale.

One of the many agricultural innovations during this period was the discovery that three-crop rotation could be replaced if farmers would replenish their soil by periodically planting nitrogen-fixing crops. This new practice spread rapidly and within a few decades the amount of acreage in crops increased substantially. At the same time, the selective breeding of animals and the practice of storing silage for winter fodder brought about striking increases in the number and the average weight of farm animals.

The revolution in English agriculture was hastened by Parliament's passage of the infamous Enclosure Acts. In this series of acts, Parliament deeded the common lands historically held by villages to the nobility that held ancient title to the land. Farmers, herdsmen, and squatters whose families had lived off this land for generations found themselves without homes or livelihood. Though social costs were staggering, the small inefficient farms were replaced by more efficient large farming estates (Mantoux, 1961, pp. 136–85).

Consequences of improved agriculture The changes in agriculture had a pervasive effect on all of English society. First, in the course of fifty years the quality and quantity of food improved dramatically. The higher quality and greater reliability of the food supply brought about significant declines in mortality that, combined with the high birth rate of the period, caused England's population to grow rapidly.

A second outcome of the changes in agriculture was a reduction in manpower needs in the countryside. The small farmer and the peasant had little choice but to migrate to nearby cities and towns.

Third, the expanding food supply and the rural-urban migration of population stimulated urban growth and development. Finally, the growth of cities and towns and the rationalization of agriculture stimulated a dramatic improvement in England's transportation network. Throughout the eighteenth century, canal and tollroad construction crisscrossed the English countryside to provide a transportation network for moving agricultural produce to urban markets (Pahl, 1970, Mantoux, 1961).

Viewed as a whole, these changes in English society formed the foundation from which an industrial society could arise. A reliable, high-quality food supply supported greater numbers of people in cities. An expanding population provided for the labor force for industry, and an efficient transportation system provided essential linkage.

Changes in Manufacturing

At the same time as the revolution in English agriculture, inventions were being made that could tap the new manpower, food surpluses, and transportation improvements. The revolution in industry—essentially the substitution of machines for hand tools and the tapping of new sources of energy—evolved over a period of decades.

Cottage industry Before 1750, manufacturing was done on a small scale, often in the form known as cottage industry whereby an entire family worked as a unit within their home handcrafting objects with their own tools. In the manufacturing of a woolen garment, for example, a middleman would purchase the wool from a merchant and in turn "let it out" to a farm or village family who would clean, dye, and spin the wool into yarn. The middleman would purchase the yarn and have it woven into cloth by another family and in turn would have the cloth fabricated into a garment. Thus the fabrication of one item was costly and inefficient, requiring the coordination of the activities of a large number of families scattered over a large geographic area. Concentration of population at one place was impractical if not impossible because of the lack of an adequate food supply, labor pool, and transportation network. Even during the early stages of the Industrial Revolution when factories were operated by water-driven machinery, the need for factories to be near running water precluded their expansion (Mantoux, 1961, pp. 47–185).

Production in factories James Watt's invention of the first practical steam engine in 1769 was a major breakthrough. The steam engine harnessed to the machine dramatically broadened the economic capacity of society and made possible the fabrication of many more commodities than the cottage system could produce. More importantly, steam power removed the locational constraints of earlier factory towns. Rather than eliminating jobs, the machines rapidly increased the demand for an urban workforce. The increase in manufacturing output stimulated the creation of jobs in other spheres of the economy (Mantoux, 1961, pp. 311–338).

The technological breakthroughs in agriculture, energy, and manufacturing made possible the transfer of all types of cottage industries to factories in urban settings. By 1800, London was the largest city in the world with a population in excess of 900,000. Birmingham, Leeds, Manchester, and Sheffield also grew rapidly, drawing vast numbers of people to work in the factories concentrated there. Living and sanitary conditions, never good in the preindustrial city, reached new lows. Filth, crowding, and disease typified the new industrial centers. The peasant, released from the tyranny of the feudal order, endured the regimentation, low wages, and oppressive working conditions of the factory.

Changes in Social Structure

England before 1700 was like any other preindustrial feudal society—class permeated the entire social order. Society consisted of two classes, the elite and the masses, and was characterized by ascribed status, little social mobility, and domination of the political, economic, educational and religious institutions by the elite.

Class in industrial society, although important, is not the all-pervasive force that it was in the preindustrial world. The most distinguishing characteristic of the social structure of industrial England was the growth of a large, influential middle class. The social structure was relatively flexible, and social mobility was not only possible but relatively common. The political, economic, religious, and educational institutions, although still influenced by social class, begin to evolve into rational bureaucratic forms wherein one's position within the organization was based on training and expertise—achievement rather than ascriptive criteria.

Conclusions

Many people narrowly define the work "revolution" as an armed confrontation with the establishment, but in sociology this word refers to any rapid change in a society's institutions. In this sense, the word "revolution" accurately describes the scope of change in English society in the eighteenth and nineteenth centuries. In terms of its overall effect, the Industrial Revolution in England was similar to the French and American Revolutions of the same period. It brought about fundamental change in the structure and character of English society and in so doing changed the course of development in all societies.

AMERICAN URBAN HISTORY

In the sixteenth century, when the first English colonists arrived in North America, they found a continent without cities. Except for the Indians of the Northwest, the North American Indian population was nomadic or lived in small agricultural villages. At this time the native population of the entire continent was estimated to be fewer than one million persons.

In the four and one-half centuries that have followed, the virgin continent has become the site of the leading urban-industrial society in the world. In 1980, more than 70 percent of the United States population lived in urban places that occupied only 1.5 percent of the land area. The history of America's social, economic, and technological changes during the last 450 years is important to other societies that hope to follow its development pattern or to avoid its mistakes.

In the following sections, the history of America's transformation to an urban society is explored. First, historians' theories on the city's role in American history are described briefly. Then the urban transformation is examined in terms of five groups of cities—the Atlantic coast cities, the river cities, the lake cities, the southern cities and the cities of the Southwest. Each group is composed of cities that are similar in time of settlement, transportation dependence, and social and economic characteristics. Each group played an important role in the development of this nation.

Historians' Perspectives

For the past thirty years, historians have been involved in a controversy over the role of the city in the history of America's national development. For much of the last century and the first quarter of this century, the original colonies of the Atlantic coast region were considered the mainspring in this development. In 1893, Fredrick Jackson Turner suggested a new interpretation of American history and declared, "the true point of view in the history of this nation is not the Atlantic Coast, it is the Great West."[5] Turner noted that the United States during the nineteenth century, in comparison with Europe, had been relatively free of communal social unrest and he contended that the availability of free land in the West acted as an escape valve contributing to domestic tranquility. Turner reasoned that people who became dissatisfied with the conditions in the urban East could simply move out and homestead in the West (Schlesinger, 1941).

Critics of the Turner thesis   Arthur M. Schlesinger in the 1940s questioned the Turner thesis and suggested that an urban reinterpretation of American history was needed. Schlesinger (1940, 1949) and others (Holt, 1953; Thernstrom, 1968) noted that the massive immigration of farmers to the cities in the last half of the nineteenth century not only contributed to the tremendous growth of cities, but also was a major factor in national development. The reason for this urban migration was the state of American farming during that period. The price of commodities fluctuated widely on the world market and currency was periodically deflated. Consequently, the nineteenth-century farmers who had secured long-term loans in good times were forced some years later to repay them in deflated dollars, that is, dollars with much greater buying power. Because the real cost of these loans had increased substantially, many farmers were no longer able to meet their obligations and were forced to sell out and move to the cities.

A noneconomic factor in the migration from farm to city was the general undesirability of farm life. The magazines and popular writings of the late nineteenth century describe the backbreaking labor involved in farming on the Great Plains and the months of deadening isolation without outside contact.

An urban reinterpretation of American history   Turner's thesis may therefore be wrong and the reverse may be true: the city rather than the Great West may have been the escape valve, not for the urbanite but for the disenchanted farmer. One reason for the general absence of social unrest in the nineteenth-century city may have been that the difficult living and working conditions of the city were still better than those on the farm.

Critics have accused Schlesinger of confusing urbanization with related phenomena such as industrialization, failing to identify the forces that created the city, and making the same mistake as Turner by attributing causality to a single factor—the city (Diamond, 1969; Lampard, 1969; Lubove, 1969). Schlesinger's work, however, marks the beginning of a major dialog among social scientists and a new direction in the field of American historiography. It is now generally agreed that urban life rivaled frontier life from the beginnings of the nation and that to understand America's history one must understand its urban history.

Atlantic Coast Cities

The Atlantic coast was the original frontier, and cities and towns had a key role in its settlement. For example, the first successful English settlements at Jamestown and Plymouth were in fact small towns. The small towns and villages that eventually dotted the landscape east of the Appalachian Mountains provided mutual protection as well as the population necessary to support a variety of occupations. In addition, these towns contributed to the settlement of the surrounding countryside. New colonists normally would spend their first months in one of these communities gathering provisions and learning the ways of the new land before moving into the countryside. Once settled, these colonists continued to depend on urban places for markets and for manufactured goods. The standard of living of the colonial farmer was greatly improved by the nails, hinges, cloth, and medicines sold in these places (Bridenbaugh, 1938, 1955; Chudacoff, 1975).

As a result of this settlement pattern, by 1690 almost 10 percent of the colonial population was concentrated in the five coastal cities of Boston, New York, Philadelphia, Newport, and Charleston.

Similarities These cities, although different in geography, were similar in time of settlement and in social, economic, and physical characteristics. First, all were seaports and became commercial centers for trade between Europe and the colonies. Second, not only goods entered these ports but also new ideas from Europe. Early in American history, the intellectual activities in science, literature, medicine, and the arts were centered in the colleges (Harvard, the College of Charleston), libraries, museums, and professional and scientific organizations of these cities. Although small by modern standards, these preindustrial cities exerted an influence on the colonies far out of proportion to their size. Third, because they were settled at about the same time, these cities were built with the same technology and not surprisingly faced similar urban problems. Fire was always a serious threat; these cities enacted building codes and other ordinances for the common welfare. Public disorder, pauperism, sanitation, and other problems led all five cities to adopt similar solutions, not by innovation but by borrowing from the great cities of Europe (Bridenbaugh, 1938). Finally, these cities were similar in social structure, which was greatly influenced by the absence of an ancestral feudal order in the New World. On the whole the leadership was Protestant, and the cultural values were drawn from the new middle class of Europe (Main, 1965).

In sum, the cities, towns, and villages of the East Coast spearheaded the settlement of the American frontier; without them colonization of the New World would not have been possible.

The River Cities

The settlement pattern in the East continued in the region west of the Appalachian Mountains. Forts and trading posts were established in advance of permanent agriculture, and the outposts pushed the frontier into the Old Northwest. By 1800, the sites of every major metropolis in this region except Chicago, Milwaukee, and Indianapolis had been cleared and surveyed (Wade, 1969, p. 100). The settlement of this region occurred in waves. In the early decades of the nineteenth century the cities along the Ohio River underwent rapid economic and population growth. Later in the century cities on the Great Lakes displaced the river cities in dominance of the political and economic affairs of the region.

The urban history of this region is marked by "city-making mania" and intense intercity rivalry. Many of the new towns were speculative ventures, the land purchased and the town platted by investors in the East. Others, with names like New London, New Baltimore, and New Philadelphia, reflected the hopes and aspirations of their founders. Some of these communities flourished briefly and then failed, leaving behind the West's first ghost towns. Wheeling, West Virginia; New Albany, Indiana; and Zanesville, Ohio are examples of towns that at one time had a chance to be a major metropolis but were surpassed by rivals such as Pittsburgh and Cincinnati and became subordinate to them (Wade, 1957).

The winners of this intense and often brutal competition were Pittsburgh, Cincinnati, Louisville, and St. Louis—the river cities. All of these cities were founded in the eighteenth century as forts or trading posts prior to the use of their land for settled agriculture. They were remarkably similar in economic, social, and physical characteristics. Each of these cities was a winner in the urban rivalry because of its strategic location on the interior river system. Pittsburgh, for example, is at the site where the Allegheny and Monongahela Rivers converge to form the Ohio River. Cincinnati was strategically located with respect to a road system in Ohio, Kentucky, and Indiana. Louisville was founded at a major series of falls on the Ohio River, and the stevedore operations that grew up there were later expanded into other areas of commerce. Finally, St. Louis is near the mouth of the Missouri River where it enters the Mississippi.

In the eighteenth century these cities were small towns with populations of fewer than 1,000 inhabitants. After 1800 growth of these cities accelerated. By 1815 Pittsburgh was a thriving center of 8,000. Cincinnati estimated its population to be 4,000, and Louisville and St. Louis were half that size. The real growth of these cities came after 1820 with the introduction of the steamboat, which permitted upriver shipment of goods for the first time. Consequently, fifty years of growth was compressed into a single decade (Wade, 1964, p. 102).

The importance of the river cannot be overstressed. Roads during this era were unpaved and few were wider than a single wagon. Rivers were the major transportation arteries, and the trade and commerce that spread through the interior river system were the economic lifeblood of the river cities. Later, such industries as glass and iron manufacturing at Pittsburgh and meat packing and brewing and distilling at Cincinnati expanded their local economies.

The river cities were laid out in a gridiron pattern with streets running perpendicular and parallel to the river. The river bank was dominated by docks, warehouses, businesses, mills, and granaries; little or no land was set aside for recreational uses. These cities were compact and densely settled and had many of the same urban problems as their eastern counterparts. Like the great cities of the East they were not innovators but borrowers. Their forms of government and solutions to the problems of fire, public safety, pauperism, and sanitation were copied largely from those of eastern cities, especially Philadelphia (Wade, 1957).

Class consciousness emerged early in the river cities. Business leaders headed the social structure, followed by professionals, working people, freemen, and slaves. A leisure class was lacking, and the dominance of the business community was reflected in all aspects of the city, especially its physical characteristics—i.e., the commercial use of the river bank.

In time, the river cities came to dominate the political and economic institutions of the region. Wade (1957) suggests that early in the history of this region two cultures emerged, one urban and the other rural. In religion, urban populations largely attended formal mainstream churches; rural populations were drawn to the tent revivals and more expressive religions. In politics, the cities provided leadership for the major state and national offices; rural constituencies controlled the state legislatures. Finally, the colleges, libraries, professional societies, museums, and theaters in the cities were dynamic cultural forces influencing the outlying rural areas.

The Lake Cities

Another wave of urbanization occurred in the north in the so-called lake cities of Buffalo, Cleveland, Detroit, Chicago, and Milwaukee. Their period of rapid economic and population growth was the 1850s, when tens of thousands of people poured into the upper Mississippi River valley. These cities were shaped by similar social, economic, and transportation forces, particularly the latter. All five cities are lake ports and owe their existence to the development of the transportation technologies of the canal and railroad. Buffalo, Cleveland, and Detroit, for example, are the end points of major canal systems; Chicago and Milwaukee grew as railroad centers (Taylor, 1951). The fact that the initial success of these cities was based on commerce led to serious economic problems, because the canals and lakes were impassable during the winter months. However, the resultant high seasonal unemployment eventually led to an increase of manufacturing and industry in all these cities (Still, 1941). The economic growth of the lake cities was spectacular, and they soon displaced the river cities in importance. For example, Chicago and St. Louis competed for markets in the same region, but Chicago had surpassed St. Louis in population by 1865 (Belcher, 1947).

The lake cities were also similar in social and political characteristics. Like the river cities before them, they were borrowers and not innovators. Their nineteenth century city charters, for example, differed only in the name of the city in the title. Local governments were of the strong mayor/council form based on Jacksonian democracy, and each city underwent a subscription stage in which voluntary groups performed the vital municipal services.

The lake cities revered the "common man," and local governments passed ordinances protecting every aspect of daily life from the sizing of bread to the cleanliness of markets and the purity of milk. Moveover, their populations were more cosmopolitan than those of the river cities; more than 50 percent of their inhabitants were foreign-born in the 1860s and 1870s. This cosmopolitan character is still evident in the rich ethnic mixture of neighborhoods in these cities (Still, 1941).

Today, these cities share similar forms of government, physical characteristics, and urban problems as a result of the forces that shaped their initial development.

The Southern Cities

Relatively little work has been done on the urban history of the South. One work, Richard Wade's (1964) *Slavery in Cities* discusses the reasons for the unusual pattern of cities in this region. Wade refers to this pattern as the South's "urban perimeter." You can see this pattern clearly in Figure 3.3. Note that there were few cities in the interior of the South before the Civil War; most were on its perimeter.

The reason given by Wade for this pattern is that the antebellum South had ties to a capitalistic society—the North—but was itself a feudal society. The South at this time was dominated by "aristocratic feudal" lords who were concerned not about the return on their investments but with maintaining their social position. Therefore, monies that might have been used for the building of railroads and industry went into land and slaves.

Although the South exported an enormous amount of agricultural products, the Northern capitalists probably made more money on cotton and other exports than the South. The Northerner provided the shipping, warehousing, insurance, processing, manufacturing, and marketing of these exports, and therein lay the profits. In many respects the South in this period could be likened to an underdeveloped country, and its economic ties to the North could be defined in terms of imperialism.

Because the economies of the Southern cities during this period were based on commerce, changes in transportation technology and world commodity markets greatly affected them. New Orleans, for example, had notable growth between 1820 and 1840 and shared economic prosperity with the river cities. New Orleans was a break-in-transportation city. Goods shipped from the Northeast via the Atlantic and the Gulf were transferred to barges there for distribution to the cities in the interior. By 1860, New Orleans was the sixth largest city in the United States, but after 1860 railroads and canals provided a more direct link between the Midwest and the Northeast, and New Orleans sank into economic decline.

The same fate befell Mobile, Savannah, and Charleston. Charleston, for example, was the fifth largest city in the United States in 1810, dropped to twenty-second in 1860, and after 1860 underwent both economic and population decline.

Before the Civil War, Richmond, Virginia, was the only Southern city

Fig. 3.3 Major cities of the South prior to the Civil War.

with an industrial base. It was leveled by the Union armies, however, and failed to regain its economic importance in the post–Civil War period.

Because of the historical background of the Southern cities, the South is estimated to lag fifteen to twenty years behind the North in urban development. The impressive economic and population gains in this region during the last decade, however, are rapidly reducing this differential.

The Cities of the Southwest

The South through much of its history served as an economic hinterland for America's industrial core, providing the major Atlantic coast, river and lake cities with raw materials, labor, and new markets. Since World War II, a new relationship has become apparent. Increasingly, large numbers of people and resources have been siphoned away from the older and now declining regions of the Northeast and North Central United States. This

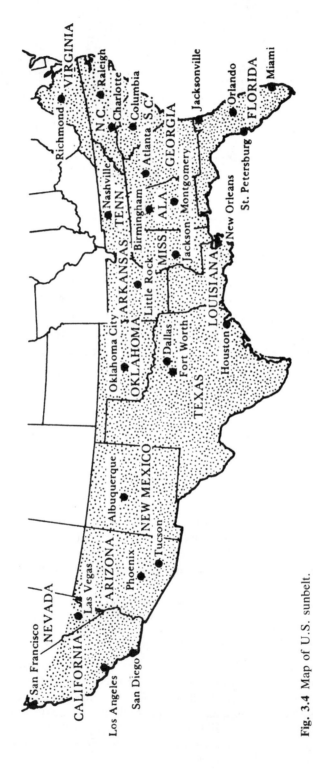

Fig. 3.4 Map of U.S. sunbelt.

Source: Goldfield-Brownell: *Urban America: From Downtown to No Town*, p. 335. Copyright © 1979 Houghton Mifflin Company. Used by permission.

process has by no means been a uniform one. Some northern cities continue to grow, especially their suburbs. In some cases, northern cities have been able to hold and even increase their populations, and the sheer inertia of historical patterns should ensure that this region continue to hold the major financial, government, and industrial centers of the United States. Many observers now, however, point to the dramatic growth and development mentioned above the "Sunbelt"—a region extending roughly from Virginia through the Southeast and Southwest to southern California (Goldfield and Brownell, 1979, p. 335). (See Figure 3.4.) Nowhere has population and economic growth been more spectacular than in the cities of the Southwest.

The Southwestern cities Southwestern cities include this nation's most rapidly growing metropolitan areas—Phoenix, Tucson, Dallas and Houston. Between 1970 and 1978, growth in and around these cities was remarkable. The Phoenix-Tucson area grew by 32.7 percent, the region around Houston grew 24.5 percent, and the Dallas–Fort Worth area 14 percent (*U.S. News and World Report,* June, 1980, p. 55). The important point is that cities differ from those in other regions in that, after years of being stable and small in size they grew to metropolitan status after World War II. For example, in 1940 Tucson and Albuquerque each had populations of approximately 35,000. Phoenix was larger but still had a population of under 100,000 in 1940. Then came the great influx of immigrants. By the mid-1970s the city of Phoenix approached a population of 800,000 (the SMSA was close to 1.3 million), and the Tucson and Albuquerque metropolitan areas had 450,000 people (Cleland, 1978, p. 89) (see Figure 3.5). These cities have been shaped by the transportation, communication and industrial technology of the twentieth century, and they differ from the older cities of other regions in their physical form, population composition, and economic base.

BOOMING SUNBELT CITIES
REACH FOR GROWTH

By Paul Van Slambrouck

Energy and other problems are casting some shadows in the Sunbelt area of the United States.

In the sunny Southwest, which this month's national census count is expected to document as one of the most rapidly expanding regions in the country, the special problems of growth are bubbling to the surface.

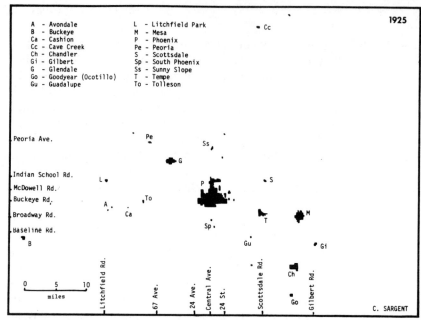

1925 The major cities and towns of the Salt River Valley were established by 1920 but most were very small and all were clearly separated one from another. The 1925 map on the title page shows the major physical and cultural features of the valley (mountains, streams, paved roads, irrigated lands and urban areas) for the same time period.

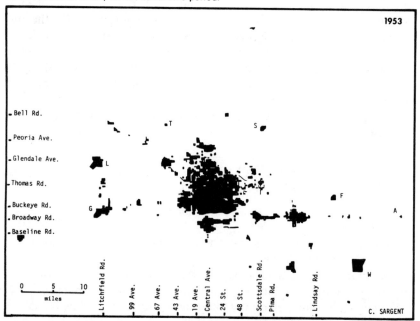

1953 The post-World War II growth of the valley is already evident, especially in Phoenix. On the periphery are the wartime air bases (L - Luke, T - Thunderbird, S - Scottsdale, F - Falcon Field and W - Williams) and a new company town, Goodyear (G). The earlier Goodyear was renamed Ocotillo. Linear development appears along Grand Ave., Scottsdale Rd., and Apache Blvd. Apache Junction (A) is established and Sunnyslope and South Phoenix are much enlarged.

Fig. 3.5 The growth of Phoenix, Arizona, 1925–1978.

Source: C. Sargent, Geography, Arizona State University.

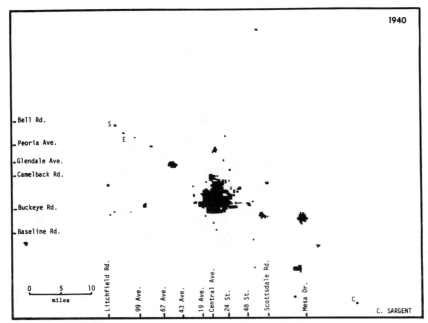

1940 The growth of existing towns was slow during the Depression of the 1930's and the only new settlements since 1925 were the cotton towns of Surprise (S), El Mirage (E) and the even smaller rural district of Chandler Heights (C). Phoenix was a city of 65,000 in 1940. Second largest was Mesa with 7,200, followed by Glendale (4,900) and Tempe (2,900)

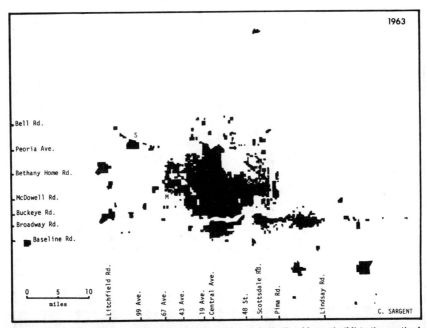

1963 Most evident is growth to the west and northwest, including Maryvale (M) to the south of Glendale, and the beginning of Sun City (S) on the site of a cotton gin. Scottsdale growth moved north into the Paradise Valley and east beyond Indian Bend Wash to the Salt River Indian Reservation boundary. Tempe and Mesa are now joined by development along Apache Blvd.

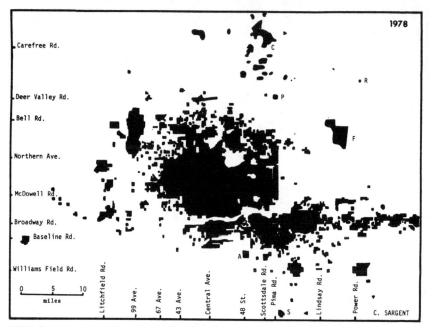

1978 Development continued on farmlands to the west of Phoenix and Glendale, to the south of Tempe and encircled Mesa. Growth north onto the desert includes portions of the Phoenix Mountains, Paradise and Deer Valleys and toward Cave Creek and Carefree (C). Some of the distant large-scale developments such as Fountain Hills (F), Rio Verde (R), Pinnacle Peak Village (P), Ahwatukee (A) and Sun Lakes (S) are easily identifiable; others are adjacent to conventional tract developments.

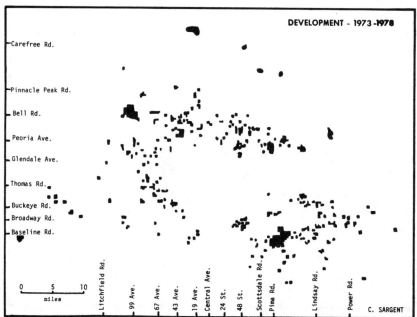

Development: 1973-1978 The pace of growth indicated by building permit data (Table 2) is further suggested by the scope of new development zones since 1973. Several growth clusters are obvious, namely, (1) To the north of Phoenix and Scottsdale in the Paradise Valley, (2) To the south of Tempe and around Mesa, particularly Dobson Ranch, (3) To the west of Phoenix along the alignment of Interstate 10, and (4) to the north of Phoenix in Deer Valley and west from Glendale, including Sun City. There are low-density developments on desert lands to the north as well.

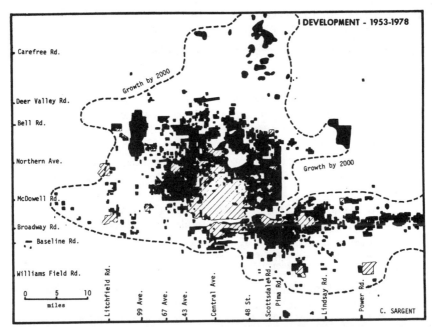

Development: 1953-1978 New lands developed between 1953 and 1978 are shown here in black while earlier development is indicated by the lighter shading. The dotted line outlines the probable extent and direction of major urban growth between 1978 and the year 2000. This is a generalized view of future growth directions and limits, for not all lands within this line will be developed by 2000.

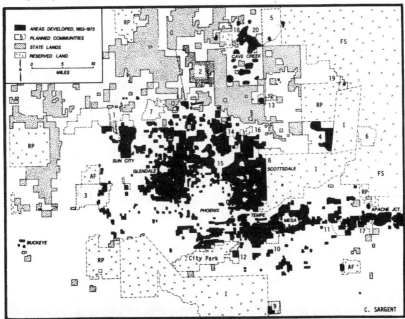

Location Factors This map indicates 20 years of growth after 1953, the location of major large-scale residential developments, the location of state-owned lands, and lands reserved for specific uses, including the Forest Service (FS), Air Force Bases (AF), Indian Reservations (I) and regional parks (RP). 1. Sun City (two parts); 2. Palo Verde Valley; 3. Litchfield Park; 4. Fountain Hills; 5. Carefree Ranch; 6. Goldfield; 7. Arrowhead Ranch; 8. McCormick Ranch; 9. Sun Lakes; 10. Dobson Ranch; 11. Leisure World; 12. Ahwatukee; 13. Pinnacle Peak Village; 14. Village of Paradise Valley; 15. Biltmore Estates; 16. Desert Springs; 17. Dreamland Village; 18. Carefree West; 19. Rio Verde; 20. Carefree (Boulders). Comparing this land-use map with others in the series will partly explain the pattern of past development. Future growth will also be affected by this land-use pattern.

Higher gasoline prices are of particular consequence in the Southwest, where cities are typically more suburban in character and heavily dependent on the automobile.

Record-high interest rates have taken the bloom off construction and real estate development, which are very important to the growth-oriented local economies of the area.

However, the most fundamental change is a growing perception that the "quality of life" that has attracted retirees, job seekers, and working adults from all over the country to the Southwest is threatened.

Interviews with pollsters, social scientists, and politicians in Texas, New Mexico, and Arizona confirm that preservation of the wide open frontier feeling and relaxed lifestyles of the region is of rising importance to its inhabitants.

"Increasing numbers of Westerners are shifting away from the exploitive mentality that usually surrounds a boom environment and are now moving toward a deep challenge to the growth ethic itself," surmises Earl De Berge, president of Behavior Research Center in Phoenix.

Here is how rapid growth is having an impact on three key metropolitan areas in the Southwest:

• Phoenix faces the possibility of a residential building moratorium later this summer because its sewer system is inadequate by federal standards for the city's booming 4.5 percent annual population growth.

The Arizona capital now sprawls over 325 square miles and will grow larger through planned annexations. The policy of expansion is aimed at keeping a solid tax base and enabling City Hall to control urban growth in the entire metropolitan region.

"We want to avoid high density and keep an open feeling about the city, which is what has made us so attractive" to newcomers, explains Mayor Margaret T. Hance.

But Mrs. Hance is the first to admit the disadvantages of having a sprawling city, including the fact that it forces residents to depend on automobiles for commuting. Phoenix has begun using an "urban village" concept of planning. Eleven centers will be established around the city, and they will be zoned for commercial and residential building. It is hoped this approach will enable people to live close to their jobs, yet in a suburban-like evnironment.

Overall, there is an attitude that Phoenix has been growing too rapidly in an unconstrained way. "Quality of life is so important here that even pro-growth advocates feel in some respects we are getting too big," says Jim Haynes, executive vice-president of the Phoenix Chamber of Commerce. "The attitude we take is: There is going to be growth . . . and we need to be sure it is quality growth, not unrestrained sprawl."

• In Albuquerque where most of New Mexico's growth is taking place, "there is a strong feeling that the city is loosing some of its intimacy and charm," Mayor David Rusk says.

Nearly one-third of Albuquerque's 430,000 residents have been in the city five years or less. These newcomers are typically white, young, and highly educated.

Businesses have flocked to the city to tap this skilled labor market, creating a prosperous local economy.

But unemployment among Hispanics and native Americans is still high, and much of the business and retail development that extends out from the city core is an eyesore against the stunning natural setting of desert and mountains.

Mayor Rusk says he believes more careful planning and encouragement of greater participation in local government by neighborhood organizations will help preserve Albuquerque's natural beauty and native character.

• Houston is not known for its physical beauty, but it is nonetheless the nation's fastest-growing major city.

But even in this growth-oriented city, where there is no zoning, inhabitants are increasingly disgruntled over the side effects of rapid expansion.

"The idea that growth is completely a good thing is dissipating," says Jan Van Lohuizen, vice-president of V. Lance Tarrance & Associates, a Houston polling and research firm.

Last summer's gasoline lines helped convince many Houstonians that the city should slow its growth so the snarl of automobile traffic does not get worse, Mr. Van Lohuizen explains.

Mass transit has received growing attention in Houston. Bus service has improved noticeably in the past year, and the Metropolitan Transit Authority has begun studying the feasibility of an inter-city commuter rail line.

There are many factors responsible for the growth of cities in the Southwest, but none are more important than the effects of cybernation. *Cybernation* is a term coined some twenty years ago that refers to the combination of automated techniques and computer technology. Examples of this technology are the computer-controlled robots that now perform over 95 percent of the spot welding in the newer automobile assembly plants. Some observers have argued that this technology is as important to twentieth-century societies as industrialization was to the nineteenth century (Gordon, 1978, p. 107).

The implications of cybernation for urban places lie in the fact that the transportation, communication, and service needs of industries based on this technology differ from those that developed at earlier stages of our industrialization. For example, the new industries operate at much higher levels of efficiency and require a small but highly skilled and well-educated work force. Smaller work forces mean that these industries no longer need to be located near the cities of the Northeast and North Central regions with their large populations of unskilled labor. Instead, a plant can be located on the basis of markets, prevailing wage and tax rates, and benign climate. This is readily apparent when examining Map 3.2. Note the strategic location of the southwestern cities in relation to the growing markets of Southern California, the South and the lower Midwest.

Other factors recognized as influencing the growth of cities in this region include (1) the growth of government military spending: world nuclear strategy has made military bases in this region vitally important to our national security; (2) the migration of large numbers of retirees (often on government pensions) drawn to the cities of the region by the warm climate and low cost of living; (3) a changing American lifestyle and an improved standard of living, which have resulted in fewer hours at work and more time at leisure—the mild climate permits year-round outdoor activity; (4) entrepreneurship and boosterism, qualities of the political and economic leadership of these cities that have motivated these leaders to take economic risks to draw industry and other economic activities into these regions.

The factors shaping the cities of the Southwest mean that they have a form and character quite different from cities of other regions. Their population mix is different, with a relatively high-skilled work force. Unlike cities of the Northeast, they do not have a large number of disadvantaged citizens who need many services. Moreover, the physical form of these cities is different. Shaped by the automobile, they have no need for a downtown central core; rather; these cities sprawl over the landscape and have low population densities. Finally, these cities face their own urban problems arising from the shortage of water, delicate arid or semiarid ecosystems, and large indigenous populations of Indians and/or Mexican Americans.

In sum, the rise of cities in the Southwest, and for that matter in all of the Sunbelt, is not an anomaly in United States urban history; rather it is a part of a long process that has continuously transformed this nation's system of cities. This urban development cannot be understood in a vacuum. Changes in our economic system and the emergence of the cybernetic age have changed the nature of regional economic and urban growth. For many reasons, cities in the Southwestern region have been better suited to take advantage of these changes (Perry and Watkins, 1977, pp. 14–15).

SUMMARY

The first cities appeared more than 5,500 years ago; they represent a revolutionary change in the way humans adapt to their physical environments. The emergence of these first cities was the outcome of a long evolutionary history in which the social and technological innovations necessary to support a large population at a permanent site were accumulated. This process began in the Mesolithic period when climatic changes enabled people to live in permanent villages through intensive hunting and gathering. The skills and knowledge of the environment gained in this epoch led to the formation of the first agricultural villages during the Neolithic period, which began around 8000 B.C. The Agricultural Revolution was an important prerequisite for the emergence of the first cities but not the only one. Human societies also needed the ability to store, transport, and distribute a food surplus and to use the surplus for varied social ends before the first cities could develop.

Therefore, the earliest cities arose as a result of the convergence of organizational and technological innovations and environmental conditions in areas of benign climate such as the valleys of the lower Tigris and Eurphrates, Nile, Indus, and Huangho Rivers. Technology modified the barriers to city building imposed by the environment and, as city-building and agricultural technology improved, cities spread to other regions of the world where conditions were less favorable. By the early centuries of the Christian Era, most of the world's continents had urban populations. The cultures of these cities differed but, as Sjoberg has shown, their ecological, institutional, and technological characteristics were similar whether they existed in early antiquity or in more recent times.

The Industrial Revolution, which began in England during the mid-eighteenth century, was an historical force that profoundly affected the course of humankind. Technological breakthroughs in agriculture, energy, and manufacturing during the eighteenth century led to the rapid growth of urban populations and the transfer of all types of cottage industries to factories in urban settings. The ability to draw upon vast numbers of people to work in factories contributed greatly to the level of human efficiency and brought about a fundamental change in the fabric of society. Class is not now the all-pervasive force that it was in the preindustrial world. A large and influential middle class arose during the Industrial Revolution, as well as social structure in which social mobility was common. The major institutions of society, although still influenced by social class, began to evolve into the rational bureaucratic forms common today in more developed societies.

The exact role of cities in the development of the United States has been a source of major debate within the field of American social history for much of this century. It now appears that the role of the "true pioneer" of folklore, who escaped the restrictions of society by carving a homestead out of the wilderness, has been exaggerated. The settlement of the West was accomplished mainly by groups. Many settlers who moved west across the Appalachian Mountains were "in search of promising towns rather than good land, their inducement being urban opportunities rather than fertile soil" (Wade, 1969, p. 100). Moreover, the settlement process was extremely conservative; most of the new settlers attempted to reproduce their old institutions as closely as possible.

The role of cities in the settlement of the United States is explored by examining five groups of cities—the Atlantic coast cities, the river cities, the lake cities, the Southern cities, and the Southwestern cities. The cities in each group were settled at about the same time, were dependent on the same type of transportation, and had similar local economies.

NOTES

1. The Agricultural Revolution may have occurred 5,000 years earlier in southeast Asia. Solheim and his associates have excavated artifacts from sites in Thailand that suggest the domestication of plants of a type very different from those of the Fertile Crescent may have begun around 13,000 B.C. See W. G. Solheim, "An Earlier Agricultural Revolution," *Scientific American* 226, no. 4 (1972):34–41.
2. For an excellent work on the transition to food production see B. Bendar, *Farming in Prehistory: From Hunter-Gatherer to Food Producer* (New York: St. Martin's Press, 1975).
3. The account is based largely on Gideon Sjoberg, *The Preindustrial City: Past and Present* (New York: The Free Press, 1960).
4. This pattern lingers on in the developing world. In Iran, for example, it is estimated that between 200 and 1,000 families dominate the political structure of the entire country on both the national and local levels (Sjoberg, 1960, p. 222).
5. For a discussion of the Turner thesis see "Epilogue: The City and the Historians," in *American Urban History: An Interpretive Reader with Commentaries*, ed. A. B. Callow, Jr. (New York: Oxford University Press, 1969).

PART TWO

The Ecology of Urban Regions

CHAPTER FOUR

Theories of Location

Statement of Objectives

1. The three major theories of city location should be looked at both as explanations of why cities locate where they do and as methodological tools.

2. The student should recognize that a city's location and subsequent growth is a historical process involving the four elements of the POET framework.

3. The student should understand the impact of changing transportation technology on the economic and social viability of a city.

4. The student should prepare to give examples of cities whose location is explained by each of the three theories of location.

5. The central place theory has limiting assumptions. The student should know these assumptions and understand how violations of them have modified the theory.

The location and distribution of human settlements have been studied by geographers, economists and human ecologists for more than a century. In this chapter the "how" and "why" of the location of cities are explored. Three commonly used theories are described. The break-in-transportation theory focuses on the role of transportation in determining the location of cities. Specialized function theory emphasizes the presence of raw materials as a determinant of city location. Central place theory, the most general of the three models, is based on the role of trade and the relationship of a city to its hinterland or trade area. Although the theories are presented separately and each theory provides a different explanation of the location of cities, the three theories complement rather than conflict with each other, since each theory explains the location of a different type of city. Together they provide a theoretical framework to describe the location of such diverse places as Pittsburgh, Las Vegas and Paris, Arkansas.

This chapter demonstrates the utility of the ecological perspective in examining the many aspects of the urbanization process. Cities represent one of the many adaptations a population can make to an environment, and why a city locates at one point and not at another is a fundamental ecological question. To answer it, the organizational, environmental, and technological factors that affect the locational process are discussed. In addition, theories of location are compared to the city typologies explored in Chapter 5.

BREAK-IN-TRANSPORTATION THEORY

Location and Transportation

The break-in-transportation theory was one of the earliest theories of city location. It can be traced to the works of a sociologist, C. H. Cooley (1894), who emphasized the importance of transportation in the location of cities. He observed that population and wealth tend to collect wherever there is a break-in-transportation (p. 313). A break-in-transportation occurs in the shipment of goods from one place to another when it is necessary to load a shipment from one form of transportation, say, an oceangoing vessel, on to another, such as a train or truck. Interrupting the shipment of goods is expensive, and specialized equipment and workers are required. Therefore a city is likely to emerge at the point where one form of transportation intersects another, e.g., where deep-water shipping intersects land transportation.

Break-in-Transportation Cities

The section of Chapter 3 on American urban history illustrates the importance of transportation in the emergence of cities. In that section the earliest American cities are categorized as either Atlantic Coast, river, or lake cities; these titles reflect the dominant forms of transportation on which the cities were depended. New York, Philadelphia, Boston, and Charleston, South Carolina—the Atlantic Coast cities—owe their existence to excellent deep-water harbors. The cargoes in incoming oceangoing vessels were loaded onto either wagons for surface transport or onto smaller sailing vessels that could navigate the inland rivers. The ability of these cities to provide a linkage between different forms of transportation ensured their economic survival.

Until the advent of the railroads, the most important highways in the American interior were the rivers. Roads in the eighteenth and nineteenth centuries were poor and travel was slow and expensive. In general, roads were passable in summer but turned into quagmires during the spring and fall rains. Because of the difficulty of land travel, rivers and other waterways were used as the primary transportation network (Wade, 1964, p. 39). The river cities of Pittsburgh, Cincinnati, Louisville, and St. Louis emerged at the points where river transportation met the primitive road system of the trans-Allegheny area.

Louisville, Kentucky, exemplifies the break-in-transportation concept of city location. From Pittsburgh to the port of New Orleans, the Ohio and Mississippi Rivers flow more than 1,000 miles with only one major obstruction—a series of falls on the Ohio River. In the twentieth century, locks were built to allow smooth movement of barge traffic past the Ohio Falls. In the eighteenth and nineteenth centuries, however, barges were forced to unload above the falls and reload below. Of the four possible settlement sites at the falls, only one afforded a natural harbor and an area of flat ground well above flood stage suitable for settlement. The stevedore operations that initially developed there eventually led to the emergence of Louisville as a commercial center (Wade, 1964, pp. 13–18).

The lake cities that developed somewhat later owed their economic success to new modes of transportation—the canal and the railroad. Buffalo and Cleveland are at the points where major canals meet Lake Erie; Chicago and Milwaukee connect lake and railroad transportation.

Effects of Technological Change

The commercial cities of the nineteenth century were much more competitive with each other than they are today. The river cities, for example, were settled at roughly the same time, had similar residential populations, depended on the same forms of transportation, and were involved in the same types of trade. Thus, it is not surprising that gains in commerce by one city were viewed with alarm by its competitors. With the development of new forms of transportation, such as the canal or railroad, a city's ability to lock itself into the new transportation network was viewed by civic leaders as a matter of economic survival. A work by Julius Rubin, *Canal or Railroad?* (1961), outlines the lengths to which cities would go to stay abreast of changing transportation technology.

The Erie Canal Rubin outlines the response of three commercial cities, Philadelphia, Baltimore, and Boston, to the competitive influences brought about by the completion of the Erie Canal in 1825. The Erie Canal stretches 364 miles from Albany to Buffalo, New York. It was not simply a success, "it was an enormous, astounding, almost unbelievable success" (1961, p. 5). New York City had access to the canal through the Hudson River and thus became the Atlantic terminus. Overnight, the canal displaced both the turnpikes and the rivers as the dominant forms of transportation in America

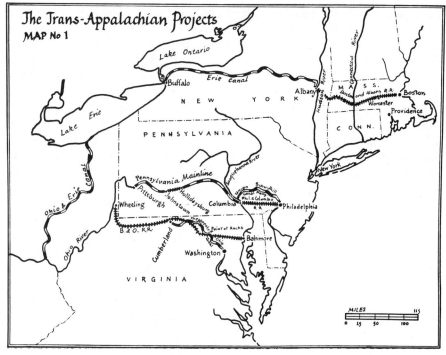

Fig. 4.1 The Trans-Appalachian Projects.
Source: From Julius Rubin, "Canal or Railroad? Imitation and Innovation in the Response to the Erie Canal in Philadelphia, Baltimore, and Boston." *Transactions of the American Philosophical Society* vol. 51, p. 7 (1961).

and placed the cities in New York State in a position to dominate the trade of the entire northern Midwest.

Note in Figure 4.1 that wherever a break in transportation occurred in the canal route, a major city developed. Cargoes from New York City were shipped to Albany where they were broken down for barge shipment along the canal to the lake port at Buffalo. There the cargoes were reassembled and loaded on sailing vessels for distribution by lake to the upper Midwest. The eastern flow of goods from the Midwest was probably more important. Cheap water transportation made possible for the first time the bulk shipment of agricultural produce to eastern markets, and thus encouraged the rapid westward expansion of the United States.

Canal and railroad technology Philadelphia, Boston, and Baltimore were forced to react to this revolution in transportation. Failure to develop competitive transportation to the West would have meant economic stagnation and ruin. All three cities faced geographic obstacles very different from those encountered by the builders of the Erie Canal. Figure 4.2 gives

Photo 4.1 This photograph shows a stretch of the Miami and Erie Canal, a canal that stretched for more than 200 miles from Toledo, Ohio, to Cincinnati, Ohio. The state of Ohio had an extensive canal system, and it was plagued by many of the same problems described by Julius Rubin in his work, *Canal or Railroad?*
Source: Courtesy of The Cincinnati Historical Society.

elevation profiles for six trans-Appalachian projects. Note that the route of the Erie Canal is over relatively flat terrain requiring only 84 locks to overcome a total rise and fall of 675 feet. In contrast, all the other projects involved crossing a mountain range that in one case required a rise and fall of more than 9460 feet! All three cities, besides being confined by mountain ranges, were commercialized coastal areas, subject to the competitive pressures created by the Erie Canal; all had access to almost identical technical information on canals and railroads; and all made their construction decisions at almost the same time. Yet, despite that many similarities among these cities, their reactions to the transportation crisis were entirely different.

By 1825, canal building technology had been well tested. Railroads, though sufficiently developed in England to indicate their engineering feasibility, had not been adequately tested. In 1825, for example, a wide, flat cast-iron rail was used rather than the modern narrow steel ribbon rail. These early rails, besides being difficult to mass-produce and lay, were brittle and prone to fatigue and fracture. This problem was exacerbated by the practice of attaching them directly to solid stone supports rather than to wooden ties, set in gravel ballast, that absorb shock and vibrations. Baltimore, like the other two cities, could have cautiously employed proven technology by building a canal or could have gambled with new technology

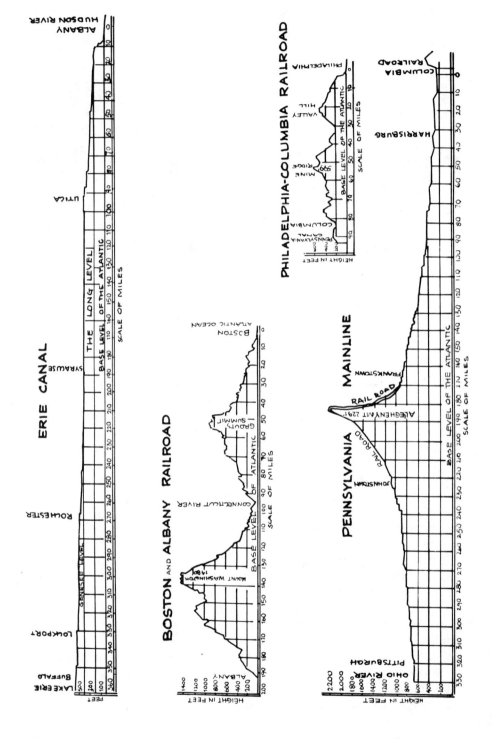

ERIE CANAL

ALBANY HUDSON RIVER
UTICA
SYRACUSE
THE LONG LEVEL
BASE LEVEL OF THE ATLANTIC
SCALE OF MILES
GENESEE LEVEL
ROCHESTER
LOCKPORT
BUFFALO
LAKE ERIE
FEET

BOSTON AND ALBANY RAILROAD

BOSTON
ATLANTIC OCEAN
GROUT'S SUMMIT
CONNECTICUT RIVER
MOUNT WASHINGTON 1480
BASE LEVEL OF ATLANTIC
SCALE OF MILES
ALBANY
HEIGHT IN FEET

PHILADELPHIA-COLUMBIA RAILROAD

PHILADELPHIA
VALLEY HILL
MINE RIDGE
COLUMBIA
PENNSYLVANIA CANAL
BASE LEVEL OF THE ATLANTIC
SCALE OF MILES
HEIGHT IN FEET

COLUMBIA RAILROAD
HARRISBURG

PENNSYLVANIA MAINLINE

FRANKSTOWN
RAIL ROAD
ALLEGHENY MT 2291'
RAILROAD
JOHNSTOWN
BASE LEVEL OF THE ATLANTIC
SCALE OF MILES
PITTSBURGH
OHIO RIVER
HEIGHT IN FEET

140

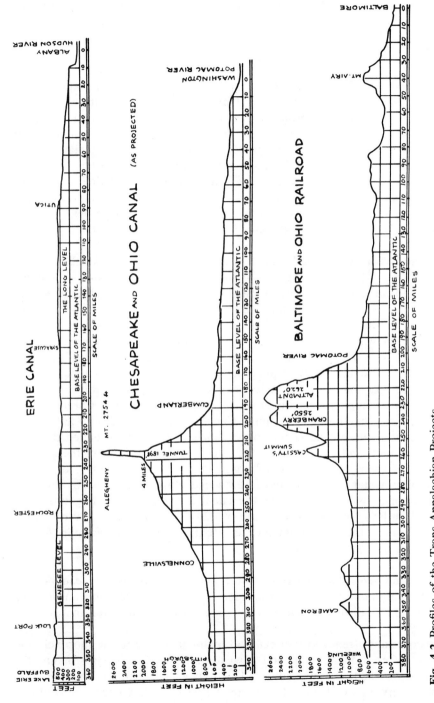

Fig. 4.2 Profiles of the Trans-Appalachian Projects.

Source: From Julius Rubin, "Canal or Railroad? Imitation and Innovation in the Response to the Erie Canal in Philadelphia, Baltimore, and Boston." *Transactions of the American Philosophical Society* vol. 51, pp. 10–11 (1961).

by building a railroad through the mountains. In an atmosphere in which the public viewed with alarm the slightest delay in making a decision, the leaders of Baltimore panicked and decided to build both (Rubin, 1961, pp. 29–35).

Baltimore's canal and railroad Construction on both the Chesapeake and Ohio Canal and the Baltimore and Ohio Railroad began in the summer of 1828. Predictably, both projects were plagued with technical and financial difficulties and both required more than twenty years to complete. After many years the Baltimore and Ohio Railroad did become a financial success. The canal, however, was from the beginning a financial disaster. The maintenance costs and the low volume of freight on the canal made it impossible to repay the bonds that had financed its construction. The State of Maryland, a major financial backer of the project, was brought to near financial collapse (Rubin, 1961, pp. 48–62).

The Pennsylvania mainland canal By 1826 the leaders of Philadelphia, with the backing of the state of Pennsylvania, decided to build a canal to compete with the Erie. The Pennsylvania Mainland and Union Schuykill Canals were completed eight years later and, as was the case in Maryland, both canals became an immediate financial liability. The reason was simply that the terrain and water resources were not suitable for the construction of a canal. Allegheny Mountain, elevation 8291 feet (Figure 4.1), was the most formidable obstacle. Early engineering studies had shown that a lock system could not economically lift a barge over the summit of this mountain. Therefore a complicated incline plane system was developed. Cargoes, after traveling the length of the Mainline Canal, were unloaded onto flatcars. A stationary steam engine at the top of Allegheny Mountain pulled the cars to the summit and then lowered them to the other side where the cargoes continued their journey to Pittsburgh. The expensive handling of goods, as well as water shortages and freezes that closed the canal for much of late summer and winter, made the canal a money loser. The enormous capital outlays for the construction of the canal and the yearly operating losses brought the state of Pennsylvania to the brink of financial ruin (Rubin, 1961, pp. 63–79).

The Boston and Albany railroad In the third city, Boston, the leaders took a more cautious approach and decided to delay their decision on building a canal or a railroad. Engineering studies strongly suggested that a canal through the mountains was simply not feasible. Moreover, the leaders of this community realized that railroad technology had to be improved and tested before it could be applied to western Massachusetts. Boston and the state of Massachusetts waited until 1832 to begin construction on the Boston and Albany Railroad, and it was completed ten years later. The railroad linked Boston to Albany, New York, and gave the city of Boston access to the Erie Canal. The construction delay allowed for the improvement of railroad technology and, unlike the projects of the other two cities, the Boston and Albany Railroad was a financial success (Rubin, 1961, pp. 80–94). Rubin points out in the analysis of these three locales the complex interplay among new technology, geography, economic competition, and public opinion that led to irrational decision making in both Baltimore and Philadelphia. Although both cities survived their folly, the financial losses on their projects crippled their economies for many years.

Effects of Technological Change in the Twentieth Century

The close relationship between changing transportation technology and patterns of human settlement is further illustrated in a classic ecological study by Cottrell (1951), "Death by Dieselization." Cottrell explores railroad technology and the changeover from steam to diesel locomotives. During the steam era, locomotives were required to stop at fixed intervals for fuel and water. These stops brought into being many small towns whose existence was wholly dependent on the railroad. After World War II, when the railroad industry changed to diesel locomotives, many of these stops were eliminated and large numbers of small railroad towns simply ceased to exist. Other communities that had developed other functions through the years continued to exist but at a smaller size.

Today, truck and air transportation is influencing the patterns of urban settlements. Akron, Ohio, for example, because of its proximity to both the large industrial centers of the East and the interstate highway system, has become a major truck transfer and dispatching center. Similarly, Atlanta's geographic location has made it the southern hub of the air transportation industry. Most commercial flights in the South and Southeast make an intermediate stop at Atlanta's Hartsfield International Airport.

A more recent example is the federal deregulation of much of the trucking and air transportation industry. Prior to the 1980s, air and truck carriers were required to file detailed route and fare schedules with federal regulatory agencies (e.g., the Interstate Commerce Commission and the Civil Aeronautics Board). Proposed changes in these schedules required a lengthy and complicated regulator procedure that was often avoided by the carriers because of the expense. With deregulation, carriers have had wide latitude in determining routes and fares, and one result has been that major trucking and air carriers have dropped unprofitable routes. Chattanooga, Tennessee provides one example. Prior to deregulation, this city was serviced by several major airlines. Since deregulation, these airlines have either dropped or drastically reduced service. The end result is that Chattanooga is now less competitive in drawing industry and business to its area. Executives faced with the prospects of depending on small and often unreliable commuter airlines for business travel will likely choose a different location, one with good air service.

Population Growth

The foregoing examples explain the reason for the location of break-in-transportation cities, but not for the high population concentrations at those locations. In the early history of all break-of-transportation cities, a dock-worker or stevedore class made up a large percentage of the city's population. Through time, however, these cities attracted additional residential populations employed in other economic activities. Because these cities are often the terminus for many shipping lines, they are natural locations for the construction and servicing of transportation vehicles. Moreover, auxiliary services to the transportation industry such as warehousing, brokering, financing, managing, and insuring employ additional people.

Because large bulky cargoes—coal, ores, and agricultural produce—are expensive to transship, processing plants are often built at break-in-transportation locations. Normally, at these locations costs of transportation and costs of materials are at a minimum and it becomes cheaper to ship a finished product than to reship raw materials. Pittsburgh, for example, because of its proximity to coal and ore fields and the availability of cheap water transportation, grew as a steel-producing center. Similarly, food-processing and flour-milling operations were established in Chicago as a result of the city's strategic location with respect to water and rail transportation and its proximity to the nation's major food-growing area, the Great Plains.

The families of the various classes of workers support secondary and tertiary functions in the local economy in the areas of retail and wholesale trade, and professional and other services. Thus, the combination of developmental forces referred to as growth inertia leads to the concentration of large populations at break-in-transportation locations.

In summary, changes in transportation technology greatly influence the patterns of urban settlements. The rise and economic decline of many cities can be attributed in part to changing transportation technology. In America's urban history, chance is often listed as the major cause for one city growing at the expense of another. More often than not, however, a city's strategic location combined with its willingness to invest heavily in innovative transportation technology offers a more meaningful explanation.

Shipping continues to be an important element in the local economies of cities originally settled as break-in-transportation centers. Today the nation's economic well-being is inextricably tied to participation in global markets. In particular, the nation must balance the costs of massive oil imports with overseas sales of finished manufactured goods and agricultural products. In the area of agricultural exports, technology has opened up large regions of the United States to international markets. Tulsa, Oklahoma, for example, was landlocked prior to 1960. With the completion of the Kerr-McClellan Waterway Project along the Arkansas River, Tulsa has become an international port with a growing grain export business serving several inland states.

SPECIALIZED FUNCTION THEORY

Location and Resources

Specialized function theory provides another explanation for the location and distribution of cities. The model, however, is not a general one and applies to those cities that are tied closely to environmental conditions or the high concentration of raw materials at one location. It applies to certain types of cities that do not fit the explanatory frameworks provided by the general theories of location. The specialized function theory, therefore, supplements rather than competes with the central place and break-in-transportation theories.

Specialized-Function Cities

The location of some cities was deliberately predetermined. For example, many state capitals—Columbus, Ohio; Indianapolis, Indiana; Jefferson City, Missouri; Springfield, Illinois—are at the geographic centers of their states. Their location was the result of a political compromise that ensured that the capital was equally accessible from all points within the state. Similar reasoning was used in the selection of county seats. In many states, statute mandated that the county seat be located at a point in the county that was accessible by all persons in the county within a half-day's wagon travel. This location enabled farmers to travel to the seat, complete their business, and return home in one day.

The location of certain other communities was totally dependent on the resources found at one strategic place. Ely, Minnesota, is a specialized mining center near massive iron ore deposits. Similarly, Scranton, Wilkes-Barre, and other cities in western Pennsylvania are coal-mining centers wholly dependent on the nearby anthracite coal deposits. Such resort cities as Miami, Florida, and Las Vegas, Nevada, emerged mainly as the result of their climate.

Subsequent Development

Edward Ullman (1941) raises the point that once a city emerges as a result of a specialized function, it develops much differently than break-in-transportation or other cities. First, there is little diversity in the local economy because of the city's dependency on one industry. Even secondary services are highly specialized and directly related to the nearby resources. Mining-equipment manufacturing and repair, ore processing, and other related activities typify these specialized function cities. As a result the fortunes of such cities are tied to the health of one industry. When the one industry fails the consequences can be catastrophic for the city. In the last century, Virginia City, Nevada, almost became a ghost town when the nearby gold deposits were exhausted. Today, Youngstown, Ohio, is suffering major financial dislocations due to the closing of the city's steel plants. Similarly, Miami, Florida, in recent years has had financial problems caused by a downturn in the local tourist industry. Many specialized function cities therefore are attempting to diversify their functions so that their local economies are protected from the financial failure of a single employer.

CENTRAL PLACE THEORY

Location and Trade and Commerce

By examining a county or state map from almost anywhere in the United States, one can see a more or less uniform distribution of many small communities. Central place theory provides an explanation for both the location and size of such towns. The central place theory can be traced to the works of Christaller (1933) and Lösch (1958), who were interested in providing a theoretical explanation for the location and size of cities in the plains area of Germany. Since they introduced the theory it has been tested in many parts of the world—Europe, North America, Australia, and New Zealand—and has been shown to have wide applicability. Interestingly, the model fits the plains states of Kansas, Iowa, and Nebraska better than it fits the plains area of Germany.[1]

The theory of central place states that a certain amount of productive land is necessary to support an urban place. The size of an urban place and the types and number of services it can support are therefore a function of the size of its trade area or, as it is often called, its "hinterland." Services oriented toward the surrounding countryside are termed central functions, and places performing those functions are known as central places.

Assumptions of the Theory

Few theories in the physical or social sciences can be applied indiscriminately; scientists normally specify the exact conditions under which a theory should work. The theory of central place is no different, and four assumptions are associated with it:

1. The geographic area under study is assumed to be flat with few geographic disturbances, such as large rivers or mountains.
2. The geographic area under study is assumed to have an agricultural rather than an industrial economy, and the dominant economic function of urban places is assumed to be trade.

Table 4.1
Economic activities found in three classes of central places—Snohomish County, Washington.

Position in central place hierarchy	Economic function	Threshold population
First-order	Filling Stations	196
	Food Stores	254
	Churches	265
	Restaurants	276
	Taverns	282
	Elementary Schools	322
Second-order	Physicians	380
	Real Estate Agencies	384
	Appliance Stores	385
	Barber Shops	386
	Auto Dealers	398
	Insurance Agencies	409
	Bulk Oil Distributors	419
	Dentists	426
	Motels	430
	Auto Repair Shops	435
	Drug Stores	458
	Beauticians	480
	Lawyers	528
	Apparel Stores	590
	Banks	610
	Farm Implement Dealers	650
	High Schools	732
	Jewelry Stores	827
	Sporting Goods Stores	928
Third-order	Sheet Metal Works	1076
	Department Stores	1083
	Optometrists	1140
	Hospital and Clinics	1159
	Undertakers	1214
	Public Accountants	1300
	Health Practitioners	1424

Source: Adapted from Brian Berry and William Garrison, "The Functional Bases of the Central Place Hierarchy." *Economic Geography*, April, Vol. 34, No. 2 (1958): p. 150.

3. The principle of least effort is assumed. That is, a farmer with the choice of shopping at two trade centers will normally exert the least effort and trade at the closest trade center. A trade center may be a village, town, or city that supplies goods and services to residents of its surrounding countryside.
4. The size of the trade area of an urban place is assumed to be a function of transportation technology. The automobile, for example, would allow a city to serve a wider area than would the horse and buggy.

The Central Place

The notion of central place and its limiting assumptions, combined with a related concept, the urban hierarchy, explain the size and location of many small communities. Urban places develop symbiotic (mutually beneficial) economic relationships with the surrounding productive farm land. Farmers find it expensive and difficult to ship their agricultural produce by road to distant markets. Small trade centers therefore develop to buy and transship agriculture products. The farmer benefits in finding a nearby market, but in turn the trade center benefits economically by supplying its surrounding trade area with goods and services.

The first order These small towns and villages are known as first-order central places, a category of towns and villages similar in size and in the type and number of services they offer. As the frontier was settled, such communities sprang up across the countryside. Normally their small size permitted them to carry out only a few economic functions; one finds in them today only a grocery, gas station, and possibly a hardware or implement store. Moreover, their small size enabled them to draw customers from only a small trade area. Therefore, the first tier of the urban hierarchy

Photo 4.2 The photographs on the opposite page were taken in southern Indiana and show first-, second-, and third-order central places. At the top is Hartsville, Indiana, which has a population of less than 100 inhabitants. Hartsville has a general store, a liquor store, a post office, and a gas station; and this village provides services to the several dozen farms in its trade area.

Spencer, Indiana (*middle*) is a county seat with a population of approximately 3000 inhabitants. Spencer, a second-order central place, has a larger trade area, and it can support doctors, lawyers, and other professionals as well as a greater variety of stores and other services.

Columbus, Indiana (*bottom*), a third-order central place, has a population of nearly 30,000 people. With an even larger trade area and industry located within its borders, it supplies goods and services to its own people and to the people living in the surrounding first- and second-order trade areas.

consists of a large number of first-order places with small trade areas, more or less evenly distributed across the landscape. These places form the foundation upon which still larger urban places depend.

The second order Certain economic functions such as wholesaling, banking, and grain storage cannot be carried out economically in small first-order places. Through time a few of the first-order centers, because of their strategic locations in space, grew in population and took on additional economic functions. These second-order functions included wholesaling to the groceries and other stores in the first-order trade centers, and also the provision of services directly to customers in the trade areas of the first-order centers. Thus the trade areas of the second-order centers overlap the trade areas of the surrounding towns; however, first- and second-order trade centers do not directly compete with each other. Second-order centers provide those goods and services that are not available in the smaller trade centers.

The third order In turn, certain activities such as milling and meat packing require even larger trade areas to be economically profitable. Third-order central places emerge because of their strategic locations, and their expanded trade areas overlap the trade areas of urban places lower in the hierarchy. Again, none of these different orders of cities directly compete with each other, even though they have overlapping trade areas. Each center has its own economic niche that permits it to survive and flourish.

Figure 4.3 gives a picture of the overlapping trade-area patterns suggested in the central-place theory. The distribution of central places resembles a pyramid. On the first tier is a large number of first-order places with small trade areas of equal size. The number of central places declines, however, as the size of their trade areas expands. Moreover, the trade areas of lower-order central places fit neatly (nest) inside the trade areas of higher-order centers. If a state were the unit of analysis, the capstone of the urban hierarchy would be the one city with a trade area the size of the entire state.

The Effects of Region and Technology

The distance between cities of the same order is a function of the transportation technology at the time of settlement, and the nature of the agriculture carried out in the region. First-order places in the Southwest, for example, are on the average farther apart than those in the Midwest. Part of the explanation is that the Midwest was settled earlier than the Southwest and transportation technology at the time of settlement was at a different stage of development. Another factor is the nature of the region's agriculture. The agriculture of the semiarid Southwest is based on the cattle industry. The low rainfall and sparse vegetation require enormous tracts

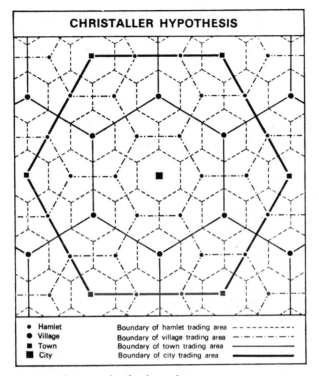

CHRISTALLER HYPOTHESIS

• Hamlet	Boundary of hamlet trading area	– – – – – – – – –
• Village	Boundary of village trading area	– · – · – · – · – ·
■ Town	Boundary of town trading area	——————
■ City	Boundary of city trading area	▬▬▬▬▬

Fig. 4.3 The hexagonal network of urban places.

of land to support the cattle herds. Ranches are large and support relatively few people. Therefore, the demands for services are such that central places tend to be few in number and far apart. The agriculture of the Midwest, in contrast, is based on intensive farming of the land in wheat, corn, and other grains. The rainfall and soil conditions permit smaller farming units, and the region supports a larger farm population. Larger populations mean greater demand for goods, and more central places that are closer together.

Once an urban place is settled and its trade niche is established, its future is determined by its location in the central place hierarchy. The Midwest is dotted with New Londons and New Philadelphias, whose founders saw their new communities as the future great metropolises of the West. However, unless these settlements were located at some strategic point in the emerging pattern, they were destined to become lower-order places.

Tests of the Theory

The central place theory has been tested in several countries. The works of both Christaller (1931) and Lösch (1958) suggest that the theory roughly fits the plains but not the mountainous areas of Germany. Ullman (1941) reports that "many nonindustrial regions of relatively uniform land surface have cities distributed so evenly over the land that some sort of central-place theory appears to be the prime explanation." Similarly, Thomlinson (1969) states that "research indicates that the scheme is not too different from existing urban networks in many of the Midwest and Great Plains states in the United States."

The concept of urban hierarchy Other researchers have tested specific elements of the theory to determine its validity. Both the notion of central places and the notion of an urban hierarchy have been systematically explored.[2] According to the central place theory, the number of cities declines at each successively higher tier in the urban hierarchy as their trade areas expand. Duncan (1960) and Zipf (1949) explored this postulated pattern and found it to be mathematically constant—as the size of cities increases their frequency decreases. Duncan tested this proposed relationship with data from the 1950 Census on cities with populations of 100,000 persons or more. Note in Table 4.2 the close agreement between the predicted and actual numbers of cities in each category.

Duncan and his colleagues also found the expected relationship between the number of functions and the size of urban places. The authors concluded that in the four regions of the United States, the position of an urban place in the urban hierarchy and the magnitude and scope of its economic functions are "more or less adequately indicated by city size" (1960, p. 56). The authors state, however, that the central place theory cannot explain all of the specialized functions that develop in the largest cities. They note that some urban centers are so large that they generate "needs and tastes

Table 4.2
The predicted* and actual number of urbanized areas of 100,000 or more in the United States, 1950.

Size of community	Calculated	Actual
1,000,000 +	12.5	12
500,000 +	12.1	13
300,000 +	15.3	17
200,000 +	20.8	18
150,000 +	19.8	22
125,000 +	15.9	16
100,000 +	23.6	21

* Predicted values from the Pareto Formula $y = 10^6 \times 9.8528X^{-.98356}$, where X = number of inhabitants, Y = number of cities of X size or larger.

Source: O.D. Duncan et al. *Metropolis and Region.* Baltimore, Md.: The Johns Hopkins Press, 1960, p. 53.

not typical of small cities." Moreover, certain specialized services emerge solely for the inhabitants of that city and do not reach out into the trade area. This phenomenon suggests that inertial forces not explained by central place theory come into play once cities in the hierarchy exceed a certain population.

The size and shape of trade areas A second test of the theory has focused on the size and shape of the trade areas themselves. Note in Figure 4.3 that the trade areas of places in the urban hierarchy are represented as hexagons with a central place at the center of each. According to von Thunen's (1826) original formulation, trade areas took the form of a circle. Later Lösch (1958) argued that the shape that best fills all of a geometric form is the hexagon.

Studies of the trade areas of various places have shown that neither shape is valid. Moreover, the size and shape of the trade area of an urban place seem to change with the type of service being studied and with the technique used to measure that service. Thus, if one were looking at

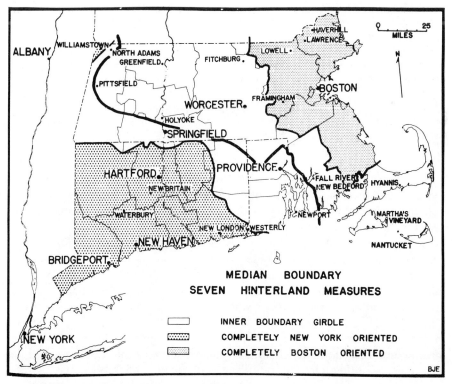

Fig. 4.4 Trade areas of New York City and Boston.

Source: H. L. Green, "Hinterland Boundaries of New York City and Boston in Southern New England." *Economic Geography* 31 (October, 1955): p. 300.

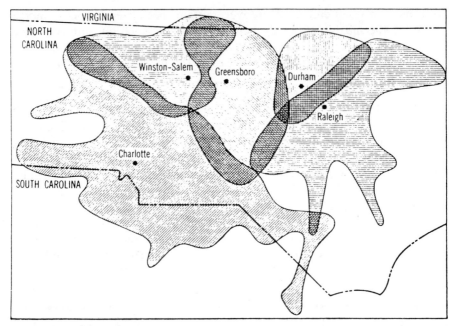

Fig. 4.5 Out-of-town accounts for selected department stores in Raleigh, Durham, Greensboro, Winston-Salem, and Charlotte. Each shaded area represents the generalized shape of the charge-account area of the indicated city based on the locations of towns of 500 or more population with at least 20 charge accounts per 1,000 inhabitants.

Source: R. W. Pfouts, "Patterns of Economic Interaction in the Crescent." In R. S. Chapin and S. R. Weiss, eds., *Urban Growth Dynamics*. Ne York: John Wiley & Sons, 1962, p. 37. Reprinted by permission of John Wiley & Sons, Inc.

wholesaling and repair services for the same city, two overlapping trade areas would probably be evident. Green (1955) showed that the areas of influence of Boston and New York City, as measured by newspaper circulation, were irregular in shape but did not overlap.

A work by Swedner (1960), *Ecological Differentiation of Habits and Attitudes*, is a study of the trade areas of urban places in Sweden. The author concludes that different urban places of the same size are related differently to their hinterlands and that the size and shape of trade areas are a function of the place under study and the specific function measured. Ullman (1941) and Pfouts (1962) found essentially the same phenomenon in the United States. Some services extend geographically much farther into the countryside than others, and their trade areas in no case could be described as either circular or hexagonal. Figure 4.5 represents the department store retail trade areas for five cities in the Piedmont area of North Carolina. The trade areas are not only irregular in shape, but in many cases overlap.

Criticisms of the Theory

The following criticisms have been made of the central place theory:

1. Central place theory is not a general theory for the location of cities. Break-of-transportation and specialized function theories are required to explain the location of certain cities.
2. The hexagonal trade areas postulated are not found in reality.
3. The assumptions of the theory limit its use in the study of much of the developed world.
4. The services carried out in the larger centers of the urban hierarchy cannot be explained fully by the central place theory. In large urban places inertial forces arise that are not related to the trade function.

Many of the criticisms are of recent origin and their appearance can be explained in part by changes that have occurred in American and other societies during the last century. The present patterns of urban places in the United States were determined between 100 and 300 years ago at the time of settlement of the various geographic regions. During the past 75 years there has been a revolution in transportation technology and a transformation of this society's economy from an agricultural to an industrial base. These changes have had a profound impact on human settlements and have set up forces not accounted for in the central place theory.

Central Place Theory Reexamined

These changes in human settlement patterns are explored in a work by Harold Mark and Kent Schwirian (1969), "Ecological Position, Urban Central Place Function, and Community Population Growth," using Iowa as their subject of study. Iowa fits the central place model extremely well, and Schwirian and Mark were interested in assessing the impact of changing transportation technology on the central place pattern.

Changing transportation technology After World War II, Iowa like many other midwestern states undertook a program to improve the state's road system. Much of this work simply involved widening and paving highways. However, the state's master plan also called for building bypasses around many small trade centers. The highway improvements and bypasses greatly increased the distance a driver could travel in an hour. *The end result was that an entirely new transportation network was superimposed over the old central place pattern.*

A farmer, for example, with access to the high-speed modern highway could avoid the high prices at the local store and travel thirty or forty miles to the supermarket in the city. During the 1950s many of the merchants in the small trade centers simply did not understand why their business was declining. Finding their town a mile or two off the main highway after the bypass had been built, they often responded by erecting a billboard on the highway—"Smallville, Nice People and a Nice Place to Shop." This gesture was fruitless because their position with respect to the new transportation network was such that they were doomed to economic decline. The new transportation technology permitted higher-order places to expand their services and trade areas to compete directly with the small trade centers. Economies of scale—the ability of high-order places to buy in volume and minimize transportation costs—dramatically changed the pattern of competition.

The effects of industrialization Industrialization was another force modifying the locational patterns of cities and towns in Iowa. Industrialization brought about the improvement of the transportation system as well as rapid economic and population growth. Mark and Schwirian found that this growth was not uniform across the state and that certain ecological classes of cities expanded but others did not. In general, cities at the top of the old urban hierarchy had a competitive edge over lower-order cities. These places already had large labor pools, good rail transportation, and other services that made them attractive to new industry. Therefore, they became the focal point for regional development at the expense of smaller trade centers.

Changing patterns of central places These changes are summarized in Table 4.3, which gives the ecological position of a sample of Iowa's cities and the changes in their populations and retail trade volume between 1950 and 1960. Note in column 1 that most of the population growth in the state during these years was centered in metropolitan areas. Growth in central cities was moderate; the suburbs absorbed most of the state's population increase. The category "metropolitan neighbors" refers to small first-order trade centers that came under the economic influence of their large neighbors. For the most part, they grew in population because they became satellite bedroom communities. Because they were within the expanding trade area of the metropolis, they ceased to be trade centers. As the metropolitan centers in Iowa continue to expand, these communities ultimately will be surrounded and absorbed into the suburban ring.

Competitive and noncompetitive trade areas are lower-order central places that have not yet come under the economic influence of the metropolitan areas. They still function as trade centers but they have made only slight gains in population.

This analysis is further strengthened by the trade volume figures in column 2 of Table 4.3. These figures give the percentage change in retail trade sales between 1950 and 1960. The metropolitan neighbors and the competitive and noncompetitive trade centers have shown large increases in dollar sales, but their economies have been stagnant and have made no real growth. They have merely kept up with inflation.

Photo 4.3 Aurora is a small trade center of 5,500 inhabitants located in southern Missouri along U.S. Highway 60. Up until thirty years ago, U.S. 60 passed through the center of town, and the highway traffic supported more than 100 merchants. Missouri, like many midwestern states, began a massive road-building program after World War II, and many communities the size of Aurora were bypassed by the new road construction. Aurora, like many other communities, erected signs along the new highway in an attempt to lure shoppers into town. This effort was unsuccessful—today only 58 merchants remain in Aurora.

The downtown areas of central cities in Iowa have held their own and have had small increases in their total volume of sales. Suburbs, in comparison, have achieved rapid expansion of their retail markets. Growth in suburban retail trade reflects the emergence of the shopping mall on a large scale in the post–World War II period. The location of malls at the periphery of the city enabled them to tap the suburban middleclass market, and their location combined with the high-speed highway system allowed them to serve a greatly expanded rural trade area. These retail sales patterns, however, are not shared by all regions. The downtown areas of many cities, including Cleveland, Detroit, Toledo, and Louisville, have had dramatic declines in the volume of sales as a result of peripheral shopping mall development.

Criticisms of the central place theory result from the inability of the theory to predict modifications of the original central place patterns caused by economic and technological changes during the last 75 years. The preceding discussion shows how new locational influences cause the growth

Table 4.3
Community ecological position by population and trade function changes 1950–1960.

Community ecological position	Population change 1950–1960 (%)	Change in trade volume 1950–1960 (%)	Number of places
Central Cities	10.0	9.1	6
Suburbs	40.4	41.5	5
Metropolitan Neighbors	12.4	2.4	17
Noncompetitive Trade Centers	3.8	.7	14
Competitive Trade Centers	0.5	.7	48

Source: Adapted from H. Mark and K. P. Schwirian, "Ecological Position, Urban Central Place Function and Community Population Growth." *American Journal of Sociology.* 73 (July 1967): pp. 37–38. Reprinted with permission of The University of Chicago Press.

and expansion of one center and the decline of another. With modifications of the basic assumptions of the theory, however, the central place theory can continue to be used in the historical analysis of the present and future patterns of human settlement.

SUMMARY

The three theories of location examined in this chapter demonstrate the utility of the ecological perspective in examining the why and how of the location of cities. The three theories complement each other because each theory explains the concentration of a population at a particular point in space in terms of different elements of the ecological complex or POET framework noted in Chapter 1.

The *Break-in-Transportation Theory* combines environmental and technological factors to explain why cities arise in a certain place. A favorable environment—a location along a navigable river or lake—is important, but the level of transportation technology at the time of settlement and at later dates is more important to this theory. The river cities, for example, came into existence because of poorly developed road transportation technology. The growth of the lake cities was closely tied to new transportation technology—the canal and the railroad. The *Specialized Function Theory* explains the initial settlement and consequent growth of a population in terms of the resources available in the environment. Subsequent growth of the economies (organization) of these cities is linked to the environmental factors responsible for their initial settlement. The *Central Place Theory* is the most general of the three because it explores the complex interaction of environment, transportation, technology, and economic organization to predict the location, size, and functions of human settlements across a region. Recent improvements in automobile technology and shifts of regional economies from agriculture to industry have caused major modifications in central place patterns.

In general, when the theories are used in conjunction with each other, they explain the reason for a location but do not explain changes in the pattern that occur through time. Combined with concepts of metropolitan growth and dominance—as in the Mark and Schwirian work—the location theories can be helpful in predicting the future direction of growth. These concepts are explored in Chapter 5.

NOTES

1. A general review of the central place theory and an annotated bibliography of empirical tests of the model is available in Brian Berry and Allen Pred, *Central Place Studies: A Bibliography of Theory and Applications* (Philadelphia: Regional Science Research Institute, 1965).
2. Berry and Garrison (1958), Berry and Pred (1965), Duncan et al. (1960), and Howard (1973) have examined the concept of an urban hierarchy. For a complete citation of each work please see the bibliography.

CHAPTER FIVE

City Typologies and the System of Cities

Statement of Objectives

1. The student should know why researchers classify cities.

2. The student should understand the techniques used to construct a single-dimension typology.

3. Harris and Nelson both found in their studies a close relationship between a city's economic function and its regional location. The student should analyze the relationship between function and location.

4. The student should understand the techniques used in constructing a multidimensional typology.

5. The student should be aware of the uses of classification schemes in policy formulation and urban planning.

6. The student should analyze the evolution of America's system of cities using Borchert's historical study of United States urban patterns.

7. The megalopolis is becoming the nation's dominant form of urban settlement. The student should know this term and the regions where the growth of this urban pattern is most rapid.

In the discussion of theories of location in Chapter 4 it was noted that cities at different locations differ in the nature of their local economies, the socioeconomic characteristics of their populations, and their physical features. These differences can be explained in part by the technology available at the time of the settlement, the local resources on which their early growth depended, regional differences in climate and resources, and changes in the competitive advantage of cities caused by changes in the national and regional economy—what a city does is closely related to where it is. The Atlantic Coast cities, for example, are deep-water ports largely involved in commerce and trade. The concentration of the petrochemical industry in Houston, Dallas, and Tulsa is a result of their proximity to gas and oil fields. Processing and distribution of agricultural products are centered in Kansas City and Omaha because those cities are in the farm belt of the Great Plains. Therefore, location and function are related and represent the complex interaction of the variables—population, organization, environment, and technology—in the ecological complex.

This chapter explores the functions of cities and the attempts of researchers to classify them and to develop city typologies. Cities differ in type. This implies that cities are not autonomous but dependent on each other for goods and services that are not produced locally. Through time some cities, because of their proximity to transportation and communication networks and other resources, emerge as a dominant force in their region and, to a degree, mandate relationships with subordinate cities. Therefore, this chapter will also explore the system of cities. An examination of this concept complements the previous discussion of theories of location and provides an understanding of the role of urban places in regional and national growth and development.

Why Classify?

Language—the ability to communicate symbolically—distinguishes the human species from the rest of the animal kingdom. Classification is a basic procedure used in language to structure and give meaning to the world. Symbols such as "man," "woman," "child," and "book," give meaning to an entire category of "things" and permit the transmission of information about these "things" from one person to another. Without classification language would be cumbersome, and science—the collection and classification of knowledge—would be impossible. Little is gained from classification alone, however; it must serve some purpose. The purpose of classifying cities into groups or types is to learn more about them and thus gain insight into urban problems and their possible solution. Specifically, city classification is done for the following reasons:

First, classifying cities summarizes large amounts of information about cities and enables one to identify the key dimensions of certain types of cities.

Second, classification enables the researcher to structure reality for the purpose of hypothesis testing. For example, a researcher might hypothesize that commercial cities have higher rates of unemployment than diversified manufacturing cities during times of recession. The researcher first would classify cities on the basis of their economic structure and then compare their rates of unemployment.

Third, the classification of cities aids in the assessment of urban problems and can contribute to better policy formation and decision making. The effectiveness of federal programs in the areas of health, housing, and poverty might be enhanced by determining the type of cities for which specific programs are the most cost-effective.[1]

Criteria Used in Classifying

Cities can be classified by any number of criteria, provided that two conditions are met. First, the measure must permit a city to be placed in only one category, i.e., the categories must be mutually exclusive. Second, the categories chosen must be all-encompassing so that every city in the sample can be classified. Such factors as age, size, and region, as well as demographic characteristics, economic function, and government structure have been used in deriving city typologies (Berry, 1972b; Hadden and Borgatta, 1965). Consequently researchers have constructed dozens of classification schemes. Basically, these schemes are of two kinds, single-dimension and multidimensional (multivariate) typologies.

SINGLE-DIMENSION TYPOLOGIES

The simplest way to classify cities is on the basis of a single characteristic such as population size, density, or types of employment. As an example, a city typology can be constructed from the figures in Table 5.1. Table 5.1 lists the percentage of the labor force employed in four types of nonagricultural jobs for eight United States SMSAs. Other categories of employment could have been included, but these four represent about 70 percent of the labor force in these cities. By scanning the table, one can see that these cities vary significantly in their employment profiles. This variation forms the basis for a classification on the single dimension of employment.

A classification scheme based on these employment figures is presented in Table 5.2. Philadelphia, Pittsburgh, and Cleveland are classified as "manufacturing type," because durable goods manufacturing is the dominant employer in each of these cities. The employment in New York City is evenly dispersed across the categories in Table 5.1; this city is labeled "diversified type." Government is the major employer in Washington, D.C.; Sacramento, California; and Columbus, Ohio; these cities are classified as "governmental." Interestingly, Miami, Florida, does not fit into any of these categories and this fact reflects some of the difficulties in constructing city typologies. Miami is heavily dependent on the tourist industry; if "service employment" had been included as a category in Table 5.1, Miami would have been so classified.

Table 5.1
Employment in nonagricultural jobs for selected U.S. SMSAs (in percent).*

SMSA	Manufacturing		Wholesale & retail trades	Finance	Government
	Durable goods	Nondurable goods			
Philadelphia, PA	*25.4*	8.0	21.8	6.0	16.2
Pittsburgh, PA	*28.5*	4.9	21.3	4.7	13.6
New York, NY	*16.5*	*12.4*	19.8	*12.1*	17.6
Washington, DC	3.5	4.2	18.8	5.8	*38.5*
Sacramento, CA	7.2	4.2	22.1	4.3	*40.9*
Miami, FL	13.7	8.2	26.3	7.6	13.9
Columbus, OH	14.0	6.5	23.5	6.9	*21.2*
Cleveland, OH	*30.2*	7.8	23.0	5.1	13.1

* Italics added.

The figures in this table show that there are similarities and differences in the employment characteristics of these cities; these similarities and differences form the basis for a classification scheme. For instance, in column 1, "durable goods manufacturing," Pittsburgh, Philadelphia, and Cleveland stand out, with significantly higher percentages of their labor force in this category than other cities. Pittsburgh and Cleveland are known for the production of steel and fabricated metal products, and Philadelphia is a major producer of machinery, electrical equipment, and other durable goods (Duncan et al., pp. 279–327). Note that New York is ranked fourth, but it is nine percentage points below Philadelphia and would not be included within this city type.

In column 2, New York is the only city with major employment in "nondurable goods manufacturing." Employment in "wholesale and retail trades" is about equal in all eight cities; the category would not be useful in classifying these cities. In column 3, New York is the only city with a high percentage of its labor force in "finance." In the last column, Washington, D.C., Columbus, Ohio, and Sacramento, California, lead the other cities in the percentage of their labor force in "government service."

On the basis of these employment figures, three types of cities are identified—manufacturing, diversified, governmental.

Source: Bureau of Labor Statistics. Employment and Earnings, States and Areas, 1939–75. Washington, D.C.: U.S. Government Printing Office, 1977.

Table 5.2
A single-dimension typology constructed with nonagricultural employment data from Table 5.1.

Manufacturing type	Diversified type	Governmental type	?
Philadelphia Pittsburgh Cleveland	New York	Washington, D.C. Sacramento Columbus	Miami

Harris's City Classification

The foregoing simple example shows how a single-dimension typology can be constructed. Harris (1943) applied the same rationale in an early classification of 605 American cities, using employment and occupation figures from the 1930 census of population and the 1935 census of business.[2] He faced many of the same problems noted in the example. In Table 5.1 each metropolitan area has some employment in each category. Harris recognized that all large cities are multifunctional to a degree and that the classification of a city as "commercial" does not indicate the absence of other employment functions. The major goal of Harris's study was to identify "critical levels" of employment that would separate cities into clearly defined functional types. As in the above example, Harris constructed his classification framework by scanning the employment profiles of cities and then intuitively setting minimum levels of employment for each functional type. At the end of this process Harris had classified 605 American cities into nine functional types.

City types Table 5.3 lists the criteria used by Harris in identifying city types. The figure at the right of each subheading is the percentage of the cities of that type in his sample. Not surprisingly, manufacturing cities were the most numerous type, comprising 44 percent of the metropolitan areas and 43 percent of the smaller cities. The high number of manufacturing cities led Harris to divide this category into two subtypes; M' type (19.5 percent), overwhelmingly manufacturing cities, and M type (23.1 percent), manufacturing cities with large numbers of people employed in support activities such as trade and wholesaling. In 1930, as today, most manufacturing cities were in an area east of the Mississippi and north of the Ohio Rivers. Harris also noted some clustering of manufacturing cities in the Piedmont region of the southeastern United States (see Figure 5.1).

Harris found fewer cities of the other functional types, but each city type had unique locational characteristics linked to its function. The majority of retail centers, R type (17.2%), were outside the manufacturing belt along a narrow band that is the eastern boundary of the farming area of the Great Plains.

Diversified cities, D type (21.5%), in which neither trade nor manufacturing was clearly dominant, were well distributed but "were particularly numerous in the transitional area between the manufacturing belt and the band of retail centers" (p. 91). The largest metropolitan areas in the nation, New York, Chicago, and Boston (each a preeminent break-in-transportation city), were included in this category.

Wholesale centers, W type (4.5%), were of two kinds, smaller centers engaged in the assembling, packing, and marketing of agricultural products, and large centers (usually the largest cities in their regions) that furnished durable and nondurable goods to their surrounding areas.

Table 5.3
Criteria used by Harris in classifying cities.

Manufacturing Cities (M')—19.5%. Principal criterion: Employment in manufacturing equals at least 74% of total employment in manufacturing, retailing, and wholesaling (employment figures). Secondary criterion: Manufacturing and mechanical industries contain at least 45% of gainful workers (occupation figures). *Note:* A few cities with industries in suburbs for which no figures were available were placed in this class if the percentage in the secondary criterion reached 50. The largest city in this group was Detroit, Michigan. The smaller cities with heavier dominance of manufacturing were Fulton, New York and Thomasville, North Carolina.

Manufacturing Cities (M)—23.1%. Principal criterion: Employment in manufacturing equals at least 60% of total employment in manufacturing, retailing, and wholesaling. Secondary criterion: Manufacturing and mechanical industries usually contain between 30% and 45% of gainful workers. Philadelphia was the largest city of this type. Pittsburgh, Rochester, Syracuse and Albany, New York are other examples.

Retail Centers (R)—17.2%. Employment in retailing is at least 50% of the total employment in manufacturing, wholesaling, and retailing and at least 2.2 times that in wholesaling alone. Tulsa, Oklahoma; Wichita, Kansas; and Shreveport, Louisiana were the largest cities classified as retail centers.

Diversified Cities (D)—21.5%. Employment in manufacturing, wholesaling, and retailing is less than 60%, 20%, and 50% respectively of the total employment in these activities, and no other special criteria apply. Manufacturing and mechanical industries with few exceptions contain between 25% and 35% of the gainful workers. New York, Boston and Chicago were the largest cities in this category. Smaller cities include Indianapolis; Columbus, Ohio; and Minneapolis–St. Paul.

Wholesale Centers (W)—4.5%. Employment in wholesaling is at least 20% of the total employment in manufacturing, wholesaling, and retailing and at least 45% as much as in retailing alone. Cities of this type were usually the largest city in their region and include such cities as Salt Lake City, Denver, Memphis, Oklahoma City, and Dallas.

Transportation Centers (T)—5.3%. Transportation and communication contain at least 11% of the gainful workers, and workers in transportation and communication equal at least one-third the number in manufacturing and mechanical industries and at least two-thirds the number in trade (occupation figures). (Applies only to cities of more than 25,000 for which such figures are available.) Harris identified rail centers and ports; among the better-known port cities were New Orleans and Portland, Maine.

Mining Towns (S)—2.3%. Extraction of minerals accounts for more than 15% of the gainful workers. (Applies only to cities of more than 25,000 for which such figures are available.) For cities between 10,000 and 25,000 a comparison was made of available mining employment by counties, using employment in the cities within such mining counties. Published sources were consulted to differentiate actual mining towns from commercial and industrial centers in mining areas.

Table 5.3 (continued)

Scranton–Wilkes-Barre and Johnstown, Pennsylvania are among the best-known mining centers.

University Towns (E)—2.8%. Enrollment in schools of collegiate rank (universities, technical schools, liberal arts colleges, and teachers' colleges) equaled at least 25% of the population of the city (1940). Enrollment figures are from *School and Society*, vol. 52, 1940, pp. 601–19. Oxford and Oberlin, Ohio; State College, Pennsylvania and Chapel Hill, North Carolina are among the most notable university towns.

Resort and Retirement Towns (X)—3.6%. No satisfactory statistical criterion was found. Cities with a low percentage of their population employed were checked in the literature for this function.

Source: Harris, C. D., "A Functional Classification of Cities in the United States." Reprinted from *The Geographical Review* 33, no. 1 (1943): p. 88, with the permission of the American Geographical Society.

Most transportation centers, T type (5.3%), railroad centers and ports, were at break-in-transportation points. Mining towns, S type (2.3%), were near the source of raw materials. University towns, E type (2.8%), were the seats of large state universities. Finally, resort and retirement towns, X type (3.6%), were either summer or winter resorts in warm southern locales, along seacoasts and lakes, or in the mountains. Harris mentioned political cities, garrison cities, professional centers, and fishing, lumbering, and farm centers, but did not include them in his typology.

Criticism Harris's typology was a benchmark work and it has been used as a model by other researchers in the construction of their own classification frameworks.[3] There were, however, serious weaknesses in this work. First, the method used by Harris in setting the criteria for the various city types was open to question. Critics challenged the validity of scanning employment profiles of hundreds of cities and then intuitively setting arbitrary employment levels for their inclusion into one of nine city types (Nelson, 1955). Second, the classification scheme was inflexible; Harris often classified a city as manufacturing even though it carried out important trade, wholesaling, and retail functions. Third, Harris's classification scheme was not used as a point of departure for further analyses (Smith, 1965).

Nelson's City Classification

In his classification of 897 U.S. cities, Nelson (1955) attempted to overcome some of the major weaknesses in Harris's earlier work. To Nelson the major question to be addressed was, "How large a percentage of the labor force must be employed in a particular service to make the performance

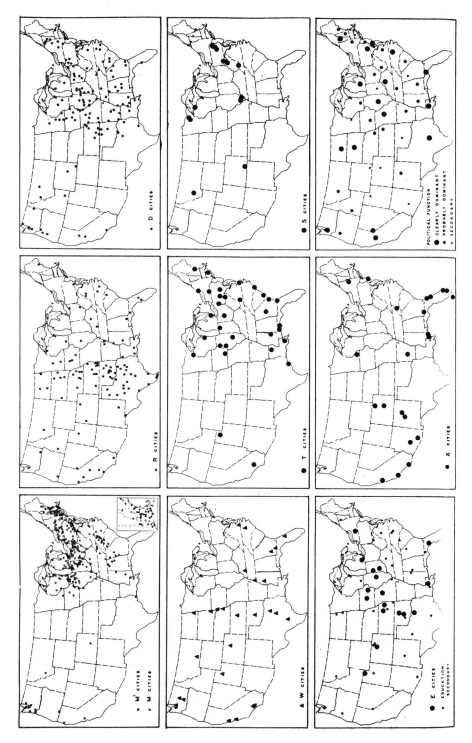

168

of the service far enough above the normal to warrant separate classification?'' (p. 194). Nelson believed that an advance in this research area could be achieved if classification were based on ''clearly stated statistical procedures'' rather than on intuition.

To this end, Nelson gathered employment figures from the 1950 United States Census of Population for nine major employment categories. These figures were expressed as a percentage of the city's total labor force. The percentages for individual cities, however, were almost meaningless without some reference point. Nelson suggested using two statistical reference points, the mean and the standard deviation (σ). The mean is simply the arithmetic average of a series of scores. The standard deviation is a simple measure of variation. It gives the researcher an idea of how far the score for a single city varies from the mean or average employment score of all cities in a particular occupational category, such as manufacturing. Both measures are widely used in social science research, are easily calculated, and provide Nelson a common set of reference points for his analysis.

Employment patterns From the frequency distributions in Figure 5.2, several patterns are discernible. First, there are some rather striking variations in the distribution of employment in the nine different occupational categories. Second, the vast majority of cities have at least some employment in all nine occupational categories. Third, three distinct patterns are apparent in the frequency distributions of the scores.

Seven of the graphs (transportation and communication; professional service; personal service; wholesale trade; mining; public administration; and finance, insurance, and real estate) have similar distribution patterns. Each of these graphs shows ''peaking around some typical percentage,'' ranging from 2 to 10%. For example, almost all cities have a low percentage of their labor force in transportation and communication—the average value or mean for this category is only 7%. In a few cities, however, the percentage of the labor force in this service is many times higher than the mean. Note in Figure 5.2 that one city has nearly 40% of its labor force in transportation and communication services. This city, at more than three standard deviations from the mean, would be classified as a highly specialized transportation center.

Retail trade shows a second and very different pattern. Most cities have a high percentage (mean = 19.2%) of their labor force in retail services and the scores do not vary much, from a low of 10% to a high of 35%.

A third pattern is seen for manufacturing. Its frequency distribution has

---

Fig. 5.1 (Opposite) The spatial distribution of cities in the United States by city types, Harris's 1943 city classification of 605 American cities.

Source: Harris, C. D., ''A Functional Classification of Cities in the United States.'' Reprinted from the *Geographical Review* 33, 1 (1943): p. 92, with the permission of the American Geographical Society.

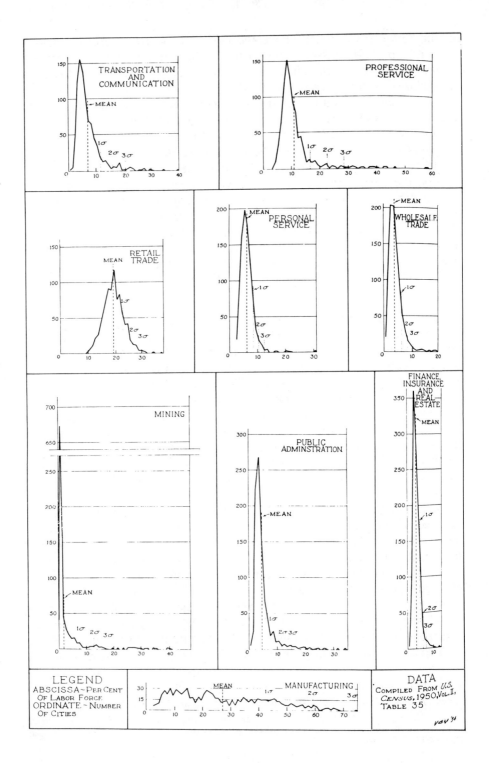

TRANSPORTATION AND COMMUNICATION

PROFESSIONAL SERVICE

RETAIL TRADE

PERSONAL SERVICE

WHOLESALE TRADE

MINING

PUBLIC ADMINSTRATION

FINANCE, INSURANCE AND REAL ESTATE

LEGEND
ABSCISSA ~ PER CENT OF LABOR FORCE
ORDINATE ~ NUMBER OF CITIES

MANUFACTURING

DATA
COMPILED FROM U.S. CENSUS, 1950, VOL. II, TABLE 35

VBV '54

the greatest variation, and its graph shows no "peaking." All cities have some manufacturing activities (mean = 27.1%), but the scores range from a low of 3% to a high of more than 65%. The graph suggests that it would be difficult to determine a "normal" level of manufacturing activity.

City types Nelson used standard deviations as the basis for his classification scheme to indicate the degree of specialization in a city's labor force. Table 5.4 is a summary of Nelson's classification of United States cities by type of activity and degree of specialization. First, note that the total number of classifications made is 1139, although only 897 cities were included in the sample. This apparent discrepancy arises from Nelson's attempt to overcome the weakness of Harris's earlier classification scheme, its inflexibility. Boulder, Colorado, for example, the seat of a major state university, was classified as a professional service and personal service center. The number of professionals employed in this city differed by more than 3σ from the mean and the percentage of its labor force employed in personal services differed by more than 2σ. This overlapping service specialization occurred in more than one fourth of the cities in the sample.

Manufacturing is the most common activity in which cities specialize, followed by retail trade, finance, transportation, and personal services. Interestingly, except for mining and to a lesser extent professional and transportation services, relatively few cities have an extreme degree of specialization in any one activity (3σ). Nearly one fourth of the cities are classified as "diversified," because they had an average or near average percentage of their labor forces in the nine occupational groupings.

Figure 5.3 shows the spatial distribution of cities in various service activities by the degree of specialization according to Nelson's city classification. By turning back to Figure 5.1 and comparing Harris's figures with Nelson's, one can see a clear correspondence between the two. Both Harris's and Nelson's city classifications show the greatest concentration of the manufacturing city type in the area east of the Mississippi and north of the Ohio Rivers. Similarities are also present in the other figures.

Means and standard deviations are understood best when seen graphically. This figure shows the means, standard deviations, and frequency distributions for 897 cities in nine occupational categories. The Y or vertical axis in each graph is the number of cities involved; the X or horizontal axis is the percentage of the labor force in each category. The means and standard deviations are represented by dotted lines and the standard deviations are labeled with the symbol σ. The standard deviation indicates how far the score of an individual city varies from the average; a score of 3σ would be an extreme variation from the "normal" or mean, 2σ less extreme, and so on. These deviations became Nelson's measure of the degree of service specialization.

Fig. 5.2 (Opposite) Labor force profiles for nine employment categories used by Nelson in constructing a city classification of 897 United States cities.

Source: Nelson, H. J., "A Service Classification of American Cities." *Economic Geography* 31 (1955): p. 192.

Table 5.4
Nelson's classification of American cities by type and degree of specialization.

	Increasing variation from the mean			
	1σ	2σ	3σ	Total
Manufacturing	153	29	1	183
Retail Trade	110	21	6	137
Professional Services	42	15	24	81
Transportation and Communication	53	18	25	46
Personal Services	62	18	12	92
Public Administration	52	15	18	85
Wholesale	60	17	13	90
Finance, Insurance and Real Estate	92	14	17	123
Mining	20	6	20	46
Diversified	206	0	0	206
			Total	1,139

Source: Adapted from Nelson, H. J., "A Service Classification of American Cities." *Economic Geography* 31, no. 3 (1955): 185–210.

Criticism Nelson's city classification appears to overcome many of the weaknesses of Harris's approach. First, it applies objective, rather than subjective, intuitive criteria for city classification. Second, the fact that it permits cities to be classified on more than one activity lends flexibility to the scheme. Nelson's approach is not without problems, however. Johnston (1968) questions the objectivity of any city classification. Nelson's choice of employment activity rather than some other criterion was subjective rather than objective. The statistical measures of central tendency and variation used by Nelson were also chosen subjectively; other measures are available. In addition, critics have argued that a single dimension cannot adequately classify cities because cities are complex and multifunctional. Finally, Nelson's city classification, like many others, was an end in itself, not a point of departure for additional analysis. Therefore, Nelson's apparently more objective method for the classification of cities is not necessarily better than Harris's approach. Both schemes need to be evaluated independently on the basis of whether they do the job for which they were intended.

Theories of Location and City Types

The different functional types of cities identified by Harris (1943) and Nelson (1955) have different locational characteristics that are well explained by

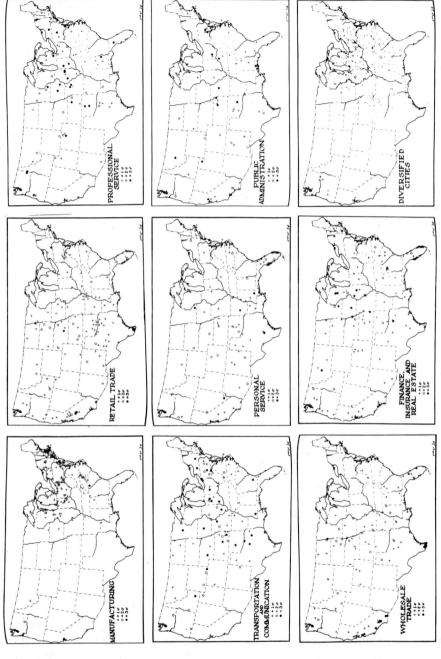

Fig. 5.3 The spatial distribution of American cities by city types, Nelson's 1955 city classification of 897 cities. *Source*: Nelson, H. J., "A Service Classification of American Cities." *Economic Geography* 31 (1955): 197–204.

173

the theories of location reviewed in Chapter 4. The distribution of the functional types of cities identified by the two researchers is presented in Figures 5.1 and 5.3.

The central place theory, which stressed the importance of a central location within a trade area, is illustrated best by the distribution of whole-sale and retail centers. Harris and Nelson both found wholesale centers normally were large cities centrally placed in large trade areas. Retail centers, in contrast, tended to be smaller in both their population and trade area. In comparison with other city types, retail centers are more evenly distributed across the United States, as would be predicted by the central place theory.

The remaining two theories of location explain the distribution of other city types. The locations of mining and resort centers, for example, are best explained by environmental influences or site factors, such as climate and the presence of mineral resources. Similarly, transportation and communication centers are normally found at break-in-transportation points.

The largest number of cities were of the manufacturing type and were concentrated in a band running from New England through Ohio, Indiana, and Illinois. The majority of these cities came into existence because of central place, break-in-transportation, or site factors. Once these cities were settled their future growth was prescribed by the availability of resources, the characteristics of the city's population, and access to regional and national markets. As a result, their present size and importance have been determined by a different set of factors than those responsible for their original settlement. This pattern of cities is explored more fully at the end of this chapter.

MULTIDIMENSIONAL TYPOLOGIES

The classification of cities on a single dimension has been done in at least two different ways, as described in the preceding section. First, several researchers have intuitively set minimum levels of employment in manufacturing and other occupations for cities as the basis for classification.[4] Second, other researchers have used arithmetic means and other statistics to set thresholds of employment for classification.[5] Although these methods of classification are straightforward, and relatively homogeneous groupings of cities have resulted, they have been overly dependent on a single classification criterion—economic function. By focusing on this single dimension these studies have ignored other facets of cities, e.g., their social, physical, cultural, ecological dimensions. Through time, social scientists have come to realize that there is more to urban places than can be explained on the basis of one economic characteristic. Researchers have begun to include other dimensions or variables in city classifications. Approaches involving more than one characteristic are known as multidimensional or multivariate city typologies.

Constructing a Multidimensional Typology

A multidimensional typology can be constructed simply by classifying cities on two dimensions rather than one. In Figure 5.4, for example, nine hypothetical cities are plotted according to the occupational and income characteristics of their populations. Note that there are three clusters, each grouping of cities having income and employment traits not shared by the others. By drawing some arbitrary cuts at the midpoints of the X and Y axes (represented by the dotted lines), a city classification with four types has been created. Cities in the upper right quadrant could be called "high manufacturing–high income type," those in the lower right quadrant "low manufacturing–low income type," and so on.

Suppose a third dimension were added, the racial characteristics of a city's population as measured by the percentage of the population that is nonwhite. Cities could again be plotted but a third axis would be added. In Figure 5.5, a single city has been plotted; its position in space has been defined by its scores on the three dimensions of manufacturing employment, median income, and racial characteristics. If the points for hundreds of

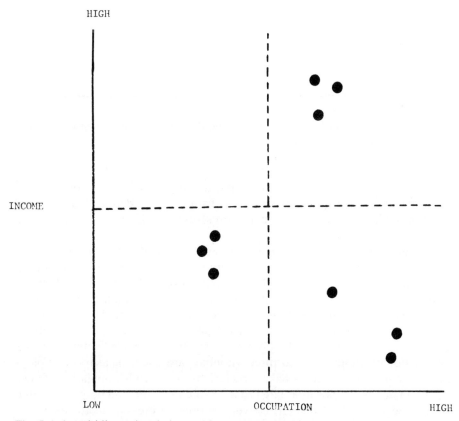

Fig. 5.4 A multidimensional city typology constructed by plotting hypothetical cities on two dimensions. The dotted lines represent the midpoints of each dimension.

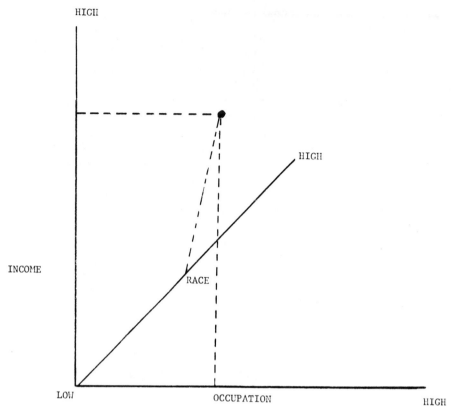

Fig. 5.5 A single hypothetical city plotted on the three dimensions of occupation, income, and racial dimensions.

other cities were added to this figure, cutting points could still be drawn, groupings of cities could be made, and a typology could be constructed. But what if a fourth, fifth, or sixth dimension were added to this analysis? Sorting out clusters of cities would be extremely difficult.

Factor analysis Multidimensional typologies are made feasible by a mathematical technique known as *factor analysis*. Factor analysis does mathematically what is done geometrically in Figures 5.4 and 5.5; it identifies clusters of similarly related dimensions or variables. Unlike these simple examples, factor analysis done with a computer has the capacity to manipulate hundreds of variables. Factor analysis sorts variables, identifies underlying similarities, and summarizes them in a single factor or index score. For example, assume three variables are used, measuring employment, income, and educational characteristics of a city's population. Types of employment are closely related to level of education, and both are related to income level. A physician, lawyer, or other professional, for example, is both highly educated and highly paid. These interrelationships can be summarized in a single factor—socioeconomic status. Factor analysis, then, is normally applied to the interrelationships among dozens of variables to identify fundamental characteristics of metropolitan centers. It summarizes a large set of seemingly unrelated variables into the smallest possible number of factors.

Price's City Classification

Price (1942) was the first to apply this technique in the construction of a city typology. Price restricted his analysis to fifteen variables (Table 5.5) and ninety-three United States cities with populations of 100,000 or more. The reason for his decision was simple. There were no computers in the 1940s and all calculations were done on slow mechanical calculators. Even in this relatively small analysis thousands of calculations were made. Analysis of the data identified the following four factors in the interrelationships among the fifteen variables.[6]

Factor I Factor I was labeled "maturity factor." It was associated with "those characteristics commonly thought of as 'typical' of the largest metropolitan centers" (Price, 1942, p. 452). The cluster of variables identified

Table 5.5
List of variables included in Price's classification of 93 United States cities.

1. Population, 1930
2. Percent gainfully employed in service industry, 1930
3. Sex ratio (males per 100 females), 1930
4. Percent increase in population, 1920–1930
5. Median monthly rental of nonfarm homes, 1930
6. Percent of total population unemployed, 1930
7. Number of census years in 100,000 class
8. Percent of total population between ages of fifteen and fifty, 1930
9. Percent of population ten years old and over, gainfully occupied, 1930
10. Percent of gainful workers who are female, 1930
11. Median size of family, 1930
12. Wholesale trade per capita, 1929
13. Retail trade per capita, 1929
14. Wages per wage earner, 1929
15. Percent of employed filing income tax returns, 1930

Source: Adapted from Price, D. O., "Factor Analysis in the Study of Metropolitan Centers." *Social Forces* 20 (1942): 450, Table 1.

by Factor I included large population (variable 1), comparatively small increases in population (4), high median rents (5), older cities (7), and high volumes of wholesale (12) and retail (13) trade. In Table 5.6, note that large cities such as New York, Chicago, Washington, Boston, and San Francisco ranked highest. Cities not shown, but that ranked lowest, were Miami, Kansas City, and Chattanooga, which were smaller, highly specialized cities in 1930.

Factor II Factor II, "occupational structure," referred to variables indicating the nature of the occupational structure of cities. This cluster of variables included percentage employed in service industry (2), low sex ratio (3), increase in population (4), low rents (5), low unemployment (9), and a high percentage of the population of working age (8). Cities such as New York, Atlanta, and Dallas, which are service centers for large areas, ranked highest on this factor. Highly specialized industrial cities such as Youngstown, Flint, Gary, and Lowell ranked low. This factor measured the extent to which a city was a service center.

Factor III Factor III was associated at the time with a high sex ratio (3), high monthly rent (5), high wages (14), and a low percentage of female workers (10). Ranked highest on this factor were Gary, Detroit, San Francisco, and New York. Ranked lowest were the textile manufacturing cities

Table 5.6
Rank according to four factor-indexes for 10 of the 93 cities having populations of 100,000 or more in 1930

Rank	Maturity factor	Occupational structure factor	Level-of-living factor	Trade volume factor
1	New York	New York	Gary	Kansas City, MO
2	Chicago	Washington	Detroit	San Francisco
3	Washington	Atlanta	San Francisco	Boston
4	Boston	Memphis	New York	Paterson
5	San Francisco	Dallas	Flint	Dallas
6	Philadelphia	Miami	Chicago	Albany
7	Pittsburgh	Los Angeles	Youngstown	Seattle
8	Newark	San Francisco	Canton	Los Angeles
9	Detroit	Kansas City, MO	Akron	Scranton
10	St. Louis	Jacksonville	Los Angeles	Oklahoma City

Source: Price, D. O., "Factor Analysis in the Study of Metropolitan Centers." *Social Forces* 20 (1942): 453.

of New England and the South. Price labeled this factor "level of living"; today it would be labeled "socioeconomic status level."

Factor IV Factor IV, labeled "trade volume," identified only two variables, wholesale (12) and retail (13) trade.

Unlike Harris (1943) and Nelson (1955), Price did not set up specific city types; rather each city in the study was given an index score on each of the four factors. The cities were ranked from high to low on each factor to allow comparisons to be made, but these data turned out to be more useful in developing city profiles. New York, for example, was ranked first on Factor I, fourth on Factor II, and forty-second on Factor IV. Cities with similar profiles could be grouped, labeled, and fitted into an elaborate city typology. Jonassen (1959, 1961), for example, constructed a "community typology" by this very method. Obviously, factor analysis greatly increased the number of possible city types, reflecting the multifunctional character of metropolitan centers.

In addition, the multidimensional studies identified some city dimensions that were similar to those derived in the earlier single-dimension studies. Factor analysis identified two dimensions that were similar to the "service" and "trade center" types identified by Harris (1943) and Nelson (1955). The presence of two additional factors associated with city age and standards of living, however, suggests that other dimensions are important in city classification.

The City Classification of Hadden and Borgatta

In the 1960s, computers became widely available for data analysis and permitted significant increases in the size and scope of multidimensional classification studies. Probably the best known study done during this period was Hadden and Borgatta's (1965) classification of 644 United States cities. The work was a report of a major research program at the University of Wisconsin entitled, "A Systematic Study of Social Factors Underlying the Classification of Communities." The goal of this program was to identify the fundamental dimensions of city structure that would facilitate their description and study (Hadden and Borgatta, 1965, p. vi).

To this end, sixty-five variables measuring income, housing, location, education, economics, demographics, employment, and other characteristics were factored and sixteen clusters of variables were identified. Table 5.7 lists, from most important to least important, thirteen of the sixteen factors identified in this analysis. Note that with the exception of Factor 4, "education center," socioeconomic and demographic dimensions were more important than purely economic functions in describing the underlying dimensions of city structure. Moreover, socioeconomic factors were found by the researchers to be only weakly related to the economic specialization of cities.

Table 5.7
The factor structures of Price, Hadden and Borgatta, and Berry's multidimensional city classification.*

Price[a]	Hadden and Borgatta[b]	Berry[c]
1 Maturity factor	1 Socioeconomic status level	1 Functional size
2 Occupational structure factor	2 Nonwhite	2 Socioeconomic status
3 Level of living factor	3 Age composition	3 Stage in family life cycle
4 Trade volume factor	4 Education center	4 Nonwhite population/ home ownership
	5 Residential mobility	5 Recent population growth
	6 Population density	6 Economic base: college town
	7 Foreign-born concentration	7 Foreign-born concentration
	8 Total population	8 Employment expansion
	9 Wholesale concentration	9 Economic base: manufacturing
	10 Retail concentration	10 Females employed
	11 Manufacturing concentration	11 Economic base: service
	12 Durables manufacturing concentration	12 Economic base: military
	13 Communication center	13 Economic base: mining
	14 Unnamed	14 Elderly males in labor force
	15 Unnamed	
	16 Unnamed	

Sample Size	97 cities	644 cities	1,762 cities
Number of Variables	15	65	97

* Ranked in order of importance.

[a] Price, D. O., "Factor Analysis in the Study of Metropolitan Centers." *Social Forces* 20 (1942): 452.

[b] Adapted from Hadden, J. K. and Borgatta, E. F., *American Cities: Their Social Characteristics*. Chicago: Rand McNally, 1965, Table 27.

[c] Adapted from Berry, B. J. L. "Latent Structure of the American Urban System, with International Comparisons." In B. J. L. Berry (Ed.), *City Classification Handbook: Methods and Applications*. New York: Wiley-Interscience, 1972, Table 1.

Berry's City Classification

Berry (1972b) replicated Hadden and Borgatta's analysis with ninety-seven variables collected on 1,762 places in the United States with 10,000 or more inhabitants in both 1950 and 1960. The factoring of these data resulted in the identification of fourteen major factors or variable clusters. In Table 5.7 both Hadden and Borgatta's (1965) and Berry's (1972) findings are listed. It should be noted that although these researchers used different samples of cities and a different number of variables, and the factors extracted in each study identify somewhat different clusters of variables, there are underlying similarities in the two lists of factors. In both studies socioeconomic, population composition, occupation, and city-function factors appear to be fundamental dimensions of United States urban places.

Implications of Berry's findings Berry (1972b), in addition, explored the interrelationships among urban places of different sizes and their spatial distribution. In this part of his analysis, he came to an important conclusion: "In nations with well developed metropolitan structures economic characteristics alone will not differentiate one metropolitan area from another" (1972, p. 47). These large centers carry out a full range of economic functions—manufacturing, transportation, communication, wholesaling, and retail trade. Only the smaller cities have the economic specialization, dependency on a single function, necessary for classification according to this system. The implications of this statement are clear. The traditional single-dimension typologies of Harris (1943), Nelson (1955), and others may have been relevant in the time when they were constructed, but today they are of minimal and declining relevance (1972, p. 47). The complex interdependence among cities in modern urban societies can only be described by means of more sophisticated multivariate research techniques.[7]

USES OF CITY CLASSIFICATION SCHEMES

Critics have argued, and justly so, that the development of different classification schemes has become an end in itself. Cities have been classified, but the classifications have not been used as a point of departure for further analysis. In addition, these schemes have been overly dependent on economic variables. Few sociological variables have been included.

In recent years, social scientists have combined city classification with research on social indicators. Social indicators are measures of social well-being. They include variables that reflect the quality of the environment (levels of air and water pollution), personal safety (crimes against persons), availability of services and public transportation, lack of stress, and political and governmental well-being. These studies differ from the earlier classification schemes not only in the types of variables included, but also in the fact that their findings are useful in policy formulation and urban planning.

Robert Angell (1941, 1947) made an early attempt to compare cities with respect to their level of social integration. Angell chose to use the community's welfare effort as an indicator of social integration, on the proposition that there would be a "more vital moral order" in communities that shoulder a larger proportion of their local welfare responsibilities. From information on the services provided in twenty-eight major cities, he derived a "Welfare Effort Index" for each place (Angell, 1941, pp. 376–77). He found wide variations among cities. Using this index with other social indicators like crime, rates of homicide, and suicide, Angell was able to classify cities into "well integrated," "moderately integrated," and "poorly integrated."

A more recent case is the research of Jones and Flax (1970), who also employed social indicators in the development of a classification scheme. The purpose of their study was threefold: (1) to determine whether living conditions in Washington, D.C. were better or worse than they used to be; (2) to see how conditions in the Washington area compared with those in the seventeen other largest metropolitan areas; and (3) to see whether conditions in Washington were improving or deteriorating faster than in other metropolitan areas. The present discussion is concerned with all eighteen cities rather than just Washington, D.C., but note the potential use of this typology for policymakers in Washington.

The authors selected fourteen "quality areas" and identified variables to measure their characteristics. They employed a city-ranking system, similar to Price's multidimensional scheme, and were able to develop city-by-city profiles. Interestingly, when overall scores were calculated, Minneapolis, Milwaukee, and Boston scored highest, and San Francisco, New York, and Los Angeles scored lowest. Thus, cities that many Americans view as highly desirable places in which to live may in reality afford a low quality of life.

This study has been replicated by others, most notably by Smith (1973). Smith expanded the number of social indicators in his study to thirty-one, and included all metropolitan areas with a population of 250,000 or more—a total of 109 SMAs. In general, Smith found that social well-being in American cities improved away from the South. Western cities performed well on criteria related to economic affluence, but poorly in areas of social pathology. Most of the midwestern and northern cities performed relatively well on most criteria, though there were some exceptions in certain industrial cities that had high rates of crime and other social pathologies.

There are a number of important policy implications in this and other studies of its type. If the quality of life in southern cities is substantially below that of other regions, then our national urban policies should funnel monies into southern cities to eliminate regional differences. This is especially true in light of the unprecedented growth of cities in the South and Southwest during the 1970s and 1980s. City classification can thus be meaningfully used to deal with pressing urban problems and policy issues.

The foregoing review of the more important attempts to classify cities should give an understanding of the purpose, methods, and problems in the classification of cities. This review also demonstrates the dynamic character of social science research. New methods were introduced as the shortcomings of earlier typologies were identified. This development was aided by the introduction of the high-speed electronic computer, which permitted previously impossible numbers of variables to be manipulated efficiently and economically. Research trends of the past will continue as new techniques are applied to uncover the underlying dimensions of urban places.

The next section of this chapter explores the interrelationships among cities implied in city typologies.

THE SYSTEM OF CITIES

The process of urbanization cannot be studied in isolation because urban places are spatial elements in the economic, social, and political organization of regions and nations. Implicit in the discussion of city typologies is the notion of interdependency. Single-dimension typologies, for example, emphasize mainly the functional specialization of cities; the classification of a city as a "retail center" implies the city's dependency on other centers (manufacturing, transportation, and wholesaling) for the goods it supplies to its trade area.
Although multidimensional typologies stress the many-faceted character of metropolitan centers (e.g., their tendency to carry out many economic functions) the city-to-city differences in functions imply an interdependency among centers.

The Concept of Economic Base

In exploring the economic ties among cities researchers have often used the concept of economic base to illustrate this relationship. *Economic base* refers to the fact that the growth of a city depends on its ability to sell goods and services beyond its own borders. The more goods and services it sells, the more growth occurs and the more active the local economy becomes. Thus a city's economy can be divided into two parts, the *basic sector,* consisting of the goods and services produced locally but sold beyond the borders of the city, and the *nonbasic sector,* consisting of those goods and services produced and sold locally. The basic sector, then, is the sector of the local economy that must expand if the city is to grow (Blumfield, 1970).

The process of urbanization in the United States in many respects is a history of urban places' attempts to expand the basic sector of their economies. These efforts are exemplified by the intense competition among cities in the nineteenth century and the attitude commonly held by the leaders of those cities—boosterism. Boosterism is the notion that the more manufacturing and commerce going on in a city, the more growth; the more growth, the larger the city's trade area; and the larger the trade area, the better the local economy.

To a degree this idea is valid, but the potential growth of a city's basic sector (as seen in Chapter 4) is determined by several specific factors. They include: (1) the city's location with respect to natural resources and other cities; (2) the transportation and resource exploitation technology at both the time of settlement and in later periods; (3) the nature of the regional and national economy; and (4) the size and composition of the regional and national population. Moreover, the relationship between a city and other cities in its region is not static but dynamic, changing in response to economic and technological changes that occur over time.

The system-of-cities concept, therefore, is important because it ties together several topics explored in this chapter and Chapter 4. First, it includes the notion of economic function and the interdependency among urban places. Second, it includes the concept of urban hierarchy and the spatial distribution of cities in the hierarchy with respect to their nested trade areas. Finally, the location of cities in this hierarchy can be described by the classical theories of location reviewed in the preceding chapter.

The Evolution of America's City System

The emergence of a system of cities and the changing relationships within this system can be understood best by examining urban and regional growth in the United States during the past 200 years. The growth of an urban center depends on its ability to expand the basic sector of its economy, or in other words its ability to collect, process, and distribute raw materials and finished goods to its hinterland. The growth of these centers therefore is closely tied to the natural resources in their hinterlands, and the levels of technology in the transportation and processing of these resources. These two factors are interrelated, however. The level of industrial technology determines what types of resources are exploited, and transportation technology determines the size of an urban center's trade area. For example, the invention of the steam and later the internal combustion engine created the need for coal and oil exploration. Demand for coal and oil led in turn to the growth of new urban centers to exploit these natural resources. Similarly, changes in transportation technology (the emergence of the automobile as the primary mode of transportation, for example) have permitted urban centers to greatly expand their trade areas.

Borchert's Historical Analysis of United States Urban Patterns

Borchert (1970) studied this relationship between transportation and industrial technology and concluded that four distinct periods or epochs can be identified in the evolution of the system of cities in the United States. Figures 5.6 to 5.10 show the growth and spread of cities during each of these four periods. In each illustration, cities are grouped by population size and a symbol for each category is shown in the legend. Note that Borchert's analysis is similar to the central place theory, but on a national scale. Borchert employs the notion of an urban hierarchy and puts cities that have approximately the same population on the same order. The size of the various groupings of cities changes through time, however. For example, Figure 5.6 shows that in 1790 a city needed a minimum population of 5,000 inhabitants to be classified as a fifth-order metropolitan area, e.g., to be part of the bottom tier of the urban hierarchy. These lower limits or threshold populations change in the figures that follow, reflecting the increase in the scale of urbanization in this country during the past two centuries. By 1960, because of the increasing scale of urbanization, a metropolitan center needed a population of 80,000 or more inhabitants to be included in the fifth-order category (see Table 5.8). Changes in the relative importance of these centers over time are also reflected in the symbols on the right side of the legends in Figures 5.7–5.10. These symbols indicate the dynamic nature of the system of cities, and the potential of a city to rise or fall in relationship to other cities in the urban hierarchy.

The sail-wagon epoch, 1790–1830 In 1790 almost all the major urban centers were either deep-water ports on the Atlantic or inland cities on one of the navigable coastal rivers. Among the eleven largest cities (third- or higher-order), only Worcester, Massachusetts, and Pittsburgh, Pennsylvania were not integrated into the Atlantic water transportation network. The major cities—Boston, New York, and Philadelphia—were of approximately the same size. Their populations, combined with those of Baltimore and Charleston, South Carolina, together made up more than half of the nation's urban population. In general, because of the poorly developed transportation technology, these cities had small trade areas and the larger port cities had economies that were tied to overseas commerce.

During the forty years of this epoch (1790–1830) virtually all urban places grew in population. The local economies of these cities were organized to exploit the products of agriculture, forests, and mineral deposits (a primary economy), but the natural resources most valued were those associated with farming—arable land and the environmental components of climate and water. The boom cities during this period (those cities that rose two or more ranks) were the lake and river cities in the old Northwest Territory. These cities grew rapidly because of their favorable sites at break-in-trans-

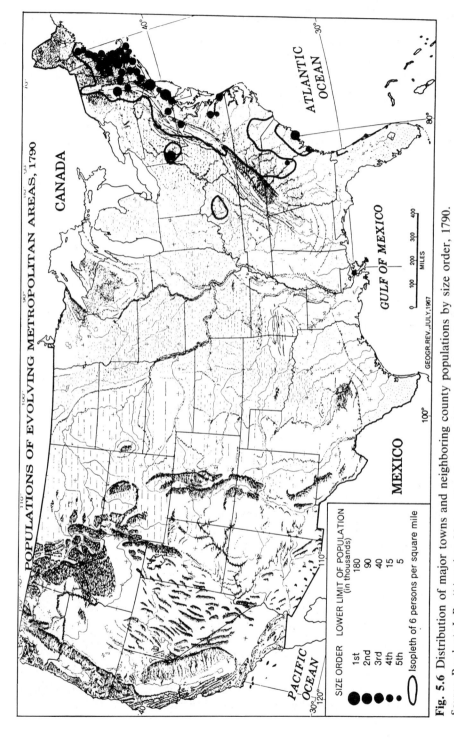

Fig. 5.6 Distribution of major towns and neighboring county populations by size order, 1790.

Source: Borchert, J. R., "American Metropolitan Evolution." Reprinted from the *Geographical Review 57* (1967): 313, with the permission of the American Geographical Society.

Table 5.8
Limits of size orders for SMSAs in 1960 and corresponding areas in earlier years.

Size order	Population threshold (thousands)				
	1790	1830	1870	1920	1960
First	180	530	1,300	4,750	8,000
Second	90	160	400	1,480	2,300
Third	40	90	130	470	820
Fourth	15	35	750	150	250
Fifth	5	15	30	60	80
Central-city minimum	1.1	3.6	11.1	29.5	50.0

Source: Borchert, J. R., "American Metropolitan Evolution." Reprinted from the *Geographical Review* 57 (1967): 302, with the permission of the American Geographical Society.

portation points combined with the exploitation of the agricultural products of their hinterlands.

As late as 1830, land transportation was slow, sporadic, and expensive, but an interdependent system of cities was evolving. For example, the opening of the Erie Canal in 1825 assured the emergence of New York as a dominant national metropolis. More important, the pattern of cities that emerged provided a framework for subsequent urban development by establishing markets, transportation routes, labor forces, and diversified economies in key or higher-order cities. Inertial forces were being set in motion that permitted cities at the top of the urban hierarchy to benefit from improvements in transportation and industrial technology (Borchert, 1970, pp. 33–43).

Iron horse epoch, 1830–1870 In 1830 all third- or higher-order centers except Pittsburgh and two cities in western New York were east of the Appalachian Mountains. In the forty years that followed, transportation routes were cut through the Appalachians and settlers poured into the Ohio River Valley and upper Great Lakes region. By 1870, settlement was continuous from the Atlantic Coast to the Mississippi River.

This growth can be attributed mainly to new forms of transportation and industrial technology. The railroad, for instance, provided the first reliable, fast land transportation, opening up areas for farming that previously had been cut off from markets. Railroad technology was still primitive, however. Tracks were formed of iron, not steel; they were brittle and prone to breakage. Steam engines were small, inefficient, and generated very little horsepower. For these reasons railroads could not economically carry bulk cargoes such as coal or grain over long distances. During this period rail lines grew to complement rather than compete with the existing inland water systems. Most rail lines converged at ports. Chicago, for example, by 1870 had grown to be the nation's largest rail center, combining the

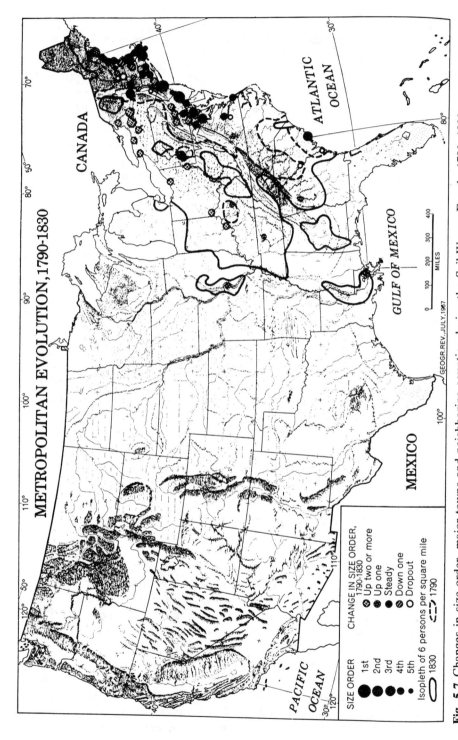

Fig. 5.7 Changes in size order, major towns and neighboring counties during the Sail-Wagon Epoch, 1790–1830.

Source: Borchert, J. R., "American Metropolitan Evolution." Reprinted from the *Geographical Review* 57 (1967): 316, with the permission of the American Geographical Society.

operations of more than thirty rail lines with its port operations on Lake Michigan.

This "age of steam" greatly influenced the emerging system of cities. The energy requirements of the steam engine, combined with the new industrial activity in cities, generated demands for new and different types of natural resources and created a new set of locational forces. The boom cities during this period were Pittsburgh, Cleveland, and Buffalo—cities where location on an inland waterway was combined with proximity to coal and ore deposits.

Figure 5.8 shows that a distinctive patterning of cities was evident by 1870. The great belt of manufacturing cities extended from New England through the lower Great Lakes region. In general, the system of cities present in 1830 was expanded. In particular, cities that had been at or near the top of the urban hierarchy in 1830 were able to take advantage of the technological innovations during this epoch.

The predominant cities in this era were in the North and the East. New Orleans was the only southern city to grow during this period, largely because of its strategic location on the Mississippi River. The pattern of cities in the South was due in part to the ravages of the Civil War, but other factors were equally important—the limited coal and ore deposits in the region, the lack of investment in railroads, canals, and industry during the antebellum period, and the dependency of this region on an agricultural export economy. By 1870, a manufacturing and marketing, transportation, and communications core had developed in the Northeast that dominated the national economy (Borchert, 1970, pp. 43–46).

Steel-rail epoch, 1870–1920 The urbanization process during this epoch was related closely to the exploitation of the agricultural and mineral resources in the lands west of the Mississippi and the further concentration of manufacturing and basic industries in the great metropolises of the upper Midwest and the East.

Figure 5.9 shows the changes in the system of cities during this third epoch. Improvements in rail technology led to the emergence of urban centers in the West and South. Tough, durable steel rails combined with heavier and more powerful equipment permitted the long haul of bulk cargoes at a cost competitive with that of water transportation. Cities in this region were smaller than their eastern counterparts. The basic sector of their economies specialized in mining, agricultural processing, or retailing and wholesaling.

Significant changes occurred in the cities in the older settled areas of the East. Economies of scale, improvements in transportation and industrial technology, expansion of manufacturing and service spheres of the national economy, and the emergence of national markets for manufactured goods benefited some centers at the expense of others. Nearly all of the higher-order cities of 1870 were able to retain their positions in the hierarchy by

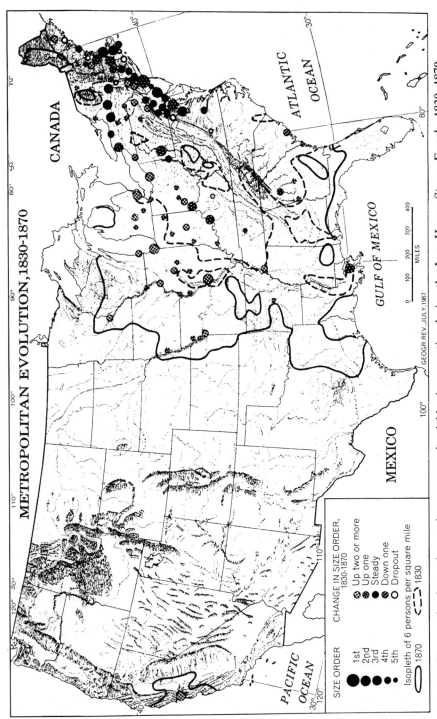

Fig. 5.8 Changes in size order, major towns and neighboring counties during the Iron Horse–Steam Epoch, 1830–1870.

Source: Borchert, J. R., "American Metropolitan Evolution." Reprinted from the *Geographical Review* 57 (1967): 317, with the permission of the American Geographical Society.

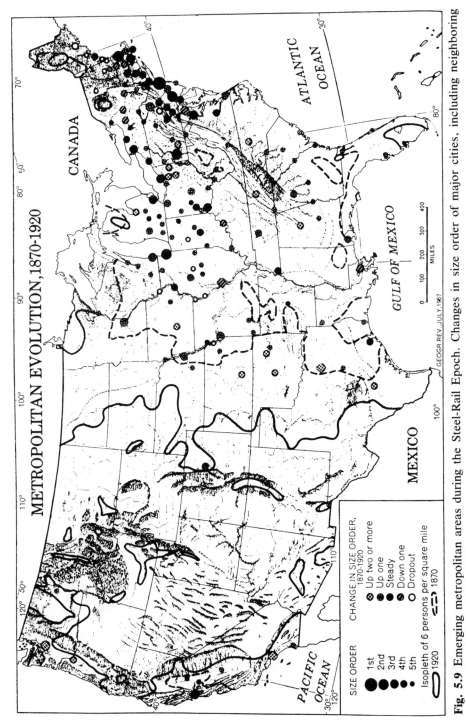

Fig. 5.9 Emerging metropolitan areas during the Steel-Rail Epoch. Changes in size order of major cities, including neighboring county populations, 1870–1920.

Source: Borchert, J. R., "American Metropolitan Evolution." Reprinted from the *Geographical Review* 57 (1967): 317, with the permission of the American Geographical Society.

making the transition from commerce to industry. Boom cities were those near the coal deposits in western Pennsylvania, West Virginia, and eastern Kentucky.

Two groups of metropolitan areas, however, dropped in size order during this period. The largest group were cities along the Ohio-Mississippi-Missouri Rivers. St. Louis, for example, was displaced by Chicago, Louisville by Cincinnati, and Wheeling by Pittsburgh. In each case, changing resource needs lowered the competitive advantage of these locations. Consequently, these cities fell in the hierarchy. A similar decline beset the older industrial cities at "historic waterpower sites" along the Hudson, Merrimack, and other coastal rivers, as well as minor ports on the Hudson and New England coast.

By 1920, the present system of cities had emerged, knit together by a standardized nationwide rail and communication network. The transportation and communication technology fused these cities and their hinterlands into a functionally integrated national economy. Moreover, within this national economy distinctive regional economic specialization occurred. Spatially, the region east of the Mississippi and north of the Ohio Rivers was the urban-industrial core of the nation. Here were concentrated the transportation and communication networks and the financing, managing, and national marketing services—the infrastructure necessary for large-scale industrial and manufacturing development.

Surrounding this urban-industrial core were the other regions, resource-rich but lacking the infrastructure necessary for large-scale industrial development. The economic relationship between the industrial core and the outlying regions was similar to that between a city and its hinterland. Natural resources and agricultural products flowed from the hinterlands to the industrial core and manufactured goods flowed back. The outlying metropolitan centers that did generate manufacturing were specialized in areas not directly competitive with the industrial core. By 1920, a symbiotic relationship had evolved among the regions, mutually beneficial to all (Borchert, 1970, pp. 46–49).

Auto-air amenity epoch, 1920–present By 1920, the present system of cities had been established but changes continued to occur within it. As in the past, new demands for resources and changes in the level of technology profoundly affected the relative importance of cities. The shift from the steam to the internal combustion engine, for example, reduced the demand for coal and increased the demand for oil. Subsequently, centers in the coal fields declined and centers near the oil and gas resources of the South and Southwest rose in rank.

During this same period, technical innovations dramatically reduced the labor requirements for farming, mining, and manufacturing, and some centers dependent on these enterprises fell from metropolitan status. In general, most Americans came to be employed in service and white-collar rather

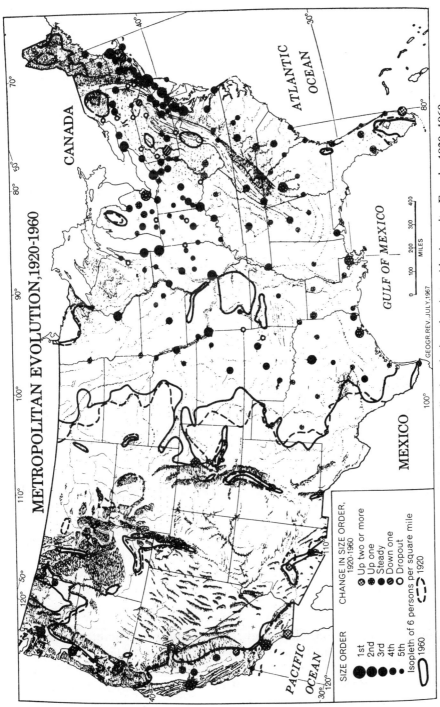

Fig. 5.10 Changes in metropolitan area size and distribution during the Auto-Air Amenity Epoch, 1920–1960.
Source: Borchert, J. R., "American Metropolitan Evolution." Reprinted from the *Geographical Review* 57 (1967): 322, with the permission of the American Geographical Society.

than in manufacturing and primary extractive occupations. Manufacturing shifted from heavy to light. Complex products such as aircraft and electronics required greater skill and higher educational levels of the labor force.

In addition, the emergence of the automobile and the truck as a dominant form of transportation in the United States removed the locational constraints on business and industry. A manufacturing operation no longer needed a rail spur; it could be located anywhere accessible by truck.

Before World War II, most manufacturing took place in "loft factories," compact three- and four-story buildings typically near the major transportation lines at a city's center. The design of a building reflected the power source available to the manufacturer—a stationary steam engine. Energy from this centralized power source was distributed by a complex series of drive shafts, pulleys, and belts, and the efficiency of the power transmission dropped off quickly with distance. The multistory compact factory therefore was the most efficient way to distribute this energy.

After the war, the invention of powerful electric motors enabled manufacturers to build factories for production efficiency rather than energy efficiency. This type of factory is normally built on one level, with electrically driven machinery along a straight assembly line. Such a layout requires large amounts of land. Manufacturing therefore moved to the city's periphery, out of its built-up center. The automobile and truck provided accessibility to the city's fringe areas for both the manufacturer and the workers.

Present trends—megalopolitan growth Examining these changes in manufacturing, the labor force, and transportation one can anticipate future modification of America's urban system. Most important is the massive movement of population and retail and manufacturing activities from central cities to their fringe areas. This movement, in turn, has led to the physical sprawl of metropolitan centers, to the point that in some regions, adjacent metropolitan areas have coalesced into one massive urban agglomeration. Jean Gottman (1961) introduced the term *megalopolis* to describe those massive urban agglomerations.

Nowhere is this new megalopolitan form more visible than along the unbroken urbanized seaboard of the United States between Boston and Washington, D.C. Officially running from Rockingham County, New Hampshire to Prince William County, Virginia, the Boston-Washington megalopolis is of staggering dimensions. Ranging in width between 100–150 miles, it runs over 600 miles in length, embracing part or all of ten states and the cities of Boston, New York, Philadelphia, Baltimore, and Washington, D.C. In 1978, the Boston-Washington megalopolis had a population of nearly 42 million or roughly one-fifth of the United States population. In addition, a significant proportion of the nation's industry, business, financial, government, and educational resources was concentrated in this megalopolis.

Through most of the 1970s and early 1980s, however, the picture in much of this region was one of economic and population decline or at best stagnation. Some 1.2 million more people left the area than moved in between 1970 and 1977. This declining population reflects the loss of large segments of important industries such as textiles and transportation. Bearing the brunt of this decline are New York City, Philadelphia, and Newark, New Jersey. New York City alone lost nearly 10 percent of its population between 1970 and 1978 (*U.S. News and World Report*, 1980, p. 55).

One factor that contributes to the population decline in the Boston-Washington megalopolis is the age of its central cities—the oldest of any region in the United States. Associated with city age are the problems of congestion, dilapidated and deteriorating housing, obsolete factories and industries, shortages of open space and recreation facilities, and a general decline in the quality of city services. This is especially characteristic of New York City. And it is, of course, in the central cities of the Northeast that one finds the greatest concentration of blacks and other deprived groups—people with the greatest need for services but with the fewest resources to pay for them. Not surprisingly, the most serious urban and social problems faced by our society are concentrated in the 55,000 square miles of this megalopolis.

There is a second major factor contributing to the population decline of this megalopolis. Since World War II, America's industry has shifted from the manufacture of basic goods, such as steel, to the manufacture of light, high-technology goods. The manufacture of light and complex products is normally limited to the final assembly of parts built by suppliers; very few components are made inside the plant. The transportation cost of such products as calculators and computers is low in comparison to the high value of the finished item. Therefore, with transportation constraints lessened, the manufacturer can select a plant location on the basis of other factors such as labor and plant construction costs, climate, and amenities for workers, for example, education. The result has been a spectacular growth of metropolitan centers in Florida, the Southwest, and Southern California—the so called Sunbelt states.

In these regions megalopolitan growth is well under way. Figure 5.11 shows the location of twenty-six emerging megalopolises in which two out of every three Americans is expected to live by the year 1980. Note in Table 5.9 that cities in the South and West are enjoying a tremendous boom in population. Southern Arizona—the area around Phoenix and Tucson—led the nation in the 1970–78 period with a 32.7 percent increase. Note also that all of the population gains in excess of 10 percent were in the southern and western regions of the United States. Stagnant or declining population growth was limited to the north central and northeastern regions of the

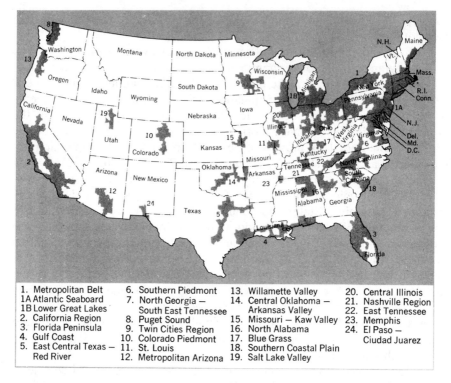

Fig. 5.11 Megalopolises, year 2000. This map shows the twenty-six growth areas of the United States that now are exhibiting megalopolitan patterns. Population projections suggest that the urban strips depicted in the map will characterize many parts of the United States in the year 2000.

Source: Adapted from *Population Growth and American Future*. Washington, D.C.: Government Printing Office.

United States. Clearly, the complex interaction of environmental resources and technological innovations has profoundly affected the relationships within the system of cities, resulting in a major redistribution of population and economic activities within and among this nation's metropolitan centers. Moreover, megalopolitan growth has emerged as "the new order in the organization of inhabited space."

The impression one gets from reading the popular press is that the cities in the northeast megalopolis are beyond hope and in a steady state of decline, and that the cities in the Sunbelt are new and without major urban problems. Pages 198–203 present two articles with contrasting views on these two regions. The article on the Northeast appeared in The Arizona Republic, *and the article on the Sunbelt in the* New York Times. *Could the region in which these two articles appeared have influenced their tone?*

Table 5.9
Emerging megalopolises.*

	1970 population	1978 population	Change, 1970–78
1. Southern Arizona	1,323,000	1,755,000	32.7%
2. Florida Peninsula	5,635,000	7,137,000	26.7%
3. Texas Gulf Coast	2,662,000	3,315,000	24.5%
4. Salt Lake Valley	822,000	1,004,000	22.2%
5. Colorado Plateau	1,687,000	2,049,000	21.4%
6. Centex	1,556,000	1,886,000	21.2%
7. Arkansas Valley	897,000	1,047,000	16.7%
8. Willamette Valley	1,194,000	1,366,000	14.4%
9. Mid-South	2,094,000	2,390,000	14.2%
10. Dalworth	2,461,000	2,804,000	14.0%
11. Carolina Coastal Plain	1,004,000	1,139,000	13.4%
12. Central Gulf Coast	2,356,000	2,666,000	13.2%
13. Northern California	6,809,000	7,555,000	11.0%
14. Southern Piedmont	2,819,000	3,120,000	10.7%
15. Southern California	11,603,000	12,819,000	10.5%
16. East Tennessee Valley	1,008,000	1,113,000	10.5%
17. Tidewater	1,742,000	1,901,000	9.1%
18. North Alabama	1,481,000	1,580,000	6.7%
19. Twin Cities	2,100,000	2,224,000	5.9%
20. Bluegrass	1,188,000	1,248,000	5.1%
21. Missouri–Kansas Valley	1,665,000	1,732,000	4.0%
22. Puget Sound	1,837,000	1,905,000	3.7%
23. Central Indiana	1,704,000	1,763,000	3.4%
24. Midlands	35,838,000	35,987,000	0.4%
25. Boswash	42,021,000	41,993,000	−0.1%
26. St. Louis	2,411,000	2,386,000	−1.0%

* Area definitions by Economic Unit of *U.S. News & World Report*. Percentages based on unrounded data.

Source: "Growth of Strip Cities: Where It's Fastest and Slowest," reprinted from *U.S. News & World Report,* June 30, 1980: p. 55. Copyright 1980, U.S. News & World Report, Inc.

Photo 5.1 This is a satellite photograph taken at night showing the eastern half of the United States. Note the emerging megalopolitan centers along the Atlantic Coast, Lake Michigan, and Lake Erie.
Source: U.S. Air Force Photo.

CAN ANYTHING SAVE BLIGHTED NORTHEAST CORRIDOR?

By Anthony Harrigan

From the window of a train moving on tracks laid down during the Grant administration, a traveler gets glimpses of an industrial and residential wasteland in Pennsylvania and New Jersey.

For mile after mile, the scene is one of derelict factories and decayed tenements. From Philadelphia to Newark the buildings along the right-of-way are blighted almost beyond belief.

The right-of-way itself is a dumping ground for abandoned refrigerators, rusted automobile parts and litter of every description.

*   *   *

It would be a mistake to describe the Northeast Corridor wholly in these terms. But this wretchedness and uglification are significant aspects of what was once the richest region of the country.

Today, this belt of decay along a once-great railroad line is a grim reminder of the proliferation of problems in an area which flourished in the 19th century and the early part of this century.

What is wrong in the troubled Northeast area along the old Pennsylvania Railroad tracks? This area is an old industrial region that dates from the steam and gaslight era.

The factories of yesteryear are unsuitable for today's operations. Public services are inadequate. Once-respectable neighborhoods have been filled with newcomers who have little self-reliance or local community spirit. Decayed areas have become breeding grounds for crime.

Mobsters and brutal, arrogant union leaders, allied or part of the same balance of forces, have created impossible conditions for industry. Indeed the entire complex of causes and problems has been catalogued many times.

These problems and conditions exist not only along this rail line but in major cities such as Newark and, most significantly, New York City. Much of the metropolis is run down and in need of replacement. The fabulous New York skyline took form largely between 1900 and 1925. That's the time frame in which the great surge of construction took place.

Now, many of the once-extraordinary buildings of Gotham are old and in need of massive reconditioning or replacement. The subway system, built many years ago, also is in need of reconstruction. Unfortunately, modernization of the metropolis is out of the question. Mismanagement of public finances leaves New York City without the resources or the credit for renewal.

What is the alternative? The alternative is deconcentration of New York City and other decayed areas in the Northeast Corridor.

The tides of development and industrial growth have flowed west and south in the last generation. The major opportunities for new energy and resource development—and industry—are in the trans-Mississippi region of the United States, in states such as Utah, Montana, and North Dakota.

*   *   *

A few years ago, Gov. Forest H. Anderson of Montana told the Federation of Rocky Mountain States, "People are going to come to the Mountain and Plains states to escape the sick cities. The exodus has already begun and it cannot be stopped."

He observed that if the nation's giant cities "continue to deteriorate, it's going to become necessary to redistribute the population of this country in order to alleviate the pressure in certain areas."

Gov. Anderson is the only prominent American to state this truth in unvarnished fashion. Redistribution of population, or deconcentration of the sick centers in the Northeast, is the only feasible alternative to repeated municipal bankruptcies and federal bailouts. The people of other regions can't afford such counter-productive assistance to decayed areas.

Under the American system, deconcentration cannot be decreed by government. But it can be encouraged by a refusal to give fiscal transfusions to terminally ill communities. It also can be encour-aged by tax incentives to people and industries that move into open lands, so to speak, in a new version of traditional homesteading.

*   *   *

Indeed a major population movement already is in progress. The New York Times News Service recently reported, "The gradual but massive shift of the American population away from the in-dustrialized North and toward the South and West documented by the 1970 Census has accelerated greatly in the last five years, according to a mid-decade estimate of state populations released by the Census Bureau."

The need for a deconcentration of population is a real one in several countries. In Great Britain, for example, much effort goes into urging companies to leave the swollen London metropolitan area and relocate in Wales, the north of England and other under-developed regions.

A free market will bring about a redistribution of population, industries and services in the United States. The federal govern-ment, however, interferes in this process when it seeks to subsidize sick cities.

Federal aid and loan guarantees cannot restore the economic health of a decayed region. Such measures only weaken the entire economy and thwart normal development on a transcontinental basis.

Source: Reprinted from *The Arizona Republic,* January 23, 1976.

THE POOR IN THRIVING SOUTHWEST CITIES

By John Herbers

PHOENIX—In this prototypically thriving Sun Belt city, whose population has risen by a third since 1970 and whose economic base is getting progressively stronger, lies a "40-mile-square pocket of poverty" larger than the entire area of many Eastern cities, according to Mayor Margaret Hance.

The cities of the Southwest are growing and the industrial cities of the North are declining, even faster than pre-census estimates had indicated. In some ways, they are facing the same troubles.

Many of the cities of this region have, in common with their poorer counterparts in the East, large areas of poverty and decay that have spread and become more isolated as the middle class has moved progressively farther from downtown sections.

Opposition to Tax Rises

Although the Sun Belt cities are fiscally stronger than those in the East, the prospect of declining Federal aid has ominous overtones here, too. The difficulty, which has been documented by several studies for the Brookings Institution in Washington, is not the lack of wealth but the means of using it to help needy areas in the face of adamant opposition to tax increases.

The tax revolt was well under way in such states as Arizona before it splashed onto the national scene in 1978, when California voted a drastic cutback in property taxes. To fill the gap, Western cities, like cities elsewhere, have become increasingly dependent on Federal grants, even as they "continuously and ritualistically condemn federalism," in the words of an Arizona State University study titled "Phoenix: The New Federal City."

Federal aid, however, has been declining slightly since 1978, and everyone agrees that more drastic reductions lie ahead. The tax revolt that was under way here five years ago has now reached every level of Government, including Washington.

Pessimism on Poverty Areas

The prospect is for reduced city services, and there are indications that the burden of cuts in many Southwestern cities will fall heaviest on the "pockets of poverty." Studies conducted for the Brookings Institution of the impact of Federal aid in Houston, Tulsa, Phoenix and New Orleans showed that much of the money went into programs for the poor.

James W. Fossett, writing on the Brookings findings in the Texas Business Review, said that minority constituent groups in Houston and New Orleans might be able to force local government to make up for at least some of the loss of Federal money in poor neighborhoods, but in Phoenix and Tulsa they "appear to lack the political strength to do so."

Mayor Hance says that if all Federal aid were stopped she would try to minimize the effect on such basic services as police work and that the city has been moving to minimize its dependence on Washington.

Poverty in Sight of Plenty

"The poor are a Federal, not a local, responsibility," she said in an interview published last summer in Fortune magazine. "If Washington cannot afford these programs, we certainly can't. Local people do not feel that welfare programs should be financed by local taxes."

The city's 40-square-mile "poverty pocket," known as South Phoenix, is home for about 125,000 people, most of them Hispanic Americans, blacks and Indians. It is an area of old farm shacks, junkyards, sagebrush, vacant lots and some recently built low-income housing, all within sight of the city's gleaming downtown skyscrapers.

South Phoenix is separated from the rest of the city by the Salt River and Interstate 17. It has few big stores, jobs or services; over the years these have moved farther away with the prospering population.

Population gains in Western cities vary widely. Census figures for 1970 and 1980 show that Houston and Tucson, for example, grew by 26 percent each and Albuquerque by 34.5 percent, while Denver lost 5 percent and is down to 488,000, even while it is booming as an energy center.

But the same phenomenon occurred almost everywhere, a thinning out of close-in neighborhoods. The cities that showed the big population gains expanded their boundaries to encompass the new areas of growth. They all face the enormous expense of providing capital improvements and services for areas of less population density and wealth.

Population Grows with Area

In 1940, Phoenix had a population of 65,000 within 10 square miles. Now it contains 325 square miles with 781,443 persons, 2,400 for each square mile, and this week the City Council was still annexing new territory. In addition, Phoenix has spawned neighboring cities of vast sprawl—Tempe, Mesa, Scottsdale, and Paradise Valley, among others.

As the city expanded in the 1970's and the cost of government rose, the introduction of Federal funds in a city that had long scorned such assistance permitted the continuing of low tax levies.

In 1972, only 8.7 percent of the city's total revenues were from Washington. But by 1978, the peak year for Federal aid, Washington was providing 25 percent of the Phoenix budget and more than 30 percent of its operating revenues.

In 1977, the City Council enacted a 1 percent increase in the sales tax, but six months later the voters nullified it in a special referendum called by a citizen initiative.

While some Sun Belt cities used Federal aid mostly for purposes other than basic services, Phoenix funneled most of its funds into such departments as police, fire and street maintenance. In a Brookings study, John Stuart Hall calculated in 1978 that the city would have had to increase its own tax effort 66 percent to replace Federal funds for operating purposes.

Social Programs Jeopardized

A portion of the Federal money has gone into South Phoenix for jobs, housing and community development. Before 1972, such programs in the area were negligible. But it is these programs that appear in jeopardy now.

City officials say they have been concerned for some time about the need for a large tax increase, should Federal aid be greatly reduced. In 1978 they began phasing out federally financed public service jobs. But the largest cuts were made in social services and recreation programs, not the more basic services.

"By adopting Federal priorities to their own image of what a local government should be," the authors of the Arizona State study concluded, "Phoenix was able to have it both ways: build a city administration on a Federal foundation while claiming a parochial orientation to crime control and maintenance of a Southwest life style. In the process, big government was co-opted by local government."

Mr. Hall said in an interview that as long as Phoenix continued its phenomenal growth—projected to 2.3 million people by the year 2000—the city could continue to be somewhat independent. Revenues from its low tax base keep increasing.

Still, the kind of reductions in Federal aid that most people here voted for Nov. 4 could bring a "fiscal crisis" of the kind facing Eastern cities, he said, and the tax revolt would really begin to hurt.

Source: Reprinted from the *New York Times,* December 21, 1980. © 1980 by the New York Times Company. Reprinted by permission.

Interrelationships within the City System

Borchert's analysis of the evolution of the system of cities in the United States focused on the population size of metropolitan centers and their spatial distribution. No attention was given, however, to the actual economic or other kinds of relationships among these centers. Such relationships were inferred from the size and position of the metropolitan centers in the transportation network linking the system of cities.

Ecologists and other social scientists in recent years have examined the intensity and volume of interaction among cities to gain a better understanding of the operation of the system. A common method is to measure the volume of various types of goods and services exchanged between centers—mail and telephone calls, commodity shipments, airline ridership, and banking and wholesale services. Such measures have been used to delineate relationships among centers and to rank urban places by their relative importance in the urban hierarchy.

Relationships measured by index scores   Vance and Smith (1954) attempted to identify metropolitan patterning in the southern region of the United States. These researchers developed an index of dominance that was the weighted sum of six variables—wholesale sales, business services receipts, number of manufacturing branch offices, retail sales, bank clearings, and value added by manufacturing (the market price of goods minus the cost of materials used to produce them). The index was designed to measure the degree to which a given metropolis was able to build and control markets in its hinterland.

On the basis of this index, Vance and Smith identified six categories of cities in the urban hierarchy. Figure 5.12 indicates how they thought these cities were linked together. The super metropolises of New York and Chicago can be thought of as having national hinterlands; metropolises of a lower order have trade areas that are nested within those of the larger metropolitan centers. This pattern is similar to the one posited in the central place theory. A weakness of Vance and Smith's work is that the linkages among the cities in the hierarchy are not based on a measure of the flow of goods and services among these centers, but are inferred from each city's index-of-dominance score.

Relationships measured by the flow and volume of money   Duncan, Scott, Liberson, Duncan, and Winsborough (1960) studied the relationships among metropolises by examining the flow and volume of credit and loans within the Federal Reserve System and its member banks, and the volume of wholesaling and commercial activity as measured by sales and receipts from business activities.

Duncan and his colleagues found in their banking study that the flow and volume of credit among members of the Federal Reserve System indicated a hierarchy of banking centers, each with its own distinct trade area. Federal Reserve Banks in the major metropolises of twelve districts made up most of the national credit and loan market. The Federal Reserve Banks made discounted loans to member banks in smaller cities that in turn made loans within their own trade areas. From the reserve banks at the top of the banking hierarchy to the member banks lower in the hierarchy, there was a decline in both the volume of loans and the size of the trade

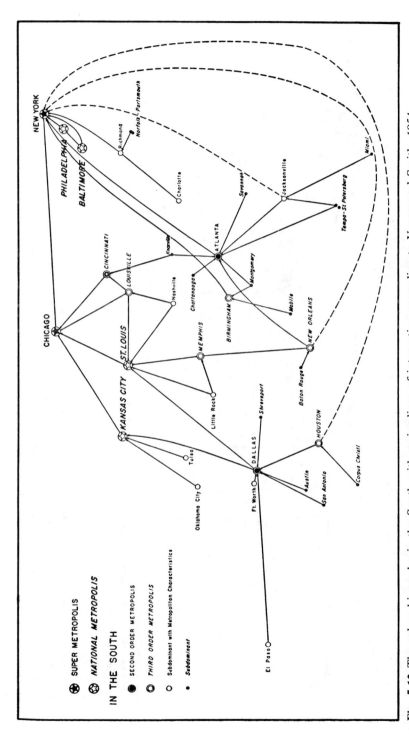

Fig. 5.12 The urban hierarchy in the South with major lines of integration according to Vance and Smith, 1954.

Source: Vance, R. B., and Smith, S., "Metropolitan Dominance and Integration." In R. B. Vance and N. J. Demerath, (Eds.), *The Urban South.* Chapel Hill: University of North Carolina Press, 1954.

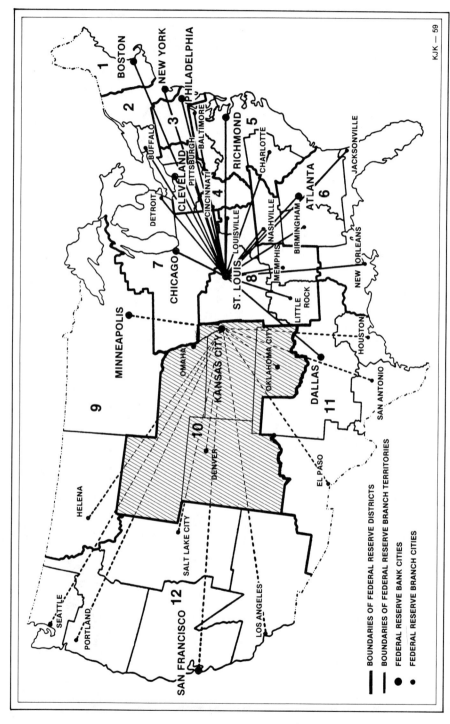

Fig. 5.13 A comparison of the flow of capital and credit between Federal Reserve District Banks in St. Louis and Kansas City and banks in outlying districts of the Federal Reserve System.

Source: Duncan, O. D., et al. *Metropolis and Region.* Baltimore: The Johns Hopkins University Press, 1960, p. 147.

areas served. Figure 5.13 illustrates the relationship between the Federal Reserve Banks in Kansas City and St. Louis and their relationships with member banks in other cities. Duncan and his co-workers found the same hierarchy in their study of business activity.

Relationships measured by industrial activity Duncan and his colleagues also constructed a city typology using "industry profiles" for all SMSAs with more than 300,000 inhabitants in 1950. These metropolises were classified into one of seven categories and ranked according to the degree to which

Table 5.10
Classification of standard metropolitan areas of 300,000 or more inhabitants according to metropolitan functions and regional relationships.

National Metropolis (N)
New York
Chicago
Los Angeles (Nd)
Philadelphia (Nd)
Detroit (Nm)

Diversified Manufacturing with Metropolitan Functions (D)
Boston (Dn)
Pittsburgh (Dn)
St. Louis
Cleveland
Buffalo
Cincinnati

Diversified Manufacturing with Few Metropolitan Functions (D−)
Baltimore
Milwaukee
Albany–Schenectady–
Troy
Toledo
Hartford
Syracuse

Specialized Manufacturing (M)
Providence
Youngstown
Rochester
Dayton
Allentown–Bethlehem–
Easton
Akron
Springfield–Holyoke
Wheeling–Steubenville
Charleston, West Virginia

Regional Metropolis (R)
San Francisco (Rn)
Minneapolis–St. Paul
Kansas City
Seattle
Portland
Atlanta
Dallas
Denver

Regional Capital Submetropolitan (C)
Houston
New Orleans
Louisville (Cd)
Birmingham (Cm)
Indianapolis (Cd)
Columbus (Cd)
Memphis
Omaha
Fort Wayne
Richmond (Cd)
Oklahoma City
Nashville
Jacksonville

Table 5.10 (continued)

Special Cases (S)
Washington
San Diego
San Antonio
Miami
Norfolk–Portsmouth
Wilkes–Barre–Hazelton
Tampa–St. Petersburg
Knoxville
Phoenix

Source: Duncan, O. D., et al. *Metropolis and Region.* Baltimore: The Johns Hopkins University Press, 1960, p. 271.

they carried out metropolitan functions and had regional relationships with other centers.

In Table 5.10, the two major National Metropolises (N), New York and Chicago, are followed closely by Los Angeles and Philadelphia. Detroit is also considered a National Metropolis but it differs from the others because of its specialized manufacturing of automobiles. Two other categories of cities, Regional Metropolis (R) and Regional Capital (C), also provide banking and other services for a hinterland. In many respects, N-R-C cities can be thought of as central places but on a larger scale than in the analysis in Chapter 4. These N-R-C cities provide banking and other functions to their hinterlands, the size of their trade areas depends on the position of the cities in the urban hierarchy, and their hinterlands are nested.

Manufacturing and Special cities, D, D-, M, and S cities, are distinctly different from the N-R-C centers. In general, the basic sectors of their economies are specialized. The goods they produce often are distributed nationally, but they produce only a few goods of this nature (tire manufacturing in Akron, for example) and they have only a limited impact on the national economy. More important, these cities depend on N-R-C centers for banking and other vital business services and can be thought of as a part of their hinterlands.

Duncan and his colleagues, therefore, combined a city typology with an analysis of the flow of banking and other goods and services to provide a clearer understanding of the system of cities.

SUMMARY

This chapter is intended to provide an understanding of the structure of cities and their interrelationship within a system of cities. The first section, a review of some of the more important attempts to classify cities, illustrates the purpose, methods, and problems in city classification.

The earliest classification methods, single-dimension typologies, were based on the economic function of cities. Harris (1943) constructed one of the first classification schemes by scanning the employment profiles of cities and then intuitively placing each city into one of nine categories—manufacturing (M type and M' type), retail, diversified, wholesale, transportation, mining, university, and resort centers. Later, Nelson (1955) employed two statistical measures (means and standard deviations) in the analysis of employment profiles to construct his classification framework. Interestingly, both researchers devised similar classification schemes, and the city types they identified had similar spatial patterns. Moreover, the spatial patterns of these city types correspond closely to patterns predicted from the general theories of location reviewed in Chapter 4. Retail and wholesale centers are centrally located in trade areas, and their spatial distribution is described by the central place theory. The location of mining centers and resorts is described by environmental influences and site factors, and transportation and communication centers by the break-in-transportation theory. Although the original settlement patterns of manufacturing centers can be described by the three theories, the subsequent growth and development of these centers result from site, resource, labor, and market factors, factors not a part of the general theories of location.

In subsequent research, it was recognized that a single dimension could not adequately describe the complex character of cities, and other dimensions were added. The resultant multidimensional typologies, facilitated by the computer and a technique known as factor analysis, showed more clearly cities' multifunctional character. In general, social factors were found to be more important than economic factors in describing cities' underlying dimensions. This research showed that single-dimension typologies were of minimal and declining relevance in the study of the structure of cities. Today, because cities carry out a full range of economic functions, it is impossible to classify them along a single economic dimension. The complex nature of cities in modern urban societies can be described only by means of more sophisticated multivariate research techniques.

The second section of this chapter examines the dynamic character of the system of cities. Borchert's analysis of the evolution of the United States system of cities demonstrates the complex interaction of elements in the ecological complex. The four historical epochs he identifies illustrate how cities rose and fell within this system in response to changing technology and resource needs that brought about the redistribution of population and industry among and within the system of cities. The research of Vance and Smith, and Duncan and his colleagues complements this analysis by identifying, through a variety of techniques, the complex economic and social relationships that weld this nation's cities into a functioning system.

NOTES

1. A review of the literature on city typologies shows that these objectives have not always been met. Critics have argued that the development of different classification schemes has become an end in itself. In other words, cities have been classified, but the classifications have not been used as a point of departure for further analysis (Duncan, 1960, p. 35; Smith, 1965, pp. 539–40). Other writers recognize the usefulness of these typologies and note that classification schemes have been sadly underemployed in urban research (Schnore and Winsborough, 1972, p. 125). Schnore and Winsborough suggest that carefully developed city typologies could be used to illuminate "the determinants, concomitants and consequences of city functions." To a degree this advice has been taken and today city typologies are used more widely for the objectives stated above (Berry and Horton, 1970; Berry, 1972a).

2. William Ogburn (1937) published a similar city classification six years before Harris's typology. In many respects, Ogburn's scheme is more sophisticated in methodology, but it has received scant attention in the literature on city typologies. For this reason, the better-known Harris work is examined here.

3. City typologies based on Harris's classification scheme are found in articles published by Forstall, 1967, 1970; Hart, 1955; Jones, 1953; Jones and Collver, 1960; Jones and Forstall, 1963; and Kneedler, 1945. A complete citation for each article is given in the references section.

4. Researchers who have set minimum levels of employment in various occupations as the basis for a city classification scheme include Forstall, 1967, 1970; Harris, 1943; Hart, 1955; Jones, 1953; Jones and Collver, 1960; Jones and Forstall, 1963; Jones, Forstall, and Collver, 1963; and Kneedler, 1945. A complete citation for each article is given in the bibliography.

5. Researchers who have used arithmetic means and other statistics to set thresholds of employment for a classification scheme include Duncan and Reiss, 1956; Nelson, 1955; Ogburn, 1937; and Pownall, 1953. A complete citation of these researchers' works is given in the bibliography.

6. Using 1960 data, Sylvia Perle (1964) replicated Price's earlier work in her master's thesis at the University of Chicago, "Factor Analysis of American Cities: A Comparative Analysis." Her results were similar to those of Price, but she found the factor "occupational structure" had grown in importance since 1930.

7. An excellent collection of works on the uses of city classifications in social and political research can be found in Brian Berry, ed., *City Classification Handbook: Methods and Applications* (New York: Wiley Interscience, 1972).

PART THREE

The Internal Structure of the Metropolis

Social Area Analysis and Factorial Ecology

Statement of Objectives

1. The importance of the Chicago School and its impact on later social area analysis should be known.

2. Three indexes—social status, family status, and ethnic status—measure basic trends in society. The student should be able to analyze the relationship of these indexes to social trends.

3. The concept of societal scale is central to the social area analysis approach. The student should know the societal changes associated with increasing societal scale.

4. The student should become aware of the link between the scale of a society and the way space is used within the society's cities.

5. The student should understand how the mathematical technique of factor analysis was used to test the social area analysis model.

6. The student should know the practical uses of social area analysis in urban research.

Much of the literature of human ecology is concerned with the distribution of population characteristics, organizations, activities, and behaviors across the urban landscape. This literature explores not only the spatial distribution of characteristics but also the processes by which these patterns emerge. Researchers in this area use a number of ecological models in studying the internal structure of the city. Two of the most important are social area analysis and factorial ecology. Both are based on the mathematical technique of factor analysis. The characteristics of a city's subareas or neighborhoods are presented as a series of variables. Factor analysis sorts these variables, identifies underlying similarities, and summarizes them on one or more factor or index scores. Factor analysis, then, is used to identify the fundamental characteristics of a city's subareas.

The major difference between social area analysis and the more general factorial ecology is in the quantity of data they use. Social area analysis is limited to seven variables that measure the social-status, family, and ethnic characteristics of subareas. Factorial ecology greatly expands the number of variables used, from seven to several dozen. This more general approach was made possible by the modern high-speed computer that became available to researchers in the 1960s.

Social area analysis was first presented in a series of books and articles written by Eshref Shevky, Marilyn Williams, and Wendell Bell in the late 1940s and early 1950s. These researchers maintained that the use of space within cities, as measured by the seven variables in their analysis, was closely related to the degree of economic development of the larger society. Shevky and Bell introduced the concept "societal scale" to refer to the extent of the division of labor within the society and the complexity of its organization and institutions. As a society modernizes or increases in scale, its degree of societal complexity increases and is reflected in increasing specialization of urban land use. In a high-scale society, neighborhoods become specialized in terms of their social-status, family, and ethnic characteristics. In a low-scale society where social organization is relatively simple, social-status, family, and ethnic characteristics are interrelated and urban land use is less specialized.

Social area analysis is important because it relates the process of urbanization to the more general process of economic development. Thus, it is based on a general theory that can be applied to the analysis of cities in both more and less developed societies. Factorial ecology, which developed out of social area analysis in the 1960s, is more inductive with little or no associated theory.

THE ORIGINS OF SOCIAL AREA ANALYSIS

The Concept of Natural Areas

Social area analysis was an outgrowth of the work of the Chicago ecologists Park, Burgess, and others, who during the 1920s and 1930s were among the first social scientists to be concerned with the internal structure of cities. In their studies of Chicago, they discovered that the city was made up of distinct areas, each one relatively homogeneous in population, housing, and other characteristics. What particularly struck the Chicago ecologists was that these areas had not been planned by a builder or large developer. Rather, the areas had evolved as the result of millions of individual decisions made by people who had different moral, political, economic, racial, and ethnic characteristics. Each "natural area" had its own special qualities, the result of its unique ethnic and racial mix, physical characteristics, and other factors including the income and occupation of its residents.

Members of the Chicago School thought of *natural areas* as concrete entities that really existed—places that could be searched for, identified, and described scientifically.[1] Yet they never agreed on how to define the boundaries of an area. McKenzie and Wirth, for example, stressed population characteristics such as race, language, income, and occupation; Zorbaugh, in contrast, was concerned largely with the areas' physical characteristics. Burgess provided the most inclusive definition of a natural area by focusing on the forces responsible for its emergence. Out of these varied approaches, three important components of a natural area emerged: (1) it is the result of the operation of ecological and social forces, (2) it is unplanned, and (3) its boundaries can be discovered by measuring the income, occupation, ethnicity, and housing characteristics of its residents.[2]

While members of the Chicago School were identifying hobohemia, the ghetto, the Gold Coast, and other areas in Chicago, researchers in Cleveland and other cities began dividing their own communities into natural areas. In the early 1930s statistician Howard Whipple Green set out to identify areas of Cleveland that were "functionally homogeneous with histories and heritages of their own" (1931, p. 7). The twenty-eight Social Planning Areas (SPAs) Green delineated are still in use in Cleveland for reporting police, fire, city health, and census statistics (see Figure 6.1), although the areas today are much different in character than when first studied by Green.

Initially, Green's goal was to use natural areas as planning units, a basis for more effective allocation of the city's limited financial resources. But the detailed housing, population, and health statistics he compiled had another important application—they could be used to describe the internal structure of the city. Data for various subareas allowed researchers to group areas into types: the slum, the ethnic enclave, the working-class and middle-class areas. Once a city's various areas had been categorized and plotted on a map, their spatial distribution gave researchers insight into the city's structure.

The concept of natural areas and the theory associated with it had limitations, however. For one thing, the natural areas concept was not consistently defined: in one study, natural areas were viewed as spatial units bounded by major streets, lakes, rivers, and parks; in others, emphasis was placed on the community—aspects of the population living in an area. Some critics claimed it was impossible to find culturally homogeneous areas in cities on the east and west coasts.[3] The most significant weakness of the work of the Chicago ecologists was that, while concentrating on areas within the city, they ignored the social, economic, and cultural changes taking place in the larger society. This problem was to restrict the usefulness of area-oriented research for nearly two decades.

The move to relate urban process to a wider range of forces and the characteristics of the larger society began as an attempt to develop a typology of subareas of the city. When in 1940 the United States Bureau of the Census began publishing data for most large American cities by census

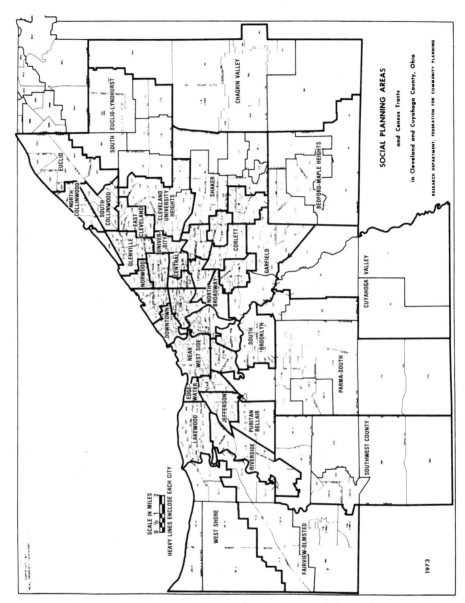

The bold lines in this map are the boundaries of Cleveland's Social Planning Areas (SPAs). SPAs were identified by the researcher Howard Whipple Green in the 1930s and they continue to be used to report fire, police, and welfare statistics. Census tract boundaries are the lighter lines that divide the SPAs into smaller units. In the city of Cleveland there are 28 SPAs but more than 200 census tracts.

Fig. 6.1 Social Planning Areas and census tracts in Cleveland and Cuyahoga County, Ohio.

Source: Research Department, Cleveland, Ohio: Federation for Community Planning, 1974.

tracts, urban researchers were faced for the first time not with too few data but with too many. The problem was that although census tracts were similar to natural areas, they were much smaller, averaging only 4,000 inhabitants. Thus, instead of twenty-eight Social Planning Areas to classify, for example, in Cleveland, social scientists were confronted with hundreds of census tracts (see Figure 6.1). A large metropolitan area might contain thousands of tracts. Urban researchers found it necessary to divide the census tracts within a city into larger categories. The approach to be known later as *social area analysis* had its beginning in one such attempt.

The Concept of Social Areas

In 1949, Eshref Shevky and Marilyn Williams published *The Social Areas of Los Angeles: Analysis and Typology*. There was an important difference between this study of the social areas of Los Angeles and earlier research by members of the Chicago School. The Chicago ecologists were interested in how a city's social organization was manifested spatially: where the very wealthy, the poor, and other groups lived in relationship to the city's center. Shevky and Williams, in contrast, were interested in the position of census tracts in "social space," regardless of their geographic location. That is, Shevky and Williams were interested in the people in the tracts, not the tracts themselves.

Social area indexes Shevky and Williams attempted to measure and describe the social differences among census tracts according to residents' scores on three indexes—social status, family status, and ethnic status.[4] Each index score represents scores for several variables combined into a single value. The indexes thus enabled the researchers to examine complex data in the form of just a few summary scores. Shevky and Williams further contended that each of their indexes tapped a basic social trend in the emerging urban society—the changing occupational structure, the declining proportion of children in the population, and the patterns of internal migration. These changes taking place in the larger society were measurable by the indexes because they were reflected first and most clearly in the distribution of tracts in social space within the city.

Social status index. The *social status index* is based on various socioeconomic attributes of American households. The most important attribute is the social value of the occupation of the head of the household. Physicians, for example, have higher occupational prestige than lawyers, lawyers higher prestige than factory workers, factory workers higher prestige than garbage collectors (see Table 6.2). Education is the second element of this index, and it is closely related to occupational prestige. Education not only provides a means of entry into occupations (a person needs a medical degree to become a licensed physician), but the status of an occupation usually is related to the amount of education required for it.

In most societies, people with similar social status tend to live near each other in fairly homogeneous areas. When these areas are classified into census tracts, they can be ranked from high to low on social status. Because of the strong relationship between status and occupation, changes in the occupation and employment characteristics of the society at large are reflected in the changing distribution of tracts according to social status. The social status index reflects the changing occupational structure in the United States and other developed nations. At present, a growing number of workers are employed in service occupations, and fewer in farming and extractive industries such as mining and forestry.

Family status index. The second index, *family status,* is based on variables such as the fertility ratio, the number of women in the labor force, and the number of single-family dwelling units in a tract. This index can be used to measure the changing economic role of the family. In the past, the extended family (more than two generations living together) was typical, and it operated as a production unit. This arrangement still can be seen on a farm: grandparents, parents, and children each contribute to the economic well-being of the family. In the city, because children have been prevented from working by child labor laws, children are no longer economic assets but economic liabilities. Today, the typical family is a consumption rather than a production unit, and its form is nuclear (two parents and their children). One can think of each nuclear family as passing through a series of stages. The "family formation" stage occurs when grown children leave their parents' household and set up households of their own, either as singles or as young married couples. Children are born into these new families and are raised to maturity—the "child-rearing" stage. Finally, grown children leave home, and the death of the parents brings the original family to an end. At each stage of the lifecycle, families have different space needs—parents with grown children no longer need a home with five bedrooms. Housing suited to these different space needs tends to be in different areas of the city: most large cities, for example, have certain areas that consist largely of apartments and are inhabited mainly by singles, retirees, or young couples with small children. In reflecting changes in the distribution of various types of living space, the family status index indicates a shift from the extended family to the nuclear family and the emergence of numerous lifestyles, each with its own space needs.

Ethnic status index. The third index, *ethnic status,* is based on variables such as the percentage of a tract's population that is foreign-born or black. The index measures the tendency of new migrants to the city to locate—

voluntarily or not—near people of their own background in a homogeneous ethnic or racial enclave. Thus the index reflects trends in internal migration whereby large numbers of members of various ethnic minorities—blacks and immigrants—concentrate in certain areas of the city. Rural to urban migration of blacks and ethnically diverse immigration from overseas were the trends described and measured by Shevky and Williams.

Shevky and Williams used the three indexes in developing a typology of social areas. First, index values for each of Los Angeles's 568 census tracts were calculated. Second, each census tract was plotted as a point on a scattergram according to its values on each of the indexes. Third, a "social area diagram" was created by adding dividing lines to the scattergram. Figure 6.2, the Los Angeles social space diagram, delineates socially homogeneous subareas within the city. Figure 6.3 shows the population and census tract distribution by social areas.

Revisions by Shevky and Bell

Shevky and Williams's approach was attacked on both theoretical and methodological grounds. Although Shevky and Williams did discuss general trends in society and the relationship of their indexes to these trends, the discussion was not presented in the form of a theory. Critics asked why these three indexes had been used. Why not some other mix of variables? Why use indexes at all? These questions were addressed six years later in a work by Eshref Shevky and Wendell Bell (1955).

In their restatement of the social area analysis approach, Shevky and Bell overcame the early narrow focus of the Chicago School by examining the sociocultural context in which urban communities are embedded. They stated:

> We conceive of the city as a product of the complex whole of modern society; thus the social forms of urban life are to be understood within the context of the changing character of the larger containing society (p. 3).

In other words, there is a close relationship between changes in the society as a whole and changes that take place in the use of space in cities. To explore this relationship, Shevky and Bell introduced the concept of *societal scale*.

The Concept of Societal Scale

The concept of societal scale was introduced in the 1950s to refer to the complex set of changes that accompany the development process. The term *high-scale societies* refers to more developed nations and *low-scale societies*

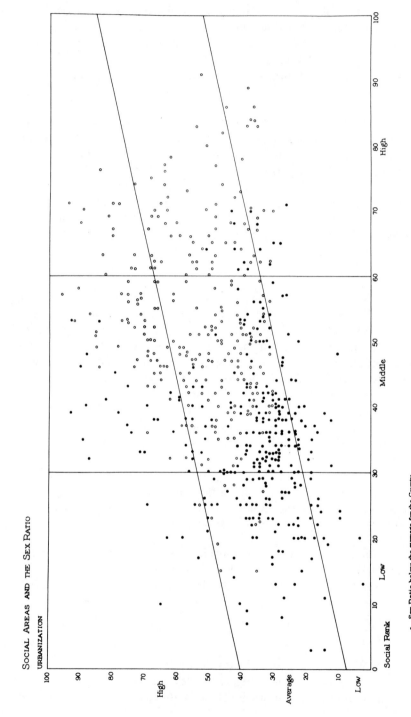

SOCIAL AREAS AND THE SEX RATIO

URBANIZATION

Social Rank

o   Sex Ratio below the average for the County
●   Sex Ratio above the average for the County

220

The figure opposite demonstrates the process Shevky and Williams used in developing a typology of social areas. First, index values for each of Los Angeles's 568 census tracts were calculated. Second, each census tract was plotted as a point on this scattergram according to its values on the indexes. Third, a social area diagram was created by adding dividing lines to the scattergram. In this figure the horizontal and vertical axes are the two dimensions of social status and family status; tracts scoring high on the third dimension, ethnic status, are represented by the symbol ⊙. Note that nine types of social areas were identified by this process.

Fig. 6.2

Source: Shevky, E. and Williams, M., *The Social Areas of Los Angeles.* Berkeley, Calif.: University of California Press, 1949, p. 60. Reprinted by permission of the University of California Press.

Total Population

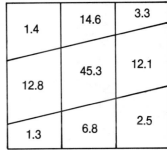

Urbanization

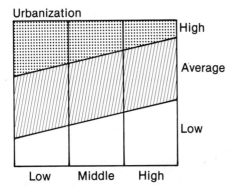

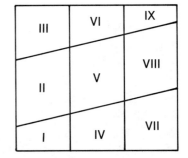

The Haynes Foundation

This figure shows the population and census tract distribution of Los Angeles by the social areas identified in Figure 6.2. Social Area I, low in social status and family status, would be similar to hobohemia in Chicago—single males and females with no children living in apartments in a state of poverty. Social Area IX, in contrast, would be characterized by high social status, few working women, large numbers of small children, and a predominance of single family dwellings—an upper-middle-class, child-oriented suburb. Social Area V, tracts with average social and family status measures, was the most common social area type, followed by Social Areas VIII and VI.

Fig. 6.3 Distribution of Los Angeles's population by social areas.

Source: Shevky, E. and Williams, M., *The Social Areas of Los Angeles.* Berkeley, Calif.: University of California Press, 1949, p. 65. Reprinted by permission of the University of California Press.

to less developed nations of the world. Shevky and Bell introduced the concept to emphasize the close relationship between the form or structure of a city and the characteristics of the encompassing society. This was a relationship often ignored by students of development. The changes that accompany an increase in the scale of a society are linked to the use of space within cities.

Effects of an increase in societal scale As a society increases in scale, basic changes occur in its organization and structure. First, economic functions become increasingly differentiated. Second, organization and structure grow more complex. Third, a change occurs in the range and intensity of human relationships. These changes, which are closely interrelated, can be seen in many areas of American society today.

Economic differentiation. A good example is the changing organization of business and industry. As the scale of American society has increased, people and machines have been integrated into a complex system for the production and transportation of goods. Sophisticated communication and transportation technology has been crucial to this development. For example, members of an organization no longer need to be in face-to-face contact to coordinate their activities; they can communicate by telephone even when they are separated by thousands of miles. Freed from many of the old spatial limitations, organizations have become more complex, and employees have become highly specialized in their skills. One result of these changes is an increase in the range and a decrease in the intensity of relationships between people in an organization. That is, people interact over greater distances, but their relationships are of an impersonal and superficial (secondary) nature.

For businesses to operate effectively and efficiently in such a high-scale society, they must depend on large numbers of people who are geographically widely dispersed. This pattern has come to characterize all of society. For example, throughout the country one out of every six Americans is employed directly or indirectly in automobile production—extraction and

---

Photo 6.1 Photographs opposite show two areas which would be classified as type 1 and type 9 on the social area diagram (see Figure 6.3). At the top is a type 1 social area, characterized by low scores on both the social, and family status dimensions. In such an area one would find people who were unmarried and childless and low in socioeconomic status. On the bottom is a photograph showing a recently built suburban neighborhood which houses people who would score high on both the social and family status dimensions. In this area one would expect to find married couples with small children, families which are also of high socioeconomic status.

Source: top, © Jon Wirce, Photo Researchers, Inc.; bottom, © Mark Stein, Photo Researchers, Inc.

refinement of raw materials, fabrication and assembly of automobiles, marketing and sales, servicing, road construction, insurance, and financing. To a degree, what happens to the automobile industry influences the economic well-being of every American.

This is especially true of the American economy in the 1980s. The automobile industry is a sick industry. In the fall of 1980, America's "Big Three"—General Motors, Ford and Chrysler—had the ignominious distinction of reporting the largest quarterly losses in the history of business. Buffeted by record interest rates, double-digit inflation, escalating gasoline prices, and intense foreign competition, two companies—American Motors and Chrysler—(at the time of this writing) were on the verge of financial collapse. A free-enterprise solution may have been found by American Motors; they merged with the French automaker Renault. In the case of Chrysler, the federal government in late 1979 recognized the devastating effects that its collapse would have on the American economy and provided a $1.5 billion loan guarantee program for the company. This nation's recent experience suggests that there is not only an interdependency within a nation but between nations on a global scale. The automobile and petroleum industries and grain production are three of dozens of examples of this international interdependence.

Increased complexity. Other areas of society also are influenced by its changing scale. As a society's scale increases, so do the range and intensity of its communication flow. In high-scale societies, mass communication—television, radio, newspapers—can influence a whole nation's tastes, ideas, and values. In the United States and other countries, the growth of mass communication combined with the power of large complex organizations has widened society's span of control over the individual.[5] The increasing sophistication of the computer has facilitated intrusion into people's personal lives by such organizations as the Internal Revenue Service, the FBI, and private credit bureaus. Increases in societal scale also have led to a loss of personal control over important choices that traditionally were individual decisions. The popular press provides numerous examples of parents who have been prevented by courts from rearing their children according to their deeply held religious or moral beliefs, terminally ill patients who have been kept alive against their will, and farmers and small businessmen who have come increasingly under the control of regulatory agencies.

Changes in human relationships. Increasing scale has also changed the form and structure of the neighborhood and the family. Neighbors and neighborhoods no longer carry out many of their traditional functions. In the past, during times of family crisis—death or unemployment—neighbors would often pitch in to help a family through their time of need. Today many of these functions have been taken over by public agencies. Similarly, the family has lost a large part of its role in the education and rearing of children. A number of social programs even bypass the family altogether to give benefits directly to children, or to protect a child from his or her family.

Changes in Use of Space

The preceding examples show how changes in the scale of society have brought about fundamental changes in the way society is organized and in the way individuals live. Urban ecologists have discovered that these social changes are reflected clearly in the use of social and physical space in cities.

Louis Wirth (1938), in his famous article "Urbanism as a Way of Life," discussed many of the changes then taking place in society. Wirth argued that increases in the size, density, and heterogeneity of America's urban populations had brought about these changes. As Table 6.1 shows, Wirth's research suggested that an increase in the size of a settlement beyond certain limits brings about a shift from primary to predominantly secondary relationships among its residents. Similarly, an increase in a population's heterogeneity leads members to depend increasingly on formal rather than informal means of social control. Wirth concluded that cities were the "prime mover" in the transformation of western society from "traditional-rural" to "urban-industrial."

Shevky and Bell agreed with Wirth that size, density, and heterogeneity are important measures in describing the character of urban life. However, they disagreed with his conclusions about causality. To them, the qualities of urbanism that Wirth attributed to the influence of size, density, and heterogeneity were not limited to cities but were characteristic of the total society. Cities simply mirror changes taking place in the society at large. In other words, increases in the scale of society bring about changes in the nature of the society's productive activity, in the distribution of occupations in the labor force, and in the composition and distribution of the society's population. These broad society-wide changes ultimately are responsible for the emergence of a predominantly urban way of life. The United States is a high-scale urban-industrial society. Even its small towns and villages reflect this fact. In a town of 10,000 people the tastes, consumption patterns, and norms and values are urban in character. Neighbors, rather than talking over the back fence, communicate by telephone. Acts of delinquency may no longer be handled informally but by the police. The unemployed and retired residents of the community collect unemployment benefits or Social Security rather than depend on neighbors for financial assistance. The dress, manners, and even language of people reflect the character of the encom-

Table 6.1
Louis Wirth's sociological definition of the city in relation to size, density, and heterogeneity

	A schematic version
	The greater the number of people interacting, the greater the potential differentiation
	Dependence upon a greater number of people, lesser dependence on particular persons
Size An increase in the number of inhabitants of a settlement beyond a certain limit brings about changes in the relations of people and changes in the character of the community	Association with more people, knowledge of a smaller proportion, and of these, less intimate knowledge
	More secondary rather than primary contacts; that is, increase in contacts that are face to face, yet impersonal, superficial, transitory, and segmental
	More freedom from the personal and emotional control of intimate groups
	Association in a large number of groups, no individual allegiance to a single group
	Tendency to differentiation and specialization
Density Reinforces the effect of size indiversifying people and their activities, and in increasing the structural complexity of the society	Separation of residence from work place
	Functional specialization of areas — segregation of functions
	Segregation of people: city becomes a mosaic of social worlds
	Without common background and common activities, premium is placed on visual recognition: the uniform becomes symbolic of the role
	No common set of values, no common ethical system to sustain them; money tends to become measure of all things for which there are no common standards

Table 6.1 (continued)

A schematic version	
Heterogeneity Cities are products of migration of peoples of diverse origin	Formal controls as opposed to informal controls. Necessity for adhering to predictable routines. Clock and the traffic signal symbolic of the basis of the social order
Heterogeneity of origin is matched by heterogeneity of occupations	Economic basis: mass production of goods, possible only with the standardization of processes and products
Differentiation and specialization reinforce heterogeneity	Standardization of goods and facilities in terms of the average
	Adjustment of educational, recreational, and cultural services to mass requirements
	In politics, success of mass appeals — growth of mass movements

passing society. Most important, the community's financial well-being is tied inextricably to the national and increasingly to the world economy. Therefore, although the community is small in size, low in density, and relatively homogeneous in population, it has characteristics that are attributable to the high-scale society of which it is a part.

From their abstract theoretical arguments, Shevky and Bell moved to indexes that measure changes on the community level. Their presentation remained similar to the earlier work of Shevky and Williams, but it was framed in more general theoretical terms. Shevky and Bell's postulates about the changes brought about by an increase in the scale of society referred to change in the range and intensity of interpersonal relations, differentiation of economic functions, and increase in the complexity of the society's organization. Figure 6.4 shows how these changes are reflected in certain specific social trends.

Changing distribution of skills The first trend Shevky and Bell identified is the changing distribution of skills in a society. As a society increases in scale, a fundamental change takes place in its system of stratification. For example, in the preindustrial city, members of the upper stratum—the governing elite—derived their station in life from inherited wealth, most of

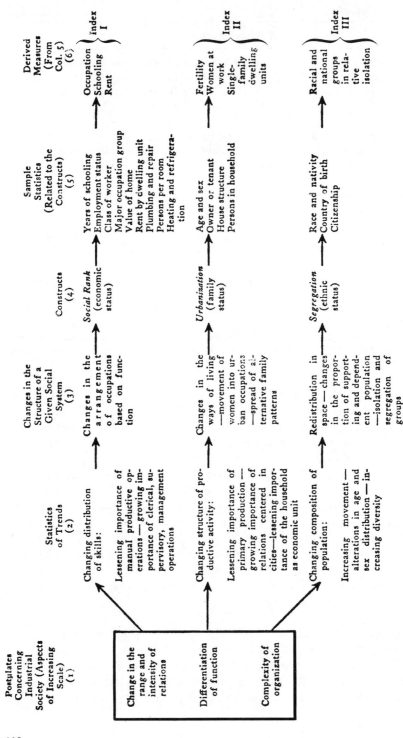

Fig. 6.4 Steps in construct formation and index construction.

Source: Reprinted from *Social Area Analysis: Theory, Illustrative Application and Computational Procedures*, by Eshref Shevky and Wendell Bell, with the permission of the publishers, Stanford University Press. Copyright © 1955 by the Board of Trustees of the Leland Stanford Junior University.

which was based in land ownership. As society increased in scale, the role of income-producing property was altered: wealth derived from land ownership became less important than wealth derived from manufacturing and commerce. Today, with the growth of stock ownership of companies, ownership of a company is less important than one's position within the enterprise. The chairman of the board of AT&T does not own the company he is directing, the shareholders do. Inherited wealth continues to be important but it is the skills of the working population that are the basis of the complex organization of high-scale society. Occupations within such a society have been regrouped and have been organized into a hierarchy along levels of skill, income, and prestige. This regrouping of skills mirrors the way consumption items are produced and distributed. In high-scale societies, automation has reduced the need for low-skilled workers and has increased the demand for people with clerical, supervisory, and management skills.

As a result, the importance of a specific skill to the society is reflected in the prestige associated with it. Table 6.2 shows the ranking of occupations in the United States by their social prestige. The most prestigious occupation is U.S. Supreme Court justice followed by physician and scientist, and ending with the least prestigious, shoe shiner. In this high-scale society, no other single characteristic tells us more about the individual and his or her position in society than the person's occupation (Shevky and Bell, 1955, p. 9). Knowing a person's occupation permits one to predict with a high degree of accuracy the person's income and education.

Therefore, *social status,* as measured by the characteristic occupation, education, and rental expenses of a society's population, indicates the scale of the society under study. In a low-scale society where technology is low and the economic system relatively simple, few types of occupations are needed and the overall skill level of the labor force is low. Moreover, because of the dominance of the elites in these societies, occupational prestige is not closely related to income and education. As the society's scale increases, the number and types of occupations increase, as does the general skill level of its labor force. As specific skills become functionally more important to a society, the level of education needed to acquire these skills increases, as does the reward for acquiring them.

Finally, changes on the societal level are manifested in the use of space within cities. Therefore, tracts high in social status have residents high in the measurable characteristics of occupational prestige, years of schooling, and rental expenses; tracts low in social status are low on all three variables.

Changes in the structure of productive activity The second trend Shevky and Bell found that resulted from scale-related social changes was change in the structure of productive activity. As societies increase in scale, fewer people are needed in production. Today, because one American farmer can produce enough food to feed fifty-four other people, fewer than five percent

Table 6.2
The prestige of selected occupations in the United States

Occupation	1963 Score	1947 Score
U.S. Supreme Court justice	94	96
Physician	93	93
Scientist	92	89
State governor	91	93
Cabinet member in the federal government	90	92
College professor	90	92
U.S. representative in Congress	90	89
Chemist	89	86
Lawyer	89	86
Diplomat in U.S. foreign service	89	92
Dentist	88	86
Architect	88	86
Psychologist	87	85
Minister	87	87
Member of the board of directors of a large corporation	87	86
Mayor of a large city	87	90
Priest	86	86
Civil engineer	86	84
Airline pilot	86	83
Banker	85	88
Biologist	85	81
Sociologist	83	82
Instructor in public schools	82	79
Captain in the regular army	82	80
Accountant for a large business	81	81
Newspaper columnist	73	74
Policeman	72	67
Radio announcer	70	75
Insurance agent	69	68
Carpenter	68	65
Manager of a small store in a city	67	69
Local official of a labor union	67	62
Mail carrier	66	66
Railroad conductor	66	67
Traveling salesman for a wholesale concern	66	68
Plumber	65	63
Automobile repairman	64	63
Barber	63	59
Machine operator in a factory	63	60
Owner/operator of a lunch stand	63	62
Corporal in the regular army	62	60
Truck driver	59	54
Clerk in a store	56	58
Lumberjack	55	53
Restaurant cook	55	54
Singer in a nightclub	54	52
Filling-station attendant	51	52
Dockworker	50	47
Night watchman	50	47
Coal miner	50	49

Occupation			Occupation		
Owner of a business that employs about 100 people	80	82	Restaurant waiter	49	48
Musician in a symphony orchestra	78	81	Taxi driver	49	49
Author of novels	78	80	Farmhand	48	50
Economist	78	79	Janitor	48	44
Official of an international labor union	77	75	Bartender	48	44
Railroad engineer	76	77	Soda-fountain clerk	44	45
Electrician	76	73	Sharecropper	42	40
Trained machinist	75	73	Garbage collector	39	35
Farm owner and operator	74	76	Street sweeper	36	34
Undertaker	74	72	Shoe shiner	34	33

Source: Adapted from data presented in Robert Hodge, Paul Siegel, and Peter Rossi, "Occupational Prestige in the United States, 1925–63." *American Journal of Sociology* 60 (1964): 290. Reprinted by permission of the University of Chicago Press.

of the labor force are employed in agricultural occupations. Because of automation, fewer workers are needed in other primary spheres of the economy, such as mining and forestry. These changes in the primary sector have led to rapid expansion of the secondary (manufacturing and industry) and tertiary (service) spheres of the economy. These economic activities require a centralized communication and transportation infrastructure that only an urban area can provide. Therefore, cities in high-scale societies assume a wider range and number of functions for the society as a whole: Shevky and Bell cited "co-ordination and control, service and promotion, and innovation" (1955, p. 12).

This transformation of productive activity affects all parts of society, but according to Shevky and Bell the family has borne the brunt of this change. In traditional agrarian or low-scale societies, the family carried out the functions of economic production, distribution and consumption; but today, in high-scale societies, the family depends on other institutions for most of these functions.

The changing functions of the family have also changed the role of women in society. Freed from large numbers of children and obligations to kin, more women enter the labor force. Consequently, women have adopted different styles of life and ways of living in high-scale societies. Specifically, in low-scale societies with their extended family forms, an unmarried female of marriage age would live with her family until she married. Today, she would probably be labeled "strange" or "peculiar" if she did not leave home, find employment, and set up her own apartment after high school or college.

Because the nuclear family is often isolated with no ties to kin in the surrounding community, a myriad of lifestyles are possible in high-scale societies for the single, the retiree, the young couple with children, the childless, and the single parent, and each lifestyle is accommodated by a different part of the city. Shevky and Bell's family status index used measures of fertility, the number of women at work, and the number of single-family dwellings in a tract to mirror these broad changes in society. A tract low on the family status index would have few young children, many working women, and mostly apartment housing; tracts high on the family status index would have large numbers of small children, few working women, and predominantly single-family dwellings.

Changes in population composition The third trend Shevky and Bell found related societal scale to changes in society's population composition. As a society increases in scale, the physical mobility of its population increases. This redistribution of a society's population over its territory is closely tied to changes in the distribution of skills and changes in the structure of productive activity. The major factor contributing to this mobility is the restructuring of productive activities. With the mechanization of agriculture, the demand for farm labor declines and surplus labor migrates from the rural to the urban areas. Similar readjustment takes place within and between cities: as industry declines in one region, opportunities may expand in another, and workers can respond to these opportunities by moving. The United States has one of the most mobile populations in the world. Roughly 20 percent of the population moves annually. This massive movement of people suggests that the labor force is closely tuned to the ebb and flow of the national economy.

Persons who migrate normally differ in important ways from the general population. Some migrants are compelled to move by "push" factors, that is, conditions where they have been living have become so bad that migration appears to be their only alternative. The "Famine Irish" who immigrated to this country in the nineteenth century were faced with the grim choice of starving in Ireland or leaving it. A more recent example is the large-scale immigration of Vietnamese to the United States with the fall of Saigon. In general, migration that results from push factors is much less selective than migration due to pull factors. The young and the old, the skilled and the unskilled overcome the obstacles of migration because their survival or the quality of their lives depends on it.

Migration caused by "pull" factors is very selective. The migrants are normally younger, with higher levels of education and training, than the general population. They are drawn from an area because of greater opportunities elsewhere. Younger workers just entering the labor market are better off economically if they "shop around" for employment. If a local employer is unwilling to pay an adequate salary, the worker can increase or maximize the return on his or her investment in education and training by moving. Many factors may impinge on an individual's decision to move—the available information on destinations, the efficiency of the search, and the monetary and psychological costs of the move. Migration because of pull factors has been dominant in the United States for much of this century; thus it has had a considerable effect on the composition of the cities' populations. It causes the percentage of the economically productive part of the population living in cities to increase and the percentage of dependent—the very young and old—to decrease.

The same forces that brought about the massive rural to urban migration in this country during the nineteenth and early twentieth centuries were at work in other countries as well. Most of these nations solved the resulting urban problems by exporting their surplus populations to such countries as the United States, Canada, New Zealand, and Australia. Since the United States began as a nation in 1776, more than 40 million Europeans have been added to its population.

The United States' first wave of immigrants, arriving before the Civil War, came from Northwestern Europe, Great Britain, Germany, Sweden, Norway, Denmark, Finland, Belgium, the Netherlands, France, and Switzerland. For the most part these immigrants have long been assimilated. The second wave of immigrants came much later, in the last quarter of the nineteenth and first quarter of the twentieth centuries. These people came predominantly from Southern and Eastern Europe, Poland, Hungary, Italy, the Balkan nations, and Russia. The second wave of immigrants, because they were predominantly Catholic or Jewish rather than Protestant, with language and customs much different from those of other immigrant groups, were not assimilated as easily into society and formed very durable ethnic enclaves within many large cities. They lived together for mutual support, and they aided each other in learning the language and customs of this country. Rather than being exclusionary, such enclaves gave immigrants a means of adapting to a new culture.

More recently, rural to urban migrants' adaptation has followed a similar pattern. These migrants have also been transported to a foreign land—the city—where the customs and even the language are different. Blacks from the rural South migrating North often seek out friends and relatives in the cities to help find employment and housing. Prejudice and discrimination have prevented this group from moving out into other areas of the city, however. In most large cities, sizable ethnic and racial enclaves still exist as viable and dynamic subcommunities. The ethnic status index reflects the racial and national groups who live in relative isolation in cities. The ethnic groups included are, for the most part, Eastern and Southern Europeans. A census tract high on the ethnic status index has large numbers of blacks and foreign-born residents within its borders; tracts low on this index have few of these residents.

Human ecologists are not the only group in American society who have developed classification schemes for subareas of the city. Banks, credit unions, gas and electric companies, and many other businesses have classified subareas along one dimension—the ability of the residents of an area to pay for goods and services. The area described by Patrick J. McCaffrey is a Type III social area (see Figure 6.3) that is low in social status, and high in family and ethnic status. Should business make this kind of judgment? How do you think you would react to treatment like this?

THE COSTS OF INNER-CITY LIFE

By Patrick J. McCaffrey

Shortly after moving into a predominantly black, inner-city neighborhood in Baltimore, I received a notice from the telephone company threatening termination of service because of late payment of a bill. I wrote the company that I had always paid my bills, even if a little late, and that in view of my credit record I was miffed at such threats. A few days later, a company public relations man invited me to lunch to explain the situation. After about $10 worth of lunch at the expense of all of us telephone users, he cautiously backed into his point.

Was I aware of the significance of my telephone exchange?

"Well, it's a downtown exchange, isn't it?"

"Yes. And most customers with that exchange are Negroes."

"So? Most inner-city dwellers are black."

"Well, the clerk just assumed from the exchange that you were black and mistakenly sent you a termination notice. She couldn't know."

"Do you mean she wouldn't have if she had known I was white?"

"Well, that and that you had a good credit record."

"Many blacks have good credit, too. That's discrimination."

"Well, not exactly. You see, generally, Negroes are poor credit risks. We have to stay on top of them to see that they pay. They're accustomed to it. Everybody does it."

And, indeed, everybody does. Utilities, banks, merchants, and even local governments code neighborhoods and quietly discriminate in the quality of services they provide. Part of the problem is the merchant mentality that equates influence with affluence. Blacks and white inner-city poor or oddballs are written off as marginal consumers. Merchants have convinced themselves that inner-city neighborhoods and people are bad credit risks and dangerous.

These attitudes are reflected especially in the harassment tactics of utilities, which have a monopoly on services. State and Federal regulatory agencies rarely check upon subtle harassment based on race, income, or address. Legal aid bureaus across the nation, however, have a dozen suits pending against such practices as discriminatory rate structures, security deposits, and arbitrary service termination.

One first notices such harassment when applying for utility service. Whether a deposit will be required, and in what amount, is determined by utility fiat. I have paid deposits ranging from nothing to $25 to utilities in various cities. I know blacks who have been required to deposit up to $150.

The phenomenon is noticed again when downtown dwellers telephone for service or repairs. The first question is not for your name or account number, but your address and whether or not it is a private residence. Utilities say they want the owner's approval, but it is the order of the questions that appears discriminatory. And the pattern of discrimination is evident in termination cases.

My black housekeeper told me one day that she would have to have the afternoon off because she had been *ordered* to appear at a hearing. It was not, as I first thought, a judicial summons to appear in court on some civil or criminal matter. It was an administrative *order* from the gas and electric company for a hearing on her bill, which was two months past due. She could not have been more frightened if she were facing a jail term.

The administrative judge, who turned out to be a service representative, was taken aback when she appeared with an attorney. He was more upset—and called in a company lawyer—when the attorney questioned his authority to *order* her appearance and suggested that the company might have violated her civil rights. It developed in the hearing that she was wrong, and confused, about the bill. The company readily agreed to a most reasonable settlement for her, "just like white folks."

The city itself is not averse to discriminating in the quality of its services. Police protection is a glaring case: Though the number of policemen assigned to our neighborhood was heavy (because of high crime-rate statistics), actual protection was erratic or poor, depending upon political pressures. The police preferred to concentrate on vice, rather than on robberies, burglaries, and assaults, because vice is more visible and makes for better statistics.

When some of my lawn furniture was stolen, I used neighborhood kids to track down the culprits—a teenaged theft ring that operated out of a garage on the edge of the ghetto. The police, who had been investigating a number of burglaries in the vicinity, were surprised at my information and amazed when it turned out that the stealing club was tied into two major fences, other burglary rings, and had information on area homicides and escaped convicts. On another occasion, neighborhood kids helped me turn up $1,200 worth of silver stolen from my home, after police had given it up as lost.

Then there are the little bureaucratic humiliations practiced by the city's health, education, and welfare agencies. These were documented by a black state legislator who, over a period of several months, dressed shabbily and visited a number of city and state agencies. He reported to the city's human relations commission that he had waited long hours, only to be ignored or snapped at by clerks and attendants. But the commission lacks the power, funds, and staff to enforce equal rights, and, of course, no one can enforce courtesy.

Mortgage money for inner-city housing has been scarce for years, and is now nonexistent. When mortgages could be found in recent years, the down payments often were prohibitive. Banks and other financial institutions would require as much as one-third down, forcing buyers to take additional loans or second mortgages at high interest rates. The effect of these policies is to choke off home purchases in inner-cities, and to trap people who already own homes there by making it difficult for them to sell their property, except to speculators.

In our neighborhood, Reservoir Hill, on the northern edge of the city's commercial area, there was a cluster of about twenty shops. A survey by the city planning department found that half of the area residents shopped at these stores, though three-quarters of the people considered them inadequate. Residents were unhappy not only with gouge-the-poor prices at some stores but with the quality and selection of merchandise. The heavy percentage of local users pointed to a lack of mobility and shopping know-how of residents.

The merchants contend their prices are higher because their shops do a smaller volume of business and are subject to high pilferage rates. But what about the shoplifting on the other side of the counter? A former employee of several neighborhood stores told me he had seen many instances. One grocery store owner, he said, always kept a new broom near the checkout counter, or several items of canned goods by the cash register. "I don't know how many times he sold that broom," he said. If the customer checked his sales slip and complained, the owner would only shrug and say, "Oh, I thought that was yours."

Inner-city residents usually distinguish between good merchants and exploiters, and even when they can't pinpoint the exploitation, they are aware they are being taken. The result is smoldering, bitter resentment. After the 1968 riots, a neighborhood improvement group attempted to pass a resolution deploring the violence against local merchants, but the attempt bogged down over a question of wording. One resident offered a compromise: "Let's say, 'We deplore the violence—but not very much.' "

Such resentment, sometimes considered reverse racism, is a predictable product of the discrimination inherent in the merchant mentality. Yet there is a distinction between white and black racism: The latter is not institutionalized. It does not threaten whites' livelihood, their living conditions, or the quality of services and products on which they depend. In short, black racism does not dictate the day-to-day course of whites' lives. By its very ineffectiveness in these areas, it often takes the course of suppressed rage or senseless violence toward immediate and visible white neighbors.

This effect of the merchant mentality, inexplicable to most whites, was best described by the previously mentioned black legislator who experienced some of the humiliations himself. "Few people know what it is to be treated as a nonperson," he said. "The few who do don't talk about it. It destroys your human dignity."

Source: Patrick J. McCaffrey, "The Costs of Inner-City Life," *The Progressive* (June 1974), pp. 39–40. Reprinted by permission from *The Progressive*, 408 West Gorham Street, Madison, Wisconsin 53703. Copyright © 1974, The Progressive, Inc.

TESTING THE SOCIAL AREA MODEL

The most persistent criticism of social area analysis was directed to the validity of the indexes themselves.[6] First, are Shevky and Bell's three indexes—social status, family status, and ethnic status—adequate to account for the social differentiation among areas of the city? Second, do the variables used to calculate these indexes result in a single dimension unrelated to the other indexes as their originators claimed? In other words, if census tracts were ranked from highest to lowest on the family status index, would their order be different—and independent—from their rank by social status?

Factor Analysis

To test the validity of the social area model, Bell (1955) used a mathematical technique known as factor analysis. Factor analysis identifies clusters of similarly related variables by sorting variables, identifying their underlying similarities, and summarizing them on a single factor or index score. In the multidimensional typologies discussed in Chapter 5, factor analysis was used in an exploratory fashion. Large numbers of variables were factored to identify the underlying characteristics of metropolitan areas. Shevky and Bell used factor analysis in a different way—to test their original hypothesis.

Shevky and Bell calculated a social status index by combining a census tract's scores on the variables of occupation, education, and rental expense. The family status index was calculated from the variables fertility ratio, number of women in the labor force, and percentage of single-family dwelling units in the tract. The ethnic status index was calculated from variables measuring the concentration of ethnics and blacks in census tracts. Bell reasoned that if the social area dimensions were valid, then the seven variables used to calculate the indexes, if factored, would yield a three-factor solution, each factor identifying a cluster of variables corresponding to the social area dimensions. Bell made twenty-one predictions on the factor solution he would expect if the social area analysis approach were valid. He predicted that the variables of occupation, education, and rent would be summarized by Factor I; Factor II would identify the variable cluster combining fertility ratio, women in the labor force, and single-family dwelling units; and Factor III would identify only one variable, segregation. (See Appendix A for a general discussion of factor analysis.)

Bell's Predictions and Findings

Using factor analysis, Bell identified three clusters of variables (See Table 6.3). Factor I identified a cluster of three variables, occupation (.482), education (.319), and rent (.653). The remaining variables were not related to this factor as indicated by their low and insignificant loadings. Factor

Table 6.3
Bell's rotated factor matrix—Los Angeles, 1940.

Measures	I	II	III
1 Occupation	(.482)	.193	−.094
2 Education	(.319)	−.044	.282
−3 Rent	(.653)	−.192	−.189
4 Fertility	.109	(.562)	.176
−5 WLF	.148	(.617)	−.193
6 SFDU	−.147	(.727)	.015
7 SEG	−.109	.004	(.576)

I Economic Status	WLF Women in the Labor Force
II Family Status	SFDU Single-Family Dwelling Units
III Ethnic Status	SEG Segregation

Source: Bell, W., "Economic, Family and Ethnic Status: An Empirical Test." *American Sociological Review* 20 (1955): p. 47. Reprinted with permission of The American Sociological Association.

II identified a second cluster of three variables; fertility (.562), women in the labor force (.617), and single-family dwelling units (.727). Again, the other variables had near-zero loadings. Factor III, interestingly, picked up two variables, segregation (.576) and education (.282), but the segregation variable has the highest loadings. The loading of the second variable, education, was not predicted by Bell.

By referring to Table 6.4, one can see that Bell made twenty-one predictions (a plus sign means a significant loading, zero an insignificant load-

Table 6.4
Bell's hypothesized factor matrix and the observed factor matrix—Los Angeles, 1940.

Measures	Predicted			Observed		
	I	II	III	I	II	III
1 Occupation	+	0	0	+	0	0
2 Education	+	0	0	+	0	+
−3 Rent	+	0	0	+	0	0
4 Fertility	0	+	0	0	+	0
−5 WLF	0	+	0	0	+	0
6 SFDU	0	+	0	0	+	0
7 SEG	0	0	+	0	0	+

I Economic Status	WLF Women in the Labor Force
II Family Status	SFDU Single-Family Dwelling Units
III Ethnic Status	SEG Segregation
0 Small Factor Loadings	
+ Large Factor Loadings	

Source: Bell, W., "Economic, Family and Ethnic Status: An Empirical Test." *American Sociological Review* 20 (1955): p. 47. Reprinted with permission of The American Sociological Association.

ing) and that in his factor analysis of Los Angeles's data, twenty of the twenty-one predictions were correct. Three factors were identified that corresponded to the three indexes developed theoretically by Shevky and Bell. Therefore, the three factors do appear to be both adequate and necessary to account for the social differentiation of the social areas of Los Angeles. In other words, each index has been shown to measure a different thing. Bell's factor analysis of the 1940 Census data for the San Francisco Bay Area had similar results.

Van Arsdol, Cammilleri, and Schmid (1958) replicated Bell's research on an additional ten regionally diverse United States cities.[7] The researchers concluded that the Shevky system had high generality for the cities included in their study, although minor variations were observed in the clustering of variables on the three factors.

Social Area Analysis and Behavior

Other studies confirmed the general empirical validity of the Shevky and Bell indexes. However, a more practical question still remained: is the social character of the subareas within a city, as defined by social, family, and ethnic characteristics, useful in predicting individual attitudes and behaviors? Shevky and Bell saw social area analysis not as an end in itself, but as a point of departure for other types of research. First, the authors saw the rigorous and systematic delineation of the subareas of a city as having great descriptive value for social scientists and city planners alike. Second, Shevky and Bell believed the use of the "social area diagram" could have practical benefits in providing a sampling frame for urban research. In other words, the type of behavior taking place in Social Area VII could differ in a predictable way from the behavior in Area III (Shevky and Bell, 1955, pp. 20–22).

A number of researchers subsequently used the social area diagram to study a wide variety of behavior, including voting behavior and neighboring.[8] Their results suggest that the social character of the local areas within a city, as defined by social, family, and ethnic status, is important in predicting individual attitudes and behavior, subcultural patterns, and social organization. Therefore, in terms of pragmatic social research, the indexes and social areas have validity.

Testing the Social Area Theory

Studies by Bell and others focused on the general empirical validity of the three social area indexes. The hypotheses tested were related to the validity of the indexes, not the general validity of the Shevky and Bell theory. Testing the theory's general validity requires examining the theoretical constructs defined in the theory. One possible test of the theory would be to determine whether the theoretical construct "societal scale" and the

Shevky indexes correspond in a predicted way. Simply, changes in the scale of society should be reflected most clearly in the use of space within cities. Therefore, one could argue that for low-scale societies, the characteristics of social, family, and ethnic status are all closely interrelated, whereas in high-scale societies these characteristics separate into independent dimensions. The reason for these differences is the dominance of the extended family in low-scale societies. In such societies the extended family controls most aspects of life. Because more than two generations live together in one dwelling, the variety of lifestyles that characterizes high-scale societies is lacking. In addition, family membership also determines one's social and ethnic status. Thus, family status alone provides an adequate basis for classifying subareas of cities in low-scale societies.

In factor analysis terms, if one were to factor the social area variables for a low-scale society, all the variables should cluster around a single factor reflecting the dominance of the institution of the family. In contrast, in high-scale societies one should find three clusters of variables, each cluster identified by the factors of social, family, and ethnic status.

Many studies have been completed to date on a variety of cities in societies at one end or the other of the development scale. High-scale societies studied include the United States, Canada, countries in Europe, and New Zealand and Australia.[9] Low-scale societies studied include India, Egypt, countries in Africa and Puerto Rico.[10] The quality of data, the number of variables included in the study, the types of cities studied, and the factor technique employed by the researchers differed among the studies. In general, the social and family status factors appear to be the most sensitive to changing societal scale.

THE CONCEPT OF
SOCIETAL SCALE—A CASE STUDY
OF PUERTO RICO

Schwirian and Smith (1974) tested the validity of the concept of societal scale in their factorial study of the internal structure of Puerto Rican cities. They predicted that both high- and low-scale societal factor patterns would be found in the cities on the island. Puerto Rico is a commonwealth of the United States, and it is undergoing the development process. As in many developing countries, the distribution of the urban population is characterized by primacy. Primacy refers to the pattern of cities in which the population of the largest city (primate city) of a nation is much greater than the population of the nation's second largest city. San Juan, like many primate cities, is the main port of the island and is its communication and transportation center. In addition, within its borders are the commonwealth's major religious, educational, and governmental institutions, a major concentration of foreigners and native migrants from the countryside, and most of the island's industry and commerce. These conditions have led to the emergence of a social stratification system similar to that of high-scale societies in which the skills of a person are more important than the prestige of his or her family (Schwirian and Smith, 1974, p. 325). Societies with large primate cities have rates of change that are not uniform across the entire society. Change in social structure first takes place in the primate city, then diffuses outward to the rest of the society. "Therefore, [the] primate city is the first to take on the changing ecological patterning. In effect, in the midst of the development process the primate city becomes ecologically very much like cities in highly developed societies. The smaller more isolated cities maintain their traditional ecological patterns for much longer time periods" (Schwirian and Smith, 1974, p. 326).

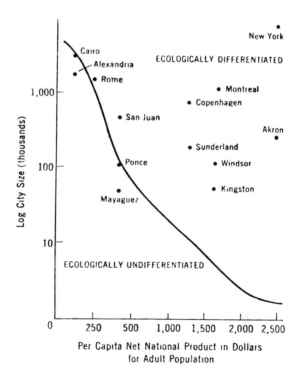

World cities by population size and scale of parent society.

Source: Schwirian, K. P. and Smith, R. K., "Primacy, Modernization and Urban Structure: The Ecology of Puerto Rican Cities." In K. P. Schwirian (Ed.), *Comparative Urban Structure.* Lexington, Mass.: D. C. Heath, 1974, p. 334. Reprinted by permission of Kent P. Schwirian.

Schwirian and Smith conducted a factor analysis of tract data from the 1960 United States Census for San Juan, Ponce, and Mayaguez on six of the Shevky variables (rent was excluded). San Juan and Ponce, the two largest cities on the island, had similar ecological structures. Four rather than three factors emerged from the analysis but it is important to note that social status, family status, and ethnic status factors were identified. The factorial structure for Mayaguez, in contrast, was undifferentiated. All the variables except dwellings correlate with a single factor. These findings, therefore, are consistent with the Shevky theory on societal scale. San Juan, a primate city, is the portal of economic development and therefore is the first to take on the ecological structure of a high-scale society. In the cities outside the region of influence of the primate city, the separation of the variables into three factors disappears and social and family status measures coalesce.

Schwirian and Smith suggest that two points must be taken into consideration in analyzing the ecological structure of cities: (1) the scale of the society containing the city under study and (2) the size of the city in relationship to the country's other cities. They found that in high-scale societies, cities in a wide range of sizes exhibited a complex internal structure that can be described by their social, family, and ethnic status dimensions. Cities in low-scale societies, in contrast, had to be of exceedingly large size before they became internally differentiated along their social area analysis dimensions (see figure above). Smaller cities in these developing nations normally exhibit simple structures that can be described by a single dimension.

Therefore, it seems well established that the emergence and separation of the social area dimensions (social, family, and ethnic status) are closely related to the scale of the society of which the city is a part. The separation of these dimensions in the cities of low-scale societies is tied closely to both the size of the city and its size in relation to the society's other cities. Although few studies have been made of the internal structure of cities in low-scale societies, it is likely that the internal structure of cities in the less-developed world will come to resemble that of the modern metropolis as the process of development continues.

The figure presents a clearer picture of the interrelationships of these variables—ecological structure, societal scale, and city size. The horizontal axis, per capita GNP, is a rough measure of the scale of society; the vertical axis is the city size. Each of the cities is plotted by its population size and by the scale of its parent society. In addition, the ecological structures of these cities have been determined by factorial ecologists in earlier research. This previous research was used as a guide in dividing the graph into two parts. The area above the curve contains those cities with complex ecological structures and the part below contains those cities generally undifferentiated in structure. In general, in low-scale societies only cities of exceedingly large size (primate cities) will have subareas that can be described by the social area analysis dimensions—social, family, and ethnic status. Note the location of Cairo, San Juan, and Rome—large cities in low-scale societies. Alexandria, the second largest city in Egypt, and Ponce and Mayaguez, the second and third largest cities in Puerto Rico, are less differentiated. The other cities are all in high-scale societies and each exhibits a high degree of ecological differentiation. Finally, the shape of the curve itself is interesting. Note that in low-scale societies, cities must be of enormous size before they exhibit complex internal structures, but in high-scale societies, cities of only a few thousand inhabitants will have an internal structure characterized by the three social area analysis dimensions.

In high-scale societies, social and family status factors are independent of each other. The reason is that the family is no longer the dominant all-encompassing institution that it once was. One's social status in adulthood can differ from the status of the family in which one is born. With the waning influence of the family, many lifestyles and living arrangements are possible and subareas of the city specialize to serve the needs of each group. As a result one can have two areas of the city inhabited by people high on the social status dimension but different in their family status.

In contrast, the family is the dominant institution in low-scale societies and this institution touches every aspect of life. The family and social status dimensions are interdependent. In these societies, one normally lives her or his entire life within the same extended family and as a result there are few alternative lifestyles. One's adult social status is normally the same as the family of origin. For these reasons, only one dimension—family status—is needed to rank the subareas in the cities of low-scale societies.

In sum, an enormous body of cross-cultural research has been completed in the past twenty-five years. This research provides general support for social area analysis, which has become a powerful analytical tool in understanding the close relationship between the form of a city and the nature of the encompassing society. In addition, through its judicious use we have gained a better understanding of present and future urban trends.

FACTORIAL ECOLOGY

Today one of the most frequently used ecological approaches in the study of the internal structure of a city is *factorial ecology*. Actually the term factorial ecology refers to a number of different approaches in which factor analysis is used to study small areas (subareas) of cities. Factor analysis is a mathematical technique that summarizes in a small number of factors the underlying similarities in a large set of research data. In social area analysis, factor analysis is limited to seven variables that measure the social, family, racial, and ethnic characteristics of a city's subareas. Factorial ecology, in contrast, is a more general approach made possible in the 1960s as a result of improvements in computer technology. The major difference between the two approaches is that factorial ecology expands the number of variables used in the analysis of a city's subareas from seven to several dozen.

Both factorial ecology and social area analysis relate the structure and form of a city to the scale or level of development of the whole society. Therefore the approaches can be applied to the cities of societies in both less and more developed countries. In addition, these approaches can be used to predict the changes that will occur in the internal structure of cities as societies undergo the development process.

Several problems are inherent in factorial ecology. The results of any factor analysis will vary according to the data used. The number and types of variables included in the analysis, the units of observation (census tracts vs. social planning areas, for example), the time span of the study, and the factorial model used all affect the results. One of the strengths of social area analysis is that the number and types of variables used as well as other parameters are similar from study to study and therefore the results from one study can be compared with those of another. The same is not true of factorial ecology.

Although the number and mix of variables differ among studies, most work in factorial ecology has emphasized the population and housing characteristics of areas; few, if any, measures of the physical and mental characteristics of individuals have been used. In the United States most factorial ecology studies have focused on these two types of variables and used census tracts as the unit of analysis; thus they are generally comparable, unlike most studies of cities outside the United States.

Studies of United States Cities

Irrespective of the number of variables included in factorial studies of United States cities, four types of factors have been reported consistently in the literature. Three of the four dimensions correspond to those drawn from the social area analysis model.[11] First, almost all studies in factorial ecology have identified a single *socioeconomic* factor closely related to Shevky and Bell's social status index. Second, one or more *family status* or lifecycle factors normally are reported. In some research, one factor will identify housing types—single-family or apartment areas of a city—and other factors will identify a cluster of variables associated with the characteristics of the population at various stages of the lifecycle. Third, factors related to the *mobility* or stability of a residential area's population, or the degree to which an area has undergone recent growth or decline in population often have been reported. Fourth, most factorial studies have identified a factor associated with the *segregation* of blacks and recently immigrated ethnic people. Studies that have included large numbers of variables on specific ethnic groups (e.g., the percentage of Italians or Poles) have identified up to five ethnic factors. In the South, a separate segregation factor has not always emerged, because race and socioeconomic status are closely interrelated in that region.

Studies of Cities in Other High-Scale Societies

Factorial studies of Canadian cities show that their structure is described generally by the same factors as the structure of cities in the United States.[12] Studies of Helsinki and Copenhagen have indicated similar factor structures.[13] Socioeconomic status, family status, and mobility factors were identified in Scandinavian cities; ethnicity factors, however, were not identified there, possibly because of the close interrelationship between ethnicity and socioeconomic status or the absence of large numbers of ethnic groups. The factor structure of English cities differs in significant ways from that found in other high-scale Western societies, but the differences are largely due to differences in the census measures and units of analysis employed there (Herbert, 1967; Robson, 1969).

Although the urban structure of the cities in high-scale Western societies can be described in terms of four main factors, one should not assume that socioeconomic status, family status, ethnic status, and mobility provide an unvarying framework for the study of all cities at all times. A detailed analysis of individual studies reveals significant differences in factor structures, reflecting the idiosyncratic characteristics of the society surrounding each city.

Studies of Cities in Low-Scale Societies

In many low-scale non-Western societies, subarea data for cities are unavailable or of questionable quality. Egypt, India and a few other nations do have adequate subarea data. Typically, in these societies the family remains the dominant institution even within the urban milieu. Therefore, social and family status factors coalesce into a single factor. Additional factors have been identified that relate to the concentration of large numbers of single males and ghettoized ethnic groups. The presence of these groups, however, is normally limited to the primate cities of these societies. In general, for social status and family status factors to dissociate from each other, broad changes must occur in the encompassing society—changes associated with the process of modernization.

SUMMARY

This chapter is a detailed review of the origins and evolution of the ecological approaches known as social area analysis and factorial ecology. The dynamic nature of research on the city is demonstrated, beginning with the "natural area" concept introduced more than fifty years ago. This concept, central to the Chicago ecologists' theories of the city, was examined critically by other researchers and was found to have serious theoretical and empirical weaknesses. A more important criticism of the Chicago School was its narrow focus; the theories and models were based on isolated studies of large American cities. The researchers ignored the characteristics of the larger encompassing society, which now are known to contribute to the form and structure of a society's cities.

Social area analysis is a logical extension of the Chicago School's pioneering work. Shevky, Williams, and Bell's work was not only based on but written in response to the works of the Chicago School. Their aim was to place the urbanization process in a broader perspective, linking the internal structure of the city to the nature and scale of the larger society. They envisioned a more practical use for their theory and methods, however—providing a sampling frame for the systematic examination of human behavior in the urban environment.

Factorial ecology is an extension of social area analysis. Though both approaches relate the internal structure of a city to the society at large, factorial ecology involves the use of many dozens of variables in addition to the seven used in social area analysis.

Used as a whole, the Shevky-Williams-Bell approach has been successful. These researchers used three indexes, social, family, and ethnic status to classify social areas of cities. For more than twenty years of research, the social, family, and ethnic status factors, when combined with a mobility factor, have provided the fundamental dimensions for the differentiation of subareas of cities in high-scale societies. In addition, key concepts such as societal scale have been validated by cross-cultural studies of city structure. The dialogue among researchers in this area has shown social area analysis to be very generalizable and relevant to the study of both high- and low-scale societies.

In this chapter the theoretical arguments associated with social area analysis and factorial ecology are presented. The major emphasis is on the close relationship between the structure of the society at large and the use of social space within cities. Chapter 7 explores how the various social areas of a city are organized into distinctive physical patterns.

NOTES

1. In a sense, Zorbaugh (1929) used this approach in his study of the Near North Side of Chicago, *The Gold Coast and the Slum,* reviewed in Chapter 1.

2. George A. Theodorson (1961) has collected many of the more important articles on the natural area concept in a reader, *Studies in Human Ecology*. It would also be valuable to read the early works of McKenzie (1923), Wirth (1928), Zorbaugh (1961), and Burgess (1964) on this topic. A complete citation for each of these works is given in the bibliography.

3. The major criticisms of the natural area concept are found in the works of Alihan (1964), Davie (1961), Form et al. (1954), and Hatt (1946). A complete citation for each of these works is given in the bibliography.

4. The terminology associated with the three social area indexes has changed over the years. For clarity, the terms "social status," "family status," and "ethnic status" are used in this text.

5. This theme is also explored in a number of popularly written books by Vance Packard e.g., *The Waste Makers* (New York: D. McKay Co., 1960) and *The Hidden Persuaders* (New York: D. McKay Co., 1957).

6. The major criticism of social area analysis is found in the works of the following researchers: Duncan (1955), Bell (1955), Hawley and Duncan (1957), and Bell and Greer (1963). Timms (1971), in his book *The Urban Mosaic*, provides a balanced presentation of the strengths and weaknesses of this approach.

7. Van Arsdol, Cammilleri, and Schmid (1958) replicated Bell's research on ten additional regionally diverse United States cities. Factoring six variables—all the original Shevky variables except rent—these researchers found that three factors were necessary to identify the clustering of variables in all ten cities. Moreover, in eight of the ten cities, the factors identified variable clusters identical to those predicted in Bell's earlier article. For two cities, Atlanta and Kansas City, the fertility variable was more highly correlated with the social status factor than with the family status factor. In these researchers' opinion this deviation was the result of these cities' relatively large proportion of blacks, combined with their location in or near the southern region of the United States. "This fact, combined especially with the unfavorable economic position of the Negroes, may indicate that the range of family forms in these cities, as described by the fertility measure, has not become dissociated from social rank" (Van Arsdol, 1958, p. 291). The researchers concluded that the Shevky system had high generality for the cities included in their study although minor variations were observed in the clustering of variables on the three factors.

8. Articles by Bell (1959, 1961, 1965), Bell and Boat (1957), Bell and Force (1956a, 1956b), Greer (1956), Greer and Kube (1959), and Kaufman and Greer (1960) represent research in which the social area diagram is used to study neighboring and other types of behavior.

9. The following is a list of some of the more important factorial studies of cities in high-scale societies—United States cities: Anderson and Bean (1961), Anderson and Egelend (1961), Rees (1970), Van Arsdol et al. (1958); Canadian cities: Berry and Murdie (1969), Murdie (1969), Schwirian and Matre (1974); cities in Europe: McElrath (1962), Herbert (1967), Petersen (1967), Robson (1969), Sweetser (1960, 1965); and cities in New Zealand and Australia: Timms (1971).

10. The following is a list of some of the more important factorial studies of cities in low-scale societies: Indian cities: Berry and Rees (1969), Berry and Spodek (1971); Egyptian cities: Abu-Lugod (1969), Latif (1974); cities in Africa: Clignet and Sween (1969); and Puerto Rican cities: Schwirian and Smith (1974).

11. The variable fertility in two of the ten cities in Van Arsdol's study rated more highly on social status than family status. Schwirian and Smith (1974), in their analysis of Puerto Rican data, reported a four- rather than three-factor solution in two of the three cities in their study. Similar patterns were found by Anderson and Bean in their analysis of data from Toledo, Ohio.
12. The major factorial studies of Canadian cities were conducted by Murdie (1969), Berry and Murdie (1969), and Schwirian and Matre (1974).
13. The major factorial studies of Scandinavian cities were conducted by Sweetser (1960, 1965) and Petersen (1967).

APPENDIX TO
CHAPTER SIX

FACTOR ANALYSIS

The following presentation is a simplified description of a very complicated mathematical technique known as factor analysis. Rather than attempt an explanation of the mathematics of factor analysis, a simpler geometric approach has been used.*

Correlations and Scattergrams

One of the most widely used statistical measures in the social sciences is correlation. A correlation simply tells the researcher whether two or more variables have a certain characteristic in common. A very useful way of portraying a correlation is the scattergram.

Suppose the researcher has a sample of census tracts and wants to find out whether there is a relationship between the size of each census tract (in acres) and the number of inhabitants living in that tract. One way of determining whether there is a relationship between these two variables is to plot the acreage and population of each tract in the sample as points on a graph and then examine the pattern of the points. If the points in the scattergram fall along a straight line running from the bottom left to upper right corner of the graph (see Figure 6A.1), this indicates that there is a direct or positive correlation between a census tract's area (horizontal axis) and its population (vertical axis). In other words, as a tract's area increases, so does its population size. Knowledge of a census tract's size would therefore aid the researcher in predicting its population.

*For an outline of factor analysis for the layman, see Dennis Child, *The Essentials of Factor Analysis* (New York: Holt, Rinehart and Winston, 1970); the more mathematically inclined reader is referred to Rudolph Rummel, "Understanding Factor Analysis," *Journal of Conflict Resolution* 11 (1967):440–80, or Rudolph Rummel, *Factor Analysis* (Evanston, Ill.: Northwestern University Press, 1970).

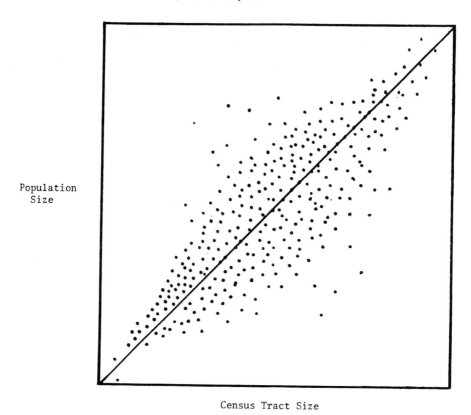

Population
Size

Census Tract Size

Fig. 6A.1 A hypothetical scattergram of points for a positive relationship.

Suppose one were interested in the relationship between the income of a tract's population and the quality of its housing, as measured by the percentage of the tract's housing that is dilapidated and deteriorating. As Figure 6A.2 shows, if the scattergram points cluster along a line running from the upper left to lower right corner of the graph, there is an inverse or negative correlation between the two variables. This means that the higher the income of the tract's population, the lower the percentage of the tract's housing that is dilapidated and deteriorating.

A third type of scattergram is represented in Figure 6A.3, where the points plotted from the scores on two variables, ethnic status and housing quality, display *no* pattern at all. Ethnic status and housing quality are unrelated; knowledge of a tract's ethnic status would not help a researcher predict the quality of its housing.

The way the points are scattered in the graph gives some idea of the sign (positive or negative) and extent of the correlation among the scores of the various tracts on whichever variables are being considered. The problem with using scattergrams is that they are imprecise. If the researcher had scattergrams for any of these sets of variables for two cities, and had

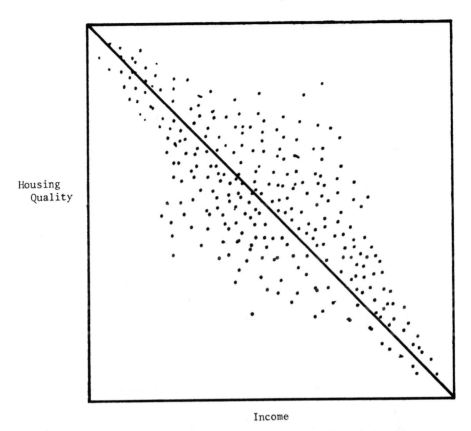

Housing
Quality

Income

Fig. 6A.2 A hypothetical scattergram of points for a negative relationship.

plotted the hundreds of tracts in each city as points by their respective scores on two separate graphs, it would be difficult to say in more than general terms which city had the stronger relationship. To overcome this imprecision, social scientists employ a mathematical measure called the *correlation coefficient.*

A correlation coefficient not only gives the sign of a relationship but also the magnitude of the relationship between two variables. Figure 6A.1 is a hypothetical scattergram in which the points fall along a straight line and indicate a strong positive relationship between census tract size and population. If the points were dispersed on the line, the correlation coefficient would be +1.0: knowledge of a census tract size would permit a perfect prediction of its population. As the points become dispersed from the straight line into a "milky-way" or elliptical pattern, the sign of the relationship remains positive but the strength of the relationship declines and the correlation coefficient takes on values less than +1.0 but greater than 0.0. The shape of the ellipse gives a clue to the size of the correlation. As the scattergram changes from points dispersed on the line to an elliptical

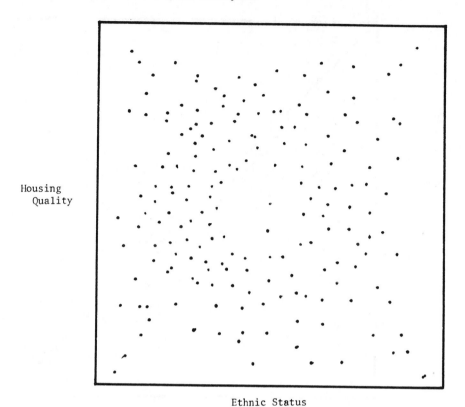

Housing
Quality

Ethnic Status

Fig. 6A.3 A hypothetical scattergram of points for no relationship.

and finally to a circular pattern, the correlation coefficient declines in magnitude, and our ability to predict one score from the other declines. If the scattering of points takes a circular distribution (Figure 6A.3), this means there is no relationship between the variables, and the correlation coefficient would be 0.0. A correlation coefficient can range from -1.0 to $+1.0$. The size of the coefficient gives the strength of the relationship, and the sign indicates the direction of the relationship.

Table 6A.1 gives the correlation coefficients for the seven measures Bell used in his study of Los Angeles. Each value in the matrix summarizes the scattergrams of the 570 census tracts included in his study. Bell found that the correlation coefficient between occupation and education was $+.730$, which indicates a fairly strong positive relationship. As the occupational prestige of Los Angeles's census tracts increases, so does the level of education. In fact the remaining correlations in this column are all positive, varying in the magnitude of their relationship with occupation. In scanning the entire table, one sees that there are only a few negative coefficients. The variable single-family dwelling units (SFDU) in column 6 and the variable segregation in row 7 are negatively related but only weakly. In other

Table 6A.1
Correlation matrix for the seven measures in Bell's 1940 Los Angeles study.

Measures	1 Occ.	2 Educ.	−3 Rent	4 Fert.	−5 WLF	6 SFDU	7 SEG
1 Occupation							
2 Education	.730						
−3 Rent	.710	.696					
4 Fertility	.810	.650	.538				
−5 WLF	.560	.277	.311	.690			
6 SFDU	.373	.047	.049	.560	.680		
7 SEG	.319	.649	.356	.383	−.063	−.030	

WLF Women in the Labor Force
SFDU Single-Family Dwelling Units
  SEG Segregation

Source: Bell, W. "Economic, Family and Ethnic Status: An Empirical Test." *American Sociological Review* 20 (1955): p. 46. Reprinted with permission of The American Sociological Association.

words, as the percentage of single-family dwelling units increases, the size of the black and other ethnic populations decreases, but this relationship is a weak one. If the values of these two variables were plotted for Los Angeles's census tracts the resulting "swarm" of points would be in a nearly circular pattern.

These simple correlation coefficients show how pairs of variables are related across a city's census tracts, but they do not show whether there is an underlying relationship among clusters of variables. This information can be obtained by means of factor analysis. To carry out a factor analysis, one must first represent each correlation graphically as a vector.

Vectors A vector is simply a line on a graph with both direction and magnitude. The magnitude of a vector is simple to calculate. A line of unit length is chosen—say, one inch—as a standard for the entire study. The correlation between occupation and education (.730) could be represented as a line segment 73/100 of an inch long. Similarly, the correlation between segregation and occupation (.319) could be represented as a line 32/100 of an inch long.

The second element of a vector is direction, which can be represented as an angle on a set of polar coordinates. A polar coordinate system is two perpendicular axes that divide a 360-degree circle into four equal quadrants of 90 degrees. Starting with 0 degrees on the X-axis in quadrant I, each successive quadrant in a counterclockwise direction identifies a different 90-degree segment, 0–90, 90–180, 180–270, 270–360 (see Figure 6A.4). The direction of the vector in this polar coordinate system can be determined by calculating the arc cosine of the correlation coefficient. The coefficient between occupation and education (.730) can be represented graphically

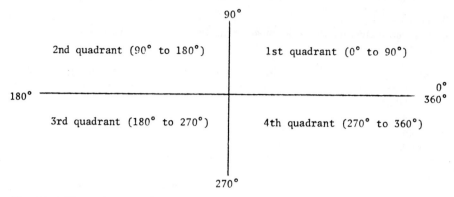

Fig. 6A.4 The polar coordinate system.

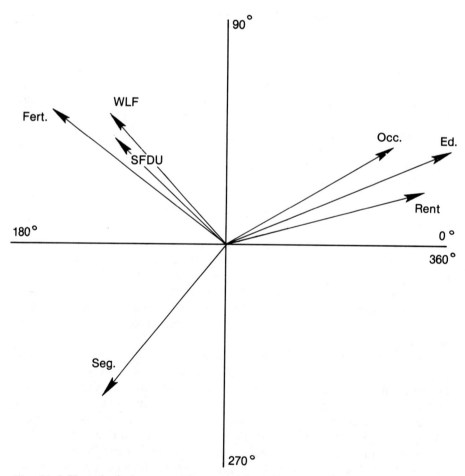

Fig. 6A.5 Hypothetical pattern of vectors of coefficients in Table 6A.1.

Table 6A.2
Bell's rotated factor matrix—Los Angeles, 1940.

Measures	I	II	III
1 Occupation	(.482)	.193	−.094
2 Education	(.319)	−.044	.282
−3 Rent	(.653)	−.192	−.189
4 Fertility	.109	(.562)	.176
−5 WLF	.148	(.617)	−.193
6 SFDU	−.147	(.727)	.015
7 SEG	−.109	.044	(.576)

I Economic Status	WLF Women in the Labor Force
II Family Status	SFDU Single-Family Dwelling Units
III Ethnic Status	SEG Segregation

Source: Bell, W., "Economic, Family and Ethnic Status: An Empirical Test." *American Sociological Review* 20 (1955): p. 47. Reprinted with permission of The American Sociological Association.

by a line 73/100 of an inch long at an angle of 43 degrees from the X-axis in quadrant I. The length of the vector gives the magnitude, and the angle gives the sign and direction of the relationship. If this process were continued for all the coefficients in Table 6A.1, a pattern similar to Figure 6A.5 would result. Once the vectors for each of the coefficients in the matrix have been projected, all that factor analysis does is search for bundles of vectors from which a reference axis or factor vector can be projected.

One reference axis is projected for each cluster of variables identified. The specific variables or variable clusters that are associated with a particular reference axis are determined by their loadings on each of the factors. A loading can range from −1.0 to +1.0 and can be interpreted in much the same way as correlation coefficients; it shows how closely a variable is related to a factor. Another interpretation is that loadings simply indicate how close a vector representing a correlation coefficient is to a factor or reference axis. A good analogy would be a partially opened umbrella; the rod to which the handle is attached is the factor vector or reference axis and the metal ribs to which the fabric is attached are the variable vectors. The loadings in Table 6A.2 indicate how close the ribs are to the central rod. If the factor umbrella were closed, the variables would be in a tight cluster and the loadings would be very high. (The higher the loading, the closer the vector is to the reference axis.) If the factor umbrella of vectors were completely open, the variable vectors would be far away from the reference axis and so the loadings would be low and near zero.

CHAPTER SEVEN

The Use of Space Within Urban Areas

Statement of Objectives

1. The importance of the work of Robert Park and other members of the Chicago School and its impact on the study of cities' internal structure should be noted.

2. The student should know and be able to give examples of these terms: dominance, competition, invasion, and succession.

3. The student should understand the theory of rents and its relationship to the classical theories of urban land usage.

4. The three classical theories of urban land usage should be understood by the student and seen as both explanations of urban land usage and as methodological tools.

5. The student should review the tests of Burgess's concentric zone model and note the continued impact of this theory on contemporary studies of the city.

6. The student should analyze the factors that influence a family's decision to move and assess the impact of high interest rates, inflated housing costs, and increasing energy costs on the decision-making process.

7. The student should recognize the factors that influence a person's search for a new home.

Chapter 6 provides a broad overview of the ecological approaches known as social area analysis and factorial ecology that link the internal structure of a city with the character and form of the larger encompassing society. However, Shevky and Williams (1949) and Shevky and Bell (1955), who introduced these terms, were concerned mainly with the nature of cities' social space, and Shevky and Bell used social area analysis to provide a framework for behavioral studies (p. 22). Although their books included maps showing the location of various subareas in the cities of Los Angeles and San Francisco, Shevky, Williams, and Bell provide little or no explanation of why one subarea type was concentrated at a city's center and another type at its periphery.

The maps do show that social differences existed between subareas of these cities and that social distance was reflected in the physical distance between them. In general, the farther apart two areas were on the social area diagram the farther apart they also were physically. This finding is not new, for as long as humankind has lived in cities, groups have been physically separated. In the preindustrial city, an internal set of walls was erected to form wards and precincts, ghettoizing Jews and other groups. Walls are not erected in the cities of high-scale industrial societies, but barriers still exist. "Living on the wrong side of the tracks" is an example of a popular saying that reflects the existence of important symbolic barriers in modern cities. Moreover, physical distance alone limits the contact between groups, reinforcing the social barriers that Shevky, Williams, and Bell identified as social status, family status, and ethnic status.

It is remarkable that land use patterns in cities are the result of millions of locational decisions made over the life of a city. These decisions are made by individuals, business, and industry in their search for space. Together these decisions determine the broad outline of land uses within a city. Moreover, past decisions determine present urban structure and hence the number of locations available for specific land uses. A decision made by a city's leaders in locating a dump, for instance, will preclude the use of adjacent land for other purposes, say, high-priced residences.

The purpose of this chapter is to explore the use of physical space within cities. In the first half of the chapter, general theories of location are examined including the three classical theories of urban land usage—Burgess's concentric zone theory, Hoyt's sector theory, and Harris and Ullman's multiple nuclei theory. This part of the discussion emphasizes not the individual, but the ecological processes that bring about the ordering of the urban landscape. In addition, the classical theories are related to the social area analysis approach.

The individual is the focus of the second half of the chapter. Ecological processes are the sum of many individual decisions, and some individuals because of their wealth or political power may have a profound impact on the spatial patterns of a city. An individual may choose to finance the building of a shopping center on the city's periphery, or, as the executive of a bank, may decide to limit loans to central-city neighborhoods. These decisions are direct and the consequences of their actions often highly visible.

In other cases, individual decision-making is more subtle and less easily observed. For example, the decision of a minority member to move into a white neighborhood or the decision of a white resident to move elsewhere is not significant in itself. But when these decisions are combined with hundreds of similar decisions the ecological process known as invasion-succession results. The second half of this chapter is a review of the research on how individuals make decisions about where to live within a city. Interestingly, although these decisions are made by individuals of different backgrounds, the decisions when combined lead to general land use patterns that correspond to the general models analyzed in the first half of the chapter.

THEORIES OF RESIDENTIAL LOCATION

The Chicago School's Theory of Residential Location

As noted in Chapter 1, the study of human ecology at the University of Chicago in the early decades of this century was profoundly influenced by the works of Darwin and the early plant and animal ecologists. As shown in Chapter 1, Park not only applied the method and the theories of plant and animal ecologists to the study of urban phenomena, but also used much of their terminology. Concepts such as invasion, succession, dominance, and symbiosis had much the same meaning for both biological ecologists and the early human ecologists. The central organizing concept for both fields was "competition." Park states:

> Competition which is the fundamental organizing principle in the plant and animal community, plays a scarcely less important role in the human community. In the plant and animal community it has tended to bring about (1) an orderly distribution of the population and (2) a differentiation of the species within the habitat. The same principles operate in the case of human population (Park, 1952, p. 109).

In other words, species of plants and animals in nature are locked in a process of impersonal competition. Within the habitat a species of plant initially competes with other species as well as with members of its own kind for the environment's scarce resources—minerals in the soil, water, air, and light. Competition leads to a process of natural selection, whereby some species of plants become dominant and other species take subordinate positions in the habitat. Implicit in this analysis is the idea that within the community certain species are segregated from others and that this segregation is the result of the process of natural selection. A clue to the basis of the segregation process can be found by examining the groups that have *dominance* within a community, because the character of the dominant group determines the basic form of the entire community. The tallest tree in the forest, for example, forces other plant species to take subordinate positions. However, ferns need the filtered light that tall trees provide in order to survive, and thus a mutually beneficial or "symbiotic" relationship is established. As the process of competition continues through time, a balance or a "natural economy" develops within this community. Each species either finds its own ecological niche or ceases to exist. The species that remain each use different parts of the habitat and, rather than competing, they complement each other—a true interdependence emerges.

Applying the Biological Model to the City

The appeal of this biological model to Park and others is understandable. Here were impersonal yet rational forces that accounted for much of the natural world. Competition, which had been identified as the key to understanding the natural world, was viewed as crucial in analyzing the sorting of groups and institutions into homogeneous subareas of cities. *Competition* within the context of a city was interpreted as a struggle by individuals for advantageous locations in geographic space, and an individual's success was determined by land values and the ability of individuals to pay rents. Thus Park defined competition narrowly—as economic competition. By this interpretation, the location within a city of ethnic, racial, and economic groups and the degree of their concentration are the result of these groups' ability to cope with such competition. The dominants in a city—usually business and industry—are able to pay the highest rents, and their concentration at the city's center (the area of highest land values) determines the form of the entire community. The location of all other groups is based both on the ability of individuals in each area to pay rents and their location with respect to the dominants. For example, it is unlikely that individuals of high socioeconomic status would choose to live downwind from a steel mill, whereas the poor may have no choice.

The dominance-competition framework and other ecological processes What struck these ecologists was the fact that cities were composed of a complex aggregation of individuals, heterogeneous in their income, racial, ethnic, and family characteristics. Through time the operation of unplanned ecological processes contributed to the emergence of areas that were homogeneous in social, family, and ethnic status characteristics. There was broad agreement among the Chicago ecologists that economic factors such as the cost of transportation and rents were responsible for the sorting of individuals into general areas of a city, e.g., the central city and the suburbs. Some members of the Chicago School, however, felt that the differentiation of these general areas into homogeneous natural areas could not be explained by economic factors alone. These ecologists pointed to other factors such as ethnic and racial identity, and to the space and housing needs of individuals and families (stage in the lifecycle) as important elements in this sorting process.

Regardless of the qualification made by some ecologists, the dominance-

*"Excuse me, sir, I am prepared to make you a rather
attractive offer for your square."*

Source: Drawing By Weber; © 1971 The New York Magazine, Inc. Reprinted by permission.

competition framework proved useful in understanding other ecological processes, such as invasion and succession. *Invasion* is the movement of an incompatible population or type of land use into a previously stable natural area of a city. Heavy industry moving into a stable residential area would be an example of this process. Conversely, *succession* is the displacement of a resident population or type of land use into other areas of a city by an invading group. The dominant population and institutions in a city are the only groups that have true freedom of location. In the absence of zoning laws, if the dominant groups decide to move into a stable subarea of a city, they are financially able to do so. The encroachment of an incompatible population or type of land use into a previously stable area normally upsets the equilibrium of that area. Stability returns only after the old uses of the area have been replaced by the new. As the original population is forced out or enters another area, they become the invaders, and a domino effect or chain reaction may occur in other parts of the city. The city, therefore, is in a continuous process of change as various types of land use compete for the most favorable location with respect to lines of transportation and markets.

Theory of Rents

Competition among individuals or different types of land use for favorable locations within a city has so far been likened to competition among species in a plant community. In this discussion, such words as "natural economy," "economic competition," and "rents" have been used. This terminology suggests that underlying Park's ecological analysis are some implicit assumptions about the economics of land use. To Park there was a close relationship between accessibility to a city's center and urban land values. This relationship is called the "theory of rents." A simplified explanation of this theory follows.[1]

Limiting assumptions   The theory of rents explains the location of a type of land use in terms of its ability to outbid all other types of land use for a particular site. Several limiting assumptions are associated with the theory: (1) the city under study is built on a flat plain with no major rivers or bluffs to distort its shape, and the city is isolated with no competing cities nearby; (2) the city's center provides the only market for manufactured goods, and industry in turn provides employment for the city residents; and (3) because the terrain is flat, transportation costs are the same in all directions from the city's center, and transportation costs increase with distance. If these assumptions are met, then the bidding process involves only two factors, the value of the commodity for sale and the cost of transporting the commodity to market. (Situations in which these conditions are not met will be discussed in Chapter 8.)

A hypothetical example   Assume that there are three factories in a hypothetical city, all manufacturing typewriters. The cost of producing these typewriters—labor, raw materials, and equipment—is the same no matter where the plants are located. The costs of land and transportation vary with location, however. Suppose that the three typewriter plants in this city are of the same size, covering one acre, and each plant has the same output. The only difference among them is their location: plant A is closest to the city's center, plant B is next closest, and plant C the farthest away (see Figure 7.1). If the price for typewriters at the only marketplace at the city's center is the same for all three factories, then their gross or total incomes will be identical, but their real incomes will differ. Why? Because the costs of transporting their finished products to market differ. A is closest to the market, its transportation cost is the lowest, and its real income is highest. B, farther away from the marketplace, has higher transportation cost and less real income, and so on.

If all three plants have the same cost of production and operate at the

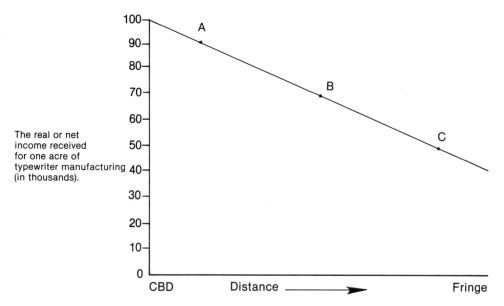

The slope of the rent curve in this figure is steep because typewriters are heavy, bulky, and expensive to transport to the central market. The high value of typewriters and the high cost of transporting them to market suggest that a location near the market is crucial for this industry.

Fig. 7.1 Rent curve for typewriter manufacturing.

same efficiency, and each plant expects the same profit, the difference in transportation costs must be offset by the rents for land. A is in a position to pay much more in rent than C because A's transportation cost is lower. This relationship is shown in Figure 7.1. The line in this figure is a rent curve illustrating that the rent for urban land decreases with distance from the city's center. The slope (steepness) of the line depends on transportation cost. In this example, as transportation cost increases, rent decreases.

Transportation costs are the key to this analysis of rents (in the real world many other factors also influence location), but transportation costs vary not only with distance but also with the weight and size of the commodity being shipped. In general, the larger and bulkier the good, the more difficult and expensive it is to transport and the steeper the slope of the rent curve.

Consider a second type of manufactured good—handheld calculators. Again, three manufacturers have plants of the same size (one acre), the same costs of production, the same output, and the same level of productivity; they differ only in their location within the city. Assume also that calculators sell for less than typewriters. If typewriter and calculator manufacturers have the same output, say 1,000 units, the total income for each acre of urban land in calculator manufacturing will be less than for that in typewriter manufacturing. Although calculators are less valuable than typewriters, they are inexpensive to transport, and their rent curve is less steep than the one for typewriters. The slope of this curve suggests that location near a city's center is less crucial than for typewriter manufacturing (see Figure 7.2).

The ability of a manufacturer to bid successfully for a particular location with respect to a city's center is determined by the slope (the steepness) of the rent curve and the market price for the commodity. Those activities with the steepest curves will be closest to the center, provided that their commodity price is the highest. The flatter the curve, the more likely it is that the activity will be at the city's periphery, if the price for the commodity is low. This pattern is evident in Figure 7.3 where the rent curves for typewriters and calculators are superimposed. At any distance from a city's center (horizontal axis) the activity with the highest price for its production (vertical axis) can outbid all other activities for a site. In this graph, a typewriter manufacturer could outbid a calculator manufacturer for a site anywhere between 0 and F_1, and calculator manufacturers win by bidding anywhere between points F_1 and F_2.

Testing the Theory of Rents

To carry out this type of analysis for each of the thousands of different land uses in a city would be impossible. Land uses can be aggregated into

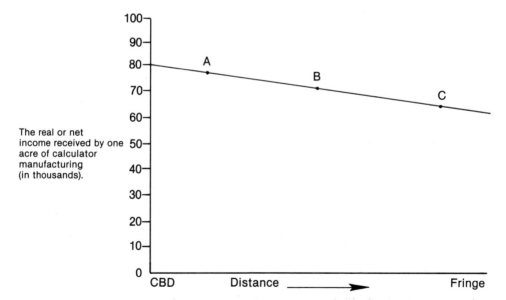

The value of the annual output of a calculator manufacturer is less than the annual output of a typewriter manufacturer, but because calculators are small and light they are inexpensive to transport to market. The flat slope of the curve suggests that transportation costs are low and that a central location for calculator manufacturing is not important.

Fig. 7.2 Rent curve for calculator manufacturing.

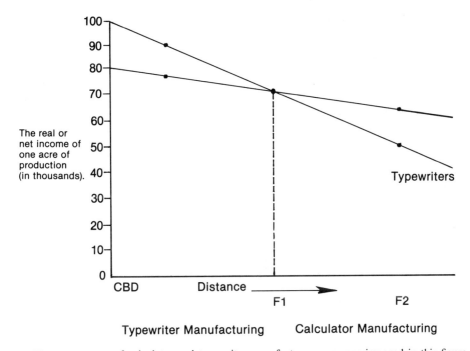

Typewriter Manufacturing   Calculator Manufacturing

The rent curves of calculator and typewriter manufacturers are superimposed in this figure. The amount each can afford to pay for rent is a function of the value of the commodity for sale and the cost of transportation. Typewriters are more valuable than calculators and are more expensive to transport to market; thus the typewriter manufacturer can outbid calculator manufacturers for any location from the central business district of a city to F_1. The opposite is true for calculator manufacturers from F_1 to F_2. Thus, the production activity with the highest curve at any distance from the central business district can theoretically outbid all other activities for the location.

Fig. 7.3 Curves for typewriter and calculator manufacturing.

general types, however, and the most common typology includes residential; manufacturing and industrial; commercial; streets, roads, and highways; public and semipublic land; and vacant land. In the most recent survey of land uses in American cities, 39 percent of all developed land was in residential usage, nearly 20 percent in streets and highways, 20 percent in public use, 11 percent in manufacturing and industry, and 4.8 percent in commercial usage. Interestingly, in this study of forty-eight large American cities, more than one-fourth of all urban land was vacant.[2] If rents decrease with distance, the location and concentration of these various activities in relation to a city's center will give some indication of the nature of their rent curves. The more centralized the activity (the closer the activity is to the city's center, on the average), the more important accessibility to the city's center is to this activity, i.e., the steeper the slope of the rent curve.

The spatial distribution of land uses A study by Browning (1964) analyzing land uses in Chicago provides the basic data needed to test such a rela-

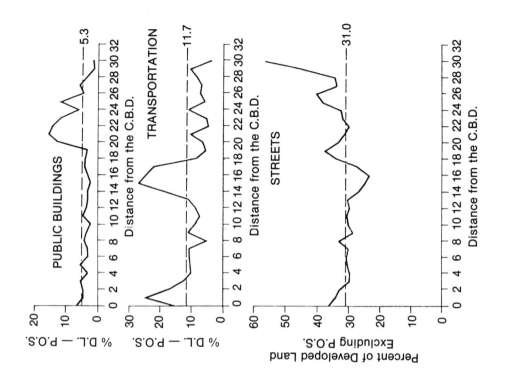

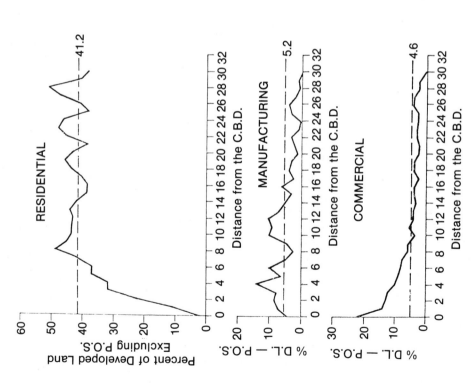

tionship. Browning used roughly the same land use categories as Niedercorn and Hearle (1964) but added a separate category for transportation activities that includes airports, rail yards, and the like. Browning mapped concentric zones for a city, each zone one mile wide, and then calculated the percentage of the developed land for each type of land use. Consistent with Niedercorn and Hearle's findings, residential use consumed the greatest percentage of the total land in Chicago, 41.2 percent; commercial uses were among the lowest, 4.8 percent. These activities, however, were not evenly dispersed across the city. Within two miles of the city's center less than 20 percent of the land was in residential use but within the city's center itself there was almost no residential usage; most of this land was occupied by streets, commercial activities, and transportation facilities. Figure 7.4 shows this relationship graphically. The peaks of the curves for transportation and commerce show that most of these activities are concentrated in or near the central business district (CBD). This pattern suggests that over time these activities have outbid all others for central locations. Manufacturing and residential activities have been less competitive because the curves of these activities peak at points away from the CBD.

Rents assessed through demand for land The land use mixes as measured by distance from the CBD give an indication of the slope of the rent curves. Another way of assessing demand for land and the rents paid is to measure the percentage of land either vacant or in nonurban or agricultural usage at different distances from the CBD. The higher the percentage of the land developed, the higher the demand and the higher the land rents. Figure 7.5 shows this relationship graphically. Between the CBD and a zone beginning at eight miles, 90 percent or more of the land is developed, largely for commercial, manufacturing, transportation, and other nonresidential uses. Outward, the proportion of developed land drops steadily. In the zone at

---

The figure opposite shows the land-use mixes at various distances from Chicago's central business district. The horizontal axis is distance (in miles) from the Chicago central business district (CBD); the vertical axis is the percentage of developed land in the activity. The fact that the residential curve does not peak until eight miles from the CBD indicates that other uses outbid this activity for central sites. Thereafter, it remains high, over 42 percent on the average, to the city's periphery. The commercial curve, in contrast, drops steadily to the ten-mile ring where it becomes relatively constant at about 4 percent. The manufacturing curve is interesting because it is irregular, having two peaks, one four to six miles and the other ten to twelve miles from the city's center. The second peak reflects the emergence of specialized manufacturing in Chicago's suburban ring. Finally, the curve for transportation land uses also is irregular with much of this activity concentrated near the city's center; the large hump on the graph at fourteen miles indicates the location of Chicago's O'Hare Field, the second busiest airport in the world. In general, these curves are supportive of the analysis of the theory of rents.

Fig. 7.4 Proportion of land in use by category.
Source: Browning, C. E., "Selected Aspects of Land Use and Distance from the City Center: The Case of Chicago." *Southeastern Geographer* 4 (1964), pp. 34–35.

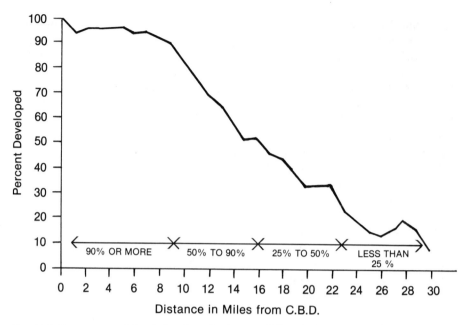

Fig. 7.5 Percentage of land developed, measured by distance from CBD.

Source: Browning, C. E., "Selected Aspects of Land Use and Distance from the City Center: The Case of Chicago." *Southeastern Geographer* 4 (1964), pp. 34–35.

twenty-three miles, 25 percent or less of the land is developed—much of this land is in agricultural usage.

The theoretical location of various land uses   To summarize the discussion of the theory of rents, rent curves for the different land use activities are combined in a single graph, Figure 7.6. Commerce has the steepest curve and therefore receives the highest price for its outputs, but it requires high accessibility to the city's central markets. The fact that the transportation and manufacturing curve is less steep indicates that accessibility is less important. The same type of analysis can be made for each activity. Remember that the curve with the highest value on the vertical axis (ability to pay rents) at any given distance from the CBD could theoretically outbid all other uses for that location. Lines drawn from the point where two curves intersect to the X-axis indicate where different activities theoretically would locate. This patterning is consistent with that based on the hypo-thetical city described previously.

Now suppose that this graph is rotated 360° forming a solid cone-shaped figure. Looking down on this graph one would see a series of concentric zones resembling Figure 7.7. In the center is the central business district, the point of greatest accessibility from anywhere within the city and the space with the highest land values. As distance increases, land values

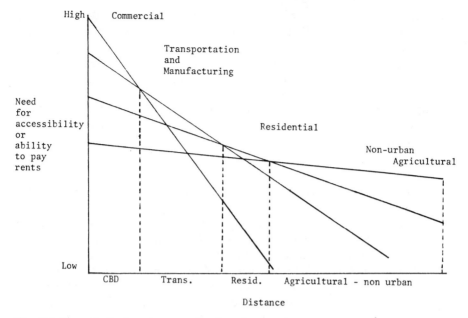

Fig. 7.6 Hypothetical rent curves for four land uses.

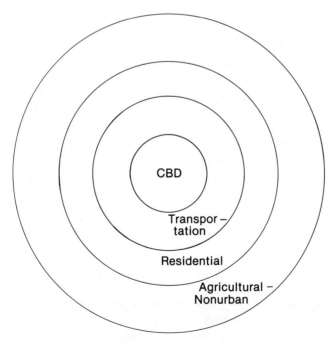

Fig. 7.7 The concentric zone pattern that results from rotating Figure 7.6, hypothetical rent curves for four land uses.

decline to the outermost zone, the zone where agriculture can compete successfully for land with urban activities. These series of zones closely resemble a general model of urban land use known as the "concentric zone theory" presented by a member of the Chicago School, Ernest Burgess, in 1925. In the following section this theory and two others, Homer Hoyt's "sector theory" published in 1939 and C. D. Harris and E. L. Ullman's "multiple nuclei theory" published in 1945, are examined. Each researcher posits a somewhat different explanation of why specific activities locate at different points in urban space.

CLASSICAL THEORIES OF URBAN LAND USAGE

Three points must be made before the general theories of urban land usage are considered. First, each theory is based on "ideal constructs" or a set of generalizations about land use patterns. Because the theories were designed to be general and to describe patterns in many cities, no one city will fit the models perfectly. Second, the theories are based on patterns found in American cities and they do not necessarily describe land use patterns of cities in other parts of the world. Finally, all three theories are concerned with ecological change or how the spatial patterns of cities change as the city grows.

Burgess' Concentric Zone Theory

The Burgess theory, first published in 1925, was one of the first attempts to describe and explain general urban land use patterns. Burgess posited that land uses in the modern city assume a pattern of concentric zones. These zones are ideal constructs, and no city will fit the pattern exactly because physical barriers such as rivers, ravines, and hills distort each zone. Major transportation lines further divide the zones into segments. Nevertheless, the distribution of land usage into zones closely resembles the pattern derived from the theory of rents as shown in Figure 7.7. The close relationship between the theory of rents and the concentric zone theory is seen by comparing Figure 7.7 with Figure 7.8 reprinted from the original Burgess article. A brief description of each zone in Figure 7.8 follows.

Zone I Zone I, the central business district or CBD, is the zone that has the greatest accessibility from any point within the city. High accessibility means high demand for land and only those activities that need a central location and can afford the high land costs are located here. Skyscrapers, department stores, hotels, restaurants, theaters, and specialty stores occupy Zone I. It is an area of retail trade, office and service facilities, light manufacturing, and commercialized recreation.

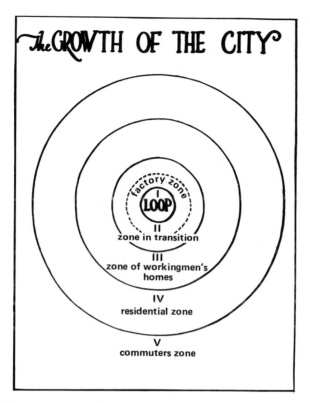

Fig. 7.8 The Burgess concentric zone model.

Source: Park, R. E., Burgess, E., and McKenzie, R. *The City.* Chicago: The University of Chicago Press, p. 55, Chart II. Reprinted with permission of The University of Chicago Press.

Zone II The zone surrounding the CBD is the zone of transition. Unlike the CBD, the zone of transition is residential, populated by groups lower on the socioeconomic scale, immigrants, and rural migrants. The Near North Side described in Zorbaugh's book *The Gold Coast and the Slum* was in this zone and, except for a small enclave of wealthy people along Lake Michigan, the majority of its population lived in poverty. Interestingly, the land usage in this zone deviates from the type one would expect on the basis of the theory of rents. Theoretically, the proximity of this zone to the CBD should cause the rents in the area to be among the highest in the city; however, its rents are among the lowest. The problem with the theory of rents as an explanation of land usage is that it assumes competition is impersonal. In human societies competition is not entirely impersonal. It is limited by custom and the culture of the larger society. The character of the zone of transition is the result of investors speculating on the future use of the land in the area. Zone II is in the path of business and industrial expansion. Investors buy land in this zone hoping that business and industry will invade the area and buy their property at a much higher price. Because

Photo 7.1 The Concentric Zone Model hypothesized by Burgess is vividly shown in this photograph. Note that the downtown highrise buildings are surrounded by the multistory buildings of the Zone of Transition. In the foreground is the densely settled Zone of Workingmen's Homes. Not shown in this photograph but farther out from the CBD are the Zone of Middle-class Homes and the Commuter Zone.

Source: © Elliott Erwitt, Magnum Photos, Inc., from the book *Crisis in America* published by Ridge Press and Holt, Rinehart & Winston.

the investors expect the structures they own to be torn down, they have little incentive to pay for their upkeep. The result is blight, and slum conditions prevail as in the Near North Side studied by Zorbaugh. Since the 1920s the rundown housing in that area has been razed and the land has been incorporated into the Loop, the central business district of Chicago.

Zone III The zone of working people's homes is superior in physical appearance to the zone of transition, but in size and quality its houses fall short of those in middle- and upper-class residential zones. Individuals who live in this zone have relatively low incomes. In comparison with wealthier families, they pay a larger part of their total budget for transportation costs. Low-income working families therefore tend to live near their place of employment in or near the CBD. This area also has a large number of neighborhoods made up of second-generation immigrants to the city, people who have escaped the slum conditions of the zone of transition but have not yet joined the ranks of the middle class.

Zone IV The zone of middle-class homes is the residential area of clerical and managerial people, professionals, and owners of small businesses. The higher incomes of this group permit them to absorb higher transportation costs and therefore escape the noise and pollution of more centrally located housing.

Zone V The commuter zone is the area of satellite towns and suburbs, sometimes thirty or forty miles from the CBD in large cities, and normally acting as bedroom communities outside the political boundaries of the central city. In Burgess's time these were the communities served by commuter railroads that carried some commuters thirty to forty miles to the CBD for employment. Because of the high transportation costs, this area is beyond the reach of most residents of the city and it is therefore limited mainly to the wealthy.

The dynamic nature of the theory The foregoing description of the concentric zone theory shows how closely it is related to the theories of the Chicago School. The concentration of the dominant groups in the CBD is the key to the entire model. Burgess noted that as a city grows, so too does the demand for land at the city's center. Through time the CBD expands, invading the adjoining zone of transition, taking over this land for nonresidential usage. Because the property in this area is largely renter-occupied, landlords can turn over their property quickly by simply evicting their tenants. The people displaced by the invading land uses must have housing, so they move outward into Zone III and the ecological process of invasion and succession continues outward toward the periphery of the city. Burgess, therefore, conceived his theory as a dynamic one that describes the process of city growth and differentiation over time. As a city grows, it must reorganize spatially and, although transportation lines, rivers, and hills introduce distortions, Burgess believed that a concentric pattern of land usage was discernible in all cities in the United States.

The Burgess theory, although first introduced more than fifty years ago, still is of great interest to students of the city. Literally hundreds of articles have been written to interpret, test, and refute the model. Reasons for this interest are numerous, but among the most important is the fact that Burgess's theory, unlike the works of Hoyt (1939) and Harris and Ullman (1945), is part of a more general theory of the city. Equally important is the fact that it was the first to be published and thus provided a point of departure for other researchers. The theories of Hoyt and of Harris and Ullman were written in response to Burgess's theory.

Hoyt's Sector Theory

The sector theory was an outgrowth of a study conducted by Homer Hoyt (1939) for the Federal Housing Administration during the Depression years of the 1930s. The study was an intensive analysis of the internal residential structure of 142 American cities, and it involved calculating the average residential rental values for each block of every city in the sample. By representing these data graphically on a map as in Figure 7.9, Hoyt found that the general spatial pattern of cities in the United States could be characterized best by sectors rather than concentric zones. Hoyt's study uncovered other important differences from the patterns suggested by the concentric zone theory. Industrial areas tended to develop along river valleys, waterways, and railroad lines rather than around the CBD. Moreover, a significant amount of this industry was at the city's periphery rather than near its center. In addition, the highest-rent areas were not in the last concentric zone but in one or more sectors usually on one side of the city. In general, these high-rent sectors were along the major axial transportation lines, which provided the residents easy access to the city's center. Low-rent areas, in contrast, tended to be more centrally located near the CBD, often in or directly opposite the highest-rent sectors. Middle-income rental areas were generally on either side of the highest rental areas or on the peripheries of low-rent residential sectors (Hoyt, 1939, pp. 72–76).

How Hoyt's theory operates On the basis of these empirical findings Hoyt rejected the concentric zone theory and proposed his sector theory. As in the case of Burgess's work, Hoyt's theory was dynamic, designed to predict where the city will expand as it grows. The key to Hoyt's theory was the changing location of the city's dominant groups—the wealthy. In his analysis of housing rents, Hoyt discovered that, the high-rent neighborhoods

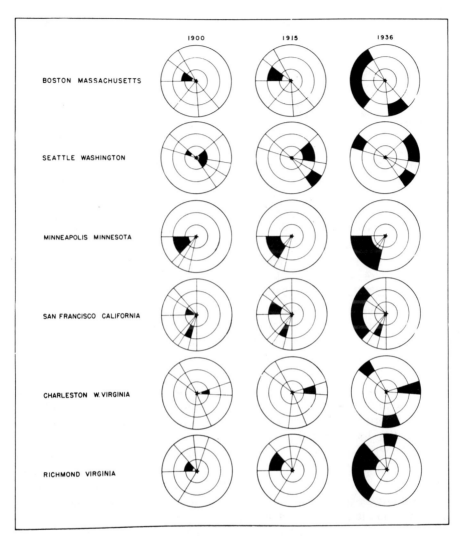

This figure from Hoyt's original 1939 work shows the shift of high-rent areas at three time intervals. Note that in most cases high-rent districts have moved from the interior of a sector to its periphery. According to Hoyt this movement was made necessary by the growth of commerce and industry in or adjacent to the central business district. It was made possible by an improved automobile technology.

Fig. 7.9 Shifts in location of fashionable residential areas in six American cities, 1900–1936 (fashionable residential areas indicated by solid black).

Source: Hoyt, H., "The Structure and Growth of Residential Neighborhoods in American Cities." Washington, D.C.: Federal Housing Administration, 1939, p. 115, Figure 40.

of the city do not skip around at random in the process of movement—
they follow a definite path in one or more sectors of the city (Hoyt, 1939,
p. 76) (see Figure 7.9). These sectors, besides being along established
transportation lines, also tended to develop on high ground, free from the
risk of floods, or along lake or river fronts not in use by industry. In
addition, high-rent residential areas tended to expand toward open country
and away from dead-end sections of the city. In general, high-rent areas
initially are near the CBD, but as the CBD expands and industry grows
the wealthy abandon these neighborhoods to escape the noise, traffic, and
pollution. As this group moves outward in the same sector toward the
newer areas at the periphery of the city, their former homes are taken over
by members of groups lower on the socioeconomic scale. These homes are
often large and multistoried and prohibitively expensive to maintain as
single-family dwellings by anyone but the wealthy. However, they are easily
converted into flats and apartments for rental purposes. Because of the age
and character of this housing as well as its proximity to the CBD, it is
typically investor-owned and is used as described in the discussion of the
zone of transition (Hoyt, 1939, pp. 72–76).

According to the sector theory, the sorting of various income groups in
the city occurs in the following way. The wealthy consume the best land—
the high ground in the open areas of the city along major transportation
lines. The low-income groups have few or no housing alternatives and either
consume the obsolete housing of the wealthy or live in other undesirable
areas. The largest group, the working- and middle-income people, consume
the remaining residential areas of the city. In sum, the theory predicts that
cities will grow axially or in only one or two directions at any one time
and that the location and movement of high-rent residential areas are the
most important organizing principles in this growth. Hoyt's theory also
reflects changes in automobile technology that made the rapid expansion
of wealthy suburbs possible in the 1920s. A major weakness of this theory
is that it largely ignores land uses other than residential and it places undue
emphasis on the economic characteristics of areas, ignoring other important
factors such as the race and ethnicity of the residents.

Harris and Ullman's Multiple Nuclei Theory

Harris and Ullman (1945) recognized the shortcomings of both the concentric zone and the sector theories and presented an alternative approach
known as the multiple nuclei theory. This theory suggests that as a city
grows it is differentiated into homogeneous areas or nuclei but these nuclei
do not necessarily form concentric zones or sectors. Harris and Ullman
contended that in many cities land use patterns do not focus on a single
center, the CBD, but on multiple centers. These centers include retail areas,
warehousing districts, concentrations of manufacturing and industry, as

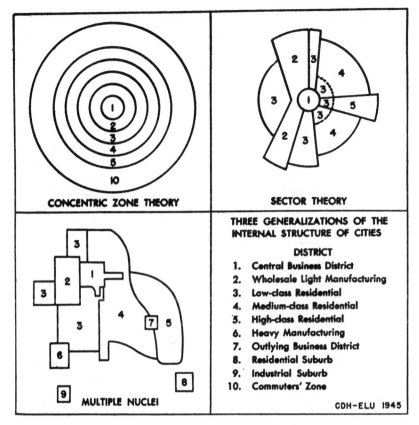

Fig. 7.10 Concentric zone, sector, and multiple nuclei models.

Source: Reprinted from "The Nature of Cities" by C. D. Harris and E. L. Ullman in volume No. 242 of *The Annals of the Academy of Political and Social Science.* © Copyright 1945, p. 107, Figure 1.

well as university, governmental, and financial centers. Moreover, these nuclei are often in different parts of the city.

Rules useful in predicting land use patterns In the presentation of their theory, Harris and Ullman identified several rules useful in predicting the location and future growth of these specialized areas. First, certain activities require specialized facilities and concentrate where these facilities are available. Industry and manufacturing, for example, require transportation facilities and these activities often locate near rail lines, waterways, and port facilities.

Second, similar activities benefit from being close to each other. Retailers locate near each other to increase the pedestrian traffic in front of their stores and hence their sales.

Third, certain dissimilar activities may be disadvantageous to each other. For example, because of its pollution, industry would be viewed as a nuisance to retailers and residents of high-income residential areas.

Finally, some activities could benefit from a centralized location in or near the CBD but cannot afford the rents. Warehousing or grocery wholesaling are examples of activities that require large structures and would benefit from a central location but must locate elsewhere because of the prohibitively high rents in the city's center (Harris and Ullman, 1945, pp. 9–12).

Harris and Ullman's theory has many of the same shortcomings as the preceding two. It is overly simplistic and does not state the limiting assumptions associated with the model. More important, Harris and Ullman are geographers and bring to this theory the unique focus of their discipline—the spatial distribution of specific land uses. Little attention is given to the process that leads to the sorting of people and institutions across the urban landscape.

Tests of the Concentric Zone Theory

Each of the three descriptive theories of urban land usage has been studied critically by urban researchers, but Burgess's model has received the most criticism. Critics of both the sector and multiple nuclei theories have been much less severe. The attention to Burgess's theory is due in part to the fact that the concentric zone theory is the only one of the three tied to a larger and more general theory of the city, and it was the first of the three published. The concentric zone theory has been tested in several ways over the years.

Attempts to identify zones The most widespread criticism of the Burgess model arises from the fact that various cities do not conform exactly to the ideal circular spatial pattern. In Figure 7.8, even Chicago fits more closely into a pattern of concentric semicircles rather than complete circles because of the distorting influence of Lake Michigan. The earliest tests of the Burgess model involved the attempt of researchers to identify homogeneous zones in cities in the United States and Canada. Quinn summarizes these findings in a 1940 article:

> The zones of Montreal, as mapped by Dawson and Gettys, take the form of irregular ovals and crescents. New Haven, as portrayed by Davie, exhibits great irregularities with no clearcut evidence of circular zones. In Long Beach, according to the map of Longmoor and Young, a circular pattern can be seen only with great difficulty, if at all. Maps of Cincinnati, Columbus, Cleveland, Minneapolis, New York, Pittsburgh, Seattle, St. Louis, and other cities all indicate characteristics of local spatial structure (p. 211).

Burgess's theory was a set of ideal constructs, and he readily admitted that transportation lines and topographic features were distorting factors. An important point raised by Quinn (1940) was the failure of critics of the Burgess zonal hypothesis to distinguish clearly between *ecological distance* and *simple linear distance* in the construction of their zones. Simple linear distance is measured in feet, yards, or miles, and it can be easily plotted on a map with a compass. Assuming the CBD to be the geographic center of the city, researchers using this measure simply drew circular zones with radii of a standard unit such as a mile. Researchers employing this measure generally have been unable to identify homogeneous zones in most of the cities studied.

Ecological distance, in contrast, is measured in terms of the cost and time of travel in any one direction from the CBD. It takes into consideration the distorting influences of a city's transportation network and topography. For example, a person who drives away from a CBD on an interstate highway could drive much farther in five minutes than a person driving on a city street. Figure 7.11 contrasts zones constructed on the basis on the

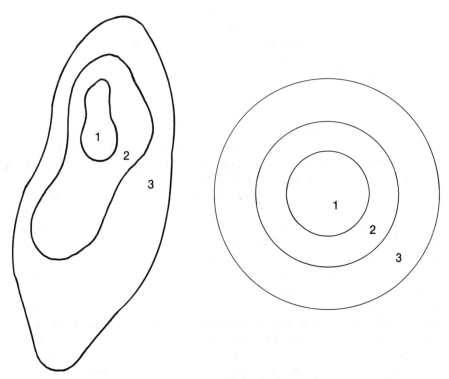

Fig. 7.11 A comparison of ecological and simple linear distance.

two distance measures. Note that in shape and width each hypothetical zone in Figure 7.11A is irregular because the graph is based on the distance one can travel across each zone in five minutes. The zones in Figure 7.11B, in contrast, are of uniform width and do not reflect distorting influences. Quinn believed that the irregularities in spatial patterns found by Dawson and Gettys, Davie, and others in cities like Montreal and New Haven would conform more closely to the pattern hypothesized by Burgess if ecological rather than simple linear distances had been applied.

Weaknesses in the theory identified Quinn (1940) agreed with critics that there were major weaknesses in the theory. The Burgess model was drawn primarily in terms of commerce, residence, and light industry and did not include the locational characteristics of heavy industry, which was thought to be an abnormal distorting influence. However, because the Burgess hypothesis presumably applied to modern American commercial-industrial cities, Quinn believed that the location of heavy industry should be included in the theory. In addition, Burgess failed to take into consideration the distorting influences of growth inertia. The present structure of any city depends on its past growth. Cities over time make enormous investments in capital improvements such as streets, parks, sewers, and water systems, and they are unlikely to abandon them as the city grows. In most cities, growth takes place in one part of the city and not another simply because an expanding area is already serviced by existing public facilities. Therefore, the inclusion of heavy industry and inertial factors were viewed by Quinn as necessary elements in a reformulation of the Burgess theory (Quinn, 1940, pp. 215–18).

Analyzing status gradients The second major type of test of the Burgess model involves analyzing status gradients (Guest, 1969, 1970; Haggerty, 1970). Students of Burgess have suggested that Burgess did not intend his work to be a rigorous theoretical frame. The concentric zone theory evolved from seminars at the University of Chicago in the early 1920s. The model was used as a general framework to organize and study Chicago's natural areas, areas being explored at that time by members of Burgess's department. Therefore the Burgess model can be applied in a different interpretation of cities' land use patterns—one based on status gradients. Hypothetically, from the CBD outward to the periphery of a city, the socioeconomic status of the zones increases. That is, as distance increases, social status increases. A variety of methods have been employed to test this relationship but probably the easiest to understand is an approach used by Schnore. Schnore simply compared the status characteristics of people living in a metropolitan area's central city with those of people residing in its fringe or suburban ring (1965, pp. 222–41). The figures in the body of Table 7.1

Table 7.1
Examples of three patterns of residential distribution of educational classes based on indexes of suburbanization, 1960 and 1970.

	Educational status				
Detroit	*1960*	*1970*	*1970/1960*		
None	141	142	1.01)		
1–4	136	158	1.16)		
5–6	126	144	1.14)		
7–8	112	121	1.08)	Centralized	
HS 1–3	99	110	1.11)		
HS 4	86	85	.99)		
C 1–3	86	77	.99)	Decentralized	
C 4	77	65	.84)		

New York City	*1960*	*1970*	*1970/ 1960*	*Tucson* *1960*	*1970*	*1970/ 1960*
None	129	130	1.01	90	91	1.01
1–4	119	125	1.05	93	97	1.04
5–6	111	122	1.10	96	99	1.03
7–8	107	108	1.01	99	100	1.01
HS 1–3	100	104	1.04	100	99	.99
HS 4	91	92	1.01	101	100	.99
C 1–3	87	89	1.02	102	102	1.00
C 4	84	86	1.02	103	101	.98

Los Angeles	*1960*	*1970*	*1970/ 1960*
None	131	126	.96
1–4	113	122	1.08
5–6	110	118	1.07
7–8	99	100	1.01
HS 1–3	94	95	1.01
HS 4	97	95	.98
C 1–3	102	101	.99
C 4	106	105	.99

Source: Adapted from Schnore, L.F., *The Urban Scene*. New York: The Free Press, 1965, p. 228; and U.S. Bureau of Census, *1970 Census: Characteristics of the Population*. Washington, D.C. Government Printing Office, 1972.

are index scores that show the degree to which a certain status group (as measured by level of education) is concentrated in the central city. A value greater than 100 means that there are more people of that educational status in the central city than in the metropolitan area as a whole; an index below

100 means fewer people of that educational status are in the central city. If the Burgess concept is correct, one would expect high index scores for the low educational categories and low index scores for the high educational categories. In other words, people with low education levels would be concentrated in the central city but not people with high levels of education—theoretically they would be in the suburbs. Examine the figures for Detroit in Table 7.1 and note that the pattern is as hypothesized. Scanning from the index value for no education to the category for college graduates, one can see that the 1960 index values decline in a regular fashion. For example, relatively few of the college graduates in the Detroit metropolitan area lived in its central city; they were in the suburbs. This pattern is even more pronounced in Detroit's 1970 figures. New York exhibits a similar pattern of index values. Now peruse the figures for Tucson and Los Angeles. In Tucson in 1960, a pattern opposite that hypothesized by Burgess is in evidence. The residents of this metropolitan area's central city had an educational status higher than that of the metropolis as a whole. In 1970, there was very little difference in educational characteristics between the residents of the central city and those in the suburban ring.

Los Angeles, in contrast, represents a completely different pattern—the highly and poorly educated are both centralized and the residents in the middle educational categories are decentralized in the suburbs.

Detroit and New York (to a lesser degree) support the Burgess zonal hypothesis. Tucson's pattern is opposite that hypothesized and the Los Angeles pattern is between these two extremes. Why are low status groups centralized as predicted in some cities and decentralized in others? The answer is provided in a study conducted by Schnore and Winsborough (1972). These researchers calculated indexes similar to those in Table 7.1 for all metropolitan areas in the United States. Interestingly, they found the pattern hypothesized by Burgess only in metropolitan areas where the central cities were older and densely populated, with large numbers of heavy industries, housing of poor quality, and a good mass transit system. These are metropolitan areas where pollution and poor housing in the central cities have driven out the middle- and upper-income groups and where this decentralization has been facilitated by good public transportation. Such characteristics describe best the older commercial-industrial cities in the heartland of the United States. Therefore, Burgess's concentric zone theory appears to have validity but only when applied to a particular type of city similar to the city on which this theory was based, Chicago.

Limiting assumptions of the Burgess theory Before passing judgment on the concentric zone theory, one must understand that theories have associated with them a series of limiting assumptions. These assumptions specify the conditions necessary for the theory to work. In a chemical theory, the theorist might specify that a reaction will occur in a certain way only if the reactants are kept at a specific temperature and pressure. Although Burgess did not state clearly the limits to his theory, the following assumptions are implicit in his work (Quinn, 1950, pp. 116–37; Schnore, 1965, pp. 353–54).

1. The city is undergoing rapid urban expansion that demands a rapidly growing population.
2. The city's population growth is the result of ethnically diverse immigration from other countries.
3. The city's population is ethnically and racially diverse with wide occupational experiences.
4. There is private ownership of property, impersonal competition, and an absence of zoning and city planning.
5. The city has a diverse commercial and industrial economic base.
6. The CBD is the point of greatest accessibility from any point within the city and accessibility declines in a regular pattern from the center.
7. Transportation is cheap and efficient and anyone can reach the city's center with ease.
8. A status hierarchy exists in the city and freedom of residential choice is limited to the upper socioeconomic strata.

Many of these conditions no longer exist. For example, there are few cities in the United States without some form of zoning and/or city planning (4). The passage of restrictive immigration quotas by the United States Congress in the late 1920s severely curtailed immigration from overseas (2). More important, with the quadrupling of oil costs in the world since 1973, one could question the assumption that transportation today is still cheap and efficient (7). Traffic congestion and inadequate mass transportation in many large metropolises limit the accessibility of the city's center (6, 7). Therefore, in applying the concentric zone theory to the study of the spatial structure of a metropolitan area, one must take into consideration the theory's assumptions and modify the theory in relevant ways as conditions change.

To a degree this modification has already been done in ecological research. Ecologists have found that distance from the CBD is useful in understanding the spatial distribution of groups, institutions, and behaviors. The importance of distance in ecological research emerges from Burgess's theory. Although Burgess's theory is seldom used today in its classical form, its influence can be found in much current ecological research.

Convergence of the Models

Each of the three models of urban land usage has supporters and critics. Recent developments in the testing of the social area analysis model suggest that, to a degree, each of the models has some validity. Anderson and Egeland (1961), in applying social area analysis to four cities (Akron, Dayton, Indianapolis, and Syracuse), found that the distribution of census tracts by their social area dimensions corresponded to the hypothesized patterns of each of the theories. Family status characteristics were distributed in a concentric zone pattern, economic status by sectors, and ethnic and racial groups were distributed in a spatial pattern resembling multiple nuclei. Studies in Rome and in Canadian cities also support these findings.

In retrospect, Anderson and Egeland's (1961) findings are not surprising. Burgess was a sociologist and his theory focused on social process and the distribution of social groups. Hoyt is an economist and his theory was based on the economic characteristics of subareas. The geographic perspective of Harris and Ullman led them to examine the spatial distribution of various institutions and urban functions. However, either by chance or as a result of the insight of Shevky, Bell, and Williams in identifying the basic dimensions underlying the structure of urban places, the three theories of urban geometry have converged under the social area analysis framework.

Conclusions

The distribution of groups and institutions within cities has been of interest to the student of the city for most of this century. Numerous theories of urban land usage have been published since 1900 and in this section the three most famous are analyzed—the concentric zone, sector, and multiple nuclei theories. Despite the narrow focus of each of the theories, each has validity in explaining the spatial distribution of groups and institutions across the urban landscape.

In the following section, discussion is shifted from general citywide processes and patterns to the family unit and the decision-making process it uses to determine where to locate within the metropolitan community.

THE DECISION TO MOVE AND THE SEARCH FOR A RESIDENCE

The city has been likened to a giant sorting machine in which individuals and families of various incomes and sizes are matched with the appropriate subareas. In most cases, individuals and families have a fair degree of freedom in choosing the location of their residence and neighborhood. The wealthy have the greatest locational freedom because their financial resources enable them to absorb transportation and housing costs at any point in the city or its periphery. As family income declines, so too does locational freedom. Thus the poor often are forced to consume the least desirable areas of the city—the slums. Slums have been appropriately defined as those areas of the city inhabited by people with no housing alternatives. Income level, however, is not the only factor influencing residential location; race, ethnicity, family size, and lifestyle are other important variables.

Regardless of the family's financial or ethnic status, choosing where to live is one of the most important decisions a family will make. First, a house is the single largest financial investment most Americans make in their lifetimes. Second, the house and neighborhood one chooses have implications for the quality of schools, the quality of the environment, the family members' personal safety, the types and number of friends and neighbors, and the availability of parks and recreation areas.

In the following section the process by which families are matched with appropriate subareas of the city is explored. The discussion is divided into two parts. First, the forces and factors that lead a family to the decision to move from their present home are examined. Second, those factors that impinge on the search process itself once the family has made the decision to move are discussed.

The Decision to Move

The decision-to-move literature began with a benchmark work by Peter Rossi entitled *Why Families Move,* published in 1955. Rossi (1955) conducted an exhaustive survey of a sample of Philadelphia residents and found that before each family moved, they had experienced significant dissatisfaction with their housing conditions that "pushed" them out of their homes. The sources of dissatisfaction included overcrowding, landlord problems, and neighborhood conditions, as well as the physical condition of the dwelling itself. Leslie and Richardson (1961) replicated Rossi's study on data gathered from a suburb of Washington, D.C. They reported that physical conditions were important in the decision to move, but other factors such as congruency of socioeconomic status between the family and neighborhood were also important. Wolpert (1965) combined Rossi's findings with those of Leslie and Richardson and constructed the first general theory on how personal, neighborhood, and housing factors interact to influence a family's decision to move.

Wolpert's (1965) basic argument is that a family's decision to move is a response to a wide range of social, psychological, and economic conditions. First, families over time undergo change and this change corresponds with the lifecycle. The size of the family first increases and then decreases as children are born and grow to maturity. Second, the head of the household may experience career and social mobility due to increased expertise in his or her job. Third, families vary considerably in their attachment to a particular house and neighborhood. These factors can be divided into four basic dimensions for use in the analysis of residential mobility: (1) the family lifecycle, (2) social mobility, (3) characteristics of the residence and neighborhood, and (4) the family's emotional attachment to and participation in the neighborhood. These dimensions vary in a generally systematic way.

Family lifecycle   The United States is one of the most mobile societies in the world with an estimated 20 percent of the population moving annually (Simmons 1968). On the average a family will move eight times in its lifetime and five of these moves are related to the lifecycle (Rossi 1955, p. 179). The stages of the family lifecycle normally include: (1) family-formation, (2) prechild (constant size), (3) child-bearing (increasing size), (4) child-rearing (constant size), (5) child-launching (decreasing size), (6) postchild (constant size), and (7) widowhood (family dissolution) stages. (Sabagh, Van Arsdol, and Butler, 1969, p. 90). The propensity to move is not constant throughout the lifecycle, however. Researchers have found that younger families in the family-formation and child-bearing stages tended to be more residentially mobile than families at other stages.[3] The major reason for their mobility was dissatisfaction with the amount of room in the old dwelling. The birth of a new child or newlyweds living in a spouse's old apartment, for example, may overtax the dwelling. Therefore, the decision of a family to move appears to be closely tied to changing space needs. The propensity to move is greatest during those stages of the lifecycle when the size of the family is either increasing or decreasing—the family-formation, child-bearing and child-launching states—and lowest during the child-rearing and postchild stages when family size remains constant. Other factors outside the lifecycle such as divorce, desertion, and remarriage also influence mobility among family members.

Social mobility   Leslie and Richardson (1961), in replicating Rossi's (1955) earlier work, found a close relationship between a family's expectations of upward social mobility and their decision to move. In their reformulation of Rossi's model they include both family lifecycle and social mobility factors. Their basic assumption was that a family's decision to move is a strategy for minimizing the social distance between the family and the group to which it belongs or wishes to belong. Because only a small percentage of Americans move out of the social class in which they are born, upward or downward mobility probably only influences the decision of a small proportion of the spatially mobile families (Lipset and Bendix 1959).

Characteristics of the residence and neighborhood   The discussion of the general models of urban geometry suggests that as a city grows it must reorganize spatially. In some cases subareas of the city undergo the process of invasion-succession as an incompatible type of land use or population displaces the original population. Hoover and Vernon (1965) suggested that neighborhoods, like people and families, have a lifecycle of five stages— development, transition, downgrading, thinning out, and renewal—corresponding with this transition process. As the neighborhood undergoes the lifecycle process, the socioeconomic status of the neighborhood or its ethnic and racial composition may change. The reactions of the current residents of these transitional neighborhoods will depend on both their view of their new neighbors and their own self-perceptions. If there is a major discrepancy between the two, these changes in the neighborhood will increase the chances that a family will move (Butler, Sabagh, and Van Arsdol, 1964). The "white flight to the suburbs" and "panic selling" are phrases used in the popular press to describe this process.

Attachment to the neighborhood environment Psychological costs are associated with any move and the degree of attachment that a family has with the immediate residential environment is an important element in their decision to move. Families who interact extensively and intimately with friends and relatives in their neighborhood are less likely to move than families with few attachments. In general, as the family's length of residence in a home increases their propensity to move decreases (Morrison, 1967; Land, 1968). This tendency reflects both increased attachment to neighbors and general satisfaction with the living environment. The converse is also true. Families who have close ties with friends and relatives may decide to move if those people move. Moreover, interaction with neighbors is not always pleasant and unresolvable conflicts with neighbors may increase the chances that a family will move (Butler, Sabagh, and Van Arsdol, 1964).

Other factors such as homeownership, ethnic status, and the housing and neighborhood aspirations of families have also been identified as important determinants in the decision to move. For example, it is much easier for a renter to move than a homeowner because of the small financial commitment of renters in their housing. Homeowners, in contrast, have a greater stake in what happens to a neighborhood and homeownership is usually a powerful deterrent to neighborhood deterioration (Speare, 1970). In addition, ethnic groups commonly have strong "symbolic attachments" to the churches, schools, meeting halls, and other institutions in their subarea, attachments that are so strong that these people will remain in an area although the structures are declining physically (Gans, 1962). Finally, family members may have definite ideas about the ideal home and neighborhood and the match between the ideal and their actual residence will affect housing satisfaction and the family's propensity to move.

The Decision-Making Process

The four sets of background variables represent the environmental and personal characteristics that influence the decision-making process. The decision-making process begins when an individual (head of household) or family compares his or her personal characteristics (space needs, emotional attachments, etc.) with the characteristics of the residential environment. If they match, there should be a high degree of satisfaction; if not, a high degree of dissatisfaction. An individual who is dissatisfied with the residential environment initiates a search for alternatives. The search does not necessarily involve a move, however. A family's space needs may be solved by adding a room or finishing an attic. The family may look for housing elsewhere but find that better housing is out of their price range. This search ultimately leads to a decision either to move out or stay. If the decision is made to move and nothing else intervenes, the family moves.

An important point made by Wolpert (1965), Speare (1974), and Bach and Smith (1977) is that dissatisfaction with the residential environment does not cause the move directly; rather, "dissatisfaction initiates a search for more satisfying alternatives and the decision to move is one such alternative" (Bach and Smith, 1977, p. 174). If families are able to reduce their dissatisfaction by some other means they are less likely to move.

A cautionary and somewhat depressing note should be added to the discussion at this time. In the final analysis housing alternatives are constrained by family income. Unfortunately, during these inflationary times, housing has been increasing in cost at a tremendous rate. In some housing markets, such as Washington, D.C., Los Angeles and San Francisco, housing costs had been increasing at a rate of 1 percent per month during the years 1979 and 1980. In December of 1980, the average cost of a single family dwelling in the United States was nearly $70,000. High housing costs combined with high interest rates mean that fewer and fewer Americans can afford to own their own homes.[4]

THE SEARCH FOR A NEW HOME

Assume that a family has reached its threshold of dissatisfaction, has evaluated all its alternatives, and has decided to move. The head of the household at this point must decide first what type of dwelling is needed and second its location within the metropolitan area. These decisions are not independent of each other. Highrise apartments, for example, are not normally found on the periphery of cities, but are more centrally located. The opposite would be true of single-family dwellings. Other factors such as the family's income, their desire for schools, recreation areas, and shopping centers as well as the dwelling's location in relation to the head of the household's place of employment are all part of this decision-making process. The final location decision, therefore, is a complex one in which a large number of personal, economic, and urban characteristics must be evaluated (Michelson, 1977). The search process involves matching the characteristics of the family with the characteristics of the available housing. The key variables in this process are summarized in Table 7.2. A short discussion of each of these variable sets follows.

Family Income-Housing Price

Of the four family characteristics listed in Table 7.2, the family's income level is by far the most important. In the final analysis a family's locational

Source: Reprinted with permission of Michael Keefe, *The Denver Post.*

decision is tied to its ability to pay both the costs of housing and the costs of transportation. The importance of housing and transportation costs in the decision-making process declines with rising family income. The rich can afford to live anyplace, and in many instances the poor have no choice. In the past fifty years, however, locational freedom has increased significantly for most income groupings as the automobile has become this nation's dominant form of transportation. In the past, the location of the working class, for example, was restricted to those areas of the city accessible to industry either by foot or mass transit. Since World War II, many industries have located on the periphery of cities. This trend, combined with the widespread use of the automobile, has extended the areas of possible location for the working person to almost the entire metropolis. The families with the least locational choice are those who cannot afford to purchase and operate an automobile (the poor and the old). The location of these

Table 7.2
Factors in the residential location decision.

Individual characteristics	Housing characteristics
Income	Price
Stage in lifecycle	Type of home
Lifestyle preferences	Neighbors; type of community institutions
Attitudes toward journey to work	Location with respect to place of employment

Source: Phillip H. Rees, "Concepts of Social Space," in *Geographic Perspectives on Urban Systems,* Berry and Horton, eds., © 1970, p. 313. Reprinted by permission of Prentice-Hall, Inc., Englewood Cliffs, New Jersey.

people is constrained by the availability of mass transit, a system that is of poor quality in most American cities.

The role of lending institutions Another important link between family income and housing is banking and lending institutions. These institutions analyze a family's income and determine the total amount they will lend. These institutions also play a crucial role in determining where a family may locate. The practice of "redlining," or the unwillingness of banks and savings and loan institutions to lend money in certain parts of a city, eliminates those areas as locational alternatives. This practice has recently come under the scrutiny of the federal government. Therefore, the availability and amount of mortgage money as well as where these monies are likely to be lent limit the housing alternatives for many families.

Stage of the Lifecycle Related to Housing Type

The stage of the family in the lifecycle determines not only the type of family dwelling but also its size. Young couples in the family-formation stage may desire an apartment or duplex near jobs and entertainment facilities in the CBD. Families in the child-producing and child-rearing stages will probably prefer single-family dwellings with yards for children and neighborhoods where families have children of the same age. Couples in the child-launching and postchild stages may desire a smaller home or an apartment. At each stage, families need different types of housing and these housing types are often found in different parts of the city. Housing type and size, combined with the price range that a family can afford to pay, limit the areas where the search will take place (Michelson, 1970, 1977).

Lifestyle—Neighborhood Preference

The flight to the suburbs of middleclass child-oriented families during the post–World War II period appears to be the result of Americans searching for a good environment in which to raise children. Therefore, the predominance of single-family dwellings on spacious lots in the suburban ring provides a physical environment conducive to the lifestyle called "familism." In the central city, however, the diversity of housing and neighborhood types provides physical environments conducive to a more varied number of lifestyles. Gans (1962b), in his article "Urbanism and Suburbanism as Ways of Life," describes some of the types of residents found in the central city. They include cosmopolites, the unmarried or childless, the deprived, the trapped, and the ethnic villagers. Each category is associated with a distinctive lifestyle; people with different lifestyles inhabit specific types of housing in different parts of the central city.

The rising costs of housing, energy, and mortgage interest mean that fewer and fewer Americans can afford to purchase their own home. Fewer home buyers mean more renters and increased costs for apartments. The social consequences of this high cost of living are reflected in this article from The Christian Science Monitor *(June 30, 1980).*

YOUNG ADULTS FLOCK HOME TO MOM AND DAD

By Victoria Irwin

The "empty nest" that parents are supposed to find as their children grow up is not so empty any more.

An increasing number of young adults in the US appear to be coming back or staying at home after high school, college, and even marriage. Although there are few statistics on the trend, everyone from sociologists to families to economists sense something in the air.

"With the high cost of homes, apartments, and automobiles, it's becoming difficult for young adults to sever family ties," says Fred Allvine, professor of economics at the Georgia Institute of Technology in Atlanta. "I think this [the "refilled" nest] will be with us for some time. Families are finding that the 'unbundling' they did when children went away to school was just temporary."

Margaret Hellie Huyck of the psychology department at the Illinois Institute of Technology in Chicago is not sure whether refilling the nest is more common today or not. But she has been hearing about it from parents and has begun to do research to find out.

Experts list several factors that keep young adults at home. Foremost are economic considerations.

Bob Macdonald, a recent college graduate who lives at home in Corona del Mar, Calif., says money is a definite reason to stay at home a while longer. He adds up the rent and food costs that he might have to pay if he lived with another young adult.

"That's $350 to $400 a month I am not paying, because I live at home," he says. "I need to raise a cash base, since I just got out of school."

Mr. Allvine points out that the middle management jobs available to college graduates in the '50s and '60s are not there for this generation.

"The independence of young adults developed between 1946 and 1970 was brought on by the rapid improvement of the standard of living and affluence," says the Georgia economist. "Now, unless the economy surges back, it's going to be increasingly difficult for younger people to break out into their own."

Lou Cottin, newspaper columnist and author of "Elders in Rebellion," says there is an increase in the number of young married couples who come to live with parents.

"The average older couple lives in a house with six or seven rooms rattling around," he says. "When young people marry and find a mortgage is unbearable, they move in with one or the other of the parents."

But some young adults say they move back home because they just enjoy living there.

Mark, a Pittsburgh salesman, has lived at home since he graduated from college in 1974. Two sisters, ages 35 and 24, also share the home with their mother.

"I am very comfortable here," says Mark. He likes the fact that his home is such a "no pressure" place. Mark's parents were divorced several years ago, another reason he has stayed at home.

"I find my home a great energy source as far as ideas go," Mark says. "My mother and sisters are really good friends that I can talk to. Our home is like a little apartment building." The only reason he would move out is if he married or took a job somewhere else in the country.

A key in the success of a refilled home is whether parents and children can have a new relationship with each other. Will mother still be expected to pick up the towels? Does the returned child have to eat what the others eat, or fix his own meals?

How can a parent deal with his son or daughter's standards of dating and relationships? What about parents who have just adjusted to life without their children and begun to enjoy their new life, only to have the children flock back home?

Parents find they have to realize they are not dealing with small children any more. Young adults must see their parents and themselves as adults.

"I think it is unhealthy if families treat each other like before the child went to college," says Bob Macdonald, who is working at a manufacturing firm until he is ready to pursue his first interests—publishing and entertainment.

Observers advise that certain guidelines need to be set down before a young adult returns. Will he or she pay rent? Who is responsible for what chores?

For example, Mr. Macdonald doesn't pay rent, but he and his parents have an agreement for him to help with chores around the house. He stresses the importance of having a schedule for these duties:

"It's a lot better than being 'on call.' Assumed responsibility can kill anything. You have to lay the cards on the table."

He adds that it's important not to become homebound. "Personally I think it would be unwise if I didn't have commitments outside the home," says Mr. Macdonald. And although he enjoys the company of his parents, he intends to stay at home for a couple more months, earn some money, and then move out.

"It is best to live on your own," he says.

To give both generations privacy while they live together, some families are converting garage space and attics into apartments for adult children, Mr. Allvine of Georgia Tech reports. Mr. Cottin recommends that an architect set up a dividing section to make a home into two separate living places.

Some parents complain that young adults sometimes "take over" when they move back home, says Mr. Cottin.

"The big problem for older people is to make sure we are not exploited," says Mr. Cottin. He points out, for example, that when grandchildren are born into these households, grandparents are recruited as babysitters.

One mother admonishes parents, "Mother-love makes it easy to overlook someone's faults. Analyze the situation to see if he or she is trying to bob from another responsibility. Make him realize that you will help out, but don't become a victim."

Source: "Young Adults Flock Home to Mom and Dad" by Victoria Irwin, January 30, 1980. Reprinted by permission from *The Christian Science Monitor.* © 1980 The Christian Science Publishing Society. All rights reserved.

Cosmopolites The cosmopolites include students, artists, writers, musicians, actors, and members of the professions. They live in the central city because they want to be near the specialized cultural facilities found there. The majority are unmarried or childless but those couples who do have children are often absentee parents, delegating much of the responsibility for the raising of their children to sitters or preschools. In general this lifestyle is incompatible with familism and an attempt to live in the suburban ring by a cosmopolite will often be of short duration.

The unmarried or childless The unmarried and childless in the past were in a transitional stage of their life, enjoying the urban core until they married or had children. Today, for millions of Americans this is no longer a transitional stage but a chosen lifestyle, a lifestyle in many respects similar to that of cosmopolites. The major difference between cosmopolites and this group is that the unmarried and childless are young white-collar workers, many of whom initially moved into an apartment to escape parental supervision. They normally locate within easy access to their place of employment and the city's entertainment facilities at the city's center.[5] People in this group who enter the family-formation and child-producing stages of the life-cycle normally return to the suburbs.

Ethnic villagers   Ethnic villagers also live in the central city by choice. The forces of tradition and kinship tie the members of these groups to their old neighborhoods. Their concentration in these areas permits them to support the schools, churches, fraternal organizations, and stores, and these institutions in turn permit this group to maintain its language, culture, and group structure.

The deprived and trapped   Unlike the cosmopolites, unmarried and childless, and ethnic villagers, the deprived and the trapped live in the central city of necessity. The deprived are the very poor, the mentally ill, and the physically handicapped. In the United States, the majority are nonwhite. Through the years, discrimination has limited their locational alternatives to specified parts of the city. A high proportion of this group are ghettoized in stable low-income areas. The transient live in flophouses in skidrow areas or, if their income permits, in the city's roominghouse district. In general, the deprived have few housing alternatives and live in the least desirable areas of the city.

The trapped, in contrast, are victims of change. In most cases they are elderly people who have raised their children and have lived most of their lives in the same neighborhood. When the area undergoes the invasion-succession process they stay in the neighborhood either because of a deep sentimental attachment or because they are too poor to move.

The urban homesteader   Recent changes in the American housing market have led to an additional category not mentioned by Gans—the urban homesteader. In 1970, the average cost of a home was $24,000; by 1980 it had soared to nearly $70,000. The result has been that the American dream of home ownership has become an elusive one for many middleclass Americans. Young couples, in particular, who are just beginning their married life find it increasingly difficult to save enough for a down payment and to meet monthly mortgage payments. Many have remained renters but others have sought the older housing in the central cities.

The urban homesteaders are people who have traditionally lived in the suburbs but who have opted for a home in the central city. They are predominantly middleclass. In many cases, they are willing to assume the risk of restoring an older house in a rundown neighborhood because it is the only kind they can afford to buy. Their efforts have led to the remarkable revitalization of older neighborhoods in Washington, D.C.; Columbus, Ohio; Minneapolis, Minnesota; and other American cities. With the prospect that both energy and housing costs will continue to spiral upward through the 1980s, the urban homesteader will, in all likelihood, become an important element in the ecology of central cities.

Lifestyle preferences, therefore, have considerable impact on the locational decision. The lifestyle of ethnic villagers would be impossible without the infrastructure provided by neighborhood facilites. The lifestyles of the cosmopolites and the unmarried and childless require easy access to the cultural and entertainment facilities of the central city as well as a high degree of personal freedom. Only the highrise or the apartment complex in the central city provides the anonymity and freedom necessary to these lifestyles. The familism lifestyle is not suited to these conditions. Parents raising children in highrise apartments find it difficult to supervise their youngsters and to exert the degree of social control needed for their socialization (Michelson, 1970). Cosmopolites would be stifled by the neighboring obligations of the suburban ring. Lifestyle preferences, therefore, reduce the areas in which the housing search process takes place.

Attitudes Toward the Journey to Work

This final category of factors influencing the search for a home is probably the most idiosyncratic. In the past this aspect of the locational decision has been based largely on the time needed for the head of the household to travel to work. In recent years, because of the increasing costs of energy, individuals more carefully assess the true costs of transportation in terms of both time and money.

The Subareas Searched

The search process involves the matching of the individual or family with housing of the appropriate type and size in an area of the city conducive to the household's lifestyle. The search process does not include the entire city, only certain well-defined areas delineated by income constraints, housing preferences, neighborhood characteristics, and geographic location. Information on these alternative areas is extremely important to the search process. People in large cities ordinarily have a general knowledge of the social status and ethnic and racial characteristics of different subareas of the city (Michelson, 1970; Hunter, 1974; Schwab, 1976). However, in the process of constructing a mental map of a city, people do an enormous amount of stereotyping. Large areas of the city with which the individual is unfamiliar may be classified inaccurately as slum, ethnic, or rich. These mental maps, if shared by a great many people, can have unintended consequences for a neighborhood. For example, a racial incident in a neighborhood school reported in the city's newspapers may lead prospective homebuyers to avoid an area although the incident may have been minor. Self-fulfilling prophecies can occur if large numbers of the city's residents share similar distortions in their mental maps. Therefore, the final choice

SOCIAL SPACE (Units: Individual or Families)

Single Small Family Childless Couples

Large Family Married with Children

Pre-School, School and Child-bearing Ages

Post Child-bearing Ages and/or Early Adulthood

High Income
High Middle Income
Average Income
Low Middle Income
Low Income

College Education
Managerial
Professional
Clerical
Sales
High School Education
Craftsman
Operative
Grade School Education
Laborers
Underemployed
Little Schooling
Unemployed

Socioeconomic Status

S_i

Stage in Life Cycle

S_i = individual i's position in social space

HOUSING SPACE (Units: Dwellings)

High Rise Apartment
Low Rise Apartment
Town House
Duplex
Single Family House

High Price or Rent
High-Medium Price or Rent
Average Price or Rent
Low-Medium Price or Rent
Low Price or Rent

Most Spacious   Luxurious
Comfortable
Spacious
Average   Average
Crowded   Could be improved
Overcrowded   Blighted

No individual lot or private yard
Smaller Lot and Yard
Small Lot and Yard
Large Lot and Yard

High Density
Medium Density
Low Density

Value and Quality

H_i

Type

H_i = individual i's home in housing space

COMMUNITY SPACE *(Units: Tracts or Larger Sub-areas)*

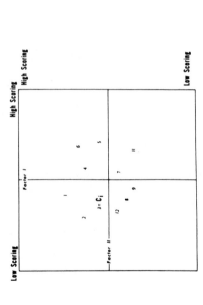

Cᵢ = the community in which *i*'s home is located

LOCATIONAL OR PHYSICAL SPACE
(Units: Tracts or Larger Sub-areas)

Lᵢ = the zone in which the community in which *i*'s home is located

Fig. 7.12 The residential location decision process.

Source: Philip H. Rees, "Concepts of Social Space," in *Geographic Perspectives on Urban Systems*, Berry and Horton, eds., © 1970, p. 313. Reprinted by permission of Prentice-Hall, Inc., Englewood Cliffs, New Jersey.

of a house may not be the best location for the household but the one perceived as the best alternative in the areas searched. The areas searched in turn depend on the information available.

Sources of information Interestingly, Rossi (1955) found that the sources of information on which the search process was based were quite varied. More than one-half of his Philadelphia sample of households found their new home through personal contacts, one-fourth found housing by "windfall" or accident, and about one-fifth found it by riding around in a car. Regardless of the source of information, distortions and biases are inevitable. The most important distortions are those of income and race. In the final analysis, residential relocation is a search for a house of a certain type in an affordable price range, but this search also includes a strategy for finding a neighborhood that minimizes the physical distance between the members of the household and the income, racial, and ethnic group to which it belongs. This is especially true of race. Although laws were enacted in the 1960s by the federal government outlawing discrimination in the sale and rental of housing, the United States remains one of the most highly segregated nations in the world. In general, whites avoid neighborhoods inhabited by blacks or areas undergoing racial transition. Whether by the restrictions placed on housing by its price or by prejudicial attitudes and discrimination, blacks and other minorities have fewer housing alternatives than other groups. The search process carried out by members of these minority groups normally takes place in those areas deemed acceptable by the dominant group in the larger society.

The Search Process

Figure 7.12 shows the residential location decision process graphically. The individual or family occupies a position in social space determined by the household's economic and family status, point S_i. The stage of the household in the family lifecycle and the occupation, education, and income of the head of the household are the determining factors. In Figure 7.12, a household located in social space at point S_i might be headed by a salesperson with some high school education and average income; it might also be the household of a single person or couple in the family-formation (childless) stage of the lifecycle. This household would be matched with a dwelling located in a parallel position in housing space, H_i. In this case, the corresponding housing would be a medium-density, lowrise apartment of average rent. The position of this dwelling in a neighborhood can be described by the "social area diagram" introduced in Chapter 6. In this figure, the neighborhood or community space is defined by the subarea's scores on the social and family status dimensions of the social area analysis model. In this case, the household is located in community space at the position C_i, a subarea average on both dimensions. Finally, from the analysis of the general models of urban geometry, the location of these subareas would resemble the fourth figure in Figure 7.12 (Rees, 1970, pp. 312–13). Family status characteristics are distributed by concentric zones, economic status characteristics by sectors. The physical location of this household would represent a compromise between price and lifestyle. Because familism is low, the dwelling could be centrally located. The price range would place it in a middle-income sector of the city. An examination of the available alternatives (dwellings at points 1.12) would lead to the final decision to locate in dwelling 3 at point L_i.

SUMMARY

This chapter explores the social, economic, and ecological processes that lead to the sorting of groups and individuals into homogeneous subareas of cities. In the first half of the chapter, general theories of location are introduced to illustrate the operation of locational forces. The economic theory of rents is used to identify the economic factors that influence the location of activities across the urban landscape. If the limiting assumptions of the theory are met, the location of an economic activity with respect to the central business district depends on the ability of this activity to pay rents. Rents are based on the cost of transporting a producer's commodity to the central market and the value of the commodity for sale. In general, distance from a city's center and rents are inversely related. From the city's center outward to its periphery, transportation costs increase and accessibility to the center decreases; rents decline accordingly.

The theory of rents underlies the classical theories of land usage—Burgess's concentric zone theory, Hoyt's sector theory, and Harris and Ullman's multiple nuclei theory. The Burgess theory was the first published and the most controversial. Burgess posits that land uses are distributed into homogeneous concentric zones through impersonal economic forces. Burgess's theory, however, focuses on the types of people that live in each zone; it has a sociological emphasis. Hoyt's theory, in contrast, is based on an analysis of housing rents; it is more empirical than theoretical and asserts that economic groups are distributed across a city in a sectoral pattern. Harris and Ullman's theory places less emphasis on groups and more emphasis on the distribution of business, industry, commerce, and other economic activities.

The Burgess and Hoyt theories are dynamic, stressing the principle that a city must reorganize spatially as it grows. Burgess points to an expanding CBD as the cause of urban change; to Hoyt both an expanding CBD and a mobile upper class are causes of change. Harris and Ullman's theory, in contrast, is more static, emphasizing present rather than future land use patterns.

The Burgess theory has come under the greatest scrutiny by students of the city and weaknesses have been discovered. Nevertheless, elements of the Burgess theory are found in present ecological research, specifically the influence of distance from a city's center. All three theories have been employed within the social area analysis framework. Family status characteristics have been found to be distributed in a concentric zone pattern, social status characteristics by sector, and ethnic status characteristics in a multiple nuclei pattern.

The decision of an individual to move and the search for a residence are explored in the second half of the chapter. The ecological processes identified in the first half of the chapter are the result of millions of individual decisions. This decision-making process is complicated, involving a wide range of factors that can be analyzed in terms of family lifecycle, social mobility, characteristics of the residence and neighborhood, and neighborhood attachment. In general, incongruency between the personal characteristics of an individual and the characteristics of his or her residential environment cause dissatisfaction. Dissatisfaction with the residential environment does not cause the move directly, but initiates a search for more satisfying alternatives. The decision to move is one such alternative.

If the individual or family decides to move, factors influencing the decision include income, stage in the lifecycle, lifestyle, and attitudes toward the journey to work. The search process involves the matching of these individual or family characteristics with an appropriate subarea of the city. The individual, however, has only limited information on the neighborhoods in the city and this information contains biases. As a result, the location finally chosen is normally not the best alternative, but the best of the sites visited.

Important is the fact that each individual decision, when combined with millions of others, leads to the emergence of homogeneous areas of the city—areas that when ranked on economic, family, and ethnic status are distributed in a patterned way corresponding with the classical models of urban land use.

NOTES

1. The following discussion is based in part on works by William Alonso, "A Theory of the Urban Land Market," *Papers and Proceedings of the Regional Science Association* 6 (1960):149–58, and William Alonso, *Location and Land Use: Toward a General Theory of Land Rent* (Cambridge, Mass.: Harvard University Press, 1965).
2. See Niedercorn and Hearle, 1964, p. 106. A complete citation of the article is in the text's bibliography.
3. See the works of Rossi (1955), Foote (1960), and Ross (1962). A complete citation for each of these works is found in the bibliography.

4. Assume that you have chosen a modest $70,000 house for your first home and you are able to make a down payment of $10,000. You need to borrow $60,000. A $60,000 loan at the present mortgage rate of 15 percent (November, 1980) for a period of thirty years would be $758.67 a month. Applying the rule-of-thumb that your housing costs should not exceed 20 percent of your gross monthly income, you would need an annual salary of $45,000 to afford this modest home. In today's housing market you need to be an upper-income family to purchase a middle-income house.

5. In older metropolitan areas of the Northeast these facilities are normally located in the CBD. Sunbelt cities of the South and Southwest have developed without a dominant CBD and these facilities may be located away from the city's center in separate nuclei.

CHAPTER EIGHT

The Suburbanization Process

Statement of Objectives

1. The student should become aware of the changing image of the suburb.
2. The student should understand the complex interaction of the elements of the POET framework that describe the rapid growth of the nation's suburbs.
3. The student should review the suburbanization process in a historical perspective—1800 to the present.
4. The student should address the following question: Is there a unique suburban way of life?
5. The student should review the analysis of the suburbanization of business and industry.
6. Social problems are not new to our cities. There are characteristics of the modern metropolis that tend to exacerbate problems, such as housing, poverty, and racism. The student should analyze these characteristics in light of our more serious urban problems.

Although the process of suburbanization has been studied by ecologists and urban sociologists for more than fifty years, it is poorly understood. A review of the literature on the suburb shows that at times suburbanization has been viewed as the solution to and at other times the cause of urban ills. For example, as early as 1905, the sociologist Charles Zueblin declared, "The future belongs not to the city but to the suburb." In a little more than fifty years, the process framed as a solution to urban problems was redefined as a problem itself. In the 1950s, authors such as Reisman (1958) voiced the concern that the movement of the middle class and their human

303

and financial resources to the suburbs was draining the vitality from central cities and aggravating the problems of poverty and racism.

In the past decade, a new generation of sociologists has begun to study suburbs and they are questioning the images of the suburb developed in the past. They ask: Are suburbs a new phenomenon or do they represent the normal fringe development of a city? Are the images of the suburb as the bastion of the well-educated, white, affluent middle class, and the central city as the haven of the poor, uneducated, and minority people correct? Are suburbs all alike or are there different suburban types? Finally, does suburban growth intensify the political, social, and economic problems of the central cities or is this a myth? These questions are addressed in this chapter. The goal of this discussion is to separate the myth of the suburban process from the reality by studying the suburbanization process in the broad perspective of the metropolitan area as a whole.

The Changing Image of the Suburb

The prevailing view of the suburbanization process has changed dramatically over the course of this century. Once considered a process that would solve urban ills, suburbanization was later thought to contribute to them. This shift in attitude can be explained by changes in the perceived nature of cities and changes in the social and intellectual biases of the researchers conducting suburban studies.

The suburban image in the 1920s Harlan Douglas published the first comprehensive book on the suburb, *The Suburban Trend*, in 1925. In this work suburbs were viewed positively. To Douglas, the suburbs represented the early stages of development of an exciting new urban form—an area that combined the amenities of the city with the low density of the countryside, a place that brought together the best of both worlds. Douglas was writing during a period of history when many of the negative byproducts of industrialization and urbanization were manifested in cities. The filth and squalor, as well as the crime, political corruption, and social disorganization found in cities suggested to him that a new urban form was needed. The suburb was thought to be the place where the traditional forms of social control could be brought to bear on these evils. Such an attitude is not surprising. Douglas and many of the other urban researchers of his era had been raised in small towns and rural areas. These were the social forms with which they were most familiar and in which they placed the greatest hope.

The suburban image in the 1950s

Ironically, a little more than twenty-five years after the publication of *The Suburban Trend*, the process framed as a solution to urban problems was redefined as a problem itself. After World War II, liberalized lending policies of the Federal Housing Authority (FHA) and the Veterans Administration (VA) made suburban housing affordable to working- and middle-class people. The explosive growth of fringe areas of cities in the decade ending in 1960 led many students of the city to worry about the future of American civic culture. Reisman voices these sentiments clearly in an article written in 1958:

> The city [before World War II] represented the division and specialization not only of labor but of attitude and opinion: by discovering like-minded people in the city, one developed a new style, a new little magazine, a new architecture. The city, that is, provided a "critical mass" which made possible new combinations—criminal and fantastic ones as well as stimulating and productive ones. Today, however, with the continual loss to the suburbs of the elite and the enterprising, the cities remain huge enough for juveniles to form delinquent subcultures; but will our cities be able to continue to support cultural and educational activities at a level appropriate to our abundant economy? (p. 382)

Reisman was part of a new generation of sociologists whose background was not in the countryside but in the great cities. These people were accustomed to the noise, filth, and social disorganization of the city, but appreciated its diversity and complexity. Rather than focusing on the negative aspects of urban life, they saw the city as a vital element of American culture. Their work is the basis of the present image of the suburb—single-family homes, crabgrass-free lawns, picture windows, familism, station wagons, backyard barbecues, and neighborliness. Suburbanization meant not only more spacious living but a more gracious lifestyle (Palen, 1977, p. 92).

In general, this group believed that the growth of suburbs was a unique phenomenon emerging for the first time in the post–World War II period. Moreover, this group viewed suburban growth as negatively affecting city life in many ways. First, these critics argued that as the middle and upper classes moved to the suburbs, the city would be deprived of its traditional leadership. Second, as these groups moved outward, leaving behind the poor, the old, and minority people, the problems of poverty and racism in the city would become worse. Third, these critics suggested that the movement of the middle class to the suburbs would cause an erosion of the tax base, and that cities would have fewer financial resources with which to solve their problems. Finally, these sociologists suggested that the financial plight of cities was worsened by suburbanites' practice of living on the city's fringe in politically autonomous communities but working at the city's center, consuming city services but not paying for them. In this sense, the poor in the central city were viewed as subsidizing the affluent in the suburban ring.

These authors also directed their criticism to the structure and lifestyle of the suburbs. Planners argued that suburbs squandered the nation's resources. Because of their low density, suburbs consumed large amounts of land in housing construction. Normally built on a modified grid pattern, they used water, sewer, gas, road, and electrical systems inefficiently. Socially, they were viewed as negatively affecting both men and women— the housewife isolated in the "Cape Cod" with the children by day was ignored at night by the breadwinner exhausted from commuting to the city. Thus, the critics thought the modern suburban lifestyle was unique, and inevitably transformed the character of suburbanites.[1]

The suburban image in the 1960s, 1970s, and 1980s During the 1960s, 1970s, and 1980s another generation of sociologists began to study the suburbs and to question the prevailing image of the suburban life. Scott Greer (1962) in the early 1960s was among the first to interject a cautionary note into the central city–suburban debate. He pointed out that suburbia, in the strictest sense, is only an artifact of the static boundary lines of the central cities. Most new construction takes place outside a city's boundaries because undeveloped land is unavailable in central locations. In addition, Greer noted that the population attributes used by Reisman and others in the 1950s to characterize suburbs (white, middle-class, and familistic) are shared by people living in many of the central city's neighborhoods (1962, pp. 82–85). Greer in other books and articles employed social area analysis in exploring the political behavior, neighboring, and community involvement of people living in different parts of the city (Greer, 1956, 1962a, 1962b, 1972; Greer and Orleans, 1962). Greer showed that the central city–suburban dichotomy was inadequate to explain the differences among social areas. In his opinion, a more elaborate conceptual framework than the central city–suburban ideal type was needed to examine these differences.

Many other researchers followed Greer's lead in challenging the assumptions about suburban life developed in the 1950s. Many members of this new group had been raised in the suburbs and their background shaped their outlook. These researchers, however, benefited from hindsight, and by testing the work of others achieved greater objectivity in their research on suburbs. The major research questions raised by this group are addressed in remaining sections of this chapter.

Suburbanization Defined

The concept of suburbanization is largely ambiguous and ill defined. Douglas defined the suburb as "the belt of population which lives under distinctly roomier conditions than is the average lot of city people, but under distinctively more crowded conditions than those of the adjoining open country, whether living within or outside the city" (p. 6). In this definition, Douglas stressed one criterion, population density. In more recent research, definitions derived from the United States Census have been employed. By one definition the suburbs are that area located within the Standard Metropolitan Statistical Area (SMSA) but outside the central city. On this basis more than 98 million Americans lived in suburbs in 1980 (Census Bureau, 1981). Another more refined census-based definition describes the suburban ring as that area located within an Urbanized Area but outside the central city. On the basis of this definition, 67 million Americans lived in suburbs in 1980 (Census Bureau, 1981). These definitions employ economic and political criteria in addition to density in delineating suburban areas. The limits of the central cities are defined by their political boundaries, whereas the outer boundaries of Urbanized Areas and SMSAs are based on a complex set of rules for population size, density and economic dependency. (See the discussion of census units in Chapter 2.) Usually the larger the metropolitan area, the smaller the central city, but the use of political boundaries to define the central city introduces distortions. Where city-county governments are consolidated there are fewer suburbs. Elsewhere, however, a suburban community may be completely surrounded by the central city. San Fernando, California, for example, is surrounded by the city of Los Angeles.

These inconsistencies have led researchers to stress additional criteria such as the housing types in an area and its proximity to the central business district, the rate of workers commuting to the central city, the proportion of an area's residents in the early stages of the family lifecycle, the socioeconomic status of residents, and the homogeneity of values and attitudes in the fringe.[2] For the purposes of this book, the deconcentration of activities and population from a city to adjacent fringe areas is called suburbanization. This definition refers to the redistribution not only of population, but also of business and industry. Thus, those communities of urban density located near large metropolitan centers are considered suburbs. Suburbs may be either incorporated or unincorporated communities but must be socially and economically dependent on the nearby city. "Their populations are urban and not rural in character; their economies are nonagricultural; their social structures reflect their interdependency with the adjacent city; and their residents usually identify with both their suburb and the city" (Schwirian, 1977, pp. 168–69).

An operational definition of suburbia The question remains how this definition can be operationalized with available public data. The two major data units available in the United States Census are the Urbanized Area and the SMSA. The SMSA consists of a group of counties economically and socially dependent on a central city of at least 50,000 inhabitants. SMSAs, however, contain many people who hardly fit the common notion of suburbanites. In 1970 more than one-quarter of the populations in SMSAs but outside central cities were classified as rural (U.S. Department of the Census, 1972, table 47). An Urbanized Area, in contrast, is a central city plus the densely populated area at its fringe. This unit of analysis more closely identifies the suburban ring as defined here. *Therefore, in the following sections the term "suburbs" refers to that area of the city outside the central city but within the Urbanized Area.*

THE SUBURBANIZATION PROCESS IN HISTORICAL PERSPECTIVE

Suburban Population Growth

Chapter 7 examines a family's decision to move and its search for a new home—that is, the process by which a household is matched with a dwelling in an appropriate subarea of a city. Factors such as stage in the lifecycle, lifestyle, socioeconomic status, race, and ethnicity are identified as important in limiting the search process to a few of the city's neighborhoods. This search can take place over the entire metropolitan area and several types of moves are possible. People in an inner-city household may decide to move to another dwelling in the same or nearby neighborhood or they may decide to move from the city to the suburban ring. Suburban dwellers, in contrast, may move to another location on the city's fringe or may choose a more centralized location in the city. In this context, suburbanization is one part of a more general process of population redistribution. Reshuffling of households is continuous within and between a city and its suburban ring, and suburbanization occurs when the city's fringe grows faster than the central city. This deconcentration of population is not a new process. It has been found to have occurred in humankind's earliest cities and it represents one way a city may grow as its population expands.

Suburban growth in the eighteenth and nineteenth centuries In the United States, cities have grown faster than rural areas since 1820, and suburbanization was an early part of this urbanization process. As early as the 1760s suburban areas near Boston and Philadelphia were populated. In 1910 one-quarter of the population of the twenty-five metropolitan districts defined by the Census Bureau lived in the suburbs (Farley, 1974, p. 99). Weber (viz., 1963), in the first comprehensive study of American cities, found that most older industrial cities in the United States had one or more suburbs as early as 1890. By 1900, the United States was well on its way to becoming an urban-industrial nation, and suburban growth around the larger metropolises during the twentieth century followed the earlier patterns.

Suburban growth in the twentieth century Table 8.1 shows interdecade rates of population increase for the total, metropolitan, and nonmetropolitan populations of the continental United States for the years 1900–1980. Metropolitan areas are subdivided into central city and urbanized fringe, and separate growth rates are provided for each. A perusal of this table shows

Table 8.1
Rates of population increase by metropolitan status, 1900–1980.

Population status	1970–80	1960–70	1950–60	1940–50	1930–40	1920–30	1910–20	1900–10
Total United States	11.3	13.4	18.5	14.5	7.2	16.1	14.9	21.0
Nonmetropolitan	3.4	5.8	8.1	6.1	6.5	6.0	6.7	13.6
Metropolitan	14.5	28.8	47.5	22.0	8.4	27.5	25.9	32.5
Central city	4.8	9.0	20.8	13.8	5.5	24.2	27.9	37.1
Urbanized fringe	18.2	45.0	81.0	26.0	8.0	42.6	35.9	49.2

Source: Adapted from Table 1 in Leo F. Schnore, *The Urban Scene.* New York: The Free Press, 1965, p. 80; Copyright © 1965 by The Free Press, a Division of Macmillan Publishing Co., Inc., and U.S. Bureau of the Census, *1970 Census, Characteristics of the Population, Vol. 1, U.S. Summary, Part 1, Section 11.* Washington, D.C.: Government Printing Office, 1972; and U.S. Bureau of the Census, 1980 Census, Provisional Data, May 1981.

that metropolitan areas have captured a disproportionately larger share of the nation's total population increase over the past eighty years. Within metropolitan areas, central-city growth has slowed while the growth rate for the urbanized fringe has progressively increased. The only exception is the decade between 1950 and 1960, a period when many central cities were annexing large parcels of adjacent developed and undeveloped land. Because the figures are uncorrected for annexation, they underestimate the amount of fringe growth in the post–World War II period (Schnore, 1965). Research published since 1970 suggests that this pattern may have changed.

MISTER BREGER

"Someday, son, all this will be yours . . !"

Source: © King Features Syndicate, Inc., 1965.

The United States Bureau of the Census in 1972 reported that nonmetropolitan areas exceeded the growth rates of metropolitan areas between the years 1970 and 1972 for the first time in this century (Beale, 1972). This statement taken at face value suggests that the nation may be on a new course of urban development. Recent articles[3] indicate that much of this population growth is centered in smaller urban places (under 50,000 inhabitants) about an hour's drive from a large metropolitan area. People in the new households in these smaller cities, though employed locally, are close enough to larger centers to enjoy the recreation, shopping, and cultural facilities found there.

Rapid suburbanization in the post–World War II period Table 8.1 indicates that the United States underwent its most rapid suburbanization in the post–World War II period. Therefore a more careful examination of metropolitan growth between 1950 and 1980 follows. Table 8.2 is a summary of the changes in the population of the central cities and urbanized fringe for the fifteen largest urbanized areas in 1980. In that year, these cities contained more than 60 million people, half of this nation's population living in urbanized areas. Because these cities are geographically dispersed, the analysis identifies regional differences that may have been masked in the summary statistics in Table 8.1.

A perusal of these data indicates that these fifteen cities followed the national trend in population deconcentration for the 1950–1980 period. Between 1950 and 1960, the nation's population grew by 17 percent but only three cities, Los Angeles, Houston, and Dallas (cities in the so-called Sunbelt), grew in excess of this rate. Note that in all cases the growth of the city's fringe greatly exceeded that of the central city. In fact, the central cities of twelve of the fifteen metropolises in the sample declined in population. The Sunbelt cities of Los Angeles, Dallas, and Houston were the only exceptions, but these cities were annexing large portions of their fringe areas during the 1950s. If the figures were corrected for annexation, Dallas and Houston and probably Los Angeles would have patterns similar to those of the other cities (Farley, 1976, p. 8). Moreover, the 1980 Census shows that these trends continued through the 1970s.

Between 1960 and 1980, the population nationally grew by 14 percent but only Houston and Dallas exceeded this percentage. As in the previous decade, central cities on the whole continued to lose population while suburban rings continued to absorb most of the urbanized areas' population growth (Farley, 1976, p. 8).

One of the stereotyped images of the suburbanization process is that it is the result of white flight to the cities' fringe. This generalization is borne out, since in both decades twelve of the cities lost whites and gained blacks. Los Angeles, Dallas, and Houston were the exceptions; both their white and black populations grew in both the central city and the urbanized fringe (Farley, 1976, p. 8).

Table 8.2
Total population of urbanized areas and decennial growth rates, 1950–1980

All urbanized areas	Total population (thousands)				Decennial growth rates (%) total		
	1950	1960	1970	1980	1950–60	1960–70	1970–80
New York*							
City	8,891	8,743	8,820	7,071	−2	+1	−19
Ring	3,405	5,372	7,387	8,513	+58	+38	+15
Los Angeles*							
City	2,221	2,823	3,175	2,950	+27	+12	−7
Ring	2,147	3,666	5,177	6,528	+70	+41	+26
Chicago*							
City	3,897	3,898	3,697	2,970	0	−5	−20
Ring	1,024	2,061	3,017	3,741	+101	+46	+24
Philadelphia							
City	2,072	2,003	1,949	1,686	−3	−3	−14
Ring	851	1,633	2,073	2,428	+92	+27	+17
Detroit							
City	1,850	1,670	1,496	1,192	−10	−10	−20
Ring	810	1,867	2,475	2,617	+131	+33	+6
San Francisco*							
City	1,160	1,158	1,077	674	0	−7	−37
Ring	862	1,273	1,911	2,518	+48	−50	+32
Boston							
City	801	697	641	563	−13	−8	−12
Ring	1,432	1,716	2,015	2,115	+20	+17	+5
Washington							
City	802	764	757	635	−5	−1	−16
Ring	485	1,045	1,725	2,127	+115	+65	+23
Cleveland							
City	915	876	751	574	−4	−14	−23
Ring	469	909	1,209	1,178	+94	+33	−2
Saint Louis							
City	857	750	622	458	−12	−17	−27
Ring	543	918	1,261	1,390	+69	+37	+10
Pittsburgh							
City	677	604	520	424	−11	−14	−19
Ring	856	1,200	1,326	1,385	+40	+10	+4
Minneapolis*							
City	833	796	744	371	−4	−7	−50
Ring	283	581	960	1,416	+105	+65	+48

Table 8.2 (Continued)

All urbanized areas	Total population (thousands)				Decennial growth rates(%) total		
	1950	1960	1970	1980	1950–60	1960–70	1970–80
Houston							
City	596	938	1,233	1,594	+57	+31	+29
Ring	104	202	445	8,118	+93	+120	+83
Baltimore							
City	950	939	906	783	−1	−4	−16
Ring	212	480	674	972	+126	+40	+44
Dallas							
City	434	680	844	901	+56	+24	+7
Ring	105	253	494	1,550	+141	+96	+214
Average							
City	1,797	1,823	1,815	1,523	+1	0	−16
Ring	906	1,545	2,143	2,565	+71	+39	+20

*More than one central city in these urbanized areas.

Source: 1950, 1960 and 1970 data from Farley, R. *Components of Suburban Population Growth.* In B. Schwartz (Ed.), *The Changing Face of the Suburbs.* Chicago: The University of Chicago Press, 1976, pp. 6–7. Provisional 1980 data from U.S. Bureau of the Census, *1980 Provisional Metropolitan Data,* 1981.

STUDY FINDS BLACKS MOVING TO THE SUBURBS

By Eugene Lowe

In a study, *Black Suburbanization at the Mid-1970's,* Eunice and George Grier say that "during the first part of the 1970's . . . there was an increase in the black suburban percentage (of households) for the first time in decades." The study was released at a plenary session ("Population Distribution Trends That Influence Housing Opportunities") of the NCDH/HUD fair housing conference.

In an analysis of data from two periodic sample surveys taken by the Bureau of Census—the Current Population Survey and the Annual Housing Survey, the Griers found that by 1976 the suburban black percentage was 5.3 percent. The 1976 statistic was an increase over a 4.8 suburban black percentage in 1960, and a 4.6 percent figure in 1970. As these figures indicate, a substantial increase of blacks living in the suburbs has occurred during the 1970's. "Between 1970 and 1974, the number of black persons living in the suburbs increased by well over twice the percentage rate of whites—19.5 percent vs. only 7.3 percent," the Griers say.

Black Suburbanization in Washington, D.C.

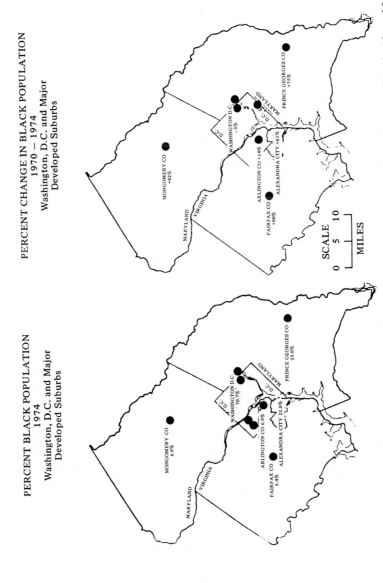

PERCENT BLACK POPULATION
1974
Washington, D.C. and Major
Developed Suburbs

PERCENT CHANGE IN BLACK POPULATION
1970 – 1974
Washington, D.C. and Major
Developed Suburbs

MARYLAND

VIRGINIA

MONGOMERY CO
6.9%

WASHINGTON D.C.
70.7%

D.C.

MARYLAND

FAIRFAX CO
5.4%

ARLINGTON CO 6.9%

ALEXANDRA CITY 22.0%

PRINCE GEORGES CO
25.0%

MARYLAND

VIRGINIA

MONGOMERY CO
+82%

WASHINGTON D.C.
−5%

D.C.

MARYLAND

ARLINGTON CO +14%

ALEXANDRA CITY +61%

FAIRFAX CO
+90%

PRINCE GEORGES CO
+75%

SCALE

0   5   10

MILES

Washington Center for Metropolitan Studies, Washington Area Census Updating System, Trends Alert, 1974.

313

But the Griers also note that even with the black suburban increase being as significant as it is, it will not equal the black percentage in the national population as a whole for decades.

Because of a lack of data, the Griers are not sure if the "recent black suburban increase represented desegregation." They concede that much of the increase might be "resegregation" where pre-existing black enclaves expand, or racial ghetto areas spill over from central cities to nearby suburbs. If this has happened, then "the prevailing pattern of segregation" has not changed at all.

Several cities were studied individually. They included: Atlanta, where the black suburban increase (of the national total) was from 5 percent in 1970 to 6.6 percent in 1975; Chicago, the increase was from 2.9 percent in 1970 to 3.7 percent in 1975; Los Angeles, the increase was from 5.1 percent in 1970 to 7.1 percent in 1974; Philadelphia, the increase was from 5.8 percent in 1970 to 6.7 percent in 1974; Detroit, the increase was from 3.2 percent in 1970 to 3.7 percent in 1974; in Washington, D.C., where the biggest increase in the nation occurred, the figures were 6.5 percent in 1970 and 10.7 percent in 1974. Of the individual cities studied, the Griers were only able to tell if Washington, D.C. had any housing desegregation. In Washington, where the Griers had the benefit of a local census updating survey, they found that both desegregation and resegregation had occurred at the same time in the suburbs.

Those black persons moving to the suburbs can be typically described (for the metropolitan areas studied) as young (two-thirds are under age 35), middle class, with high incomes and small households (three persons or less). "Most are renters—ranging from 70 to 88 percent depending on the area."

Much can be learned from recent experience "that will advance housing desegregation elsewhere." Washington, D.C., where there is some data and a good deal of black suburban movement, is especially helpful, say the Griers. Two forms of intervention might be undertaken. First, the market for housing could be strengthened by "improving incomes and job prospects" of minorities. In Washington, "the size and relative affluence of the black community" has no doubt led to some housing desegregation. Second, fair housing groups can help minorities take advantage of the protections provided by law and can see to it that these protections are enforced. In Washington, the Griers believe that "a vigorous citizen fair housing program . . . played an important role in encouraging desegregation under the federal law." A summary of the report is available from NCDH.

Source: From *Trends in Housing*, May 1978. Used by permission of Eugene T. Lowe.

Changes in the types of people living in today's central cities and suburbs Farley (1976) carried out a detailed analysis of the age, racial, educational, and income characteristics of the populations of these fifteen cities and drew the following conclusions:

1. All cities must respond to population growth, and suburbanization was the process by which these cities expanded between 1950 and 1970. Suburbs grew rapidly during the entire period, growing by 71 percent in the 1950s but slowing to 39 percent in the decade ending in 1970. In general, central cities lost population by the out-migration of whites, a deconcentration of people that greatly exceeded the growth of the central cities' nonwhite population.
2. The people moving from the central cities to the suburbs were found to be in their late twenties and early thirties, on the average. Central cities, in contrast, attracted younger people regardless of race, and this finding supports the analysis of lifestyles and location decisions in Chapter 7.
3. Levels of education and income rose for both central city and suburban residents for the 1950–1970 period, but the increases were greater for populations living in the urban fringe. In all fifteen urbanized areas the suburban populations were of a higher socioeconomic status than their counterparts in the central cities.
4. Migrants into these urbanized areas between 1950 and 1970 tended to be of higher socioeconomic status than the nonmover resident population. A high percentage of whites who moved into these urbanized areas for the first time located directly in the suburban ring. Moreover, the few whites who did move directly into the cities were of high socioeconomic status suggestive of a "cosmopolite" lifestyle orientation. In general both whites and nonwhites who moved to the suburbs were of higher socioeconomic status than the central-city residents left behind.
5. Finally, Farley notes that urbanized areas have become increasingly heterogeneous in their population characteristics since 1950, making it difficult for investigators to predict future demographic trends in the urbanized fringe.

The last point is important, especially in terms of the stereotyped image of the suburb as the subarea of a city most conducive to the lifestyle "familism." Long and Glick (1976), in their analysis of SMSA data, found that during the 1960s central cities continued to "attract single persons in their early twenties" but lost them to the suburbs as they reached their late twenties and early thirties (p. 52). This pattern is explored in some detail in Chapter 7. Higher-income suburbs are still characterized by the familism lifestyle. Moderate-income suburbs, however, show a greater diversity of family types. In general, during the 1960s these suburbs included "more persons in the 'singles' category, fewer married couples, more working wives, and more working mothers" (Long and Glick, 1975, p. 52). Therefore, if one compares cities and suburbs on the dimension of family status, these places are seen to have become more alike during the 1960s. Significant differences continue, however, if one compares their socioeconomic and racial characteristics.

Socioeconomic and Racial Characteristics of Cities and Suburbs

The socioeconomic and racial characteristics of cities and suburbs are summarized in Table 8.3. First, note that in 1970 the percentage of the urbanized-area population living on a city's fringe was nearly equal to that living in the central city. This pattern was due solely to the growth rate in the fringe, which exceeded that of the city by four times. The percentage of nonwhite population in the fringe, 5.7 percent, is much lower than that in the city, 22.5 percent, but this pattern has remained unchanged since 1950. Recent research indicates that the suburbanization of blacks is occurring

Table 8.3

Social characteristics of city and fringe populations of United States urbanized areas, 1970.

Characteristic	City	Fringe
Percentage of population growth, 1960–1970	11.7	44.0
Percentage of population that is nonwhite (black and other groups)	22.5	5.7
Percentage of population under 18 years of age	31.5	35.4
Percentage of population 65 years of age and older	10.7	7.8
Fertility ratio	336.0	342.0
Percentage of females 14 years and older who are married	56.1	63.8
Average number of persons per household	2.90	3.25
Median number of school years completed by males 25 years of age and older	12.0	12.4
Median number of school years completed by females 25 years of age and older	12.0	12.3
Percentage of all population 25 years of age and older with 4 years of high school and 1–3 years of college completed	66.3	70.0
Percentage of females 16 years of age and older who are in the labor force	44.5	42.5
Percentage of males 16 years of age and older with occupations classified as professional, technical and kindred, and managers	22.8	27.9
Median family income	$9,519.00	$11,771.00

Source: 1970 Census, *Characteristics of the Population, Vol. 1, U.S. Summary, Part 1, Section 1.* Washington, D.C.: U.S. Government Printing Office, Tables 99, 101, 102, 119.

in the nation's largest areas but at a very slow rate (Schnore, Andre, Sharp, 1976, pp. 69–94).

In general, fringe populations are younger than cities', as indicated by the larger percentage of people under eighteen and the lower percentage of people sixty-five years and older, but these differences are not great. A larger percentage of females in fringe areas are married but they have lower levels of fertility and somewhat larger households. Differences in the educational characteristics of both males and females are relatively minor. The most striking contrast is in median family income; the average income levels in cities and fringe areas differ by more than $2,200.

These summary data suggest that, except in race and income characteristics, cities and suburbs are becoming more alike. General metropolitan-wide data tend to mask important differences, however. For example, aggregated data for all United States central cities suggest enormous heterogeneity in the racial, family, and socioeconomic characteristics of their residents. Summary statistics indicate a population that is large, heterogeneous, and densely settled. Upon closer scrutiny, however, one finds the effects of these factors mediated by the emergence of homogeneous subareas as described in Chapters 6 and 7. (See also the discussion of Claude Fisher's work in Chapter 1.)

Suburban Types

The same forces are at work in fringe areas as in the central cities, and the spatial complexity normally associated with a central city now characterizes the fringe. This spatial complexity is reflected in the research on suburban types. Boskoff (1970), for example, identified twelve types of suburbs but only two, the "traditional suburb" and the "identity-conscious suburb," are middleclass and familistic. Herbert Gans (1967), in his study *The Levittowners*, found a great diversity of people living in this "mass-produced suburb." Similarly, in his monograph *Working-class Suburb*, Bennett Berger (1960) examined the experiences of autoworkers and their families in an industrial suburb of San Jose, California. Clearly there are fundamental differences among suburbs in both their function and their social, family, and ethnic status. Although Boskoff (1970) and others have presented elaborate typologies, researchers usually distinguish between two general suburban types—employing suburbs and satellites or residential suburbs (Schnore, 1957, 1965).

Residential suburbs Residential suburbs are dormitory communities made up of homeowners and in a few cases renters. In general, the only economic activities within their borders are retail and personal services that fill the needs of local residents; i.e. dry cleaners and grocers. In fact, residents in these suburbs want to keep manufacturing and industry out and preserve the residential character of their community. Park Forest, Illinois, a suburb of Chicago studied by Whyte (1956); Levittown, New Jersey, a suburb of Philadelphia studied by Gans (1967); and Crestwood Heights, a suburb of Toronto studied by Seeley, Sim, and Loosley (1956) are examples of this suburban type.

Employing suburbs Employing suburbs, in contrast, have employment as their key function. Normally, they have large manufacturing or industrial operations within their borders, and their principal function is to provide goods and services to consumers outside the suburb. These communities provide jobs to large numbers of local residents, but they also attract a large workforce of commuters who are employed there on a daily basis (Schnore, 1957, 1965). Many of the suburbs around the nation's older industrial cities are of the employing type. Norwood, a suburb of Cincinnati, Ohio, employs thousands of workers in the General Motors assembly plant located there. Similarly, Euclid, Ohio, and many of the other suburbs around Cleveland have large numbers of industries within their borders.

Residential and Employing Suburbs Compared

Schwirian (1977) illustrates the differences between these two suburban types in his analysis of the larger fringe communities (10,000 and over) of the Chicago Urbanized Area. He distinguishes between these suburban types by using an index called the E/R ratio. The numerator, E, in this ratio is the number of jobs in manufacturing and trade within a particular suburb. The denominator, R, is the number of residents in the suburb who are employed in these activities. Dividing R into E gives a value that indicates the degree to which residents are employed locally. A high index, one exceeding 116, indicates that many more jobs in manufacturing and trade are available than are filled by local residents, and as a result large numbers of workers must come into the community each day for employment. Fringe communities with index values of 116 or greater are considered employing suburbs. The opposite is true of suburbs with index values of 85 or less. These communities are categorized as "residential suburbs." Suburbs that have index values between 86 and 115 have a mixed pattern and are difficult to classify (Schwirian, 1977, p. 178).

Differences in social characteristics Table 8.4 summarizes Schwirian's findings of the social characteristics of the employing and residential suburbs of the Chicago Urbanized Area in 1970. In the first column are the average scores of selected social characteristics for the twenty-three employing suburbs identified by Schwirian. The data in column 2 are the average scores for the fifty residential suburbs included in the study. Scanning both columns and comparing the figures for each suburban type, one can see that they do not differ much in their social, economic, and racial characteristics. Employing suburbs are larger on the average than residential

Table 8.4
Social characteristics of employing suburbs and residential suburbs of the Chicago Urbanized Area, 1970.

Characteristic	All employing suburbs N = 23	All residential suburbs N = 50	Selected residential suburbs			
			Summit	Berwyn	Glen Ellyn	Winnetka
Average population	28,067	23,650	11,569	52,502	21,909	13,998
Average growth 1960–1970	41.6	91.8	11.5	−3.2	37.2	4.7
Percentage of adults with 4 years of high school or more	62.7	66.8	37.5	46.0	85.2	90.0
Percentage of families with incomes of $15,000 or more	39.3	42.8	20.2	29.7	61.5	79.3
Cumulative fertility women 35–44 years of age	2,842	2,924	2,882	2,214	2,910	2,882
Percentage of married women with young children and husband present who work	21.8	19.3	27.6	17.6	13.9	11.6
Percentage of the population who are foreign-born	28.5	26.7	26.7	45.2	17.4	20.8
Percentage of the population who are nonwhite	3.0	2.9	19.5	0.4	0.7	1.3

Source: Schwirian, K. P., *Contemporary Topics in Urban Sociology*. Morristown, N.J.: General Learning Press, 1977, p. 179.

suburbs, but the latter's growth rate was more than double that of employing suburbs in the decade ending in 1970. Their education and income characteristics differ, the socioeconomic status of residential suburbs exceeding that of employing suburbs, but the differences are not great. The fertility of women in the residential suburbs is slightly higher than that in employing suburbs but fewer women are married with young children and employed husbands. Finally, the ethnic and racial characteristics of both are roughly the same.

Though the figures in the first two columns of Table 8.4 indicate that the differences between these two suburban types are not great, summary statistics average extreme scores and thus may hide major differences among individual suburbs. This fact is clear in the figures in the right half of the table for four residential suburbs selected from the original sample of fifty. Summit and Berwyn are of low socioeconomic status; a low percentage of their residents have four years or more of high school and family incomes are relatively low. Glen Ellyn and Winnetka, in contrast, are of high socioeconomic status with high scores on both variables. But even this distinction between low- and high-status suburbs is imprecise because they differ in significant ways in population size, population growth, and social, economic, racial, and ethnic characteristics.

Suburban persistence These suburbs differ greatly in their socioeconomic characteristics, but how do individual suburbs develop their unique character? Research by Farley (1974), Stahura (1978), Guest (1978), and others suggests that in the early stages of settlement a suburb's socioeconomic character and function are fixed and persist although the community may undergo rapid population growth at some later date. The character of a suburb is shaped initially by its niche in the ecological structure of the metropolis, that is, its proximity to transportation lines, the central business district, industry, and ammenities such as schools, recreation areas, and cultural facilities. Farley, in commenting on the persistence of suburban types, writes:

> Evanston and Hammond are approximately equal in population size, at the same distance from Chicago's Loop, comparable in age, and both have Lake Michigan frontage. Yet the inhabitants of these suburbs have quite different characteristics. A meat packing plant was the first establishment to attract residents to Hammond, and an excellent rail facility fostered later industrial growth, while the history of Evanston was dependent upon Methodist institutions including Northwestern University (1974, p. 108).

The reasons for this persistence are many and varied but the most important factors appear to be related to the vested interests of homeowners and other users of land as well as banking and lending institutions. A change in the socioeconomic character of an area would adversely affect the investments of these groups; economic self-interest leads them to preserve the character of the area. Thus, not only are there great differences in the character and function of these communities in the urban fringe, once their character is determined it persists through time.

THE *POET* FRAMEWORK USED TO ANALYZE SUBURBAN GROWTH

Factors in Suburban Growth

The unprecedented growth of the nation's urban fringe in the post–World War II period represents the interaction of a complex set of social, economic, historical, and technological factors. These forces, at work for more than a century, made the suburb as it is known today both possible and in many respects necessary. By examining these forces one can better understand the general population shifts associated with the suburbanization process discussed in the preceding section. In the following analysis of the ecological complex, the POET framework introduced in Chapter 1 is used to structure the discussion and to demonstrate the utility of the ecological perspective.

The American city of the twentieth century differs significantly from the city of the nineteenth century in both form and function, yet the cities in both eras grew and expanded by the same process. A city can respond in one of three ways to population growth. First, its boundaries can remain stable and it can grow by increasing its overall population density. Second, its population can expand outward, spilling over the city's political boundaries into satellite communities or the urbanized fringe—the suburbanization process. Third, a city can grow by a combination of the two processes. The form that this expansion takes can be understood by examining the interrelationship among the four variables in the ecological complex—population, organization, environment, and technology. A metropolis viewed from this perspective is a system, and a change in any one element of the ecological complex results in a change in the direction of the metropolis's growth. Factors associated with each element of the POET framework are considered in the following.

Population The most obvious factor influencing the overall suburbanization process is population growth. In the United States, cities have grown faster than rural areas since 1820, but rapid expansion of the metropolitan areas did not occur until after 1850 with the emergence of an integrated national industrial economy. The components of this urban growth are threefold—natural increase (births exceeding deaths), rural to urban migration, and ethnically diverse migration from overseas. Different components affected urban growth at different times in history. For example, cities in the nineteenth century were unhealthy places and deaths normally exceeded births;

thus migration rather than natural increase was the more important element of this growth. In the twentieth century the reverse is true. Immigration quotas have slowed the influx of people from overseas and public health measures have lowered mortality nationwide; thus natural increase has become a more important factor in urban population growth. Concomitantly, the mechanization of American agriculture has brought about a continuation of the nineteenth-century trend of rural to urban migration (McKelvey, 1963, pp. 3–86).

In examining the numerical aspect of the nation's population, urban researchers often overlook another important aspect—the values held by citizens. As discussed in Chapter 7, the value individuals place on lifestyle, housing type, and neighborhood character influences their locational decision. The decision-making process, however, takes place within the alternatives provided by the larger society, alternatives made possible by changes in other elements of the ecological complex.

Organization Institutions ultimately determine how and where the resources of the nation are to be used. Their decisions have profoundly influenced the suburbanization process. Since the 1940s, the federal government has in effect subsidized fringe development with its FHA and VA loan programs, categorical grants to suburbs for water and sewer system construction, and intrametropolitan highway construction programs. The private institutional sphere has been equally important in influencing fringe growth. Banking and lending institutions, large-scale developers, and the real estate industry have actively promoted this form of urban development.

Environment The supply and cost of resources are another factor in the suburbanization process. The geographic distribution of resources has influenced both the location of cities and their potential growth. The availability and costs of fossil fuels, ores, and wood products have also been key factors in population diffusion. In many of the older industrial centers of the Northeast the only available land was in the fringe; thus both the availability and accessibility of this land influenced the suburbanization process.

Technology Technology is the fourth element in the ecological complex influencing the suburbanization process. Just as the elevator, telephone and telegraph, and structural steel made possible skyscrapers and central business districts as they are known today, inventions such as the septic tank, efficient electrification, and the internal combustion engine made the modern suburb a reality. Of all the technological innovations of this century, those in transportation have been the most important in influencing the spatial structure of cities. The cost and time involved in moving goods and people ultimately set the limits on how densely a city will be populated and how its population can be dispersed. Cities bring people together at one point, but the better the available transportation, the greater the dispersal of population that is possible.

Technology has also brought about increased efficiency in American industry and consequently a higher per capita income that has enabled more Americans to absorb the higher costs of housing and transportation in the urban fringe.

Interaction of the POET elements Population, organization, environment, and technology are the key factors in the analysis of suburban growth. A change in one element of the POET framework influences all the other elements and causes a change in the degree and pattern of suburbanization. A dramatic drop in population would have significant consequences for the suburbanization process. Similarly, another depression of the same magnitude as the one in the 1930s would bring urban and suburban growth to a standstill. To clarify the complex interaction of these four factors, the evolution of suburbs is examined in the following temporal sequence: early industrialization 1800–1890, 1890–World War I, World War I–World War II, and the post–World War II period.

Stages of United States Suburban Development

Early industrialization 1800–1890 The conditions for the growth of large urban areas did not occur until the Agricultural and Industrial Revolutions. The Agricultural Revolution, 8,000 years ago, freed individuals from food production and permitted the rise of the first cities. Not until the eighteenth century in England did agricultural technology reach a level that enabled a few farmers to produce surpluses large enough to support large urban populations. Although a cause-effect relationship has not been established between improved agriculture and the Industrial Revolution, the changes in agriculture produced a surplus rural workforce that provided the workers for the newly emerging industries in the cities. Before the Industrial Revolution, cities were small and few in number, and their population made up only about 10–15 percent of the society's total. After the Industrial Revolution this relationship changed drastically, as was shown in Chapter 3.

The effects of primitive transportation technology During the years 1800–1890, the United States was undergoing the early stages of the Industrial Revolution. In fact, by 1890 several American cities had become very large. Chicago had grown to 1.1 million, New York to 1.5 million. Although large, these cities were quite compact. Transportation technology was primitive, and the cost of moving goods and people was very high. In short, transportation technology defined the geographic possibilities of American cities. Because of their dependency on humans and horses as sources of power, cities like Chicago and New York had a radius of densely built-up area of only four and six miles, respectively (McKelvey, 1963, pp. 35–60).

The limitations imposed on cities by primitive transportation technology affected many other aspects of life. Weber (viz., 1963), writing in this period, remarked with alarm on the appalling congestion of cities. High density combined with the lack of elementary sanitation led to dreadful levels of mortality during the more or less regular epidemics of cholera, typhus, influenza, and other diseases. The visitations of these diseases to New York City can be seen clearly in the graph in Figure 8.1. Note the extreme fluctuations in the graph during most of the nineteenth century and the decline and flatness of the curve in the twentieth century. Public health measures, especially the chlorination of drinking water, greatly influenced this mortality decline, but the lowering of density levels (decongestion) was also an important factor (Rosenberg, 1962).

The internal structure of cities   The internal structure of cities was shaped by transportation technology. In the early stages of the Industrial Revolution only the wealthy and the small middle class could afford a ride on the omnibus or horsecar. Most people lived either in the building where they worked or within a short walking distance of their place of employment. Transportation, therefore, did not permit much spatial separation between social classes. Then, as today, the wealthy could absorb the costs of transportation and many of them lived in the suburbs or satellite towns serviced by steam railroads. Only a small minority of a city's population could afford to commute and therefore the railroad had little impact on the spatial structure of the city. The horsedrawn trolley or horsecar was a common means of urban transport but only the middle and upper classes who could afford the fares escaped to other parts of the city. In general, the wealthy, the poor, the artisan, and the factory worker lived near each other and near the factories, wharves, and offices of the city (Warner, 1962).

1890–World War I

Before 1890, residential cities were built primarily within the limits of horsepower. This limitation combined with the spectacular growth rates of cities like Chicago and New York led to severe congestion. In 1888 the diffusion of cities' population was made possible by a technological innovation—the electric streetcar.

The introduction of the electric streetcar on the Richmond Union Passenger Railway in 1888 was so successful that within three years more than 175 systems were in operation in the United States. In 1890 60 percent of all street railways (by mileage) were operated by horses; by 1902 this figure had dropped to 1 percent even though the street railway mileage in this country had more than doubled (Tobin, 1976, p. 99). This new and efficient form of transportation lengthened the radius of the densely built-up areas of cities like Boston and Chicago to ten miles.

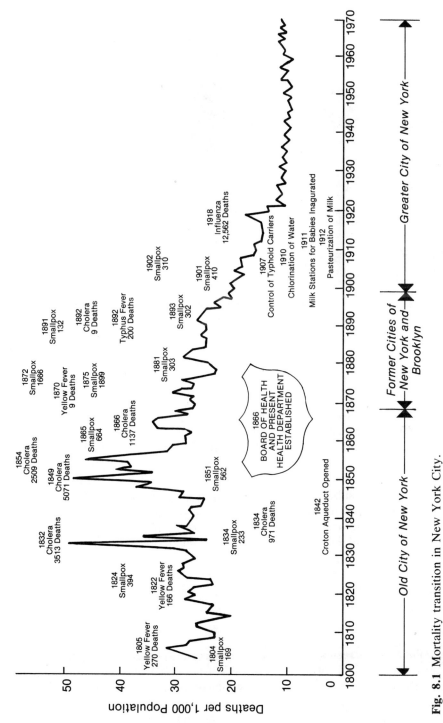

Fig. 8.1 Mortality transition in New York City.

Source: New York City Department of Health, *Summary of Vital Statistics, 1965: The City of New York.* New York: City Department of Health, 1965.

Photo 8.1 The electric streetcar, introduced in American cities in the last quarter of the 19th century, permitted the first real decentralization of population from the central city. The middle class could now afford to live in the suburbs and commute to work in the CBD. This photograph taken at the turn of the century shows a streetcar line that connected Cincinnati, Ohio, to its outlying suburbs.
Source: Courtesy of the Cincinnati Historical Society.

The United States during the decade ending in 1900 was growing at a rate of 1.3 million persons per year, and most of this growth was centered in cities. New York grew from 1.5 million to 3.5 million inhabitants and Chicago from 1.1 to 1.7 million. Similar growth rates characterized many other cities in the "heartland" region of the United States. As these cities grew so did their suburbs. Warner (1962), in his analysis of the streetcar's impact on Boston's suburban development, gives an estimate of the effect of this new transportation form on population diffusion. In 1850, one of every four Bostonians lived in suburbs; by 1900 more than one-third were suburbanites. Boston's population had grown by fourfold between 1850 and 1900, but the population in its suburbs was six times as large in 1900 as in 1850. This pattern was shared by many American cities. The electric streetcar enabled urban populations to spread out and dramatically reduced residential densities.

The influence of streetcar technology Transportation technology greatly influenced the physical form of cities. Pedestrian cities were usually circular because any place on the periphery could be reached from the center by foot or horse in about the same time. Streetcars, in contrast, ran on rails that are expensive to build and maintain, and they were economically feasible only if they were built between points of ridership demand. Initially, streetcar lines were built to connect the central business district with out-lying satellite towns eight to ten miles from a city's center. During the early years of a line's operation the trolleys would travel outside a densely settled city and pass through several miles of undeveloped farmland before reaching their destination. These satellite communities, then, provided the necessary ridership to justify the lines' initial construction. Through time the unde-veloped land between the city and satellite was settled in a pattern pre-scribed by the transportation technology.

The satellite towns had come into existence originally because of the steam locomotive. Because their economics of operation demanded that a string of cars be pulled, steam engines were not suited to schedules requiring frequent stops. As a result, large expanses of undeveloped land extended between a city and its satellites. Homes in the satellite towns were clustered around a small retail center dominated by the railway station, within easy walking distance. The streetcar, in contrast, was not only based on a more efficient power source—electricity—but was quiet and fast. Cars could be run separately or in tandem depending on ridership demand. Because power could be applied uniformly to the wheels, frequent stops were possible. Therefore, because of the streetcar's speed and its ability to make frequent stops, residential construction could occur on land ad-jacent to the line between a city and its satellite towns.

In general, the new streetcar technology led to the emergence of the following spatial pattern. Initially, streetcar lines radiated from a city's center in a pattern resembling the spokes of a wheel. Housing construction in the city's undeveloped fringe was limited to areas within easy walking distance of a trolley stop; the stops were frequent and more or less uniformly spaced along the entire line. Through time, the city changed from a circular pedestrian form to a star-shaped form made up of a densely populated core and appendages of streetcar suburbs. The areas between the built-up street-car corridors were largely undeveloped; they were inaccessible because of the limitation of this form of transportation technology (Warner, 1962; Ward, 1964).

The growth of suburbs This new transportation technology permitted a much needed decongestion of American cities. For example, Baltimore grew by 10 percent between 1900–1910 but its suburbs grew by 45 percent; Chicago grew by 29 percent and the area surrounding the city grew by 88 percent; Los Angeles tripled in size during the decade but its suburbs grew by 533 percent. Many of the nation's cities, especially in the Northeast, underwent similar suburban growth (Tobin, 1976, p. 100).

The internal structure of cities Another and equally important change in the nature of cities resulted from the electrified streetcar—the spatial differ-entiation of cities according to their social area dimensions. As discussed in preceding chapters, groups that differ in socioeconomic, racial, and ethnic character have always been separated from each other in cities, but pri-

Photo 8.2 The "mass-produced" suburbs, built in the post–World War II period, were the product of the complex interaction of population, organizational, environmental, and technological changes in American society.

Source: Photograph by Elliott Erwitt © Magnum Photos, Inc.

mitive technology kept these groups in relatively close proximity to each other. The internal structure of the American city was transformed between 1890 and World War I by several interrelated trends. First, the metamorphosis of society from rural agrarian to urban-industrial was completed. This increase in the scale of society was accompanied by changes in the social structure, especially in the percentage of society considered middle-class. Second, industrialization brought about more efficient exploitation of natural resources, greater per capita wealth, and housing and other amenities previously impossible to provide. Third, transportation technology permitted the interaction of these two trends and thus led to the greater spatial and functional differentiation of the cities. Therefore, in the quarter of the century ending with the opening years of World War I, American cities were transformed from a preindustrial to a modern metropolitan form.

Suburbanization during this period primarily benefited the middle class, and the city and its fringe began to differ in its social, family, and ethnic characteristics. Although the suburbanized fringe was predominantly middle class, the housing in the area was graded into price and style groupings. The populations in these suburbs were differentiated spatially by income and occupational characteristics. Cities changed in turn and by the start of World War I, American cities were spatially more complex, social distance between groups was reflected in greater physical distance between them, and subareas of the city could be identified by the social area analysis dimensions—a pattern associated with high-scale societies (Warner, 1962).

World War I–World War II

It is difficult to define specific periods for any process, but in this analysis dates that correspond to cataclysmic national events are used for good reason. During war, resources that normally would go into housing construction and other areas of the economy are diverted to the war effort. In postwar periods, a nation must undergo major economic and social readjustments as industry shifts from war production and millions of men and women leave the military service and join the civilian workforce. In the post–World War I years this readjustment included the most rapid expansion of suburbs that had ever occurred in America. In the 1920s, for example, central cities grew at a rate of 19.4 percent from 29 million to more than 34 million people while suburban areas grew by 39.2 percent from 11 million to more than 15 million inhabitants. This development was nationwide in scope—suburbs grew faster than central cities in 70 percent of all United States metropolitan districts. Tobin (1976), commenting on this suburban growth, writes:

> Many cities experienced rates of suburban growth that would never again be equaled in these urban areas. The central city of Boston grew by 4%, the suburbs by 20%. Cleveland showed a 12% population increase, while its suburbs grew by 125%. New York gained over 1.5 million inhabitants between 1920 and 1930, some 23%, even as the suburbs gained 400,000 persons, a growth of 67%. Saint Louis grew by 5% while the population of the suburbs increased by 107% (p. 103).

Suburbanization slowed dramatically during the Depression but the metropolitan growth that did occur followed the patterns established during the previous decade, "with new residential construction primarily taking place in the suburbs" (Tobin, 1976, p. 104).

The effects of automobile technology This large-scale suburbanization occurred simultaneously with the widespread adoption of the automobile. The undeveloped areas between the streetcar corridors in the city's fringe finally were accessible by means of this transportation innovation. The automobile during this period first competed with and then began to displace the streetcar as the dominant form of urban transportation. The reasons were varied, but cost was a major factor. After World War I, mass production lowered the unit cost of the automobile into the price range of the middle class. Cars also became more reliable and convenient. By the 1920s, the electric starter had replaced hand cranks and technical improvements reduced the number of breakdowns that had so often plagued the automobile a few years earlier. Also, more gas stations and garages had been built, and more mechanics had been trained to keep the machines running.

The automobile was readily adopted by an urban population that disliked public carriers. "Mass transit was characterized by crowding, discomfort, and inconvenience . . . streetcars remained crowded and dirty, routes were fixed, service was irregular, and unpleasant social intermingling persisted" (Tobin, 1976, p. 101). The private automobile enabled the owner to avoid all these problems and provided other benefits as well. It was a multipurpose vehicle that could be used for commuting, recreation, and shopping. Moreover, it gave the owner a high degree of mobility and access to a more varied choice of goods and services, while at the same time providing privacy and segregation from undesirable groups. Most important was the fact that the automobile was fast, comfortable, and permitted the owner to schedule his or her activities at will (Tobin, 1976, p. 10).

The automobile became dominant in this period as the major form of intraurban transportation in the United States. Although rates of adoption differed among cities, figures for St. Louis indicate how rapidly this shift from public to private transportation occurred. "In 1916, 83% of the persons entering the central business district of Saint Louis came by streetcar, with 17% coming in automobiles. By 1937, 45% used cars, 12% buses and 27% streetcar" (Tobin, 1976, p. 105). Even earlier, in both Kansas City and Washington, D.C., the majority of persons entering central business districts used the automobile.

Post–World War II

In terms of sheer numbers, the post–World War II period was the decade of the greatest suburban expansion in United States history. Most of this suburbanization was based on no other transportation than cars, trucks, and buses. An indication of this dependency is reflected in the number of registered motor vehicles. In 1945 about 25 million motor vehicles were registered in the United States; by 1973 this number had grown to more than 100 million vehicles (Tobin, 1976). It would be wrong to suggest that the automobile and other motor vehicles were solely responsible for this suburban development, however. Cars, trucks, and buses permitted the low-density development of retail, manufacturing, and residential areas in the urban fringe, and thus transportation technology set the broad parameters within which this expansion could take place. Changes in other spheres of society, however, determined how metropolitan areas would develop within these limits.

Changes in the POET framework Specifically, in the post–World War II period several interrelated changes took place in American society in terms of the ecological complex. In *population* the socalled "baby boom" between 1945 and 1958 generated demands for housing that simply could not be met in the existing housing market. Because little housing construction had taken place during the Depression years and World War II, the nation was faced with a critical housing shortage.

Organizationally, the federal government through the FHA and VA housing programs made long-term, low–down payment mortgage money available for the first time. These model programs were copied by saving and lending institutions that provided twenty-year loans to the general public for the first time. Previously, the purchase of a home had required a large down payment and a loan period of only four or five years. These changes made homeownership a reality to many socioeconomic groups previously priced out of the housing market. The new mortgage availability also permitted the building of the nation's first "mass-produced suburbs," suburbs of hundreds and in some cases thousands of homes with a standard floor plan and architecture.

Environmentally, the central areas of many older, industrial cities were undesirable in several respects. First, the housing was old and lacked the modern conveniences that the middle class had come to expect in a suburban home. In the city of Cleveland, for example, the average age of a home was forty-five years in 1960. Second, the pollution from industry and the high density made a central-city location undesirable in some cities. Third, in many cities the only available land was in the fringe (Schwab, 1976).

Technology affected many aspects of urban life, especially the workplace. A revolution in the technological level of American industry in the post–World War II period enabled fewer workers to produce larger outputs of goods and services which in turn created higher per capita income. This income provided the additional capital necessary for the rapid expansion of the urban fringe.

In sum, suburbanization is a process that involves the complex interaction of the factors in the POET framework. Technology, especially in transportation, set the broad limits for what the city could become. The manner in which the city changed within these limits depended on other spheres in the metropolitan and national system. Suburbanization in the post–World War II period differed from that of early eras in the rate of growth, but not in the kind of growth. In all likelihood, it was the rate of suburban growth combined with the new affluence of society that led Reisman and others to view this growth as something new and unique to the American experience. However, was there something in fact unique about the suburban way of life?

The Suburban Way of Life

To this point, the POET framework has been used to analyze the broad societal changes that have shaped this nation's suburbs. In general, this analysis shows that despite gross changes in the economic and demographic characteristics of cities and suburbs over the past two decades, major differences continue to exist between cities and suburbs. Although Kasarda (1976) demonstrates the dramatic movement of blue-collar occupations to the suburbs, others have shown that suburbs are becoming industrialized without a resident industrial population (Schwartz, 1976). Farley (1976), moreover, demonstrates that the gap in the income and educational levels between cities and suburbs has remained quite stable over the last decade.

Finally, Long and Glick (1976) show that differences between city and suburb with regard to family structure are about the same as they were in 1970. In spite of the major redistribution of economic activity and population since World War II, suburbs remain predominantly white, more affluent, and more likely than the city to contain upwardly mobile families engaged in the process of child rearing.

Political fragmentation From an ecological point of view, can the massive redistribution of economic activity and population have occurred without fundamentally changing the suburban way of life? The answer is a complicated one, but it appears that the highly fragmented political structure of the American metropolis has been able to suppress the social consequences of metropolitan growth and change. In most American metropolises, the central city is surrounded by many suburbs, smaller in size and politically autonomous. In 1970, the thirty-three largest metropolitan areas contained an average of 200 suburban non–school-system decision-making bodies. These political units have broad discretionary powers in the areas of taxation, zoning, and land-use planning. In other words, suburbs are in a position to control the size and quality of their population and produce a socially homogeneous community. Although differences between central city and suburb have diminished since 1950, the political structure of the metropolis has minimized these differences by compartmentalizing groups similar in socioeconomic and racial characteristics.

The consequences of these residential patterns are straightforward. The more homogeneous a community, the more likely that a person will find others nearby whose interests and tastes are similar to his or her own. This, in turn, contributes to the development of social networks ("coffee klatching," for example) that often lead to the emergence of beliefs, values and lifestyle preferences that are associated with suburban living. Therefore, it is not surprising that the behavior of people living in relatively homogeneous suburbs differs from similar groups living in central cities where they are more exposed to groups that differ in their socioeconomic and racial characteristics (Schwartz, 1976, pp. 330–31).

The status of housing The above analysis is consistent with the discussion of "The Decision to Move and the Search for a Residence" in Chapter 7. Why do people choose a suburban house over one in the central city? One factor is the status-conferring aspect of housing. Human ecologists have long observed that people use housing as an instrument in "keeping up with the Joneses." For example, Michelson (1977), in a survey study of residential choice in Toronto, found that those moving to single-family houses in the suburbs put a priority on their homes and on the characteristics of their neighbors. The status-enhancing quality of the suburban home was brought out by the fact that most persons in the study buying a new home were already homeowners in other suburban locations. Their new homes were larger than their old ones in more socially acceptable neighborhoods.

Moreover, they were people who felt personally similar, although economically superior, to their old neighbors and moved to a new residence where
more of their neighbors were like themselves (pp. 172–76).

Familism A second factor that appears to be important in attracting certain
people to the suburbs is the familism lifestyle. Familism refers to a lifestyle
that emphasizes activities centered around home and children. The values
associated with this lifestyle stand in sharp contrast to alternative American
value systems centered on career success and conspicuous consumption.
Since American culture stresses all three value systems, there must be a
trade-off among them; if a person vigorously pursues a career he or she
will find less time for enjoyable consumption and family life.

*As noted in the discussion on the suburban way of life, familism, ca-
reerism, and consumerism lifestyles seldom coexist in the same family.
When they do, interpersonal conflict often results, as suggested in this
letter to Ann Landers.*

COLUMNIST IS NOT HOUDINI

Ann Landers

DEAR ANN: Every now and then I see a letter in your column I
can relate to. Especially when a woman complains about a husband
who doesn't spend enough time with her and the children. I have
not yet seen you give a helpful answer.

"Logansport Lu" is a good example. Lu says she hated playing
second fiddle to bowling, hunting, union meetings and Friday-
night poker. You told her, "Don't nag or beg for his company.
Keep busy. And turn on the heat."

Do you honestly believe you helped that woman? What you
told her to do was "leave him alone." Don't you understand that
this poor, lonely soul desperately wants a relationship with her
husband? She didn't marry him to take over where his mother left
off.

My husband is a workaholic. He is so involved with business
that he hardly knows our two boys. I have expressed my feelings
about his lack of interest in his family—not in a nagging way, but
enough so that he knows I feel he should spend more time with
us.

The heat? Yes, it's on. I am an eager and loving bed partner,
but he is usually too tired or he works until I've fallen asleep.

My husband has an excellent job in a big company and does
well financially. He is determined to make it to the top, so he
takes classes two evenings a week, attends business seminars regularly and buries himself in paperwork every week end.

He says he is preparing himself so we can have all the good things in life later. I've told him I'm satisfied with the "things" we already have and that we need him NOW.

Please try a little harder to come up with some practical advice, Ann. Women who are married to men like this need it.

—My Name is Legion

DEAR LEGION: You want me to tell you how to transform a driven, self-centered, upwardly mobile overachiever into a home-loving, concerned father and husband? I wish I could pull a magic formula out of a hat, dear, but Houdini I am not.

Trying to get a workaholic to change his pace is like making love to a gorilla. They slow down when THEY want to—not when YOU want to.

Women pick these types because they are attracted to the very qualities they later complain about. The gung-ho guys are bright, aggressive, outgoing, hard-working and hellbent on making it. What the woman doesn't realize is that her super-achiever has his priorities all figured out, and she and the kids are pretty far down on the list.

The man will not change—unless he works himself to a frazzle, comes apart at the seams and must resort to professional help. If his doctor tells him he must either change his way of living or pay a terrible price, he just might listen.

My advice to you is keep yourself busy. Develop interests of your own. Stay off his back, and try to expose the boys to suitable role models—an uncle or neighbors who have kids the same age as yours.

Of course, you could tell Mr. Upwardly Mobile to shove his ego-centered lifestyle because you are leaving and taking the boys with you—but you might wind up sorry and even more lonely.

Source: *Arkansas Gazette*, Oct. 14, 1980. Reprinted with permission of Ann Landers and The Field Newspaper Syndicate.

Bell (1958) examined these three value systems in a study of several Chicago suburbs. He found that suburban residents placed greater emphasis on familistic values than on the other two value systems. For example, when respondents were asked, "why did you move from the city?" 83 percent gave responses such as "more healthy for children," "nicer children for playmates," "better schools," and "home ownership provides greater security for children than living in an apartment." Only 10 percent gave responses involving upward social mobility, and only 43 percent gave responses involving consumerism.

It should be noted that Greer and others stress that these are not uniquely suburban values. Bell's study does show that people who hold familistic values prefer suburbs. Still, some people with the same values live in the central city but in lesser concentrations.

Neighboring Another force, selectively drawing people into certain suburbs is a desire for neighboring. Fava (1975) describes most suburbanites as "locals" in her analysis of suburban attitudes. These people's span of interests is limited principally to their immediate residential environment, in contrast to those living in the cities, who more often have interests in national and world affairs. Fava also reports that suburbanites are likely to have neighboring relations with those who live in the same area and that their involvement with local concerns is greater than city dwellers'.

The question remains whether the suburbs are to be understood simply as the product of ecological processes resulting from metropolitan growth or whether they represent a subculture with distinctive values, beliefs, and lifestyle preferences. In truth, there is probably an interaction between the two. American suburbs are usually age- and class-graded. That is, residents of a suburb will often manifest similar demographic characteristics—age, ethnicity, homeownership, and family lifecycle. Young homeowners with children in school will obviously be pursuing familistic lifestyles and have a more direct concern in local rather than national problems. The characteristics of these homogeneous, class-compartmentalized suburbs give rise to suburban values and provide an environment supportive of these attitudes.

In sum, ecological processes such as the decentralization of population from a city's center to its fringe are the result of millions of locational decisions made by individuals searching for housing. Why do people choose suburban housing over locations in the central city? Our discussion suggests that the availability of modern housing and schools unaffected by court-ordered school busing, as well as residential environments insulated from the urban ills associated with more centrally located communities, are major determining factors. Equally important is the presence of a residential environment conducive to a "local" and/or familistic lifestyle.

THE SUBURBANIZATION OF BUSINESS AND INDUSTRY

National Trends

To this point the discussion of the suburbanization process has focused on the decentralization of the nation's residential population. In the post–World War II period conditions enabled large numbers of businesses and industries to relocate in the urbanized fringe.[4] This trend is viewed with alarm by the leadership of many cities. Examples of the exodus of major corporations from the city are numerous. New Orleans does not keep statistics on the business and industry it loses, but in the early 1970s it lost the Elmer Candy

Company, the Diebert-Bancroft Machinery Works, automobile dealers, and numerous distributors of national products. The city of Atlanta has lost the corporate offices of Sinclair Oil, Shell Oil, Continental Can Company, Avon Cosmetics, Piedmont Life Insurance Company, and Monsanto Chemical Company to suburban office parks (Masotti and Hadden, 1974, p. 88). In 1970, St. Louis lost forty-three companies to the suburbs. Boston lost seventy-five firms in two years and the trend continues in Chicago, Milwaukee, Cleveland, and Detroit (Berry and Kasarda, 1977, pp. 255–56). A more vivid picture of this decentralization of business and industry can be seen in a partial list of companies that in 1974 had moved or planned to move all or part of their operations out of New York City to the surrounding suburbs (Berry and Kasarda, 1977, p. 255):

> *To Connecticut:* American Can Company; Lone Star Cement Corporation; Bangor Punta Corporation; Howmet Corporation; U.S. Tobacco Corporation; Olin Corporation (chemicals division); Hooker Chemical; Chesebrough-Pond's, Incorporated; Technicolor, Incorporated; Christian Dior Perfumes Corporation; General Telephone and Electronics Corporation; Consolidated Oil; and Stauffer Chemical.
>
> *To Westchester County:* IBM, Incorporated; Pepsico, Incorporated; Dictaphone Corporation; General Foods Corporation; Flintkote; and AMF.
>
> *To Northern New Jersey:* CPC International; Union Camp; and the American Division of BASF. Even Fantus Company, the relocation firm that helped plan many of these moves, has taken up new offices in Englewood Cliffs, New Jersey (population 5,810)—along with CPC, Thomas Lipton, Scholastic Magazine, and Volkswagen.

Employment Patterns

The pattern of decentralization of business and industry is national in scope, as is apparent in the data in Table 8.5 for the fifteen largest metropolitan areas in the United States. Between 1960 and 1970 the total civilian employment of the central cities of these SMSAs shows a net loss. In Table 8.5, note that eight central cities lost employment, five had slight or moderate increases, and two cities, Dallas and Houston, had significant employment growth. Because these figures are uncorrected for annexation, the gains for Houston and Dallas are artificially high. These two cities reached metropolitan size in the twentieth and not the nineteenth century, and their character and form were shaped by the automobile rather than other forms of transportation. They are multicentered metropolitan areas, and in their form and the timing of their suburbanization they differ from the other cities in the sample.[5] Nevertheless, the figures for suburban growth indicate that the suburbs have gained rapidly in employment during the decade ending in 1970. These trends have undoubtedly continued into the 1980s. Even in Dallas and Houston, the increase of civilian employment in the suburbs greatly exceeds that of the central city during this decade.

Table 8.5
Percentage increase in total civilian employment, in the cities and suburbs of the 15 largest metropolitan areas, 1960–70.

Metropolitan area	Central city percentage change	Suburban employment percentage change	Percentage of total employment in the suburbs		
			1960	1970	change 1960–70
New York	−9.7	24.9	28.8	35.9	7,.1
Los Angeles	−10.8	16.2	47.8	54.3	6.5
Chicago	−13.9	64.4	32.2	47.5	15.3
Philadelphia	−11.3	61.5	37.0	51.8	14.8
Detroit	−22.5	61.5	43.3	61.4	18.1
San Francisco	0.4	22.7	44.9	50.0	5.1
Boston	8.6	20.2	55.5	62.2	6.7
Washington, D.C.	1.9	117.9	36.2	54.9	18.7
Cleveland	−15.3	82.5	28.3	46.0	17.7
Saint Louis	−15.2	80.4	39.3	58.0	18.7
Pittsburg	4.4	2.5	64.0	63.7	−6.3
Minneapolis–St.Paul	0.3	126.2	23.6	41.1	17.5
Houston	49.2	164.2	15.7	24.4	8.7
Baltimore	−5.6	76.6	34.1	49.9	15.8
Dallas	37.6	73.5	24.4	29.0	4.6
Total	−6.9	43.6	37.0	47.6	10.6

Source: New York Times analysis of U.S. Census Bureau data, October 15, 1972, pp. 1, 58.

Decentralization of employment Table 8.6 indicates the types of employment decentralizing to the suburban ring. The central cities of ten of the fifteen metropolitan areas in the sample declined in manufacturing employment between 1953 and 1967, a trend that has continued into the 1970s and 1980s. Only five cities—Los Angeles, Washington, D. C., Minneapolis, Houston, and Dallas—recorded any gains. As in the preceding table, Dallas and Houston had impressive gains (42 percent), whereas in the other three cities growth was moderate. But note that in all metropolitan areas, except Houston, the employment growth rates for the suburbs far exceeded those of the central city. Again the only exception is one of the newer metropolises in the Sunbelt region of the South and Southwest.

Retail sales figures show that retailers have followed the consumer to the suburbs. In some cases, the large suburban shopping mall has spearheaded suburban development, permitting a number of large-scale developers to direct and therefore shape urban development. The Sunbelt cities

Table 8.6
Percentage increase in manufacturing employment and retail sales in the 15 largest metropolitan areas, 1958–1967

| | Manufacturing | | Retail sales | |
	Central city	Suburbs	Central city	Suburbs
New York	− 10.3	36.0	9.7	60.2
Los Angeles	10.3	23.0	22.2	75.4
Chicago	− 4.0	51.6	5.3	86.6
Philadelphia	− 11.6	30.0	6.2	65.4
Detroit	− 1.8	47.6	0.7	86.4
San Francisco	− 23.5	29.3	16.3	81.6
Boston	− 11.8	17.0	− 1.4	79.2
Washington, D.C.	8.5	141.8	10.5	134.8
Cleveland	− 5.3	42.6	− 15.2	269.1
Saint Louis	− 14.9	41.4	− 7.6	76.2
Pittsburgh	− 13.8	3.7	7.8	28.7
Minneapolis–St. Paul	8.9	146.2	7.9	149.7
Houston	41.6	12.6	55.9	63.3
Baltimore	− 5.9	22.0	4.9	128.2
Dallas	41.9	131.0	33.6	119.2

Source: Adapted from data presented in Berry, B.J.L. and Kasarda, J.D., *Contemporary Urban Ecology*. New York: MacMillan, 1977, Tables 13.1 and 13.2, pp. 256–57. Copyright © 1977 by Macmillan Publishing Co., Inc.

of Los Angeles, Dallas, and Houston are the only metropolitan areas having significant retail growth within their central cities.

Blue-collar vs. white-collar employment Kasarda (1977) explored a different facet of the decentralization of business and industry. This researcher examined the distribution of white-collar and blue-collar workers in both the central city and suburbs of 101 SMSAs. Noteworthy is the fact that in 1970 the overall occupational composition of the suburban ring (51 percent white-collar and 49 percent blue-collar) was the same as the central-city composition in 1960. The SMSAs that had reached metropolitan status in the nineteenth century, the older industrial cities of the Northeast, had the most rapid expansion of both their blue-collar and white-collar employment functions (Kasarda, 1977, pp. 237–38). In general, in the post–World War II period commerce and industry made significant shifts beyond central cities into the suburban ring. This drift of commerce and industry to fringe areas reaffirms the observation that the suburbs now have the spatial complexity previously characteristic of the central city.

The Suburb's Impact on the Central City

Over the years the news media have presented the broad changes in the structure of metropolitan areas as a serious national problem. Is pessimism justified? Are the central cities of the largest and oldest metropolitan areas beyond help? The answers to these questions are neither simple nor definitive, but the tendency to define the changes as an "urban crisis" is perhaps shortsighted. In addressing these questions one must remember two very important points. First, American cities are in a state of becoming, in a process of continuous change. Second, there is an important difference between the lifespan of a city and the lifespan of an individual. In reference to the first point, the character and spatial form of cities today were shaped by growth during early eras. Schnore (1965) and Berry and Kasarda (1977) have demonstrated that the timing and character of a metropolitan area's suburbanization are tied closely to the period when the city reached metropolitan status. For example, cities that reached metropolitan size in the nineteenth century were shaped by the transportation technology of the horse and the streetcar. These cities were more densely settled in the first place, and when the technology became available, their suburbs grew rapidly. Cities like Dallas and Houston reached metropolitan status in the twentieth century and were shaped by automobile technology. Their initial population densities were lower, and decentralization of their inhabitants was less crucial.

In reference to the second point, people often confuse an institution's time span with personal time frames. The average human lifespan of seventy years is insignificant in comparison with that of cities such as Rome and Athens that have been in existence for more than three millennia. The suburbanization of the residential population, business, and industry represents the response of these land uses to broad changes in society's transportation, communication, and energy technology, as well as in the size and composition of the population and the organization of society.

The reasons for business and industrial decentralization Business and industry have decentralized for many reasons. First, the development of the motor vehicle has dramatically reduced the need for a central location. Because travel to most parts of a metropolis is fast and travel time is not necessarily tied directly with distance, retailers and businesses need be less concerned with geographic location. In fact, if one measures the cost of travel in terms of the time it takes to travel door to door—including the time it takes to find parking and walk to the office or shop—it is often less costly to drive twenty-five miles on a city's "outerbelt highway" to a shopping mall than to travel eight to ten miles to the central business district. Second, the CBD is not the only point within the metropolis where major transportation lines converge. The geographic point where two major interstate highways cross is as accessible from within the metropolitan area as the CBD. Third, dramatic changes in communication and energy technology have further reduced the need for a location at the city's center.

Modification of Land-Use Model

According to the classical land-use model introduced in Chapter 7, the point of greatest accessibility and hence the point of highest land rents would be at a city's center. Theoretically, the center would be the location of businesses and offices, and the periphery would be the location of low-density residential housing. With the removal of locational constraints, the metropolitan areas in the United States have become multinucleated. Business and industry still require good highways and rail access, but these facilities are available at many locations besides a city's center. Consequently industries, regional shopping centers, and large service facilities have begun to include a different set of factors in their locational calculus—low tax rates, a high level of public services, availability of land, suitable topography, a benign political climate, good schools and recreation facilities for their employees, and an existing labor force with the appropriate mix of skills (Logan, 1976, p. 337).

As large numbers of manufacturing and retail activities moved to the suburban ring, blue-collar workers left the central city and were replaced with white-collar workers. Kasarda (1977) aggregated central-city and suburban employment data for 101 central cities and found that between 1960 and 1970 blue-collar employment declined by 825,000 jobs, but white-collar jobs increased by 500,000. Blue-collar jobs declined by 12.7 percent but this loss was counterbalanced by a 7.2 percent increase in white-collar employment.

New locational forces   In the past urbanization has been viewed as a concentrating process. The traditional land economics model posited that metropolitan growth resulted from a growing central business district and the balancing of external factors such as transportation and labor costs. In reality, what the metropolitan areas of this nation have undergone in the past thirty years is a reshuffling or a resorting of urban functions as many businesses and industries reoptimize their location in response to the new transportation, communication, and energy technologies. Although central cities will continue to lose jobs to the suburban ring, they will continue to attract a large share of a metropolis's office space, elite functions such as banking, and the legal and medical arts. In fact, as the peripheral areas of metropolises have grown, this growth has been matched by an increase in the organizational functions at a city's center that ensure the coordination of activities throughout the metropolis (Kasarda, 1972, Berry and Kasarda, 1977). Many activities will continue to benefit from a centralized location. Also, it is unlikely that society can afford to abandon the buildings and transportation facilities in cities' centers. Cities such as Pittsburgh, Cincinnati, St. Louis, and many others have made defensive investments in sports complexes, convention centers, and downtown malls to protect the value of the property already there.

Urban-Suburban Problems

Suburbanization must be seen as a part of a larger process, one that in the final analysis will continue until cities cease to exist. Cities, large and small, continue to evolve. Just as there were negative byproducts of urbanization in the past, problems will be created at each successive stage of urban development.

Members of the Chicago School more than fifty years ago wrote about the problems of social disorder, crime, and poverty in cities. These problems still exist but in different form and greater scope. Moreover, characteristics of the modern metropolis tend to magnify the problems associated with poverty and race. For instance, the rapid expansion of office employment in central cities requires a labor force with specific skills that do not always match the skills of the population living in the central city. Therefore, a large number of white-collar workers must commute to the central business district to fill these jobs. Similarly, manufacturing and industry require a different type of worker, one who is often not found in the suburb but in the central city.

Blacks, in particular, have been adversely affected by this pattern. This group remains highly segregated in central cities; only 5.7 percent of suburban rings' population is black. Because of the lack of housing for blacks near suburban employment, a disproportionate number of blacks employed in the suburbs must commute from the central city. In 1970, 49 percent of all blacks employed in a suburban ring commuted from the central city, compared with only 13.7 percent of all white suburban workers (Berry and Kasarda, 1977, p. 243). Ironically, thousands of white workers commute to a city center to fill office jobs, and thousands of black workers commute in the opposite direction. Because the black population is overrepresented in the lower socioeconomic status groups, low-skill jobs traditionally found in central cities apparently now are in the suburbs. The lower incomes of these workers make commuting to the suburbs difficult, especially where public transportation is unavailable.

The Costs of Suburbs

What effect does a large and growing suburban population have on the public services provided by central-city governments? Research on this question has produced contradictory findings. Weicher (1972), in an analysis of metropolitan data, found that retail and office functions require far fewer public services than manufacturing and industry. In general, the cost of providing public services to manufacturing and industry exceeds the amount of tax revenue generated by these functions. For retail and office functions, the tax revenue exceeds the cost to government of providing services. Weicher concludes that the decentralization of manufacturing and industry to the suburbs has been beneficial to central-city governments because they are no longer burdened with these service obligations. Moreover, the centralization of office and retail activities should improve the financial outlook of many central cities. Weicher believes that the suburbanite who commutes to the central city daily is probably paying more than her or his fair share in city income tax and sales tax in relation to the services consumed.

Berry and Kasarda (1977) and Kasarda (1972) come to a completely different conclusion. In a more comprehensive analysis of the relationship between suburban population growth, the commuting population, and the cost of central-city services, these researchers concluded that there is a close relationship between service demands and suburban growth. As suburban areas continue to expand, suburban residents continue to use central-city services and facilities. This usage has substantially increased the costs of providing central-city services, often beyond the ability of the central-city's tax base to pay for them. Berry and Kasarda conclude:

> Suburban populations may thus be exploiting central cities to the extent that, by regularly using central-city services and public facilities, they are imposing marginal costs on the central cities without providing full repayment for those costs. Although partial payments are made by suburbanities (*sic*) to central cities in the form of income taxes, user changes (*sic*), and sales taxes levied by some central cities, limited research has shown that these sources do not generate the necessary revenue to cover the additional costs (Berry and Kasarda, 1977, p. 226).

This research suggests that central-city populations, which have a higher percentage of poorly educated minorities, the unemployed, and the aged—the segment of the population with the fewest financial resources—are required to provide services to those best able to pay, the population outside the political boundaries and thus outside the taxing jurisdiction of the central city. What are the implications of this research for future metropolitan growth? First, consolidated metropolitan government perhaps could distribute more fairly the costs of public service to all user groups. Second, because this solution is politically infeasible in most metropolitan areas, central-city leaders should be increasingly sensitive to future population growth in the suburban fringe. User charges, city income tax increases, and other short-term solutions could be used to more fairly distribute the costs of central-city public services.

SUMMARY

This chapter is intended to provide an understanding of the internal structure of the city and the complex interrelationship between the central city and its suburban fringe. The first section of the chapter is an historical overview of the suburbanization process.

Suburbanization has occurred here since the inception of the United States more than 200 years ago. Suburban development was most rapid in the decades following this century's two major wars, and it slowed significantly during the Depression of the 1930s. Between World War II and 1970, the rate of suburban growth was unprecedented. This growth was due to the outward migration of central-city residents to a suburban ring and the tendency of migrants from outside an Urbanized Area to move directly into the fringe rather than to the city itself. Research by Farley (1976) and Long and Glick (1976) indicates that the families and individuals moving into the suburbs are in their late twenties and early thirties on the average and are predominantly white, but do not necessarily pursue the "familism" lifestyle. Moderate-income suburbs, in particular, have a much more heterogeneous population that makes generalizations about suburban trends difficult. Finally, although the suburbanization process has been somewhat selective, differences between central city and fringe in the nation's Urbanized Areas have diminished during the past thirty years. More important, the spatial complexity normally associated with central cities now characterizes their urban fringe.

In the second section of this chapter, factors contributing to suburban growth are examined within the POET framework first introduced in Chapter 1. The suburbanization process is described during four periods spanning nearly 200 years, from 1800 to the present. During each stage of this development, the elements of population, organization, environment, and technology interacted in unique ways to prescribe the nature and direction of urban growth. In the earliest period, early industrialization—1800–1890, most people walked; as a result one's place of residence and employment were close together. Because of the primitive state of transportation technology cities were settled at high density and took a circular shape. Moreover, groups that differed in socioeconomic status lived near each other. Only the wealthy could escape to the urban fringe.

In the periods that followed, the introduction of new transportation technology, first the electric streetcar and later the automobile, changed American cities into its present-day form. The streetcar era, spanning the years from 1890 through World War I, permitted the first decentralization of the middleclass to the suburbs. Later, improvements in automobile technology accelerated the process. In the post–World War II period, in particular, rapid population growth combined with environmental constraints, organizational changes, and technological breakthroughs in transportation and communiction led to unprecedented growth of urban fringe areas. These changes also enabled groups other than the middle class to move to the suburban fringe. Today suburbs resemble central cities in their employment and socioeconomic-status characteristics. Black Americans, however, have not fully participated in this process and they continue to be highly segregated in the central cities.

In the last section of the chapter, the decentralization of business and industry is examined. The rapid decentralization of business and industry in the post-World War II period was a predictable response to changes in transportation and in other spheres of society. This movement represented a reoptimization of the location of these land uses in response to the removal of locational constraints during this period. Such decentralization is part of a larger process. As business and industry move to the suburbs, other activities begin to locate in central cities. All urban areas are undergoing a process of continuous change. The rate of change in the post–World War II period has created serious problems that are intensified by the fact that central cities are surrounded by politically autonomous suburbs outside their taxing jurisdiction.

Finally, the discussion of the suburbanization process is designed to show how central cities and their outlying fringe areas have become inseparable parts of a single system, a system whose structure can be understood within the general theoretical frameworks provided in Chapters 6 and 7.

NOTES

1. These points of view are expressed not only in the works of Reisman (1958), but also in the works of Spectorsky (1955), Seeley, Sim, and Loosley (1956), Martin (1958), Fava (1956), and Mowrer (1958).
2. See the works of Martin (1958), Hoover and Vernon (1959), Schnore (1965), Glenn (1973), and Shyrock and Siegel (1973). A complete citation for each work is found in the bibliography.
3. See the articles by Fuguitt and Zuiches (1975) and DeJong (1977).
4. See the articles by Struyk (1972), Dean (1973), Berry and Cohen (1973), Guest and Cluett (1974), Manners (1974), and Berry and Kasarda (1977). A complete citation for each article is found in the text's bibliography.
5. See the articles and citations by Schnore (1965) and Berry and Kasarda (1977) listed in the text's bibliography.

PART FOUR

Social Consequences and Social Responses to Urbanization

CHAPTER NINE

The Community—The Social Aspect of Urban Life

Statement of Objectives

1. The student should become aware of the contributions of Maine, Tönnies, and Durkheim to the contemporary study of community.

2. Robert Park's work was profoundly influenced by the theories of Emile Durkheim. Both researchers developed theories to explain how society and a community maintain order. The student should know how the works of the two theorists are related and the explanations they use to explain society's ability to maintain order.

3. The student should review the criticism of Robert Park's theory.

4. The student should become aware of the changing nature of local communities and the relationship between societal scale and a local community.

5. The student should become aware of the importance of the symbolic community in day-to-day life in a city.

Though the concept of community has been of concern to sociologists for nearly 200 years, there continues to be disagreement on its exact definition. Early ideas about community were developed before cities had reached their present-day size and scope, at a time when societies were smaller and less complex and large population centers were few. The early concepts of community focused on the relationship of individuals and groups to their society. How societies maintained order and the forces that produced and maintained rules of conduct were the central concerns in the perspective of the nineteenth-century sociologists.

Societies have changed radically since the nineteenth century and the concept of community has changed also, but not to the same degree. Though in many respects the nineteenth century sociologists' concepts of community are not relevant to today's communities, these concepts continue to shape current expectations of the ideal community. This cultural heritage combined with the fact that what constitutes a "good" or "ideal" community is a subjective evaluation leads to definitional problems.

The problem of defining the concept of "community" is highlighted in a 1955 article by the sociologist George Hillery entitled, "Definitions of Community: Areas of Agreement." Hillery conducted a thorough review of the sociological literature on community and found ninety-four separate definitions in use. The only point of total agreement among them was that communities "deal with people!" The diversity of definitions is due to the fact that sociologists work from several different theoretical perspectives, study a wide variety of phenomena, and adopt the definition that is most compatible with their theoretical approach.

Although Hillery concluded that there was no overall agreement beyond the fact that community involves people, he did find substantial agreement among the majority of the authors on three points. First, community involves groups of people who reside in a geographically distinct area. Second, community also refers to the "quality" of the relationships within this group. The idea that members of a community are bound together by common characteristics such as culture, values, attitudes, and the like was shared by a majority of the authors. Third, community refers to a group of people who are engaged in sustained social interaction—neighboring, for example. Therefore, for the purposes of this text, a *community* is defined as a group of people who share a geographic area and are bound together by common culture, values, race, or social class.

In this chapter the evolution and present usage of the concept of "community" are examined. In the first section, the contributions of the nineteenth-century community theorists Maine, Tönnies, and Durkheim are explored in terms of the historical factors that shaped their works. Next the works of Robert Park and other members of the Chicago School are discussed in relation to the influence of both the nineteenth-century community theorists and factors in American society. The chapter ends with an examination of the community as a social unit in contemporary society. This section complements the discussion of social areas in Chapter 6.

EVOLUTION OF THE CONCEPT OF COMMUNITY

Although an operational definition of community has been established, what level of community is meant? A city? A small town? A neighborhood? The concept of community has evolved from earlier concepts. To understand its present usage and the types of geographic units to which it refers, one must understand its evolution.

The concept of community was a central element in the works of most of the founders of sociology—Comté, de Tocqueville, Maine, Tönnies, LePlay, Marx, and Durkheim (Nisbet, 1966, pp. 47–60). These men were living and writing during the nineteenth century, a period of profound change in western society. Change was so rapid and pervasive that it can best be described as revolutionary. Industrialization, urbanization, and bureaucratization were the forces shaping society. Many negative by-products of transformation were manifested. In this atmosphere the modern concept of community first emerged. Community during this era was often thought of in romantic terms as a way of life destroyed by the forces of the modern world. Community was equated with the good life and industrial society was often contrasted with the community of the past. Thus, the concept of community first was used for the purpose of contrast—the past versus the present—and examples of this usage can be found in the works of Maine, Tönnies, and Durkheim (Bell and Newby, 1972, pp. 21–27).

Sir Henry Maine: Family vs. Individual Status

Maine, an Englishman writing in the middle of the nineteenth century, was primarily interested in the origins of codified or written law.[1] His book, *Ancient Law*, was not concerned with community as such but his work greatly influenced other thinkers of his age, especially Tönnies. The major contribution of Maine is his demonstration that one cannot understand a society's legal system without first understanding its social system. The contrast he makes between societies of different ages is based primarily on ascribed status and tradition vs. achieved status and contract.

The family and tradition Maine describes these differences clearly in the following statement:

> Society in primitive times was not what it is assumed to be at present, a collection of individuals. In fact, and in view of the man who composed it, it was an aggregation of families. The contrast may be most forcibly expressed by saying that the unit of ancient society was the family, of a modern society an individual (1870, p. 126).

In many ancient societies, the individual was not recognized in law; the family was the legal entity. The individual's position in society was based on the family into which he or she was born. Stated another way, the status of the individual in society was ascribed by family membership. In addition, solutions to the problems of day-to-day living were drawn from the experience of past generations or tradition rather than based on reason.

In contrast, the individual, not the family, is the important unit under law in modern society. Some modern societies even protect the individual from her or his family (e.g., in cases of child abuse)—a practice unknown to "society in primitive times." The individual's position in modern society, although influenced by family membership, depends mainly on the person's skills, training, and education. Ideally, the individual rises to a social status based on his or her achievements rather than family membership.

The contract The contract is another important element of modern society. To Maine, the contract was a revolutionary social invention that made possible an entirely different form of society. A *contract* is simply a binding agreement between two or more individuals or parties. The agreement states certain terms and conditions that, when fulfilled, relieve both parties of any further obligation. It permits two strangers to come together, carry out a business transaction, and then go their separate ways once the terms of the agreement have been fulfilled. Contractualism makes possible an ordered society composed of individuals.

Maine's distinctions between the legal systems of "primitive" and "modern" societies were explicitly recognized and taken into account by sociologists who later attempted to understand and explain change in the social relationships among persons in industrial societies. The influence of Maine is clear in the writings of Tönnies and Durkheim.

Ferdinand Tönnies: Gemeinschaft and Gesellschaft

Tönnies's book *Gemeinschaft and Gesellschaft* (usually translated as *Community and Society*) was first published in 1887. It has provided a constant source of ideas for students of community ever since. Drawing on the earlier works of Sir Henry Maine, Otto von Gierke, and Fustel de Coulanges, Tönnies described several dimensions along which European society had changed (Nisbet, 1966, pp. 72–73). The basic changes were threefold. First, the basis of one's social status had changed from ascription to achievement. In other words, a person's position in society was becoming less dependent on the family into which he or she had been born and more dependent on the individual's accomplishments. Second, the individual was increasingly viewed as the basic unit of society. As Maine noted, by the nineteenth century the individual was recognized in the legal system of western societies as a person rather than simply a member of a communal organization. Third, the character of societies themselves had changed from sacred-communal to the secular-associational (Nisbet, 1966, p. 73).

Tönnies, like many nineteenth- and twentieth-century theorists, employed a technique known as "ideal types" to structure his analysis. Ideal types do not exist in reality but represent the essential qualities of the phenomenon being studied. Researchers construct ideal types by examining a category of things and then identifying those qualities that set the members of that grouping apart from all others. For example, psychologists use this technique to develop profiles of potential airline highjackers, bank robbers, or child abusers. The ideal type "highjacker" does not really exist; rather, it represents those qualities shared by all persons who are highjackers.

Tönnies employed the ideal types Gemeinschaft and Gesellschaft to describe the characteristics of two different types of societies, the human relationships within those societies, and the process by which society is transformed from one type to another. These ideal types are at polar extremes of a continuum and represent the essential characteristics of traditional vs. modern communities. "Gemeinschaft" translates easily into "community." "Gesellschaft" is more difficult to interpret; its translation is "society." The problem is that community is a part of society, but the concept becomes clear when one examines the types of societies to which Tönnies was referring.

Gemeinschaft Gemeinschaft refers to communities that are small and relatively homogeneous. Members of the community normally spend their entire lives in the same locale and have very little geographic mobility. The social structure is relatively simple but rigid. Each person has a clear understanding of where he or she belongs in society and this position is determined by the social status of the family of the person's birth. Gemeinschaft leads to a communal life based on tradition, with strong sentimental attachments to the moral code and conventions of the place. There is nearly universal agreement among the members on the way things should be done. Deviations from this code are punished informally. Because people, places, and things are familiar to everyone, the individual cannot escape this collectivity. The basic unit of the social structure is the family. The individual's life has meaning only in the context of the family and the larger community. Therefore, the moral code is clear, strongly held, and enforced by the family and the church.

The social structure of Gemeinschaft is made possible by the nature of day-to-day interaction among its members. In Gemeinschaft, social relationships are warm and personal, with strong ties among individuals and between the individual and the community. The members of Gemeinschaft are like a family and, as in a family, the rules of conduct are understood, not codified into law. "Harmony," "naturalness," "depth," and "fullness" are words often used to describe the intimacy and pervasiveness of the relationships among members of Gemeinschaft (Nisbet, 1966, p. 75). Obviously, under these conditions, individualism and privacy are at a minimum.

Gesellschaft In polar extreme to the ideal type of Gemeinschaft is the ideal type of Gesellschaft. Tönnies saw Gesellschaft as a new phenomenon, the end product of social change occurring in the nineteenth century. Gesellschaft refers to large, complex, heterogeneous societies composed of individuals who differ in their racial, ethnic, and socioeconomic characteristics. The social structure is complex and fluid. The individual has been freed from the constraints of the family and ideally may rise in the social structure to her or his own level of achievement. Gesellschaft is a rational, willed society that one can join or leave at will. The basic unit of the social structure is the individual and as a result the traditional means of social control—the family and the church—are supplanted by what is called "rational-legal authority" the police and court system, for example. Deviations from the normative order are no longer sanctioned informally but are penalized by formal institutions such as the courts and police.

In Gesellschaft each individual is guided by her or his self-interest. Human relationships become impersonal; egoism and competition begin to dominate interpersonal relationships. Sharing and concern for others are minimal. Because economic self-interest guides the relationships between individuals, a formal device—the contract—must be used to ensure that both parties abide by an agreement. Moreover, in Gesellschaft, the size and complexity of the social structure make it impossible to know the social status of each person. Tangible symbols of a person's social standing therefore become important, e.g., cars, clothing, and homes.

Gesellschaft is a contractual, individualistic society in which the accumulation of property has a greater importance than close personal ties between individuals. Gesellschaft is symbolized best by the modern corporation and its complex economic and legal relationships with the larger society. Relationships are based not on kinship and friendship, but on rationality, calculation, and contractualism.

Gesellschaft refers not just to a concept of society, but also to a process. Gesellschaft describes the process by which society is transformed from one type to another. As a society is transformed from Gemeinschaft to Gesellschaft the nature of its social organization is changed. Social relationships become more contractual, based on self-interest. Consequently, communal ties are weakened, social solidarity decreases, and the individual is more isolated and potentially more alienated.

Gemeinschaft and Gesellschaft are concepts that reflect a great many factors—legal, economic, cultural, and intellectual—but at the core of each concept is an image of a type of social relationship and a state of mind. As Nisbet (1966) notes, the importance of Tönnies' work is not simply classification of community types but rather his historical and comparative use of these types which gives insight into the fundamental social change caused by the processes of urbanization, industrialization, and bureaucratization (p. 78).

To Tönnies, Gemeinschaft was humankind's natural habitat, and it was the basis of what he thought "modern society" should be. Tönnies considered the industrial society of his day to be dehumanizing and artificial, in contrast to the natural structure of Gemeinschaft. This viewpoint was a major source of disagreement between Tönnies and his contemporary

Emile Durkheim, who held that industrial society could be as satisfactory as western societies had been before the Industrial Revolution.

Emile Durkheim—Mechanical and Organic Solidarity

Durkheim shared with Tönnies many concerns about the direction of modern society. He differed from Tönnies, however, in that he believed modern society could be as natural and organic as the Gemeinschaft societies of the past. A major theme in Durkheim's work is social solidarity. If modern societies are large, complex, and heterogeneous, what is the social "glue" that holds individuals together to form a functioning society? Durkheim's work covers a broad spectrum of topics, but for the student of community his analysis of the types of social solidarity is the most important.

Mechanical solidarity Durkheim made a distinction between two types of social solidarity—mechanical and organic.[2] Mechanical solidarity is found in small homogeneous societies, similar to Tönnies' Gemeinschaft. In such societies, the division of labor is simple and each family unit can carry out most of the functions necessary for society. The division of labor is based on the age and the sex of individuals. Moreover, each member knows every other member and people agree on what society should be. Durkheim called this agreement the collective conscience—the values, beliefs, and sentiments held in common by the members of society. The operation of the collective conscience is reflected most clearly in society's norms or rules of conduct and the types of punishment used when these rules are violated. Durkheim agreed with Maine that law reflects the underlying character of society, its institutional structure, and the form of social solidarity.

In societies based on mechanical solidarity, legal rules are repressive; violation of rules demands retaliation and punishment. In general in such societies, offenses against the collective conscience evoke an immediate and direct response, and this punishment guarantees conformity in other members. Such punishment serves to reinforce the collective conscience. In the context of a Gemeinschaft society, deviants serve a positive social function. Deviation from a norm elicits an immediate response from society. It reinvigorates the collective conscience, and increases the solidarity among the members.

Organic solidarity In small societies, an individual can know the roles of every other member. Modern societies, in contrast, are large and complex, composed of diverse groups of people of which an individual has little or no knowledge. In these societies, the division of labor is complex, based in many cases on specialized skills learned through years of formal training. Because society is composed of diverse groups, there is much less agreement on what society should be. For example, few crimes in these societies would be viewed as "a crime against society." Treason is one, but no one has been tried and convicted of that crime in the United States in more than twenty years. The question posed by Durkheim was, if this type of society is composed of individuals and diverse groups of people and if there is no single unifying collective conscience, what keeps it together? Durkheim suggests that modern societies have a special type of social cohesion—organic solidarity.

In modern complex societies, an individual is dependent on a great many other people for day-to-day existence. An urbanite, for example, depends for basic sustenance—food, clothing, and shelter—on thousands of other people with whom he or she has no personal contact. Organic solidarity occurs in societies in which separate groups perform many different functions. A good analogy of how organic solidarity works is a living organism. The functioning of each organ in the body depends on the functioning of every other part. Each organ is composed of specialized cells that collectively carry out a specific function. All organs work together to accomplish a single purpose—life. A similar interdependency among diverse groups in society (cooperation necessary for survival) provides social cohesion.

The change in the nature of a society's solidarity is reflected in law. With organic solidarity, law is no longer repressive but restitutive. Civil lawsuits, for example, attempt to bring parties together, to reconcile differences so that society can work more smoothly. Contractualism and the legal system that emerges to enforce it exemplify this new form of organic solidarity. However, the collective conscience does not cease to exist. Durkheim notes that although a contract is often made between strangers, a contract cannot exist unless it is built on an explicit social foundation. The parties to a contract know when they enter such a relationship that society will enforce it. Therefore, a collective conscience is present—a set of beliefs and sentiments—but it operates indirectly on an individual through modern society's institutional structure. In societies characterized by mechanical solidarity, the individual is bound directly to society without this intermediary. In addition, mechanical solidarity continues to exist within modern societies, not in society as a whole but within specialized groups. In metropolitan areas, for example, the viability of tight-knit ethnic neighborhoods is based largely on mechanical solidarity.

The preceding brief review of the works of three sociologists of diverse national origins—French, English, and German—shows that each explored the changing nature of human association. Questions raised by these theorists are still central to the discipline of sociology, especially the literature on community. Collectively they had an important influence on all of sociology, but particularly on the works of Robert Park and other members of the Chicago School. The influence of the European social philosophers on Robert Park and the contributions of the Chicago ecologists to the study of community are examined in the following section.

ROBERT PARK AND THE CHICAGO SCHOOL

The preceding section is a brief overview of the theoretical roots of the present concept of community. In general, Tönnies, Maine, Durkheim, and other European theorists documented both the destruction of the small, tightly integrated community and the emergence of community in its modern form. The works of these sociologists give a negative impression of urban life—a life in which egoism, isolation, and anomie pervade the community. Interestingly, early American sociology continued in this tradition, as is particularly evident in the works of Robert Park and other members of the Chicago School.

Wirth, in his 1938 essay, "Urbanism as a Way of Life," summarized the major viewpoint of this school: city growth with its concomitant increases in the size, density, and heterogeneity of population leads to a substitution of secondary relations for primary ones and a greater dependency on formal means of social control (see Chapter 1). Moreover, the traditional sources of community solidarity and control (the family and the church) were believed to be largely ineffective in the urban setting and social disorganization was thought to be a predictable outcome of these underlying changes. Through the works of these sociologists, social disorganization became a central theme in the theoretical and empirical works in American sociology for the next two decades. The obsession of the Chicago ecologists with disorganization is reflected in the titles of their works: Thrasher's *The Gang*; Anderson's *The Hobo*; Shaw's *Delinquency Areas*, *The Jack-Roller*, and *Brothers in Crime*; Zorbaugh's *The Gold Coast and the Slum*; Wirth's *The Ghetto*; and Faris and Dunham's *Mental Disorders in Urban Areas*.

The Influence of Nineteenth-Century Community Theorists

There is an important difference between the sociology of Tönnies, Maine, and Durkheim and that of the Chicago ecologists, however. The nineteenth-century theorists used the concept of community in a broad sense and considered whole societies. The Chicago School was referring to cities like Chicago. Thus, "community" is synonymous with "city" in much of their work. In addition, the concept of community was defined ecologically as the "patterns of symbiotic and communalistic relations that develop in a population; it is in the nature of a collective response to the habitat; it constitutes the adjustment of organisms to the environment" Hawley, 1950, p. 2). Although community was defined narrowly by these ecologists, both groups wrestled with essentially the same problem—the problem of order in society. Park's sociology in particular attempted to identify the "control mechanism through which a community composed of several quite different subcommunities can arrange its affairs so that each of them maintains its

own distinctive way of life without endangering the life of the whole"
(Stein, 1972, p. 17). This statement is reminiscent of Durkheim's work,
because Durkheim greatly influenced Park. Durkheim addressed the same
problem in his interpretation of the transition from mechanical to organic
solidarity as the basis for order in society. Like Park, Durkheim saw a role
for each type of solidarity in modern society: subgroups within society
were held together by the bonds of mechanical solidarity, whereas in the
larger society the cohesive forces of organic solidarity prevailed. Park examined the relationships between subcommunities (natural areas) and the
encompassing community. The major thrust of both of their works, therefore, was how organic solidarity can be achieved (Stein, 1971, pp. 17–18).[3]

Achieving solidarity in the modern community To Durkheim, the integration
of complex societies was based on the role of occupational subgroups. Each
subgroup—physicians, lawyers, tradesmen, and skilled workers—would
develop their own code of ethics through which the behavior of their members would be restricted. Moreover, in order to survive, each subgroup had
to integrate its functions with the larger society. In this way the self-interest
of the occupational subgroup and the necessities of "organic solidarity"
could be reconciled (Stein, 1972, p. 20).

Park approached the same problem but from a somewhat different perspective, subcommunities. Subcommunities were simply another type of
subgroup in society that were defined spatially. The behavior of the members of these subcommunities could be controlled either through a complex
set of social institutions (police, courts, welfare agencies) or through the
operation of the informal control mechanisms of the residential subgroups.
The operation of these informal control mechanisms within subcommunities
was of greatest interest to the members of the Chicago School.

Natural areas As noted in previous chapters, the urban landscape is not
homogeneous and undifferentiated, but is composed of a mosaic of social
worlds. These subcommunities, or natural areas as they were called by
Park, are often strikingly different in makeup, but most large cities share
many of the same types of subareas. For example, every large city has a
central business district, slums, ghettoes, middle- and working-class areas.
Most large cities have a "skidrow," a "bright lights district," and a "Greenwich Village" where "life is freer, more adventurous and lonely than elsewhere" (Stein, 1972, p. 21). To Park, these areas were the product of
unplanned biotic forces; the product of the sorting of individuals and groups
into homogeneous subareas based on common culture and language, race,
or occupational and socioeconomic status. The reason for their emergence
was framed in purely ecological terms. Natural areas emerged simply because they helped a group of people with similar characteristics satisfy
"fundamental needs and solve fundamental problems." Park reasoned that
as long as the problems remained, natural areas would continue to exist.

There is another important characteristic of natural areas according to Park. Through time, each natural area develops its "own peculiar traditions, customs, conventions, standards of decency and propriety, and, if not a language of its own, at least a universe of discourse, in which words and acts have a meaning which is appreciably different for each local community" (Park, 1952, p. 201). New residents of the natural areas through time are socialized and take on the norms of their new community. Therefore, once a natural area comes into existence it has a tendency to perpetuate itself. Thus, Park, like Durkheim, saw subgroups—defined spatially within the larger community—as developing a moral code to regulate the behavior of the members. In addition, natural areas must make a contribution to the functioning of the encompassing community. This functional interdependence among subareas of the city was the basis for the integration and solidarity of the larger community.

Why social disorganization was emphasized The question remains of why Park and the Chicago School emphasized social disorganization. The answer relates to Park's notion of natural area. Natural areas were not viewed as static but as dynamic phenomena. Park reasoned that within a city, individuals, groups, and institutions are constantly being sorted and relocated. During periods of rapid population growth, especially when there is an influx of large numbers of diverse ethnic or racial groups, the stability of certain natural areas is upset as the subareas undergo the invasion-succession process. As a result of this transition the mechanisms for social control within the natural areas are weakened and social disorganization occurs. Most natural areas maintain their solidarity, but in some areas the control mechanisms break down.

In the 1920s, Chicago gained more than one-half million people. This rapid growth affected all areas of the city to a degree, but nowhere was the effect greater than in the slums. In the slum, ghetto and hobohemia the Chicago ecologists saw an absence of any effective means of social control. In these areas the traditional forms of social control—the family, the church, and the neighborhood—had been undermined and such "secondary agencies as the police, courts, newspapers, schools and settlement houses" had taken their place.

Criticism of the Natural Area Concept

The image of a community (a city) as a planless outgrowth of ecological segregation, along with the view that homogeneity and stability characterize a city's subcommunities or natural areas, has persisted and influences the present image of community. Is this image correct? Did natural areas, as the concept was advanced by the Chicago School, exist in the 1920s and, if so, do they exist today?

The social order of the slum and ghetto ignored A review of the works published by the Chicago School in the 1920s and the research on sub-communities completed since that decade suggests that Park and the Chicago ecologists may have overstated their case. First, were the slums, ghettoes, and hobohemias as devoid of social order and institutional structures as this school suggests? In *The Gold Coast and the Slum* (1929), Zorbaugh begins with this general statement on the slum, which he characterizes as a collection of isolated individuals:

> The slum is an area of freedom and individualism. Over large stretches of the slum men neither know nor trust their neighbors. Aside from a few marooned families, a large part of the native population is transient: prostitutes, criminals, outlaws, hobos. Foreigners who come to make a fortune, as we used to go west, and expect to return to the Old Country as soon as they make "their stake," who are not really a part of American life, and who wish to live in the city as cheaply as possible, live in the lodging-houses of the slum. Here, too, are the areas of immigrant first settlement, the foreign colonies. And here are congregated the "undesirable" alien groups, such as the Chinese and the Negro (p. 128).

Zorbaugh in this paragraph lumps a number of diverse groups under one heading—slum dwellers. Moreover, he implies that they are unorganized. But it is interesting to note that within a few pages he describes the manner in which the immigrant community is organized!

> As the colony grows, the immigrant finds in it a social world. In the colony he meets with sympathy, understanding and encouragement. There he finds his fellow-countrymen who understand his habits and standards and share his life-experience and viewpoint. In the colony he has status, plays a role in a group. In the life of the colony's streets and cafes, in its churches and benevolent societies, he finds response and security. In the colony he finds that he can live, be somebody, satisfy his wishes—all of which is impossible in the strange world outside (p. 141).

Commenting on other areas, Zorbaugh notes:

> The life of this area is far from unorganized. The Gold Coast has its clubs; intimate groups gather in "village" studios; the foreign areas have numerous lodges and mutual benefit societies; the slum has its "gangs . . ."
> And these groups may play an enormously important role in the lives of their members (p. 192).

During the same period other researchers, including H. A. Miller (1920), Robert Park, Fredrich Thrasher (1926), and Louis Wirth (1928), identified similar organizations within the slum, but their attention continued to be focused on social disorganization. Why were findings of organization in slums reported by the Chicago ecologists and then ignored? Suttles (1972) and Whyte (1943) suggest that the theoretical and political perspectives as well as the class and social backgrounds of the researchers themselves biased their research.[4] Whyte (1943) observes:

> Apparently Zorbaugh began his study with the conviction that the slum represents the Gesellschaft ideal type. (This idea is expressed in the first quote.) His discussion of the evidences of social organization does not fit the ideal type. However, by calling them (organizations) interstitial phenomena, he manages to dismiss them from further consideration (p. 36).

Zorbaugh found that lower-class organizations were closely bound to the local area and had no "community-wide loyalties." Because these organizations were very different from the middle-class ones with which he was familiar, he dismissed them as unimportant. More recent ethnographic works, however, have outlined in detail the social organization and the normative order in these districts. Whyte's *Street Corner Society* (1955), Liebow's *Tally's Corner* (1967), Gans's *The Urban Villagers* (1962), and Suttles's *The Social Order of the Slum* (1968) are four of the dozens of community studies that have reported in detail the social processes operating within slums.

Park's influence on research Apparently Park's influence at the University of Chicago over both the types of research and the researchers themselves led to biases in the school's works. Park looked back with nostalgia to the days when the family, the church, and the neighborhood provided a natural order for a community. In the present, he looked to secondary institutions such as schools, newspapers, and social agencies as potent forces in reconstituting a community, e.g., a city. Within this scheme, natural areas were viewed as a social unit that could provide a social order similar to that of an earlier and simpler time. Therefore, Park saw the combining of two worlds, the Gemeinschaft in the subcommunity within the encompassing Gesellschaft society.

Difficulty of identifying natural areas The natural area concept has a second weakness. Natural areas were viewed by the Chicago School as emerging through the operation of basic ecological or biotic forces. To these ecologists, the most distinctive characteristic of these areas was that they were not planned or artificially constructed, but developed out of millions of individual decisions based on different moral, ecological, political, and economic positions. The city from this perspective was a mosaic of social worlds loosely organized by larger political and administrative structures of the metropolis. In other words, each natural area had a unique quality that was the result of the unique combination of the area's ethnic and racial mix, physical characteristics, and other factors including the income and occupation of its residents.

The reader of this literature is left with the impression that all one need do to delineate the boundaries of each natural area is examine the racial, ethnic, income, and occupational characteristics of a city's population or examine its housing and land-use characteristics. That is, a city is seen as a gigantic jigsaw puzzle and natural areas are the pieces. In this scheme, boundaries do not overlap and the world is neat and ordered.

In the 1930s, 1940s, and 1950s, research was published that called into question the validity of the natural area concept. For example, Davie (1938), Hatt (1946), and Form et al. (1954) were unable to find clearly bounded culturally homogeneous areas in the cities they examined. By the mid-1940s the concept of natural areas and the theoretical foundation of the Chicago ecologists had been seriously undermined.

As a result of these findings, most research since the 1940s has shifted from the physical characteristics of urban subareas to the social character of these areal units. Although the term "natural area" is seldom used, Keller (1968) suggests that many of the key components of this concept have been integrated into the popular term "neighborhood." Since the 1940s, the major areas of sociological research on the neighborhood have been urban-rural differences in neighborhoods, formal and informal participation in neighborhood activities, family adaptation to new residential environments, social networks in urban areas, propinquity, and neighboring and symbolic communities.[5]

THE SOCIAL CONSTRUCTION OF COMMUNITIES

Much recent research is directed to identifying the present nature of the communities. Janowitz (1961), Greer (1962), Suttles (1968, 1972), and Hunter (1974) address two questions about the modern community. First, what is the relationship of communities to changes in the scale of the larger society? Second, do local communities have recognizable names and boundaries, and are these names and boundaries known to their residents and members of the larger metropolis as well?

Societal Scale and the Local Community

A consensus seems to have developed about the relationship between societal scale and the nature of a local community. Increasing societal scale—indicated by increasing use of nonhuman energy and increased per capita output—results in a loss of autonomy and fragmentation of local groups and increased dependency on secondary and formal institutions, especially in the area of crisis intervention. Concomitantly, increasing societal scale leads to greater social and physical mobility and a decreasing dependency on the local community.

The separation of physical and social neighborhoods The validity of this point is found in the research of Morris and Mogey (1965). These authors found in their studies on neighboring a decreasing correspondence between social and physical groupings in urban areas. They concluded that the growth of secondary institutions, such as schools and welfare organizations, and increased physical mobility have led to a separation between physical and social neighborhoods. As Keller (1968) states, these changes have altered the social relationships among neighbors from "neighboring of place to a neighboring by taste" (p. 55). Transportation innovations, in particular, have drastically changed the nature of human relationships within urban areas. In the past, because of poor transportation, people either worked within the home or lived within walking distance of their place of employment. The individual was closely tied to the subcommunity because there were no alternatives. Today, the automobile gives Americans great physical mobility. The place of employment is normally far from one's place of residence. The automobile gives individuals many alternatives. The urbanite has been released from the constraints of the local area, and he or she can be very selective in choosing friends. Ties to the local community have been weakened but new forms of social relationships have emerged (Meier, 1968; Tobin, 1976).

Social networks These new forms of social relationships include social networks. Kasarda and Janowitz (1974), Fischer (1976), Wellman (1979), and others suggest that because of the high rates of residential mobility; cheap, effective transportation and communication; the scale, density, and diversity of the city; and the spatial distribution of primary ties, it is very unlikely that the urbanite will be closely tied to a neighborhood.[6] *Social networks* are primary relationships that are spatially dispersed rather than concentrated in a single locale like a neighborhood (Wellman, 1979, p. 1207). These networks of friends can span an entire metropolitan area, and because friends in one network may have friends in others, a complex interconnected social network emerges across the metropolis. The implication for the study of subcommunities is that if this pattern does exist, there is little basis for solidarity of either the mechanical or the organic kind within the local community. Moreover, the starting point for analyzing community would be to examine the limited involvement of people in the local community, and the structure of this local community.

The community of limited liability Janowitz (1961) in contrast explored in detail the effect of an increasing societal scale on the subareas of the city. To Janowitz the most important change brought about by increasing societal scale was the metamorphosis of community from a primary grouping to a more voluntary and less involving institution. Janowitz (1961) introduced the concept of "community of limited liability" to describe this phenomenon and defined it as the "intentional, voluntary, and especially the partial and differential involvement of residents in their local community" (p. 47).

Janowitz discovered this pattern in specific areal units while studying the local community press. He found that neighborhood newspapers sold weekly within the metropolis's subcommunities provided not only an advertising medium for the local merchants, but also a communication mechanism for the social and cultural integration of the local area. During the same period, Hawley and Zimmer (1970), Axelrod (1957), and others found large numbers of voluntary associations operating within local areas, organized to argue their community's position on metropolitan issues. The Clintonville area of Columbus, Ohio, provides a good example. In 1975, the city of Columbus decided to widen and thus destroy a beautiful tree-lined street in the Clintonville area known as Northwest Boulevard. The local area's weekly, *The Booster,* in a series of front-page stories, publicized the city's plans. As a result, several local concerned citizens' groups were formed, monies were collected for attorneys' fees, and the city's plans were blocked in the courts. The point that Janowitz and others have made is that the neighborhood or "the community of limited liability" is no longer a primary group but it is still an important source of social contacts for a large proportion of the metropolis' residents.

These articles are from a series on the neighborhood that ran in the Christian Science Monitor *during 1977, and they focus on an area called Southeast Baltimore. The reporter calls this area a neighborhood; human ecologists would prefer the term community of limited liability. Regardless of the term used, inner-city communities of limited liability in many cities have reemerged in recent years as a potent political force. The grass-roots character of this movement is explored in the following articles, "Bootstrap Efforts Revive a City," and "They Fought a Highway and Formed a Congress."*

BOOTSTRAP EFFORTS REVIVE A CITY

By Stewart Dill McBride

Journalist H. L. Mencken once asked James Thurber to "drop off in Baltimore some day and let me show you the ruins of a once great medieval city." Baltimore has been called "Mobtown" and "Factorytown"; W. C. Fields might well have said of it, "I spent a week there one afternoon." It has never attracted many tourists; and it remains one of the few East Coast cities without a Gray Line tour office.

Recently, however, Baltimore has been staging a quiet comeback. The renovation of its dilapidated waterfront, and a creative "urban homesteading" housing program, are luring "back to the city" pioneers to reclaim large tracts of urban wasteland. Not long ago the National Municipal League even named Baltimore an "All-American City."

The town's second wind results largely from the revival of its neighborhoods.

Southeast Baltimore is a proud working-class conglomerate. Its people are second- and third-generation descendants of Ukrainians, Poles, Greeks, Italians, and Germans, who sweated in the steel mills and canneries, saved every possible penny, always paid cash, and each Saturday morning scrubbed down their marble steps with brush and pumice.

One of the oldest sections of the city, southeast Baltimore has always been the welcome mat for immigrants. Of the 94,000 people living there now, most are of Eastern European descent. There is a small colony of Lumbee Indians from the Carolinas and a scattering of Koreans and Filipinos. The median income here is less than $8,000—well below the metropolitan average of $10,-577. More than half of southeast residents have not gone beyond the ninth grade; three in a hundred have college degrees. Nearly one-fifth of the population is over 60 years old. Half of the houses are owner-occupied.

A decade ago this unpretentious section of town decided to take on City Hall and the federal government and fight an expressway scheduled to slice through the neighborhood. The "concrete issue" in turn spawned a remarkable coalition of church groups, block clubs, ethnic fraternities, "hard hats" and "longhairs," Republicans and Socialists, Little League baseball coaches and welfare mothers—all working under an "umbrella" called Southeast Community Organization (SECO). Together they have revived the oldest, and one of the most blighted, sections of the inner city.

When it was formed six years ago, SECO possessed a few picket signs and an underpaid community organizer working out of a church basement. Today SECO has a staff of 41 and a budget of $650,000. It also is responsible for another $16 million in neighborhood programs—including a "land bank," a neighborhood housing corporation, a research and planning office, health clinics, tutoring programs, and a senior citizen center. SECO has restored entire blocks of row houses; it has restored community pride.

In short, southeast Baltimore has become a classic model for reviving the inner city.

THEY FOUGHT A HIGHWAY AND FORMED A CONGRESS

By Stewart Dill McBride

The Route 40 downtown overpass was bumper to bumper with steelworkers from west Baltimore. They were making their daily pilgrimage through inner-city blight and dusty afternoon heat to the swing shift at Bethlehem Steel's Sparrows Point mill. Striding along the sidewalk next to the overpass, a grandmotherly woman in canary pants and flowered blouse fluffed her graying hair and glared at the rush-hour traffic on the expressway below. Downtown Baltimore was exhaling businessmen and bureaucrats in air-conditioned cars bound for the northern suburbs of Pikesville and Towson.

"The fight started right here," the woman bellowed over the drone of passing cars. "And that's the monster I was telling you about." She pointed down at Interstate 83. "It still makes me angry just to look at it."

Gloria Aull's "monster" is an unfinished expressway. Eleven years ago the city announced that I-83 would cut an eight-lane swath through her neighborhood—southeast Baltimore—a fiercely proud, white, working-class section of the city where home ownership and control of "turf" are synonymous with personal freedom.

Gloria Aull's neighbors had little use for an expressway. They could walk to the corner store, to church, to school. Nearly half of them didn't own cars.

Highway Tangled in Courts

So Mrs. Aull and her neighbors fought the highway, and so far have won; today it stops in downtown Baltimore as abruptly as the end of a diving board. Its progress has been tangled in the courts for nearly a decade by Mrs. Aull and a ragtag band of her neighbors, who took on City Hall and the federal government and emerged as one of the most sophisticated and powerful community organizations in the country.

Mrs. Aull and her family live on the borders of the Canton and Highlandtown sections of southeast Baltimore, in a row house her German grandmother bought at the turn of the century with a $5 bill as down payment. Her grandmother came from Hamburg back when Canton was being developed as the nation's "first industrial park," and broadsides throughout Europe were luring peasant stock from abroad to southeast Baltimore. The broadsides offered free passage, together with housing and jobs—jobs in the copper works, packing houses, and canneries lining the harbor. The immigrants landed in Fells Point and worked their way east into Canton, Highlandtown, and eventually to the county," as the size of their paychecks grew with promotion. Southeast Baltimore is still ringed with industry, and to this day the working-class pecking order is sacred: steelworkers live in Canton, their foremen live in Highlandtown and their supervisors reside in the suburbs of Essex and Dundalk.

A few blocks from the Aulls' house is Patterson Park, the beginning of Highlandtown—the "town within a city." Like much of southeast Baltimore, it is a clannish sort of place, where self-sufficient neighborhoods are knit as tight as a sweater, and nearly everyone pays cash. People here save. Everything. The bleak anonymity of formstone facade row houses belies five-figure bank accounts and parlors cluttered with figurines and knickknacks.

The purest strain of "Bawlmarese"—the city's hybrid accent is spoken in Highlandtown ("Hollandtayon") where "drucksstrewer" is a place to buy toothpaste, "paramoore" is what your suburban uncle cuts the grass with, and a "mixed marriage" is one between a German and a Pole. Residents of Highlandtown rarely venture downtown but shop at Ma and Pa grocery stores with names like "Bach's" or "Kaczorowski's." The proprietors offer ethnic specialties such as homemade mustard and Polish sausage, together with information on houses up for sale; you'll rarely see a "for sale" sign on a house here. Advertising is done through word of mouth. They like to "keep things in the family."

After World War II, something changed in Highlandtown and the rest of southeast Baltimore. The most educated and affluent young adults began moving out to the suburbs, leaving behind parents and grandparents on fixed incomes. Absentee landlords and speculators started to subdivide three-family homes into rooming houses of 9 and 10 apartments. Suspicion spread. Neighbors, afraid of the crime and blight that began to claim their turf, retreated behind their aluminum screen doors. Southeast Baltimore was referred to as the "white ghetto." Many banks stopped mortgage loans to the area.

In January, 1966, without a whimper from this community, the Baltimore City Council passed an ordinance laying out condemnation lines for the new expressway system. The system was designed to divert Philadelphia-Washington traffic from downtown Baltimore along a "path of least resistance" through the deteriorating southeast neighborhoods like Fells Point and Canton.

Gloria Aull was then working with a group of Protestant pastors, counseling teen-agers. Through her volunteer church work she met Barbara Mikulski, a young social worker from Highlandtown. They were both outraged by the highway. And out of their friendship and this outrage was born a small group known as the Southeast Committee Against the Road (SCAR).

Says Barbara Mikulski: "We knew how to organize. Most of the people here work in places that are unionized. They knew how to deal with the big boys, whether it was in the old sweat shops that our grandparents worked in, or whatever. There are two sources of power: money and large numbers. We didn't have lots of money. All we had was each other, and our strength rested in activating those large numbers." Not that the numbers interested in fighting the highway were large at first. "We got started with about eight of us meeting seven times a week in groups under different names to create the illusion of power."

Unbeknown to SCAR, a group of preservationists was meeting in Fells Point to plan how to keep the proposed road from destroying hundreds of 18th- and early 19th-century buildings on the historic waterfront. The group was headed by Jack Gleason, one of the first of the "new people" to move into Fells Point. Cultured and comfortable, Mr. Gleason bought and renovated an old brick house in Fells Point, and found himself in the middle of the highway fight. His house was less than a foot from the demolition corridor. "Getting involved in fighting the road was the furthest thing from my mind. I'd never been a joiner or an advocate. The idea of carrying a picket sign was a little foreign to me."

Nevertheless, soft-spoken Jack Gleason soon became known as "Mr. Anti-highway" and joined forces with SCAR. Armed with a survey of all the historic buildings in Fells Point, he sidestepped City Hall, went directly to Washington, and got Fells Point listed on the National Register of Historic Places. He knew that 90 percent of the highway construction funds were coming from the federal government, which legally could not damage historic sites. As an extra safeguard, SCAR filed suit against the federal government. The case is still in court.

The SCAR activists took on, and won, other neighborhoodwide issues: they defeated an ordinance which would have down-zoned much of southeast Baltimore for industrial use; they stopped the closing of a library in Canton; and they blocked the termination of health services for some senior citizens.

Block clubs and improvement associations began forming to fight for a streetlight here, better garbage pickup there.

In 1970, a southeast Baltimore steering committee hired a community organizer for $6,000 a year. He in turn demanded 15 hours a week volunteer time from a core of 15 neighborhood leaders. Each was asked to bring a friend to each monthly meeting. With each meeting the numbers grew, until by April, 1971, the "network" had evolved into a "congress" of more than 1,000 neighborhood representatives. Thus the formation of the Southeast Community Organization (SECO)—an umbrella organization governed by elected "senators" from each member-group in the federation.

Political Tremors

Baltimore's "machine" politicians felt their political base threatened by such an independent grass-roots organization. Some labeled SECO members as "nigger lovers," "Communists," "blockbusters."

After early victories, community activity lulled as SECO searched for neighborhoodwide issues to fight for. SECO's first organizer, Joe McNeely, resigned and was replaced by someone whose "confrontation organizing" eventually led to an internecine power struggle. This ended with a third of the member association walking out and forming a splinter group, Neighborhoods United, which survived through the next year.

Simultaneously, with the aid of a Ford Foundation grant, SECO was founding a subsidiary community development corporation. The "senators" of SECO functioned as stockholders of Southeast Development Inc. (SDI), and SDI's early successes cast a protective shadow on the parent SECO while the latter licked its wounds and recuperated under the leadership of an energetic housewife named Betty Hyatt.

Meanwhile, SECO organizers were knocking on the doors of as yet uninvolved neighbors who were eventually to take over the organization's leadership:

—**Elaine Smith** had lived on Washington Street in Upper Fells Point for 42 years. "I would look out the window and cry to see the neighborhood go downhill. You could smell it. You could taste it. It got so bad people were sending their garbage airmail—just throwing it out the window. Five houses on the street were abandoned, and the rats were having a ball."

About that time, three years ago, a SECO organizer came to her door. "I told him I just wanted a tree in front of my house to hide the garbage. And he said, 'Let's do something about the garbage.' "

A few days later 15 neighbors met in Mrs. Smith's living room to discuss their sanitation problems. In a matter of months they had organized 14 other blocks to negotiate with city officials involved with health, sanitation, highways, and zoning.

The National Guard hauled away 78 truckloads of refuse from

a block area. And now Mrs. Smith and her brigade of housewives took city officials on inspection tours of the neighborhood. The officials, in turn, issue fines to homeowners who are not keeping up property.

Mrs. Smith has no qualms about picketing the office of a landlord to embarrass him into cleaning up his property. She has even had a health inspector to fine her own husband for not bringing in the garbage cans.

Prodded by Mrs. Smith and the new Upper Fells Point Planning Council, the city inspected some 410 houses in this neighborhood and found 383 violations; 208 houses have since been brought up to code.

Seventy-eight houses have been painted. The city has channeled into the area $500,000 in federal community development block grant money to pay for sanitation services and the hiring of neighborhood residents to inspect the three neighborhoods involved.

SDI, with the help of the planning council, formed a "land bank" which has already purchased 40 properties in Upper Fells Point. The intention was to encourage home ownership and so protect the neighborhood against real estate speculation. The non-profit bank sets aside $30 a month from the tenant's rent, and at the end of 18 months the tenant has accumulated a $500 minimum down payment. He can then buy the property with mortgage assistance from the "land bank."

Home ownership in Upper Fells has soared in the last few years.

Matilda Koval grew up in the Ukrainian enclave of Glenlyon, Pennsylvania. Moving to Baltimore, she fell in love with a radio repairman at a Polish dance, married him, and settled in a row house north of Patterson Park. She used to spend her days crocheting by the window. In 1973 Mrs. Koval attended her first SECO meeting. She then formed a block club and eventually became president of Community Taking Action (CTA)—a coalition of block clubs. Mrs. Koval now is vice-president of the Neighborhood Housing Services (NHS).

Modeled after an experiment in Pittsburgh, the Baltimore NHS has a board of residents and representatives of local lending institutions. It has generated some $3.5 million in loans to an area previously "redlined" (cut off from credit) by downtown banks. In the NHS "model block" on Fayette Street, home ownership has skyrocketed from 4 percent to 83 percent.

"SECO and NHS," says Howard Scaggs, president of a local savings and loan association, "are getting back to the very basis on which this country was founded: people doing things for themselves."

Mr. Scaggs is also the voluntary chairman of the NHS board,

and a booster for southeast Baltimore. His bank, which three years ago made 10 suburban loans for every one in the city, now is filtering most of its loans into the city.

Bill Kelch calls himself the "typical second-generation success story." Of Polish-German extraction, he grew up in southwest Baltimore, married, moved to the suburbs, "only to find myself trapped into mortgage payments for a $30,000 home and spending all my time painting the house and cutting the lawn so I could have a cookout on Sunday."

Life in suburbia didn't last long for Mr. Kelch. He was glad to move back into Canton near his family scrap-iron business. When an SEO organizer asked him to help do something about the abandoned house behind his, Mr. Kelch organized a neighborhood meeting at the local pigeon-racing club, and eventually got the city to move in a "homesteader" who put in $30,000 in renovations. Mr. Kelch then formed the West Canton Improvement Association, which opposed the state's plans to moor a World War II troop carrier for use as a "prison ship," at the foot of Clinton Street.

Seeing the need for publicity, Mr. Kelch entered a hog-calling contest in downtown Baltimore wearing a "No Prison Ship" T-shirt. He didn't win the contest, but he got his picture in the papers. This launched him as the chief spokesman for prison-ship opposition.

A trade-school dropout, Bill Kelch became a self-trained expert on the ship and its potential impact on the neighborhood. He appeared on radio and television talk shows; he debated state and federal officials; and, with a lawyer hired by the neighborhood, he discovered a legal loophole requiring an act of Congress before the ship could be turned over to the state.

Mr. Kelch was also one of the first foremen hired in the new Baltimore Homes program, started by the SDI as a low-cost home-repair service. For a fee of $10 a month, homeowners receive a "preventive maintenance" package that includes an annual inspection of their homes, plus the labor and materials needed for basic home maintenance. In addition, Baltimore Homes offers monthly home improvement workshops, an equipment purchasing cooperative, and a tool lending service.

Over the past several years, SECO has gained the ear and respect of city officials downtown, and has shed its early reputation as a mob of "rabble rousers" and "off-the-wall radicals." The current epithet is "efficient" or "shrewd."

SECO's young executive director, Bill Ariano, still wears blue jeans to work; but many, like Baltimore City Council President Walter S. Orlinksy, think SECO may have become too respectable.

"It is a government partner—a municipal and federal fund-seeker. SECO has joined the 'establishment' and succeeded." If SECO hasn't "joined" the "establishment," it is certainly hitchhiking along with it.

So, somewhat ironically, SECO now is faced with the problem of success. Except for the continuing fight against urban blight, the dramatic issues have vanished. The democratic process is often laborious, and interest hard to maintain.

In Fells Point a different dilemma is developing. Having stopped the highway, this old working waterfront neighborhood is being invaded by the tassled-loafer crowd which is buying up the historic houses and renovating them; and the indigenous old-timers, many on fixed incomes, are being forced out by soaring property values and taxes which have increased as much as eightfold in 10 years.

Some claim SECO has yet to face the issue of race. Southeast Baltimore is only 11 percent black. Many blacks have not forgotten the 1968 riots and the crosses burned on their lawns. They remember the Nazi bookstore which opened for a while on Eastern Avenue across from the fashionable Housner's restaurant. Some even charge that renewed ethnic pride in the southeast Baltimore sector is simply undercover racism in a city that is 57 percent black overall.

Not all agree. Black City Councillor Clarence Burns, representing the predominantly black neighborhood bordering on SECO's northern edge, hopes for beneficial windfalls: "SECO knows how to organize, to withstand outside hostility, to penetrate the system, pick up grants, deliver good programs. Every organization in the city is looking at SECO and asking them questions, and SECO is giving them the answers. What more can you ask for?"

Perhaps the best measure of SECO is how it has altered the lives of the individuals who worked with it:

Barbara Mikulski, "the trumpet of Highlandtown" and the "godmother of SECO," ran for City Council on a neighborhood platform, defeating a highway proponent. Now she represents southeast Baltimore in the U.S. House of Representatives.

Betty Hyatt, a housewife who never finished high school, and former president of SECO, was recently appointed by the Mayor to sit on the nine-member Baltimore City School Board, which controls an annual budget of $300 million.

Bill Kelch, who spearheaded the prison ship fight, now is vice-president of SECO and talking about running for City Council.

Elaine Smith was recently elected as the new president of SECO.

Gloria Aull was elected SECO's second vice-president. After 11 years, she says, people on her block "still don't understand why I go to all these meetings."

Robert Embry Jr., Baltimore's enlightened housing commissioner during the revival of southeast Baltimore, has gone on to become an assistant secretary of the federal Housing and Urban Development (HUD) agency.

Joe McNeely, SECO's first community organizer, has taken a job at HUD as consultant on neighborhoods.

Jack Gleason is president of SDI.

Bill Ariano, who used to make leather belts for a living, now is executive director of SECO.

SECO succeeded because it could weather internal dissension and external attacks. It emphasized issues, not personalities. Says Barbara Mikulski: "We knew we had to be tough and militant. But the *issue* was always the enemy. And we knew the very institutions that we challenged were the ones that we would have to work with when peace broke out. So it was never 'The mayor is the enemy' or 'The City Council is the enemy.' We never attacked people. We attacked issues."

Symbolic Communities

Suttles (1968, 1972) provided additional support for the concept of the community of limited liability and also addressed the question of whether local communities have recognizable boundaries that are known both to their residents and to members of the larger metropolis.

Suttles's research suggests that the individual simplifies and makes comprehensible the complexity of the metropolis by developing a simplified mental or cognitive map of the city. In large cities, those mental maps were found to consist of three symbolic structures—the face-block, the defended neighborhood, and the community of limited liability.

The face-block The most elementary grouping in urban areas is a network of acquaintances known as the face-block. "These are acquaintances who are recognized from face-to-face relations or encounters and seen regularly because they live on the same block, use the same bus station, shop at the same stores, and for any number of reasons continually cross one another's pathways" (Suttles, 1972, p. 55). The basis for this association is not ethnicity, race, or socioeconomic status but rather familiarity, because in the back of each person's mind "is the knowledge that this person lives close by or uses the same facilities" (Suttles, 1972, p. 55).

Face-blocks are only loosely organized and do not constitute a neighborhood because the boundaries of these units are normally known only to the residents living within them and remain unknown to outsiders. The areal unit is real and important for the people living within its boundaries, however. Parents often use the face-block as the area in which their children are permitted to play. As a result, these units become the basis of the child's peer-group activities. In addition, adults use this unit to organize block clubs, "a common adult form of organization for acquiring better public services" (Suttles, 1972, p. 56).

Social processes carried out in the face-block Thus, the face-block that surrounds the household is an important and inescapable part of any household's environment. Here the problems of social order are clearest because this is the areal unit in which the play of children as well as child-adult and adult-adult relations must be regulated. If misunderstanding and conflict arise, the orderly performance of the household may be interrupted. In addition, the social interaction that takes place on this level is in many respects determined by the nature of the physical environment. In apartment-house districts the communication level is low because of the lack of common or overlapping space and a separation of the work and leisure routines of the residents. In these areas greater dependence generally is placed on the rules of the building and the formal authorities that enforce them.

In familistic areas, social interaction is greater. As Suttles notes, it occurs among persons whose paths must cross—in adjoining backyards, bus stops, schools, on sidewalks, and in playgrounds. Interaction with one's neighbors is unavoidable (Michelson, 1970).

Although the face-block is a social unit for both adults and children, Suttles believes that it is not based on the ties suggested by Park in the natural area concept. Although age, race, and ethnic and socioeconomic status characteristics do bring about the general sorting of individuals into subareas of the city, physical closeness and small area are the basis of the face-block.

The defended neighborhood The defended neighborhood is composed of numerous face-blocks. It is commonly the smallest area within the metropolis that has an identity known to both its residents and outsiders. Suttles (1972) defined it as that area outside the face-block in which residents have a high degree of familiarity and a relative degree of security on the streets compared to adjacent areas (p. 57). These units vary considerably in size depending on the characteristics of the area's inhabitants, but normally include the schools, churches, and grocery and retail stores that an area's residents use on a day-to-day basis.

Zorbaugh's *The Gold Coast and the Slum* and many of the other works by the Chicago School explored the operation of defended neighborhoods. Park and his followers give the impression that these areas were homogeneous, occupied by a single ethnic, racial, or occupational grouping. Suttles, however, suggests that very few of these defended neighborhoods now have, or ever have had, homogeneous populations and that most inner-city neighborhoods have undergone a continuous process of invasion-

Photo 9.1 Although the neighborhood is now less important than in the past to people, their lives and behavior are still influenced by their propinquity. Living together in physical proximity requires social structures and social functions to sustain life in the neighborhood and provide the satisfactions people seek.
Source: © 1977 Paul Sequeira, Photo Researchers, Inc.

succession during the past forty years. Interestingly, although these areas' populations have completely turned over, the character and boundaries of many of the areas have remained the same. This persistence is due to the fact that these units have been incorporated into the cognitive maps of residents of the larger community. As Suttles remarks:

[Some neighborhoods] may be known as snobbish, trashy, tough, exclusive, dangerous, mixed or any number of other things. Some neighborhoods may simply be unknown, and reference to one's residence may arouse only puzzlement and necessitate one's explaining one's guilt or virtue by residential association. In any case, neighborhood identity remains a stable judgemental reference against which people are assessed, and although some may be able to evade the allegations thrown their way, they nonetheless find such evasions necessary (1972, p. 35).

These units are also used in the cognitive maps of city residents to guide other types of behavior, specifically travel. In large metropolitan areas one must be concerned about one's personal safety. In many areas of a city it is not safe to travel day or night. The cognitive map held by individuals simplifies the choices he or she makes on spatial movement within the city, e.g., areas of travel, time of day, type of transportation, and appropriate number of people in the group.

Finally, although some people may have strong sentimental attachments to a defended neighborhood, this feeling is not the basis for social cohesion in these areas. Though there may be underlying similarities in race, ethnicity, and income, solidarity appears to be simply a matter of common residence. Defended neighborhoods are a grouping and as in any other grouping "members are joined in a common plight whether or not they like it" (Suttles, 1972, p. 37). The fate of a defended neighborhood often depends on city planners, realtors, politicians, and industry. This common fate and common experience provide the cohesion of the neighborhood. A threat to the neighborhood will lead to a defensive response that generates cohesive solidarity.

The community of limited liability   A defended neighborhood may or may not be known to members of the larger community. A community of limited liability, in contrast, is a unit of analysis that research has shown to be symbolically important to residents of an area and to members of the larger metropolis as well. More important is the fact that in some cities the boundaries of these units are reinforced by governmental agencies on the federal, state, and local levels. Physical and symbolic boundaries of these areas do not always reinforce each other. However, such physical characteristics of a city as parks, railroads, waterways, highways, and major distorting features in the terrain normally lead to a clear demarcation of these areas.

The formation of communities of limited liability   One aspect of the boundary-forming and boundary-maintenance process that Suttles believes has largely been ignored by sociologists, is the role of external organizations in defining residential groupings. Both Suttles (1972) and Hunter (1974) report that the boundaries, as well as the names used by residents to identify their communities, have often been imposed by planners, developers, booster organizations, and realtors. "Once symbols and boundaries come into existence numerous 'external' adversaries or advocates . . . are anxious to claim a constituency or market and keep it intact" (Suttles, 1972, p. 49). Unlike the other cognitive structures identified by Suttles, a community of limited liability has an official identity that requires its name and boundaries to be institutionally secured by governmental acknowledgment. More important, although this official identity is imposed by an external force, the boundaries and symbols are often incorporated into the cognitive models of the residents of the neighborhood and the wider metropolis as well (Hunter, 1974, p. 25).

The validity of the concept can be seen in Hunter's research on the community areas first delineated by Burgess and his students in the 1920s. At that time, Chicago was mapped into seventy-five exhaustive and mutually exclusive areas. Kitagawa and Tauber outlined the criteria used in this

"Welcome to 457 East Sixty-third."

Source: Drawing by Whitney Darrow, Jr.; © 1964 The New Yorker Magazine, Inc. Reprinted by permission.

mapping process in the introduction to the 1960 edition of *Local Community Fact Book for Chicago Metropolitan Area.* They state:

> when community area boundaries were delineated . . . the objective was to define a set of subareas of the city each of which could be regarded as having a history of its own as a community, a name, an awareness on the part of its inhabitants of community interests, and a set of local businesses and organizations oriented to the local community (Kitagawa and Tauber, 1963, p. xiii).

Although the names and boundaries were imposed on these areas nearly fifty years ago, for a large proportion of Chicago's residents these community areas still operate as meaningful symbolic communities or natural areas (Hunter, 1974, p. 25). A significant percentage of the residents sampled were able to name the community area and its boundaries in a way consistent with the *Fact Book*.

In terms of the mechanisms by which these symbols were transmitted from generation to generation, Hunter points to the role of local community organizations, neighborhood newspapers, government agencies, and real estate interests as crucial in maintaining symbolic stability through time. The gradual socialization of a new member of a community into an area through initial contacts with schools, shops, realtors, and neighbors is another dimension of this process. Both Hunter and Suttles provide general support for the existence of these areal units in the city of Chicago. Similar units are found in many other cities. A map of Cleveland's planning areas is provided in Figure 6.1.

A community of limited liability develops when the similar interests of residents are transformed into common interests based on the degree to which the vital resources of a household are involved—e.g., public schools and government services. The residents of a community of limited liability are therefore functionally interdependent, often with a single adversary. Communication in a community of limited liability takes place through two channels—the community press and local voluntary organizations. Organizations such as homeowner associations are more important in ordering behavior, whereas the press is the more effective channel of communication.

Participation in Local Community Affairs

What is the relationship of local voluntary associations and the community press to the residents of an area? The interaction of the community press and the local voluntary associations is examined in detail by Greer and Orleans (1962), Greer (1970), and others in their studies of the participation of residents in local community affairs. These authors suggest that approximately 90 percent of a city's population fits into one of three categories: isolates, neighbors, and community actors.

Isolates Isolates are people who are literally disengaged from the organizational structure of a local community. They operate as neighbors slightly if at all, and belong to none of the voluntary organizations in the area. In general, they rarely vote. They seldom read the local community newspaper except to see the advertisements. As a result, they are generally ignorant of most of the local community affairs. For example, they are unable to name local leaders or important current issues in the community.

Neighbors Neighbors are the second largest group. They are involved in their immediate social environment. Generally, they live in the small world of the face-block, and their social life revolves around casual social interaction and family friendships. They tend to be young families and, like isolates, they have low rates of participation in politics, but are likely to read the local community newspaper and to know the names of local community leaders. They participate in the local area, but this participation is limited to their face-block or defended neighborhood.

The intensity of neighboring activity varies considerably from one area of a metropolis to the next. John Ciardi questions the value of neighboring in the metropolis, in general:

NEIGHBORING

If the anonymity New York grants us is a problem, it is also a blessing. In small towns it is natural and easy to be passing friendly with everyone nearby, and in a small town it works. But in New York there are too many people nearby. Just try being friendly to everyone you meet there! Not only would you never get where you are going, but you would be making a nuisance of yourself to thousands of people with their own errands to run. The very multitude of people makes it necessary for us to stare through and beyond one another.

Were I living in an apartment house, I would not care to know who lives above me, below me, or in the next apartment on either side. I want to choose my friends. I do not care to have them thrust upon me by the rental agent. And I do not want people dropping in to borrow whatever people borrow, nor to chitchat whatever neighbors chitchat . . . It can be lonely at times inside that anonymity, but let a small-town friendliness echo through those canyons and the future would be chaos forever, bumper to bumper and nose to nose from here to infinity (John Ciardi, "Manner of Speaking," *Saturday Review,* Feb. 12, 1966, pp. 16–17).

Community actors Community actors are the smallest group but are the most influential because of their involvement in local organizations. Generally they are "joiners" involved in voluntary associations at many levels—a church group, the Chamber of Commerce, the Lions Club. They are a disproportionately large part of the local electorate (approximately 70 percent of them vote versus 30 percent of the isolates) and they are the most knowledgeable on local issues. Interestingly, this group, which carries out most of the public affairs in a local community, is self-selected. Interest in local community affairs is so low that literally anyone who has the time and the interest can be a community leader. Therefore, it is the community actors who speak for the interests of the local community, normally through a community-based voluntary association. This group could be likened to a ruling class who through their influence have a disproportionate role in determining the outcome of local community issues.

The other less interested groups benefit from the actions of these self-chosen community actors, however, and frequently identify with them. The community actors serve an important watch-dog function in the community and defend it from outside adversaries. If a threat to the local area is particularly severe, this group uses the local community press and their overlapping memberships in voluntary associations to publicize the problem. In certain circumstances they can elicit the help of neighbors and in extreme circumstances even of the isolates.

Transition in Local Communities

Although face-blocks, defended neighborhoods, and communities of limited liability appear to be present in Chicago or other cities, these units are in a process of continuous change. In a face-block, for instance, a dispute among the block's central clique may cause members to switch their loyalties to other adjacent areas. Likewise, the defended neighborhoods in inner cities regularly undergo the invasion-succession process that may influence both their solidarity and identity. The boundaries and identity of a community of limited liability may also change as groups of advocates and adversaries compete for influence over the constituencies of these areas. The identification of the areas is complicated by the fragmentation of authority on the local level. Municipal governments are often familiar with the natural or symbolic communities but seldom use their boundaries explicitly to determine the jurisdictions of various public agencies. Suttles (1972) and Hunter (1974) found very little overlap in the boundaries of Chicago's community areas, political wards, school districts, and police districts. Residents often are members of more than one community of limited liability. In one case, the boundaries may coincide with a school district, in another an improvement district. The split loyalties that result from the fragmentation of local authority partly explain the high failure rate of local community groups. It is difficult to raise interest in a particular issue when residents of an area are involved in other issues.

In general, when one examines how an urbanite defines and uses space, a somewhat confusing picture of the urban landscape emerges. Boundaries between the various areal units are not clear and sharply delineated but instead overlap and in some cases are superimposed over one another. The pattern contrasts to the neat patchwork that results from social area analysis. Social area analysis provides a tool for examining the broad structural form of a city, but it is less useful in analyzing the actual operation of a city on the social level.

This is not to say that the social area dimensions are unimportant in analyzing the social basis of community life. Family status, ethnic status, and social status have each been identified as important factors influencing social interaction and the size of the various symbolic community units. In lower socioeconomic areas of the city, for example—areas characterized as low in both ethnic and social status—distrust among residents is often high and the defended neighborhood may be a single building (Suttles, 1968). Suburban areas, in contrast, are characterized by high family, ethnic, and social status, and normally their defended neighborhoods are very large, covering many square blocks.

Relationship of a Community to the Larger Society

The discussion of community suggests that local communities, whether they be face-blocks, defended neighborhoods, or communities of limited liability, are best described as partial communities unable to perform within their boundaries all the functions traditionally carried out in Gemeinschaft communities. In the past, the services provided by local merchants, bankers, and schools were important in generating a sense of community. Today, most local communities depend on numerous institutions and organizations outside their borders for basic, day-to-day services. Most local communities, for example, have chain stores, branch banks, schools, and churches that serve the local community but are affiliated with metropolitan or national organizations. These ties that Warren (1978) calls "vertical patterns of integration" are important in that they integrate the local area into citywide and national social and economic systems. There are, however, costs. Because of these ties, subcommunities do not perform a full range of community functions on their own, those functions often necessary to generate a sense of community. However, there are mechanisms and institutions within the local community that promote cohesiveness. Ideally, the community press, local voluntary organizations, locally based networks of friends and kin, as well as awareness of a common fate bring about the internal integration of a local community. This horizontal pattern of integration combined with vertical patterns leads to the orderly operation of a local community in the metropolitan system.

An optimistic outlook for local communities The nature, scope, and functions of local communities have changed dramatically in the past century, and these changes mirror the underlying scale of society. Increasing societal scale has brought major improvements in transportation, communication, and energy technology that make the all-encompassing Gemeinschaft communities of the past unnecessary. A common human failing is to remember the past selectively—remembering the good and discounting the bad. In many respects, this is precisely what has happened to the concept of community. The Gemeinschaft type of community is romanticized and continues to be described by the words "harmony," "naturalness," "depth," "fullness," and "family-like." Such communities, however, are not without social costs. They preclude free expression and individualism. The local community as it is known today in urban America is neither better nor worse than those of the past, just different.

Social critics suggest that the crime, isolation, poverty, and alienation in the urban setting are the result of the destruction of community. Is this a fair criticism? The city is truly composed of a mosaic of social worlds, each subcommunity serving the needs of a special subgroup in society. Certainly, problem conditions are severe in some of these subcommunities, but for the majority of Americans living in urban areas the partial communities in which they reside provide a satisfactory and satisfying solution to the recurring problems of day-to-day life in a large and complex society.

SUMMARY

In this chapter the evolution of the concept of community is traced from its use by nineteenth-century social philosophers to its present usage in American community studies. The nineteenth-century community theorists Maine, Tönnies, and Durkheim used the community concept to analyze the changing relationship between the individual and society. Community was also applied as an ideal by which life in industrial societies could be compared with life in communities of the past. Although the concept of community is a theme in many of their works, each theorist explored a different aspect of this phenomenon. Maine explored the legal systems of societies, contrasting the family-centered traditional societies with the individual-centered modern societies.

Tönnies employed the ideal types Gemeinschaft and Gesellschaft to analyze the qualities of past and present societies. Gemeinschaft refers to small, homogeneous communities based on tradition, communities in which an individual is guided by the norms and conventions of the community and is tied to the institutions of family and church. Gesellschaft stands in polar extreme to Gemeinschaft and refers to large, complex, heterogeneous societies composed of individuals. In these societies reason prevails and contracts define the relationships between people.

Durkheim's concern was with the "social glue" that holds society together. He identified two types of social solidarity: mechanical and organic. Mechanical solidarity is found in small homogeneous societies in which there is near universal agreement on the values, beliefs, and norms of the community—a collective conscience. Organic solidarity prevails in modern societies that have large, heterogeneous populations and a complex division of labor. The all-encompassing collective conscience cannot exist in such societies because of their size, but the functional interdependency that develops among specialists forms the basis for social solidarity.

In general, these sociologists concluded that three basic changes had occurred in community. First, the basis of one's social status had changed from the family's status to one's individual achievement. Second, an individual was increasingly viewed as the basic unit of society. Third, the character of societies had changed from sacred-communal to secular-associational.

Park and the Chicago School were influenced by the writings of the nineteenth-century sociologists. Their interest, however, was not in "community" in a broad sense, but in cities and their subcommunities. Although this school's unit of analysis differed from that used in the earlier works of Durkheim, Tönnies, and Maine, both groups were interested in essentially the same problem—order in society. Park, in particular, combined the ecological notion of natural areas with Durkheim's concepts of mechanical and organic solidarity to explain how a community composed of several different subcommunities could allow each of them to maintain its own distinctive way of life without endangering the life of the whole community (Stein, 1972, p. 17).

Durkheim greatly influenced Park. Like Durkheim, Park felt that the city was held together by both mechanical and organic solidarity. Park viewed natural areas as homogeneous in their family, social, or racial and ethnic characteristics. Their mechanical solidarity was based on their commonly held norms, values, and beliefs. However, each of these specialized natural areas made a functional contribution to the operation of the entire city, that produced organic solidarity. Major weaknesses in Park's approach have been identified. The natural areas concept has been called into question as has the emphasis of the Chicago School on social disorganization. These notions, nevertheless, continue to influence the present image of community.

Recent research by Suttles, Hunter, and others suggests that areal units continue to influence life in urban places. Face-blocks, the most elementary grouping in urban areas, are based on the familiarity among people who live on the same block, or use the same parks, stores, or other local facilities. This unit is important because it is where children play and where adult-child and adult-adult relationships are regulated.

The defended neighborhood corresponds to the areas identified by Zorbaugh and the other members of the Chicago School. It is the larger area outside the face-block that people use on a day-to-day basis.

The most distinguishing characteristic of the community of limited liability, the largest of the three symbolic communities, is that it is normally known by the people who reside within it and by the larger community as well. These units are normally composed of numerous defended neighborhoods and come into existence through the actions of builders, planners, or booster groups. Most residents of these areas are classified as isolates or neighbors and have little involvement in community affairs. The few community actors who hold membership in many community organizations provide the political direction for the community.

The concept of community, like many of the other concepts introduced in this text, has a long evolutionary history. Many elements in the present concept of community reflect ideas introduced more than half a century ago. Although social ties to local communities have been weakened, these social units remain important despite their different form and functions. Moreover, these units reflect the scale of society at large.

NOTES

1. The following discussion of Maine, Tönnies, and Durkheim is based in part on the following books: Robert A. Nisbet, *The Sociological Tradition* (New York: Basic Books, Inc., Publishers, 1966); Lewis A. Coser, *Masters of Sociological Thought* (New York: Harcourt Brace Jovanovich, Inc., 1971); David A. Karp, Gregory P. Stone, and William C. Yoels, *Being Urban: A Social Psychological View of City Life* (Lexington, Mass.: D. C. Heath and Co., 1977), Chapter 1.

2. The following material is based in part on Chapters 3, 4, 5, 6, and 8 of *Emile Durkheim: Selected Writings,* edited and translated by Anthony Giddens, published by Cambridge University Press, 1972.

3. The following material is based in part on Maurice Stein, "Robert Park and Urbanization in Chicago," in *The Eclipse of Community: An Interpretation of American Studies* (Princeton, N. J.: Princeton University Press, 1972) (expanded edition).

4. The following material is based in part on an article by William F. Whyte, "Social Organization in the Slums," *American Sociological Review* 8 (1943): 34–39.

5. Contributors to the major areas of sociological research on the neighborhood are: *Urban and Rural Differences*—Wirth (1938), Redfield (1947, 1953), Lewis (1949), Redfield and Singer (1953), and Dewey (1960); *Formal and Informal Participation in Neighboring*—Dotson (1951), Foley (1952), Bell and Force (1956), Axelrod (1957), Bell and Boat (1957), Greer (1962), Babchuk and Edwards (1965), Greer and Orleans (1968), Nohara (1968), Litwak (1970), and Edwards and Booth (1973); *Family Adaptation to New Neighborhoods*—Simey (1954), Young and Willmott (1957), Bott (1957), Frankenburg (1965), Gans (1967), and Bardo (1973); *Social Networks in Urban Areas*—Mitchell (1969), Craven (1973), Kasarda and Janowitz (1974), Fischer (1976), Fischer et al. (1977), Taub (1977), Wellman (1979), and Wellman and Leighton (1979); *Propinquity and Neighboring*—Festinger et al. (1950), Caplow and Forman (1950), Morris and Mogey (1965), Michelson (1970), and Timms (1971); *Symbolic Communities*—Stein (1960), Janowitz (1961), Greer (1962), Suttles (1968, 1972), and Hunter (1974).

6. A few of the contributors to the sociological research on social networks include: Mitchell (1969), Craven (1973), Granovetter (1978), Kasarda and Janowitz (1974), Fischer (1976), Taub (1977), Wellman (1979), and Wellman and Leighton (1979). Refer to the bibliography for a citation for each article.

CHAPTER TEN

The Segregation and Location of Groups in United States Cities

Statement of Objectives

1. The student should become aware of the reasons for studying racial segregation.
2. The social distance between groups is invariably reflected in the spatial distance between them. The student should employ this ecological rule to the text's analysis of social status and ethnic and racial segregation patterns.
3. The student should know how segregation is measured.
4. Ecological, voluntary, and involuntary factors are responsible for the segregation patterns found in cities. The student should assess the importance of each factor in the study of social status and ethnic and racial segregation.
5. The student should become aware of the social costs associated with the high levels of segregation among black Americans.

In Chapter 6, the social area analysis model is used to explore the process by which individuals, groups, and institutions are sorted into more or less homogeneous areas of a city. Empirical studies in the United States and abroad have shown that the degree of differentiation in the internal structure of a city is tied closely to both the scale of the encompassing society and the position of the city in the society's urban hierarchy. In general, subareas of cities in high-scale societies can be described by several dimensions (social, family, and ethnic status), whereas in low-scale societies differences between subareas are based on only a single dimension. The material in Chapter 6 is framed in terms of the properties of areas, e.g., census tracts and social planning areas. In the following discussion the focus is shifted to the properties of groups and the degree to which they are concentrated and located in specific areas of a city.

TYPES OF GROUPS

Very few individuals live in isolation; most people belong to groups, of all types. A person is a member of some groups through the circumstances of statistical arrangement (statistical groups). A person is a member of other groups because he or she is conscious of having something in common, some shared attribute or characteristic, with other people (societal groups). A person is a member of still other groups as a result of entering into social relationships with them (social groups). Finally, a person is a member of certain groups because he or she has joined them, paid dues, and has been added to their membership rolls (association groups) (Bierstedt, 1974, p. 285). The characteristics of each of these groups are summarized in Table 10.1.[1]

Statistical groups are formed not by the members themselves but by social scientists. In general, members of these groups are unaware of membership and do not interact. Such groups have no organizational structure. A label is simply applied to a group by a researcher for the purpose of scientific study. An example of a commonly used statistical group is the cohort. A cohort is a group of people who have experienced a similar event at approximately the same time—for instance, the birth cohort of 1960, or all women giving birth to their first child at age twenty-one. This aggregation of individuals into groups based on similar characteristics has been found to be a powerful tool in predicting a wide range of behavior.

Societal groups differ from statistical groups in one important respect—consciousness of kind. Members of these groups are aware of their similar traits, such as age, sex, skin color, language, and dress, but although they are aware of their similarities, they do not interact (form social relationships). These groups do not have a formal organizational structure.

The last two groups—social and associational—are similar to societal groups in that there is a consciousness of kind, but they are different in that social interaction takes place among members. *Social groups* are often unstructured and include friendships, cliques, members of a classroom, and neighborhood groups. *Associational groups* differ from social groups in that

Table 10.1
The characteristics of four kinds of groups.

	Consciousness of kind	Social interaction	Social organization
Statistical	No	No	No
Societal	Yes	No	No
Social	Yes	Yes	No
Associational	Yes	Yes	Yes

Source: From *The Social Order* by R. Bierstedt, p. 309. Copyright © 1974, McGraw-Hill Book Company. Used with the permission of McGraw-Hill Book Company.

they are organized, normally having a constitution and a formal structure with officers. The NAACP, the League of Women Voters, and Rotary, Lions, and Kiwanis clubs as well as social fraternities and sororities on college campuses are examples of associational groups.

The Types of Groups Studied in this Chapter

All four types of groups are important to social scientists in the understanding of society, but for the purposes of this text the primary consideration is the degree to which certain statistical and societal groups are segregated in American cities.[2] By segregation is meant the process of separating two or more groups and preventing them from using common facilities or enjoying common facilities. Specifically, to what degree are social status (statistical), ethnic, and racial groups (societal) segregated in American society and to what degree are they concentrated in certain parts of cities?

In addition to the patterns of segregation, other related topics are addressed in this chapter. Why does segregation occur in the first place? How is segregation measured? What are the present patterns of segregation in American cities and how have they changed through time? Finally, in the discussion of racial segregation, the implications of these patterns for housing and neighborhood change are explored.

Why Study Segregation?

More than fifty years ago Robert Park stated:

> It is because social relationships are so frequently and so inevitably correlated with spatial relationships; because physical distances so frequently are, or seem to be, the indexes of social distances that statistics have any significance whatever for sociology. And this is true, finally, because it is only as social and physical facts can be reduced to, or correlated with, spatial facts that they can be measured at all (Park, 1926, p. 18).

The notion that the social distance between groups is reflected in the spatial distance between them is therefore a venerable ecological principle. This principle is implicit in most of the ecological studies reviewed in this text, especially the research on the social area analysis model. However, in the preceding discussion of the broad structural characteristics of cities little was said about the social implications of these patterns.

In general, the sorting of groups and individuals into more or less homogeneous areas of a city leads to spatial isolation. This segregation reduces the personal contacts between dissimilar groups and causes social isolation. Without close day-to-day interaction, contact between such groups tends to be formal and is confined principally to the market and workplace. The segregation of a population therefore influences the patterns of relationships between people and can have positive and negative consequences for a community.

Positive effects of segregation On the positive side, as long as there have been cities, people who are similar in social position, language, race, and religion have tended to live together in specified areas of the city. If this segregation is voluntary, residents may find that living with others of similar physical, cultural, or psychological attributes is satisfying and contributes to a sense of belonging and security. A group consciousness may emerge, based not only on similar group attributes but also on common residence. Segregation of a neighborhood therefore may affect the behavior of the resident group in a positive way. Similar characteristics may provide "common ground" for the formation of social groups—neighbors or friendships—or even locally based associational groups such as ethnically based fraternal organizations or political action groups.

Negative effects of segregation The involuntary segregation of groups, however, can have negative consequences for the community and society. The concentration of individuals with similar characteristics in certain parts of a city can form the social basis for the emergence of community, but it can also act as a barrier that negatively affects the life chances of individuals and that thwarts national policies such as racial integration. For example, a high percentage of United States blacks—one of the most segregated groups in American society—are ghettoized in the least desirable areas of cities where housing is poor and public services are inadequate. The children of these areas are often forced to attend the worst schools in the city, a practice that has been found to perpetuate inequality (Coleman, 1966; Armour, 1972). (The same is true of Mexican-Americans and Puerto Ricans who are also highly segregated groups in American cities.)

Federal courts, in attempting to overcome the negative aspects of segregation, have relied on school busing, a controversial policy that has been actively resisted in many of the largest metropolitan areas. Thus, the group consciousness that emerges in segregated areas may lead to extreme forms of collective behavior such as the civil disorders that erupted in many cities during the 1960s and the early 1970s.

Reasons for studying segregation Residential segregation in American society is of interest for several reasons. First, the degree of segregation between groups is a good indicator of the degree of social inequality in society. Second, measuring residential segregation gives policy makers an indication of the effectiveness of specific programs or social legislation in addressing the problems of social inequality, e.g., open housing legislation and the 1964 Civil Rights Act. Third, the study of segregation gives ecologists insight into the basic ecological processes that lead to the internal structuring of cities. Finally, the segregation or integration of neighborhoods in different parts of a city leads to the emergence of communities with different characteristics and institutional structures and different behavioral patterns among residents. Understanding the complex linkages of process, social structure, and behavior is a common goal of all social science.

Why Does Segregation Occur?

For more than fifty years sociologists and ecologists have been trying to determine why segregation occurs. Social scientists have identified three sets of factors that appear to influence segregation—ecological, voluntary, and involuntary.

Ecological segregation If a large concentration of population is heterogeneous in terms of lifestyle, race, social status, and culture, it is reasonable to assume that persons will sort themselves from other persons on the basis of some subjectively important criterion. In general, the ecologist looks to the operation of impersonal economic and biotic forces such as the cost and types of housing and its location in relation to the CBD to explain residential segregation. The Burgess concentric zone model (reviewed in Chapter 7) is a good example of an ecologist's attempt to explain and describe the segregation of groups within industrial cities. The model, which involves simple land-use patterns, is based on the assumption that the operation of impersonal economic forces results in the segregation of groups in various zones of a city.

Voluntary segregation According to another school of thought, segregation is the result of voluntary factors—what might be called factors of self-selection—that bring about the concentration of similar groups in certain parts of a city. A group with a common language or culture would probably have common problems or common needs that could be addressed best if the members lived close to each other. Moreover, children raised in these voluntarily segregated local communities may develop deep emotional or sentimental attachments to the streets, buildings, and institutions of the area.

Timms (1971) posits another explanation for the voluntary segregation of groups in the city. He suggests that a person's identity is closely interwoven with the people with whom he or she interacts. In other words, a person's peers provide an important reference point for the evaluation of the individual's behavior. Moreover, a person's public identity, the social class to which he or she belongs, is based largely on the types of associates with whom that person is seen. "This is especially true in the case of those more primary relationships which imply the status-equality of the participants. Because physical distance between people is a major factor in determining association, who associates with whom, choosing a:

"proper" residential location may be regarded as a strategy for optimizing the probability of desired association. Individuals who wish to interact with each other are likely to wish to live in close proximity. In this way the time and costs of interaction are kept to a minimum and the chance of associational identification is maximized. Individuals who do not desire to interact, on the other hand, are likely to wish to live far apart. In this way the chances of accidental contact are minimized and there is little possibility of an unwanted identification (Timms, 1971, p. 100).

This statement has two implications. First, it describes the individual psychological factors that influence residential choice. Second, it explains why areas keep their social, racial, or ethnic character over time although individuals are constantly moving in and out. Once areas become associated with certain types of social groups, individuals who wish to identify with those groups tend to move into those areas and thus perpetuate the pattern of segregation.

Involuntary segregation Involuntary segregation can occur in several ways. A group may be required by law or custom to live in designated areas of a city. The apartheid policy in South Africa is an example of governmental action that creates a totally segregated society. Involuntary segregation may also be the result of collective action of individuals or institutions within a community. So-called "white-flight" (white individuals moving out of a neighborhood as blacks move in) is an example of how individual acts, when combined, tend to perpetuate racial segregation.

The role of realtors. Institutions also have an important impact on land uses and hence the levels of segregation in a city. Realtors have traditionally been singled out as a major force in perpetuating segregation. As late as the 1950s, the National Association of Real Estate Brokers included in their code of ethics the following statement:

A realtor should never be instrumental in introducing into a neighborhood, by character of property or occupancy, members of any race or nationality, or any individual whose presence would be clearly detrimental to property values in a neighborhood (U.S. Commission on Civil Rights, 1975, p. 11).

Although this statement can no longer legally appear in the association's code of ethics, Baressi (1968) reports that such attitudes still were held by many realtors in the Buffalo, New York area as late as the 1960s.

Realtors have a central role in the operation of the urban housing market. Palmer (1955) refers to real estate agents as one of several "gate keepers" in modern industrial cities who channel and control the activities of individuals seeking a new residential location. Normally, a realtor is one of the first persons with whom a new resident of a city comes in contact. The realtor therefore can exercise a control function through selection of clients, the selection of houses to be shown prospective buyers, the prices at which properties are offered for sale, and the price at which the sale is made. The realtor may even intervene into the source and type of mortgage the buyer secures. Palmer found that members of the New Haven Real Estate Board used various techniques, both ethical and nonethical, in an attempt to match the social class level of the buyer to the social level of the area. Baressi (1968), Helper (1969), House (1977) and others found similar practices in other United States cities. Although the scope of these practices is difficult to assess, they appear to be widespread. A recent United States Supreme Court ruling makes realtors legally responsible for their actions in steering prospective buyers to selected neighborhoods.[3]

The role of government and lending institutions. Other institutions also greatly influence residential segregation. The Federal Housing Authority (FHA) for many years would not loan money to blacks if their purchase of a home would upset the racial balance of an area. The practice of redlining by banks and lending institutions, as well as the decisions of planning commissions, zoning boards, and other agencies on the local level, whether acting individually or in concert, profoundly influence residential land uses and therefore the patterns of segregation in society.

Interaction of factors A complex and interrelated set of factors, some personal but most impersonal, operate to segregate groups from each other. The three sets of factors identified as influencing residential patterning—ecological, voluntary, and involuntary—are not mutually excluding. For example, ecological and voluntary factors may interact and prescribe the areas of the city in which people of high social status will reside. A wealthy person is unlikely to choose to live in an area of slum housing. Thus the distribution of housing types combined with the desire of high-status individuals to live near members of their own group would contribute to the social segregation of this group in cities. One goal in the following discussion is to identify those factors that seem to be most responsible for patterns of segregation. These factors interact in different ways depending on the particular social-status, ethnic, or racial group.

Measuring Segregation

Sociologists and ecologists have used three different approaches in studying residential segregation in the United States. The first method is participant observation, whereby the researcher moves into the area of interest and studies its social patterns and processes first-hand. Liebow's *Tally's Corner,* Gans's *The Urban Villagers,* and Suttles's *The Social Order of the Slum* are examples of studies in which this method was used to describe social

Table 10.2
Causes of segregation.

Ecological
- operation of impersonal economic and biotic forces
- cost, quality, and type of housing
- location of housing in relationship to the central business district, industry, and other important features in the urban landscape

Voluntary
- individual or group's sentimental attachment to a neighborhood
- common characteristics (i.e., culture or race) that lead to common needs and common problems
- sense of belonging and security that comes from living with your own "kind"

Involuntary
- forced exclusion by law or custom
- institutional action by: realtors, government, business and industry

class, ethnic, or racial differences and segregation patterns in United States cities.

The second approach is social area analysis and factorial ecology (described in Chapter 6). This approach, however, focuses on the characteristics of areas rather than groups. In many studies the factors of social status, family status, and ethnic status have been found adequate to describe the various subareas of cities.

Most studies, however, have been based on the third approach, which involves the use of various segregation indexes calculated from census data. The most commonly applied measure is the *index of dissimilarity*. This index compares the residential location of pairs of groups, whites and blacks for example, and gives a measure of net percentage of one population who would have to relocate in order to reproduce the residential pattern of the other.[4] The index (D) has values that range from 0 to 100. If, for example, blacks and whites were evenly distributed in all census tracts of a city (if their proportion were the same in all census tracts of the city), the index would be 0. No one would have to change his residential location to maintain a social balance. If all census tracts were inhabited exclusively by blacks or whites, the index would be 100. In general, an index value of more than 50 is considered a high index of dissimilarity. Sorenson et al. (1975), in a study of racial desegregation of 109 United States cities, found the index to range from a low of 62.9 in Berkeley, California to a high of 97.4 in Shreveport, Louisiana. The vast majority of metropolitan areas, however, had index of dissimilarity sources above 80, meaning that 80 percent of the black or white population would have to move to eliminate segregation.

In the following discussion the third approach is followed, and the index of dissimilarity is used to compare the concentrations of various groups in United States cities.

SOCIAL STATUS SEGREGATION

The overall distribution of wealth and income in American society is extremely unequal. Though more than 25 million Americans are living below the poverty line, 1 percent of the population controls more than a third of the nation's wealth and 2 percent of private stockholders own about two-thirds of all stocks held by individuals (Gans, 1972, p. 43). Additional data presented in Table 10.3 show the percentage of this nation's income received by each fifth of the nation's families for the years 1947–1972.

In 1972, the poorest fifth of the families in the United States received only 5.4 percent of the nation's annual income, whereas the richest fifth received over 41 percent. This pattern of income distribution has remained virtually unchanged since the end of World War II in spite of the massive federal poverty programs carried out over the past three decades. Moreover, Kolko's (1972) research suggests that this general pattern may not have changed appreciably since the 1920s. Other measures of social status—education and occupation—show similar distributions. Therefore, given the gross inequalities in American society, it would not be surprising to find at least some segregation among statistical groups that differ in their occupation, income, and education.

Research on Status Segregation

Ecological theories The degree to which members of different status groups are residentially segregated from each other has been of long-standing interest to students of the city. Burgess, one of the early Chicago ecologists, posited in his concentric zone model that lower-status groups are centralized near the central business district, whereas upper-status groups are decentralized near a city's periphery. To Burgess, the residential segregation of these groups was the result of impersonal ecological and economic factors operating within the city. As Hawley (1950) notes, "Familial units are

Table 10.3
Percent of income received by each fifth of families in the United States, 1947–1972.

Income	Rank	1947	1950	1960	1966	1972
Lowest	Fifth	5.1	4.5	4.8	5.6	5.4
Second	Fifth	11.8	11.9	12.2	12.4	11.9
Third	Fifth	16.7	17.4	17.8	17.8	17.5
Fourth	Fifth	23.2	23.6	24.0	23.8	23.9
Highest	Fifth	43.5	42.7	41.3	40.5	41.4
Total Families		100.0	100.0	100.0	100.0	100.0

Source: Executive Office of the President: Office of Management and Budget, *Economic Report of the President.* Washington, D.C.: U.S. Government Printing Office, 1974.

distributed with reference to land values, the location of other types of (familial) units and the time and cost of transportation to centers of activity . . . the influences of these factors are combined in a single measure, namely rental value for residential use" (pp. 280–82). The family would attempt to maximize its housing satisfaction while minimizing its costs by balancing the costs of transportation with costs of rent (cost of housing and land) within the constraints of the family budget. Theoretically, a citywide pattern of land rents would be high rents and low transportation costs near the city's center and the reverse situation at the city's periphery. Only high-status families would have true locational freedom, because only they have sufficient income to absorb the costs of transportation and rent. Because high-status families often prefer large houses on spacious lots in areas where there is little congestion or business and industry, they would commonly select locations at the city's periphery. The concentric zone model has been widely tested and it appears to have descriptive utility in older industrial cities (see Chapter 6).

The Duncans' research If the concentric zone patterns are correct, one would expect a close relationship between the characteristics of the social structure and the degree and form of residential segregation. In a famous study, Otis Duncan and Beverly Duncan (1955) examined the segregation of occupational groups in the Chicago metropolitan district in 1950. They used the index of dissimilarity to examine the differences in the residential distribution of eight major occupational groups. The prestige of each occupational category was determined by using national survey data from the National Opinion Research Center studies on occupational prestige (see Table 6.1) and each category was ranked from highest prestige (professional), to lowest (laborers).

The Duncans found that as the differences in prestige of any two occupational groups increased, a corresponding increase was evident in their index of dissimilarity. Replications of this original study in other cities in the United States and abroad suggest that the residential dissimilarity between status groups is a universal phenomenon.[5]

Simkus's replication of the Duncans' study Simkus (1978) partially replicated the earlier Duncan and Duncan (1955) study on ten urbanized areas in the United States for the years 1950–1970.[6] The major occupational categories used in the study were the same as those in the Duncan and Duncan (1955) study: (1) professionals; (2) managers, officials, and proprietors; (3) salesmen; (4) clerical workers; (5) craftsmen; (6) operatives; (7) service workers; and (8) nonfarm laborers. Table 10.4 is a summary of Simkus's findings for the decade ending in 1970. Above the diagonal are the indexes of dissimilarity among employed males in each of the eight occupational groups. Below the diagonal are the changes that have occurred in the indexes

Table 10.4
Indexes of residential dissimilarity among employed males in major occupational groups, averaged across the ten urbanized areas, 1970 and change from 1960 to 1970.[a]

Major occupational group	Professional	Managerial	Sales	Clerical	Craft	Operative	Service	Laborers
Professional		16	16	28	36	45	40	46
Managerial	0		14	30	36	46	42	48
Sales	0	0		27	34	44	39	45
Clerical	− 1	0	3		20	25	22	29
Craft	0	1	3	3		20	25	29
Operative	− 2	− 1	1	0	0		19	19
Service	− 8	− 7	− 6	− 9	− 8	− 4		19
Laborers	− 11	− 11	− 10	− 12	− 11	− 7	− 4	

[a] Above diagonal, 1970; below diagonal, change from 1960 to 1970.

The setup of this table permits the reader to find the index value of any pair of occupations. First, note that the left column contains the same categories of occupations as those across the top of the table. Comparing the occupational category "professionals" (the top category in the left column) with the category "managers" (the second category along the top of the table) yields an index value of only 16. Thus, there is very little difference between those two groups in their residential patterning. As one compares professional with other occupational categories across the top of the table, the index scores increase regularly. Under the heading "laborers" the index value is 46. This score means that 46 percent of this occupational group would have to be relocated to eliminate differences in residential patterning between professionals and laborers. The overall pattern in this table suggests that the most markedly segregated groups are those at the top and the bottom of the occupational hierarchy. The fact that those in the middle of the hierarchy (sales, clerical, and craft workers) have relatively low indexes means that they tend to live near each other. This pattern is observable in the U-shaped curve in Figure 10.1.

The figures below the diagonal are the changes in the indexes during the 1960s. Note that the degree of segregation between each of the six highest occupational categories remained roughly the same, averaging less than one point of change. The indexes of dissimilarity between service workers and the six higher categories decreased by an average of 7.6 points, whereas the indexes between laborers and the six highest categories averaged an 11.0 point decline. The finding that service workers are less segregated from the five highest occupational categories than operatives suggests that measurable changes in the occupational prestige of these two categories may be observable on the national level in the near future. Except for the changing residential segregation patterns of service workers, Simkus (1978) indicates that the patterns have remained stable since 1950. On the whole, these figures suggest only a moderate degree of residential dissimilarity among groups.

Source: Simkus, A., "Residential Segregation by Occupation and Race in Ten Urbanized Areas, 1950–1970." *American Sociological Review* 43 (1978): p. 84. Reprinted with permission of The American Sociological Association.

between 1960 and 1970. The figures represent the average scores across the ten urbanized areas included in the study.

The figures above the diagonal in this table show that the most markedly segregated groups are those at the top and the bottom of the occupational hierarchy. Groups in the middle of the hierarchy have relatively low indexes, which means that they tend to live near each other. This pattern is observable in the U-shaped curve in Figure 10.1.

The figures below the diagonal on the whole show that segregation patterns among occupational groups have changed little since 1960. The only exception is the change in the index of dissimilarity of service workers. Service workers became less segregated from the top five occupational categories during the decade ending in 1970. This shift in residential patterns suggests that the relative importance of service workers has changed in American society. The table on the whole shows that there is only a moderate degree of residential dissimilarity.

Indexes based on educational attainment Farley (1977) used a different measure of social status—educational attainment—in twenty-nine urbanized areas in the United States. Figure 10.2 summarizes one of Farley's important findings. First, note that Figure 10.1 is similar to Figure 10.2 and shows again that groups at the top and bottom of the status hierarchy have the greatest residential dissimilarity, whereas those groups in the center of the distribution have the lowest. Second, observe in Figure 10.2 that the pattern holds true regardless of whether it is whites or blacks, central cities or the suburban rings, that are compared. This pattern has been found in the United States, Canada, England, India, Puerto Rico, Egypt, and other countries.[7]

Location of Status Groups

Residential dissimilarity among social status groups appears to be a universal phenomenon, but the degree and magnitude of the differences vary from society to society. The differential location of status groups in relation to the central business district is also a universal characteristic, but whether it is the highest or the lowest status groups that are centralized (concentrated near a city's center) depends on the scale of the society, as well as the position of the city in the country's urban hierarchy. In high-scale societies, the classical models of urban geometry indicate that low-status groups should be centralized near the city's center and high-status groups concentrated in the urban fringe. Conversely, the preindustrial pattern should prevail in low-scale societies where the positions of the two status groups are reversed.

Low-scale societies In countries undergoing the modernization process, cities at the top of the country's urban hierarchy, especially primate cities,

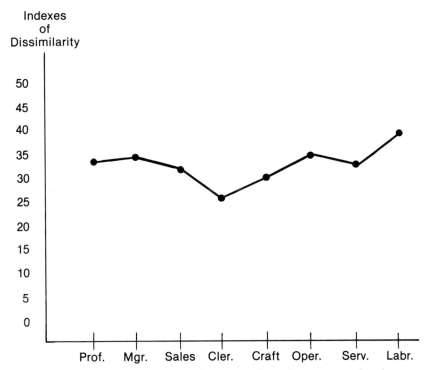

Fig. 10.1 Average indexes of residential segregation of one occupational group to that of all others.

Source: Prepared from data presented in Simkus, A.A., "Residential Segregation by Occupation and Race in Ten Urbanized Areas, 1950–1970." *American Sociological Review* 43 1978: Table 2, p. 84. Reprinted with permission of The American Sociological Association.

modernize before others. Thus centralization patterns differ among cities; some cities have an industrial pattern and others a preindustrial pattern. For example, in Table 10.5 data for Puerto Rico's three metropolitan areas are provided. The data for San Juan suggest that this city follows the pattern of a high-scale society with low-status groups closer to the city's center than high-status groups. In the case of Ponce and Mayaguez the opposite pattern is in evidence. The data are for 1960, and by 1980 it is likely that the United States Census will show both Ponce and Mayaguez to have a high-scale pattern.

High-scale societies Even within high-scale societies variations in centralization are evident. In Table 10.6, the residential distribution of educational groups in Detroit, New York City, Tucson, and Los Angeles for the years 1960 and 1970 are presented. The figures in the body of Table 10.6 are index scores that show the degree to which a certain status group is concentrated in the central city. A value greater than 100 means that there are

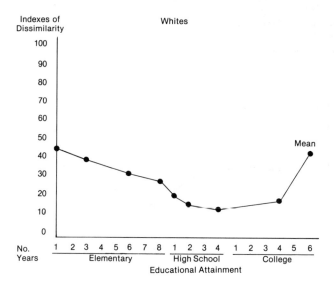

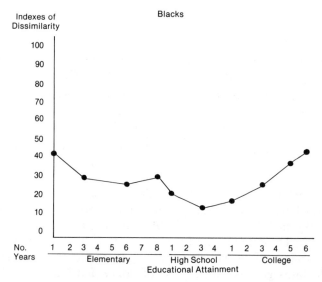

Fig. 10.2 Average indexes of the residential segregation of educational attainment groups for whites and blacks. Urbanized areas: 1970[a].

---

[a] These indexes compare the residential distribution of one attainment group to that of all others. The figure shows the unweighted means of the indexes based on data for 29 urbanized areas. Source: U.S. Bureau of the Census, Census of Population and Housing: 1970, Fourth Count (Population) Summary Tape, File A. Washington, D.C.: U.S. Government Printing Office.

Source: Adapted from Figure 1 in Farley, R., "Residential Segregation in Urbanized Areas of the United States in 1970: An Analysis of Social Class and Racial Differences." *Demography* 14 1977: 497–518.

Table 10.5
Average number of miles distance from the center of the city of each educational status group, San Juan, Ponce, Mayaguez, Puerto Rico, 1960.

Educational status group		Average number of miles from city center		
		San Juan	Ponce	Mayaguez
None		2.30	.92	.68
Grade:	1–4	2.31	.90	.68
	5–7	2.39	.88	.65
	8	2.41	.82	.64
High:	1–3	2.53	.84	.60
	4	2.58	.82	.61
College		2.67	.82	.53

Source: Adapted from Tables 4 and 5 in Schwirian, K. P. and Rico-Velasco, J., "The Residential Distribution of Status Groups in Puerto Rico's Metropolitan Areas." *Demography* 8 (1971): p. 87.

more people of that educational status in the central city than in the metropolitan area as a whole—the group is centralized. An index score below 100 means fewer people of that educational status are in the central city and thus the group is decentralized. By scanning the figures for all four cities in Table 10.6 one can see that Detroit and New York have a pattern of index values consistent with Burgess's model and the other classical models for high-scale societies, whereas Tucson and Los Angeles have patterns that diverge from the pattern normally associated with cities in high-scale societies.

The major reason why these cities diverge from the Burgess model is that they reached metropolitan status in the twentieth century and thus were shaped by the technology and economic organization of this century. Tucson and Los Angeles have CBDs, but the CBDs have never operated as the central organizing element of those cities. Automobile technology, in particular, has allowed these cities to develop in a way best described by Harris and Ullman's multiple nuclei theory.

As noted in Chapter 7, the classical pattern best describes older commercial-industrial cities in the heartland region of the United States. The younger cities of the South and Southwest have different patterns. It is difficult to make broad generalizations on the location of status groups within cities, regardless of the scale of the society.

Factors Influencing Social Status Segregation

Ecologists have long debated the actual causes of social-status segregation. Such segregation is probably the result of multiple factors. In addition,

Table 10.6
Examples of three patterns of residential distribution of educational classes based on indexes of suburbanization, 1960 and 1970.

Detroit Educational status	Educational status 1960	1970	1970/1960	
None	141	142	1.01	)
1–4	136	158	1.16	)
5–6	126	144	1.14	)
7–8	112	121	1.08	) Centralized
HS 1–3	99	110	1.11	)
HS 4	86	85	.99	)
C 1–3	86	77	.99	) Decentralized
C 4	77	65	.84	)

	New York City 1960	1970	1970/1960	Tucson 1960	1970	1970/ 1960
None	129	130	1.01	90	91	1.01
1–4	119	125	1.05	93	97	1.04
5–6	111	122	1.10	96	99	1.03
7–8	107	108	1.01	99	100	1.01
HS 1–3	100	104	1.04	100	99	.99
HS 4	91	92	1.01	101	100	.99
C 1–3	87	89	1.02	102	102	1.00
C 4	84	86	1.02	103	101	.98

Los Angeles	1960	1970	1970/1960
None	131	126	.96
1–4	113	122	1.08
5–6	110	118	1.07
7–8	99	100	1.01
HS 1–3	94	95	1.01
HS 4	97	95	.98
C 1–3	102	101	.99
C 4	106	105	.99

Source: Adapted from Schnore, L. F., *The Urban Scene.* New York: The Free Press, 1965, p. 228, copyright © 1965 by The Free Press, a Division of Macmillan Publishing Co., Inc.; and U.S. Bureau of Census, *1970 Census: Characteristics of the Population.* Washington, D.C.: Government Printing Office, 1972.

measures of social status are confounded by the effects of both race and ethnicity. Blacks and other minorities in American society are overrepresented in the lower socioeconomic strata. As a result, cities with large black, Mexican-American, Puerto Rican, or other minority populations will have, overall, more extreme social-status segregation than cities with small minority populations.

Ecological and voluntary factors appear to be most important in explaining social-status segregation. Persons of high social status have the purchasing power to select houses and neighborhoods in accordance with their tastes. Much research supports this position, demonstrating that social-status segregation is largely the result of occupation and income.[8] Guest (1971) further supports this position in his study of the distribution of white- and blue-collar workers in seventeen SMSAs in 1960. Guest shows that the location of these groups is very dependent on the types of housing in census tracts, and suggests that higher-status groups use their income to purchase a particular type of housing. To the degree the type of housing is segregated, the occupational groups will be aggregated.

Even if the effects of occupation, income, and education are removed mathematically, a "residual segregation" remains among these groups, segregation that simply cannot be explained by ecological factors. Such segregation is in all likelihood the result of voluntary factors of self-selectivity that are difficult to measure statistically.

In sum, residential dissimilarity among status groups appears to be a universal phenomenon. The pattern of residential dissimilarity is U-shaped (see Figures 10.1 and 10.2), the groups at the high and low ends of the status hierarchy being the most markedly segregated. The centralization of high- and low-status groups, however, is difficult to predict. Factors such as city age, position in the urban hierarchy, and the scale of the encompassing society appear to influence the centralization or decentralization of particular status groups in the urban landscape.

ETHNIC SEGREGATION

Immigration to the United States was the largest mass migration in the history of the world. Precise data are lacking but in the period between 1820 and 1920 roughly 45 million people immigrated to the United States. Immigration to this country peaked between 1900 and World War I and then slowed to a trickle with the passage of restrictive immigration quotas in the 1920s (Smith and Zopf, 1976, pp. 478–80). Since the early 1960s immigration laws have been liberalized, and approximately 25 percent of this nation's annual population growth is now estimated to be the result of immigration—the figure ranges annually from 250,000 to 290,000 people[9] (see Figure 10.3). Not included, however, are the estimated 1 million illegal

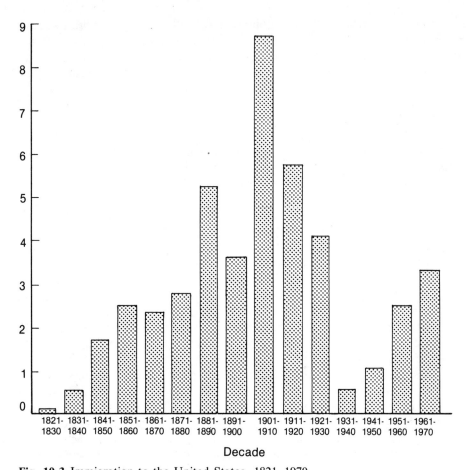

Fig. 10.3 Immigration to the United States, 1821–1970.

Source: U.S. Department of Justice, *1973 Annual Report of the Immigration and Naturalization Service*. Washington, D.C.: Government Printing Office, 1974, p. 25.

aliens who yearly enter this country, largely across the southern border with Mexico (Smith and Zopf, 1976, pp. 478–82). In 1970, the Bureau of the Census estimated that approximately 4.7 percent of the United States population was foreign-born and an additional 11.8 percent were second-generation ethnics, that is, persons with one or both parents foreign-born (U. S. Census Bureau, 1972, Table 1). Moreover, a large percentage of this group is concentrated in the nation's urbanized areas, making up 7.5 percent of central-city populations and 5.8 percent of the population in the urban fringe (U. S. Census Bureau, 1972, Table 97).

Therefore, roughly one of every twenty persons living in the United States is foreign-born, and their segregation and location in the metropolis continue to be of interest to ecologists.

Theories of Ethnic Assimilation

In the 1950s and early 1960s most ecologists and sociologists treated ethnicity simply as one aspect of social-status segregation. In other words, the segregation of ethnics was seen as nothing more than an artifact of their low social status in American society. Moreover, most sociologists thought that this social-status standing was a temporary phenomenon and that as the members of an ethnic group began to improve their standing in American society their segregation would gradually disappear. Ecologically, a four-stage process of assimilation was hypothesized. (1) Initially new arrivals would seek cheap accommodations because of their poverty and desire to accumulate savings. The tenements in the zone of transition were cheap and close to jobs, and became centrally located ethnic ghettoes. (2) After an extended length of time, the immigrants individually and collectively would improve their socioeconomic status. Higher incomes would permit them to pursue better housing and they would begin to move outward into other areas of the city. (3) The redistribution of this group in other areas of the city would lead to less physical concentration and a breakdown of the old cultural solidarity. (4) Subsequent movements would result in further dispersion of group members and their assimilation into the surrounding society.

The melting-pot thesis In general, most sociologists saw this process occurring in as few as three generations and identified problems of adjustment associated with each. The first generation or the actual immigrants to this country formed the initial ethnic enclaves in the cities and struggled to learn the new language and culture.

The second generation has been characterized in both the professional and popular media as a generation caught between two cultures. *West Side Story,* a successful Broadway musical and later a movie, dramatized the conflict faced by second-generation Puerto Rican youth in their assimilation into the urban culture of New York City. Raised at home in the "old way," they attended public schools that, at the time, deprecated their Puerto Rican culture while praising American culture, language, and values. Such experiences were thought to be shared by many ethnic groups.

The third generation was viewed as being well on its way to assimilation. Normally, they were thought to know only one language, English, and to have little knowledge of the foreign subculture of their grandparents. In other words, they had become Americans.

This ideal pattern is known as the melting-pot thesis. It has been taught in American high school history and civics classes for decades. The assimilation process was believed to have led to the emergence of the American culture. Moreover, much research suggested that this process was indeed occurring.[10] The segregation of foreign-born groups from the native population was found to decrease over time, although for some groups this decline was not great.

Unmeltable ethnics? Several books written in the 1960s and early 1970s called into question the traditional melting-pot notion. Three of the better known books are Glazer and Moynihan's *Beyond the Melting Pot,* first published in 1963, Kantrowitz's *Ethnic and Racial Segregation in the New York Metropolis* (1973), and Novak's *The Rise of the Unmeltable Ethnics* (1971). These authors pointed to the durable ethnic divisions that persisted in New York City after many generations and suggested that these groups represent major cleavages within the city; cleavages particularly important in the resolution of emotion-laden political issues.

Today, most ecologists agree that the melting-pot phenomenon has not occurred as predicted and that ethnic enclaves form durable and resilient subcommunities within urban areas even after four and five generations. Research has shifted from the study of the assimilation process to an examination of the factors responsible for the continued existence of these segregated areas. Specifically, the major question addressed is the degree to which ethnic segregation is the function of the social-status characteristics of the group rather than voluntary and involuntary segregation factors.

Factors Influencing Ethnic Segregation

Region of origin and time of arrival Region of origin and time of arrival are known to influence the level of segregation of an ethnic group. Two distinct waves of immigrants came to this country. The first wave of immigration to the United States spanned the years from the first settlements in the New World through the first half of the nineteenth century, ending roughly with the depression of 1857.[11] This wave was composed largely of people from western and northern Europe. Their Anglo-Saxon physical features and predominantly Protestant religion reinforced the characteristics of the native population. Large numbers of this group settled on farms, but those who settled in cities normally chose cities in the Midwest, including the lake and river cities.

The second wave of immigration The second and greatest wave of immigration to American cities occurred roughly between 1860 and 1930. By the end of the nineteenth century, although Germans and Scandinavians continued to immigrate as well as millions of Irish, the origins of most of the immigrants to this country had shifted from western and northern Europe to eastern and southern Europe. The vast majority of these groups settled in Atlantic Coast and lake cities. Because of their language, culture, and dress they were highly visible and formed ethnic enclaves. These groups differed from the native population in physical features, culture, and, most

Photo 10.1 This photo of a business in a Polish neighborhood in Chicago was taken in 1903. It is interesting that ethnic neighborhoods like this one can still be found in many American cities. Ethnicity continues to be an important factor shaping the modern metropolis.
Source: Courtesy of the Chicago Historical Society DN #729.

important, religion—they were predominantly Catholic and Jewish. To native Americans, this new group often seemed "foreign" or "alien" to the American culture, and prejudice and discrimination hindered their movement into the mainstream of society. Therefore, in the following discussion, a distinction is made between old immigrant groups (from Germany, Ireland, Sweden, United Kingdom) and new immigrant groups (from Czechoslovakia, Hungary, Italy, Poland, USSR). This old-new dichotomy refers to the approximate time of arrival of the group in the United States, and not to the time of arrival of an individual.

Comparing residential patterns of new and old ethnics The data in Table 10.7 suggest that this distinction between new and old groups has validity. Note that consistently the values for the index of dissimilarity are higher for those pairs of ethnic groups whose origins and time of arrival differ. For example, if the Irish and English are compared, both old immigrant groups, the index is only 28. But if English and Russians are compared, the index value increases to more than 50. Averaging the index of dissimilarity for the two types of immigrants produces a predictable pattern. Comparison of the residential patterns of different old immigrant groups yields a mean index of dissimilarity of 41.1. A similar comparison between new immigrant groups yields a mean index of 38.9. However, if old groups are compared with new groups, the index jumps to 51.6, suggesting that in New York City the residential dissimilarity between them is relatively great (Kantrowitz, 1969, p. 692).

Ethnic Segregation Due to Social-Status Factors

How does one account for the continued segregation of these ethnic groups? Is it the result of their income and occupational characteristics or are other factors involved? The United States Bureau of the Census collects information only on first- and second-generation ethnics or persons of foreign stock. It is therefore difficult to examine the interaction of the ecological, voluntary, and involuntary factors responsible for ethnic segregation after the second generation. Fortunately, the Canadian census provides extensive data on ethnicity on all citizens of Canada and several researchers have used these data to study ethnic segregation in that country. Although the factors responsible for ethnic segregation in Canada may differ from those in the United States, one such study by Darroch and Marston (1971) provides insights that may be applicable to ethnic segregation in American cities.

The Canadian case Darroch and Marston (1971) were interested in finding the degree to which the segregation of ethnic groups in Toronto was the result of social-status factors. In using 1961 Canadian census data, they were able to determine through a process of indirect standardization the percentage of an ethnic group's segregation that was the result of the income and occupational characteristics of its members. Table 10.8 is a summary of their findings. The first column of the table is the actual segregation of each group. Groups from western Europe and the United States have lower scores than groups from eastern and southern Europe. The second column in the table gives the segregation of each group that is due to the distribution of occupations among its members. Except for Italians, these figures are very low. Finally, the third column gives the percentage of each ethnic group's residential segregation that can be explained by the group's occupational characteristics. Note that these percentages are low and that a

Table 10.7

Indexes of residential segregation in 1960, between selected ethnicities (foreign stock), New York City standard metropolitan statistical area.

Ethnic population	1	2	3	4	5	6	7	8	9	10	11	12	13
1. United Kingdom													
2. Eire	28.1												
3. Norway	51.4	58.7											
4. Sweden	31.8	41.3	45.8										
5. Germany	25.6	33.3	56.4	38.2									
6. Poland	45.0	51.7	67.9	57.9	47.1								
7. Czechoslovakia	39.5	44.5	65.6	51.1	39.5	41.7							
8. Austria	40.2	47.1	68.0	54.2	40.4	20.3	39.9						
9. Hungary	39.1	44.2	68.3	52.9	38.7	31.3	33.9	24.7					
10. U.S.S.R.	50.2	57.1	72.9	62.2	52.1	20.0	49.0	19.0	32.7				
11. Italy	44.9	48.0	60.2	51.9	45.6	52.7	51.6	53.0	53.9	60.5			
12. Black	80.3	80.3	88.4	83.7	80.6	79.7	81.9	81.1	80.4	81.8	80.5		
13. Puerto Rican	79.8	76.5	88.2	83.9	79.7	75.5	78.6	76.6	76.3	78.1	77.8	63.8	

Source: Reprinted from "Ethnic and Racial Segregation in the New York Metropolis, 1960," by N. Kantrowitz in *American Journal of Sociology* 74, 1969, p. 693 by permission of The University of Chicago Press.

Table 10.8
Actual and expected indexes of residential dissimilarity between the British and each of the other origin groups, based on indirect standardization for education, occupation, and income: ratios (in %) of expected to actual indexes, Toronto, 1961.

			Expected index based on				
Origin group	Actual index	Edu-cation	% Expected/ Actual	Occu-pation	% Expected/ Actual	Income	% Expected/ Actual
Scandinavian	14.40	0.87	6.0	1.85	12.8	1.24	8.6
German	17.13	0.67	3.9	4.07	23.8	5.25	30.6
French	22.19	3.72	16.7	6.17	27.8	6.62	29.8
Netherlands	17.21	1.30	7.6	2.04	11.9	3.18	18.5
Other	26.16	1.81	6.9	2.59	9.9	3.71	14.2
Asiatic	34.93	2.62	7.5	3.57	10.2	8.05	23.0
Other European	32.27	3.73	11.6	4.97	15.4	10.25	31.8
Ukrainian	44.05	5.47	12.4	7.15	16.2	9.77	22.2
Polish	48.09	4.30	8.9	3.13	6.5	7.73	16.1
Russian	53.61	2.84	5.3	8.07	15.1	2.89	5.4
Italian	56.20	12.30	21.9	14.08	25.1	15.72	28.0
Jewish	78.8	1.40	1.8	10.01	12.7	2.98	3.8

Source: Reprinted from "The Social Class Basis of Ethnic Residential Segregation: The Canadian Case," by A. B. Darroch and W. G. Marston in *American Journal of Sociology* 77, 1971, Table 3, p. 499 by permission of The University of Chicago Press.

relatively small percentage of any group's actual segregation can be explained by its status characteristics. Therefore, these groups are either segregated involuntarily through law or custom or have voluntarily chosen to live near each other in metropolitan Toronto. In Canadian society, the latter situation rather than the former probably explains the segregation of ethnic groups.

Research on American ethnics Guest and Weed (1976) conducted a study similar to the Canadian one on data from three United States cities: Cleveland, Boston, and Seattle. The patterns between old and new groups were similar to those found by Kantrowitz (1973) and Darroch and Marston (1971) in New York and Toronto. Moreover, these patterns have remained relatively constant since 1960. Table 10.9 provides the average indexes of dissimilarity for the ethnic groups included in the study. Guest and Weed found that a high percentage of the observed segregation of old and new ethnic groups was a function of group social-status differences and that "future changes in relative group status among ethnic groups should affect the degree of ethnic segregation between them[12] (Guest and Weed, 1976, p. 1109). However, even with the effects of social-status differences removed, in Cleveland any two ethnic groups "would still have a residential

Table 10.9
Average indices of residential dissimilarity for ethnic groups.

Group	Cleveland 1960	Cleveland 1970	Boston 1960	Boston 1970	Seattle 1960	Seattle 1970
Old:						
1 Canada	47.3	50.5	48.2	48.7	37.8	37.4
2 Germany	45.6	46.5	48.8	49.2	36.2	37.2
3 Ireland	52.0	56.1	53.2	52.4	40.8	42.1
4 Sweden	56.5	60.1	53.5	53.5	39.7	39.9
5 United Kingdom	46.6	48.8	47.6	47.4	37.2	37.9
New:						
6 Austria	47.7	48.5	52.0	53.5	40.8	41.9
7 Czechoslovakia	53.4	52.3	59.8	66.5	44.6	47.7
8 Hungary	52.7	53.2	59.8	63.8	48.4	51.3
9 Italy	54.7	55.4	59.0	58.2	46.6	44.1
10 Poland	56.8	58.7	55.2	53.4	40.8	43.3
11 USSR	58.9	60.6	61.6	58.0	39.8	40.7
Other:						
12 Mexico	69.9	74.6	82.6	78.6	57.3	52.6
13 Negro	86.0	85.5	82.3	81.3	80.4	74.9
14 Other Nonwhite	60.3	56.1	63.6	58.4	57.8	49.6
15 Puerto Rico	76.8	77.9	78.6	77.6	77.9	82.0
Average:						
Old vs. old	30.2	38.8	29.6	30.8	19.4	22.2
Old vs. new	46.5	48.3	48.3	49.3	31.3	34.6
Old vs. other	73.5	72.1	73.8	71.1	67.9	62.1
New vs. new	45.4	47.0	51.9	55.2	37.1	40.7
New vs. other	74.2	72.7	77.4	75.5	66.8	62.8
Other vs. other	70.8	77.4	80.3	75.7	72.0	73.3

Source: Reprinted from "Ethnic Residential Segregation: Patterns of Change," by A. M. Guest and J. A. Weed in *American Journal of Sociology* 81, 1976, p. 1096, Table 3 by permission of The University of Chicago Press.

dissimilarity index of 33.6, if they did not differ at all on the measures of income, occupation and education. Although in Boston and Seattle the indices would be lower, ethnic segregation would still clearly exist in the absence of status differences between groups" (Guest and Weed, 1976, pp. 1102–3).

The Function of Ethnic Enclaves

Recent research strongly suggests that ethnic segregation in American cities will continue into the foreseeable future. Given the rise of ethnic and racial consciousness in the United States since the Black Power movement of the

1960s, this finding is not surprising. Because voluntary factors appear to explain a high proportion of the segregation of ethnic groups in this society, one might ask why ethnic enclaves continue to exist. At least two factors are involved. First, as Glazer and Moynihan (1963) observed, ethnic groups continue to serve as important political interest groups locally and nationally. The attempts of both presidential candidates "to get the ethnic vote" in the 1976 election illustrate the importance of Poles and other groups in national politics. Second, ethnic groups probably serve another important function, that is, to provide an "identity" as well as "associational and residential ties . . . which may counterbalance some of the less agreeable aspects of urban life" (Guest and Weed, 1976, p. 1109).

Ethnic enclaves in many of this nation's metropolises continue to be durable and resilient, resisting change for many generations. Although structural factors such as income, occupation, and education explain a high percentage of this residential segregation, a certain residual variance can be explained only through the operation of voluntary factors. Is American society a melting pot of diverse racial and culture groups? The answer is both yes and no. For the vast majority of Americans, one's ethnic origins are of little importance, but for a significant percentage of this nation's urban population, ethnic enclaves that may include stores, churches, parochial schools, meeting houses, and lodges continue to provide a source of identity and an important source of associational ties.

There are both positive and negative consequences of segregating large numbers of ethnic and racial groups in homogeneous subareas of the city. This article published in The Washington Post *in 1976 shows that one's self-image can be shaped by the people and institutions of one's residential surroundings.*

POLISH-AMERICANS' SELF-IMAGE IS LOW

Boston—The stereotype of the Polish-American man is so ingrained in our culture that even Polish-American men believe it.

"The men view themselves as unintelligent factory workers unworthy of respect and incapable of anything worthwhile except supporting a family through hard work," Dr. Paul Wrobel of Detroit's Merrill-Palmer Institute told the annual meeting of the American Association for the Advancement of Science on Sunday. "The men are fully aware of what society says about them. It is tragic that so many believe it."

Over 16 months, Wrobel interviewed and studied several hundred second-generation Polish-Americans working in Detroit's automobile plants, living in the same neighborhood and worshiping at the same Roman Catholic church.

Wrobel said most of the men had dropped out of high school for blue-collar jobs, which they regard as the only thing they can do. They dismiss their workaday lives as little more than a means of earning enough money to support families. Their whole goal in life is to send their children to college so they won't be like them.

"Me?" one man told Wrobel. "I just work in a factory, nothing special. Same old thing day after day now for 20 years. But it pays the bills. So I can't complain."

None of them complain about their status, Wrobel said. In fact, they wonder why anybody complains about status in life. "All I expect is decent pay for hard work," another man said in what Wrobel called a typical attitude. "Now it's gettin' so that young kids and black folks are always asking for more and more benefits. What the hell do they expect? Something for nothing?"

The men's wives do little to help the men feel differently, Wrobel said. Their first concern about their husbands is how hard they are willing to work.

"I tell my niece to look for a guy that's willing to sacrifice, a guy that will work overtime without complaining," one woman told Wrobel. "Because that's what it takes for a man to make it today. Sacrifice."

"Just give me a man who loves to work," another said, "and everything else will take care of itself."

Many of the marriages Wrobel observed were unhappy, but the men and women all endured them even though they said they believed in divorce.

"You don't have to know that much about a man, just make up your mind that you can put up with anything," one woman said. "That's what makes a successful marriage."

"Getting along with my husband on a day-to-day level is one helluva trial," another said. "But I make it. By God, I make it. I go to church. I pray. I go to communion. And it all helps, I guess. After all, we're in this for life."

Wrobel said the men and women appeared to exist solely "to raise children whose lives will be significantly different from their own."

"You're asking me how I would feel if my sons followed in my footsteps? Are you kidding? That's the last thing I would want to happen," one man told Wrobel. "My kids are going to wear suits and ties to work. And they're not gonna come home all smelly and dirty like me. No sir, you can bet on that."

What this means, Wrobel said, is that sons take fathers' lives as warnings instead of models. Wrobel said that young boys in the families he observed are encouraged to be different from their fathers, a condition that often results in total estrangement between fathers and sons.

"A son views his father as a failure, a person unable to rise above the work he despises," Wrobel said. "When this happens, sons turn to their mothers for advice and emotional support, feeling she is the stronger of the two parents."

The surprising thing about all this, Wrobel said, is that the men don't lose their identities. "The men don't ask 'Who am I?' " Wrobel said, because they know who they are.

"He is a husband, a father, a factory worker, a Roman Catholic, a parish member, and a homeowner concerned about maintaining the safety of his home and the security of his family," Wrobel said. "His attitude towards life is 'Nobody owes me nothing'. This point of view allows him to work long hours of overtime without complaining, for the future of his family is worth everything, even himself."

Source: From *The Washington Post,* February 23, 1976; reprinted with permission. © 1976 *The Washington Post.*

RACIAL SEGREGATION

The more than 22 million black Americans are this country's largest and one of its most segregated minority groups. The nation's Mexican-American population is also large and segregated but it has been little noticed until recent years. Blacks were among the first nonnative Americans and their experiences are an integral part of the nation's social history. For these reasons the urban experience of blacks is the focus of this section.

The Rural to Urban Migration of Black Americans

Historically, America's black population has been mostly rural and southern. During the past seventy years, however, a major redistribution of population occurred in America as blacks moved to urban areas in the North and the South. The magnitude of this migration can be seen in the figures in Table 10.10. In 1900, 76 percent of this nation's black population lived in rural areas and nearly 90 percent in the South. By 1970, only about 20 percent of this nation's black population lived in rural areas and approximately 47 percent lived in regions outside the South.

The reasons for this movement are reflected in the figures in Table 10.11, which give the percentage change in the racial makeup of populations of metropolitan areas for the years 1900–1970. The first significant outmigration of blacks from the South began with World War I and continued through the 1920s. The primary attraction of northern cities to southern

Table 10.10
Population location by race 1900–1970 (percentage distribution).

	Northeast	North Central	South	West
White				
1900	30.9	38.5	24.7	5.8
1920	30.5	35.0	25.4	9.0
1940	29.2	32.7	26.8	11.3
1960	26.2	30.3	27.4	16.1
1970	25.0	29.1	28.4	17.4
Black				
1900	4.4	5.6	89.6	0.3
1920	6.5	7.6	85.2	0.8
1940	10.6	11.0	77.0	1.3
1960	16.0	18.3	60.7	5.7
1970	19.2	20.2	53.1	7.4

Source: Irene B. Taeuber, "The Changing Distribution of the Population of the United States in the Twentieth Century." In Vol. 5 of Commission Research Reports, *Population Distribution and Policy*, ed. Sara Mills Mazie, U.S. Commission on Population Growth and the American Future. Washington, D.C.: Government Printing Office, 1972, pp. 44–45.

blacks was jobs. The war cut off the immigration of cheap European labor to northern industries, creating a severe labor shortage. At the same time the mechanization of farming was creating a surplus of unskilled farm labor in the South. Black Americans in the 1920s and following decades therefore became a new source of cheap industrial labor.

The Depression of the 1930s dramatically lowered the number and percentage growth of blacks in metropolitan areas. Later with the rapid expansion of American industry during World War II, the flow of immigrants accelerated and this trend continued into the 1950s and 1960s.

Table 10.11
Racial change in metropolitan areas in the twentieth century (% change).

Decade	Inside central cities		Outside central cities	
	White	Black	White	Black
1900–1910	36.2	46.3	25.2	19.3
1910–1920	24.7	93.7	39.0	33.7
1920–1930	25.9	107.8	67.4	77.9
1930–1940	4.2	27.6	17.1	20.8
1940–1950	4.4	74.2	42.3	62.3
1950–1960	−6.9	55.7	70.4	73.3
1960–1970	−7.6	41.7	24.7	57.6

Source: Irene B. Taeuber, "The Changing Distribution of Population in the United States in the Twentieth Century," in Volume 5 of Commission Research Reports, *Population Distribution and Policy*, ed. Sara Mills Mazie, U.S. Commission on Population Growth and the American Future. Washington, D.C.: Government Printing Office, 1972, page 89.

Migration streams Between 1900 and 1970 more than 5 million blacks left the South, largely for the cities of the North. Moreover, this migration occurred along well-defined migration streams. Blacks from the South Atlantic states of Virginia, North and South Carolina, Georgia, and Florida generally migrated to the metropolises of the Northeast and Middle Atlantic states including Washington, D.C., Philadelphia, New York, and Boston. Blacks from Alabama, Mississippi, Tennessee, Arkansas, and Louisiana tended to follow migration streams along the valleys of the Mississippi and Ohio Rivers to the lake and river cities. Finally, blacks from Texas and western Louisiana usually chose cities in the West (Smith and Zopf, 1976, pp. 141–45).

Residential patterns in the 1970s By 1970, 80.7 percent of all blacks were urban, a percentage that exceeds that of their white counterparts—72.5 percent. The black migration from the South was predominantly a migration to the central cities of metropolitan areas (Taeuber, 1972, p. 90). By 1970, although the population of Standard Metropolitan Statistical Areas of 250,000 or more persons had become 14 percent black, blacks made up less than 7 percent of these areas' suburban rings (Taeuber, 1972, Table 21). The massive shift of more than 5 million black people during this century must be viewed in perspective, however. Although this is a great number of people, it hardly compares with the waves of European immigrants who arrived during the first years of this century (Palen, 1975, p. 212). For example, although nearly 5 million black Americans migrated from 1900 to 1970, in just the ten-year period from 1901 to 1911 8.8 million European immigrants entered the United States (U.S. Census Bureau, 1975, Table 153).

Rural to urban migration of black Americans has ceased to be an important factor in metropolitan growth. Today, the vast majority of moves made by blacks in this society are within and between metropolitan areas, and the growth of the black populations within metropolitan areas is due largely to natural increase (births exceeding deaths). This population increase, however, has been contained in well-defined areas of the city, as black Americans remain one of the most segregated groups in American society.

Trends in Racial Segregation

The degree of residential segregation of urban blacks in the United States is shown in the results of a comprehensive study of residential segregation done by the Taeubers (1965). These researchers calculated an index of dissimilarity from census data for 207 cities and found scores that ranged from a low of 60.4 to a high of 98.1 with an average of 86.1. That is, on the average, 86 percent of the blacks or whites in the cities included in the study would have had to move from their present to another residential location to produce an index of zero—an unsegregated distribution.

These scores are averages and there were some interesting variations. The black populations in cities of the North and West were somewhat less segregated than those in southern cities, the average indexes being 83 and 90.9, respectively. The scores for central cities of Standard Metropolitan Statistical Areas were found to be somewhat higher (86.8) than those for suburbs (82.3). The overall distribution of these scores, however, showed clearly that blacks are markedly segregated in American cities, more so than any other ethnic, status, or racial group. For example, 80 percent of the cities in the Taeubers' sample had index scores above 80, whereas only 4 percent of the cities had scores below 70.

Changes in racial segregation, 1940–1970 Sorenson and his colleagues (1975) examined trends in residential segregation in 109 cities for which comparable data were available for the thirty-year period from 1940 to 1970. A selected sample of these data is presented in Table 10.12. The researchers found the average indices of racial segregation to be 85.2 in 1940, 87.3 in 1950, 86.1 in 1960, and 81.6 in 1970; no clear straight-line trend is indicated (Sorenson et al., 1975). Interestingly, the South had the greatest regional gains in racial segregation over the span of the study; its index score increased from 84.9 in 1940 to 88.0 in 1970.

Changing segregation patterns in the South To explain this pattern in the South, Schnore and Evenson (1966) explored the relationship between the age of southern cities and the degree of their residential segregation. Schnore and Evenson's findings suggest that the increase in segregation is due in large part to the changing social relationships between races in the South. In many of the older southern cities during the post–Civil War period, blacks continued to live in servant quarters on alleys or side streets near the homes of their white employers. As the "New South" became industrialized, the old pattern of race relations disintegrated and blacks and whites began to live in their "own neighborhoods." In the historic "South of Broad" section of Charleston, South Carolina, for example, many of the servants' quarters were renovated into "carriage houses" that are rented to white people. In addition, the court-ordered desegregation of southern schools in the 1950s and 1960s further stimulated residential segregation, as white parents sought neighborhoods where their children would not have to attend schools with large numbers of blacks.

Recent data therefore suggest that even with the massive civil-rights movement of the last twenty years, residential segregation has not decreased but has actually increased in some regions. Although the levels of racial segregation vary from region to region and city to city, the United States remains one of the most segregated societies in the world.

Table 10.12
Residential segregation of nonwhites in United States cities, 1940–1970.

City	1940	1950	1960	1970
Akron, OH	82.2	87.6	88.1	81.2
Asheville, NC	88.6	89.2	92.3	88.5
Atlanta, GA	87.4	91.5	93.6	91.5
Baltimore, MD	90.1	91.3	89.6	88.3
Birmingham, AL	86.4	88.7	92.8	91.5
Boston, MA	86.3	86.5	83.9	79.9
Buffalo, NY	87.9	89.5	86.5	84.2
Canton, OH	89.9	89.3	81.5	82.4
Charleston, SC	60.1	68.4	79.5	86.5
Charlotte, NC	90.1	92.8	94.3	92.7
Chicago, IL	95.0	92.1	92.6	88.8
Cincinnati, OH	90.6	91.2	89.0	83.1
Cleveland, OH	92.0	91.5	91.3	89.0
Columbia, SC	83.0	88.1	94.1	86.7
Dallas, TX	80.2	88.4	94.6	92.7
Denver, CO	87.9	88.9	85.5	77.6
Des Moines, IA	87.8	89.3	87.9	79.2
Detroit, MI	89.9	88.8	84.5	89.0
Greensboro, NC	93.1	93.5	93.3	91.4
Houston, TX	84.5	91.5	93.7	90.0
Indianapolis, ID	90.4	91.4	91.6	88.3
Jacksonville, FL	94.3	94.9	96.9	92.5
Kansas City, MO	88.0	91.3	90.8	88.0
Little Rock, AR	78.2	84.5	89.5	89.7
Los Angeles, CA	84.2	84.6	81.8	78.4
Louisville, KY	81.7	86.0	89.2	88.9
Memphis, TN	79.9	86.4	92.0	91.8
Miami, FL	97.9	97.8	97.9	89.4
New Orleans, LA	81.0	84.9	86.3	83.1
New York, NY	86.8	87.3	79.3	73.0
Oklahoma City, OK	84.3	88.6	87.1	81.8
Philadelphia, PA	88.0	89.0	87.1	83.2
Pittsburgh, PA	82.0	84.0	84.6	83.9
St. Louis, MO	92.6	92.9	90.5	89.3
St. Paul, MN	88.6	90.0	87.3	76.8
San Francisco, CA	82.9	79.8	69.3	55.5
Savannah, GA	84.2	88.8	92.3	91.2
Seattle, WA	82.2	83.3	79.9	69.2
Washington, DC	81.0	80.1	79.7	77.7
Wichita, KS	92.0	93.3	91.9	85.0

Source: Annemette Sorenson, Karl E. Taeuber, and Leslie J. Hollingsworth, Jr., "Indexes of Racial Residential Segregation for 109 Cities in the United States, 1940–1970." *Sociological Focus* 8, April, 1975. Reprinted with permission.

Patterns of Racial Segregation in Cleveland, Ohio

In the preceding discussion racial segregation is examined in general terms. The index figures cited indicate the degree of segregation in American society, but do not describe the impact of the large numbers of black immigrants on the social and economic life of cities. The impact can best be understood by studying the patterns of racial segregation in a single city. Cleveland, Ohio serves as a useful example.

Growth of Cleveland's black population Table 10.13 gives the number of and change in the total and nonwhite populations of the city of Cleveland for the years 1910–1970. Notice that between 1910 and 1930 the city's total population increased by roughly a third of a million people. But since the 1930s, the city's population has actually declined by 150,000. During this same seventy-year period, Cleveland's black population grew rapidly, particularly in the 1940s after World War II. In 1940, for example, the 84,504 blacks in Cleveland were 9.6 percent of its total population. During the decade ending in 1950, this number grew by more than 64,000—an increase of over 76 percent. In absolute terms, Cleveland's black population posted the greatest gains during the 1950s, when more than 103,000 people were added to its number. As a result, by 1960, 30 percent of Cleveland's total population was black. That proportion exceeded 50 percent in the 1980 census. Cleveland is not an isolated example of black population growth. If present central-city growth patterns continue, the central cities of Philadelphia, Atlanta, St. Louis, Detroit, Cleveland, Oakland, Baltimore, New Orleans, Richmond, Jacksonville, Washington, D.C., Newark, and Gary will have populations that are more than 50 percent black (Downs, 1968, p. 1333).

Cleveland's residential patterns The rapid growth in Cleveland's black population has had a major impact on the city's residential patterns. Blacks have always been segregated in Cleveland. As early as 1910, the segregation index for blacks in the city was 69 (Taeuber, 1965, p. 53). Much of this population was concentrated in a centrally located ghetto east of and adjacent to the city's central business district (see Figure 10.4). From 1910 to 1940 the growth of Cleveland's black population was relatively constant and was predictably and easily absorbed in the traditional "black areas" of the city. However, the rapid expansion of the city's black population in the 1940s and post–World War II period, along with the city's segregated housing market, led to critical housing shortages for blacks in the 1960s. This shortage was intensified by the federal government's urban renewal program. The program was initially designed to rid central cities of older, blighted housing, but the vast majority of Cleveland's projects were centered in the traditional "black areas." Most of the land cleared by demolition of housing was used subsequently for commerce and industry; little

Table 10.13
Population and number and percent nonwhite Cleveland, 1910 to 1970

	1910	1920	1930	1940	1950	1960	1970	1980
Cleveland								
Population	560,663	796,841	900,429	878,336	914,808	876,050	750,903	573,822
Nonwhite	8,560	34,611	72,469	84,504	147,847	253,108	287,841	251,347
% Nonwhite	1.5	4.3	8.1	9.6	16.2	28.9	38.3	43.8

Source: For 1910, 1920, 1930 figures: Green, H. W. Population Characteristics by Census Tracts, Cleveland, Ohio: The Plain Dealer Publishing Co., 1931. For 1940 figures, U.S. Census of Population and Housing: 1940. For 1950 figures, U.S. Census of Population and Housing: 1950. For 1960 figures, U.S. Census of Population and Housing: 1960. For 1970, U.S. Census of Population and Housing: 1970. For 1980, U.S. Census of Population (provisional data).

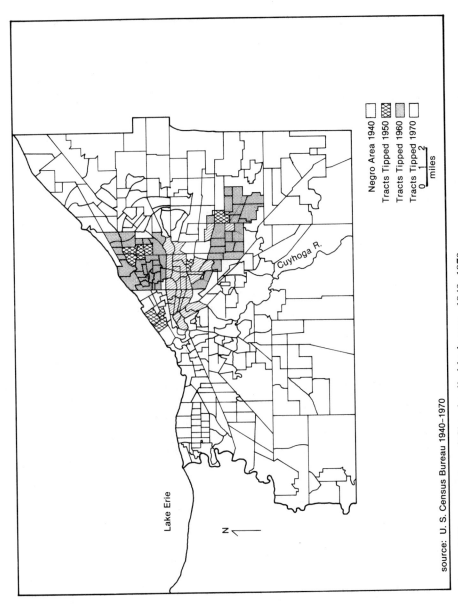

Legend on map:

☐ Negro Area 1940
▨ Tracts Tipped 1950
▨ Tracts Tipped 1960
☐ Tracts Tipped 1970

0 1 2
miles

Lake Erie

N

Cuyhoga R.

source: U. S. Census Bureau 1940–1970

Fig. 10.4 The expansion of Cleveland's black area, 1940–1970.

417

was used for low-income housing. The end result was that the black population's demand for housing was intensified and could not be met within the existing black community.

Expansion of Cleveland's black community Consequently, in the early 1950s many blacks had little choice but to move into other areas of the city to find housing. In Cleveland, as in other cities, these movements did not take place across the entire metropolis but in well-defined areas of the city. As Figure 10.4 shows, Cleveland's black population has historically moved to the east. Expansion into adjacent areas on the west was blocked by the central business district and industry. Moreover, Cleveland's ethnic populations were concentrated on the west side. The housing in these ethnic neighborhoods was largely owner-occupied and, through custom, vacant residences were simply not made available to prospective black buyers. In contrast, much of the housing in the older white neighborhoods on the east side was renter-occupied and was declining physically. These factors, combined with the expanding housing market in Cleveland's eastern suburbs made possible by the federal government's FHA and VA housing programs, led many east-side whites to move out when blacks moved in. Rather than trying to accommodate the new black residents of these neighborhoods, Cleveland's white population chose to maintain a separation of the races. The outcome was that Cleveland, like many United States cities, has two separate housing markets—one black and one white—and the degree to which the races are segregated is reflected in the city's index of dissimilarity.[13] The index was 92.0 in 1940, 91.5 in 1950, 91.3 in 1960, and 89.0 in 1970 (Sorenson et al., 1975). The slight downward trend in these indices is probably only a transitory phenomenon. Cleveland's black community expanded so rapidly in the 1960s that many whites simply have not had the opportunity to move, and thus a slight degree of integration seems to have occurred. Through time, the few remaining whites will be replaced and Cleveland's index should move gradually upward.

Neighborhood Change

Invasion-succession The situation in Cleveland is typical of American cities. In fact, the invasion-succession process has been studied intensively since the initial work on the subject was done by the Chicago ecologists in the 1920s. Invasion-succession refers specifically to the process in which a group moves into an area (invasion) already occupied by a second group that differs in significant ways from the invaders. Over time, the second group moves out and, when the cycle is completed, the original inhabitants are completely displaced (succession). To the Chicago ecologists, the driving force in the process was the impersonal economic competition among groups for land. Initially, an ethnic or racial group is concentrated in specific areas of a city, but as their numbers rise and their aggregate demand for housing increases, they move outward and purchase housing in adjacent areas of the city.

In a study of racial change in Chicago, Duncan and Duncan (1957) argued that the invasion-succession process occurs in a sequence of five stages: invasion, early consolidation, consolidation, late consolidation, and piling up. In the final stage the neighborhood becomes predominantly black. Duncan and Duncan conclude that once the process has begun, it is seldom checked.

The Duncans found that in the beginning stage—invasion—the first blacks to move into an area are usually comparable in socioeconomic characteristics to the whites who have left. As an area passes through the next three stages, the social-status level of the area, as measured by the proportion of the adult population with some high school education, actually increases slightly. The final stage—piling up—begins only after the transition of the area from a totally white to totally black population has taken place. In spite of an area's population turnover, the socioeconomic characteristics of the population appear to remain the same and thus the area maintains elements of stability. If the ecological position and site characteristics of an area remain the same over time, the new residents will probably adopt the norms of the older residents. Thus, the Duncans conclude that "the residential structure of an urban community is in good part independent of the social makeup of the community's inhabitants" (p. 239). Although people are constantly moving in and out of an area, a degree of continuity is maintained by a core of "nonmover residents."

The tipping point model Research on the invasion-succession process has also led to the development of a model of neighborhood change based on the notion of a tipping point. The tipping point model posits that once a white area reaches a certain percentage of black residents, the area will inevitably become completely black. Researchers disagree, however, on whether tipping actually occurs. For example, Wolf (1965), Taeuber and Taeuber (1965), and Pryor (1971) found that the racial turnover of an area proceeds in a more or less orderly fashion at fairly stable rates on a block-by-block basis. In general these researchers discovered that the distance of a neighborhood from the black community rather than the percentage of blacks in a neighborhood is the better predictor of racial turnover.

Moltoch (1969) found another argument against tipping in a study of two Chicago neighborhoods, one changing racially and the other white and stable (c.f., Aldrich, 1976; Bruckner, 1977). Moltoch notes that urban neighborhoods have a high turnover of residents each year, roughly 20 percent, and in the normal operation of the housing market, the racial characteristics of a neighborhood's population can turn over in less than a decade. He found that the racial composition of a neighborhood can change when whites simply move out at normal rates and are then replaced by new residents who are predominantly black. That is, the racial change of a neighborhood in his study is due to whites' refusal to buy into the neighborhood, rather than white flight.

Guest and Zuiches (1971) replicated Moltoch's (1969) Chicago study with data from Cleveland, Ohio. They found that the majority of racially changing census tracts had only a slightly higher rate of out-mobility than would be predicted by knowing the housing and socioeconomic characteristics of the area. They did find a few transition neighborhoods where rates of racial turnover were much higher than predicted and suggested that a "tipping" or white-flight phenomenon may have occurred.

In contrast, research by Grodzins (1957), Schelling (1972), Steinnes (1977), and Schwab (1979) suggests that in certain parts of larger metropolitan areas, tipping may indeed be occurring. The findings indicate that the tipping point ranges from 10 to 20 percent, the actual percentage depending on the characteristics of the city and area under study. Variables that appear to influence tipping are the boundaries, size, and location of an area in relation to the existing black community, the normal rate of turnover in a neighborhood, the housing alternatives for those whites who leave as well as the alternatives for those minority members seeking entrance, prevailing racial attitudes in the community, and the region and size of the city under study (Schelling, 1971, 1972; Steinnes, 1977; Schwab, 1979).

Factors that influence tipping. The actual mechanisms involved in the tipping point phenomenon, however, are not well understood. It is known that the first blacks to move into a segregated neighborhood are usually of the same socioeconomic status as their white neighbors (Duncan and Duncan, 1957; Taeuber and Taeuber, 1965). Moreover, if the black families are widely dispersed within an area, they may go unnoticed by the area's white population (Smith, 1959; Schelling, 1972). If black families form a "subneighborhood" on a single street, however, their high visibility appears to contribute to the process of white succession (Schelling, 1972). Whites appear to be concerned about the future racial balance of their neighborhood. They are concerned about becoming a minority numerically in the neighborhood in which they live (Aldrich and Reiss, 1977). Therefore, two factors appear to affect tipping: (1) the number, rate, and visibility of black families entering a segregated area and (2) the number of blacks entering a neighborhood, which leads whites to believe that the percentage of blacks will become "intolerable," plus the number of whites leaving a neighborhood, which reinforces the belief among the remaining white families in the "inevitability of the process." The final outcome is the complete racial turnover of an area.

Research has also shown that animosity toward black expansion is greatest on the edge of an expanding black area where whites live in fear of invasion (Schelling, 1972). Moreover the whites who remain once the invasion-succession process has begun are usually low-income and financially unable to move. This group generally expresses more racial prejudice than those who do move (Schelling, 1972). However, evidence does not support the idea that racial attitudes are the key to understanding why whites move out or fail to replace those who have moved out (Aldrich and Reiss, 1977). Apparently whites' fear of being isolated in a predominantly black neighborhood is the major factor in determining the racial change in an area.

Misconceptions About Neighborhood Change

In general, the dynamics of racial change in neighborhoods is not well understood. Enough is known, however, to address some of the more widely held misconceptions about the racial transition of neighborhoods. One commonly held belief is that blacks who invade neighborhoods are of lower socioeconomic status than the present residents. Research by Duncan and Duncan (1957), Taeuber and Taeuber (1965), and Edwards (1972) has shown that blacks in transition census tracts often have more education and are more likely to be homeowners than the whites in these tracts, both before and after invasion. In fact, the work of these researchers suggests that the racially changing areas of central cities attract the same type of individuals as white suburbs: young blacks who are in the family formation-stage of the lifecycle and who usually have high socioeconomic status.

Race and housing values This first misconception is closely related to a second, the notion that blacks moving into a neighborhood negatively affect housing values. Although more studies in this area are needed, research over the past twenty years suggests that blacks pay as much, and in many cases more, than whites for comparable housing.

The most comprehensive study of the relationship between property values and race was done in the 1950s by Laurenti (1960). Laurenti studied single-family neighborhoods matched in social and housing characteristics with some of the racially changing neighborhoods in San Francisco, Oakland, and Philadelphia. During the one-year study, Laurenti found no noticeable upward or downward trends in housing prices; in 44 percent of the comparisons, the housing price in changing neighborhoods was significantly higher.[14]

In a more recent study, Kain and Quigley (1972) analyzed a sample of approximately 1,200 dwelling units in St. Louis and concluded that blacks pay between 5 and 10 percent more than whites in that city for comparable housing. Kain and Quigley, however, contend that many researchers, in their concern about estimating the magnitude of price discrimination, have overlooked a much more serious consequence of housing market discrimination: "In asking whether blacks pay more than whites for the same kind of housing, [researchers] have failed to consider adequately the way in which housing discrimination has affected the kind of housing consumed by Negro households" (Kain and Quigley, 1972, p. 265). Their evidence shows that nonwhites often have difficulty in obtaining housing outside the ghetto. Most blacks, in fact, limit their housing search to all-black areas of the city, where fewer housing services are available regardless of one's willingness to pay for them. For example, Kain and Quigley found a substantial difference in the probability of black and white homeownership even after controlling for differences in the socioeconomic status of the two groups. It was their opinion that the lower rates of homeownership among blacks, in all likelihood, reflect restrictions on the location or types of housing available to blacks.

Thus, the findings of Kain and Quigley suggest that black households at all income levels are impeded by housing discrimination from purchasing and owning single-family homes. These findings have significant policy implications. For most low- and middle-income Americans, homeownership is the most important means of accumulating wealth. It is one of the few "hedges against inflation" available to low- and moderate-income groups. Additionally, homeowners are given a sizable "tax break" by being permitted to deduct the annual interest on mortgage payments from their federal income taxes. The difficulties of homeownership experienced by black Americans therefore significantly affect blacks' housing costs, income, and welfare. The authors conclude that black Americans pay 5 to 10 percent more for housing (direct costs), and that when the indirect costs are included (inflation and tax breaks), the limitations on homeownership can increase the true housing cost to blacks by more than 30 percent (Kain and Quigley, 1972).

A Community within a Community

The impact of segregation forces blacks of widely different social status to live closer to each other than do their white counterparts. Because of the persistence of segregation in American society, the "black community" in most large American metropolises has taken on some of the characteristics of the total metropolis of which it is a part. The most interesting of these is residential segregation according to class within the black community.

This pattern is shown clearly in Table 10.14, in which indexes of residential dissimilarity for employed males are listed by occupation and race. These figures, calculated from the 1970 Census, are the average index scores of ten urbanized areas.[15] In the top third of the table (10.14A) the residential patterns of whites of different occupational status are compared. As noted in the discussion of social-status segregation, as the social distance between any two status groups increases, the average physical distance between their residences as reflected in the indexes of dissimilarity also increases. In comparing white professionals with other white occupational groups across the top line of this table, one sees that the index scores increase in a regular fashion as social-status differences increase.

In the middle of the table (10.14B), the indexes of dissimilarity for non-whites are presented. Interestingly, the same patterns are observed, but these index scores are consistently higher than the white scores. In other words, although blacks are segregated as a group, their racial communities are clearly differentiated internally with respect to social status.

The bottom of the table (10.14C), which compares whites of different occupational status with blacks in the same occupational categories, is very informative. Comparing blacks and whites of the highest occupational status—professionals—produces an index score of 70. The rest of the table shows clearly that within the ten urbanized areas included in Simkus's (1978) study, two entirely different communities exist—one white and one nonwhite (c.f., Marston, 1969; Cottingham, 1975).

Social consequences of these patterns The figures in Table 10.14 show that indexes of dissimilarity between socioeconomic groups were roughly comparable for whites and nonwhites in 1970. What the figures do not show is the physical closeness (propinquity) between the various occupational groupings. Erbe (1975) investigated this relationship among different status groups in both the white and black populations of the Chicago SMSA in 1970. She discovered that the residential propinquity between high- and low-status persons differed dramatically between racial groups. Though white professionals and managers lived in census tracts with others of comparable status, black professionals and managers "lived in tracts with occupational composition comparable, on the average, to that of tracts where unskilled white workers live" (Erbe, 1975, p. 811). Erbe (1975) notes that

> for the black middle class, residential segregation by socioeconomic status means living in neighborhoods with an occupational, educational and income level above that of all blacks in the Chicago SMSA. It may mean avoidance of the inner ghetto and public housing. It does not mean isolation from the black lower class. . . . To the extent that neighborhood context affects individual behavior and attitudes independently of individual characteristics by circumscribing and channeling individual experiences, the implications of these findings for the study of race and social class are important (pp. 811–12).

When a family purchases a home, it purchases a cluster of housing services in addition to the structure and the land. These housing services include the subcommunity's schools, parks, and public services, as well as the status that is associated with the area and its housing. Erbe's research suggests that high-status blacks, in particular, receive less in return for their housing dollars than whites of comparable status. Not only do they pay more for housing, but their very restricted housing alternatives allow them

Table 10.14

Indexes of residential dissimilarity calculated between employed males categorized by occupation and race, averaged over ten urbanized areas, 1970.

	Professional	Managerial	Sales	Clerical	Craft	Operative	Service	Laboring
A.				White				
Professional		15	15	26	36	43	34	39
Managerial			14	28	36	43	35	41
Sales				25	33	40	32	38
Clerical					19	25	18	24
White Craft						14	18	20
Operative							20	19
Service								21
Laboring								
				Nonwhite				
B.								
Professional		43	45	38	46	46	44	50
Managerial			46	39	42	42	43	47

Nonwhite					
Sales	37	40	39	40	44
Clerical		26	25	28	33
Craft			18	24	24
Operative				21	21
Service					22
Laboring					22

White

C.								
Professional	70	80	79	77	79	78	76	77
Managerial	84	86	85	84	85	84	83	84
Sales	89	90	89	88	89	88	87	87
Clerical	87	88	87	85	85	84	83	84
Nonwhite								
Craft	87	87	86	84	83	82	81	81
Operative	88	89	88	86	86	84	83	83
Service	87	88	87	84	84	82	81	84
Laboring	89	89	89	87	86	84	81	83

Source: Adapted from Table 3 in Simkus, A. A. "Residential Segregation by Occupation and Race in Ten Urbanized Areas, 1950–1970." *American Sociological Review* 43, 1978, p. 86. Reprinted with permission of The American Sociological Association.

"THE COLOREDS ARE COMING! THE COLOREDS ARE COMING!"

In this cartoon, Doug Marlette is satirizing Boston's resistance to court ordered school busing, but it could just as well reflect the resistance black Americans face when attempting to buy or rent housing in white areas of the city. (Doug Marlette, © *The Charlotte Observer*)

fewer housing services, especially the intangible status recognition that comes from living in an exclusive area.

Why Racial Segregation?

Ecological factors In this discussion of social status and ethnic segregation, three factors—voluntary, involuntary and ecological—have been identified as being responsible for the segregation of racial and ethnic groups. In the case of racial segregation, involuntary factors appear to be the most important. This notion is supported in a paper by Karl Taeuber, "The Effect of Income Redistribution on Racial Residential Segregation" (1968). In his hypothetical study, Taeuber was interested in the effect that the elimination of race as a basis for assigning housing would have on residential patterns in Cleveland, Ohio. In other words, he pretended that all lower- and middle-class housing was available to whoever could afford to live in given areas of Cleveland. (Since 1940, the city's index of dissimilarity has remained near 90.) Interestingly, when Taeuber carried out his redistribution—assigning whites and blacks of equal income to the available housing in their income range—Cleveland's segregation index dropped dramatically to 10. Thus, in Cleveland, only 11 percent of segregation of blacks could be explained by ecological factors.

Photo 10.2 Although the majority of black Americans live in the central cities, an increasing number of blacks now live in the suburbs. This decentralization of our black population, however, has not been accompanied by integration. Black Americans continue to be highly segregated whether they live in the city or the suburbs. *Source:* © Allen Green, Photo Researchers, Inc.

A similar pattern is found in other cities. For example, in 1970, only 14.0 percent of the segregation in Atlanta was due to the economic characteristics of the black population; in Baltimore 5.6 percent; Dallas 10.5 percent; Houston 9.8 percent; Washington, D.C. 6 percent; Detroit 4.7 percent; and so on (U.S. Census Bureau, 1971). The economic position of blacks in American society improved significantly in the post–World War II period, and more than half of all black families are now categorized as middleclass. The preceding figures, however, strongly suggest that the improving economic status of blacks is unlikely, by itself, to alter the prevailing patterns of racial residential segregation in the United States.

Voluntary and involuntary factors Even if involuntary and ecological factors in residential patterning could be eliminated completely, the segregation of races would persist for voluntary reasons—blacks might still choose to live near blacks. However, the nation's history gives many examples of how violence, rumor, prejudicial insinuation, and racial threats of declining property values and block busting have been used to ghettoize black Americans involuntarily. Racial minorities, because of their high visibility, are the most easily manipulated real estate client groups. Because their housing options have been limited by prejudicial feelings, a segregated market, and the undemocratic rules to which they are subject, racial minorities have traditionally had little choice in the matter of residential location. Nearly a century ago William Graham Sumner, a founding father of American sociology, stated, "stateways cannot change folkways." It is probably true that federal legislation cannot change attitudes (prejudices), but it can stop overt behavior (discrimination). The 1964 Civil Rights Act and subsequent legislation have had a measurable impact on the economic well-being of black Americans—these laws have reduced discrimination in the economic sphere. For example, the gap between average family income for blacks and whites has decreased significantly since the laws' passage. Unfortunately, this legislation has had little impact on residential patterns, and blacks continue to live in a community within a community in the nation's urban places.

SUMMARY

This chapter addresses the segregation and location of socioeconomic, ethnic, and racial groups in United States cities. Ecologists have discovered that the social distance between groups is reflected in the spatial distance between them in their residential locations. These patterns can have both positive and negative consequences for society. Voluntary segregation can positively affect society by contributing to the solidarity of societal groups and directly enhancing the individual members' sense of belonging and security. Segregation can also lead to the physical and social isolation of a group and form a barrier to their full participation in society.

Segregation in American society is studied for several reasons. First, the degree of segregation between groups is an indicator of the degree of social inequality in society. Second, understanding residential segregation gives policy makers an indication of the effectiveness of social programs and government policies in reducing segregation. Third, the study of segregation gives the ecologist insight into basic ecological processes that affect the overall structure and functioning of society.

Three sets of factors have been identified as influencing the segregation process. Ecological factors include impersonal economic and ecological forces such as the location of housing types in the city and the socioeconomic characteristics of groups. Voluntary factors are ones of self-selection. Individuals of common culture, because of common problems and needs, willingly choose to live near each other. Involuntary segregation occurs as the result of law or customs that prescribe where certain groups can live. These three types of factors can operate alone but are usually interrelated.

The degree to which members of different status groups are residentially segregated from each other has been of long-standing interest to students of cities. Social-status segregation is a universal phenomenon; the gross inequality in the distribution of income in the United States is reflected clearly in the residential patterns of its status groups. When the indexes of dissimilarity are plotted, a U-shaped curve is produced that shows that the members of the highest and lowest status groups are the most segregated. The location of these high- and low-status groups in a city depends on the scale of the society and the age and region of the city under study. Voluntary and ecological rather than involuntary factors are indicated in the segregation of status groups.

Ethnic segregation continues in many United States cities in spite of the melting-pot theory that predicts the assimilation of ethnic groups. Although ecological factors such as income, occupation, and education explain a high percentage of this residential segregation, voluntary factors also appear to contribute to the durability and resiliency of ethnic enclaves in American cities.

Black Americans are the largest and one of the most segregated minority groups in the United States. Blacks lived in mostly southern and rural areas until this century, when more than 5 million black Americans left the rural South for the cities. A majority of these migrants moved to the central cities of the North, where they formed durable racial communities. These communities have isolated black Americans, however; the high degree of racial segregation in this country has remained constant for the past thirty years.

The invasion-succession process and the tipping point model have been proposed to explain neighborhood change. Although the process of neighborhood change is poorly understood, once a neighborhood begins to change racially the process is seldom checked. The initial black "invaders" of an area are typically of the same or higher status as their white neighbors. Moreover, it is estimated that the high demand of blacks for housing often leads to their paying between 5 and 10 percent more than whites pay for housing. The decline of housing values as the result of racial change in an area appears to be a myth.

Finally, although voluntary factors cannot be eliminated, research has shown that ecological factors have little effect. In all probability racial segregation in the United States is due to involuntary factors. Although the

1964 Civil Rights Act has increased economic opportunities for black Americans, it has not increased the number of housing alternatives. Therefore, racial segregation will persist in most United States cities for the foreseeable future.

NOTES

1. Bierstedt's inclusion of statistical groups with societal, social, and associational categories is not universally accepted. Other sociologists do not consider a statistical group as a true group but as a grouping. However, Bierstedt's scheme is appropriate for the purposes of this text and is used in the analysis of the segregation of groups.
2. The segregation of other groups has been studied. Guest (1972), for example, investigated the distribution of groups in similar stages in the lifecycle and Pampel and Choldin (1978) studied the location and segregation of the aged. Social status, ethnic, and racial groups, however, form major cleavages in American society and are important not only ecologically but politically and socially.
3. For more information on the sociology of real estate agents, see J. D. House, *Contemporary Entrepreneurs: The Sociology of Real Estate Agents* (Westport, Conn.: Greenwood Press, 1977).
4. The formula of the index is:

$$D = 1/2 \sum_{i=i}^{k} (x_i - y_i)$$

5. Replication of the Duncans' research by Wilkens (1956), Uyeki (1964, 1975), Fine (1971), Guest (1971), Farley (1977), and Simkus (1978) confirms this earlier research.
6. Simkus's study included the cities of Hartford, Syracuse, Chicago-Gary, Cleveland, Columbus, Indianapolis, Fort Worth, Atlanta, Memphis, and Richmond.
7. Dotson and Dotson (1956), Collism and Mogey (1959), Mehta (1968), Guest (1969), Schwirian and Rico-Velasco (1971), and Latif (1972) are a few of the more important studies on residential dissimilarity among status groups in cities outside the United States. Refer to the bibliography for a complete citation of each research article.
8. For a further discussion of the role of occupation and income in social status segregation see Duncan Timms, *The Urban Mosaic: Towards a Theory of Residential Differentiation.* Cambridge, England: The University Press, 1971.
9. The nation's current immigration law still follows the framework of the Immigration and Nationality Act of 1952, which established a national quota system. However, with major revisions in 1965, the national-origins emphasis in this law was replaced by the governing themes of family reunification and the admission of aliens with needed skills. The current law establishes a worldwide annual ceiling of 250,000 people.
10. The research is by Cressey (1938), Ford (1950), Duncan et al. (1959), Lieberson (1961, 1962, 1963), and Kiang (1968).

11. Smith and Zopf identify five distinct periods in the history of immigration to the United States. "The first embraces the years from establishment of the first settlements to the emergence of the national state in 1783; the second period of free immigration, ended about 1830; the third extending until 1882 was the period of state regulation; the fourth, beginning with the passage of the first national immigration act in 1882 and lasting until 1917, was a period of federal regulation with individual selection; and the fifth, the present stage of restricted immigration began in 1917" (Smith and Zopf, 1976, p. 473). The periods chosen for this book are related to the ethnic composition of immigrants to the United States.

12. Guest and Weed (1976) employ regression analysis in their study of the effects of social-status characteristics on levels of ethnic segregation in the three United States cities. Because this statistical approach is beyond the level of most students using this text, the discussion is presented in nontechnical language.

13. This analysis of Cleveland's patterns of racial segregation is based on Chapter 2 of the author's dissertation, *A Test of the Neighborhood Life-Cycle Model of Hoover and Vernon*.

14. A recent work by George S. Rent and J. Dennis Roof, "Neighborhood Racial Transition and Property Value Trends in a Southern Community," suggests that the racial change of neighborhoods adversely affected housing values in the Piedmont region of the South. Approximately a $2,000 decline in the market value of houses was attributable to the racial transition of the area's housing.

15. For a more detailed discussion of the Simkus study, see the review of his research in the section on social-status segregation.

CHAPTER ELEVEN

Density and Its Consequences

Statement of Objectives

1. The student should understand the density-distance relationship.

2. The student should analyze how the distance-density relationship changes over time in the cities of high- and low-scale societies.

3. The student should employ the POET framework in analyzing the reasons for shifting density-distance patterns.

4. The student should become familiar with the theories of Georg Simmel and Louis Wirth on the relationship of population density and pathology.

5. The student should know the five theories of the density-pathology relationship.

6. Ecologists have empirically studied the relationship between density and human pathology since the 1920s. The student should analyze the strengths and weaknesses of the studies reviewed in the text.

In the preceding chapters the internal structure of cities was examined from several different yet complementary perspectives. For example, the theoretical approach known as social area analysis was introduced in Chapter 6 to explore the relationship between societal scale and the use of space within cities. In Chapter 7, the models of Burgess, Hoyt, and Harris and Ullman were used to describe macropatterns of urban geometry. Suburbanization was discussed in Chapter 8 with special emphasis on the forces leading to the rapid growth of the fringe in the older metropolitan areas as well as the broad differences in land use and populations of central cities and their suburban rings. This chapter describes another approach to the study of the form and growth of human settlements—the analysis of population density.

Ecologists and other social scientists have studied population density using at least two different approaches. First, some researchers have systematically studied the so-called density-distance relationship. More than twenty-five years ago, Colin Clark (1951) discovered that as one moves from a city's center to its periphery, residential population density declines in a regular fashion. Subsequently ecologists and geographers described this relationship with a high degree of mathematical precision.[1] Because this mathematical approach is beyond the scope of this text, a simpler graphic approach is used to explain the findings. Density-distance curves are presented that describe the patterns found in most of the cities of the world. A historical analysis of density patterns in United States cities serves to emphasize the population, organization, environmental, and technological factors that influence residential density. Finally, differences in the density patterns of cities of the more- and less-developed countries are examined, with special attention given to the ecological factors responsible for their divergence.

The second approach used by ecologists in studying population density explores the possible relationship between high density and human pathology. In the early decades of this century, research suggested a close relationship between high residential density and increased levels of crime, mental disorders, mortality, and other social and physical ills. This early research was flawed because it did not take into consideration the effects of social class. The poor more than other economic groups live in high-density situations and it was impossible to determine whether class or density factors caused human pathology. The second half of this chapter is an overview of the literature on this relationship. First, the theoretical works of Georg Simmel and Louis Wirth are examined. Their findings indicated that the concentration of large numbers of people in urban places has negative social and psychological consequences. Second, the density research conducted with animals that has been inappropriately applied to the study of human populations is discussed. Third, a general overview is given of the major theories of crowding and density. Finally, the more important ecological studies on this subject are described with a brief caveat about the strengths and weaknesses of this type of research. In this section special emphasis is given to research that takes into account the effects of socioeconomic status. The major purpose of this section is to review objectively the available literature on the relationship between density and human pathology and to assess the policy implications for the future development of cities.

THE DENSITY-DISTANCE RELATIONSHIP

As is emphasized throughout this text, metropolises are constantly changing. Chapters 6 to 8 show that as a metropolis's population increases, the

Photo 11.1
Source: Photograph by © Mark Godfrey. Magnum Photos, Inc.

distribution of people within its urban area changes accordingly. There are only two sources of metropolitan population growth. One is net in-migration, the change that occurs when the number of people moving into a city exceeds the number moving out. The other source of population growth is natural increase, the change that occurs when births exceed deaths. In the past, metropolises have grown largely through net in-migration, but in recent years a larger proportion of this growth has been the result of natural increase. Regardless of the source of population growth, a metropolitan area accommodates the additional people by changes in its residential structure. Viewed as a general process, this accommodation can take place in one of three ways. First, the metropolis can accommodate population increase by expanding at its fringes (deconcentration). Second, the outer boundaries of a metropolis can remain the same, and new population can be housed by increasing the overall density (congestion). Third, population increases can be accommodated by a combination of the two processes (Winsborough, 1963).

Density-Distance Models

Urban population patterns and processes have been systematically studied for more than a quarter-century. Past studies of residential density patterns have shown a systematic tendency for density to decline with increasing distance from a city's core. Clark (1951) suggested that the density-distance relationship can be described by what is called a negative exponential relationship. It is negative because distance and density are inversely related: as distance increases, density decreases. It is an exponential relationship because of the nature of the mathematical function relating density

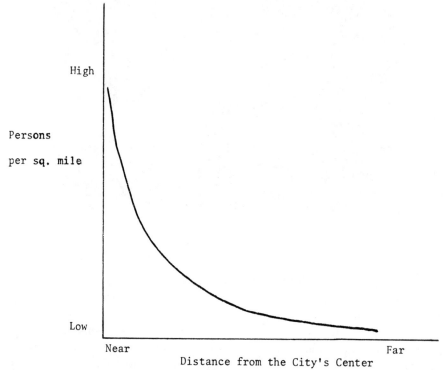

Fig. 11.1 Population density and distance from the center of a city.

to distance.[2] This relationship is represented graphically in Figure 11.1. The vertical axis in this figure is the number of persons per square mile; the horizontal axis is the distance from a city's center. The curve is produced simply by plotting the average population density at various distances from the city's center.

Chicago's Density Pattern

The Chicago pattern is seen clearly in the three-dimensional contour map in Figure 11.2. In constructing this map, researchers divided Chicago into seven pie-shaped sectors and then plotted curves for each sector. Note that, despite some variations in the density curves of the sectors, Chicago fits the general negative exponential pattern. Population density declines sharply from a peak, equivalent to seventy-eight families per residential acre, to between four and five families at the city's periphery. Of interest is the fact that this density pattern is consistent with the pattern predicted by Burgess in the concentric zone model fifty years earlier.

Fig. 11.2 The sectoral pattern of net population densities. Population density declines sharply from a peak equivalent to 78 families per net residential acre to between 4 and 5.

Source: Chicago Area Transportation Study, Final Report, I: Survey Findings. Chicago: Western Engraving and Embossing Co., 1959.

Comparing Density-Distance Curves

Because it is difficult to compare curves visually, assume that the curve in Figure 11.1 has been transposed into the straight-line form in Figure 11.3.[3] Between-city differences thus can be seen by simply comparing two basic dimensions of the line—measures of congestion and deconcentration. *Congestion* refers to the average number of persons per square mile at a city's center. In Figure 11.3, congestion is the expected population density at the point where the line crosses the vertical axis (Winsborough, 1963). In Figure 11.3, City A is much more congested than City B. That is, central density is significantly higher in City A than in City B. *Deconcentration* is indicated by the pitch of the slope. This measure is negative because density declines with distance, and the magnitude or size of the measure is represented by the steepness of the line's slope. The larger the value for deconcentration, the steeper the slope. In the example in Figure 11.3, City B is more deconcentrated than City A.

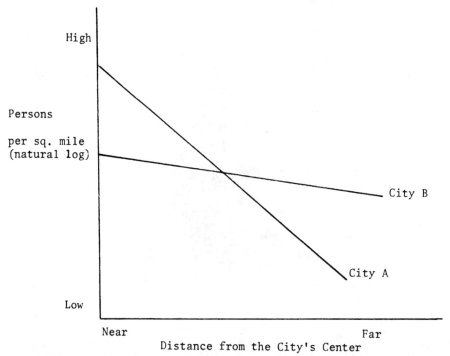

The curve for City A is typical of metropolises that reached metropolitan status in the nineteenth century—the industrial cities of the North and Northeast. The horse and trolley were the forms of transportation that shaped their early development. Past and present density levels are relatively high. Cities reaching metropolitan status in the twentieth century were shaped by the automobile, which permitted low-density settlement patterns. Cities in the South and Southwest have density curves that resemble those of City B.

Fig. 11.3 The density-distance curves for two cities (linear form).

United States comparisons The form of the density-distance curve seems to hold for cities in both more- and less-developed societies.[4] The values for the two measures, however, vary considerably from city to city at any one time. Table 11.1 gives values for the measures of congestion and deconcentration for fifteen United States cities. Note that in 1960 Cincinnati had 72,000 persons per square mile at its center, whereas New Orleans had a figure roughly half as great (30,000 persons), and central density in Los Angeles was only 7,900 persons per square mile. Similar variations are found in the measures of deconcentration. Bridgeport, Connecticut has the largest value in the table— − .66; for every mile outward from the city's center there is a 66 percent decline in a unit of population density. In contrast, Spokane's measure is − .01, meaning that there is virtually no relationship between distance and density. The population density in Spokane's central core (2,500 per square mile) is roughly the same as the density at its fringe. If this relationship were plotted in Figure 11.3, it would be a straight line running parallel with the horizontal or X-axis.

Changes in the Density-Distance Relationship Over Time

Despite considerable variation in the density-distance relationship (congestion and deconcentration) among United States cities, they all have density patterns that fit the general negative exponential curves. This analysis, however, shows only the pattern existing at a single time. The question

Table 11.1
Measures of congestion and deconcentration for fourteen metropolitan areas.

Metropolitan area	Congestion[a]	Deconcentration[b]
Baltimore	41.1	− .32
Boston	24.2	− .18
Bridgeport	21.9	− .66
Chicago	56.0	− .12
Cincinnati	71.9	− .29
Cleveland	18.2	− .20
Detroit	18.8	− .10
Kansas City	10.5	− .12
Los Angeles	7.9	− .02
New Orleans	30.1	− .38
Philadelphia	9.5	− .15
Pittsburgh	11.0	− .12
Spokane	2.5	− .01
Washington	6.6	− .06

[a] Actual density in thousands of persons per square mile
[b] Change in density per mile of distance from the central business district

Source: Adapted from Guest, A.M., "Urban Growth and Population Density." *Demography* 10 1973: p. 65, Table 4.

remains of how cities accommodate a growing population over time. New-ling (1969) outlined four stages of urban development that are reflected in unique density-distance curves. These stages of growth are represented in Figure 11.4. In young cities (Stage I) just attaining metropolitan status (50,000 population or more), density declines very quickly with distance; central-city density (congestion) is high and the slope (concentration) is steep. Early growth (Stage II) is accommodated both by increasing central congestion and by deconcentration at the city's periphery. As a city attains maturity (Stage III), the increased demand for space in the metropolitan core by business and industrial users drives residential users out, and central congestion declines. Old metropolitan areas (Stage IV) are characterized by low central-city density (congestion) and a relatively flat curve.

An Alternative Approach to the Study of Density-Distance Patterns

In reviewing Newling's curves, one notices a "cratering" or a density crest in most of them. Examination of the position of the crest in the curve—the distance from a city's core where the residential density is highest—is another approach to the study of density-distance gradients. In Table 11.2 these data are provided for the city of Chicago for the years 1860 through 1970. In the first column of the table, the position of the crest is given in number of miles from the city's center; the second column gives the pop-ulation density at that distance. Since 1860, Chicago has consistently been one of the nation's most rapidly growing metropolitan areas. The city has accommodated this growth during the past century in two distinctively

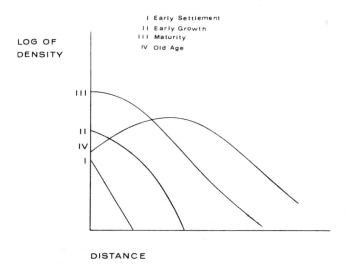

Fig. 11.4 Density-distance relationship according to Newling.

Table 11.2
Measures of concentration and decongestion for the Chicago metropolitan area, 1860–1970

Year	Concentration[a]	Congestion[b]
1860	1.09 miles	30,000 persons per sq. mile
1870	1.14	70,800
1880	1.26	96,600
1890	1.97	86,300
1900	2.41	100,000
1910	2.71	100,000
1920	4.36	51,200
1930	5.60	49,100
1940	5.85	46,200
1950	6.51	46,500
1960	8.24	38,100
1970	8.46	32,100

[a] Location of the crest in miles from the city's center
[b] Density as measured at the crest

Source: Reprinted from,"An Ecological Approach to the Theory of Suburbanization," by H. Winsborough in *American Journal of Sociology* 68 (1963): p. 568, Table 1, by permission of the University of Chicago Press. Measures of concentration and congestion for 1960 and 1970 were calculated from a sample of census tracts drawn from the *U.S. Census of Population: Characteristics of the Population* for Chicago Standard Metropolitan Statistical Area, 1960 and 1970.

different ways. Prior to 1900, because of Chicago's inefficient transportation network, population growth had to be accommodated through a piling-up process (increased congestion). Note that in the forty-year period from 1860 to 1900 the location of the crest shifted outward only one and one-half miles, but density levels at the crest increased threefold from 30,000 persons per square mile to 100,000!

After 1900, the internal combustion engine permitted the rapid deconcentration and decongestion of Chicago's population. In the seventy-year period ending in 1970, the crest shifted from 2.4 to 8.4 miles and congestion decreased dramatically.

Cleveland's Changing Density Patterns

The patterns can be seen more clearly in the density-distance curves for the city of Cleveland, Ohio for the years 1930–1970 (see Figure 11.5). Changes in the patterns were the result of the interaction of several important social, economic, and ecological factors that are examined in the following discussion of the curves.[5]

1930 curve By 1930 Cleveland already had a "classical" mature-city density-distance curve (see Stage III in Figure 11.4). The curve for this year

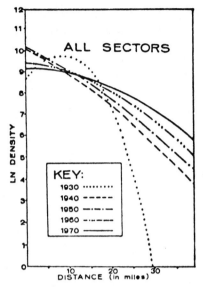

Fig. 11.5 Density-distance curves for Cleveland, 1930–1970.

Source: Arnold, J. W., Schwab, W. A., and Schwirian, K. P., "Spatial and Temporal Aspects of the Density-Distance Relationship." *Sociological Focus* 10 (1977) p. 121, figure 2.

shows a distinctive central-city cratering with a rim of high density that drops abruptly toward the periphery of the city. Cleveland in 1930 was relatively compact, with a density of 18,000 at the crest, which was 7.5 miles from the city's center. This pattern is normally associated with cities where relatively inefficient mass transportation makes suburban living prohibitively expensive in both time and cost. Also, Cleveland's inner-city neighborhoods, although high in residential density, remained desirable residential locations because of their proximity to the central business district and the relatively low age of their housing.

1940 curve The depression of the 1930s brought marked changes in the density-distance curve for Cleveland. Not only did many inner-city neighborhoods begin to decline due to lack of repairs on their aging dwellings, but many families were forced to double up or take in roomers to make up for their dwindling income (Steiner, 1969, p. 23). These changes are clearly reflected in the density-distance curve of 1940. The most noticeable changes are the disappearance of the central cratering, the most distinctive part of the 1930 curve, and the central-city density increase over the 1930 level. These changes are due not only to the doubling-up phenomenon, but also to the lack of new housing construction during much of the Depression.

1950 curve Cleveland's 1950 density-distance curve reflects events of the preceding decade that worsened an already tight housing market. The 1950 curve is a continuation of the 1940 pattern with a distinctive absence of central cratering and an upward shift in citywide population density. This pattern can be explained in part by several national trends in housing. First, capital and other resources that normally would have been invested in the housing market were diverted to the war effort. More important was the national housing policy of rent control that continued into the post–World War II period. Landlords under rent control, unable to raise rents on individual apartments, often compensated for lost revenue by subdividing structures into smaller units to produce greater profits per structure (Steiner, 1969, p. 121). The chronic shortage of single-family dwellings during this period led to essentially the same outcome in the owner-occupied sector of the housing market. The result was an overall upward shift of the density-distance curve.

1960 curve The 1960 curve is flattened and is considerably more linear than the curves for previous years. This change is due to dramatic decreases in central-city density and marked increases in the population density of the suburban ring. The pattern can be explained in part by the centrifugal forces operating in most United States cities. Automobile technology, an improved highway system, and the availability of large amounts of capital for home construction made the periphery of cities both accessible and affordable for large numbers of American families. In addition, by 1960 federal urban renewal monies had enabled Cleveland and many other cities to turn interior central-city residential areas to different land use. Therefore, the rapid growth of Cleveland's suburban ring and the normal turnover of residential property adjacent to the central business district largely explain the changes in the 1960 density-distance curve.

1970 curve The city of Cleveland proper underwent an absolute drop in population between the years 1960 and 1970 as a result of several factors (U.S. Bureau of the Census, 1962, 1972a). First, many of Cleveland's older, interior neighborhoods were becoming increasingly undesirable because of the age and condition of their housing. For example, in the Central Social Planning Area, immediately adjacent to Cleveland's Central Business District, the mean age of housing in 1970 was over fifty years, and more than 60 percent of the units were deficient in plumbing and heating (Welfare Federation, 1974, p. 1). This fact, taken in conjunction with the racial metamorphosis of many of Cleveland's older neighborhoods and the concomitant "flight" of Cleveland's white population to the suburban ring, gives some explanation of the density-distance curve of 1970. In general, the 1970 curve continues the trend from 1960, with marked decreases in central density and continued increases in the area of the curve associated with suburbia.

1980 curve During the 1970s, the number of households in the Cleveland metropolitan area rose by more than 40,000, but the number of new housing units granted building permits was over 71,000. That equals 1.8 new units for every additional household. Subtracting the 18,000 units that were abandoned or demolished during the decade leaves approximately 53,000 units, or 1.3 units per additional household (Cleveland Planning Commission, 1980). Since most of this new construction occurred in the suburbs, increasing numbers of Cleveland residents left the central city for newer homes in the suburbs. As a result, the 1980 curve continues the trend from the previous two decades with marked decreases in central density and continued increases in density in the area of the curve associated with suburbia.

In brief, the density-distance curves for Cleveland over the past fifty years have changed from a "mature" city pattern in 1930 with distinctive cratering to a linear pattern with high central density that peaked in the curve of 1950. If the trends in the 1960, 1970, and 1980 curves continue, the cratering phenomenon may appear again when the 1990 Census data are plotted. The curves reflect both metropolitan and national events and forces that influence the distribution of a city's population.

Societal Scale and the Density-Distance
Relationship in High-Scale Societies

From Cleveland's density-distance curves in Figure 11.5, note that during the past fifty years the city has accommodated its population growth through the process of deconcentration—the slope of the curve has progressively flattened. This process, however, is only one of three ways in which the accommodation could have taken place. According to Berry, Simmons, and Tennant (1963) the particular way in which a city's population growth is accommodated is a function of the scale of the society. Cities in high-scale societies typically accommodate population growth through the process of deconcentration. Cities in low-scale societies accommodate growth by increased congestion and concentration.

As shown graphically in Figure 11.6, density-distance curves for cities in a high-scale society progressively flatten from time 1 (early development) through time 3 (late development). This pattern of change can be attributed to several related factors analyzed within the POET framework. The elements of Duncan's ecological complex are introduced in the order of their importance.

Technology One factor is advances in transportation technology that have provided access to vast areas of a city's fringe for residential development. The degree to which a city deconcentrates is tied closely to its age and its particular mix of modes of transportation (e.g., mass transit; automobile). Table 11.3 shows the location of the density crest (in miles from a city's core) and per capita mass transit ridership for the years 1890 and 1950 for eight United States cities. From the 1890 figures one can see that the most deconcentrated cities—that is, those for which the density crest is farthest

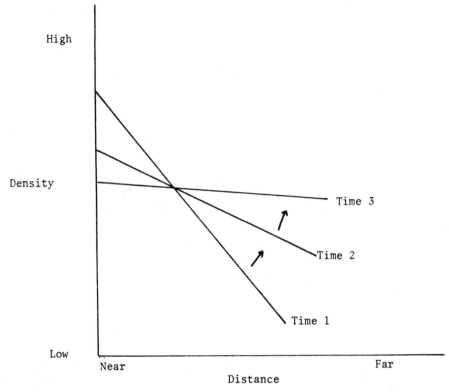

Fig. 11.6 Changes in the density-distance curve over time in a high-scale society.

Table 11.3
Measures of concentration and mass transit ridership for eight United States cities, 1890 and 1950.

City	*1890* Concentration[a]	Transit ratio[b]	*1950* Concentration	Transit ratio
Boston	3.31	252	3.38	164
Cincinnati	.85	128	1.45	114
Detroit	1.87	111	10.00	102
Kansas City	1.37	286	3.85	105
Philadelphia	1.95	158	2.50	148
Pittsburgh	1.10	134	11.11	85
St. Louis	1.08	150	3.57	136
Washington	2.02	153	3.70	135

[a] Location of the crest in miles from a city's center
[b] Annual per capita mass transit ridership

Source: Reprinted from "An Ecological Approach to the Theory of Suburbanization," by H. Winsborough in *American Journal of Sociology* 68 (1963): p. 570, Table 3, by permission of the University of Chicago Press.

from the central core—also have the highest transit ratio. Boston is the best example. In the late nineteenth century, mass transit was the most efficient mode of transportation and its intensive use made possible the deconcentration of a city's population.

In the twentieth century the reverse is true. Cities with the highest transit ratios are the most concentrated, and vice versa. Compare Boston with Pittsburgh and Detroit. Differences in the patterns are due largely to changing transportation technology. In 1890, a city's residential structure was influenced by the availability of mass transit. Subways and other forms of mass transit require enormous capital investments, and once a system was built it shaped the growth of a city for generations to come. Boston, for example, still has an extensive subway system, whereas the mass transit systems in Detroit and Pittsburgh are now poorly developed. Therefore, in the twentieth century the automobile became the more efficient mode of transportation. It made possible the large-scale but low-density development of an urban fringe. In general, the density patterns of older cities of the North and East were shaped by streetcars, subways, and commuter rail lines. Those cities are now both more congested and less deconcentrated than the newer cities of the West and the South where the automobile had a more important role (Guest, 1978).

Environment A second factor is related to the first. Cheap undeveloped land at a city's fringe was made accessible by automobile technology. In the past, most of a city's transportation network converged at its center, and thus land in and near the center was the most accessible. Good accessibility led to high demand, and high demand created high land costs. Only through the intensive use of this land could returns exceed costs. The intensity with which residential land was used produced high central residential density (Alonso, 1960).

Today, although cities in high-scale societies no longer have transportation networks that converge at a single center, land prices still decline with increasing distance. Moreover, the average size of land parcels consumed increases with distance, thereby creating lower peripheral density. The suburbanization process that is so characteristic of cities in high-scale societies therefore is an apparently normal process whereby an urban population expands into the surrounding low-density fringe.

Population A third factor is related to the social stratification system in high-scale societies. Only the wealthy have true locational freedom because only they can absorb the costs of transportation and land at any point within a city. In the older and larger cities of high-scale societies the concentration of industry and commerce in the inner city makes the central city less attractive than the fringe for residences. Thus, the middle- and upperclasses have been able to preempt the more attractive fringe locations because of these groups' financial resources (see Chapter 7).

Organization A fourth factor that cannot be overlooked is the role of government in encouraging fringe development. The federal government in the United States, through a series of direct and indirect subsidies, has made fringe development comparatively cheap in relation to other development patterns. Numerous examples of these subsidies can be cited. The Federal Housing Authority and Veterans Administration have made low-downpayment and low-cost home mortgages available to millions of Americans, opening the single-family housing market to families heretofore excluded. Massive federal categorical grants to suburban communities for sewer and water systems have provided additional incentive for fringe development. Finally, the federal government's interstate highway system has made these areas accessible.

Therefore, for cities in high-scale societies, the interaction of population, organizational, environmental, and technological factors has led to a density-distance relationship in which deconcentration continues to the limits imposed by the level of transportation technology. Transportation technology determines the limits to which a city can expand spatially; population, organizational, and environment factors determine whether these limits are reached.

Low-Scale Societies

Population growth in cities in low-scale societies is accommodated by increasing congestion and a constant degree of concentration. This pattern is represented in Figure 11.7. As a city grows, the slope of the curve remains the same, even though the total area of the settlement expands. Thus, the city remains compact and population growth leads to increasing congestion.

Factors responsible for the pattern Two factors largely explain the pattern for low-scale societies. One is the low level of transportation technology in the cities of these societies. Automobile ownership is prohibitively expensive for the vast majority of the people, and mass transportation is often inadequate. Because most residents of a city must rely on the pedestrian mode of transportation, a central location is most desirable.

The second factor is the location of the upperclass. Typically the upperclass is centralized near a city's central plaza, the site of government and religious buildings, while the poor live on the city's fringe (Sjoberg, 1960; Mehta, 1968; Schwirian and Rico, 1971; Vaughan and Schwirian, 1978). This pattern is particularly evident in the Spanish colonial cities in Latin America, which were laid out according to a standardized plan provided by the Spanish government called the Bill of the Indies. At the center of these cities was a plaza, typically surrounded by the cathedral and government buildings. Upperclass families of Spanish birth were given land adjacent to the plaza complex. Persons of lower status—Indians, slaves,

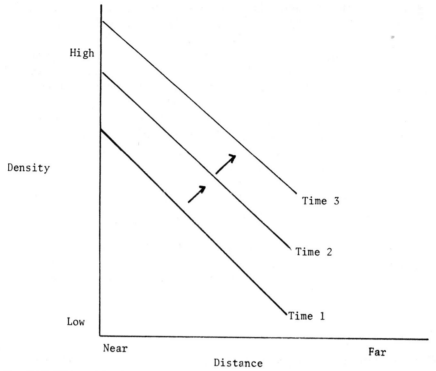

Fig. 11.7 Changes in the density-distance curve over time in a low-scale society.

and racially mixed populations—were housed in specified quarters on the land that remained. Today, squatter settlements have spread to the fringe of these cities. As a result of both the transportation factor and the class location factor, density patterns in the cities of low-scale societies are not likely to change in the foreseeable future.

A Link Between the Two Models of Urban Density Patterns

Two models of urban residential patterning have been identified. In high-scale societies, a city's population growth is accommodated by a continued deconcentration and decongestion made possible by transportation technology; because industrial and commercial development near the core makes a centralized residential location undesirable, the inner core is left to the lower socioeconomic classes. In low-scale societies, a city's population is accommodated by increasing congestion and compactness; the upperclasses are centralized and the poor are crowded into slums and squatter settlements on a city's fringe.

Though these models are presented separately, recent research suggests that they may be part of a more general model of urban growth and development. If the analysis of societal scale is correct, one would expect that as societal scale increases the density-distance pattern would shift from that of a low-scale society to that of a high-scale society (Schnore, 1965; Hawley, 1971; Schwirian and Rico, 1971; Vaughan and Schwirian, 1978).

The experiences of Kingston, Jamaica Colin Clark (1951, 1975) found just such a pattern in his studies of Kingston, Jamaica. His results clearly show that as the scale of the society increased, a shift occurred in the way in which Kingston accommodated its population growth. Before 1911, this city had the residential development pattern of a city in a low-scale society. Since that year the trend has been to decongestion and deconcentration, with the movement of high-status families to the fringe—a high-scale society pattern.

Research on the cities of Puerto Rico Vaughan and Schwirian (1978) found a similar pattern in their study of Puerto Rico. Before 1930, San Juan's density pattern closely approximated the pattern for low-scale societies. Since 1930, the pattern has been one predicted for cities in high-scale societies. In this case, however, the investigators found that both the scale of the city's encompassing society and the city's position in the common-wealth's urban hierarchy were important in predicting how the city accommodated population growth. In the Puerto Rican study, San Juan, the commonwealth's primate city, had a high-scale density pattern, whereas the smaller cities of Ponce and Mayaguez continued the more traditional patterns.

The Reason for Shifting Density-Distance Patterns

According to Hawley (1971) the shift from one pattern to another as the development process proceeds is the result of the increasing participation of a society in the world community. "Participation requires adoption of new technologies, a reorientation toward resources, a realignment and reconstruction of social and economic institutions that enable the society to interact with institutions in other societies, and a major redistribution of the country's population: the effects of such massive adjustments become reflected in all aspects of life including the way urban growth is absorbed by the settlement pattern" (Vaughan and Schwirian, 1978, pp. 7–8).

Why Study Urban Density Patterns?

One question remains: Why study urban density patterns? The major reason is that they more clearly describe the dynamic nature of all urban places. Although a number of descriptive and analytical theories have been reviewed in this text—the theory of rents, central place theory, the descriptive models of Burgess, Hoyt, and Harris and Ullman—these are all primarily static models. The density-distance models, in contrast, take into account the dynamic nature of metropolitan growth and describe how cities accommodate increases in population over time. Moreover, the models clearly show how transportation and communication technology, a city's economic base, and the scale of the encompassing society prescribe the nature and direction of growth. Knowledge of these basic mechanisms are critical both for sound planning purposes and for general understanding of a metropolis. For this reason, empirical models drawn from this literature have been developed for use by planning practitioners, models that permit prediction of future population shifts and an anticipation of the problems and service needs of various parts of a city.

DENSITY AND THE QUESTION OF PATHOLOGY

In the first half of this chapter, the general patterns of residential density in cities were explored. This section addresses some negative consequences of living in cities—the possible relationship between high residential density and human pathology.

In "no previous age has such a large proportion of our citizenry been so directly and so vocally concerned with environmental deterioration and the threat to the quality of life" (Hawley, 1972, p. 521). The fact that much of this concern has been directed to urban conditions is understandable because American society consists mostly of city dwellers. Moreover, many of the most difficult social problems are urban problems. In recent years some of these problems have been attributed to the crowding of people into the limited spaces available, to density. On the surface, this conclusion would appear to be correct. Anyone who has experienced "rush hour" in Manhattan would conclude that the frenzied rush of people, the crowding of 1.5 million persons onto an island of only 23 square miles, will necessarily produce tension and anxiety and some physiological or psychological effect (U.S. Bureau of the Census, 1972b, Table 6). National statistics also seem to bear out this intuitive conclusion because divorce and crime rates, as well as levels of neuroses and psychoses, are higher in urban than in nonurban places. But is there really a clear relationship between density and human pathology?

The study of density and behavior has expanded in the last ten to fifteen years, capturing the attention of a wide variety of social and natural scientists including ecologists, psychologists, sociologists, anthropologists, geographers, and biologists. In addition, practitioners such as city planners, architects, and interior designers have actively pursued this topic in striving for a more livable urban environment. The study of the relationship between density and human pathology is therefore an interdisciplinary effort. The purpose of this section of the chapter is to provide an overview of the literature in this field.

Photo 11.2
Source: © Jan Lukas from Rapho/Photo Researchers, Inc.

Definitions of Terms

Density is a complex variable in both its definition and its effects. The term is often used synonymously with the term "crowding," but the two words have different referents. *Density* in this text refers strictly to the number of people per unit of space, i.e., persons per room. Moreover, density involves two separate components—number of people in a given space and the amount of space per person. For example, consider two situations in which six square feet are available per person. In one case, 10,000 people are in a concert hall, and in the other case six people are in a jail cell. Socially and psychologically, these situations are very different, even though each may be designated as a "high-density" situation (Saegert, 1978, pp. 259–60).

Crowding, in contrast, is a psychological concept based on the experiences of an individual. In the above example, the high density of the concert hall adds to the thrill and pleasure of the performance, whereas the prison environment would undoubtedly be perceived as unpleasant. Several factors must be kept in mind about crowding. First, crowding is a personal, subjective state and not a physical state. For example, Saegert (1975) and her associates found in a study of a Manhattan train station that subjects described the station as crowded even at a low-density time when the station was almost empty. Second, crowding is normally a negative mental state—a discomfort—involving a feeling of too little space. Third, crowding often leads to behavior by an individual to relieve this discomfort. The need to "get some fresh air" is one of many behavioral manifestations of crowding (Stokols, 1972).

Pathology is a deviation from a normal state. For an individual, the term refers to a structural or functional change induced by disease, stress, or some other factor. In the study of cities such measures as mortality, rates of specific types of mental disorders, and prevalence of certain types of diseases (such as cardiovascular disease) are used to identify pathologies of a physiological or psychological nature (see Schmitt, 1963, 1966).

Social pathology, in contrast, is a more difficult term to define. Social pathology has been defined as a significant number of people who deviate from the norm(s) of society. It is estimated that over a third of all Americans have tried marijuana at one time or another. Is this activity pathological? The term "social pathology" contains both an objective and a subjective dimension. First, a significant number of people must violate a norm (objective). Second, this deviation must be defined as harmful or injurious to society (subjective). Measures commonly used include rates of juvenile delinquency, crimes of violence, number of illegitimate births, and prevalence of venereal disease (see Schmitt, 1957, 1963, 1966; Winsborough, 1965; Galle, Gove, and McPherson, 1972).

The vast majority of ecological studies in this field have explored the statistical relationship between density and some measures of human pathology. Few ecological studies, however, have included measures of crowding. Most such work has been done by psychologists in the laboratory or on a small scale in the field. Before the ecological research is examined, a brief explanation of some early theories on the relationship between density and human pathology is presented.

Early Concerns About Population Density

For nearly a century, concerned observers have concluded that high residential density negatively affects both the individual and the family. For example, the muckrakers—a group of journalists and writers in the late nineteenth and early twentieth centuries who wrote exposés on a wide variety of urban ills—publicized the deplorable conditions of slum housing. Jacob Riis (1906), in his famous book *How the Other Half Lives,* combined a journalistic writing style with vivid photography to bring this serious problem to the attention of the American public. Through his efforts and the work of such people as New York City's Lawrence Veiller, tenement reform and public housing projects became a reality. This public housing contained many families, often in highrise apartments, but there was a major attempt to provide sufficient space for families within their own apartments (Lubove, 1962). The assumption that too many people create unhealthy conditions also guided the work of town planners and legislators. Zoning ordinances designed to control land use and density levels were first introduced in New York City in the 1920s and were widely adopted by most American cities (Lubove, 1967).

Early Sociological Concerns

The notion that high population density creates poor social conditions also influenced sociologists. Durkheim (1972) concluded that large concentrations of people lead to changes in the structure and form of a society, in particular to occupational specialization and a complex division of labor.

Georg Simmel Simmel (1950) believed that a city's increasing size, density, and heterogeneity lead to the deterioration of relationships among its inhabitants. Simmel's discussion of cities might best be called the study of the urban personality type. Simmel's major interest was discovering how an individual living in a city copes with diversity. Simmel's main point was that because of the concentration of large numbers of people at high densities in cities, an individual is constantly bombarded by physical and social stimuli. These stimuli are so numerous and diverse that an individual exposed to them simply cannot respond to them all. Therefore, the urbanite must have some sort of screening device that enables her or him to respond appropriately to the most important stimuli. One major screening device is the money economy, an invention of cities. In day-to-day life, an urbanite is constantly involved in the exchange of dollars and cents. To survive in a world where the common denominator is money, an individual must respond to the world not with the heart but with the mind. To Simmel, a heightened awareness of the world, a degree of cynicism, and rationality are the most obvious personality manifestations of the urban way of life.

Simmel noted another personality change wrought by the urban setting, the blasé attitude, promoted by the intense stimulation of the metropolis and the predominance of its money economy. The incessant bombardment of incompatible stimuli upon individuals ultimately exhausts their mental energies, making it impossible for them to respond to new situations. This process, he believed, is reinforced by a money economy. In the day-to-day process of economic exchange, a person is constantly reminded of the purchasability of things. "Things" include not only material goods but also the services of people. This evaluation process influences all other aspects of life; individuals are evaluated for what they have, not for what they are. Outward signs of one's status—dress, grooming, and the like—become the basis on which a person is evaluated by others. Therefore, the essence of the blasé attitude consists of the "blunting of discrimination . . . and . . . money with all its colorlessness and indifference becomes the common denominator of all values; irreparably it hollows the core of things, their individuality, their specific value, and their incomparability" (Simmel, 1950, p. 414).

The stimulus overload, the dehumanizing aspects of a money economy, and the inability of urbanites to respond to new situations might explain, in part, some of the bizarre and often tragic personal events that occur in the largest cities. A good example is the 1964 case of Catherine Genovese who was brutally murdered in full view of thirty-eight residents of a respectable New York City neighborhood. Not one person helped her or even bothered to call the police until after she was dead. This absence of a response by bystanders might be attributed to stimulus overload that causes people to ignore communications not personally directed to them (Milgrim, 1970, p. 1462).

According to Simmel, the ability of an urban individual to absorb and process stimuli decreases as the size of the city increases. Moreover, as the size and density of a city increase, each individual is less able to comprehend and control situations and thus develops feelings of powerlessness, isolation, social withdrawal, alienation—characteristics that have been the concern of sociologists through most of this century and that are thought to be at the root of many urban problems.

Louis Wirth Simmel (1950) described what he thought to be the deterioration of social relations among inhabitants of cities brought on by the cities' size and density. Wirth (1938), a member of the Chicago School, restated Simmel's ideas in ecological terms. He argued that city growth with the concomitant increases in size, density, and heterogeneity of population leads to a substitution of secondary relationships for primary ones and a greater dependency on formal means of social control. With respect to population density, Wirth notes that as a city grows a person increasingly lives among strangers (heterogeneity) and at the same time is forced to live close to other people (density). Heterogeneity combined with increased physical proximity, according to Wirth, is a source of tension and a contributing factor to interpersonal and group conflict, e.g., a factor contributing to social disorganization.

Wirth's negative view of the city was not original. His work was deeply influenced by Simmel and other European social philosophers. Moreover, his writing was in tune with a general antiurban bias that pervaded the American culture in the nineteenth and early twentieth centuries.[6] This antiurban tradition started with Thomas Jefferson and continued through the nineteenth century in the writings of such men as Thoreau, Emerson, and Melville. In the late nineteenth century the antiurban tradition was apparent in the efforts of American city planners to provide open space in place of physical structures and environments that deconcentrate populations. The parks and parkway programs undertaken by many American cities in the nineteenth and early twentieth centuries are a product of this tradition (Hawley, 1972, p. 521–23).

Animal Studies

The early concerns of sociologists and ecologists about the relationship between density and pathology were framed in theoretical terms that had not been verified by empirical research.[7] Several decades would pass before the density-pathology relationship would undergo serious scientific scrutiny, not by social scientists but by natural scientists—biologists. Their research with animals has been uncritically and incorrectly applied to human studies.

Probably the most famous animal studies on the relationship between density and pathology were conducted by John Calhoun (1961, 1962) in the early 1960s. Calhoun found that when a population of laboratory rats was allowed to increase in a confined space, the rats developed acutely abnormal patterns of behavior that might even have led to the extinction of the population. This phenomenon has been studied by others (Southwick, 1955; Freedman, 1975) but the procedures used have been the same. A number of animals are placed in an enclosed space and given all the food and water they need, then are left alone and observed. Within this protected environment, the rat colony thrives and increases rapidly until the cage is overcrowded with animals. At some point, just as in natural environments, the colony ceases to increase in size and suddenly begins to decline. What causes this sharp population decline? It cannot be a lack of food or water, or disease, or predators, because these conditions have been carefully controlled by the researchers. It seems to follow that the decline must be caused by something in the animals themselves.

Calhoun observed that an increase in population density brought on abnormal animal behavior, behavior that caused a sharp increase in infant mortality. Under normal conditions, a male rat collects a small harem, designates a section of the cage as his territory, and mates only with his females. Males roam the cage freely but respect the territory of other males. Moreover, they do not mate with other females and seldom fight. Females, in contrast, seldom leave the nesting area and concentrate on building their nests and rearing their litters.

Once the population density of a cage exceeds a certain threshold, normal behavior begins to break down. A few dominant males continue to live a normal life and with their harems continue to raise healthy offspring, but the majority of the animals do not. Some male rats, not strong enough to secure their own harems and territories, become marauders and indiscriminantly attack females, disturbing their nests and upsetting the rearing of the young. Others become recluses and do not interact with other animals or reproduce. The largest group in the colony is composed of males and females who mill around on the floor of the enclosure, frequently fight, and indulge in promiscuous and indiscriminate sexual behavior. They normally live their lives without nesting or reproducing.

Interestingly, the decline in these populations did not occur because of a decrease in the number of pregnancies, but as a result of a marked increase in infant mortality—a rate that more than doubled under crowded conditions. A young rat needs good care for the first few weeks of life to survive. High density upsets the normal nesting behavior of females, and the nests that are built are often trampled by other animals simply because of their numbers. Although high density appears to produce increased aggressiveness, sexual promiscuity, cannibalism, withdrawal, and other types of abnormal behavior, the disturbance of normal nesting behavior seems to have the greatest effect on population decline. Researchers have uncovered physiological changes in animals that are due to high density (enlarged adrenal glands, abnormally small testes), but the breakdown of the rats' social structure and the disruption of normal mating and rearing appear to be the major factors contributing to the animals' population decline (Freedman, 1965, pp. 12–23).

The dangers of an analogy between human and animal behavior The abnormal behavior that resulted from crowding animals together in unusually large numbers was labeled a "behavioral sink" by Calhoun. Within a few years an analogy was made between the living conditions of Calhoun's caged rats and what were generally held to be the conditions of life in American inner cities. The urban equivalent of the behavioral sink is the behavior in human slums. Analogies also were drawn between Calhoun's behavioral types—dominant males, recluses, normless roaming juvenile rats—and the juvenile gangs and other groups found within inner cities.

It is both difficult and risky to generalize directly from the behavior of one animal to that of another. For example, a biologist would be unwilling to say that a dog or cat would act in the same way as a rat under the same density conditions. A biologist certainly would be unwilling to make an analogy between the behavior of a rat and that of a human. Humans are animals, but humans have a complex social structure, the ability to reason, the use of language, and most important, culture. Culture, more than anything else, separates humankind from the rest of the animal world by providing greater flexibility and adaptability. It is therefore surprising that social scientists have been so willing to draw an analogy between the findings of Calhoun and other students of animal behavior (ethologists) and the behavior of human populations (Hawley, 1972, p. 522). Animal studies, however, have contributed to the development of theories on the relationship between high density and pathology in human populations. The five most widely known theories follow.

Theories on the Density-Pathology Relationship

The theory of social overload This theory, the simplest of the five, posits that high density creates problems of interference in the operation of normal

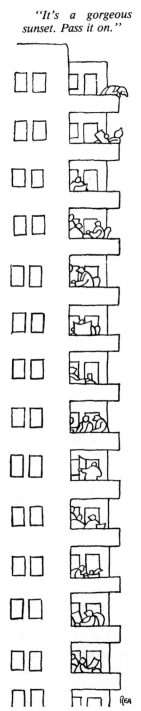

social processes. The theory argues that the greater the number of persons in a limited area, the more likely they are to interfere with each other, and the more subdivided the available resources—food, water, air, and shelter— must be. The negative effects are due to the interference in normal processes and the confusion that ensues (Altman, 1975; Saegart, 1978). This theory is supported by Calhoun's rat studies.

The theory of territoriality According to this theory, high density creates stress because human beings, like many other animals, have a territorial instinct. Conclusions on human behavior are drawn directly from the behavior of other animals. Moreover, the theory is based in large part on books written for a mass market and not for the scientific community. Examples are former playwright Robert Andrey's *Territorial Imperative* and *Beyond Aggression*, and zoologist Desmond Morris's *The Naked Ape* and *The Human Zoo*. These authors hold that the more people there are in a place, the more likely it is that any individual's area will be invaded, and thus natural reactions such as aggression will occur.

Examples of territorial behavior have been found among humans. Gerald Suttles (1968), in his participant-observation study of a Chicago slum, found that juvenile gangs had clearly delineated territories that they defended from outside encroachment by other gangs. It is very doubtful that this behavior is the result of a territorial instinct, however. An instinct is a pattern of behavior biologically fixed in a species. Instincts, such as nest building in birds, evolve in a species because they are advantageous to its survival. A territorial instinct usually serves to distribute a species more or less evenly over terrain so that scarce food and water resources are not overtaxed. Humans, in contrast, historically have worked best in groups, and humans as well as other primates show few signs of territorial instinct. The human territorial behavior that has been observed—a gang protecting its turf—is more likely an artifact of culture, the aspect of the human species that separates it from all the other animals and gives it enormous adaptability (Altman, 1975, pp. 126–45).

Theory of stimulus overload This theory states that the presence of many members of a species at high density in crowded conditions produces a stimulus overload and has negative physiological and psychological consequences. The theory is based largely on animal studies.

Physiological studies of rats and mice have shown that overstimulating animals (by keeping them at high density) causes adrenal glands to enlarge, physical size to diminish, miscarriages to increase, and behavioral abnormalities to occur. Studies of humans suggest that overcrowding raises levels of anxiety and causes irritability, weariness, and withdrawal (Michelson, 1970; Mitchell, 1971).

The Milgram article explores in greater detail one of the five theories of density and human pathology—the theory of stimulus overload. Milgram does not question the theory but rather looks at the costs of being insensitive to many things that humans normally find of interest.

THE EXPERIENCE OF LIVING IN CITIES

By S. Milgram

When I first came to New York it seemed like a nightmare. As soon as I got off the train at Grand Central I was caught up in pushing, shoving crowds on 42nd Street. Sometimes people bumped into me without apology; what really frightened me was to see two people literally engaged in combat for possession of a cab. Why were they so rushed? Even drunks on the street were bypassed without a glance. People didn't seem to care about each other at all.

This statement represents a common reaction to a great city, but it does not tell the whole story. Obviously cities have great appeal because of their variety, eventfulness, possibility of choice, and the stimulation of an intense atmosphere that many individuals find a desirable background to their lives. Where face-to-face contacts are important, the city offers unparalleled possibilities. It has been calculated by the Regional Plan Association that in Nassau County, a suburb of New York City, an individual can meet 11,000 others within a ten-minute radius of his office by foot or car. In Newark, a moderate-sized city, he can meet more than 20,000 persons within this radius. But in midtown Manhattan he can meet fully 220,000. So there is an order-of-magnitude increment in the communication possibilities offered by a great city. That is one of the bases of its appeal and, indeed, of its functional necessity. The city provides options that no other social arrangement permits. But there is a negative side also, as we shall see.

Granted that cities are indispensable in complex society, we may still ask what contribution psychology can make to understanding the experience of living in them. What theories are relevant? How can we extend our knowledge of the psychological aspects of life in cities through empirical inquiry? If empirical inquiry is possible, along what lines should it proceed? In short, where do we start in constructing urban theory and in laying out lines of research?

Observation is the indispensable starting point. Any observer in the streets of midtown Manhattan will see (1) large numbers of people, (2) a high population density, and (3) heterogeneity of population. These three factors need to be at the root of any sociopsychological theory of city life, for they condition all aspects of our experience in the metropolis. Louis Wirth (1938), if not the first to point to these factors, is nonetheless the sociologist who relied most heavily on them in his analysis of the city.[1] Yet, for a psychologist, there is something unsatisfactory about Wirth's theoretical variables. Numbers, density, and heterogeneity are demographic facts, but they are not yet psychological facts. They are external to the individual. Psychology needs an idea that links the individual's *experience* to the demographic circumstances of urban life.

One link is provided by the concept of overload. This term, drawn from systems analysis, refers to a system's inability to process inputs from the environment because there are too many inputs for the system to cope with, or because successive inputs come so fast that input A cannot be processed when input B is presented. When overload is present, adaptations occur. The system must set priorities and make choices. A may be processed first while B is kept in abeyance, or one input may be sacrificed altogether. City life, as we experience it, constitutes a continuous set of encounters with overload, and of resultant adaptations. Overload characteristically deforms daily life on several levels, impinging on role performance, the evolution of social norms, cognitive functioning, and the use of facilities.

The concept has been implicit in several theories of urban experience. In 1903 George Simmel (1950) pointed out that, since urban dwellers come into contact with vast numbers of people each day, they conserve psychic energy by becoming acquainted with a far smaller proportion of people than their rural counterparts do, and by maintaining more superficial relationships even with these acquaintances. Wirth (1938) points specifically to "the superficiality, the anonymity, and the transitory character of urban social relations."

One adaptive response to overload, therefore, is the allocation of less time to each input. A second adaptive mechanism is disregard of low-priority inputs. Principles of selectivity are formulated such that investment of time and energy are reserved for carefully defined inputs (the urbanite disregards the drunk sick on the street as he purposefully navigates through the crowd). Third, boundaries are redrawn in certain social transactions so that the overloaded system can shift the burden to the other party in the exchange; thus, harried New York bus drivers once made change for customers, but now this responsibility has been shifted to the client, who must have the exact fare ready. Fourth, reception is blocked off prior to entrance into a system; city dwellers increasingly use unlisted telephone numbers to prevent individuals from calling them, and a small but growing number resort to keeping the telephone off the hook to prevent incoming calls. More subtly, a city dweller blocks inputs by assuming an unfriendly countenance, which discourages others from initiating contact. Additionally, social screening devices are interposed between the individual and environmental inputs (in a town of 5000 anyone can drop in to chat with the mayor, but in the metropolis organizational screening devices deflect inputs to other destinations). Fifth, the intensity of inputs is diminished by filtering devices, so that only weak and relatively superficial forms of involvement with others are allowed. Sixth, specialized institutions are created to absorb inputs that would otherwise swamp the individual (welfare departments handle the financial needs of a million individuals in New York City, who would otherwise create an army of mendicants continuously importuning the pedestrian). The interposition of institutions between the individual and the social world, a characteristic of all modern society, and most notably of the large metropolis, has its negative side. It deprives the individual of a sense of direct contact and spontaneous integration in the life around him. It simultaneously protects and estranges the individual from his social environment.

Many of these adaptive mechanisms apply not only to individuals but to institutional systems as well, as Meier (1962) has so brilliantly shown in connection with the library and the stock exchange.

In sum, the observed behavior of the urbanite in a wide range of situations appears to be determined largely by a variety of adaptations to overload. I now deal with several specific consequences of responses to overload, which make for differences in the tone of city and town.

SOCIAL RESPONSIBILITY

The principal point of interest for a social psychology of the city is that moral and social involvement with individuals is necessarily restricted. This is a direct and necessary function of excess of input over capacity to process. Such restriction of involvement runs a broad spectrum from refusal to become involved in the needs of another person, even when the person desperately needs assistance, through refusal to do favors, to the simple withdrawal of courtesies (such as offering a lady a seat, or saying "sorry" when a pedestrian collision occurs). In any transaction more and more details need to be dropped as the total number of units to be processed increases and assaults an instrument of limited processing capacity.

The ultimate adaptation to an overloaded social environment is to totally disregard the needs, interests, and demands of those whom one does not define as relevant to the satisfaction of personal needs, and to develop highly efficient perceptual means of determining whether an individual falls into the category of friend or stranger. The disparity in the treatment of friends and strangers ought to be greater in cities than in towns; the time allotment and willingness to become involved with those who have no personal claim on one's time is likely to be less in cities than in towns.

Bystander Intervention in Crises

The most striking deficiencies in social responsibility in cities occur in crisis situations, such as the Genovese murder in Queens. In 1964, Catherine Genovese, coming home from a night job in the early hours of an April morning, was stabbed repeatedly, over an extended period of time. Thirty-eight residents of a respectable New York City neighborhood admit to having witnessed at least a part of the attack, but none went to her aid or called the police until after she was dead. Milgram and Hollander, writing in *The Nation* (1964), analyzed the event in these terms:

> Urban friendships and associations are not primarily formed on the basis of physical proximity. A person with numerous close friends in different parts of the city may not know the occupant of an adjacent apartment. This does not mean that a city dweller has fewer friends than does a villager, or knows fewer persons who will come to his aid; however, it does mean that his allies are not constantly at hand. Miss Genovese required immediate aid from those physically present. There is no evidence that the city had deprived Miss Genovese of human associations, but the friends who might have rushed to her side were miles from the scene of her tragedy.
>
> Further, it is known that her cries for help were not directed to a specific person; they were general. But only individuals can act, and as the cries were not specifically directed, no particular person felt a special responsibility. The crime and the failure of community response seem absurd to us. At the time, it may well have seemed equally absurd to the Kew Gardens residents that not one of the neighbors would have called the police. A collective paralysis may have developed from the belief of each of the witnesses that someone else must surely have taken that obvious step.

Latané and Darley (1969) have reported laboratory approaches to the study of bystander intervention and have established experimentally the following principle: the larger the number of bystanders, the less the likelihood that any one of them will intervene in an emergency. Gaertner and Bickman of The City University of New York have extended the bystander studies to an examination of help across ethnic lines. Blacks and whites, with clearly identifiable accents, called strangers (through what the caller represented as an error in telephone dialing), gave them a plausible story of being stranded on an outlying highway without more dimes, and asked the stranger to call a garage. The experimenters found that the white callers had a significantly better chance of obtaining assistance than the black callers. This suggests that ethnic allegiance may well be another means of coping with overload: the city dweller can reduce excessive demands and screen out urban heterogeneity by responding along ethnic lines; overload is made more manageable by limiting the "span of sympathy."

In any quantitative characterization of the social texture of city life, a necessary first step is the application of such experimental methods as these to field situations in large cities and small towns. Theorists argue that the indifference shown in the Genovese case would not be found in a small town, but in the absence of solid experimental evidence the question remains an open one.

More than just callousness prevents bystanders from participating in altercations between people. A rule of urban life is respect for other people's emotional and social privacy, perhaps because physical privacy is so hard to achieve. And in situations for which the standards are heterogeneous, it is much harder to know whether taking an active role is unwarranted meddling or an appropriate response to a critical situation. If a husband and wife are quarreling in public, at what point should a bystander step in? On the one hand, the heterogeneity of the city produces substantially greater tolerance about behavior, dress, and codes of ethics than is generally found in the small town, but this diversity also encourages people to withhold aid for fear of antagonizing the participants or crossing an inappropriate and difficult-to-define line.

Moreover, the frequency of demands present in the city gives rise to norms of noninvolvement. There are practical limitations to the Samaritan impulse in a major city. If a citizen attended to every needy person, if he were sensitive to and acted on every altruistic impulse that was evoked in the city, he could scarcely keep his own affairs in order.

Willingness to Trust and Assist Strangers

We now move away from crisis situations to less urgent examples of social responsibility. For it is not only in situations of dramatic need but in the ordinary, everyday willingness to lend a hand that the city dweller is said to be deficient relative to his small-town cousin. The comparative method must be used in any empirical examination of this question. A commonplace social situation is staged in an urban setting and in a small town—a situation to which a subject can respond by either extending help or withholding it. The responses in town and city are compared.

One factor in the purported unwillingness of urbanites to be helpful to strangers may well be their heightened sense of physical (and emotional) vulnerability—a feeling that is supported by urban crime statistics. A key test for distinguishing between city and town behavior, therefore, is determining how city dwellers compare with town dwellers in offering aid that increases their personal vulnerability and requires some trust of strangers. Altman, Levine, Nadien, and Villena of The City University of New York devised a study to compare the behaviors of city and town dwellers in this respect. The criterion used in this study was the willingness of householders to allow strangers to enter their home to use the telephone. The student investigators individually rang doorbells, explained that they had misplaced the address of a friend nearby, and asked to use the phone. The investigators (two males and two females) made 100 requests for entry into homes in the city and 60 requests in the small towns. The results for middle-income housing developments in Manhattan were compared with data for several small towns (Stony Point, Spring Valley, Ramapo, Nyack, New City, and West Clarkstown) in Rockland County, outside of New York City. As Table 1 shows, in all cases there was a sharp increase in the proportion of entries achieved by an experimenter when he moved from the city to a small town. In the most extreme case the experimenter was five times as likely to gain admission to homes in a small town as to homes in Manhattan. Although the female experimenters had notably greater success both in cities and in towns than the male experimenters had, each of the four students did at least twice as well in towns as in cities. This suggests

Table 1
Percentage of entries achieved by investigators for city and town dwellings (see text)

| | Entries achieved (%) | |
Experimenter	City*	Small town†
Male		
No. 1	16	40
No. 2	12	60
Female		
No. 3	40	87
No. 4	40	100

* Number of requests for entry, 100.
† Number of requests for entry, 60.

that the city-town distinction overrides even the predictably greater fear of male strangers than of female ones.

The lower level of helpfulness by city dwellers seems due in part to recognition of the dangers of living in Manhattan, rather than to mere indifference or coldness. It is significant that 75 percent of all the city respondents received and answered messages by shouting through closed doors and by peering out through peepholes; in the towns, by contrast, about 75 percent of the respondents opened the door.

Supporting the experimenters' quantitative results was their general observation that the town dwellers were noticeably more friendly and less suspicious than the city dwellers. In seeking to explain the reasons for the greater sense of psychological vulnerability city dwellers feel, above and beyond the differences in crime statistics, Villena points out that, if a crime is committed in a village, a resident of a neighboring village may not perceive the crime as personally relevant, though the geographic distance may be small, whereas a criminal act committed anywhere in the city, though miles from the city-dweller's home is still verbally located within the city; thus, Villena says, "the inhabitant of the city possesses a larger vulnerable space."

Civilities

Even at the most superficial level of involvement—the exercise of everyday civilities—urbanites are reputedly deficient. People bump into each other and often do not apologize. They knock over another person's packages and, as often as not, proceed on their way with a grumpy exclamation instead of an offer of assistance. Such behavior, which many visitors to great cities find distasteful, is less common, we are told, in smaller communities, where traditional courtesies are more likely to be observed.

In some instances it is not simply that, in the city, traditional courtesies are violated; rather, the cities develop new norms of noninvolvement. These are so well defined and so deeply a part of city life that *they* constitute the norms people are reluctant to violate. Men are actually embarrassed to give up a seat on the subway to an old woman; they mumble, "I was getting off anyway," instead of making the gesture in a straightforward and gracious way. These norms develop because everyone realizes that, in situations of high population density, people cannot implicate themselves in each others' affairs, for to do so would create conditions of continual distraction which would frustrate purposeful action.

In discussing the effects of overload I do not imply that at every instant the city dweller is bombarded with an unmanageable number of inputs, and that his responses are determined by the excess of input at any given instant. Rather, adaptation occurs in the form of gradual evolution of norms of behavior. Norms are evolved in response to frequent discrete experiences of overload; they persist and become generalized modes of responding.

Overload on Cognitive Capacities: Anonymity

That we respond differently toward those whom we know and those who are strangers to us is a truism. An eager patron aggressively cuts in front of someone in a long movie line to save time only to confront a friend; he then behaves sheepishly. A man is involved in an automobile accident caused by another driver, emerges from his car shouting in rage, then moderates his behavior on discovering a friend driving the other car. The city dweller, when walking through the midtown streets, is in a state of continual anonymity vis-à-vis the other pedestrians.

Anonymity is part of a continuous spectrum ranging from total anonymity to full acquaintance, and it may well be that measurement of the precise degrees of anonymity in cities and towns would help to explain important distinctions between the quality of life in each. Conditions of full acquaintance, for example, offer security and familiarity, but they may also be stifling, because the individual is caught in a web of established relationships. Conditions of complete anonymity, by contrast, provide freedom from routinized social ties, but they may also create feelings of alienation and detachment.

CONCLUSION

I have tried to indicate some organizing theory that starts with the basic facts of city life: large numbers, density, and heterogeneity. These are external to the individual. He experiences these factors as overloads at the level of roles, norms, cognitive functions, and facilities. These overloads lead to adaptive mechanisms which create the distinctive tone and behaviors of city life. These notions, of course, need to be examined by objective comparative studies of cities and towns.

NOTE: 1. Wirth's ideas have come under heavy criticism by contemporary city planners, who point out that the city is broken down into neighborhoods, which fulfill many of the functions of small towns. See, for example, H. J. Gans, *People and Plans: Essays on Urban Problems and Solutions* (Basic Books, New York, 1968); J. Jacobs, *The Death and Life of Great*

American Cities (Random House, New York, 1961); G. D. Suttles, *The Social Order of the Slum* (Univ. of Chicago Press, Chicago, 1968). ·

Source: Excerpted and reprinted by permission from S. Milgram, "The experience of living in cities." *Science*, 13 March 1970, 167, 1461–64, 1468. Copyright 1970 by the American Association for the Advancement of Science.

Theory of personal space This theory emerges from a book written by an anthropologist, Edward Hall (1966), entitled *The Hidden Dimension*. Hall pointed out the fact that people in all cultures make very active use of space in communicating with one another and that different cultures have different norms of space utilization. From personal experiences, one is aware that each person maintains a more or less constant distance from others. Hall's work suggests that each individual is surrounded by personal "space bubbles," the invasion of which produces anxiety and distress. (In your next conversation with a friend, try moving six inches closer to the other person than you normally would and observe the results.) This theory argues that high density generates stress because it leads to violations of the personal space that surrounds each human being (Altman, 1975, pp. 52–102).

Theory of spatial constraint The most obvious consequence of limited space and high density is the reduction of freedom of physical movement. Although this restriction need not lead to stimulus or social overload, it can severely limit the behavior patterns that can be selected from an individual's repertoire of roles. In other words, certain space standards are adopted by all cultures that permit individuals to carry out specific aspects of their lives. When these space standards are violated by high density, when the ability to carry out certain behavior is thwarted, stress occurs (Saegert, 1978).

One example is reported by Michelson (1970). He notes that married couples with children living in highrise apartments find it difficult to carry out the lifestyle of familism. Mothers find it exceedingly difficult to supervise the play of small children and the husbands often find it difficult to carry out their traditional role. That is, without grass to mow, repairs to make, or room for a workshop to carry out hobbies, the husband becomes a "star boarder" without a useful function in the home. Constraints on behavior created by limited space cause stress and may lead to pathology.

The five theories are not mutually exclusive and in fact several complement each other. The two biologically based theories—territoriality and stimulus overload—imply that high density necessarily leads to pathology. The other three theories are more sociological and suggest that the manipulation of the physical and social environment may reduce the negative aspects of high density. The description of these theories provides a basis for understanding ecological research studies of the density-pathology relationship.

Ecological Studies of the Relationship between Density and Human Pathology

Early Ecological Studies

The earliest work on the density-pathology relationship was done by sociologists who, beginning in the 1920s, tried to identify the social consequences of population density with such indicators of social pathology as mental health, disease, crime, and various forms of social disorganization. For example, Schmid (1933) found high population densities and high crime rates in ghettos and central-city areas of Minneapolis and Seattle and lower rates in the surrounding suburbs. In Honolulu, Schmitt (1957, 1966) found a high correlation between population density and juvenile and adult crime. Farris and Dunham (1939) reported similar relationships between mental illness and density. Many other studies have confirmed these types of relationships in other cities.

Weaknesses in the Early Research

Major weaknesses in the early studies detracted from the validity of the results. First and most important, the density measures were contaminated by the variable of social class. For example, ghettos and slums are normally of high density but they are also inhabited by people of low socioeconomic status. Is it the social status of the inhabitants or the density at which they live that influences the levels of social pathology? There is no way to tell from the early studies. Second, the variable of density was used in an uncritical manner. Density measures used in the early studies included persons per acre or census tract and gave little indication of the number of people per dwelling or room.

Ecological Research Since 1960

In the 1960s, the methodological strategies of ecological studies shifted in several ways. First, population density was viewed more critically; the density measures did make sense when applied to interpersonal relationships (i.e., number of persons per room, number of rooms per dwelling unit). More important, the researchers specifically controlled the confounding effects of race, ethnicity, and social status when examining the line between population density and social pathology.

An example A classic example of this type of study was conducted by Galle, Gove, and McPherson (1972) in Chicago. Chicago is divided into census tracts and for each tract information is available on the number of residents, the number of houses, the number of apartments in each apartment house, and the number of acres covered by the tract. Also available from city, police, and hospital records is information on births, deaths, crimes, and hospital admissions. Using this information, Galle and his colleagues devised indices of population density and pathology. The investigators developed five measures of density—persons per room, rooms per housing unit, housing units per structure, and structures per acre—and then correlated these measures with five standardized rates of social pathology—standard mortality ratio, general fertility rate, public assistance rate, juvenile delinquency rate, and admissions to mental hospitals. The effects of ethnicity and social class were statistically controlled. The highest correlations were between people per room and the four measures of social pathology. Thus, the density measures that relate most closely to the social theories discussed previously (social overload, stimulus overload, spatial constraint) are the most important. These results must be interpreted with caution, because in the above study when the effects of ethnicity and social class were removed, the statistical relationships were found to be very weak. Moreover, other investigators have been unable to find statistical relationships between density and a variety of measures of human pathology, including rates of infant mortality, crime rates, rates of public assistance, deviant sexuality, and psychological disorders (Winsborough, 1965, Mitchell, 1971, Freedman, 1975).

Weaknesses in All Ecological Research

Several explanations can be given for the negative results of ecological studies. First, there may be no negative consequences of high residential density. Freedman (1975) and others argue this point convincingly. Second, the negative findings of many of the ecological studies may be due to built-in weaknesses in this type of research. Each of the theories on crowding is framed in individual terms. They are all based on interpersonal relationships. But the data employed in these studies are aggregated or group data—the unit of analysis is the census tract. Thus, the relationship being examined is between an area's density and the area's indices of pathology, not between individuals and pathology. Therefore, ecological correlation can inflate or suppress relationships among variables, making their interpretation chancy at best (Robinson, 1950). More important, theories on the density-pathology relationship suggest an interaction among psychological, social, and physical variables. Ecological correlations, because of the restricted data available, do not permit one to consider the effects of density independently from other related factors. In addition, correlation studies do not enable one to specify the exact causes of human pathology and may not adequately reflect the relationship between density and pathology. Therefore any effort to determine a statistical relationship between indices of density and pathology must proceed with caution. Moreover, the negative effects of crowding in all likelihood result from an interpersonal process, a process that is difficult to measure with aggregate data. Alternative research strategies were needed to overcome these weaknesses.

Recent Research

Gove, Hughes, and Galle (1979) introduced two innovations that specifically addressed the major objections to the previous ecological research. First, because of the strong relationship between the social structure and crowding, the researchers selected 80 of Chicago's more than 1,000 census tracts in such a way as to minimize the confounding influence of class, race, and ethnicity. Second, the researchers entered each tract and scientifically selected a sample of residents for interviews. In other words, they measured the personal experiences of individuals while controlling socioeconomic status and race with ecological variables. Using this sample, the investigators found that both density measured by the ecological variable of persons per room and a measure of crowding indicated by the personal experiences of the subjects in their interviews were strongly related to poor mental health, poor social relationships in the home, and poor child care and were less strongly but significantly related to poor physical health and poor social relationships outside the home. More important, these research findings clearly support the theories of social overload and spatial constraint.

The results of this study, combined with others, have several important policy implications. First, the negative effects of high density and crowding appear to be the result of social processes rather than the biological character of the human species. Second, the effects of density appear to be mediated by culture. Schmitt (1963), for example, found that the Chinese in Hong Kong live in residential areas where the density is more than four times that of the most densely populated census tracts in American cities— more than 2,000 persons per acre of ground space! Yet Hong Kong has very low levels of most measures of social pathology. Death and disease rates, except for tuberculosis, are relatively low. Juvenile delinquency and adult crime are likewise lower than in the United States. Cases of murder and manslaughter in Hong Kong occur at about one-sixth the rate in the United States, and serious crimes are committed at less than half the American rate (Schmitt, 1963, pp. 215–16). These findings suggest that through increased knowledge of urban population dynamics and the imaginative manipulation of the urban environment, the negative effects of high population density can be reduced.

SUMMARY

As cities grow, they must reorganize their residential patterns accordingly. Regardless of the scale of the encompassing society, all cities show a negative exponential distance-density residential pattern. The nature of the distance-density curve, however, is closely tied to both the scale of the encompassing society and the location of a city in the nation's urban hierarchy. In this century most high-scale societies have adopted to population growth through the processes of deconcentration and decongestion. Overall residential density levels have dropped as increasing numbers of families have moved to fringe areas. Cities in low-scale societies, in contrast, because of a poorly developed transportation system and a rigid class structure, have traditionally remained compact settlements accommodating growth through a piling-up process—congestion. In each case, a unique combination of factors (analyzed through the POET framework) proves insights into the density-distance patterns. Recent research suggests that as the scale of a society changes, density patterns may change from the traditional to a more developed societal form. This possible developmental sequence may provide researchers additional insight into the complicated process called economic development.

The second half of this chapter explores the relationship between density and human pathology. Density is a complex variable in both its definition and its effects. The term "density" in this text refers strictly to the number of persons per unit of space, and it differs from the term "crowding" that is the personal experience of high density. Pathology refers to a deviation from a normal state. Measures of pathology commonly used in ecological research include rates of mortality and morbidity as well as indices of crime, illegitimate births, and the prevalence of venereal disease.

In the United States concern about the effects of high density has been expressed since the nineteenth century, but animal studies done in the early 1960s generated the present interest in the topic. Calhoun (1961, 1962) and others found in their studies of rats and other mammals that high population density leads to abnormal behavioral and physiological responses that ultimately lead to dramatic population declines. Though it is risky to generalize from animal behavior to human behavior, animal studies have suggested some fruitful lines of research for social scientists.

Specifically, several theories on the density-pathology relationship have been developed. Three are based on social-psychological factors—social overload, personal space, and spatial constraint. Two are biologically based—territoriality and stimulus overload. Which theory is correct? Ecological research done in the 1960s and early 1970s showed only a weak relationship between density and human pathology. These findings, however, could be attributed to weaknesses in ecological types of research. Recent works by Gove and his colleagues (1979) in which statistical controls were applied for social class, race, and ethnicity, have shown that density and crowding may be related to certain types of pathology. Moreover, this research supports the social rather than the biological theories on crowding.

In general the effects of high density appear to be moderate and those that do occur appear to be the result of social processes mediated by culture. Consequently, the effects of density may be controllable through architectural and urban planning innovations.

NOTES

1. For an excellent brief overview of population density theory see J. W. Arnold, W. A. Schwab, and M. P. Schwirian, "Spatial and Temporal Aspects of the Density-Distance Relationship," *Sociological Focus* 10 (1977): 117–32.
2. Clark (1951) suggested that the relationship is described by the negative exponential equation:

$$D_x = D_o{}^{e-bx}$$

where:

D_x = population density at distance x from a city's center
D_o = population density at the center of the city
e = base of the Napierian or natural logarithm 2.71823
x = distance from the city's center

3. The curve in Figure 11.1 represents the curve that results from plotting the equation in Note 2. This curve can be transposed into a linear form through the logarithmic transformation of the equation in Note 2 to $\ln D_x = \ln D_o - bx$
4. The major theoretical framework for these studies is presented in B. J. L. Berry, J. W. Simmons, and R. J. Tennant, "Urban Population Densities: Structure and Change," *Geographic Review* 53 (1963): 389–405.
5. This analysis is based in part on Chapter 2 of the author's dissertation, *A Test of the Neighborhood Life-Cycle Model of Hoover and Vernon*, The Ohio State University, 1976.
6. Morton and Lucia White explore the antiurban attitudes in American social history in "The American Intellectual versus the American City," *Daedalus* (1961): 166–79.
7. Several studies carried out by Chicago ecologists indirectly dealt with the density-pathology relationship, i.e., R. E. Faris and H. W. Dunham, *Mental Disorders in Urban Areas* (Chicago: The University of Chicago Press, 1939). This research, although of an empirical nature, did not directly address the density-pathology relationship.

CHAPTER TWELVE

The Structure and Role of Government in the Metropolis

Statement of Objectives

1. The student should become aware of the fact that cities are products of a higher governmental authority.

2. The student should identify the major factors responsible for the fragmentation of municipal government. The negative aspects of this fragmentation should also be identified.

3. The student should become aware of the changing relationship between federal and local governments.

4. Increasingly, central-city governments have found it difficult to meet their financial responsibilities. Identify the major factors responsible for this fiscal crisis.

5. Students should become aware of the role of big business in the fiscal problems of cities.

6. An ecological perspective is used to analyze the reasons for and responses to fragmented local government. The student should carefully read this section.

7. The student should weigh the merits of the three policy alternatives presented in the text.

In the past decade a series of critical and interrelated problems have afflicted many of America's major cities. Among them are physical blight of the inner cities; a shortage of safe, decent housing; an inadequate and poorly conceived transportation network; an increasingly troubled educational system; and an unacceptable level of violent personal and property crime. Because such problems are public in their impact, their solution depends largely on government at the federal, state, or local level. Since World War II, however, the increasing scale of American society has brought about

473

a dramatic metamorphosis of cities—changes in their structure and scale that make them difficult to manage. Moreover, solutions to the cities' problems require enormous financial investments in facilities and services that may greatly exceed the metropolis's ability to provide. The recent situations in New York City and Cleveland, Ohio are notable examples of problems that surpass a city's financial and organizational ability to solve them.

The purpose of this final chapter is to examine the role of government in addressing the problems of cities. First, the past and present structure of city government and its position in the nation's federal system are explained. Second, the changing relationships between and within the levels of government are explored and the increasingly important role of the federal government in urban affairs is surveyed.

Third, the relationship between the structure of metropolitan government and its fiscal affairs is examined with special emphasis on the problems of taxation, spillover of services, and the fragmentation of local government. The role of big business in the fiscal problems of cities is also discussed.

Fourth, ecological theories are employed to critically analyze present metropolitan government structure and recent research on the organiza-

Photo 12.1 The modern metropolis. Its size and complexity seem, at times, to overwhelm our government's ability to govern it.
Source: Bruce Davidson © 1970 Magnum Photos

tional response of cities to the fragmentation of local government is discussed.

Fifth, the policy alternatives available to the nation's urban areas are explored. Should the administration of cities be centralized in Washington and in regionalized programs or should control be returned to local governments (decentralization)? Knowledge of the internal structure of cities gained through an ecological perspective is used to evaluate the policy alternatives.

Finally, the ecological perspective is used to look at the problems that can be anticipated for urban areas in the 1980s.

THE STRUCTURE OF CITY GOVERNMENT
IN THE UNITED STATES

The Source of Local Governmental Authority

The decision of the Founding Fathers to create a federal state has had important implications for American governments, particularly in terms of the relations among the levels of government—national, state, and local. According to Webster, a federal system is "formed by a compact between political units that surrender their individual sovereignty to a central authority but retain limited residuary powers of government" (1977, p. 420). In this nation, the document setting forth the distribution of powers in the several levels of government is the United States Constitution. The Tenth Amendment states that all powers not conferred on the federal government are "reserved" to the states. Municipalities and other local governments are not mentioned explicitly in the Constitution, and therefore are assumed to be under the jurisdiction of state governments. A fundamental point that must be kept in mind about cities and other local governments is that they are products of a higher authority. They can exercise only those powers explicitly granted them by the state government. Moreover, whereas the United States Constitution has been interpreted liberally by the Supreme Court, city charters and related documents of incorporation traditionally have been interpreted very narrowly—local government's powers are clearly circumscribed. The classic formulation of the legal position of cities was stated by a famous jurist, Judge John F. Dillon, in a work first published in 1872:

> It is a general and undisputed proposition of law that a municipal corporation possesses and can exercise the following powers, and no others; First, those granted in express words; second, those necessarily or fairly implied in or incident to the power expressly granted; third, those essential to the accomplishment of the declared objects and purposes of the corporation,— not simply convenient, but indispensable. Any fair, reasonable, substantial

doubt concerning the existence of power is resolved by the courts against the corporation, and the power is denied (Dillon, 1911, Vol. 1, Sec. 237).

"Dillon's Rule" has been tested over the years and has been upheld by state courts and the United States Supreme Court. The doctrine means that cities can be chartered only by the state, which sets forth a city's form of government, rights, and powers. In legal theory, states control cities, but city governments actually exercise considerable autonomy. In fact, over the years states have granted vast powers to cities. One type of charter known as a "home rule charter" is drafted by a city itself and then is approved by the state legislature. These charters grant the municipal corporation a high degree of independence in making charter changes and revisions. Because state governments seldom take punitive action against cities, the state is supreme in theory but in reality cities govern themselves (Stedman, 1972, pp. 41–45).

The United States System of Local Government

Counties and municipalities Since the inception of the federal system more than 200 years ago, local government in the United States has rapidly expanded in terms of the number, size, and scope of governmental units. The expansion is directly attributable to the problems associated with rapid urban growth and to America's conception of the kinds of functions that local governments should perform (Bromley, 1977, p. 470).

Although there are some regional variations, originally the basic forms of local government in this nation were counties and municipalities.[1] Like all forms of government, they came into existence to perform basic functions. Because most states in the United States are too large geographically to carry out services on a statewide basis, states subdivided themselves into conveniently sized administrative units—counties. Counties carry out numerous services to local populations including court services, the registration of vital events (birth, deaths, and marriages), the recording of transfers of property, the assessment and collection of taxes, the supervision of state and county elections, the maintenance of county roads and highways, as well as the preservation of public safety through the sheriff and county health and social service agencies. Similarly, municipalities came into existence to supply local services but to more densely populated places. Though counties together serve an entire state population, municipalities primarily serve residents in urban areas that include only a small portion of the state. In most states the boundaries of these two basic local governments overlap, although each normally provides a different set of services to the population (Stedman, 1972, pp. 46–58).

Special districts The explosive growth of the nation's urban places in the nineteenth and twentieth centuries literally overwhelmed local governments. For example, Chicago, which had a population of only 30,000 in 1850, had grown to more than 300,000 by 1870 and a million by 1890. In the next forty years this city was to absorb more than a half-million persons per decade, and the service resources of the city were strained to the limit (Bromley, 1977, p. 471). Chicago is not an isolated example. Many American cities had similar rates of growth. It was imperative that these communities find means to preserve the public safety and maintain social control; improve transportation and communication; assimilate and acculturate vast numbers of immigrants; educate the young; and provide for the basic health, safety, and welfare of community members. In response to these problems a new form of local government was created to fill the needs not being met by counties and municipalities—the special district.

School districts, the earliest special districts, were created "because of the strong conviction that public education was of such importance to the society as to warrant its own local financing and its freedom from the politics of other local governments" (Bollens and Schmandt, 1975, p. 48). Generally school-district organization is similar to that of a municipality with a city manager–council form of government. A small elected school board appoints a superintendent who runs the school system.

Other types of special districts are water, sewer, fire, transit, park, library, and police districts. They differ considerably in size. Some are so small that they cover only a few city blocks (a city's historic preservation district, for example), whereas others are gigantic. The revenues from the Chicago Sanitary District, for instance, exceeded $65 million in 1970 and in the same year the city's transit authority had an income of more than $138 million. One of the largest special districts in United States local government is the New York Port Authority, which has jurisdiction in both New York and New Jersey and in 1970 had more than 5,000 employees and an annual revenue of about $150 million (Flinn, 1970, p. 15).

Special districts also differ in terms of organization. Some districts have elected boards that are responsible for their operations. Other districts have appointed boards whose members are selected by local government authorities to serve long, overlapping terms. In this case, local elected officials have little control over the activities of the special district and the district's board exercises great authority (Stedman, 1972, pp. 55–56).

In the twentieth century special districts proliferated to meet the needs of a rapidly expanding urban population. As populations grew in and around urban centers, in many cases it was politically more expedient to set up special districts than to reorganize local government. This trend, combined with legal technicalities in many states that made it easier for a suburb to incorporate than to be annexed to a central city, led to an increase in the number of government units at the local level.

The Fragmentation of Metropolitan Government

Trends in the number and type of local governmental units are summarized in Table 12.1. On the local level there were 79,867 governmental units at the beginning of 1977. The 25,962 special districts and 15,174 school districts accounted for a little more than half of this total. The remaining units were 3,042 counties, 18,862 municipalities, and 16,822 townships. The average number of governmental units per state was 1,598, but Illinois had 6,620 and Hawaii had only 19. States with more than 3,000 governmental units were California (3,806), Illinois (6,620), Kansas (3,725), Minnesota (3,437), Nebraska (3,485), New York (3,309), Ohio (3,285), Pennsylvania (5,246), and Texas (3,883). Together these nine states accounted for nearly half (46 percent) of all government units in the nation (U.S. Bureau of the Census, 1978, pp. 1–4). Although the present number of local governments is enormous, it is substantially smaller than the number thirty-five years ago. In 1942, there were twice as many units—155,155. The reduction is due mainly to the consolidation and reorganization of state school systems. In 1942 there were 108,579 school districts and in 1977 only 15,174. However, during the same period the number of other special districts increased threefold to 25,962 districts in 1977, and the number of counties, townships, and municipalities remained approximately the same.

Reasons for the change in the number of special districts Why did the number of local governmental units change? School districts were responding to changing transportation technology. In the past, because of transportation, a school could draw its student body only from a relatively small area; thus school districts were small in size but large in number. In recent years,

Table 12.1
The number of local governments.

Government type	1942	1952	Year 1962	1972	1977
School districts	108,579	67,355	34,678	15,781	15,174
Special districts	8,299	12,340	18,323	28,855	25,962
Municipalities, counties, and townships	38,237	37,111	38,235	38,582	38,731
Total number of governmental units	155,115	116,806	91,236	78,218	78,867
Average number of governmental units per state	3,231	2,433	1,825	1,565	1,597

Source: U.S. Bureau of the Census, *Census of Government, 1977, Government Organization.* Washington, D.C.: U.S. Government Printing Office, 1978, Tables 1–3 and pp. 1–17.

improved transportation has enabled small districts to be consolidated into larger and more efficient units. The boundaries of these units, however, generally do not coincide with those of other local governments. In municipalities, school districts normally serve not only a city but also its unincorporated fringe areas. Structuring school districts in this way minimizes the risk that they will be taken over by municipal governments.

Though the number of school districts has declined, other types of special districts have become more numerous. One reason for this increase is that special districts have filled the void left by the inaction of municipal and county governments. Special districts have the advantage of being extremely flexible units not tied to the traditional boundaries of county and municipal governments. Water and sewer districts can span two or more counties or municipalities, and special districts can be formed to supply a particular service within a city or county. In addition to its spatial flexibility, the special district has the advantage of having its own budget. Because special districts are normally service providers, they generate their operating revenue through user charges. Consequently their programs do not compete with other programs when a municipality or county draws up its annual budget.

Negative aspects of fragmentation Although the structure and flexibility of special districts are advantageous, the fragmentation associated with the proliferation of government jurisdictions may be more negative than positive in its effect.

First, the logistical difficulty of coordinating the activities of dozens of government units makes rational policy planning in an urban area almost impossible. Figure 12.1, a map of St. Louis, shows a typical "governmentally crowded" modern metropolis. Involved in the operation of this single Standard Metropolitan Statistical Area are one federal, two state, and seven county governments, 194 municipalities (dark-shaded part), plus adjoining unincorporated territory and 615 special districts—270 in Missouri and 345 in Illinois (U.S. Bureau of the Census, 1978, pp. 204–5).

A second negative effect of fragmentation is that in large cities, governmental authority is so dispersed among federal, state, county, city, and other local governments that no single entity has the power to exercise effective leadership. Frank Yorty, the former mayor of Los Angeles, complained that the mayor of that city has no authority over many important urban policy areas. The school board is independently elected, the welfare program is county-operated and state-funded, the city housing authority is an independent unit, transit system development is under state authority, and the health department is part of a county structure. In Los Angeles, as in many cities, authority is dispersed among the mayor, the council, and various independent officials, boards, and commissions that run the myriad of special districts. In addition, a rigid civil service system with stringent rules covering entrance to positions, promotion, and seniority further re-

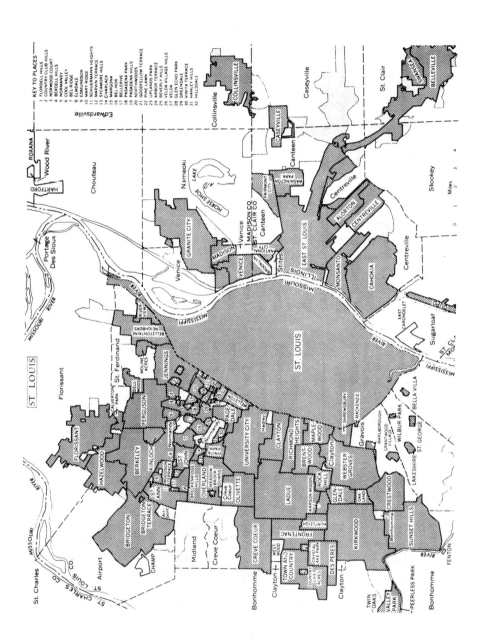

duces the policy options available to the city's leadership (Palley and Palley, 1977, pp. 62–63). The entrenched civil service combined with the increasing militancy of city police and fire fighters has led one political analyst to comment that local government bureaucracies have led many cities to "become well-run, but ungoverned" (Lowi, 1967, p. 86).

Finally, the fragmentation of government dissipates managerial and leadership ability. In any society only a limited number of people have the managerial and leadership skills necessary to run a metropolis. Fragmentation of government authority diminishes the effective application of such skills.

INTERGOVERNMENTAL RELATIONSHIPS

In general, the rapid growth of urban population in this century and the decentralization of people and activities outward from central cities to their suburban fringe have brought about a corresponding decentralization and proliferation of local governments. A major problem of many cities is simply to coordinate the activities of the numerous local government units in order to provide basic services. Interaction between governmental units on the same level (e.g., municipality-municipality or county-county) is called a *horizontal pattern* of intergovernmental relationship. Municipalities and other forms of local government also interact with higher government units (e.g., with the state or the federal government) in a *vertical pattern* of intergovernmental relationship. Since the Depression years of the 1930s, the vertical relationships between a city and higher levels of government have changed dramatically, especially the link between the national and local governments. This change is interesting because technically cities are not recognized in the United States Constitution as part of the federal system. However, cities have had a significant role in the federal system for many years, mainly as a result of the structure of state government.

State and Local Government Relations

State governments are structured by state constitutions, most of which are outmoded and inflexible. Though the federal constitution was written in such a way as to provide wide latitude in its interpretation by the United States Supreme Court, state constitutions are written rigidly and can be changed only by amendment—a time consuming and politically difficult procedure. Whereas the United States Constitution has been amended

---

Fig. 12.1 (Opposite) The St. Louis urbanized area. One example of the "governmentally-crowded" modern metropolis.

Source: Advisory Commission on Intergovernmental Relations. *Urban America and the Federal System: Commission Findings & Proposals.* Washington, D.C.: U.S. Government Printing Office, 1969, Figure 1.

twenty-six times, Arkansas's constitution, for example, has been amended fifty-seven times. In addition, the makeup of state legislatures normally does not reflect accurately the distribution of population in the state; state legislatures tend to overrepresent the interests of a rural minority. Ohio, for example, has more cities of 50,000 people or more than any state in the nation, yet rural interests continue to exert an enormous influence in Ohio's legislature. Why? A major reason is that state elections are based on the county system and urban populations are concentrated only in a few of the state's many counties. Therefore, because of state constitutions and the political realities built into a state's legislative branch, financial resources available to cities are often inadequate by design and new programs that address urban problems are difficult to implement.

Federal and Local Government Relations

The United States Senate has traditionally been responsive to urban constituencies because senators are elected on a statewide basis. In the 1960s, the court-ordered reapportionment of United States congressional districts according to the "one man one vote" principle gave urban populations proportionally greater representation in the United States House of Representatives. At the national level, therefore, government has come to recognize that the major problems facing the nation are basically urban problems, and has generated federal policies and programs to address them. The concept of "dual federalism" (the vertical intergovernmental relationship between the national and state governments) has given way to what might be called "cooperative federalism"—the sharing of public responsibility by two or more levels of government.

The expanding role of the federal government on the local level Prior to the 1930s, national-local relations were few. The Depression, however, brought about a dramatic change in the relationships between federal and local governments. Cities, confronted with heavy relief costs and high unemployment, turned to states for help. But the states, which normally operate under a legal debt limit, were hard pressed to meet their own financial obligations. Only the federal government had the flexibility to raise the money needed to cope with the cities' critical problems.

During the Depression, Congress authorized funds to be spent on the local-government level for direct relief purposes. As with many other federal programs, what began as a temporary program eventually was expanded into other areas. By the closing years of the Depression, state and local governments were receiving direct grants and loans for schools, hospitals, highways, and other projects (Stedman, 1972, pp. 58–63).

Federal-local intergovernmental relationships have expanded tremendously since the Depression. The federal government channels money to the cities through a variety of grant-in-aid programs; a grant-in-aid is defined as a payment of federal funds to a lower level of government for a specified purpose, usually with some supervision or review (Caputo, 1975, p. 116). The two main types of federal grants-in-aid are *categorical grants* and *block grants*. Categorical grants are given for a specific purpose (the provision of public housing, the construction of highways) whereas block grants are given for broadly defined purposes such as "community development." In general, federal controls tend to be much more extensive for categorical grants than for block grants. To obtain a categorical grant a local government may have to provide "matching funds" or a detailed proposal for funding. In contrast, block grants permit local governments great latitude in program development and budgeting. For example, the federal government's Community Development Block Grant Program gives cities enormous leeway in assessing needs and developing programs. Monies can be spent on housing assistance, redevelopment, sewers, sidewalks or streets, social services, and many other projects. The only restraint is that these monies must be spent in low- and moderate-income areas of the city, areas deemed appropriate by the federal government's Department of Housing and Urban Development (Caputo, 1975, pp. 116–88).

Federal-city relations were initiated during the 1930s, and New Deal Programs institutionalized the notion of federal responsibility to cities. In general, the federal government used categorical grants almost exclusively from the Depression years through the early 1970s. During the Kennedy and Johnson administrations in the 1960s these types of grant programs were rapidly expanded. For example, the number of categorical grant programs is estimated to have grown from 100 in 1960 to more than 600 by 1969, and from a total dollar amount of $7 billion to almost $30 billion (Caputo, 1975, p. 120).

THE FISCAL PROBLEMS OF METROPOLITAN GOVERNMENTS

The vertical and horizontal intergovernmental relationships between a single central city and the hundreds of surrounding governments on the local level, and the numerous agencies and departments on the state and federal levels, form a tangled web of government. Closely tied to the problems created by the fragmentation of governmental jurisdiction are the increasingly serious fiscal problems of many of the nation's largest metropolitan areas. A growing crisis of urban government financing was recognized in 1968 by the presidentially appointed National Commission on Urban Problems. According to the commission, the impending crisis was brought about by (1) an increased demand for urban services; (2) a rapid rise in overall urban expenditures, (3) mounting opposition to urban taxation, and (4) the inability of most cities to tap the economic resources of the entire metropolitan area (1968, p. 355). These financial problems can be divided into two broad categories: problems associated with the costs of providing services and problems in raising revenues to pay for city services.

"Come on, you guys! This is the place."

Source: Drawing by Ed Fisher; © 1972 The New Yorker Magazine, Inc. Reprinted by permission.

Services and the City Budget

In the discussion of "The City and Its Fringe" in Chapter 8, the ecological factors responsible for the decentralization of people and industry are examined. Changing transportation technology is identified as a major factor permitting many activities to locate in the urban fringe. Other factors such as the availability of affordable undeveloped land, a labor force, low taxes, and good schools and other institutions also are considered in the locational decisions of individuals and business and industry. In many of the largest metropolises in the Northeast, heavy industry and an aged and obsolete housing stock have contributed to the flight of middleclass residents to the suburban rings. Business and industry have followed their markets and labor forces to the urban fringe areas, leaving behind the poor and minority groups in central cities. Because suburbs are outside the taxing jurisdictions of most central cities, the metropolis's central-city government is often faced with both diminishing tax resources and increasing service requirements of low-income residents.

The Problem of High-Cost Citizens

The financial dilemmas of central cities in providing services to their "high-cost" citizens are exemplified by the situation in Essex County, New Jersey, which serves the city of Newark. In 1971, this city spent 27 percent of its local revenues on public welfare in comparison with the 9 percent of general revenue spent on welfare throughout the state. Moreover, the children of the poor require special education services that further strain the local government's limited financial resources. Newark is not an isolated example. In New York City general expenditures for education in 1971–1972 were more than $2.3 billion and public education expenditures were over $2.2 billion; in Baltimore, Maryland, public welfare expenditures exceeded $221 million and welfare exceeded $132 million during the same period; in Washington, D.C. public welfare expenditures exceeded $145 million and public education exceeded $248 million (Palley and Palley, 1977, p. 52). In the four states where education is a municipal rather than a state or county function and in the three states where public welfare is a municipal function, substantial state support has been necessary to help meet the costs of providing these services (Advisory Commission on Intergovernmental Relations, 1974).

Local Governmental Expenditures

Table 12.2 is a summary of the local expenditures of seventy-two of the nation's largest metropolitan areas and the expenditures of all local governments for the years 1972 and 1973. Note that educational and public welfare expenditures take up more than half of metropolitan and local government expenditures. Note also that services such as sewerage, fire protection, parks and recreation, and sanitation make up a higher percentage of SMSA than local government expenditures. These slight percentage differences, if multiplied into the billions of dollars spent by local governments annually, represent tens of millions of more dollars spent by large metropolitan governments on basic services. These budgetary differences hint at the financial problems created by "spillover."

Spillover

Spillover refers to municipal services that are provided directly and indirectly to suburban populations, services for which the central city is never fully reimbursed. Examples are police, fire, sanitation, and sewer services that are provided to commuters while they work in central cities. Parks, museums, and libraries are often supported through municipal budgets, though they are facilities that benefit an entire metropolis. Consequently, municipalities have a substantially higher per capita outlay for services than their suburban counterparts. In 1977, for example, the thirty-seven largest

Table 12.2
Local expenditures, 1972–1973 (percent).

Purpose	72 largest SMSAs	All local governments
Education	40.6	45.1
Local schools	(38.0)	(42.5)
Higher education	(2.6)	(2.6)
Public welfare	10.4	8.3
Health and hospitals	6.6	6.4
Police protection	5.7	5.0
Highways	4.4	5.7
Interest on general debt	4.1	3.7
Sewerage	3.4	3.2
Fire protection	2.7	2.4
Parks and recreation	2.7	2.3
Sanitation	1.7	1.5
Financial administration	1.2	1.3
Other	16.5	15.1
Total	100.0	100.0

Source: U.S. Bureau of the Census, *Finances in Selected Metropolitan Areas and Large Counties, 1972–1973.* Washington, D.C.: U.S. Government Printing Office, 1974, p. 2.

central cities had a service outlay (excluding school expenditures) of $408 per person, a figure $100 greater than the service outlays of their neighbors.[2]

This pattern is shown vividly in Chapter 8 in the discussion of Berry and Kasarda's research on the impact of suburban population growth on the costs of central-city services. These investigators clearly demonstrate that suburban populations greatly influence the costs of providing police, fire, highway, sanitation, recreation, and general-administration functions to central cities. The pattern remains strong even when statistical controls are applied for city size, city age, per capita income, and percentage of a city's population that is nonwhite. Although suburban residents do partially reimburse central cities through employment and sales taxes, such revenues do not appear to be adequate to cover costs. The implication to city officials is clear: attention must be given to trends in population growth in outlying areas when demand for city services is being projected.

Financing Local Governments

Between 1945 and 1977 state and local revenue increased by more than 500 percent from $30 billion to over $189 billion (U.S. Bureau of the Census, 1978, p. 16). Though the amount sounds large, such revenue has not been adequate to meet urban needs. Weighing the cities' needs against their expected income for the year 1972, Maxwell S. Stewart projected a "revenue gap" of about $35.5 billion (1972, p. 3). Interestingly, public officials have known for years of impending revenue shortfalls. For example, the National Committee for Economic Development projected that between 1965 and 1975 urban revenues would increase by 87 percent and urban expenditures would increase by 103 percent (Rasmussen, 1973, p. 141). Although this financial dilemma has long been predicted, little or nothing has been done to prevent it from reaching crisis proportions as in Cleveland, New York, and other cities.

Revenue Sources

Where does the money come from to finance local governments? Most comes from general revenues generated locally. The largest single source of locally originated tax money is the property tax, which accounted for nearly 39.9 percent of local general revenues in 1970–71. Special charges for services provided an additional 10.7 percent, sales taxes provided 4 percent, and income taxes provided an additional 1.9 percent (see Table 12.3). The remaining local general revenues come from federal and state aid to local governments.

The property tax Whereas federal revenues are derived largely from individual and corporate income taxes and states have increasingly relied on sales and income taxes, property taxes still are the largest source of locally collected revenues, constituting two-thirds of the total. This tax, however, has always been unpopular, partly because of inequitable tax rules and also because tax payments normally must be made in one lump sum (Stedman, 1972, p. 66). Property taxes apply to real property, such as land and buildings. The tax is based on an "assessment," which is an estimate of the "cash value" of a property. For example, a person's house may be appraised at a cash value of $50,000. The rate of assessment may be 10

Table 12.3
Sources of municipal revenue 1976–1977 (in percent).

Fiscal aid[a]	39.6
Property taxes	25.7
Sales taxes[b]	9.6
Income taxes[c]	3.1
Current charges[d]	11.2
Other revenues[e]	10.8

[a] Includes both federal and state aid to local governments
[b] Includes general and specific taxes and gross receipts taxes
[c] Includes business and personal income taxes
[d] Includes such charges as those for education, hospitals, and sewerage
[e] Includes, for example, miscellaneous taxes; special assessments; interest income

Source: Adapted from U.S. Bureau of the Census, *1977 Census of Governments: Finances of Municipalities and Township Governments.* Washington, D.C.: U.S. Government Printing Office, 1978, p. 9.

percent of the cash value or $5,000. If the rate of taxation is 5 percent of the assessed value ($50,000), then the property tax would be $250. Property taxes, however, usually are erroneously assessed below real property values and are often assessed so as to place the greatest burden on a private homeowner, thereby favoring business and industry (Goodall, 1968).

Other tax revenues Inequities are also built into other taxes used on the local level. A local sales tax not only increases the price of any retail item, but also is regressive in that the poor must pay the same rate as the wealthy (Netzer, 1970). Local income taxes also favor the wealthy if they are based on one's federal income tax. Finally, some cities tax utilities. Large users of these utilities, such as industry, are usually charged at a lower rate than an average citizen (La Greca, 1977, p. 387).

Revenue Limitations

The revenues that can be raised by locally based taxes are limited. In the case of property taxes certain properties such as churches, state and federal buildings, universities, and military bases are exempt from local tax rules. High local income taxes and sales taxes fall most heavily on poor families and may accelerate the movement of the middleclass and business to the suburbs where taxes are lower. However, the greatest financial problem facing central cities is the fiscal fragmentation that typifies most metropolitan areas. Although residents of suburbs utilize a central city for shopping, employment, and recreation, the central city has no effective way of taxing these separately incorporated areas. Clearly, local sources of tax revenues lack the flexibility of state and federal income taxes. The higher levels of government have wider taxing authority, and their ability to tax such intangible assets as savings accounts, bonds, and stocks gives them resources that are simply unavailable to local jurisdictions. As a result, central cities and local governments have increasingly turned to state and federal governments for assistance. In 1970–71, 37.5 percent of local general revenues came from state and federal sources (see Table 12.5).

At the state level, the largest expenditures have been for education, public welfare, and highway construction and maintenance. As the costs of these services have increased, the states have tapped new sources of revenue. From 1959 to 1969 state governments introduced thirty-six new taxes and raised existing taxes 376 times (Berman, 1975, p. 204). Many state constitutions limit the total revenue that can be raised and the amount of money that can be transferred to local governments. Consequently, in the late 1960s and 1970s both states and local governments began to turn to the federal government for financial help. Since 1972 much of this help has come in the form of revenue sharing.

The Role of Big Business in the Fiscal Problems of the City

No analysis of a city's fiscal problems would be complete without recognizing the importance of big business to urban America.[3] For example, it would be impossible to conceive of America's major cities without America's largest business firms. In 1965, Robert Heilbroner (1965) described what would happen to America's cities if this nation's 150 largest firms were suddenly obliterated:

> Not only would the Union and the Southern Pacific, the Pennsylvania, the New York Central, and a half dozen of the other main railroads of the nation vanish, [since 1965 they have been part of the federally subsidized Conrail System] leaving the cities to starve, but the possibilities of supplying the urban population by truck would also disappear as the main gasoline companies and the tire companies—not to mention the makers of cars and trucks—would also cease to exist. Meanwhile, within the nine largest concentrations of urban population all activity would have stopped with the termination of light and power, as the utilities in these areas would break down with the disappearance of the telephone company (pp. 11–12).

The above gives a somewhat disturbing picture of the close tie between the large corporation and the well-being of the American city. It gives only a partial picture; it fails to show the pervasive influence of corporations on the entire economy. At present, the corporate sector of the American economy employs nearly half of all those gainfully employed. Moreover, 56 percent of the national income is generated by corporations, and this pattern has remained stable since the 1950s. These figures are for all corporations, and do not show the influence of this nation's largest corporations. In 1970, "the top 100 industrial firms accounted for about a third of the value added by manufacturing, a third of the manufacturing payroll, a fourth of the manufacturing labor force, about 40 percent of all capital expended for new purchases and approximately half of the assets of all manufacturers" (Larson and Nitchel, 1979, p. 113). Put another way, less than 2 percent of all manufacturing firms in the United States accounted for 88 percent of all net profits in manufacturing. As the Committee for Economic Development states it, "the large corporations are the dominant producers in the industries in which they operate, and their influence is pervasive throughout the business world and much of society" (1971, pp. 18–19).

Since the influence of this nation's largest corporations is so pervasive in the American political economy, it is little wonder that the decisions they make are closely related to the fate of the cities. It appears corporate decision making influences American cities in at least two major ways: (1) In the redistribution of population and jobs, and (2) in the erosion of a city's tax base.

Redistribution of population and jobs Americans are the most mobile population in the world, with approximately 20 percent of us moving annually. Of these forty million Americans who move to a different home annually, more than half the moves are the result of job changes or corporate transfers. For cities, this movement is a mixed blessing. On the positive side, high rates of residential mobility mean a more open housing market. On the negative side, those leaving a city are usually the most affluent. This loss, of course, can be balanced if there is an equal number of in-migrants with the same or higher economic status, but this is usually not the case in America's older central cities, where large numbers of less affluent minorities, especially blacks, have been concentrating.

Closely related to this redistribution of population is the redistribution of jobs within and between metropolitan areas. Here corporate decisions directly affect the fiscal well-being of a city. Since World War II, as noted in Chapter 8, corporations have found it in their best interests to locate manufacturing and industry in urban fringe areas. As blue-collar jobs were created in the suburbs, white-collar job opportunities rose in the central cities, since corporation doing business in finance, insurance, real estate, and various services invested in downtown locations. These processes have led to a mismatching of job skills and places of residence. The poor and minorities who live in a central city need suburban blue-collar jobs but often are unable to afford the costs of commuting to the suburban ring.

This is only part of the story. Corporate decision making contributes to the redistribution of population and jobs between metropolitan areas in different regions. The dramatic growth of the Sunbelt cities (see Chapter 5) is in large part the result of corporate growth in this region. In all employment areas, except service jobs, there have been declines of employment in manufacturing, wholesaling, and retailing in the Northeast, while in the Sunbelt states all metropolitan areas have experienced dramatic increases in each category. Since the poor are the least able to migrate from one region to another, these corporate decisions may have contributed to the creation of a permanent unemployed "underclass" in many of the mature cities of the Northeast.

Decentralization of business and erosion of the tax base The decentralization of business and industry make it clear that central cities are not in a position to influence large corporations. In the few cases where local officials have formally challenged the policies and actions of businesses, corporations have seldom found it difficult to get higher levels of government or the courts to interfere on their behalf.

To maintain and bolster their economies, local officials have had to make concessions in the form of tax incentives to businesses in order to induce them to remain or relocate within the city's borders. Dayton, Ohio, after years of economic stagnation and physical decline in its central business district, instituted a series of tax incentives to attract business to its downtown. The corporations that moved to Dayton have usually been exempt from property taxation. The result is that other property owners, especially homeowners, must pay a disproportionate share of the costs of running the city. Thus, the ability of corporations to move freely between cities and across state lines makes it impossible to compel large businesses to be more financially responsible to local areas. They are free to exact whatever financial concessions they can from cities and states.

In general, this chapter shows that many metropolitan areas have problems that greatly transcend their financial ability to deal with these problems. A partial solution in recent years has been to increase the role of the federal government in city finances. Revenue sharing is one mechanism whereby the federal government can use its broad taxing authority to lessen central-city financial problems. A second is to create a national policy compelling large businesses to be more financially responsible to local areas. The federal chartering of corporations and the imposition of tax penalties on corporations that abandon a community are two of the many solutions under consideration. Thus, the fiscal problems of a city are multifaceted and require not only the cooperation of federal, state and local governments but also a new relationship with big business given its influence over our political and social institutions.

THE ECOLOGICAL STRUCTURE OF THE METROPOLIS AND ITS RELATIONSHIP TO FRAGMENTED LOCAL GOVERNMENTS

The chapter to this point shows that the present fragmented structure of metropolitan government is the end-product of a long evolutionary process. That is, the present structure of metropolitan government represents the accumulated effect of decisions made by community leaders in the past in an attempt to solve urban problems. It is important to note that this decision-making process took place within the limits imposed by the organizational structure, technology, and environmental resources of the time. Present metropolitan structure can be understood best by examining the ecological processes that shaped it.

The City in the Nineteenth Century

Through most of the nineteenth century, the fragmentation of local government authority was not a problem because cities were compact, densely settled places, usually no more than three or four miles in diameter. This settlement pattern was dictated by the primitive transportation of the time—horse and foot travel—and groups and institutions were located close to each other out of necessity. Moreover, this was the century in which the nation was transformed from an agrarian-rural to an industrial-urban society. This process drew millions of rural Americans and foreign immigrants to the cities in search of industrial employment, and by accommodating these masses, cities increased in overall population density. The transportation technology to move people cheaply and efficiently within a city had not yet been invented. As a result, in the second half of the nineteenth century, population densities in cities like Chicago and New York exceeded 100,000 persons per square mile. Not surprisingly, many of this century's most serious urban problems have been related to high population density, and the solution most favored has been to decentralize population.

The many problems we face as a society in the 1980s tend to narrow our field of interest to the present, cutting us off from the experiences and lessons of the past. Read closely this article from The Literary Digest *(1921) written over sixty years ago. New Yorkers then, as today, were searching for solutions to their urban problems.*

THE CITY PROBLEM

Two startling editorials, separated by only a week's time, appeared not long ago in the New York *Tribune,* and a glance at their opening paragraphs will reveal how grave is the city problem. Says one: "The 1920 census shows that the country's urban population has at last overtopped its rural population. There are 54,318,082 persons living in cities and 51,390,739 outside them." Says the other: "Six million witnesses can testify to the fact that a drastic investigation into conditions in New York City is a vital and immediate necessity. The evidence is on every hand. You can see it in the gross incompetency of city officials. You can see it in the utter breakdown of the Police Department. You can see it in the graft that has flourished." True, this is Republican criticism of a Democratic city administration, but it has a familiar ring. And not in New York alone, but in many of our great cities. And when the question arises, "What are we going to do about it?" a newspaper answers: "Run and tell the legislature. Demand a drastic investigation." For, as Mr. Arthur William Dunn reminds us in "The Community and the Citizen": "Cities receive their right of self-government from the State. Their form of government and the powers they may exercise are prescribed in a charter granted by the legislature just as some of the colonies received charters from the King."

So, when a city gets into trouble, it turns to the legislature. No wonder! As Mr. Dunn goes on to explain, the legislature is often responsible for the trouble—or to a large extent responsible. "The city does not always have even the right of ratifying the charter. Since the charters are often long and detailed, and since the legislature usually holds the right to change them at will, the amount of self-government left to the city may be very limited," tho it is clear that "legislators from all parts of the State, many of them from rural districts, can not know the peculiar needs of the city so well as the people of the city themselves," and tho "it is much easier for scheming politicians and corrupt corporations to exercise an influence over a few legislators than over the citizens of the city."

Convinced that their troubles result from something wrong with their charters, a number of our cities are demanding new charters, always with a view to simplifying the machinery of city government. When a city is ruled by an old-fashioned "council of two chambers—an upper chamber, or board of aldermen, and a lower chamber, or common council," with the mayor "little more than a presiding officer for the council," there is "difficulty in fixing responsibility," and the "elective council members are frequently incompetent to direct the business of the various city departments."

Some of the revised charters granted to cities have greatly reduced the powers of the council while greatly increasing those of the mayor, and many new charters provide a "commission form," under which "the government is placed wholly in the hands of a commission of from three to nine men (most often five), who are elected by the people at large. One member of the commission is mayor, but he has no powers different from those of the other members," each of whom "is placed at the head of one of the main departments. Thus there is a commissioner of public works, a commissioner of finance, a commissioner of public safety, and so on."

This arrangement, first put into practise at Galveston, Texas, is said (1) to "prevent the concentration of too much power in the hands of one man, the mayor; (2) supplant the large council with the small commission, which makes it easier for the people to hold their legislative body responsible for its acts; (3) fix the responsibility for the management of each department upon one man; and (4) facilitate the transaction of the city's business."

When objections are raised to the commission plan it is on the ground that it is considered "unwise to combine legislative and administrative powers in one body," and also because there are people who believe that "the commission plan tends to break up the city government into three, five or more parts without sufficient provision for unity." So there are cities—several of them now—that prefer the "city-manager plan."

This, too, provides for a commission. But "the commission becomes a board of directors for the city, and the city manager is their expert superintendent, to whom is given full power to administer, or manage, the city's business in all its departments and to appoint his own subordinates." Generally the commission is allowed "to seek its manager wherever he may be found." When Sumter, S.C., which was the first city to adopt the plan, sought a manager, it advertised widely throughout the country. "One hundred and fifty replies were received, mostly from trained civil engineers, and from this list the commission made its choice."

Now this growing insistence upon the simplification of city government is not only a demand for efficiency in the business sense, it is still more a demand for efficiency in the moral sense. The great—in fact, the greatest—need is that of honesty. Enormous sums of money are raised by taxation, and passages in "The New Civics," by Roscoe Lewis Ashley, recount the activities these sums should adequately support. "We find first that of preserving order, since disorder, evasion of law, and crime increase as population becomes more congested. Fully as important is the subject of health. The larger the city the greater the menace to health from epidemics, from the spread of ordinary contagious diseases, and from the accumulation of filth and waste. In self-protection cities must make and enforce strict plumbing and sewerage regulations, they must provide a supply of pure water, they must prevent the use of preservatives in milk and meats, and must have careful inspection of all foods which are offered for sale."

Meanwhile, "the proper paving and care of streets constitutes a task of no mean proportions. The construction of public school buildings, the maintenance of schools of every grade, from kindergartens to high schools or even colleges, and the selection of teachers require the best thought and effort of one of the city's most important departments, the Board of Education. Almost as essential for the social well-being of the people is the work of education, culture, and recreation furnished by city libraries, parks, and playgrounds.

"Possibly the greatest problem confronting our city governments is the question of public utilities. There are five public utilities which are needed in every city: these are water, gas, electricity, transportation, and telephone service. In cities the householders can not furnish their own supply of water, and most of them must depend on others for light, transportation, and telephone service. Among a municipality's necessary duties is that of deciding whether these utilities shall be provided by private corporations or by the city, in other words, whether the city shall have municipal ownership of any or all of these utilities." If the answer is "Yes," then the city has added to the already long list of things for which money raised by taxation must be spent.

We say "must be," but is it in reality so spent—all of it? Not only can city officials waste the city's money in foolish ventures, they can steal it—lay out a portion of it on genuine work for the city and pocket the rest, or pay for things purchased at prices far beyond what they are worth and make the dealer divide the extra amount with them, or even, as has happened in many American cities, put imaginary names on pay-rolls and, with the sums thus expended for "wages," fill their own purses. When such men get control of a city that city becomes dangerous. Its police force is depraved, its building laws unobserved, its health laws violated. Its streets go dirty. Its schools decline. Its entire morale deteriorates. Happily, our cities are finding that out. While a great deal still remains to be accomplished in the struggle for better government in the cities, it is at least an enlightened struggle and one that grows increasingly hopeful.

A breakthrough in transportation technology The technological breakthrough needed to decongest America's cities came in the last quarter of the nineteenth century with the introduction of the electric trolley. It provided relatively cheap and efficient short distance travel and enabled large cities to expand from a diameter of three to four miles to a diameter of seven to eight miles. Later in that century, rapid-transit trains extended the distance a person could conveniently commute to the city to between ten and twenty miles.

The application of rail technology to cities signaled the beginning of the widespread decentralization of urban population and the emergence of the present-day metropolitan structure. Improved transportation meant that people no longer needed to live within walking distance of their place of employment. Places of employment and places of residence became increasingly separated. Similarly, services no longer needed to be distributed across each district of the city, as they had been in the pedestrian city. They could now be concentrated in a specialized subarea—the central business district. The central business district, as a result, became the organizational hub of the city. Rail lines spreading outward from a city's center began to bring outlying small towns and villages under the city's economic and social influence. Although these outlying communities were transformed into suburbs and bedroom communities by the nearby city, they usually retained their political autonomy. They were governmentally independent, but were part of the metropolitan structure. Thus the seeds of metropolitan government fragmentation were sown.

The Twentieth-Century Metropolitan Community

As noted in Chapter 8, the intraurban rail system was inflexible and restricted the expansion of a city to those areas near the rail lines. Cities took on a star-like shape with a central core and suburban appendages. The widespread adoption of the motor vehicle in the twentieth century permitted the development of the previously inaccessible fringe areas between the rail lines. The speed and flexibility of the automobile combined with a complex intraurban highway system led to a rapid decentralization of population and the present-day metropolitan structure. The car also expanded the commuting distance to up to fifty miles.

The impact of automobile technology on metropolitan structures   Automobile technology enabled central cities to draw increasing numbers of small towns and villages under their influence, and as these communities grew they took on specialized functions. Some communities that were once low-order central places became bedroom communities. Others were transformed into industrial suburbs. Still others, because of their strategic ecological position became commercial satellites. All of these communities, however, now have two features in common. First, they are integral parts of a metropolitan community. They are often specialized in a particular function that contributes to the operation of the entire metropolitan system. Second, they are communities with histories and governments of their own. Although under the social and economic influence of a central city, they normally retain their own political identity. Thus, they are economically dependent but politically autonomous.

The process whereby the metropolis expands outward and envelops already existing communities is only one aspect of fringe development. Fringe growth does not always take place around existing towns and villages. Much of it occurs in new suburbs built in unincorporated and undeveloped areas of the fringe. These areas spring up because of nearby employment in a central city (or employing suburb), but the ability of central cities to annex these adjacent areas is severely limited in most states by state constitutions and public laws.

Factors Contributing to Metropolitan Government Fragmentation

The present fragmented nature of metropolitan government is the result of a number of interrelated factors. One factor is normal ecological processes. Much of the decentralization of population, business, and industry that has occurred in the post–World War II period is the normal response of these activities to changing transportation and industrial technology and to expanding regional and national markets.

A second factor is the decision of this nation's leadership, at all levels of government, to use decentralization as the major solution to urban problems. FHA and VA loans, categorical grants by the federal government for suburban water and sewerage systems, and a high-speed intraurban highway system financed by the Highway Trust Fund are examples of direct subsidies to urban areas that encouraged fringe development.

A third factor is recalcitrant and unresponsive state legislatures and rigid and inflexible state constitutions and public laws. Their combined effect has been to make annexation and governmental consolidation impossible.

A fourth factor is the sheer inertia of historical patterns and the unwillingness of small suburban governments to relinquish control to a central authority.

Finally, the social, racial, and ethnic cleavages in American society also contribute to governmental fragmentation of metropolitan areas. Present political structures represent a century of compromises that have formalized the relations between groups, and have limited their social interaction.

The Metropolis—An Ecological System

A major theme in the second half of the text is the integrated nature of a metropolitan community. Changes in the scale of American society have led to the emergence of specialized subareas of a city—a mosaic of social worlds. Each subarea specializes in a particular function that contributes to the overall functioning of the metropolis. Together they form an ecological system. In this context, the discussion of the suburbanization process in Chapter 8 is particularly relevant. The most recent literature on the suburbs clearly shows that suburbs represent one of the ways cities can grow. Cities can accommodate population growth by maintaining boundaries and increasing population density or by populating fringe areas. In America the latter process prevails. This process has been viewed as unique because a highly fragmented political structure has been superimposed over the metropolitan community. It is not fringe development that is unusual, but rather the system that has evolved to govern it.

Institutional and Ecological Responses to Governmental Fragmentation

The hundreds of government units that operate within most large metropolitan areas and the complex intergovernmental relations that have developed among them might appear to be an unworkable system. But this nation's metropolises do work. A number of structures have developed over the years to link political units and aid them in their operation. In the public sphere the rapid increase in the use of special districts and the expanding role of the federal government in urban affairs are two examples. In the private sphere, managerial and coordinating functions have become more concentrated in the central cities.

Special districts The use of special districts has increased rapidly in this century because they are flexible governmental units that can effectively span political boundaries. An independent water district is a formal and politically safe way for a central city and suburban government to come together to solve a common problem. Special districts, therefore, provide important linkages between governments on the metropolitan level that permit them to coordinate certain service functions.

The expanding role of the federal government Since the 1930s, the relationship between the federal and local governments has changed dramatically; it is becoming another institutional response to the fragmentation of metropolitan government. A major problem faced by many central-city governments is the large number of "high-service-cost citizens" who live in a city that has a shrinking tax base: the financial resources are concentrated in the suburban ring outside the taxing jurisdiction of the central city. In response to this problem, President Nixon signed into law the 1972 State and Local Fiscal Assistance Act, commonly known as general revenue sharing. Under this act, $6 billion a year was to be turned over to state and local governments. One-third of the money was to be given to the states and two-thirds to local government units. Under the provisions of this legislation, states can spend their funds for any normal and customary purpose, whereas local governments are required to spend their funds for "priority expenditures" and necessary and ordinary capital expenditures (Caputo, 1976, p. 143)—fire and police services, environmental protection, public transportation, health and hospitals, recreation and culture, libraries, financial administration, and social services. Obviously, these categories are so broad that local governments have been able to use considerable discretion in the allocation of funds.

Revenue sharing enables a central city to tap the wealth of its surrounding suburban ring. Ironically, however, these monies that could travel directly only a few miles from suburb to city, instead travel indirectly thousands of miles from the suburban community to the central city via Washington, D.C.

The expanding role of the metropolis's center A third response to governmental fragmentation often is overlooked by students of a metropolis—the expanding role of the metropolis's center. Berry and Kasarda (1977) found in their study of 157 SMSAs that the expansion of the peripheral areas of metropolitan communities is matched with a parallel development of organizational functions in their centers. Central cities are much more developed in their coordinative and integrative functions than their suburban rings, and the number of these functions increases as the size of the suburban ring expands (p. 209). Thus, changes in both the private and governmental spheres have helped to link and coordinate the operation of the metropolitan community.

POLICY ALTERNATIVES

Public policy does not occur in a vacuum. It is shaped by the political, social, and economic climate of the times. Moreover, past decisions limit the alternatives available to present decision makers in their search for solutions to urban problems. For example, the nation's inability to become less dependent on foreign oil is directly related to past policies that have made the automobile the dominant form of intraurban transportation in the United States. These policies, formulated decades ago, were based on the assumption that energy supplies would always be cheap and plentiful. Therefore, the central issue facing policy makers at all levels of American society is the impact their decisions will have on the quality of life in the future. "This issue is extremely important at the urban level, because policy decisions made by urban leaders inevitably will have a direct and measurable influence on the life styles and individual alternatives and destinies of the citizens residing in their particular urban area" (Caputo, 1975, p. 12).

If individuals do exercise some control over their own destiny and the destiny of their society, three broad policy alternatives are available to the leaders who must address the problems of administrative and fiscal fragmentation of the metropolis.

Policy Alternative I—The Status Quo

One alternative is for leaders to do nothing, to accept the status quo and continue to work within the tangle of governmental jurisdictions on the local level. This approach appears to have been chosen in most large metropolitan areas, possibly because it was the only alternative. Even if a city is on the verge of total financial collapse, the structure of local government normally is not changed. Rather, cosmetic changes are made in the existing structure. New York City, for example, in recent years has had difficulty in meeting its payroll and other financial obligations and has been on the verge of bankruptcy. In 1978, Mayor Abraham Beame was faced with a variety of alternatives, all of them unpleasant. After several unsuccessful attempts to obtain more revenue from both state and federal sources, Mayor Beame slashed city programs, laid off or fired city employees, and drew up an austerity budget that put the city on firmer financial ground.

Similarly, the city of Cleveland, after years of financial mismanagement, went into bankruptcy in 1979 after defaulting on $15 million of municipal bonds held by a group of local banks. Federal marshals actually tagged city vehicles and property for sale at public auction. This ignominious end was averted only when Mayor Denis Kocinich announced an austerity budget and city voters approved a sizable increase in local taxes. Of necessity these cities have begun to live within their means, but cuts in services have negatively affected their quality of life. Typically, the cuts have had the greatest impact on minority groups and the economically disadvantaged.

Policy Alternative II—Centralization and Consolidation

A second policy alternative is to centralize fiscal and governmental jurisdictions in a single governmental unit on the local level and in some cases (e.g., transportation, water, and sewer) on the regional level. This alternative was recommended by the Advisory Commission on Intergovernmental Relations. They suggested the following steps (1974, p. 17–18):

1. The equitable distribution of the costs and benefits of elementary and secondary education and public welfare requires broadening the geographic base of support. State governments should assume the costs of financing education, whereas the federal government should assume the responsibility for public assistance.
2. Because the federal government has the widest tax base and the greatest fiscal power, the commission recommended that intergovernmental fund transfers, in the form of revenue sharing, be increased.
3. A more rational and ordered approach should be taken to both local and state tax efforts, including the rehabilitation of the property tax and an equilization of taxes between local governmental units such as central cities and their suburbs.

In terms of consolidating governmental jurisdiction, the commission recommended (1974, p. 84–87):

1. In the short run, new regionalized agencies should be superimposed over the existing government structures to plan and coordinate transportation and other activities that have a true regional character.
2. All functions and responsibilities should be expanded to the broadest governmental units possible—e.g., metropolitan government.

The solutions suggested in the commission's recommendations refer to consolidation, that is, the entire metropolitan area or the county of which it is a part should be consolidated under one government. Most consolidations, however, have not been so all-encompassing. In the United States most consolidations have been designed to cope with a specific problem shared by all communities in a particular metropolis, a problem that requires the coordination of all major governmental units in the metropolitan area. Examples are problems in transportation, pollution, and water and sewer systems.

Regional committees In the 1960s, Washington, D.C. established a regional metropolitan committee on transportation problems composed of delegates from the District of Columbia, Maryland, and Virginia. On the whole this committee was unsuccessful in alleviating the traffic congestion caused by people commuting into the District. The committee was unable to coordinate the activities of highway departments, bus companies, airport authorities, and the numerous local governments in two states and one federal district (Martin, 1970).

Nationally, such consolidation in transportation and other areas has met with mixed success. Typically, boards have been hampered by organizational problems and limited jurisdictions.

Successful consolidation The notable exception to unsuccessful consolidation in the United States occurred in Jacksonville, Florida. In 1967, by voter approval, Jacksonville established a consolidated government that covered all but four small communities in Duval County. As a result Jacksonville is now the largest city of developed land in the Western Hemisphere, covering 827 square miles. Consolidation has eliminated the duplication of personnel and services throughout Duval County, but with mixed results.

Table 12.4 compares Jacksonville's revenue during the fiscal year before merger and the revenue five years later. Total revenue increased from $118 million to $193 million (70 percent) though revenue raised locally, largely from property taxes, declined sharply from 50 percent of the total revenue in 1966 to about 35 percent in 1972. The greatest revenue change was in intergovernmental transfer. Note that this metropolitan government has been very successful in attracting funds from both state and federal government sources.

Expenditures for human services (such as public safety, health and welfare, and housing) doubled between 1966 and 1972. Expenditures in some other areas, notably parks and recreation, actually declined.

Jacksonville's consolidation, on the whole, has been a successful merger, but it would be unwise to hold it up as a model for the rest of urban America. First, most states have stringent laws governing consolidation. Second, it is nearly impossible to persuade suburban voters to approve consolidation. "Most communities surrounding a central city either have been there for generations or were developed by people who 'fled' the

Table 12.4
Annexation and revenue in Jacksonville, Florida (in millions).

Source of revenue	1966–1967	1971–1972
Taxes (all types)	$ 57	$ 71
Charges: licenses, permits, etc.	7	17
Intergovernmental transfers	33	82
Other and miscellaneous	21	23
Total	$118	$193

Source: Adapted from Carver, J., "Responsiveness and Consolidation." *Urban Affairs Quarterly* 9 (1973): p. 111.

problems of the central city" (La Greca, 1977, p. 388–89). These people see little or no advantage to coming under the jurisdiction of one central government. Their attitude probably has been strengthened as a result of court-ordered school busing. The Supreme Court ruled on July 25, 1974 that buses cannot cross school-district boundaries. Suburban school districts are therefore insulated from this program.

Policy Alternative III—Decentralization

The third possible alternative is to decentralize urban governments. This idea is based on the assumption that when a city grows to more than some critical size, say 100,000 people, the population becomes too large for the city government to be both responsive and representative. Major proponents argue that decentralization would "contribute to improved urban governance by achieving a greater sense of community, redressing an imbalance of power, making public services more effective, promoting the public order, and opening more opportunities for personal development (Hallman, 1974, p. 12).

There is a long tradition of employing neighborhoods as the geographical basis for city organization. In Chapter 9, the community theory of Robert Park was reviewed. Park analyzed "natural areas" (a term synonymous with neighborhood), seeing them as important spatial units that helped groups of people with similar characteristics to satisfy "fundamental needs and solve fundamental problems." In addition, the functional interdependency that developed among these homogeneous subareas was viewed by Park as the basis for the integration and solidarity of a city.

In the late nineteenth and early twentieth centuries neighborhoods were the basis for political organization. Urban political machines in New York, Chicago, and elsewhere were built on a foundation of precinct committees. Political reform in this century has stressed nonpartisan elections carried out on a city-wide rather than a precinct basis, thus diminishing the political influence of neighborhoods.

Finally, planners, educators and social welfare workers have long seen neighborhoods as an important social element of a city. Settlement houses, first organized in the United States in the 1880s, served their surrounding neighborhoods. Similarly, community planners and educators have stressed the role of schools as multiple-use centers, drawing residents of a neighborhood together as a community.

The role of the neighborhood declined in the 1930s, 1940s, and early 1950s, largely because there was a national trend towards the centralization of city authority in an elected chief executive and in city departments headed by professional experts. This trend has changed in recent years as the federal government has exerted increasing influence over city affairs. For example, in 1964 the enactment of the Economic Opportunity Act required the "maximum feasible citizen participation" in many community programs. This program element is also present in the more recent federal revenue-sharing programs. The result has been that neighborhoods in many cities in the United States have begun to take on an expanded role in their own political and administrative affairs.

Regardless of the historical precedent for using neighborhoods as the basis for city organization, there also appear to be some very pragmatic reasons for considering this use. First, neighborhoods are usually shared by people with similar racial, ethnic and socioeconomic characteristics. Second, their neighborhood, not their city, is the reference point for most residents. Third, each neighborhood has a unique combination of needs and problems brought on by the characteristics of its people, the age of its housing, and its proximity to the central city. Kotler (1969) and others argue that only neighborhood government can be sensitive to these needs and problems.

In recent years there have been attempts by many cities to decentralize political and administrative functions. These attempts fall into three broad categories. The first has been the decentralization of administrative and management functions to neighborhoods with retention of political control in central-city government. New York City, in December 1971, began an experimental program of decentralized administration of municipal services. The eight communities finally selected for the experiment represented a wide range of social and economic groups. The program included redistricting of police, fire, sanitation, and other service boundaries; formal delegation of increased powers to district personnel; formation of district service cabinets; and appointment of district managers along with small staffs. The district manager served as chairman of the "district service cabinet" that consisted of field supervisors from city agencies such as city planning, environment protection, fire, housing, health services, police, and transportation. The rationale for the program was that the district manager and his cabinet were closer to the community that they serve and therefore had a better grasp of the needs of people and were more likely to be responsive to citizen demands. Similar programs have been tried in San Antonio and Washington, D.C. (Hallman, 1974, pp. 88–103).

A second approach has been to decentralize political functions while central-city government retains administrative control over basic city services. A number of cities, most notably Los Angeles, Houston, Boston, and Baltimore, opened neighborhood city halls or multiservice centers. In Boston, for example, Little City Halls emerged as neighborhood extensions of the mayor's office. Each Little City Hall was headed by a manager, whose primary role was to serve as the mayor's representative. Although these representatives provided information and referral service, they were not administrators of municipal services carried out on the neighborhood level. The majority of their time was spent in dealing with community issues, meeting with civic groups, conferring with residents, talking with the staff of city agencies, and developing plans for community schools. In general, they emerged as community leaders, acting as spokespeople for city government's interest while also identifying with neighborhood opinion when they communicated with the main city hall. Thus, rather than being neighborhood city managers, they functioned more as neighborhood mayors (Hallman, 1974, pp. 106–17).

A third approach, tried in Columbus, Ohio; Washington, D.C.; and many other American cities, has been the formation of nonprofit neighborhood corporations outside of the political and administrative structure of city government. The majority of these organizations were organized to take advantage of federal grants that provided funds to pay the costs of administration and neighborhood service programs.

The East Central Citizens Organization (ECCO) in Columbus, Ohio is one example. ECCO began in 1965 when a neighborhood church decided to turn a community center over to neighborhood control (Kotler, 1969). Early efforts to include neighborhood residents in a "general assembly" were successful and this led to a larger grant from the United States Office of Economic Opportunity. By 1967, ECCO was carrying out a wide variety of service programs for the neighborhood: preschool activities, tutoring, adult education, family counseling, legal services, employment counseling and other service activities. When federal funding ended in the early 1970s, most of the neighborhood services came to an end.

The problems of ECCO have been shared by many other neighborhood corporations. Outside of the normal structure of city government they have operated as a "special interest group" and often have little support from city officials. More importantly, without formal ties to city government they have had no direct and legitimate access to a city's financial and other resources.

This third policy alternative, decentralizing city functions, has been tried in a number of American cities with mixed success. This policy alternative looks at problems in relation to the concept of neighborhood. Neighborhoods as conceived by Kotler (1969) and Hallman (1974) simply do not exist in large metropolitan areas. As explained in Chapter 9, social and psychological attachments to local areas are now of a partial and very fragmented character. Secondly, autonomous neighborhood governments probably could not generate the financial resources necessary to provide basic services. Finally, neighborhood controls could thwart efforts to achieve racial integration and other national goals.

Which Policy Alternative?

The question remains of which policy alternative would be most effective. Theoretically, consolidation would be the most judicious. As is stressed throughout the second half of this text, a metropolis is an ecological system. It is impossible to separate the operation of one area of a city from all others. This interdependence among the various elements of a metropolitan system is evident in the daily ebb and flow of people between the central city and its suburban ring. White-collar workers commuting to a central city for work often pass blue-collar workers traveling to their jobs in the factories in the suburban ring. Moreover, the locations of the factories, offices, and businesses are tied to changes in the ecological complex—population, organization, environment, and technology—forces operating across a metropolis as a whole, not just in one area.

Theoretically, it would make sense to remove political boundaries that often impede, if not distort, the rational distribution of people and institutions across the metropolitan landscape. Realistically, consolidation is seldom a feasible policy alternative. First, no two metropolitan governments have exactly the same ecological and political structures, so a structure of government well-suited to the needs of one unit may be unsuited to another. Second, major economic, social, racial, and political cleavages exist in American society that cannot be ignored. The present governmental structure of the metropolis is one means of resolving the conflict among these groups. Third, any system constructed by human beings will be imperfect. Finally, in a democracy, ideally the majority prevails. The present patterns of intergovernmental relationships on the local level, as well as at higher levels, are the result of political compromises made since the conception of the nation more than 200 years ago. Their evolution is a continuing process. Local governmental units will continue to respond to metropolitan needs, modifying their functions and structures, although at a rate slower than many Americans would like.

Metropolitan Change in the 1980s

But what of the future? What changes in metropolitan areas can be expected in the decade of the 1980s? The question can be examined systematically by using the Duncans' POET framework.

The Ecological Complex

Population The size and composition of America's population are changing and these changes have consequences for all spheres of society. First, the socalled "baby boom" cohorts (those children born in the late 1940s through the early 1960s) are now adults. Many of these people are now entering the family-formation and child-rearing stages of the family lifecycle. Fewer children were born in the 1960s and 1970s, and as a result the average age of the population is rising.

Second, the American family is becoming smaller—the average family has fewer than two children. Although there are a tremendous number of women in the baby boom cohorts, they are having fewer children.

Third, the nature of American households has changed dramatically. More people than ever are living alone, and an increasing number of unmarried couples are living together. In addition, the typical American family household is one in which both parents work.

Fourth, Spanish-speaking Americans will soon displace blacks as this nation's largest minority.

Fifth, the United States is still the world's most spatially mobile society. Large numbers of Americans will continue to move to the Sunbelt cities of the South and the Southwest. Nonmetropolitan areas (urban places with fewer than 50,000 inhabitants) will probably continue to grow at a rate faster than metropolitan areas in the 1980s. Spiraling costs of energy and energy-supply shortfalls, however, will probably reduce the nation's spatial mobility.

What predictions can one make from these population trends? The changing size and composition of America's population have already had an impact on certain spheres of society. City school systems, for example, are closing elementary and secondary schools because there are fewer young children. Gerber's baby food commercials no longer say, "Babies are our only business." The company has been forced to diversify into other areas. In terms of cities, a number of problems and changes can be anticipated in the 1980s as a result of these population trends.

First, the increased cost of housing in the 1970s was in large part due to the tremendous demand for housing generated by the baby boom cohorts. Because fewer children were born in the 1960s and 1970s, demand for housing should level off. The prevalence of smaller families and of singles and childless couples suggests that demand will increase for apartments and townhouses. Different housing needs combined with the high costs of home ownership will mean that more Americans will be renters and fewer will be homeowners.

Second, in the 1980s race and ethnicity will continue to cause deep divisions in American society that will be reflected in the use of space in cities. Blacks, Spanish-speaking Americans, and other minorities will remain highly segregated in the cities.

Third, intergroup conflict may increase as energy and housing costs draw large numbers of suburban middleclass people into the central city. As areas of the central city are "reclaimed" by the middleclass, the poor will be displaced and minorities, in particular, will face more severe housing problems.

Finally, as the cost of energy and energy-supply shortfalls make society less mobile, the decentralization of population to urban fringe areas should cease. As outward expansion stops, overall population densities should increase.

Organization Irrespective of the taxpayer revolts in California and other states in the late 1970s, the role of government will expand in the 1980s. American cities have been built on the assumption that energy would always be plentiful and cheap. This assumption is no longer correct. Painful readjustments will be necessary in the future ("odd-even" gasoline rationing was only the beginning) and only government can mobilize the financial resources and legislative action to implement such changes.

However, in terms of metropolitan government structure, the sheer inertia of the present system will ensure that no dramatic change will occur in the foreseeable future.

Environment America is entering an age of scarcity. The end of the Petroleum Age is imminent. However, changing energy and resource costs will have only a minimal impact on the structure of American metropolises. The present physical structure of America's cities will continue to influence urban development for generations to come. It is simply not feasible to abandon the highways and streets, water and sewerage systems, schools, hospitals, and residential areas that now exist. The future of the older industrial cities in America's heartland will be interesting to observe. These cities were built originally at high population densities and many have well-developed mass transit systems. They may therefore be able to cope with the resource limitations of the 1980s. Conversely, the automobile-dominated cities of the South and Southwest should prepare for major dislocations in the decade to come.

Technology America has traditionally placed its trust in technology to solve any problem. Several events in closing months of the 1970s may have shaken that trust. The Three Mile Island nuclear accident, Skylab's uncontrolled descent to earth, possible engineering and design flaws in the DC-10 aircraft, and an uncontrollable oil-well spill in the Gulf of Mexico vividly demonstrated the weaknesses of uncontrolled and poorly applied technology. Technology in the 1980s will probably produce many useful inventions, such as energy-saving vehicles, synthetic fuels, and computer-based urban control systems. However, solutions to urban problems in the 1980s will require an understanding of social and political factors, rather than technological innovation alone.

Many Americans look to the 1980s with a sense of foreboding. Unchecked inflation, spiraling housing and energy costs, and less disposable income threaten the traditional way of life. The structure and form of cities and the way people use and live within them will change in the 1980s in response to changes in the elements of the ecological complex. Therefore, the ecological perspective that is the organizational theme of this text will provide a powerful tool for identifying and understanding these changes. The city in the 1980s will provide a unique laboratory in which to test theories and to examine more closely the process called urbanization.

SUMMARY

This chapter is an overview of government's structure and role in metropolises and government's impact on urban problems. The American governmental structure originally was set forth in the Tenth Amendment to the

United States Constitution, which delegates all powers not conferred on the federal government to the states. Municipalities and other local governments are not mentioned in the Constitution and therefore they are under the jurisdiction of the states. Local government units are created by the states through a charter, a document setting forth a city's form of government, powers, and duties to its citizens. Because charters have been strictly interpreted, a city's powers are limited, in some cases to the point of a city's inability to solve its problems.

Originally, the basic units of American government were counties and municipalities, except in the Northeast where many county functions are carried out by townships. Counties are subdivisions of a state and provide services (such as courts, tax collection, elections, and road maintenance) to a local population. Similarly, municipalities provide essential services, such as water, sewer, sanitation, and police and fire protection, to densely populated areas of a state. Though county and municipal boundaries commonly overlap, the two forms of government usually provide different services to the population.

Special districts are another form of local government. School districts were the first special districts. They were formed in the nineteenth century to provide public education to a state's school-age population. Other types of special districts are water, sewer, fire, park, library, and police districts. They range in size from a few city blocks to several counties and differ considerably in organization. Their boards may be elected or appointed. Their great flexibility is one reason for their appeal, and they have grown rapidly in number in the twentieth century as a means of addressing many urban problems.

The proliferation of special districts and the separate incorporation of suburban communities adjoining a metropolis's central city has led to a fragmentation of local government. The negative aspects of fragmentation include: (1) problems in coordination of the numerous governments in a single metropolis, (2) problems of exercising effective leadership and setting coherent policy, and (3) the underutilization of the nation's limited managerial talent by the dispersal of capable individuals throughout the metropolis.

The relationships among governments on the same local level are called horizontal intergovernmental relations. Local governments also have ties to both the state and national governments. These ties, called vertical intergovernmental relations, have changed dramatically in the twentieth century.

During the Depression of the 1930s, states and cities turned to the national government for funds. Programs designed to be temporary later became the basis of massive federal programs to the states and cities. These programs involve fund transfers of two major types—categorical grants and block grants. Categorical grants are usually provided for a single specific purpose such as public housing or urban renewal and require a detailed grant application, a tedious review process, and federal government audits to assure compliance with the guidelines set forth in the legislation creating the program. The red tape, high administrative costs on both the local and national levels, and abuses of the guidelines and goals of many programs have led to the creation of block grant programs.

Block grants permit great latitude in local needs assessment, program development, and budgeting. They give local leaders, those closest to the problems of cities, wide discretionary power in how the monies are used and minimize the federal government's role in the program. The Community Development Block Grant Program is one example of this type of fund transfer.

The fragmentation of local governmental juridications, combined with the decentralization of population, business, and industry to politically autonomous suburbs, has created severe fiscal problems for central cities. In general, the problems of central cities can be divided into two broad categories—providing services and raising revenues.

One of the major problems of central cities is providing services to low-income residents. These people are "high-cost citizens" requiring services not demanded by middle- and upper-income groups. Central cities also are forced to provide services to commuters from the suburbs for which they are never fully compensated. The large number of these citizens combined with the spillover of services adds to the financial plight of cities.

In terms of revenue, the amount of tax money that can be collected locally is limited. First, a central city has no taxing jurisdiction in areas outside its boundaries. Raising property, sales, and local income taxes only drives more businesses and middleclass persons out to the suburbs and unfairly taxes the poor. For this reason central cities and other local governments have increasingly turned to the federal government, which has a broader tax base and taxing authority, to generate funds that can be channeled to the local level. General and special revenue sharing are examples of this intergovernmental transfer of funds.

From an ecological perspective, the rapid expansion of the nation's fringe areas is viewed as a normal response of urban areas to changes in the elements of the POET framework. In the nineteenth century, trolleys and high-speed trains permitted the first decentralization of population. In the twentieth century, this process continued, aided by the flexibility and low cost of the automobile. From an ecological perspective, it is clear that it is not the evolution of the physical form of today's metropolitan community that is unique, but the means that have evolved to govern it.

Three policy alternatives have been applied to solve the problem of metropolitan governmental fragmentation. The first alternative is to maintain the status quo. The second is to consolidate or centralize the administration of cities in a metropolitan government. The third is to decentralize or return control of many urban functions to a local neighborhood unit.

Consolidation appears to be the most reasonable policy alternative. As is stressed throughout the text, the metropolis is an ecological system in which one element or area cannot be separated from another. The boundaries between central city and suburb are artificial and often hinder the orderly and rational structuring of the metropolis. Realistically, however, consolidation is seldom achievable. Politically, suburbs are reluctant to give up power to a central government. The present government structure of metropolitan areas represents decades of compromise among various competing interest groups and this process continues. The present structure of government in metropolitan areas will continue to change in the future in response to changing problems.

Finally, the ecological complex can be used to analyze and anticipate urban problems in the 1980s. Two major points are clear. First, rising energy costs will profoundly influence the future development of this nation's cities. Second, the present physical structure of metropolises and the rigid and inflexible nature of urban government will limit the options available to leaders in addressing urban problems in the 1980s.

NOTES

1. Townships in New Jersey and Pennsylvania and towns in New England are administratively more important than counties, and records and data are compiled locally for such minor governmental units.
2. Calculations are based on data from the U.S. Bureau of the Census, *Local Government Finances in Selected Metropolitan Areas and Large Counties: 1970–71* (Washington, D.C.: U.S. Government Printing Office, 1972) p. 57.
3. The following is based in part on Chapters 5 and 6 of C. J. Larson and S. R. Nikkel, *Urban Problems: Perspectives on Corporations, Governments, and Cities* (Boston: Allyn and Bacon, Inc.).

References

2*   Abu-Lughod, J. "Migrant Adjustment to City Life: The Egyptian Case." *American Sociological Review* 67 (1961):22–32.

6   ———. "Testing the Theory of Social Area Analysis: The Ecology of Cairo, Egypt." *American Sociological Review* 34 (1969):189–212.

3   Adams, R. M. "The Origin of Cities." *Scientific American* 203, no. 3 (1960):153–68.

3   ———. *The Evolution of Urban Society: Early Mesopotamia and Pre-Hispanic Mexico*. Chicago: Aldine, 1966.

12   Advisory Commission of Intergovernmental Relations. *Urban America and the Federal System: Commission Findings and Proposals*. Washington, D.C.: U.S. Government Printing Office, 1969.

10   Aldrich, H. "Ecological Succession in Racially Changing Neighborhoods: A Review of the Literature." *Urban Affairs Quarterly* 10 (1975):327–48.

10   Aldrich, H., and Reiss, A. J., Jr. "Continuities in the Study of Ecological Succession: Changes in the Race Composition of Neighborhoods and Their Businesses." *American Journal of Sociology* 81 (1977):846–66.

1, 6   Alihan, M. A. *Social Ecology: A Critical Analysis*. New York: Cooper Square, 1964. (Originally published by Columbia University, 1938.)

7, 11   Alonso, W. "A Theory of the Urban Land Market." *Papers and Proceedings of the Regional Science Association* 6 (1960):149–58.

11   Altman, I. *The Environment and Social Behavior*. Monterey, Calif.: Brooks/Cole, 1975.

1   Anderson, N. *The Hobo*. Chicago: University of Chicago Press, 1923.

2   ———. "Urbanism and Urbanization." *American Journal of Sociology* 65, no. 1 (1959):68–73.

* Relevant text chapters

511

6   Anderson, T. R., and Bean, L. "The Skevky-Bell Social Areas: Confirmation of Results and a Reinterpretation." *Social Forces* 40 (1961):119–24.

6, 7   Anderson, T. R., and Egelend, J. A. "Spatial Aspects of Social Area Analysis." *American Sociological Review* 26 (1961):392–99.

5   Angell, R. C. "The Social Integration of Selected American Cities." *American Journal of Sociology* 44 (1941):575–92.

5   Angell, R. C. "The Social Integration of American Cities of More Than 100,000 Population." *American Sociological Review* 12 (1947):335–42.

10   Armor, D. J. "The Evidence of Busing." *The Public Interest* 20 (1972):90–126.

2   Arriaga, E. A. "A New Approach to the Measurement of Urbanization." *Economic Development and Cultural Change* 18, no. 2 (1970):206–18.

1, 9   Axelrod, M. "Urban Structure and Social Participation." In *Cities and Society,* edited by P. K. Hatt and A. J. Reiss. Glencoe, Ill.: Free Press, 1957.

9   Babchuk, N., and Edwards, J. "Voluntary Associations and Integration Hypothesis." *Sociological Inquiry* 2 (1965):149–62.

7   Bach, R. L., and Smith, J. "Community Satisfaction, Expectations of Moving and Migration." *Demography* 14 (1977):147–67.

10   Barresi, C. M. "The Role of the Real Estate Agent in Residential Location." *Sociological Focus* 4 (1968):1–13.

1   Barzun, Jacques. *Darwin, Marx, Wagner.* New York: Doubleday, 1958.

8   Beale, C. L. "Rural and Nonmetropolitan Population Trends of Significance to National Population Policy." In *Commission on Population Growth and the American Future: Vol. 5, Population, Distribution, and Policy,* edited by Sara M. Mazie. Washington, D.C.: Government Printing Office, 1972.

3   Belcher, W. W. *The Economic Rivalry Between St. Louis and Chicago, 1850–1870.* New York: Columbia University Press, 1947.

9, 4   Bell, C., and Newby, H. *Community Studies: An Introduction to the Sociology of the Local Community.* New York: Praeger Publishers, 1972.

6   Bell, W. "The Social Areas of the San Francisco Bay Region." *American Sociological Review* 18 (1953):29–47.

8   ———. "Social Choice, Life Styles, and Suburban Residence." *The Suburban Community,* edited by R. Dobriner. New York: G. P. Putnam's Sons, 1958.

6   ———. "Comment on Duncan's Review of Social Area Analysis." *American Journal of Sociology* 61 (1955a):260–61.

6   ———. "Economic, Family and Ethnic Status: An Empirical Test." *American Sociological Review* 20 (1955b):45–52.

6   ———. "Social Areas: Typology of Urban Neighborhoods." In *Community Structure and Analysis,* edited by M. Sussman. New York: Thomas Crowell, 1959, 61–92.

6 ———. "The Utility of the Shevky Typology for the Design of Urban Subarea Field Studies." In *Studies in Human Ecology,* edited by G. A. Theodorson. New York: Harper & Row, 1961.

6 ———. "Urban Neighborhoods and Individual Behavior." In *Problems of Youth,* edited by M. Sherif and C. W. Sherif. Chicago: University of Chicago Press, 1965, 235–64.

6, 9 Bell, W., and Boat, M. "Urban Neighborhoods and Informal Social Relations." *American Journal of Sociology* 62 (1957):391–93.

6, 9 Bell, W., and Force, M. "Urban Neighborhood Types and Participation in Formal Associations." *American Sociological Review* 21 (1956a):25–34.

6 ———. "Social Structure and Participation in Different Types of Formal Associations." *Social Forces* 34 (1956b):345–50.

6 Bell, W., and Greer, S. "Social Area Analysis and Its Critics." *Pacific Sociological Review* 5 (1962):79–86.

3 Bender, B. *Farming in Prehistory: From Hunter-Gatherer to Food Producer.* New York: St. Martin's Press, 1975.

8 Berger, B. M. *The Working-Class Suburb: A Study of Auto Workers in Suburbia.* Berkeley, Calif.: University of California Press, 1960.

12 Berman, D. R. *State and Local Politics.* Boston: Holbrook Press, 1975.

2 Berry, B. J. L. "City Size Distributions and Economic Development." *Economic Development and Cultural Change* 9, no. 2 (1961):573–87.

5, 6 ———. *City Classification Handbook: Methods and Applications.* New York: Wiley-Interscience, 1972a.

5 ———. "Latent Structure of the American Urban System, with International Comparisons." In *City Classification Handbook: Methods and Applications,* edited by Brian Berry. New York: Wiley-Interscience, 1972b.

8 Berry, B. J. L., and Cohen, Y. S. "Decentralization of Commerce and Industry: The Restructuring of Metropolitan America." In *The Urbanization of the Suburbs,* edited by Louis H. Masetti and Jeffrey K. Hadden. Beverly Hills: Sage Publications, 1973.

4 Berry, B. J. L., and Garrison, W. "The Functional Basis of the Central Place Hierarchy." *Economic Geography* 34 (1958):145–54.

5 Berry, B. J. L., and Horton, F. E. *Geographic Perspectives on Urban Systems.* Englewood Cliffs, N.J.: Prentice-Hall, 1970.

8, 12 Berry, B. J. L., and Kasarda, J. D. *Contemporary Urban Ecology.* New York: Macmillan, 1977.

6 Berry, B. J. L., and Murdie, R. A. *Socioeconomic Correlates of Housing Condition.* Toronto: Metropolitan Planning Board, 1969.

6 Berry, B. J. L., and Rees, P. H. "The Factorial Ecology of Calcutta." *American Journal of Sociology* 74 (1969):447–91.

11 Berry, B. J. L., Simmons, J., and Tennant, R. J. "Urban Population Densities: Structure and Change." *Geographical Review* 53 (1963):389–405.

6 Berry, B. J. L., and Spodek, H. "Comparative Ecologies of Large Indian Cities." *Economic Geography* 47 (1971):266–75.

10 Bierstedt, R. *The Social Order.* New York: McGraw-Hill, 1974.

5 Blumenfeld, H. "The Economic Base of the Metropolis." In *A Geography of Urban Places,* edited by R. G. Putnam, F. J. Taylor and P. G. Kettle. Toronto: Methuen, 1970.

12 Bollens, J. C., and Schmandt, H. J. *The Metropolis.* New York: Harper & Row, 1975.

5 Borchert, J. R. "American Metropolitan Evolution." *Geographical Review* 57 (1967):301–23.

8 Boskoff, A. *The Sociology of Urban Regions.* New York: Appleton-Century-Crofts, 1970.

9 Bott, E. *Family and Social Networks.* New York: Free Press, 1971.

3 Braidwood, R. J. "The Agricultural Revolution." *Scientific America* 203, no. 3 (1960):131–48.

3 ———. "The Iraq Jarmo Project." In *Archaeological Research in Retrospect,* edited by G. R. Willey. Cambridge, Mass.: Winthrop, 1974.

2 Breeze, G. *Urbanization in Newly Developing Countries.* Englewood Cliffs, N.J.: Prentice-Hall, 1966.

3 Bridenbaugh, C. *Cities in the Wilderness.* New York: Knopf, 1938.

3 ———. *Cities in Revolt.* New York: Capricorn Books, 1955.

12 Bromley, D. G. "Power, Politics and Decision Making." In *Contemporary Topics in Urban Sociology,* edited by K. P. Schwirian. Morristown, N.J.: General Learning Press, 1977.

3 Brownell, B. A., and Goldfield, D. R., eds. *The City in Southern History: The Growth of Urban Civilization in the South.* Port Washington, N.Y.: Kennikat Press, 1977.

7 Browning, C. E. "Selected Aspects of Land Use and Distance from the City Center: The Case of Chicago." *Southeastern Geographer* 4 (1964):29–40.

10 Brueckner, J. "The Determinants of Residential Succession." *Journal of Urban Economics* 4 (1977):45–59.

7 Burgess, E. W. "The Growth of the City: An Introduction to a Research Project." In *The City,* edited by Robert E. Park, Ernest Burgess and R. D. McKenzie, pp. 47–62. Chicago: University of Chicago Press, 1925.

6 Burgess, E. W., and Bogue, D. J., eds. *Contributions to Urban Sociology.* Chicago: University of Chicago Press, 1964.

7 Butler, E. W.; Sabagh, G.; and Van Arsdol, D. "Demographic and Social Psychological Factors in Residential Mobility." *Sociology and Social Research* 48 (1964):139–54.

11 Calhoun, J. B. "Phenomena Associated with Population Density." *Proceedings of the National Academy of Sciences* 47 (1961):429–49.

11 ———. "Population Density and Social Pathology." *Scientific American* 206 (1962):139–48.

9 Caplow, T., and Forman, R. "Neighborhood Interaction in a Homogeneous Community." *American Sociological Review* 15 (1950):357–66.

12 Caputo, D. A. *Urban America: The Policy Alternatives*. San Francisco: W. H. Freeman, 1976.

2 Casetti, E., and Demko, G. J. *A Diffusion Model of Fertility Decline: An Application of Selected Soviet Data: 1940–1965*. Unpublished manuscript, Ohio State University, 1975.

3 Chang, K. *The Archaeology of Ancient China*. New Haven: Yale University Press, 1968.

3 Childe, G. "The Urban Revolution." *Town Planning Review* 21 (1950):3–17.

4 Christaller, Walter. *Die Zentralen Orte in Suddeutschland*. Jena, Germany: Gustav Fisher Verlag, 1933.

3 Chudacoff, H. P. *The Evolution of American Urban Society*. Englewood Cliffs, N.J.: Prentice-Hall, 1975.

11 Clark, C. "Urban Population Densities." *Journal of the Royal Statistical Society* 114 (1951):490–96.

11 ———. *Kingston, Jamaica—Urban Growth and Social Change, 1692–1962*. Berkeley: University of California Press, 1975.

3 Clark, G., and Piggott, S. *Prehistoric Societies*. London: Hutchinson, 1965.

12 Cleland, D. B. "Community Organization and Problems in the American Arid-Zone City." In *Urban Planning for Arid Zones*, edited by Gideon Golany. New York: John Wiley and Sons, 1978.

6 Clignet, R., and Sween, J. "Accra and Abidjan: A Comparative Examination of the Theory of Increasing Scale." *Urban Affairs Quarterly* 4 (1969):297–324.

10 Coleman, J. *Equality of Educational Opportunity*. Washington, D.C.: U.S. Government Printing Office, 1966.

10 Collison, P., and Mogey, J. "Residence and Social Class in Oxford." *American Journal of Sociology* 64 (1959):599–605.

12 Committee for Economic Development. *Social Responsibilities of Business Corporations*. New York: Committee for Economic Development, 1971.

4 Cooley, C. H. "The Theory of Transportation." *Publications of the American Economic Association* 9 (1894):312–22.

10 Cottingham, P. H. "Black Income and Metropolitan Residential Dispersion." *Urban Affairs Quarterly* 10 (1975):273–96.

4 Cottrell, W. F. "Death by Dieselization: A Case Study in the Reaction to Technological Change." *American Sociological Review* 16 (1951):358–65.

3 Coulborn, R. *The Origin of Civilized Societies*. Princeton: Princeton University Press, 1959.

9 Craven, P., and Wellman, B. "The Network City." *Sociological Inquiry* 43 (1973):57–88.

1 Cressey, P. B. *The Taxi Dance Hall*. Chicago: University of Chicago Press, 1932.

10   ———. "Population Succession in Chicago 1898–1930." *American Journal of Sociology* 44 (1938):61–65.

10   Darroch, A. G., and Marston, W. G. "The Social Class Basis of Ethnic Residential Segregation: The Canadian Case." *American Journal of Sociology* 77 (1971):491–510.

1   Darwin, Charles. *Origin of Species*. London: J. Murray, 1859.

3   Davidson, B. *African Kingdoms*. New York: Time, 1966.

6, 9   Davie, M. R. "The Pattern of Urban Growth." In *Studies in the Science of Society,* edited by G. D. Murdock. New Haven: Yale University Press, 1938. (Also in *Studies in Human Ecology,* edited by G. A. Theodorson. New York: Harper & Row, 1961.)

2   Davis, K. *World Urbanization 1950–1970, Vol. I: Basic Data for Cities, Countries, and Regions*. Berkeley: University of California Press, 1969.

2   ———. *World Urbanization 1950–1970, Volume II: Analysis of Trends, Relationships and Development*. Berkeley: University of California Press, 1972a.

2   ———. "The Urbanization of the Human Population." In *Cities,* edited by D. Flanagan. New York: Knopf, 1972b.

3   ———. "The First Cities: How and Why Did They Arise?" In *Cities: Their Origin, Growth and Human Impact,* edited by K. Davis. San Francisco: Freedman, 1973.

2   Davis, K., and Golden, H. H. "Urbanization and the Development of Pre-Industrial Areas." *Economic Development and Cultural Change* 3 (1954):6–26.

8   Dean, R. D. *The Suburbanization of Industry in the U.S.: An Overview*. Oak Ridge, Tenn.: *Southern Regional Demography Group,* 1973.

3   Deevey, E. S. "The Human Population." *Scientific American* 203, no. 3 (1960):195–205.

8   DeJong, G. F. "Residential Preferences and Migration." *Demography* 14 (1977):169–78.

9   Dewey, R. "The Folk-Urban Continuum: Real but Relatively Unimportant." *American Journal of Sociology* 56 (1960):60–66.

3   Diamond, William. "On the Dangers of an Urban Interpretation of History." In *American Urban History,* edited by A. B. Callow, pp. 609–31. New York: Oxford University Press, 1969.

12   Dillon, J. F. *Commentaries on the Law of Municipal Corporations*. Boston: Little, Brown, 1911.

3   Dixon, J. E.; Cann, J. R.; and Renfrew, C. "Obsidian and the Origins of Trade." *Scientific American* 218, no. 3 (1968):38–46.

8   Dobriner, W. M., ed. *The Suburban Community*. New York: G. P. Putnam's Sons, 1958.

9   Dotson, F. "Patterns of Voluntary Associations Among Urban Working Class Families." *American Sociological Review* 16 (1951):687–93.

10   Dotson, F., and Dotson, L. O. "Urban Centralization and Decentralization in Mexico." *Rural Sociology* 21 (1956):41–49.

8   Douglas, P. H. *The Suburban Trend*. New York: Century, 1925.

2, 10   Downs, A. "Alternative Futures for the American Ghetto." *Daedalus,* Fall (1968):1331–78.

6   Duncan, O. D. "Review of Social Area Analysis." *American Journal of Sociology* 61 (1955):84–85.

1   ———. "From Social System to Ecosystem." In *Population, Environment, and Social Organization: Current Issues in Human Ecology,* edited by Michael Micklin, pp. 107–17. Hinsdale, Ill.: Dryden Press, 1973.

10   Duncan, O.. D., and Duncan, B. "Residential Distribution and Occupational Stratification." *American Journal of Sociology* 60 (1955):493–503.

10   ———. *The Negro Population of Chicago.* Chicago: University of Chicago Press, 1957.

10   Duncan, O.; Duncan, B.; and Lieberson, S. "Ethnic Segregation and Assimilation." *American Journal of Sociology* 64 (1959):364–74.

5   Duncan, O. D., and Reiss, A. J., Jr. *Social Characteristics of Urban and Rural Communities.* New York: John Wiley and Sons, 1956.

4, 5   Duncan, O. D.; Scott, W. R.; Lieberson, S.; Duncan, B.; and Winsborough, H. H. *Metropolis and Region.* Baltimore, Md.: Johns Hopkins Press, 1960.

9, 11   Durkheim, E. *Emile Durkheim: Selected Writings.* Edited and translated by A. Giddens. Cambridge: Cambridge University Press, 1972.

2   ———. *The Division of Labor in Society.* Translated by G. Simpson. New York: Free Press, 1949.

9   Edwards, J. A., and Booth, A., eds. *Social Participation in Urban Society.* Cambridge: Schenkman, 1973.

10   Edwards, O. "Family Composition as a Variable in Residential Succession." *American Journal of Sociology* 77 (1972):731–41.

2   Eldridge, H. T. The Process of Urbanization. In *Demographic Analysis,* edited by J. J. Spengler and O. D. Duncan. Glencoe, Ill.: Free Press, 1956.

10   Erbe, B. M. "Race and Socioeconomic Segregation within a Metropolitan Ghetto." *American Sociological Review* 40 (1975):801–12.

1   Faris, R. E. *Chicago Sociology: 1920–1932.* San Francisco: Chandler Publishing Co., 1967.

11   Faris, R. E., and Dunham, W. *Mental Disorders in Urban Areas.* Chicago: University of Chicago Press, 1939.

8   Farley, R. "Suburban Persistence." In *Comparative Urban Structure,* edited by K. P. Schwirian. Lexington, Mass.: D. C. Heath, 1974.

8   ———. "Components of Suburban Population Growth." In *The Changing Face of the Suburbs,* edited by B. Schwartz. Chicago: University of Chicago Press, 1976.

10   ———. "Residential Segregation in Urbanized Areas of the United States in 1970: An Analysis of Social Class and Racial Differences." *Demography* 14 (1977):497–518.

8   Fava, S. F. "Contrasts in Neighboring: New York City and a Suburban Community." In *The Suburban Community,* edited by William M. Dobriner. New York: G. P. Putnam's Sons, 1958.

8 ———. "Beyond Suburbia." *The Annals* 422 (1975):10–24.

9 Festinger, L.; Schachter, S.; and Back, K. *Social Pressures in Informal Groups.* Oxford: Oxford University Press, 1950.

10 Fine, J.; Glenn, N. D.; and Monts, J. K. "The Residential Segregation of Occupational Groups in Central Cities and Suburbs." *Demography* 8 (1971):91–101.

1 Firey, W. *Land Use in Central Boston.* Cambridge, Mass.: Harvard University Press, 1947.

1 ———. "Sentiment and Symbolism as Ecological Variables." *American Sociological Review* 10, no. 6 (1945):140–48.

1 Fisher, C. "Toward a Subcultural Theory of Urbanism." *American Journal of Sociology* 80, no. 6 (1975):1319–51.

9 Fischer, C. *The Urban Experience.* New York: Harcourt Brace Jovanovich, 1976.

9 Fischer, C.; Jackson, R. M.; Steuve, C. A.; Gerson, K.; and Jones, L. M. with Baldassare, M. *Networks and Places.* New York: Free Press, 1977.

12 Flinn, T. A. *Local Government and Politics.* Glenview, Ill.: Scott, Foresman, 1970.

9 Foley, D. *Neighbors or Urbanites? A Study of a Residential Rochester District.* Rochester, N.Y.: University of Rochester Press, 1952.

7 Foote, N., et al. *Housing Choices and Housing Constraints.* New York: McGraw-Hill, 1960.

10 Ford, R. "Population Succession in Chicago." *American Journal of Sociology* 56 (1950):150–60.

6, 9 Form, W. H.; Smith, J.; Stone, G. P.; and Cowhig, J. "The Compatibility of Alternative Approaches to the Delimitation of Urban Sub-Areas." *American Sociological Review* 19 (1954):176–87.

5 Forstall, R. L. "Economic Classification of Places Over 10,000, 1960–1963." In *The Municipal Year Book, 1967.* Chicago: International City Managers Association, 1967.

5 ———. "A New Social and Economic Grouping of Cities." In *The Municipal Year Book, 1970.* Washington, D.C.: International City Managers Association, 1970.

9 Frankenburg, R. *Communities in Great Britain: Social Life in Town and Country.* Hammondsworth, Middlesex: Pelican Books, 1965.

11 Freedman, J. L. *Crowding and Behavior.* San Francisco: W. H. Freeman, 1975.

2 Frisbie, W. P. "The Scale and Growth of World Urbanization." In *Cities in Change,* edited by J. Walton and D. E. Carnes. Boston: Allyn and Bacon, 1977.

8 Fuguitt, G. V., and Zuiches, J. J. "Residential Preferences and Population Distribution." *Demography* 12 (1975):491–504.

11 Galle, O. R.; Gove, W. R.; and McPherson, J. H. "Population Density and Pathology: What Are the Relations for Man?" *Science* 176 (1972):23–30.

1, 7, 9 Gans, H. J. *The Urban Villagers: Group and Class in the Life of Italian Americans.* New York: Free Press, 1962a.

7 ———. "Urbanism and Suburbanism As Ways of Life: A Re-evaluation of Definitions." In *Human Behavior and Social Process*, edited by Arnold Rose. Boston: Houghton Mifflin, 1962b.

8, 9 ———. *The Levittowners*. New York: Pantheon Books, 1967.

10 ———. "The New Egalitarianism." *Saturday Review*, May, (1972):625–48.

1 Gehlke, C. E., and Biehl, K. "Certain Effects of Grouping Upon the Size of the Correlation Coefficient in Census Tract Material." *Journal of the American Statistical Association* 24 (1934):169–70.

1 Gettys, W. E. "Human Ecology and Social Theory." *Social Forces* 18 (1940):469–76.

2 Gibbs, J. P. *Urban Research Methods*. New York: Van Nostrand, 1961.

2 ———. "Measures of Urbanization." *Social Forces* 45, no. 2 (1966):170–77.

2 ———. "Types of Urban Units." In *Contemporary Topics in Urban Sociology*, edited by K. Schwirian. Morristown, N.J.: General Learning Press, 1977.

2 Gibbs, J. P., and Browning, H. L. "The Division of Labor, Technology and the Organization of Production in Twelve Countries." *American Sociological Review* 31, no. 1 (1966):81–92.

2 Gibbs, J. P., and Martin, W. T. "Urbanization and Natural Resources: A Study in Organizational Ecology." *American Sociological Review* 23 (1958):266–77.

2 ———. "Urbanization, Technology and the Division of Labor: International Patterns." *American Sociological Review* 27 (1962):667–77.

2 Gibson, C. "Urbanization in New Zealand: A Comparative Analysis." *Demography* 10, no. 1 (1973):71–84.

10 Glazer, N., and Moynihan, D. *Beyond the Melting Pot: The Negroes, Puerto Ricans, Jews, Italians and Irish of New York City*. Cambridge, Mass.: M.I.T. Press, 1963.

8 Glenn, N. "Suburbanization in the United States Since World War II." In *The Urbanization of the Suburbs*, edited by Louis H. Masetti and Jeffrey K. Hadden. Beverly Hills, Calif.: Sage Publications, 1973.

3, 5 Golany, G. *Urban Planning for Arid Zones*. New York: John Wiley and Sons, 1978.

3, 5 Goldfield, D. R., and Brownell, B. A. *Urban America: From Downtown to No Town*. Boston: Houghton Mifflin, 1979.

2 Goldstein, S. "Urbanization in Thailand, 1947–1967." *Demography* 8, no. 2 (1971):205–23.

12 Goodall, L. *The American Metropolis*. Columbus, Ohio: Charles E. Merrill, 1968.

5 Gordon, L. *Social Issues in the Arid City*. In *Urban Planning for Arid Zones*, edited by Gideon Golany. New York: John Wiley and Sons, 1978.

5 Gottman, J. *Megalopolis: The Urbanized Northeastern Seaboard of the United States*. New York: Twentieth Century Fund, 1961.

11 Gove, W. R.; Hughes, M.; and Galle, O. R. "Overcrowding in the Home: An Empirical Investigation of Its Possible Pathological Consequences." *American Sociological Review* 44 (1979):59–80.

9 Granovetter, M. "The Strength of Weak Ties." *American Journal of Sociology* 78 (1973):1360–80.

4 Green, H. L. "Hinterland Boundaries of New York City and Boston in Southern New England." *Economic Geography* 31 (1955):283–300.

6 Green, H. W. *Characteristics of Cleveland's Social Planning Areas.* Cleveland, Ohio: Welfare Federation of Cleveland, 1931.

6, 9 Greer, S. "Urbanism Reconsidered: A Comparative Study of Local Areas in a Metropolis." *American Sociological Review* 21 (1956):19–25.

2, 6, 9, 12 ———. *The Emerging City: Myth and Reality.* New York: Free Press, 1962a.

8 ———. *Governing the Metropolis.* New York: John Wiley and Sons, 1962b.

9 ———. "The Social Structure of Political Process of Suburbia." In *Neighborhood, City, and Metropolis: An Integrated Reader in Urban Sociology,* edited by Robert Gutman and David Popenoe. New York: Random House, 1970.

8 ———. *The Urbane View.* New York: Oxford University Press, 1972.

6 Greer, S., and Kube, E. "Urbanism and Social Structure: A Los Angeles Study." In *Community Structure and Analysis,* edited by M. Sussman. New York: Thomas Crowell, 1959.

6, 9 Greer, S., and Orleans, P. "The Mass Society and the Parapolitical Structure." *American Sociological Review* 27 (1962):634–46.

10 Grodzins, M. "Metropolitan Segregation." *Scientific American* 197 (1957):33–41.

12 ———. "Federal and State Impacts." In *Urban Government,* edited by E. C. Banfield. New York: Free Press, 1969.

7, 10 Guest, A. M. "The Applicability of the Burgess Zonal Hypothesis in Urban Canada." *Demography* 6 (1969):271–77. (Correction on p. 493.)

7, 10 ———. "Retesting the Burgess Zonal Hypothesis: The Location of White-Collar Workers." *American Journal of Sociology* 76 (1970):1094–1108.

10 ———. "Patterns of Family Location." *Demography* 9 (1972):159–71.

8, 11 ———. "Suburban Social Status: Persistence or Evolution." *American Sociological Review* 43 (1978):251–63.

8 Guest, A. M., and Cluett, C. "Metropolitan Retail Nucleation." *Demography* 11 (1974):493–507.

10 Guest, A. M., and Weed, J. A. "Ethnic Residential Segregation: Patterns of Change." *American Journal of Sociology* 81 (1976):1088–1112.

10 Guest, A. M., and Zuiches, J. J. "Another Look at Residential Turnover in Urban Neighborhoods: A Note on 'Racial Change in a Stable

Community' by Harvey Moltoch." *American Journal of Sociology* 77 (1971):457–67.

6, 8   Hadden, J. K., and Borgatta, E. F. *American Cities: Their Social Characteristics*. Chicago: Rand McNally, 1965.

2   Hagen, E. E. *The Economics of Development*. Homewood, Ill.: Richard D. Irwin, 1968.

2   Hagerstrand, T. *Innovation Diffusion as a Special Process*. Translated by A. Pred. Chicago: University of Chicago Press, 1967.

7   Haggerty, L. J. "Another Look at the Burgess Hypothesis: Time As an Important Variable." *American Journal of Sociology* 76 (1970):1084–93.

12   Hallman, H. W. *Neighborhood Government in a Metropolitan Setting*. Beverly Hills, Calif.: Sage Publications, 1974.

3   Halloway, R. L. "The Casts of Fossil Hominid Brains." *Scientific American* 231, no. 7 (1974):106–15.

3   Hammond, N. "The Earliest Maya." *Scientific America* 236, no. 3 (1977):116–33.

5   Harris, C. D. "A Functional Classification of Cities in the United States." *Geographical Review* 33, no. 1 (1943):86–99.

7   Harris, C. D., and Ullman, E. L. "The Nature of Cities." *The Annals of the American Academy of Political Science* 242 (1945):7–17.

3   Harris, D. R. "New Light on Plant Domestication and the Origins of Agriculture: A Review." *Geographical Review* 57 (1967):90–107.

3   Harrison, H. S. "Discovery, Invention and Diffusion." In *A History of Technology: Volume I*, edited by C. Singer, E. J. Holmyard and A. R. Hall. New York: Oxford, 1954.

5   Hart, J. F. "Functional and Occupational Structures of Cities of the American South." *Annals of the Association of American Geographers* 45, no. 3 (1955):269–86.

6, 9   Hatt, P. K. "The Concept of Natural Area." *American Sociological Review* 11 (1946):423–28.

1, 9, 10   Hawley, A. H. *Human Ecology: A Theory of Community Structure*. New York: Ronald Press, 1950.

3, 11   ———. *Urban Society*. New York: Ronald Press, 1971.

11   ———. "Population Density and the City." *Demography* 9 (1972):521–29.

6   Hawley, A. H., and Duncan, O. T. "Social Area Analysis: A Critical Appraisal." *Land Economics* 33 (1957):337–45.

9   Hawley, A. H., and Zimmer, B. *The Metropolitan Community*. Beverly Hills, Calif.: Sage Publications, 1970.

12   Heilbroner, R. L. *The Limits of American Capitalism*. New York: Harper & Row, 1965.

10   Helper, R. *Racial Policies and Practices of Real Estate Brokers*. Minneapolis: University of Minnesota Press, 1969.

2   Henderson, J. W. *Area Handbook for Thailand* (Da Pam 550–53). Washington, D.C.: U.S. Government Printing Office, 1971.

6   Herbert, D. T. "Social Area Analysis: A British Study." *Urban Studies* 4 (1967):41–60.

9 Hillery, G. A. "Definitions of Community: Areas of Agreement." *Rural Sociology* 20 (1955):111–23.

1 Hinkle, G. J., and Hinkle, R. C. *The Development of Modern Sociology: Its Nature and Growth in the United States.* New York: Random House, 1954.

1 Hollingshead, A. B. "A Re-examination of Ecological Theory." In *Studies in Human Ecology,* edited by G. A. Theodorson, pp. 108–14. New York: Harper & Row, 1961.

3 Holt, W. S. "Some Consequences of the Urban Movement in American History." *Pacific Historical Review* 22 (1953):337–51.

4 Hoover, Edgar M. *The Location of Economic Activity.* New York: McGraw-Hill, 1963.

7, 8 Hoover, E. M., and Vernon, R. *Anatomy of a Metropolis.* Cambridge, Mass.: Harvard University Press, 1959.

2 Hoselitz, B. F. "Generative and Parasitic Cities." *Economic Development and Cultural Change* 3 (1955):278–94.

10 House, J. D. *Contemporary Entrepreneurs: The Sociology of Real Estate Agents.* Westport, Conn.: Greenwood Press, 1977.

4 Howard, William. "An Approach to a Functional Classification of Cities." Paper presented at the Annual Meeting of the Southern Sociological Society, April, 1973, Atlanta, Georgia.

7 Hoyt, H. *The Structure and Growth of Residential Neighborhoods in American Cities.* Washington, D.C.: Federal Housing Administration, 1939.

9 Hunt, G. J., and Butler, E. W. "Migration, Participation and Alienation." *Sociology and Social Research* 56 (1972):440–52.

7, 9 Hunter, A. *Symbolic Communities: The Persistence and Change of Chicago's Local Communities.* Chicago: University of Chicago Press, 1974.

2 Irwin, P. H. "An Operational Definition of Societal Modernization." *Economic Development and Social Change* 23, no. 4 (1975):595–613.

2 Jackson, J. C. "Urban Squatters in Southwest Asia." *Geography* 59 (1974):24–30.

3 Jacobsen, T. W. "17,000 Years of Greek Prehistory." *Scientific American* 234, no. 6 (1976):76–87.

9 Janowitz, M. *The Community Press in an Urban Setting: The Social Elements of Urbanism.* Chicago: University of Chicago Press, 1961.

2 Jefferson, M. "The Law of the Primate City." *Geographic Review* 39 (1939):226–32.

5 Johnston, R. J. "Choice in Classification: The Subjectivity of Objective Methods." *Annals of the Association of American Geographers* 58 (1968):575–89.

1 Jonassen, C. T. "Cultural Variables in the Ecology of an Ethnic Group." *American Sociological Review* 14, no. 5 (1949):32–41.

5 ———. *The Measures of Community Dimensions and Elements.* Columbus, Ohio: Ohio State University, 1959.

5 ———. "Functional Unities in Eighty-Eight Community Systems." *American Sociological Review* 26 (1961):398–407.

5   Jones, M. V., and Flax, M. J. *The Quality of Life in Metropolitan Washington, D.C.: Some Statistical Benchmarks*. Washington, D.C.: Urban Institute, 1970.

5   Jones, V. "Economic Classification of Cities and Metropolitan Areas." In *Municipal Year Book, 1953*. Chicago: International City Managers Association, 1953.

5   Jones, V., and Collver, A. "Economic Classification of Cities and Metropolitan Areas." In *Municipal Year Book, 1960*. Chicago: International City Managers Association, 1960.

5   Jones, V., and Forstall, R. L. "Economic and Social Classification of Metropolitan Areas." In *The Municipal Year Book, 1963*. Chicago: International City Managers Association, 1963.

5   Jones, V.; Forstall, R. L.; and Collver, A. "Economic and Social Characteristics of Urban Places." In *Municipal Year Book, 1963*. Chicago: International City Managers Association, 1963.

10 Kain, J. F., and Quigley, F. "Housing Market Discrimination, Home Ownership and Savings Behavior." *American Economic Review* 62 (1972):263–77.

10 Kantrowitz, N. "Ethnic and Racial Segregation in the New York Metropolis, 1960." *American Journal of Sociology* 74 (1969):685–95.

10 ———. *Ethnic and Racial Segregation in the New York Metropolis: Residential Patterns Among White Ethnic Groups, Blacks and Puerto Ricans*. New York: Praeger, 1973.

8   Kasarda, J. D. "The Impact of Suburban Population Growth on Central City Service Functions." *American Journal of Sociology* 17 (1972a):1111–24.

8   ———. "The Theory of Ecological Expansion: An Empirical Test." *Social Forces* 51 (1972b):165–75.

9   Kasarda, J. D. and Janowitz, M. "Community Attachment in Mass Society." *American Sociological Review* 39 (1974):328–39.

6   Kaufman, W. C., and Greer, S. "Voting in a Metropolitan Community: An Application of Social Area Analysis." *Social Forces* 38 (1960):196–204.

9   Keller, S. *The Urban Neighborhood: A Sociological Perspective*. New York: Random House, 1968.

10 Kiang, Y. "The Distribution of Ethnic Groups in Chicago." *American Journal of Sociology* 74 (1968):292–95.

3   Kimber, G., and Athwal, R. S. "A Reassessment of the Course of Evolution of Wheat." *Proceedings of the National Academy of Sciences* 69, no. 4 (1972):912–15.

9   Kitagawa, E. M., and Taeuber, K. E., eds. *Local Community Fact Book for Chicago Metropolitan Area, 1960*. Chicago: Chicago Community Inventory, University of Chicago, 1963.

5   Kneedler, G. "Economic Classification of Cities." In *Municipal Year Book, 1945*. Chicago: International City Managers Association, 1945.

10 Kolko, G. *Wealth and Power in America: An Analysis of Social Class and Income Distribution*. New York: Praeger, 1962.

12 Kotler, M. *Neighborhood Government*. Indianapolis: Bobbs-Merrill, 1969.

12 La Greca, A. J. "Critical Urban Problems." In *Contemporary Topics in Urban Sociology,* edited by K. P. Schwirian. Morristown, N.J.: General Learning Press, 1977.

3 Lamberg-Karlovsky, C. C., and Lamberg-Karlovsky, M. "An Early City in Iran." *Scientific American* 225, no. 6 (1971):102–11.

3 Lampard, E. E. "American Historians and the Study of Urbanizations." In *American Urban History,* edited by A. B. Callow, Jr. New York: Oxford University Press, 1969, 631–42.

7 Land, K. C. "Duration of Residence and Prospective Migration: Further Evidence." *Demography* 6 (1969):133–40.

10 Latif, A. H. *Residential Segregation and Location of Status and Religious Groups in Alexandria, Egypt.* Research Paper, Department of Sociology, University of Manitoba, 1972.

6 ———. "Factor Structure and Change Analysis of Alexandria, Egypt, 1947 and 1960." In *Comparative Urban Structure: Studies in the Ecology of Cities,* edited by K. P. Schwirian, pp. 338–49. Lexington, Mass.: D. C. Heath, 1974.

10 Laurenti, L. *Property Values and Race.* Berkeley, Calif.: University of California Press, 1960.

3 Leaky, L. S. B. *Olduvai Gorge 1951–1961, Volume 1: A Preliminary Report on the Geology and Fauna.* Cambridge, England: Cambridge University Press, 1967.

2 Lerner, D. *The Passing of Traditional Society.* New York: Macmillan, 1958.

7 Leslie, G. R., and Richardson, A. H. "Life Cycle, Career Patterns and Decision to Move." *American Sociological Review* 26 (1961):894–902.

2 Levy, M. J. *Modernization and the Structure of Societies.* New York: Harcourt, Brace, and World, 1967.

9 Lewis, O. "Further Observations on the Folk-Urban Continuum." In *The Study of Urbanization,* edited by P. Hauser and L. Schnore. New York: John Wiley and Sons, 1949.

10 Lieberson, S. "The Impact of Residential Segregation in Ethnic Assimilation." *Social Forces* 40 (1961):52–57.

10 ———. "Suburbs and Ethnic Residential Patterns." *American Journal of Sociology* 68 (1962):673–81.

10 ———. *Ethnic Pattern in American Cities.* New York: Free Press, 1963.

9 Liebow, E. *Tally's Corner.* Boston: Little, Brown, 1967.

2 Linsky, A. S. "Some Generalizations Concerning Primate Cities." In *The City in Newly Developing Countries,* edited by G. Breeze. Englewood Cliffs: Prentice-Hall, 1969.

7 Lipset, S. M., and Bendix, R. *Social Mobility in Industrial Society.* Berkeley, Calif.: University of California Press, 1959.

9 Litwak, E. "Voluntary Associations and Neighborhood Cohesion." In *Neighborhood, City, and Metropolis: An Integrated Reader in Urban Sociology,* edited by Robert Gutman and David Popenoe. New York: Random House, 1970.

8   Logan, J. R. "Industrialization and the Stratification of Cities in Suburban Regions." *American Journal of Sociology* 82 (1977):333–48.

2   London, B. *Urban Growth and Regional Urban Decentralization in Thailand, 1947–1970.* Paper presented at the meeting of the Southwestern Social Science Association, April, 1978, Houston.

7   Long, L. H. "The Influence of Number and Ages of Children on Residential Mobility." *Demography* 9 (1972):371–82.

8   Long, L. H., and Glick, P. C. "Family Patterns in Suburban Areas: Recent Trends." In *The Changing Face of the Suburbs,* edited by Barry Schwartz. Chicago: University of Chicago Press, 1976.

4   Losch, A. "The Nature of Economic Regions." *Journal of Sociology* 5 (1958):71–78.

12 Lowi, T. J. "Machine Politics—Old and New." *The Public Interest* 9 (1967):84–98.

11 Lubove, R. *The Progressive and the Slums: Tenement House Reform in New York City, 1890–1917.* Pittsburgh: University of Pittsburgh Press, 1962.

3   ———. "The Urbanization Process: An Approach to Historical Research." In *American Urban History,* edited by A. B. Callow, Jr., pp. 642–45. New York: Oxford University Press, 1965.

11 ———. *The Urban Community: Housing and Planning in the Progressive Era.* Englewood Cliffs, N.J.: Prentice-Hall, 1967.

3   Main, J. T. *The Social Structure of Revolutionary America.* Princeton, N.J.: Princeton University Press, 1965.

9   Maine, H. S. *Ancient Law.* London: John Murray, 1870.

2   Mangrin, W. T. "Squatter Settlements." *Scientific American* 217 (1967):21–29.

8   Manners, G. "The Office in Metropolis: An Opportunity for Shaping Metropolitan America." *Economic Geography* 50 (1974):93–110.

3   Mantoux, P. *The Industrial Revolution in the Eighteenth Century: An Outline of the Beginnings of the Modern Factory System in England.* New York: Macmillan Co., 1961.

4   Mark, H., and Schwirian, K. P. "Ecological Position, Urban Central Place Function, and Community Population Growth." *The American Journal of Sociology* 73 (1967):30–41.

10 Marston, W. G. "Socioeconomic Differentials within Negro Areas of American Cities." *Social Forces* 48 (1969):165–76.

12 Martin, R. C. *The Cities and the Federal System.* New York: Atherton Press, 1970.

8   Martin, W. T. "The Structuring of Social Relationships Engendered by Suburban Residence." In *The Suburban Community,* edited by William M. Dobriner. New York: G. P. Putnam's Sons, 1958.

2   ———. "Urbanization and National Power to Requisition External Resources." *Pacific Sociological Review* 5 (1962):227–84.

8   Masetti, L. H., and Hadden, J. K. *The Urbanization of the Suburbs.* Beverly Hills, Calif.: Sage Publications, 1973.

2   Meadows, D. H. *The Limits of Growth.* New York: Signet, 1972.

2   Mehta, S. K. "The Correlates of Urbanization." *American Sociological Review* 28, no. 4 (1963):609–16.

10, 11   ———. "Patterns of Residence in Poona (India) by Income, Education and Occupation (1937–1965)." *American Journal of Sociology* 73 (1968):496–508.

2   ———. "Some Demographic and Economic Correlates of Primate Cities: A Case for Reevaluation." In *The City in Newly Developing Countries,* edited by G. Breeze. Englewood Cliffs, N.J.: Prentice-Hall, 1969.

9   Meier, R. L. "The Metropolis as a Transaction-Maximizing System." *Daedalus* 97 (1968):1293–1313.

7, 9, 11   Michelson, W. *Man and His Urban Environment.* Reading, Mass.: Addison-Wesley, 1970.

7, 11   ———. *Environmental Choice, Human Behavior, and Residential Satisfaction.* New York: Oxford University Press, 1977.

11   Milgrim, S. "The Experiences of Living in Cities." *Science* 167 (1970):1461–70.

9   Mitchell, J. C. "The Concept and Use of Social Networks." In *Social Networks in Urban Situations,* edited by J. C. Mitchell. Manchester: University of Manchester Press, 1969.

11   Mitchell, R. E. "Some Social Implications of High Density Housing." *American Sociological Review* 36 (1971):18–29.

10   Moltoch, H. "Racial Change in a Stable Community." *American Journal of Sociology* 75 (1969):226–38.

2   Moore, W. E., and Hoselitz, B. F., eds. *Industrialization and Society.* New York: UNESCO, 1963.

9   Morris, R. N., and Mogey, J. *The Sociology of Housing.* London: Cambridge University Press, 1965.

7   Morrison, P. A. "Duration of Residence and Prospective Migration: The Evaluation of a Stochastic Model." *Demography* 4 (1967):553–61.

2   Mountjoy, A. B. "Urbanization, the Squatter, and Development in the Third World." In *Systems of Cities: Readings on Structure Growth and Policy,* edited by L. S. Bourne and J. W. Simmons. New York: Oxford University Press, 1978.

8   Mowrer, E. R. "The Family in Suburbia." In *The Suburban Community,* edited by William M. Dobriner. New York: G. P. Putnam's Sons, 1958.

3   Mumford, L. *The City in History.* New York: Harcourt, Brace, and World, 1961.

6   Murdie, R. A. *Factorial Ecology of Metropolitan Toronto, 1951–1961: Research Paper 116, Department of Geography.* Chicago: University of Chicago Press, 1969.

6, 7   McElrath, D. "The Social Areas of Rome: A Comparative Analysis." *American Sociological Review* 27 (1962):376–91.

8   McKelvey, B. *The Urbanization of America, 1860-1915.* New Brunswick, N.J.: Rutgers University Press, 1963.

6   McKenzie, R. D. *Neighborhood.* Chicago: University of Chicago Press, 1923.

12 The National Commission on Urban Problems. *Building the American City: Report to the Congress and to the President of the United States*. Washington, D.C.: U.S. Government Printing Office, 1968.

5   Nelson, H. J. "A Service Classification of American Cities." *Economic Geography* 31 (1955):189–210.

12 Netzer, D. "Tax Structures and Their Impact on the Poor." In J. P. Creline, ed., *Financing the Metropolis: Urban Affairs Annual Reviews, No. 4,* Beverly Hills, Calif.: Sage Publications, 1970.

11 Newling, B. E. "The Spatial Variation of Urban Population Densities." *Geographical Review,* 59 (1969):242–52.

6   Nicholson, T. G., and Yeates, M. "The Ecological and Spatial Structures of the Socio-Economic Characteristics of Winnipeg, 1961." *Canadian Review of Sociology and Anthropology* 6 (1969):162–78.

7   Niedercorn, J. H., and Hearle, E. F. F. "Recent Land Use Trends in 48 Large American Cities." *Land Economics* 40 (1964):105–10.

9   Nisbet, R. A. *The Sociological Tradition*. New York: Basic Books, 1966.

9   Nohara, S. "Social Context and Neighborliness: The Negro in St. Louis." In *The New Urbanization,* edited by S. Greer, D. L. McElrath, D. W. Minor, and P. Orleans. New York: St. Martin's Press, 1968.

10 Novak, M. *The Rise of the Unmeltable Ethnics*. New York: Macmillan, 1971.

2   Ogburn, W. F. *Social Change*. New York: B. W. Huebsch, 1922.

5   Ogburn, W. F. *Social Characteristics of Cities*. Chicago: International City Managers Association, 1937.

2   Owen, C., and Wilton, R. A. "National Division and Mobilization: A Reinterpretation of Primacy." *Economic Development and Cultural Change* 21 (1973):325–37.

3   Pahl, R. E. *Patterns of Urban Life*. New York: Humanities Press, 1970.

8   Palen, J. J., ed. *City Scenes: Problems and Prospects*. Boston: Little, Brown, 1977.

12 Palley, M. L., and Palley, H. A. *Urban America and Public Policies*. Lexington, Mass.: D. C. Heath, 1977.

10 Palmer, S. H. "The Role of the Real Estate Agent in the Structuring of Residential Areas: A Study in Social Control." Ph.D. dissertation, Yale University, 1955. (Reported in Barresi, 1968)

10 Pampel, F. C., and Choldin, H. M. "Urban Location and Segregation of the Aged." *Social Forces* 56 (1978):1121–39.

1   Park, R. E. "The City: Suggestions for the Investigation of Human Behavior in the Urban Environment." *American Journal of Sociology* 20 (1916):577–612.

1   ———. "Human Ecology." *American Journal of Sociology* 42 (1932):1–15.

1, 7,   ———. *Human Communities*. Glencoe, Ill.: Free Press, 1952.
9, 10

9   Park, R., and Miller, H. A. *Old World Traits Transplanted*. New York: Harper and Bros., 1921.

5 Perry, D. C., and Watkins, A. J. *The Rise of the Sunbelt Cities.* Beverly Hills, Calif.: Sage Publications, 1977.

6 Peterson, P. O. "An Empirical Model of Urban Population Structure in Copenhagen." *Proceedings of the First Scandinavian-Polish Regional Science Seminar.* Warsaw: Polish Scientific Publishers, 1967.

4 Pfouts, R. W. "Patterns of Economic Interaction in the Crescent." In *Urban Growth Dynamics,* edited by F. S. Chapin, and S. R. Weiss, pp. 31–58. New York: John Wiley and Sons, 1962.

3 Piggott, S. *Prehistoric India: To 1000 B.C.* New York: Barnes and Noble, 1962.

3 Polgar, S., ed. *Population Ecology, and Social Evolution.* Chicago: Aldine, 1975.

3 Pownall, L. L. "The Functions of New Zealand Towns." *Annals of the Association of American Geographers* 45, no. 4 (1953):332–50.

3 Pred, A. R. *The Spatial Dynamics of U.S. Urban-Industrial Growth, 1800–1914: Interpretative and Theoretical Essays.* Cambridge, Mass.: M.I.T. Press, 1966.

5, 6 Price, D. O. "Factor Analysis in the Study of Metropolitan Centers." *Social Forces* 20, no. 4 (1942):449–55.

10 Pryor, F. L. "An Empirical Note on the Tipping Point." *Land Economics* 47 (1971):413–17.

7 Quinn, J. A. "The Burgess Zonal Hypothesis and Its Critics." *American Sociological Review* 5 (1940):210–18.

7 ———. *Human Ecology.* Englewood Cliffs, N.J.: Prentice-Hall, 1950.

12 Rasmussen, D. W. *Urban Economics.* New York: Harper & Row, 1973.

9 Redfield, R. "The Folk Society." *American Journal of Sociology* 52 (1947):293–308.

9 ———. "The Natural History of the Folk Society." *Social Forces* 31 (1953):224–28.

9 Redfield, R., and Singer, M. "The Cultural Role of Cities." *Economic Development and Cultural Change* 3 (1953):206–33.

7 Rees, P. H. "Concepts of Social Space: Toward an Urban Social Geography." In *Geographical Perspectives in Urban Systems,* edited by B. J. L. Berry and Frank E. Horton. Englewood Cliffs, N.J.: Prentice-Hall, 1970.

6 ———. "The Factorial Ecology of Metropolitan Chicago." In *Geographical Perspectives on Urban Systems,* edited by B. J. L. Berry and F. E. Horton. Englewood Cliffs, N.J.: Prentice-Hall, 1970.

6 ———. "Problems of Classifying Subareas Within Cities." In *City Classification Handbook: Methods and Applications*, edited by B. J. L. Berry. New York: Wiley-Interscience, 1972.

8 Reisman, D. "The Suburban Sadness." In *The Suburban Community,* edited by William M. Dobriner. New York: G. P. Putnam's Sons, 1958.

3 Renfrew, C. "Carbon 14 and the Prehistory of Europe." *Scientific American* 225, no. 10 (1971):63–72.

3 Renfrew, J. M. *Paleoethnobotany: The Prehistoric Food Plants of the Near East and Europe.* New York: Columbia University Press, 1973.

10 Rent, G. S., and Lord, J. D. "Neighborhood Racial Transition and Property Value Trends in a Southern Community." *Social Science Quarterly* 59 (1978):51–59.

11 Riis, J. A. *How the Other Half Lives: Studies Among the Tenements of New York.* New York: C. Scribner's Sons, 1906.

2 Rios, J. A. "The Growth of Cities and Urban Development." In *Modern Brazil,* edited by J. Saunders. Gainesville: University of Florida Press, 1971.

2, 11 Robinson, W. S. "Ecological Correlations and the Behavior of Individuals." In *Studies in Human Ecology,* edited by G. A. Theodorson, pp. 115–20. New York: Harper & Row, 1961.

6 Robson, B. T. *Urban Analysis: A Study of a City Structure with Special Reference to Sunderland.* Cambridge: Cambridge University Press, 1969.

2 Rogers, E. M. *Diffusion of Innovations.* New York: Free Press, 1962.

8 Rosenberg, C. E. *The Cholera Years, The Disease in America, 1832, 1846, 1867.* Chicago: University of Chicago Press, 1962.

7 Ross, H. L. "The Local Community: A Survey Approach." *American Sociological Review* 27 (1962):75–84.

6, 7 Rossi, P. H. *Why Families Move: A Study in the Social Psychology of Urban Residential Mobility.* New York: Free Press, 1955.

4 Ruben, Julius. "Canal or Railroad?: Imitation and Innovation in the Response to the Erie Canal in Philadelphia, Baltimore, and Boston." *Transactions of the American Philosophical Society,* 51 (1961), Part 7.

7 Sabagh, G.; Van Arsdol, M. D.; and Butler, E. W. "Some Determinants of Intrametropolitan Residential Mobility: Conceptual Considerations." *Social Forces* 48, no. 1 (1969):88–98.

11 Saegert, S. "High Density Environments: Their Personal and Social Consequences." In *Human Response to Crowding,* edited by A. Baum and Y. Epstein. Hillsdale, N.J.: Lawrence Erlbaum Associates, 1978.

11 Saegert, S.; Mackintosh, E., and West, S. "Two Studies of Crowding in Urban Public Spaces." *Environment and Behavior* 7 (1975):159–84.

2 Saunders, J., ed. *Modern Brazil: New Patterns and Development.* Gainesville: University of Florida Press, 1971.

10 Schelling, T. C. "Dynamic Models of Segregation." *Journal of Mathematical Sociology* 1 (1971):143–86.

10 ———. "A Process of Residential Segregation: Neighborhood Tipping." In *Racial Discrimination in Economic Life,* edited by A. H. Pascal. Lexington, Mass.: D. C. Heath, 1972.

3 Schild, R. "The Final Paleolithic Settlements of the European Plain." *Scientific American* 235, no. 2 (1976):88–99.

3   Schlesinger, A. M. "The City in American History." *Mississippi Valley Historical Review* 27 (1940):43–91.

3   ———. *Paths to the Present*. New York: Macmillan, 1949.

11   Schmid, C. "Suicide in Minneapolis, Minnesota 1928–1932." *American Journal of Sociology* 39 (1933):30–49.

11   Schmitt, R. C. "Density, Delinquency and Crime in Honolulu." *Sociology and Social Research* 41 (1957):274–76.

11   ———. "Implications of Density in Hong Kong." *Journal of the American Institute of Planners* 24 (1963):210–17.

11   ———. "Density, Health and Social Disorganization." *Journal of the American Institute of Planners* 32 (1966):38–40.

8   Schnore, L. F. "Satellites and Suburbs." *Social Forces* 36 (1957):121–27.

7, 8, 10   ———. *The Urban Scene*. New York: Free Press, 1965a.

7   ———. "On the Spatial Structure of Cities in the Two Americas." In *The Study of Urbanization,* edited by Philip M. Hauser and Leo F. Schnore. New York: John Wiley and Sons, 1965b.

8   Schnore, L. F.; Andre, C.; and Sharp, H. "Black Suburbanization, 1930–1970." In *The Changing Face of the Suburbs,* edited by Barry Schwartz. Chicago: University of Chicago Press, 1976.

10   Schnore, L. F., and Evanson, P. E. "Segregation in Southern Cities." *American Journal of Sociology* 72 (1966):58–67.

5, 7   Schnore, L. F., and Winsborough, H. H. "Functional Classification and the Residential Location of Social Classes." In *City Classification Handbook,* edited by B. J. L. Berry. New York: Wiley-Interscience, 1972.

7, 8   Schwab, W. A. "A Test of the Hoover and Vernon Neighborhood Life-Cycle Model." Dissertation, Ann Arbor, Mich.: University Microfilms, 1976.

10   ———. "The Tipping Point Model: Prediction of Change in the Racial Composition of Cleveland, Ohio's Neighborhoods, 1940–1970." *Environment and Change A,* March, 1980.

8   Schwirian, K. P., ed. *Contemporary Topics in Urban Sociology*. Morristown, N.J.: General Learning Press, 1977.

1   ———. "Some Recent Trends and Methodological Problems in Urban Ecological Research." In *Comparative Urban Structure: Studies in the Ecology of Cities,* edited by K. P. Schwirian. Lexington, Mass.: D. C. Heath, 1974.

6, 7   Schwirian, K. P., and Matre, M. "The Ecological Structure of Canadian Cities." In *Comparative Urban Structure: Studies in the Ecology of Cities,* edited by K. P. Schwirian. Lexington, Mass.: D. C. Heath, 1974.

10, 11   Schwirian, K. P., and Rico-Velasco, J. "The Residential Distribution of Status Groups in Puerto Rico's Metropolitan Areas." *Demography* 8 (1971):81–90.

6   Schwirian, K. P., and Smith, R. K. "Primacy, Modernization and Urban Structure: The Ecology of Puerto Rican Cities." In *Comparative Urban Structure: Studies in the Ecology of Cities,* edited by K. P. Schwirian. Lexington, Mass.: D. C. Heath, 1974b.

8   Seeley, J. R.; Sim, R. A.; and Loosley, E. W. *Crestwood Heights*. New York: Basic Books, 1956.

1   Shaw, C. *Delinquency Areas*. Chicago: University of Chicago Press, 1929.

1   ———. *The Jackroller*. Chicago: University of Chicago Press, 1930.

6, 7   Shevky, E., and Bell, W. *Social Area Analysis: Theory, Illustrative Application and Computational Procedures*. Stanford, Calif.: Stanford University Press, 1955.

6, 7   Shevky, E., and Williams, M. *The Social Areas of Los Angeles: Analysis and Typology*. Berkeley, Calif.: University of California Press, 1949.

8   Shryock, H. S. and Siegel, J. S. *The Methods and Materials of Demography, Volume 2*. Washington, D.C.: U.S. Government Printing Office, 1973.

9   Simey, T. S. *Neighborhood and Community*. Liverpool: University of Liverpool Press, 1954.

10   Simkus, A. A. "Residential Segregation by Occupation and Race in Ten Urbanized Areas, 1950–1970." *American Sociological Review* 48 (1978):81–93.

11   Simmel, G. "The Metropolis and Mental Life." In *The Sociology of Georg Simmel*, edited and translated by K. Wolff. New York: Free Press, 1950.

2   ———. *The Sociology of Georg Simmel*. Translated by K. H. Wolff. New York: Free Press, 1950.

6, 7   Simmons, J. "Changing Residence in the City: A Review of Intra-Urban Mobility." *Geographical Review* 58 (1968):622–51.

3, 11   Sjoberg, G. *The Preindustrial City: Past and Present*. New York: Free Press, 1960.

2   ———. "The Rise and Fall of Cities: A Theoretical Perspective." In *The City in Newly Developing Countries*, edited by G. Breeze. Englewood Cliffs, N.J.: Prentice-Hall, 1963.

3   ———. "The Origin and Evolution of Cities." In *Cities*, edited by D. Flanagan. New York: Alfred A. Knopf, 1972.

2   Smelser, N. J. "Essays in Sociological Explanation." In *Industrialization and Society*, edited by W. E. Moore and B. F. Hoselitz. New York: UNESCO, 1963.

10   Smith, B. "The Reshuffling Phenomenon: A Pattern of Residence of Unsegregated Negroes." *American Sociological Review* 24 (1959):77–79.

5   Smith, D. M. *The Geography of Social Well-Being in the United States*. New York: McGraw-Hill, 1973.

3   Smith, P. E. L. "Stone-Age Man on the Nile." *Scientific American* 235, no. 8 (1976):30–41.

5   Smith, R. H. T. "Method and Purpose in Functional Town Classification." *Annals of the Association of American Geographers* 55, no. 3 (1965):539–48.

10   Smith, T. L., and Zopf, P. E. *Demography: Principles and Methods*. Port Washington, N.Y.: Alfred, 1976.

3   Solheim, W. G. "An Earlier Agricultural Revolution." *Scientific American* 226, no. 4 (1972):34–41.

10 Sorenson, A.; Taeuber, K. E.; and Hollingsworth, L. J., Jr. "Indexes of Racial Residential Segregation for 109 Cities in the United States: 1940–1970." *Sociological Focus* 8 (1975):125–42.

11 Southwich, C. H. "The Population Dynamics of Confined House Mice Supplied with Unlimited Food." *Ecology* 36 (1955):212–25.

2   Sovani, N. V. "The Analysis of Over-Urbanization." *Economic Development and Cultural Change* 12 (1964):113–22.

7   Speare, A. "Home Ownership, Life Cycle Stage, and Residential Mobility." *Demography* 7 (1970):449–58.

7   ———. "Residential Satisfaction As an Intervening Variable in Residential Mobility." *Demography* 11 (1974):173–88.

8   Spectorsky, A. C. *The Exurbanites.* New York: Berkeley, 1955.

8   Stahura, J. M. "The Evolution of Suburban Functional Roles." *Pacific Sociological Review* 21, no. 4 (1978):423–439.

12 Stedman, Fr., M. S. *Urban Politics.* Cambridge, Mass.: Winthrop, 1972.

9   Stein, M. R. *The Eclipse of Community: An Interpretation of American Studies, Expanded Edition.* Princeton, N.J.: Princeton University Press, 1972.

11 Steiner, H. D. *The Crisis in Welfare in Cleveland: Report of the Mayor's Commission.* Cleveland, Ohio: Case-Western Reserve University, 1969.

10 Steinnes, D. N. "Alternative Models of Neighborhood Change." *Social Forces* 55 (1977):1043–57.

12 Stewart, M. S. *Money for Our Cities: Is Revenue Sharing the Answer?* New York: Public Affairs Committee, 1971.

3   Still, B. "Patterns of Mid-Nineteenth Century Urbanization." *Mississippi Valley Historical Review* 28 (1941):187–206.

11 Stokols, D. "On the Distinction Between Density and Crowding: Some Implications for Future Research." *Psychological Review* 79 (1972):275–77.

8   Struyk, R. J. "Spatial Concentration of Manufacturing Employment in Metropolitan Areas: Some Empirical Evidence." *Economic Geography* 48 (1972):189–92.

2   Subramanian, M. "An Operational Measure of Urban Concentration." *Economic Development and Cultural Change* 20, no. 1 (1971):105–15.

9, 11   Suttles, G. *The Social Orders of the Slums.* Chicago: University of Chicago Press, 1968.

9   ———. *The Social Construction of Communities.* Chicago: University of Chicago Press, 1972.

4   Swedner, Harold. *Ecological Differentiation of Habits and Attitudes.* Lund, Sweden: CWK Cleerup, 1960.

6   Sweetser, F. L. "Factor Structure As Ecological Structure in Helsinki and Boston." *Acta Sociologica* 8 (1965a):205–25.

6 ———. "Factorial Ecology, Helsinki, 1960." *Demography* 2 (1965b):372–85.

10 Taeuber, I. "The Changing Distribution of the Population of the United States in the Twentieth Century." In *U.S. Commission on Population Growth and the American Future: Volume 5*. Washington, D.C.: U.S. Government Printing Office, 1972.

10 Taeuber, K. E. "The Effect of Income Redistribution on Racial Residential Segregation." *Urban Affairs Quarterly* 4 (1968):5–14.

10 Taeuber, K. E., and Taeuber, A. R. *Negroes in Cities*. Chicago: Aldine, 1965.

9 Taub, R. P.; Surgeon, G. P.; Lindholm, S.; Otti, P. B.; and Bridges, J. "Urban Voluntary Organizations, Locality Based and Externally Involved." *American Journal of Sociology* 83 (1977):425–42.

3, 8 Taylor, G. R. *The Transportation Revolution, 1815–1860*. New York: Rinehart, 1951.

3 Thernstrom, S. "Urbanization, Migration, and Social Mobility in Late Nineteenth-Century America." In *Towards a New Past: Dissenting Essays in American History*, edited by B. J. Bernstein. New York: Pantheon, 1968.

4 Thomlinson, Ralph. *Urban Structure: The Social and Spatial Character of Cities*. New York: Random House, 1969.

4 Thompson, W. R. *A Preface to Urban Economics*. Baltimore: Johns Hopkins Press, 1965.

1, 9 Thrasher, F. *The Gang*. Chicago: University of Chicago Press, 1926.

1, 6 Timms, D. W. G. *The Urban Mosaic: Towards a Theory of Residen-*
9, 10 *tial Differentiation*. Cambridge: Cambridge University Press, 1971.

8, 9 Tobin, G. A. "Suburbanization and the Development of Motor Transportation: Transportation Technology and the Suburbanization Process. In *The Changing Face of the Suburbs*, edited by Barry Schwartz. Chicago: University of Chicago Press, 1976.

9 Tonnies, F. *Community and Society*. New York: Harper Torchbook, 1957.

2 Turner, J. F. C. "Squatter Settlements in Developing Countries." In *Toward a National Urban Policy*, edited by D. P. Moynihan. New York: Basic Books, 1970.

11 U.S. Bureau of the Census. *U.S. Census of Population and Housing: 1960 Census Tracts. Final Report PHC (1)–28, Cleveland, Ohio SMSA*. Washington, D.C.: U.S. Government Printing Office, 1962.

10 ———. *The Social and Economic Status of Negroes in the United States, 1970*. Washington, D.C.: U.S. Government Printing Office, 1971.

10 ———. *Census of Population, 1970: General Social and Economic Characteristics, Final Report PC (1), United States Summary*. Washington, D.C.: U.S. Government Printing Office, 1972a.

11 ———. *Census of Population, 1970: Characteristics of the Population, (1)–34–(1)*. Washington, D.C.: U.S. Government Printing Office, 1972b.

2   ———. *Census of the Population, 1970: Characteristics of the Population: Number of Inhabitants [PC (1)–A–1]. Washington, D.C.: U.S. Government Printing Office, 1972c.*

8   ———. *Census of the Population, 1970. PC(1)–B1.* Washington, D.C.: U.S. Government Printing Office, 1972d.

11   ———. *U.S. Census of Population and Housing: 1970 Census Tracts, Final Report PHC (1)–45, Cleveland, Ohio SMSA.* Washington, D.C.: U.S. Government Printing Office, 1972e.

8   ———. *Our Cities and Suburbs: We the Americans, Report #7.* Washington, D.C.: U.S. Government Printing Office, 1973.

10   ———. *Statistical Abstract of the United States: 1974.* Washington, D.C.: U.S. Government Printing Office, 1975.

12   ———. *1977 Census of Governments: Governmental Organization 1–(1).* Washington, D.C.: U.S. Government Printing Office, 1978a.

12   ———. *1977 Census of Governments: Finances of Municipalities and Township Governments 4–(4).* Washington, D.C.: U.S. Government Printing Office, 1978b.

10   U.S. Commission on Civil Rights. *Twenty Years After Brown: Equal Opportunity in Housing.* Washington, D.C.: U.S. Governmental Printing Office, 1975.

4   Ullman, Edward. "A Theory of Location for Cities." *American Journal of Sociology* 46 (1941):853–64.

10   Uyeki, E. S. "Residential Distribution and Stratification, 1950–1960." *American Journal of Sociology* 69 (1964):491–96.

10   ———. "Occupation and Residence: Cleveland 1940–1970." Paper presented at the Annual Meeting of the American Sociological Association, 1975, San Francisco.

6   Van Arsdol, M. D.; Camilleri, S. F.; and Schmid, C. F. "The Generality of Urban Social Area Indexes." *American Sociological Review* 23 (1958):277–84.

5   Vance, R. B., and Smith, S. "Metropolitan Dominance and Integration." In *The Urban South,* edited by R. B. Vance and N. J. Demeratn. Chapel Hill: University of North Carolina Press, 1954.

11   Vaughan, S., and Schwirian, K. P. "A Longitudinal Study of Metropolitan Density Patterns in a Developing Country: Puerto Rico, 1899–1970." Paper presented at the Annual Meeting of the North Central Sociological Association, April, 1978, Cincinnati, Ohio.

3   Wade, R. *The Urban Frontier: 1790–1830.* Cambridge, Mass.: Harvard University Press, 1957.

3   ———. *Slavery in the Cities: The South 1820–1860.* New York: Oxford University Press, 1964a.

4   ———. *The Urban Frontier: Pioneer Life in Early Pittsburgh, Cincinnati, Lexington, Louisville, and St. Louis.* Chicago: University of Chicago Press, 1964b.

3   ———. "Urban Life in Western America, 1790–1830." In *American Urban History,* edited by A. B. Callow, pp. 99–112. New York: Oxford University Press, 1969.

8   Ward, D. "A Comparative Historical Geography of Streetcar Suburbs in Boston, Massachusetts and Leeds, England: 1850–1920." *Annals of the Association of American Geographers* 54 (1964):1477–89.

8   Warner, S. B. *Streetcar Suburbs: The Process of Growth in Boston.* Cambridge, Mass.: Harvard University Press, 1962.

9   Warren, R. L. *The Community in America.* Chicago, Rand McNally, 1978.

8   Weber, A. F. *The Growth of Cities in the Nineteenth Century: A Study in Statistics.* Ithaca, N.Y.: Cornell University Press, 1963.

3   Weber, M. *The Protestant Ethic and the Spirit of Capitalism.* Translated by T. Parsons. New York: Scribner, 1958.

12   *Webster's New Collegiate Dictionary.* Springfield, Mass.: G. & C. Merriam, 1977.

8   Weicher, J. C. "The Effect of Metropolitan Political Fragmentation on Central City Budgets." In *Models of Urban Structure,* edited by David Sweet. Lexington, Mass.: D. C. Heath, 1972.

2   Weil, T. E. *Area Handbook for Brazil.* (Da Pan 550–20) Foreign Area Studies Division of American University. Washington, D.C.: U.S. Government Printing Office, 1975.

11   Welfare Federation of Cleveland. *Area Facts: By Social Planning Area for Cuyanoga County and Cleveland, Ohio.* Cleveland: Federation for Community Planning, 1974.

9   Wellman, B. "The Community Question: The Intimate Networks of East Yorkers." *American Journal of Sociology* 84 (1979):1201–31.

9   Wellman, B., and Leighton, B. "Networks, Neighborhoods and Communities: Approaches to the Study of the Community Question." *Urban Affairs Quarterly* 15 (1979):369–93.

9   Whyte, W. F. "Social Organization in the Slums." *American Sociological Review* 8 (1943a):34–39.

1, 9   ———. *Street Corner Society.* Chicago: University of Chicago Press, 1955.

8   ———. *The Organization Man.* Garden City, N.Y.: Doubleday, 1956.

10   Wilken, A. H. *The Residential Distribution of Occupation Groups in Eight Middle-Sized Cities of the United States in 1950.* Ph.D. dissertation, University of Chicago, 1950.

11   Winsborough, H. "An Ecological Approach to the Theory of Suburbanization." *American Journal of Sociology* 68 (1963):565–70.

11   ———. "The Social Consequences of High Population Density." *Law and Contemporary Problems* 30 (1965):91–98.

1, 2, 6, 9, 11   Wirth, L. "Urbanism As a Way of Life." *American Journal of Sociology* 44 (1938):1–24.

1, 6, 9   ———. *The Ghetto.* Chicago: University of Chicago Press, 1928.

10   Wolf, E. T. "The Tipping-Point in Racially Changing Neighborhoods." *Journal of the American Institute of Planners* 15 (1963):217–22.

7   Wolpert, J. "Behavioral Aspects of the Decision to Migrate." *Papers of the Regional Science Association* 15 (1965):159–69.

9   Young, M., and Willmott, P. *Family and Heirship in East London.* Harmondsworth, Middlesex: Pelican Books, 1957.

1   Young, P. *Scientific Social Surveys and Research: An Introduction to the Background, Content, Methods and Principles and Analysis of Social Studies.* Englewood Cliffs, N.J.: Prentice-Hall, 1956.

4   Zipf, G. K. *Human Behavior and the Principle of Least Effort: An Introduction to Human Ecology.* Reading, Mass.: Addison-Wesley, 1949.

1, 6, 9   Zorbaugh, Harvey. *The Gold Coast and the Slum.* Chicago: University of Chicago Press, 1929.

6   ———. "The Natural Areas of the City." In *Studies in Human Ecology,* edited by G. A. Theodorson. New York: Harper & Row, 1961.

Glossary

This glossary contains words or terms that appeared in the text. Included are terms that are central to an understanding of the study of human ecology. The chapter notation in parentheses refers to the chapter in which the term is first discussed in detail.

achieved status   membership in a social group which may be elective or striven for by an individual. Ideally, the individual rises to a social status based on her/his achievements. (Chapter 9)

Agricultural Revolution   the domestication of plants and animals which made possible a new form of human adaptation to the environment—agricultural villages and cities. (Chapter 3)

ascribed status   membership in a social group imposed on the individual by society without the individual's consent. (Chapter 9)

associational groups   highly organized groups normally having a constitution and formal structure with officers, i.e., NAACP, The Rotary Club. (Chapter 10)

basic sector   the part of the economic base of a city in which goods and services are produced locally but sold beyond the borders of the city. Growth in this sector of the urban economy is necessary for urban population growth and economic growth. (Chapter 5)

biological division of labor   the ecological pattern in which many species of plants and animals use the same environment but each is adapted to slightly different parts of it. (Chapter 1)

biotic level or sphere   introduced by Robert Park to refer to that part of society in which the ecological principles of competition and symbiosis operate. The biotic level is where humans either learn to adapt to the environment or become extinct. (Chapter 1)

block grants   one of the two major types of federal grants-in-aid given to municipalities for general purposes such as community development. See categorical grants. (Chapter 12)

break-in-transportation   occurs in the shipment of goods from one place to another when it is necessary to offload a shipment from one form of transportation to another. (Chapter 4)

categorical grants one of the two major types of federal grants-in-aid given to municipalities for a specific purpose, i.e., housing or sewer construction. See block grants. (Chapter 12)

Central Business District (CBD) the city's center and point of greatest accessibility from anywhere within the city. The urban space with the highest land values. (Chapter 7)

central place an urban place which provides services to the surrounding countryside or a trade area. (Chapter 4)

centralization the extent to which groups are concentrated in the central city or are dispersed toward the city's periphery. (Chapter 1)

classical models the Burgess' Concentric Zone Model, Hoyt's Sector Model, and Harris and Ullman's Multiple Nuclei Model. The first models that attempted to explain citywide land use patterns. (Chapter 1)

cohort any group that experiences some event at the same time, i.e., all persons born in 1960 would form the 1960 birth cohort. (Chapter 2)

congestion the average number of persons per square mile at the city's center. (Chapter 11)

commensalism competition and cooperation among members of the same species. (Chapter 1)

community a group of people who share a geographic area and are bound together by common culture, values, race, or social class, a cohesion which is the result of frequent social interaction (Chapter 9); or, defined ecologically, the complex system of interdependence that develops as a population collectively adapts to an environment. (Chapter 1)

community actors urbanites who are members of numerous voluntary associations and who carry out most of the public affairs of the local community. (Chapter 9)

community of limited liability intentional, voluntary and especially the partial and differential involvement of residents in their local community. (Chapter 9)

competition the process that results when members of different species vie for the same food and other scarce resources in the environment. (Chapter 1)

contract a binding agreement between two or more individuals or parties setting forth certain terms and conditions which, when fulfilled, relieve both parties of any further obligation. (Chapter 9)

crowding a psychological concept based on the experiences of the individual. Crowding is a negative mental state—a discomfort—which often leads to behavior by the individual to relieve this discomfort. (Chapter 11)

cultural level or sphere a term introduced by Robert Park to refer to that part of society built upon the biotic level—society's foundation. The cultural level is composed of a structure based on customs, norms, laws, and institutions. See biotic level. (Chapter 1)

deconcentration a measure which indicates the rate at which population density declines as one moves from the city's center to its periphery. (Chapter 11)

defended neighborhood composed of numerous face-blocks. It is that area of the city which holds the schools, churches, grocery and retail stores which an area's residents use on a day-to-day basis. (Chapter 9)

degree of urbanization a measure of urbanization; the percentage of a country's total population in cities of 100,000 or more. (Chapter 2)

density the number of people per unit of space, i.e., persons per room. (Chapter 11)

density models describe the density patterns of urban populations at various points in the city. (Chapter 1)

diffusion one of the ways urbanization is defined in the urban literature. The process whereby urban characteristics spread through time from urban to non-urban areas. (Chapter 2)

Dillon's Rule a legal position which states that cities have only those powers granted to them by the state which sets forth the city's form of government, rights and powers. (Chapter 12)

dominance a species of plants or animals with such definite relations to climate and such significant reactions upon the habitat as to control the community and assign to other species a subordinate position of varying rank. (Chapter 1)

E/R ratio a measure used to determine the degree to which residents of a suburb are employed locally. (Chapter 8)

ecological complex a term introduced by Otis Duncan to refer to the four reference variables: population, organization, environment and technology (POET). These categories of variables provide the ecologist with a means of simplifying and identifying clusters of relationships in the initial exploration of any ecosystem. (Chapter 1)

ecological distance measured in terms of the cost and time of travel in any one direction from the CBD. (Chapter 7)

ecological segregation results from the operation of impersonal economic and biotic forces such as the costs and types of housing and their location in relation to the CBD. (Chapter 10)

ecology the branch of science concerned with the interrelationship of organisms and their environment and the interdependency that develops between members of the same and different species. (Chapter 1)

economic base refers to the fact that city growth depends on its ability to sell goods and services beyond its own borders. See basic and non-basic sector. (Chapter 5)

economic development or modernization increases in the aggregate output of a society and the social and cultural changes which occur in the development process. (Chapter 2)

ecosystem the environment and the species of plants and animals that have adapted to it. (Chapter 1)

employing suburbs communities located in the urban fringe which have employment as their key function. Normally, they have large manufacturing or industrial operations within their borders and their principle function is to provide goods and services to consumers outside the suburb. (Chapter 8)

environment an element of the ecological complex (POET). Refers to all phenomena external to a population which influence it—including raw materials and other social systems. (Chapter 1)

ethnic status index a social area analysis index. The index is based on variables such as the percentage of a tract's population that is foreign born or black. This index can be used to measure the changing composition of a society's population. (Chapter 6)

face-block the most elementary symbolic grouping in urban areas composed of a network of acquaintances. A unit based on familiarity gained from face-to-face relations or encounters. (Chapter 9)

factor analysis   a mathematical technique which identifies clusters of similarly related variables and summarizes them on a single factor or index score. (Chapter 5)

factorial ecology   one of the basic ecological approaches used to study the internal structure of the city. Factorial ecology is a more general approach than social area analysis because it includes dozens of variables in the analysis of a city's subareas. (Chapter 6)

factorial models   models based on a mathematical technique called factor analysis which enable researchers to determine the underlying characteristics of neighborhoods in cities around the world. (Chapter 1)

familism   the lifestyles associated with the child-rearing stage of the lifecycle. (Chapter 8)

family status index   one of the social area analysis indexes. The index is based on variables such as the fertility ratio, the number of women in the labor force and the number of single family units in a tract. This index can be used to measure the changing economic role of the family. (Chapter 6)

Federal system   formed by a compact between political units that surrender their individual sovereignty to a central authority but retain limited residuary powers of government. (Chapter 12)

Gemeinschaft   a German term meaning community, generally referring to a folk-like society. (Chapter 9)

Gesellschaft   a German term meaning society and used in opposition to Gemeinschaft or folk-like society. Generally referring to modern-industrial society. (Chapter 9)

group location models   explain the physical location of populations in urban space, usually in relationship to the city's central business district. (Chapter 1)

high scale societies   synonymous with the term "more developed nations." Societies in which economic functions are highly differentiated, organization and structure are complex and the range and intensity of human relationships are primarily secondary and segmental in character. (Chapter 6)

hinterland   the countryside surrounding a central place which forms its trade area. (Chapter 4)

homo sapiens   the present physical form of the human species. (Chapter 3)

horizontal pattern of intergovernmental relationship   interaction between governmental units on the same level, i.e., municipal to municipal. (Chapter 12)

human ecology   the branch of sociology concerned with the study of the collective adaptation of human populations to their environment. (Chapter 1)

ideal types   a form of analysis in which the essential qualities of a phenomenon are identified for study. Researchers construct ideal types by examining a category of things and then identifying those qualities which set the members of a grouping apart from all others. (Chapter 9)

index of dissimilarity   a frequently used index to measure the degree of segregation of two groups. The index compares the residential location of pairs of groups, whites and blacks, for example, and gives a measure of the net percentage of one population who would have to relocate in order to reproduce the residential pattern of the other. (Chapter 10)

Industrial Revolution rapid change in the social, cultural, organizational and population elements of a society brought about by the invention of complex machines and the tapping of inanimate sources of energy. (Chapter 3)

industrialization the reorganization of the labor force into more efficient forms which provide a greater output of goods and services for consumption by society. (Chapter 2)

intensification one of the ways urbanization is defined in the urban literature. The situation found in urban areas in which the concentration of diverse ethnic, racial and occupational groups leads to an environment conducive to rapid social change. (Chapter 2)

invasion-succession the sequence of changes by which one dominant species replaces another in an environment. (Chapter 1)

involuntary segregation occurs when a group is required by law or custom to live in designated areas of the city. (Chapter 10)

isolates urbanites who are socially disengaged from the organizational structure of the local community. (Chapter 9)

less developed countries see low scale societies. (Chapter 2)

low scale societies synonymous with the term "less developed nations." Societies in which economic and social organization and structure are relatively simple and follow traditional patterns. The family is the dominant institution. Human relationships are predominantly personal and primary in nature. (Chapter 6)

mean the arithmetic average of a series of scores. (Chapter 5)

mechanical solidarity group solidarity based on sharing common attitudes and sentiments, as found in folk society, contrasted with organic solidarity. (Chapter 9)

melting pot thesis the process of assimilation of ethnic groups into American society thought by some social scientists to take as few as three generations. (Chapter 10)

Mesolithic a transition period of the Stone Age lasting from 10,000 to 8000 B.C. in the Near East. Characterized by village life based in intensive food gathering. (Chapter 3)

modernization see economic development. (Chapter 2)

more developed countries see high scale societies. (Chapter 2)

multidimensional typology the classification of cities into groups or types using more than one criteria. (Chapter 5)

natural areas introduced by Robert Park to refer to slums, rooming house districts, wealthy suburbs and other homogeneous areas of the city which result from unplanned ecological forces operating on the biotic level of society. (Chapter 1)

negative exponential relationship a mathematical relationship which reflects the universal pattern that as one moves from a city's center to its periphery, population declines in a regular fashion. The relationship is negative because distance and density are inversely related and it is exponential because of the nature of the mathematical function relating density to distance. (Chapter 11)

neighbors urbanites who are involved in their immediate social environment (face-block) and who organize their social life around casual social interaction and family friendship. (Chapter 9)

Neolithic or New Stone Age   lasting from 8000 B.C. to the appearance of the first cities in the Near East around 3500 B.C. The first villages based in agriculture appear during this period. (Chapter 5)

Neoorthodox Approach   the school in contemporary human ecology which clarified concepts and worked out the theoretical weaknesses of the classical or Chicago school of human ecology. This school emphasizes the role of ecological processes in explaining the location of groups and institutions in cities. (Chapter 1)

nonbasic sector   refers to the part of the economic base of a city in which goods and services are produced and sold locally. (Chapter 5)

organic solidarity   social cohesion based on mutual dependence of members of a society upon each other. Used in contrast to mechanical solidarity of folk society. (Chapter 9)

organization   the element of the ecological complex (POET) which refers to those structures developed by a population to sustain itself in an environment. (Chapter 1)

output   the total number of objects produced by a country. (Chapter 2)

overurbanized   those nations whose urban population is too large in relation to the level of economic development. (Chapter 2)

Paleolithic or Old Stone Age   one of the three periods of human prehistory lasting from 500,000 to 10,000 B.C. A period in which humans lived in societies based on hunting and gathering. (Chapter 3)

population   the element of the ecological complex (POET) which refers to a structured group of human beings which functions routinely as a unit. (Chapter 1)

population concentration   a definition of urbanization found in the urban literature which is based on demographic criteria. This view of urbanization refers to the process of population concentration and redistribution. (Chapter 2)

primacy   a pattern of cities in which one large city dominates all other cities in a country. Primacy is measured by comparing the population of a nation's largest city with that of its second largest city. (Chapter 2)

primary relationships   close, intimate, and non-transferable relationships between two people, i.e., father and son relationship. (Chapter 1)

primate city   one large city which dominates all other cities in a country and through time draws away from all of them in character as well as size. (Chapter 2)

pull factors   migration conditions which draw people from one area because of greater opportunities elsewhere. (Chapter 6)

push factors   conditions conducive to migration which result when conditions in a geographical area become so bad that migration becomes the only alternative, i.e., the Vietnamese boat people. (Chapter 6)

residential suburbs   dormitory communities located in the urban fringe with economic activities within their borders limited to retail and personal services that fill the needs of local residents. (Chapter 8)

scale of urbanization   a measure of urbanization introduced by Jack Gibbs useful in making international comparisons of the urbanization process. The index is sensitive to different settlement patterns and the distribution of both the urban and total population. (Chapter 2)

secondary relationships impersonal, easily transferable relationships between two people, i.e., the relationship between a customer and clerk. (Chapter 1)

segregation the act of separating two or more groups and preventing them from common use of facilities or enjoying common opportunities. See ecological segregation, voluntary segregation, involuntary segregation. (Chapter 10)

segregation models models which focus on the degree of spatial concentration and isolation of racial, ethnic and status groups across residential areas of the city. (Chapter 1)

single dimension typology the classification of cities into groups or types using a single criterion, i.e., employment characteristics. (Chapter 5)

social area analysis one of the basic ecological approaches used to study the internal structure of the city. Social area analysis introduced by Shevky and Bell analyzes the basic dimensions of cities with seven variables measuring social, family and ethnic characteristics of a city's subareas. (Chapter 6)

social class a body of persons who occupy a position in a social hierarchy by reason of similar kinship, power, achievements, wealth or moral and personal attributes. (Chapter 3)

social groups have a "consciousness of kind" and social interaction takes place among members. These groups are often unstructured and include friendships, cliques, members of a classroom and neighborhood groups. (Chapter 10)

social networks primary relationships between two or more people that are spatially dispersed rather than concentrated in a single area like a neighborhood. (Chapter 9)

social pathology occurs when a significant number of people deviate from the norm(s) of society and this deviation is defined as harmful or injurious to society. (Chapter 11)

social space the location of a census tract on the social area diagram (see Figures 6.2 and 6.3) according to its scores on the social, family, and ethnic status indexes. (Chapter 6)

social status index one of the social area analysis indexes. The index is calculated from U.S. census tract data and is based on various socioeconomic attributes of households, e.g., occupation, education and income characteristics. The index can be used to measure the changing distribution of skills in a society. (Chapter 6)

social stratification the ordering of social classes which results in the unequal distribution of valued material and nonmaterial items in society and the emergence of institutional mechanisms to perpetuate this structural inequality. (Chapter 3)

societal groups have members who are aware of their similar traits, such as age, sex, skin color, language and dress, but they do not interact or have a formal organizational structure. (Chapter 10)

societal scale refers to the extent of the division of labor within a society and the complexity of its organization and institutions. (Chapter 6)

sociocultural approach the school of contemporary human ecology which emphasizes the role of culture and values in explaining the location of groups and institutions in cities. (Chapter 1)

spillover municipal services that are provided directly and indirectly to suburban populations, services for which the central city is never fully reimbursed. (Chapter 12)

Standard Consolidated Area (SCA) a U.S. census definition used to refer to large metropolitan complexes composed of several SMSAs, i.e., the New York-Northwestern New Jersey SCA. (Chapter 2)

standard deviation a measure of variation which tells the researcher how far a score varies from the mean or average score. (Chapter 5)

Standard Metropolitan Statistical Area (SMSA) a U.S. census definition used to identify central cities of 50,000 or more inhabitants and the counties in which they are located and those adjoining counties which have economic or social relationships to the central city. (Chapter 2)

statistical groups the aggregation of individuals into groups based on similar characteristics. Such groups have no organizational structure and members of these groups are unaware of membership and do not interact. Statistical groups are formed by social scientists for research purposes. (Chapter 10)

status gradient the relationship between distance from the CBD and the socio-economic status of the inhabitants of a city's subareas. The Burgess Concentric Zone Theory posits that as the distance from the CBD increases, social status increases. (Chapter 7)

subareas relatively small geographical units within cities which are homogeneous in population, land use or function. (Chapter 1)

subcommunities synonymous with natural area. (Chapter 9)

subpopulations groups of humans living in cities who are similar in their racial, ethnic and income characteristics. (Chapter 1)

suburbanization the deconcentration of activities and population from the city to its adjacent fringe areas. This definition refers to the redistribution of not only population but also business and industry. (Chapter 8)

suburbs the area of the city outside the central city but within the urbanized area. (Chapter 8)

symbiosis the competition and cooperation among members of different species. (Chapter 1)

technology the element of the ecological complex (POET) which refers to the skills, tools and artifacts employed by a population in adapting to its environment. (Chapter 1)

theory of personal space the theory that high density generates stress because it leads to violations of the personal space which surrounds each human being. (Chapter 11)

theory of rents a theory which examines the close relationship between accessibility to the city's center and urban land values. (Chapter 7)

theory of social overload posits that density creates problems of interference in the operation of normal social processes which may lead to social pathology. (Chapter 11)

theory of spatial constraint posits that constraints on the normal behavior of an individual created by limited space causes stress and may lead to pathology. (Chapter 11)

theory of stimulus overload states that the presence of many members of a species in crowded conditions produces a stimulus overload and has negative physiological and psychological consequences. (Chapter 11)

theory of territoriality posits that high density creates stress because human beings like many other animals have a territorial instinct. (Chapter 11)

tipping point model   posits that once the population of a white subarea of a city reaches a certain percentage of black residents, the invasion-succession process becomes irreversible and the area will become completely black. (Chapter 10)

urban   a measure of the degree of urbanization of a country based on each country's official definition. There are more than 30 types of definitions of urban now in use in the world, but most are based on population size, legal or government criteria or the combination of several criteria. In the U.S., urban refers to incorporated or unincorporated places with 2,500 inhabitants or more. (Chapter 2)

urban hierarchy   the distribution of central places according to their size and economic functions. The higher an urban place is in the urban hierarchy the larger its population, and the more numerous its economic or central functions. (Chapter 4)

urbanism   life styles, changes in social structure and modifications of interpersonal relationships that result from urbanization. (Chapter 2)

urbanization   the process of population concentration. (Chapter 2)

Urbanized Area   a U.S. census definition referring to a central city of 50,000 or more inhabitants and surrounding closely settled territory. (Chapter 2)

vertical pattern of intergovernmental relationship   interaction between governmental units on different levels, i.e., municipal, state. (Chapter 12)

voluntary segregation   factors of self selection which bring about the concentration of similar groups in certain parts of the city. A group with a common language or culture has common problems and needs and may chose to live in a specific area. (Chapter 10)

web of life   introduced by Charles Darwin to refer to the delicate balance that exists between many species of plants and animals that share the same environment. (Chapter 1)

zone of transition   the residential zone surrounding the CBD populated by the lower socioeconomic strata—immigrants and rural migrants. (Chapter 1)

Author Index

Abu-Lughod, J., 83n
Adams, R. M., 88n, 89n, 90n, 91n,
    94n, 96, 96n
Aldrich, H., 419n, 420n, 421n
Alihan, M., 23, 25, 31
Alonzo, W., 446n
Altman, I., 458n, 467n
Anderson, N., 12, 13, 355
Anderson, T. R., 35n, 283–84
Andre, C., 317
Andrey, R., 458
Angell, R. C., 182n
Arnold, J. W., 442, 472n
Arriaga, E. A., 40n
Axelrod, M., 362, 382n

Babchuck, N., 382n
Bach, R. L., 288
Bardo, J., 382n
Baressi, C. M., 388, 389
Barzun, J., 5n
Beale, C. L., 310
Belcher, W. W., 119n
Bell, C., 349
Bell, W., 214, 219, 223, 225, 227–32,
    238–40, 245, 253, 255, 257–58,
    284, 334, 382n
Bender, B., 88n, 94n, 132n
Bendix, R., 286
Berger, B. M., 317
Berman, D. R., 488n
Berry, B. J. L., 85n, 147, 159n, 163n,
    180–81, 336–38, 339, 340–41,
    444, 472n, 498
Biehl, K., 23
Bierstedt, R., 384n
Blumfield, R., 183
Boat, M., 382n
Bollens, J. C., 477n
Booth, A., 382n
Borchert, J. R., 185–94, 203
Borgatta, E. F., 179–80, 181n
Boskoff, A., 317

Bott, E., 382n
Braidwood, R., 92, 94n
Breeze, G., 83n
Bridenbaugh, C., 117n
Bromley, D. G., 476n, 477n
Brownell, B. A., 122, 123n
Browning, C. E., 265–68
Bruckner, J., 419n
Burgess, E. W., 214–15, 270–74,
    278–80, 374–75, 391, 433, 437,
    449
Butler, E. W., 286–87

Calhoun, J., 455, 456, 458, 471
Callow, A. B., 132n
Cammilleri, S. F., 240n
Caplow, T., 382n
Caputo, D. A., 483n, 498n, 499n
Carver, J., 501
Casetti, E., 36n, 37
Chang, K., 102n, 103n
Child, D., 249n
Childe, G., 95n, 95
Choldin, H. M., 430n
Christaller, W., 146, 151
Chudacoff, H. D., 117n
Ciardi, J., 377
Clark, C., 434, 436, 449
Clark, K., 88n, 90n, 103n
Cleland, D. B., 123n
Coleman, J., 386n
Collison, P., 430n
Cooley, C. H., 136
Comte, A., 349
Coser, L., 382
Cottingham, P. H., 423n
Cottrell, W. F., 143
Coulburn, R., 100n
Craven, P., 382n
Cressey, P. B., 13, 17, 430n
Critchfield, R., 61

Darroch, A. G., 404, 406
Darwin, C., 5, 6, 7, 8, 31, 32n

Davis, K., 39, 40, 52n, 67, 72, 73, 76, 89n, 95n, 99n
Davie, M. R., 360
Deevey, E. S., 90n, 91n
Dempko, G. J., 36n, 37
Dewey, R., 382n
Diamond, W., 116n
Dillon, J. F., 475, 476n, 476
Dixon, J. E., 95n
Dotson, F., 382n, 430n
Dotson, L. O., 430n
Douglas, H., 304, 306
Downs, A., 35n, 415n
Duncan, B., 392, 419, 420n, 421n, 430n, 444, 505
Duncan, O. D., 25, 25n, 152, 159n, 204, 206–08, 392, 419, 420n, 421n, 430n, 444, 505
Dunham, H. W., 13, 355, 468, 472n
Durkheim, E., 36, 36n, 84n, 353–54, 356, 453

Edwards, J. A., 382n
Edwards, O., 421
Egeland, J. A., 283–84
Eldridge, H. T., 35n, 36, 37
Emerson, P. E., 413
Emerson, R. W., 454
Erbe, B. M., 423

Faris, R. E., 13n, 13, 355
Farley, R., 308, 310–12, 315, 320, 331, 396, 430n
Farris, R. E., 468, 472n
Fava, S. F., 335
Festinger, L., 382n
Fine, J., 430n
Firey, W., 24
Fischer, C., 22, 23, 317, 361, 382n
Flax, M. J., 182
Flinn, T. A., 477n
Foley, D., 382n
Foote, N., 300n
Force, M., 382n
Ford, R., 430n
Form, W. H., 360
Forman, R., 382n
Frakenburg, R., 382n
Freedman, J. L., 455n, 456n, 469n, 469
Frisbie, W. P., 71

Galle, O. R., 452n, 468, 469, 470
Gans, H. J., 22n, 24, 287, 290, 317–18, 359, 382n, 389, 391

Garrison, W., 147, 159
Gehlke, C. E., 23
Gettys, W. E., 23
Gibbs, J. P., 40n, 79, 80
Gibson, C., 54n, 55, 58
Giddens, A., 382
Glazer, N., 402, 408
Glick, P. C., 315, 331
Golden, H. H., 52n
Goldfield, D. R., 122, 123n
Goldstein, S., 49, 50, 51, 53
Goodall, L., 488n
Gordon, L., 129n
Gottman, J., 194
Gove, W. R., 452n, 468, 470, 471
Granovetter, M., 382n
Green, H. L., 153, 154
Green, H. W., 215–7, 416
Greer, S., 76, 84n, 306, 360, 376, 382n
Grodzins, M., 420
Guest, A. M., 280, 320, 406–07, 408, 420, 430n, 431n, 439, 446

Hadden, J. K., 179–80, 181n, 336
Haeckle, E., 6
Hagen, E. E., 76n
Haggerty, L. J., 280
Hall, E., 467
Hallman, H. W., 502n, 503n, 504n, 504
Halloway, R. L., 88n, 89n
Hammond, N., 104n
Harrigan, A., 198–200
Harris, C. D., 165–67, 276–78, 284, 433, 449
Harris, D. R., 94n
Harrison, H. S., 89n, 94n
Harsch, J., 46, 47, 48
Hatt, P. K., 23, 360
Hawley, A., 7n, 25, 99, 355, 362, 391–92, 449n, 449, 450n, 454n, 456n
Headerson, J. S., 50
Hearle, E. F. F., 267, 300n
Heilbroner, R., 489
Helper, R., 389
Herbers, J., 200–3
Herbert, D. T., 246
Hillery, G. 348
Hinkle, G. J., 17n
Hinkle, R. C., 17n
Hodge, R., 230–31
Hollingshead, A., 23, 25
Holt, W. S., 116n
Hoselitz, B. F., 85n

House, J. D., 389, 430n
Howard, W., 159n
Hoyt, H., 274–76, 433, 449
Hughes, M., 470
Hunter, A., 295, 360, 374, 375, 376, 378, 382n

Irwin, P., 77, 78
Irwin, V., 291–93

Jackson, J. C., 83n
Jacobsen, T. W., 88n, 90n
Janowitz, M., 360, 361–62, 382n
Jefferson, M., 52, 52n, 85n
Jefferson, T., 454
Jonassen, C. T., 22n, 24, 179n
Jones, M. V., 182

Kain, J. F., 421, 422n
Kane, T. T., 67
Kantrowitz, N., 402, 404–05, 406
Karp, D. A., 382
Kasarda, J. D., 331, 336–38, 338–39, 340–42, 361, 382n, 498
Keller, S., 360, 361
Kiang, Y., 430n
Kimber, G., 94n
Kitagawa, E. M., 375
Kolko, G., 391
Kotler, M., 503, 504, 504n

LaGreca, A. J., 488n, 502n
Lamberg-Karlovsky, C. C., 88n
Lamberg-Karlovsky, M., 88n
Lampard, E. E., 116n
Land, K. C., 287
Landers, A., 333
Latif, A. H., 403n
Larson, L. J., 489n, 510n
Laurent, L., 421
Leakey, L. S. B., 88n
Leighton, B., 382n
LePlay, F., 349
Lerner, D., 76, 85n
Leslie, G. R., 285–86
Levy, M. J., 76n
Lewis, O., 382n
Lieberson, S., 430n
Liebow, E., 357, 389
Linsky, A. S., 85n
Lipset, S. M., 286
Litwak, E., 382n
Locke, H. J., 13
Logan, J. R., 340

Losch, A., 146, 151, 153
Loosley, E. W., 318
Long, L. H., 315, 331
Lowe, E., 312–14
Lowi, T. J., 481n
Lubove, R., 116n, 452n, 453n

Main, J. T., 117n
Maine, H., 349–50, 353
Mangrin, W. T., 83n
Mantoux, P., 112n, 113n, 114n
Mark, H., 155, 156, 158, 159
Marston, W. G., 423n
Martin, W. T., 79, 80
Martin, R. C., 501n
Masotti, L. H., 336
Marx, K., 349
McBridge, S. D., 362–371
McCaffrey, P. J., 234–37
McKelvey, B., 322
McKenzie, R. D., 215
McPherson, J. H., 452n, 468
Meadows, D. H., 76n
Mehta, S. R., 40n, 85n, 430n, 447n
Meier, R. L., 361
Melville, H., 454
Michelson, W., 288, 290n, 295, 332, 372n, 382n, 458n, 467
Milgrim, S., 454n, 459, 460, 461, 462, 463, 464, 465, 466, 467
Miller, H. A., 358
Mitchell, J. C., 382n
Mitchell, R. E., 458n, 469n
Mogey, J., 361, 382n, 430n
Moltoch, H., 419
Moore, W. E., 75n
Moris, R. N., 361
Morris, D., 458
Morrison, P. A., 287
Morton, 472n
Mountjoy, A. B., 82
Moynihan, D., 402
Mumford, L., 111
Myers, P. F., 67

Netzer, D., 488n
Nelson, H. J., 167–74
Newby, H., 349
Nikkel, S. R., 489n, 510n
Newling, B. E., 440
Nisbet, R., 349n, 350n, 351n, 352n, 382
Novak, M., 402
Nohara, S., 382n

Niedercorn, J. H., 267, 300n

Ogburn, W., 53, 53n
Orleans, P., 376, 382n
Owen, C., 85n

Pahl, R. E., 113n
Palen, J. J., 305, 412n
Palley, H. A., 481n, 485n
Palley, M. L., 481n, 485n
Palmer, S. H., 388
Pampel, F. C., 430n
Park, R., 3, 4, 6n, 8, 9, 10n, 10, 11n,
    11, 12, 13, 17, 23, 25, 31, 32n,
    214, 259–65, 355, 356, 357n, 358,
    359, 385, 502
Perry, D. C., 130n
Pfouts, R. W., 154
Piggott, S., 101n
Pikaplow, C., 84n
Polgar, S., 89n
Pred, A., 159n
Price, D. O., 177–79
Pryor, F. L., 419

Quigley, F., 421, 422n
Quinn, J. A., 278–80, 283

Rasmussen, D. W., 487n
Redfield, R., 382n
Rees, P. H., 289, 297, 299
Reiss, A. J., 420n, 421n
Reisman, D., 303, 305
Renfrew, C., 88n, 94n
Rent, G. S., 482n
Richardson, A. H., 285–86
Rico-Velasco, J., 397, 430n
Riis, J., 32n, 452
Rios, J. A., 447n, 449n
Robinson, W. S., 23, 469n
Robson, B. T., 246
Roof, J. D., 482n
Rosenberg, C. E., 325
Ross, H. L., 300n
Rossi, P., 230–31
Rubin, J., 137, 138, 139n, 139, 140,
    141, 142, 142n
Russell, J. C., 109

Sabagh, G., 286–87
Sargent, C., 124, 125, 126, 127
Saegert, S., 451n, 451, 458n, 467n
Schelling, T. C., 420n, 421n
Schild, R., 88n

Schlesinger, A. M., 116
Schmandt, H. J., 477n
Schmid, C. F., 240n, 468
Schmitt, R. C., 452n, 468, 470, 470n
Schnore, L. F., 281–82, 283, 309,
    317–18, 339, 398, 413, 449n
Schwab, W. A., 295, 331, 420n, 442,
    472n
Schwartz, B., 331–2
Schwirian, K. P., 33n, 155, 156, 158,
    159, 241–44, 307, 318–20, 397,
    430n, 442, 447n, 449n, 449, 472n
Seeley, J. R., 318
Sharp, H., 317
Shaw, C., 13, 17, 355
Shaw, G. B., 107
Shevky, E., 214, 217–19, 219–23, 225,
    227–32, 240–41, 245, 257–58, 284
Siegel, P., 230–31
Sim, R. A., 318
Simey, T. S., 382n
Simkus, A. A., 392–94, 423, 430n
Simmel, G., 433, 434, 453, 453n, 454
Simmons, J., 444, 472n
Sinclair, U., 32n
Singer, M., 382n
Sjoberg, G., 85n, 89n, 97n, 98, 99n,
    100n, 102n, 104n, 105n, 106,
    111, 131, 132n, 447n
Slambrouch, P. V., 123, 125, 128, 129
Smelser, N. J., 76n
Smith, B., 420n
Smith, D. M., 182
Smith, J., 288
Smith, M. P., 33n
Smith, R. H. T., 167n
Smith, R. K., 241–44
Smith, P. E. L., 88n, 90n
Smith, S., 204–05
Smith, T. L., 400n, 412
Solheim, W. G., 94n
Sorenson, A., 413, 414
Southwich, C. H., 455n
Sovani, N. V., 52n
Speare, A., 287–88
Stahura, J. M., 320
Stedman, F., 476n, 477n, 482n, 487n
Steffens, L., 32n
Stein, C., 356n
Stein, M. R., 381, 382n
Steiner, H. D., 442n, 443n
Steinnes, D. N., 420n
Stewart, M. S., 486
Still, B., 119n, 120n

Stokols, D., 452n
Stone, G. P., 382
Subramanian, M., 40n
Sutherland, E. H., 13
Suttles, G., 358, 359, 360, 371, 371n, 372, 372n, 373, 374, 374n, 376, 378, 382n, 389, 458
Swedner, H., 154

Taeuber, I. E., 411, 412n, 419, 420n, 421n
Taeuber, K. E., 412, 415n, 420n, 421n, 426
Taub, R. P., 382n
Tauber, K. E., 375
Taylor, G. R., 119n
Tennant, R. J., 444, 472n
Theodorson, G. A., 24n
Thernstrom, S., 116n
Thomlinson, R., 152
Thoreau, H. D., 454
Thrasher, F., 13, 355, 358
Timms, D. W. G., 24n, 382n, 387
Tobin, G. A., 325, 327, 329–30, 361
Tocqueville, A., 349
Tonnies, F., 350–53
Turner, F. J., 115, 116
Turner, J. F. C., 83n

Ullman, E., 145, 151, 154, 276–78, 284, 433, 449
Uyeki, E. S., 430n

Van Arsdol, M. D., 240n, 286–87
Vance, R. B., 204–5
Van Valey, I., 84n
Vaughan, S., 447n, 449n, 449
Veiller, L., 452

Wade, R., 117n, 118n, 119n, 120, 132n, 137n
Ward, D., 327
Warner, S. B., 325, 327–28
Watkins, A. J., 130n
Warren, R., 379
Weber, A. F., 308
Weber, M., 18, 111
Weed, J. A., 406–07, 408
Weicher, J. C., 341–42
Weil, T. E., 59, 60, 60n, 65n
Wellman, B., 361, 361n, 382n
White, L., 472n
Whyte, W. F., 22n, 318, 359, 382
Willhelm, S. M., 33n
Wilkens, A. H., 430n
Williams, M., 214, 217–19, 221, 257–58
Willmott, P., 382n
Wilton, R. A., 85n
Winsborough, H., 436n, 438n, 441, 445, 452n, 469n
Wirth, L., 3, 13, 18, 19, 20, 21, 22, 31, 33n, 38n, 215, 225–27, 355, 358, 382n, 433, 434, 454
Wolf, E. T., 419
Wolpert, J., 285, 288

Yoels, W. C., 382
Young, M., 382n

Zimmer, B., 362
Zipf, G., 152
Zopf, P. E., 400n, 430–31n
Zorbaugh, H., 13, 13n, 14, 15, 16, 17, 17n, 215, 271, 273, 355, 358, 359, 372
Zorbaugh, L. H., 372
Zueblin, C., 303
Zuiches, J. J., 420

Subject Index

Agricultural revolution, 92–94
American urban history, 115–30
  regional development, 116–30
    Atlantic coast cities, 116–17
    lake cities, 119–20
    river cities, 117–19
    southern cities, 120–21
    southwestern cities, 121–31
  Turner thesis, 115
    critics of, 116
    urban reinterpretation, 116
Anomie, 21
Auto-air amenity epoch, 192–94; *see
  also* system of cities

Baby boom, 505–6
Baltimore, Maryland, 362–71
  "Bootstrap Efforts Revive a City,"
    362–63
  "They Fought a Highway and
    Formed a Congress," 364–71
Biological ecology, 516; *see also* ecol-
  ogy, human ecology
Biotic and cultural, 10; *see also* Chi-
  cago School, Park, R. E.
  critics of, 23
Blasé attitude, 20; *see also* Simmel, G.
Block grants, 483
Boosterism, 184
Boston and Albany Railroad, 142–43;
  see also theories of location
Break-in-transportation theory, 136–45;
  see also theories of location
Burgess' concentric zone theory,
  270–74; *see also* theories,
  classical

Canal or Railroad?, 137–43
Categorical grants, 483; *see also* block
  grant
Central place theory, 146–58; *see also*
  theories of location

Chesapeake and Ohio Canal, 142; *see
  also* theories of location
Chicago School, 8–18; *see also* Park,
  R. E.
  biological ecology, influence of, 9–10
  areas of agreement, 9
  biotic and cultural spheres, 23
  critics of, 21–22
  Park, R. E., 3, 4, 6, 8–13, 17, 23,
    25, 31, 32, 214, 259–65, 357n,
    358–59, 385, 502
  "The City," 11–12
  research program, 11–12
  social survey movement, 30n
  publications, 12–13
  research program, 12
  social disorganization, interest in,
    355
  theories, 17
  Wirth, L., 3, 13, 18–22, 31–33n,
    38n, 215, 225–27, 355, 358,
    382n, 433–34, 454
  Zorbaugh, H., 13, 215, 271, 273,
    355, 358, 359, 372
    The Gold Coast and the Slum,
      14–17
Cities, earliest, 95–106
  China, 102
  Egypt, 100
  evolution of social organization, 96
  India, 101
  Mesoamerica, 103–05
  Mesopotamia, 97–99
    ecological organization, 97
  vulnerability, 97–98
  overgrown village, 95–96
  preconditions for cities, 87–90
  role of trade, 95
  spread of urban revolution, 105
Cities, fiscal problems, 483–91
  big business, role of, 489–91
  high-cost citizens; problem of,
    484–85

revenue limitations, 488
revenue sources, 487–89
City government structure, 475–81
City typologies, 161–83
  criteria used, 163
  multidimensional, 174–83
    Berry's typology, 180–81
    construction of, 175–77
    factor analysis, use of, 176–77
    Hadden & Borgatta's typology,
      179–80
    Price's typology, 177–79
  single-dimension, 163–74
    construction of, 163–64
    Harris' typology, 165–67
    Nelson's typology, 167–72
  uses of, 181–83
  why classify, 162–63
Classical theories; *see* theories,
    classical
Cohort, 69–70, 505
Collective conscience, 353–54; *see
    also* theories of community
Commensalism, 7
Community; *see also* theories of
    community
  black, 422–26
  changes in, 378–79
  Chicago School, 356–60
    natural areas, 356–59
    social disorganization in, 359–60
  concept, 348–55
  definition, 248
  in 19th century thought, 347–48
  participation, 376–78
  relations to larger society, 379
  social networks, 361
  social construction of, 361–62
  societal scale, related to, 360–61
  symbolic, 361–73
    defended neighborhood, 372–73
    face block, 371–72
    limited liability, 361–62, 374–76
  theories; *see* theories of community
Community Development Block Grant
    Program, 483
Competition, 7, 10, 259, 260
Concentric Zone Theory; *see* theories,
    classical
Congestion, 438
Contemporary human ecology, 28–30
  areas of research, 28–30
    internal structure, 28–29
    urbanization process, 28

Contract, 350; *see also* theories of
    community
Cooperation, 10
Crowding, 451
Cultural level, 10; *see also* Chicago
    School, biotic level
Cybernation, 130; *see also* southwest-
    ern cities

Darwin, C., 5–6
  Origin of Species, 5
  theory of evolution, 5
Decentralization, 502–04; *see also*
    suburbanization
Decision-to-move
  decision-making process, 287–88
  factors influencing, 286–87
  importance of decision, 285
  pull factors, 285
Deconcentration, 200, 438; *see also*
    density-distance relationship
Defended neighborhood, 372–73; *see
    also* community, symbolic
Density, 451
Density-distance relationship
  Chicago's pattern, 437–38
  Cleveland's pattern, 441–44
  congestion, 438
  curves, 438–41
    changes over time, 439–41
    U. S. cities, 438–39
  deconcentration, 438
  models of, 436–37
  reasons for studying, 449–50
  sources of change, 434–36
  societal scale, related to, 444–49
Density and pathology, 451–70
  animal studies, 455–56
    analogy with humans, 456
  crowding, defined, 451
  density, defined, 451
  studies of, 452–71
    early studies, 452–53
    ecological, 468–70
    recent research, 470–71
  theories of, 456–68
    personal space, 467
    social overload, 456–58
    spatial constraint, 467–68
    stimulus overload, 458–59
    territoriality, 458
Dillon's rule, 475–76
Dominance, 7–8, 259

Dominance-competition framework, 260–61

Durkheim, E., 36, 353–54, 356, 453

Dynamic density, 36; *see also* theories of community, Durkheim, E.

East Central Citizens Organization, 504

Ecological complex, 25–28, 444–47, 505–07
  critics of, 33n
  reference variables, 25–28

Ecological distance, 279

Ecological process, 259–61

Ecological system, the metropolis, 497–98

Ecology, 5–6

Economic base, 183–84
  basic sector, 183–84
  nonbasic sector, 183
  relationship to urbanization, 184

Economic competition, 260

Economic development, 75–76; *see also* modernization

Economy, sectors, 232

Ecosystem, 7

Electric streetcar, 325

Erie Canal, 137–38; *see also* theories of location

"The Experience of Living in Cities," 459–66

Face block, 371–72; *see also* communities, symbolic

Factor analysis, 213, 238, 249–55
  technique described, 249–55
    correlation coefficients, 251–52
    reference axis, 255
    vectors, 253

Factorial ecology, 214, 244–47
  defined, 244–45
  related to social area analysis, 245
  studies, 245–46

Familism, 333–35

Family life cycle, 218

Fertile crescent, 91

Fiscal problems; *see* cities, fiscal problems

Fragmentation, 491–98; *see also* suburbanization
  ecological factors, 491–96
  factors influencing, 496–97
  responses to, 497–98

Gemeinschaft, 350–51; *see also* theories of community, Tonnies, F.

Gessellschaft, 351–53; *see also* theories of community, Tonnies, F.

The Gold Coast and the Slum, 358–72; *see also* Chicago School, Zorbaugh, H.

Groups, types, 384–85
  associational, 384–85
  social groups, 384
  societal groups, 384
  statistical groups, 384

Harrison & Ullman's Multiple Nuclei Theory; *see* theories, classical

Heartland, 192; *see also* system of cities

Hinterland, 192; *see also* system of cities

Hoyt's Sector Theory; *see* theories, classical, Hoyt

Human ecology, 4, 6; *see also* ecology, Chicago School
  contemporary, 28–30
    areas of research, 28–30

Human prehistory, 90–92
  Paleolithic, 90
  Mesolithic, 90–91
  Neolithic, 91–92

Ideal type, 18, 350

Immigration, 399–400

Index of dissimilarity, 390; *see also* segregation, measuring

Industrial Revolution, 111–115
  changes in agriculture, 112–113
  changes in manufacturing, 113–114
  changes in social structure, 114
  reasons for, 111–12

Intensification, 36

Intergovernmental relationships, 481–83
  federal & local, 482–83
  horizontal, 481
  state & local, 481–82
  vertical, 481

Invasion, 7–8, 261

Invasion-succession, 418–19; *see also* succession

Iron-Horse Epoch, 187–89; *see also* system of cities

Jacksonville, Florida, 501

Lake cities, 119–20; *see also* American urban history
Law, 354
The Levittowners, 317
Lifestyles, 293–95; *see also* decision to move, search for a home
  cosmopolites, 293
  deprived & trapped, 294
  ethnic villagers, 294
  urban homesteader, 294
  unmarried and childless, 253–94
Local government, 475–77
  sources of authority, 475–76
  system of, 476–77
    counties & municipalities, 476
    special districts, 477

Mechanical solidarity, 353
Megalopolis, 194–95
Megalopolitan Epoch, 194–97; *see also* system of cities
Melting-pot thesis, 401–02; *see also* segregation, ethnic
Metropolitan change 1980s, 505–07
  POET, analyzed with, 505–07
Metropolitan government, 478–81
  fragmentation, 478–81; *see also* fragmentation
    reasons, 478–79
    negative aspects, 479–81
  policy alternatives, 499–505
    centralization, 500–02
    decentralization, 502–05
    status quo, 499–500
  problems, fiscal, 483–86
    expenditures, 485
    financing, 486
    high cost services, 485
    services, 484
    spillover, 485–86
Miami, Florida, 501
Migration, 233–34
  black urban, 234
  immigration, 233–34
    first wave, 233
    second wave, 234
  pull factors, 233
  push factors, 233
  rural to urban, 233
Modernization
  changing role of urbanization, 80–81
  defined, 76
  Irwin's Model, 77–78
  less developed countries, 68–69, 76

more developed countries, 68–69, 76
  related to urbanization, 79–80
Multidimensional typologies; *see* city typologies
Multiple Nuclei Theory; *see* theories, classical

Natural areas; *see also* Chicago School
  Chicago School, 214–15
  Cleveland, map of areas, 215–16
  concept, 10, 214–27, 357, 502
  criticism of, 357–58
  defined, 215
  difficulty identifying, 359
  limitations of, 215
Natural economy, 260
Natural selection, 259; *see also* Darwin
Neighborhood, 502–03
  racial change, 421
    misconceptions, 421–22
    housing values, 421–22
Neighborhood Lifecycle Model, 286
Neighboring, 335–77
Neoorthodox approach, 25; *see also* sociocultural, contemporary human ecology
Northeast corridor, 198–200
New York City, 503

Occupational prestige, 230–31; *see also* social area analysis
Organic solidarity, 353–54; *see also* theories of community, Durkheim, E.
Origin of cities; *see also* cities, earliest
  collection of evidence, 88–89
  preconditions, 89–90
    social change, 90
    technology & environment, 89

Park, R. E.; *see* Chicago School
Pennsylvania Mainland Canal, 142; *see also* system of cities
Phoenix, Arizona, 200–03
  dependency on federal government, 201
  population growth, 202–03
  problems, 201–02
Plant and animal, 259–60; *see also* ecology
POET; *see* ecological complex
Policy alternatives; *see* metropolitan government

Population concentration, 36
Preconditions for cities, 89–90; *see also* cities, earliest
Preindustrial city, 106–11
  demography and ecology, 108–11
  prevasiveness of class, 106–07
  physical structure, 108–11
  social institutions, 107–08
Primacy, 52–53; *see also* modernization
Primacy index, 85n

Realtors, 388–89
Redlining, 290, 389
Regional development; *see* American urban history, system of cities
Revolution, agricultural; *see* agricultural revolution
Revolution, industrial; *see* industrial revolution
Revolution, urban; *see* urban revolution

The search for a new home, 288–99
  factors influencing, 288–95
    summary table, 289
  search process, 298–99
  subareas searched, 295–99
    summary table, 296–97
Sector theory; *see* theories, classical, Hoyt
Segregation
  effects, negative & positive, 386
Segregation, ethnic, 399–410
  assimilation, theories of, 401–02
    melting-pot thesis, 401–02
  enclaves, function of, 407–410
  factors influencing, 402–07
    region and time of immigration, 402–03
    social status factors, 404–07
Segregation, measuring, 389–90
  index of dissimilarity, 390
Segregation racial, 410–28
  black migration, 410–11
    migration streams, 411
  Cleveland, Ohio, case study, 415–18
    residential patterns, 415–16
    black community, 418
  factors influencing, 426–28
    ecological factors, 426–27
    voluntary & involuntary, 428
  neighborhood change, 418–22

  invasion-succession, 418–19
  tipping, 419–21
  trends, 412–15
    1940–70, 413
    1970s & 1980s, 412
    summary table, 414
Segregation, social status, 391–99
  factors influencing, 397–99
  location of wealthy & poor, 394–97
  research on, 391–94
    Duncan, 392
    Farley, 394
    Simkus, 392–93
Segregation, types, 387–89
  ecological, 387
  involuntary, 388–89
  summary table, 390
  voluntary, 387
Segregation, why study?, 385–87
Shanty towns, 82
Shevky, E., 214, 217–19, 219–23, 225, 227–32, 240–41, 245, 257–58, 284
Simmel, G., 433, 434, 453, 454
Simple linear distance, 279
Single dimension typologies; *see* city typologies
Slum, 358–59
  social order in, 358
SMSA, 84–85n; *see also* Standard Metropolitan Statistical Area
Social area analysis
  assumptions of, 214
  business uses, 234–37
  changes on community level, 227–34
  changes on societal level, 223–25
  classical models, relationship to concept of, 217
  criticism of, 219, 238
  importance, 214
  index construction, 227–34; *see also* social area indexes
    summary table, 228
  origins, 214–23
  revisions by Shevky & Bell, 219–37
  testing, 238–44
    factor analysis used, 238
    Bell's predictions & findings, 239–40
    societal scale, 240–44
Social area diagram, 220
Social area indexes
  ethnic status, 219
  family status, 218–19

social status, 218
operationalized, 238
Social area analysis and behavior, 240
The Social Areas of Los Angeles:
Analysis and Typology, 217
Social networks, 361
Societal scale
changes in land use, 225–27
concept of, 223
effects on complexity, 224
effects on economy, 223–24
effects on human relationships,
224–25
impact on the family, 232
impact on women, 232
relationship to urbanism, 225–27
summary table, 226–27
social status, 214, 229
Sociocultural approach, 24; *see also*
contemporary human ecology,
neoorthodox approach
Southern cities, 120–21
Southwestern cities, 121–30
Specialized function theory, 145–46;
see also theories of location
Spillover, 485–86
Squatter settlements, 81
Standard Metropolitan Statistical Area,
42–3, 307
Status gradients, 282
Stimulus overload, 453–54; *see also*
density and pathology
Subcommunities, 356; *see also* communities, symbolic
Suburban development, stages of,
323–31
early industrial, 323–25
1890-WWI, 325–28
WW I – WW II, 328–30
post World War II, 330–31
POET analysis, 330–31
Suburban growth, 321–23
ecological analysis, 321–23
Suburban image, 304–08
during 1920s, 304
during 1950s, 304–06
during 1960–80, 307–08
Suburbanization-business and industry,
335–41
decentralization of employment,
337–39
employment patterns, 336–37
national trends, 335–36

new locational forces, 340–41
reasons for decentralization, 339–40
Suburbanization—demographic patterns, 315–16
Suburbanization, history of, 308–11
18th & 19th century, 308
20th century, 308–09
post WW II period, 310–12
Suburbanization-impact on central city,
337
Suburbanization-operational definition,
306–08
Suburban persistence, 320
The Suburban Trend, 304
Suburban types, 317–20
employing suburbs, 318–20
residential suburbs, 317
comparisons, 319–20
summary table, 319
working class suburbs, 317
Suburban way of life, 331–35
effects of fragmentation, 332
familism, 333–35
neighboring, 335
status of housing, 332–33
Succession, 7–8, 261
Sunbelt, 200–03
Symbiosis, 7, 10, 259
Symbolic communities, 371–76, *see*
also communities, symbolic
Systems of cities, American, 183–203
historical analysis, 185–97
map of, 186, 188
stages of development, 185–97
Sail-Wagon Epoch, 185–97
Steel-Rail Epoch, 189–92
Auto-Air Amenity Epoch, 192–93
Megalopolitan Epoch, 194–97
interrelationships between cities,
203–08
by index scores, 204
by industry, 207–08
by money flow, 204–07

Theories, classical, 270–78
Burgess Concentric Zone Theory,
270–74
dynamics of, 273
limiting assumptions, 282–83
map of, 271
tests of, 278–83
weaknesses, 280
convergence of theories, 283–84

Harris and Ullman's Multiple Nuclei
    Theory, 276–78
  description of, 276–77
  dynamics of, 177–78
Hoyt's Sector Theory, 274–76
  dynamics of, 274–76
  map of, 275
  methodology, 274
  relationship to social area analysis,
    283–84
Theories of community; *see also*
    community
  Durkheim, E., 353–55
    mechanical solidarity, 353
    organic solidarity, 353–54
  Maine, H., 349–50
    contract, 350
    family and tradition, 349–50
  Park, R. E., 355–60; *see also* Chi-
    cago School
    achieving solidarity, 355
    definition of, 355
    influence of Durkheim, 355–56
  Tonnies, F., 350–53
    ideal types, 350–53
Theories of location
  break-in-transportation
    Canal or Railroad? case study,
      137–43
    cities, examples of, 136–37
    population growth, 143–44
    technological change, 137, 143
  Central Place Theory, 146–58
    assumptions, 147–58
    central place, defined, 148
    changing patterns, 156–58
    critics of, 155
    industrialization, effects of, 156
    reexamination, 155–58
    region and technology, effects of,
      150–51
    test of, 151–52
    trade areas, 153–54
    transportation technology, effects
      of, 155–56
    urban hierarchy, 152
Theories of residential location, 259–70
  applying biological models, 260
Theory of Rents, 262–70
  assumptions, 262
  hypothetical examples, 262–64
  land uses
    spatial distribution, 265–66

    theoretical location, 268–69
  rents assessed, 267–68
Tipping-point model, 419–21

Urban development, early; *see* cities,
    earliest
Urban revolution, spread of, 105
Urban history; *see* American urban
    history
Urban sociology, 3
Urbanism, 18, 36
"Urbanism as a Way of Life," 18–21,
    355; *see also* Wirth, L.
  consequences of
    density, 19
    heterogeneity, 20
    size, 18
Urbanization
  age of scarcity, during, 74–75
  concept of, 36–38
  criteria of, 39–40
  delineating boundaries, 40–41
  industrial-age, during, 73–74
Urbanization, global patterns, 48–75
  approaches to the study, 68–75
  Brazil, 58–65
    primacy, 55–56
    urban growth, 54
  New Zealand, 54–58
    primacy, 55–56
    urban growth, 54
  Thailand, 48–54
    primacy, 52–53
    urban growth, 49–52
Urbanization, measuring, 38–41
Urbanization, overurbanization,
    53–54
Urbanization and economic develop-
    ment, 75–83
Urbanization and natural resources,
    79–80
U.S. Census
  history of, 84n
  definitions, 41–46
    extended city, 42
    Standard Consolidated Statistical
      Area, 43
    Standard Metropolitan Statistical
      Area, 42–43
    urban, 41
    urbanized area, 41–42
    usefulness of definitions, 44–45

Why families move, 285
Wirth, L., 3, 13, 18–22, 31, 33n, 38n,
    215, 225–27, 355, 358, 433, 434,
    454
  "Urbanism as a Way of Life,"
    18–21

critics of, 22–23
summary table, 226–27

Zorbaugh, H., 13–17, 215, 271, 273,
    355, 358, 359, 372
  The Gold Coast & the Slum, 13–17